# Option Theory

# Wiley Finance Series

# Option Theory

**Peter James**

**WILEY**

Published   2003      John Wiley & Sons Ltd, The Atrium, Southern Gate, Chichester,
West Sussex PO19 8SQ, England

Telephone   (+44) 1243 779777

Transferred to digital printing, 2005

Email (for orders and customer service enquiries): cs-books@wiley.co.uk
Visit our Home Page on www.wileyeurope.com or www.wiley.com

***Other Wiley Editorial Offices***

John Wiley & Sons Inc., 111 River Street, Hoboken, NJ 07030, USA

Jossey-Bass, 989 Market Street, San Francisco, CA 94103-1741, USA

Wiley-VCH Verlag GmbH, Boschstr. 12, D-69469 Weinheim, Germany

John Wiley & Sons Australia Ltd, 33 Park Road, Milton, Queensland 4064, Australia

John Wiley & Sons (Asia) Pte Ltd, 2 Clementi Loop #02-01, Jin Xing Distripark, Singapore 129809

John Wiley & Sons Canada Ltd, 22 Worcester Road, Etobicoke, Ontario, Canada M9W 1L1

***British Library Cataloguing in Publication Data***

A catalogue record for this book is available from the British Library

ISBN 0-471-49289-2

Typeset in 10/12pt Times by TechBooks, New Delhi, India
Printed & bound by Antony Rowe Ltd, Eastbourne

This book is printed on acid-free paper responsibly manufactured from sustainable forestry
in which at least two trees are planted for each one used for paper production.

To Vivien

To Vivien

# Contents

# Preface

Options are financial instruments which are bought and sold in a market place. The people who do it well pocket large bonuses; companies that do it badly can suffer staggering losses. These are intensely practical activities and this is a technical book for practical people working in the industry. While writing it I have tried to keep a number of issues and principles to the forefront:

- The emphasis is on developing the theory to the point where it is capable of yielding a numerical answer to a pricing question, either through a formula or through a numerical procedure. In those places where the theory is fairly abstract, as in the sections explaining stochastic calculus, the path back to reality is clearly marked.
- An objective of the book is to demystify option theory. An essential part of this is giving explanations and derivations in full. I have (almost) completely avoided the "it can be shown that . . . " syndrome, except for the most routine algebraic steps, since this can be very time-wasting and frustrating for the reader. No quant who values his future is going to just lift a formula or set of procedures from a textbook and apply them without understanding where they came from and what assumptions went into them.
- It is a sad fact that readers do not start at the beginning of a textbook and read every page until they get to the end – at least not the people I meet in the derivatives market. Practitioners are usually looking for something specific and want it quickly. I have therefore tried to make the book reasonably easy to dip in and out of. This inevitably means a little duplication and a lot of signposts to parts of the book where underlying principles are explained.
- Option theory can be approached from several different directions, using different mathematical techniques. An option price can be worked out by solving a differential equation or by taking a risk-neutral expectation; results can be obtained by using formulas or trees or by integrating numerically or by using finite difference methods; and the theoretical underpinnings of option theory can be explained either by using conventional, classical statistical methods or by using axiomatic probability theory and stochastic calculus. This book demonstrates that these are all saying the same thing in different languages; there is only one option theory, although several branches of mathematics can be used to describe it. I have taken pains to be unpartisan in describing techniques; the best technique is the one that produces the best answer, and this is not the same for all options.

The reader of this book might have no previous knowledge of option theory at all, or he might be an accomplished quant checking an obscure point. He might be a student looking to complement his course material or he might be a practitioner who wants to understand the use of stochastic calculus in option theory; but he will start with an intermediate knowledge of calculus and the elements of statistics. The book is divided into four parts and a substantial mathematical appendix. The first three parts cover (1) the basic principles of option theory, (2) computational methods and (3) the application of the previous theory to exotic options. The mathematical tools needed for these first three parts are pre-packaged in the appendix, in a consistent form that can be used with minimal interruption to the flow of the text.

Part 4 has the ambitious objective of giving the reader a working knowledge of stochastic calculus. A pure mathematician's approach to this subject would start with a heavy dose of measure theory and axiomatic probability theory. This is an effective barrier to entry for many students and practitioners. Furthermore, as with any restricted trade, those who have crossed the barrier have every interest in making sure that it stays in place: who needs extra competition for those jobs or consulting contracts? This has unfortunately led to many books and articles being unnecessarily dressed up in stochastic jargon; at the same time there are many students and practitioners with perfectly adequate freshman level calculus and statistics who are frustrated by their inability to penetrate the literature.

This particular syndrome has been sorted out in mature fields such as engineering and science. If you want to be a pure mathematician, you devote your studies to the demanding questions of pure mathematics. If you want to be an engineer, you still need a lot of mathematics, but you will learn it from books with titles such as "Advanced Engineering Mathematics". Nobody feels there is much value in turning electrical engineering or solid state physics into a playground for pure mathematicians.

It is assumed that before embarking on Part 4, the reader will already have a rudimentary knowledge of option theory. He may be shaky on detail, but he will know how a risk-free portfolio leads to the risk-neutrality concept and how a binomial tree works. At this point he already knows quite a lot of useful stochastic theory without realizing it and without knowing the fancy words. This knowledge can be built upon and developed into discrete stochastic theory using familiar concepts. In the limit of small time steps this generalizes to a continuous stochastic theory; the generalization is not always smooth and easy, but anomalies created by the transition are explicitly pointed out. A completely rigorous approach would lead us through an endless sea of lemmas, so we take the engineer's way. Our ultimate interest is in option theory, so frequent recourse is made to heuristic or intuitive reasoning. We do so without apology, for a firm grasp of the underlying "physical" processes ultimately leads to a sounder understanding of derivatives than an over-reliance on abstract mathematical manipulation.

The objective is to give the reader a sufficient grasp of stochastic calculus to allow him to understand the literature and use it actively. There is little benefit to the reader in a dumbed down sketch of stochastic theory which still leaves him unable to follow the serious literature. The necessary jargon is therefore described and the theory is developed with constant reference to option theory. By the end of Part 4 the attentive reader will have a working knowledge of martingales, stochastic differential equations and integration, the Feynman Kac theorem, local time, stochastic control and Girsanov's theorem.

A final chapter in Part 4 applies all these tools to various problems encountered in studying equity-type derivatives. Some of these problems had been encountered earlier in the book and are now solved more gracefully; others are really not convincingly soluble without stochastic calculus. Of course the most important application in this latter category is the whole subject of interest rate derivatives. However, the book stops short at this point for two reasons: first, the field of derivatives has now become so large that it is no longer feasible to cover both equity and interest rate options thoroughly in a single book of reasonable length. Second, three or four very similar texts on this subject have appeared in the last couple of years; they are all quite good and they all launch into interest rate derivatives at the point where this book finishes. Any reader primarily motivated by an interest in interest rate options, but floundering in stochastic calculus, will find Part 4 a painless way into these more specialist texts.

Peter James
option.theory@james-london.com

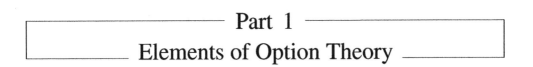

# Part 1
# Elements of Option Theory

# 1

## Fundamentals

The trouble with first chapters is that nearly everyone jumps over them and goes straight to the meat. So, assuming the reader gets this far before jumping, let me say what will be missed and why it might be worth coming back sometime.

Section 1.1 is truly jumpable, so long as you really understand continuous as opposed to discrete interest and dividends, sign conventions for long and short securities positions and conventions for designating the passing of time. Section 1.2 gives a first description of the concept of arbitrage, which is of course central to the subject of this book. This description is rather robust and intuitive, as opposed to the fancy definition couched in heavy mathematics which is given much later in the book; it is a practical working-man's view of arbitrage, but it yields most of the results of modern option theory.

Forward contracts are really only common in the foreign exchange markets; but the concept of a forward rate is embedded within the analysis of more complex derivatives such as options, in all financial markets. We look at forward contracts in Section 1.3 and introduce one of the central mysteries of option theory: risk neutrality.

Finally, Section 1.4 gives a brief description of the nature of a futures contract and its relationship with a forward contract.

### 1.1 CONVENTIONS

(i) **Continuous Interest:** If we invest $100 for a year at an annual rate of 10%, we get $110 after a year; at a semi-annual rate of 10%, we get $100 \times 1.05^2 = \$110.25$ after a year, and at a quarterly rate, $100 \times 1.025^4 = \$110.38$. In the limit, if the interest is compounded each second, we get

$$\$100 \times \lim_{n \to \infty} \left( 1 + \frac{0.1}{n} \right)^n = \$100 \times e^{0.1} = \$110.52$$

The factor by which the principal sum is multiplied when we have continuous compounding is $e^{r_c T}$, where $T$ is the time to maturity and $r_c$ is the continuously compounding rate.

In commercial contracts, interest payments are usually specified with a stated compounding period, but in option theory we always use continuous compounding for two reasons: first, the exponential function is analytically simpler to handle; and second, the compounding period does not have to be specified.

When actual rates quoted in the market need to be used, it is a simple matter to convert between continuous and discrete rates:

$$\text{Annual Compounding:} \quad e^{r_c} = 1 + r_1 \quad \Rightarrow r_c = \ln(1 + r_1)$$

$$\text{Semi-annual Compounding:} \quad e^{r_c} = \left( 1 + \frac{r_{1/2}}{2} \right)^2 \Rightarrow r_c = 2 \ln \left( 1 + \frac{r_{1/2}}{2} \right)$$

$$\text{Quarterly Compounding:} \quad e^{r_c} = \left( 1 + \frac{r_{1/4}}{4} \right)^4 \Rightarrow r_c = 4 \ln \left( 1 + \frac{r_{1/4}}{4} \right)$$

(ii) **Stock Prices:** This book deals with the mathematical treatment of options on a variety of different underlying instruments. It is not of course practical to describe some theory for foreign exchange options and then repeat the same material for equities, commodities, indices, etc. We therefore follow the practice of most authors and take equities as our primary example, unless there is some compelling pedagogical reason for using another market (as there is in the next section).

The price of an equity stock is a stochastic variable, i.e. it is a random variable whose value changes over time. It is usually assumed that the stock has an expected financial return which is exponential, but superimposed on this is a random fluctuation. This may be expressed mathematically as follows:

$$S_t = S_0 \, e^{\mu t} + RV$$

where $S_0$ and $S_t$ are the stock price now and at time $t$, $\mu$ is the return on the stock and $RV$ is a random variable (we could of course assume that the random fluctuations are multiplicative, and later in the book we will see that this is indeed a better representation; but we keep things simple for the moment). It is further assumed that the random fluctuations, which cause the stock price to deviate from its smooth path, are equally likely to be upwards or downwards: we assume the expected value $E[RV] = 0$.

It follows that

$$E[S_t] = S \, e^{\mu t}$$

which is illustrated in Figure 1.1.

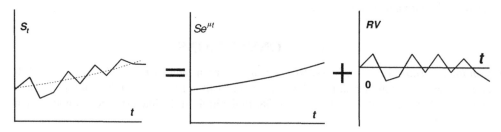

**Figure 1.1**   Stock price movement

A word is in order on the subject of the stock return $\mu$. This is the increase in wealth which comes from investing in the stock and should not be confused with the dividend which is merely the cash throw-off from the stock.

(iii) **Discrete Dividends:** Anyone who owns a stock on its ex-dividend date is entitled to receive the dividend. Clearly, the only difference between the stock one second before and one second after its ex-dividend date is the right to receive a sum of money $d$ on the dividend payment date. Market prices of equities therefore drop by the present value of the dividend on ex-dividend date. The declaration of a dividend has no effect on the wealth of the stockholder but is just a transfer of value from stock price to cash. This suggests that before an ex-dividend date, a stock price may be considered as made up of two parts: $d \, e^{-rT}$, which is the present value of the known future dividend payment; and the variable "pure stock" part, which may be written $S_0 - d \, e^{-rT}$. In terms of today's stock price $S_0$, the future value of the stock may then be written

$$S_t = (S_0 - d \, e^{-rT}) e^{\mu t} + RV$$

We could handle several dividends into the future in this way, with the dividend term in the last equation being replaced by the sum of the present values of the dividends to be paid before time $t$; but it is rare to know the precise value of the dividends more than a couple of dividend payment dates ahead.

Finally, the reader is reminded that in this imperfect world, tax is payable on dividends. The above reasoning is easily adapted to stock prices which are made up of three parts: the pure stock part, the future cash part and the government's part.

(iv) **Continuous Dividends**: As in the case of interest rates, the mathematical analysis is much simplified if it is assumed that the dividend is paid continuously (Figure 1.2), and proportionately to the stock price. The assumption is that in a small interval of time $\delta t$, the stock will lose dividend equal to $q S_t \delta t$, where $q$ is the dividend rate. If we were to assume that $\mu = 0$, this would merely be an example of exponential decay, with $E\langle S_t \rangle = S_0 e^{-qt}$. Taking into account the underlying stock return (growth rate)

$$E[S_t] = S_0 e^{(\mu - q)t}$$

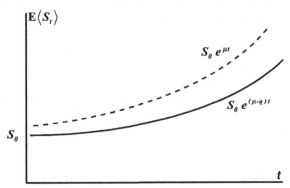

**Figure 1.2**  Continuous dividends

The non-random part of the stock price can be imagined as trying to grow at a constant exponential rate of $\mu$, but with this growth attenuated by a constant exponential rate of "evaporation" of value due to the continuous dividend.

It has been seen that for a stockholder, dividends do not represent a change in wealth but only a transfer from stock value to cash. However, there are certain contracts such as forwards and options in which the holder of the contract suffers from the drop in stock price, but does not benefit from the dividends. In pricing such contracts we must adjust for the stock price as follows:

$$S_0 \to S_0 - \text{PV[expected dividends]} \quad \text{(discrete)}$$
$$S_0 \to S_0 e^{-qt} \quad \text{(continuous)}$$

(v) **Time**: As the theory is developed in this book, it will be important to be consistent in the use of the concept of time. When readers cross refer between various books and papers on options, they might find mysterious inconsistencies occurring in the signs of some terms in equations; these are most usually traceable to the conventions used in defining time.

The time variable "$T$" will refer to a length of time until some event, such as the maturity of a deposit or forward contract. The most common use of $T$ in this course will be the length of time to the maturity of an option, and every model we look at (except one!) will contain this variable.

Time is also used to describe the concept of date, designated by $t$. Thus when a week elapses, $t$ increases by $1/52$ years. "Now" is designated by $t = 0$ and the maturity date of one of the above contracts is $t = T$.

This all looks completely straightforward; $t$ and $T$ describe two different, although interrelated concepts. But it is this inter-relationship which requires care, especially when we come to deal with differentials with respect to time. Suppose we consider the price today ($t = 0$) of an option expiring in $T$ years; if we now switch our attention to the value of the same option a day later, we would say that $\delta t = 1$ day; but the time to maturity of the option has *decreased* by a day, i.e. $\delta T = -1$ day. The transformation between increments in "date" and "time to maturity" is simply $\delta t \leftrightarrow -\delta T$; a differential with respect to $t$ is therefore equal to *minus* the differential with respect to $T$, or symbolically $\partial/\partial t \Rightarrow -\partial/\partial T$.

(vi) *Long and Short Positions*: In the following chapters, the concepts of long and short positions are used so frequently that the reader must be completely familiar with what this means in practice. We take again our example of an equity stock: if we are long a share of stock today, this simply means that we own the share. The value of this is designated as $S_0$, and as the price goes up and down, so does the value of the shareholding. In addition, we receive any dividend that is paid.

If we are short of a share of stock, it means that we have sold the stock without owning it. After the sale, the purchaser comes looking for his share certificate, which we do not possess. Our remedy is to give him stock which we borrow from someone who *does* own it.

Such stock borrowing facilities are freely available in most developed stock markets. Eventually we will have to return the stock to the lender, and since the original shares have gone to the purchaser, we have no recourse but to buy the stock in the market. The value of our short stock position is designated as $-S_0$, since $S_0$ is the amount of money we must pay to buy in the required stock.

The lender of stock would expect to receive the dividend paid while he lent it; but if the borrower had already sold the stock (i.e. taken a short position), he would not have received any dividends but would nonetheless have to compensate the stock lender. While the short position is maintained, we must therefore pay the dividend to the stock lender from his own resources.

The stock lender will also expect a fee for lending the stock; for equities this is usually in the region of 0.2% to 1.0% of the value of the stock per annum. The effect of this stock borrowing cost when we are shorting the stock is similar to that of dividends, i.e. we have to pay out some periodic amount that is proportional to the amount of stock being borrowed. In our pricing models we therefore usually just add the stock lending rate to the dividend rate if our hedge requires us to borrow stock.

The market for borrowing stocks is usually known as the **repo market**. In this market the stock borrower has to put up the cash value of the stock which he borrows, but since he receives the market interest rate on his cash (more or less), this leg of the repo has no economic effect on hedging cost.

A long position in a derivative is straightforward. If we own a forward contract or an option, its value is simply designated as $f_0$. This value may be a market value (if the instrument is traded) or the fair price estimated by a model. A short position implies different mechanics depending on the type of instrument: take, for example, a call option on the stock of a company. Some call options (warrants) are traded securities and the method of shorting these may be similar to that for stock. Other call options are non-traded, bilateral contracts (over-the-counter options). A short position here would consist of our writing a call giving someone the right to buy stock from us at a fixed price. But in either case we have incurred a liability which can be designated as $-f_0$.

Cash can similarly be given this mirror image treatment. A long position is written $B_0$. It is always assumed that this is invested in some risk-free instrument such as a bank deposit or treasury bill, to yield the interest rate. A short cash position, designated $-B_0$, is simply a borrowing on which interest has to be paid.

## 1.2 ARBITRAGE

Having stated in the last section that most examples will be taken from the world of equities, we will illustrate this key topic with a single example from the world of foreign exchange; it just fits better.

Most readers have at least a notion that arbitrage means buying something one place and selling it for a profit somewhere else, all without taking a risk. They probably also know that opportunities for arbitrage are very short-lived, as everyone piles into the opportunity and in doing so moves the market to a point where the opportunity no longer exists. When analyzing financial markets, it is therefore reasonable to assume that all prices are such that no arbitrage is possible.

Let us be a little more precise: if we have cash, we can clearly make money simply by depositing it in a bank and earning interest; this is the so-called risk-free return. Alternatively, we may make rather more money by investing in a stock; but this carries the risk of the stock price going down rather than up. What is assumed to be impossible is to borrow money from the bank and invest in some risk-free scheme which is bound to make a profit. This assumption is usually known as the no-arbitrage or no-free-lunch principle. It is instructive to state this principle in three different but mathematically equivalent ways.

(i) *Equilibrium prices are such that it is impossible to make a risk-free profit.*
Consider the following sequence of transactions in the foreign exchange market:

(A) We borrow \$100 for a year from an American bank at an interest rate $r_\$$. At the end of the year we have to return \$100 $(1 + r_\$)$ to the bank. Using the conventions of the last section, its value in one year will be $-\$100\,(1 + r_\$)$.

(B) Take the \$100 and immediately do the following three things:

- Convert it to pounds sterling at the spot rate $S_{\text{now}}$ to give $£\frac{100}{S_{\text{now}}}$;
- Put the sterling on deposit with a British bank for a year at an interest rate of $r_£$. In a year we will receive back $£\frac{100}{S_{\text{now}}}\,(1 + r_£)$;
- Take out a forward contract at a rate $F_{1\,\text{year}}$ to exchange $£\frac{100}{S_{\text{now}}}\,(1 + r_£)$ for $\$\frac{100}{S_{\text{now}}}\,(1 + r_£)\,F_{1\,\text{year}}$ at the end of the year.

(C) In one year we receive $\$\frac{100}{S_{\text{now}}}\,(1 + r_£)\,F_{1\,\text{year}}$ from this sequence of transactions and return \$100 $(1 + r_\$)$ to the American bank. But the no-arbitrage principle states that these two taken together must equal zero. Therefore

$$F_{1\,\text{year}} = S_{\text{now}}\frac{(1 + r_\$)}{(1 + r_£)} \tag{1.1}$$

(ii) *If we know with certainty that two portfolios will have precisely the same value at some time in the future, they must have precisely the same value now.*
We use the same example as before. Consider two portfolios, each of which is worth \$100 in one year:

(A) The first portfolio is an interest-bearing cash account at an American bank. The amount of cash in the account today must be $\$\frac{100}{(1+r_\$)}$.

(B) The second portfolio consists of two items:

- A deposit of $£\frac{100}{(1+r_£)F_{1\,\text{year}}}$ with a British bank;
- A forward contract to sell $£\frac{100}{F_{1\,\text{year}}}$ for \$100 in one year.

7

(C) The value of the forward contract is zero [for a rationale of this see Section 1.3(iv)]. Both portfolios yield us $100 in one year, so today's values of the American and British deposits must be the same. They are quoted in different currencies, but using the spot rate $S_0$, which expresses today's equivalence, gives

$$\frac{1}{(1+r_£)}\frac{100}{F_{1\,\text{year}}}S_0 = \frac{100}{(1+r_\$)}$$

or

$$F_{1\,\text{year}} = S_0\frac{(1+r_\$)}{(1+r_£)}$$

(iii) *If a portfolio has a certain outcome (is perfectly hedged) its return must equal the risk-free rate.*

Suppose we start with $100 and execute a strategy as follows:

(A) Buy $£\frac{100}{S_0}$ of British pounds.

(B) Deposit this in a British bank to yield $£\frac{100}{S_0}(1+r_£)$ in one year.

(C) Simultaneously, enter a forward contract to sell $£\frac{100}{S_0}(1+r_£)$ in one year for $£\frac{100}{S_0}(1+r_£)F_{1\,\text{year}}$.

We know the values of $S_0$, $r_£$ and $F_{1\,\text{year}}$ today, so our strategy has a certain outcome. The return on the initial outlay of $100 must therefore be $r_s$:

$$\frac{\$\frac{100}{S_0}(1+r_£)\,F_{1\,\text{year}}}{\$100} = (1+r_\$)$$

or

$$F_{1\,\text{year}} = S_0\frac{(1+r_\$)}{(1+r_£)}$$

## 1.3   FORWARD CONTRACTS

(i) A forward contract is a contract to buy some security or commodity for a predetermined price, at some time in the future; the purchase price remains fixed, whatever happens to the price of the security before maturity.

Clearly, the market (or spot) price and the forward price will tend to converge (Figure 1.3) as the maturity date is approached; a one-day forward price will be pretty close to the spot price.

In the last section we used the example of a forward currency contract; this is the largest, best known forward market in the world and it was flourishing long before the word "derivative" was applied to financial markets. Yet it is the simplest non-trivial derivative and it allows us to illustrate some of the key concepts used in studying more complex derivatives such as options.

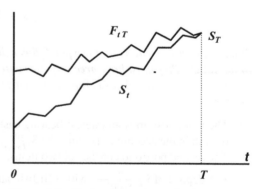

**Figure 1.3**   Stock price vs. forward price

(ii) Consider some very transitory commodity which cannot be stored – perhaps some unstorable agricultural commodity. The forward price at which we would be prepared to buy the commodity is determined by our expectation of its market price at the maturity of the contract; the higher we thought its price would be, the more we would bid for the future contract. So if we were asked to quote a two-year contract on fresh tomatoes, the best we could do is some kind of fundamental economic analysis: what were past trends, how are consumer tastes changing, what is happening to area under cultivation, what is the price of tomato fertilizer, etc.

However, all commodities considered in this book are non-perishable: securities, traded commodities, stock indexes and foreign exchange. What effect does the storable nature of a commodity have on its forward price?

Suppose we buy an equity share for a price $S_0$; in time $T$ the value of this share becomes $S_T$. If we had entered a forward contract to sell the share forward for a price $F_{0T}$, we would have been perfectly hedged, i.e. we would have paid out $S_0$ at the beginning and received a predetermined $F_{0T}$ at time $T$. From the no-arbitrage argument 1.2(iii), this investment must yield a return equal to the interest rate. Expressed in terms of continuous interest rates, we have

$$\frac{F_{0T}}{S_0} = e^{rT} \qquad \text{or} \qquad F_{0T} = S_0\, e^{rT}$$

This result is well known and seems rather banal; but its ramifications are so far-reaching that it is worth pausing to elaborate. Someone who knows nothing about finance theory would be forgiven for assuming that a forward rate must somehow depend on the various characteristics of each stock: growth rate, return, etc. But the above relationship shows that there is a fixed relationship between the spot and forward prices which is the same for all financial instruments and which is imposed by the no-arbitrage conditions. The reason is of course immediately obvious. With a perishable commodity, forward prices can have no effect on current prices: if we know that the forward tomatoes price is $1 million each, there is nothing we can do about it and the current price will not be affected. But if the forward copper price is $1 million, we buy all the copper we can in the spot market we can, put it in a warehouse and take out forward contracts to sell it next year; this will move the spot and forward prices to the point where they obey the above relationship.

We express this conclusion rather more formally for an equity stock, since it is actually the cardinal principle of all derivative pricing theory: *the relationship between the forward and spot rate is absolutely independent of the rate of return $\mu$.* This is known as the principle of risk neutrality. The reader must be absolutely clear on what this means: if it suddenly became clear that the growth rate of an equity stock was going to be higher than previously assumed, there would undoubtedly be a jump in both the spot and forward prices; but the relationship of the forward price to the spot price would not change. In a couple of chapters, we will show that risk neutrality holds not only for forwards but for all derivatives.

(iii) **Forward Price with Dividends**: A forward contract to buy stock in the future at a price $F_{0T}$ makes no reference to dividends. At maturity one pays the price and gets the stock, whether or not dividends were paid during the life of the contract. In order to calculate the forward price in the presence of dividends, we use the same no-arbitrage arguments as before: buy a share of equity for a price $S_0$ and simultaneously write a forward contract to sell the share at time $T$ for a price $F_{0T}$. Our total receipts are a dividend $d$ at time $\tau$ and the forward price $F$ at time $t$. Taking account of the time value of money, this gives us a value of $F_{0T} + d\, e^{r(T-\tau)}$ at time $T$.

Using the no-arbitrage argument as before, we have

$$\frac{\left(F_{0T} + d\,e^{r(T-\tau)}\right)}{S_0} = e^{rT} \qquad \text{or} \qquad F_{0T} = (S_0 - d\,e^{-r\tau})e^{rT}$$

This is confirmation of the rule that dividends can be accommodated by making the substitution $S_0 \to S_0 - \text{PV[expected dividends]}$ which we examined in Section 1.1(iv). Several dividends before maturity are handled by subtracting the present value of each dividend from the stock price. In the same section, we saw that continuous dividends require the substitution $S_0 \to S_0\,e^{-qt}$. The forward price is then given by

$$F_{0T} = S_0\,e^{(r-q)T}$$

(iv) **Generalized Dividends**: At this point it is worth extending the analysis to forward contracts on foreign exchange and commodities; these behave very similarly to equities, but the concept of dividend must be re-interpreted.

In Section 1.2 the power of arbitrage arguments was illustrated with a lengthy example using forward foreign exchange contracts. We used simple interest rates to derive a relationship between the forward and spot US dollar/British pound exchange rates. This is given by equation (1.1) but may be re-expressed in terms of continuous interest rates as

$$F_{0T} = S_0\,e^{(r_{\$}-r_{\pounds})t}$$

Comparing this with the previous equation, the interest earned on the foreign currency ($\pounds$) takes the role of a dividend in the equity model. The analogy is, of course, fairly close: if we buy equity the cash throw-off from our investment is the dividend; if we buy foreign currency the cash throw-off is the foreign currency interest.

Commodities are slightly more tricky. Remember the argument of Section 1.1(iv) used in establishing the continuous dividend yield formula: it was assumed that the equity is continually paying us a dividend yield. Storage charges are rather similar, except that they are a continual *cost*: these charges cover warehousing, handling, insurance, physical deterioration, petty theft, etc. If it is assumed that storage charges are proportional to the value of the commodity, they can be treated as a negative dividend. The reader is warned that this analysis is scoffed at by most commodities professionals, and it must be admitted that the relationships do not hold very well in practice. The main interest for the novice is that it provides an intellectual framework for understanding the pricing.

(v) **Forward Price vs. Value of a Forward Contract**: Suppose we take out a forward contract to buy a stock. A couple of weeks then go by and we decide to close out the contract. Clearly we do not just cancel the contract and walk away; some close-out price will be paid by or to our counterparty, depending on how the stock price has moved. The reason is that the forward price $X$ specified in the original contract is no longer the no-arbitrage forward price $F_{0T}$.

The value of an off-market forward contract can be deduced using the same no-arbitrage arguments as before: suppose we have a portfolio consisting of one share of stock and a forward contract to sell this share at time $T$ for a price $X$. If the value of a contract to buy forward at an off-market price $X$ is written $f_{0T}$, the value of the portfolio is $S_0 - f_{0T}$ (the negative sign arises as our portfolio contains a contract to *sell* forward). The value of the portfolio at maturity will be $X$, so that the no-arbitrage proposition (1.1) may be written

$$\frac{X}{S_0 - f_{0T}} = e^{rT} \quad \text{or} \quad f_{0T} = S_0 - X e^{-rT} \tag{1.2}$$

(vi) *Value of a Forward Contract with Dividends*: The analysis of the last section is readily adapted to take dividends into account. If there is a single discrete dividend at time $\tau$, the numerator in the first part of equation (1.2) becomes $X + d\, e^{r(T-\tau)}$, giving a forward contract value

$$f_{0T} = S_0 - X e^{-rT} - d\, e^{-r\tau} \tag{1.3}$$

For continuous dividends, we simply make the substitution $S_0 \to S_0\, e^{-qt}$ into equation (1.1) to give

$$f_{0T} = S_0\, e^{-qT} - X e^{-rT} = e^{-rT}(F_{0T} - X) \tag{1.4}$$

## 1.4 FUTURES CONTRACTS

In the last section it was seen that after a forward contract has been struck, it can build up very substantial positive or negative value depending on which way the forward price subsequently moves. This means that substantial credit exposure could build up between counterparties to transactions. This may be acceptable in a market like the forward foreign exchange market where the participants are usually banks; but it will be a constraining factor in opening the market to players of lower credit standing. Hence the futures contract was devised: it has substantially the same properties as the forward contract but without leading to the build up of value which makes forwards unsuitable for exchange trading.

(i) Futures and forwards are quite similar in many ways so it is very easy to confuse them. However, the two types of contract are cousins rather than twins, and it is important to be clear about their differences. The essential features of a futures contract are as follows:

- A futures contract on a commodity allows the owner of the contract to purchase the commodity on a given date. Like a forward contract, a futures has a specified maturity date.
- When the contract is first opened, a futures price (which is quoted in the market) is specified. This can loosely be regarded as the analog of the forward price $F_{0T}$.
- Here the two types of contract diverge sharply. A forward contract provides for the commodity to be bought for the price $F_{0T}$ which is fixed at the beginning; a futures contract states that the commodity will be bought for the futures price quoted by the market at the end of the contract. But one second before the maturity of the contract, the futures price must equal the spot price. Where then is the benefit in a contract which allows a commodity to be bought at the prevailing spot price?
- The answer is that a futures contract is "settled" or "marked to market" each day. If we enter a futures contract at a price $\Phi_{0T}$, we receive an amount $\Phi_{1T} - \Phi_{0T}$ one day later (or pay this away, if the price went down). The following day we are paid $\Phi_{2T} - \Phi_{1T}$; and so on until maturity. In a sense, the futures contract is like a forward contract in which the party who has the credit risk receives a collateral deposit so that the net exposure is zero at the end of each day.
- A futures contract may be compared to a forward contract which is closed out each day and then rolled forward by taking out a new contract at the prevailing forward rate: enter a

contract at a price $F_{0T}$. One day later, when the forward price is $F_{1T}$, close out the existing contract and take out a new one at $F_{1T}$. The amount owed from the close out of the first day's contract is $F_{0T} - F_{1T}$, which would normally be payable at maturity (but which could be discounted and paid up front).

Without getting into the mechanical details, it is worth knowing that for some types of futures contracts the last leg of this sequence is the delivery of the commodity against the prevailing spot price (physical settlement); others merely settle the difference between the spot price and yesterday's futures price (cash settlement).

(ii) **Futures Price**: We now consider the price of a futures contract to buy a commodity in time $T$. The number of days from $t = 0$ to $t = T$ is $N$; for convenience we can write $\delta t = T/N = 1/365$. We now perform the following armchair experiment:

1. At the outset we enter two contracts, neither of which involves a cash outlay:

   - Enter a forward contract to sell one unit of a commodity at the forward price $F_{0T}$ in time $T$.
   - Enter a futures contract at price $\Phi_{0T}$ to buy $e^{-r(N-1)\delta t}$ units of the commodity at time $T$ (remember $\delta t = $ one day).

2. After the first day, close out the futures contract to yield cash $(\Phi_{1T} - \Phi_{0T})\,e^{-r(N-1)\delta t}$:

   - Place this sum on deposit with a bank until maturity in $N - 1$ days, when it will be worth $(\Phi_{1T} - \Phi_{0T})$. If $\Phi_{1T} < \Phi_{0T}$, we borrow from the bank rather than depositing with it.
   - Enter a new futures contract at price $\Phi_{1T}$ to buy $e^{-r(N-2)\delta t}$ units of the commodity at time $T$.

3. After the second day, close out the futures contract to yield cash $(\Phi_{2T} - \Phi_{1T})\,e^{-r(N-2)\delta t}$:

   - Place this sum on deposit with a bank until maturity in $N - 2$ days, when it will be worth $(\Phi_{2T} - \Phi_{1T})$. If $\Phi_{2T} < \Phi_{1T}$, we borrow from the bank rather than depositing with it.
   - Enter a new futures contract at price $\Phi_{1T}$ to buy $e^{-r(N-3)\delta t}$ units of the commodity at time $T$.

4. And so on. . . .

Suppose the futures and forward strategies are both cash settled. The amount of cash resulting from the futures strategy will be

$$(\Phi_{1T} - \Phi_{0T}) + (\Phi_{2T} - \Phi_{1T}) + (\Phi_{3T} - \Phi_{2T}) + \cdots + \left(\Phi_{NT} - \Phi_{(N-1)T}\right)$$
$$= \Phi_{NT} - \Phi_{0T} = S_T - \Phi_{0T}$$

since $\Phi_{NT}$ is just equal to the commodity price $S_T$ at time $T$.

If the forward contract is cash settled, we will merely receive the difference between the original forward price and the current spot price, i.e. a sum $F_{0T} - S_T$. Our total cash at the end of this exercise will therefore be $F_{0T} - \Phi_{0T}$. The whole strategy yields a profit which was determinable at the beginning of the exercise; we started with nothing and have manufactured $F_{0T} - \Phi_{0T}$. The only way this can be squared with the no-arbitrage principle is if the profit is zero, i.e. if

$$\Phi_{0T} = F_{0T} \qquad \left(= S_0\,e^{(r-q)T}\right) \tag{1.5}$$

(iii) *Effect of Interest Rates*: Many students gloss over the last results with a shrug: after all, "forwards and futures are kinda the same so the prices gonna be the same". This view, which is surprisingly widely held even in the trade, misses the important difference between the two instruments. In fact, the last pricing relationship is by no means obvious and only holds in certain circumstances.

We return to the futures armchair strategy of the last subsection. This depended on the fact that interest rates were constant, so that we knew exactly how many futures contracts to enter each day. But if interest rates change from day to day, the armchair experiment no longer works and the equality of the forwards and futures prices breaks down. The effect is particularly marked if the commodity price is correlated with the interest rate. Consider, for example, the case where the commodity is a foreign currency. It is well known that the foreign exchange rate can be strongly correlated with the interest rate. We may then find in our armchair arbitrage strategy that each day when $(\Phi_{(n+1)T} - \Phi_{nT})$ is large and positive, the interest rate at which we invest funds is high; but when $(\Phi_{1T} - \Phi_{0T})$ is large and negative, the interest rate is low. This would create a systematic bias and equation (1.5) would no longer hold.

# 2

## Option Basics

It is unlikely that a reader will pick up a book at this level without already having some idea of what options are about. However it is worth establishing a minimum base of knowledge and jargon, without which it is not worth proceeding further. All the material in this chapter was well known before modern option theory was developed.

### 2.1 PAYOFFS

(i) A call option on a commodity is a contract which gives the holder of the option the right to buy a unit of the commodity for a fixed price $X$ (the strike price). The key feature of this contract is that while it confirms the *right*, it does not impose an *obligation*. If it were a contract which both allowed and obligated the option holder to buy, we would have a forward contract rather than an option. The difference is that the option holder only exercises his right if it is profitable to do so. For example, suppose an option holder has a call option with $X = \$10$. If the price of the commodity in the market is $12, the option can be exercised for $10 and the underlying commodity sold for $12, to yield a profit of $2; on the other hand, if the market price is $8, the option will not be exercised.

The outcome of this type of option contract can be summarized mathematically as follows:

$$\text{Payoff} = \max\left[0, (S_T - X)\right] \qquad \text{or} \qquad (S_T - X)^+$$

which means that the payoff equals $S_T - X$, but only if this is positive; otherwise it is zero.

The payoff may equally be regarded as the *value* of the call option at exercise $C_{\text{payoff}}$. Much of this book is dedicated to the following problem: if we know $C_{\text{payoff}}$, how can we calculate the value of the option now?

A put option gives the holder the right (but not the obligation) to sell a unit of a commodity for a strike price $X$. This type of option is completely analogous to the call option. The payoff (option value at exercise) can be written

$$P_{\text{payoff}} = \max[0, (X - S_T)] \qquad \text{or} \qquad (X - S_T)^+$$

(ii) The payoff of a call, a put and a forward contract are shown in Figure 2.1. These are the so-called "hockey-stick" diagrams which show the value at exercise or payoff of the instruments as a function of the price of the underlying commodity.

(iii) An option is an asset with value greater than or equal to zero. If we buy an option we own an asset; but someone out there has a corresponding liability. He is the **option writer** and is said to be short an option in the jargon of Section 1.1. An option is only exercised if it yields

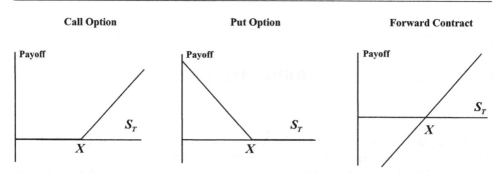

**Figure 2.1**   Payoff diagrams

a profit to the holder, i.e. if the option writer incurs a loss. The payoff diagrams of such short positions are shown in Figure 2.2 and are reflections of the long positions in the $x$-axis.

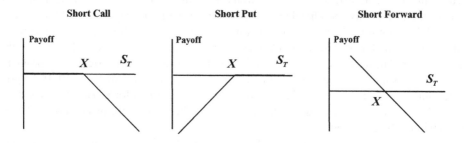

**Figure 2.2**   Payoff diagrams for short positions

(iv) Put and call options exist in two forms: European and American. A European option has a fixed maturity $T$ and can only be exercised on the maturity date. An American option is more flexible; it also has a fixed expiry date, but it can be exercised at any time beforehand. American options are the more usual in the traded options markets.

Looking back at the payoff diagrams of the previous paragraphs, these apply to European options on the maturity dates of the options. On the other hand, the payoff diagrams for American options could be achieved whenever the holder of the option decides to exercise. In general, European options are much easier to understand and value, since the holder has no decision to make until the maturity date; then he merely decides whether exercise yields a profit or not. With an American option, the holder must decide not only *whether* to exercise but also *when*.

## 2.2   OPTION PRICES BEFORE MATURITY

(i) *Put-Call Parity for European Options*: Consider the following two portfolios:

- A forward contract to buy one share of stock in time $T$ for a price $X$.
- Long one call option and short one put option each on one share of stock, both with strike price $X$ and maturity $T$.

The values of the portfolios now and at maturity are shown in Table 2.1. It is clear that whatever the maturity value of the underlying stock, the two portfolios have the same payoff

**Table 2.1**   Initial and terminal values of two portfolios

| | Value now | Value at $t = T$ $S_T < X$ | Value at $t = T$ $X < S_T$ |
|---|---|---|---|
| Forward purchase of stock at $X$ | $f_0(T) = S_0 - X\,e^{-rT}$ | $S_T - X$ | $S_T - X$ |
| Long call; short put | $C_0(X, T) - P_0(X, T)$ | $C_{\text{payoff}} - P_{\text{payoff}}$ $= -P_{\text{payoff}} = S_T - X$ | $C_{\text{payoff}} - P_{\text{payoff}}$ $= C_{\text{payoff}} = S_T - X$ |

value. Therefore, by the no-arbitrage proposition 1.2(ii), the two portfolios must have the same value now. This important relationship is known as put–call parity and may be expressed as

$$f_{0T} = C_0(X, T) - P_0(X, T)$$

or equivalently

$$P_0(X, T) + S_0 = C_0(X, T) + X\,e^{-rT} \tag{2.1}$$

If dividends are taken into account, the last equation may be written

$$P_0 + (S_0 - d\,e^{-r\tau}) = C_0 + X\,e^{-rT} \qquad \text{discrete dividend at } \tau$$
$$P_0 + S_0\,e^{-qT} = C_0 + X\,e^{-rT} \qquad \text{continuous dividend rate } q$$

(ii) Consider the value of a put option prior to expiry, if the stock price is much larger than the strike price. Clearly the value of this asset cannot be less than zero since it involves no obligation; on the other hand, its value must be very small if $S_0 \to \infty$, since the chance of its being exercised is small. The same reasoning applies to a call option for which $S_0 \to 0$. These can be summarized as

$$\lim_{S_0 \to \infty} P_0 \to 0; \qquad \lim_{S_0 \to 0} C_0 \to 0$$

Using both these results in the put–call parity relationship of equation (2.1) gives the following general result for European options without dividends:

$$\lim_{S_0 \to \infty} C_0 \to f_{0T} = S_0 - X\,e^{-rT}; \qquad \lim_{S_0 \to 0} P_0 \to -f_{0T} = X\,e^{-rT} - S_0 \tag{2.2}$$

These results are illustrated in Figure 2.3. The dotted lines and the $x$-axes provide the asymptotes for the graphs of $C_0$ and $P_0$ against $S_0$, for European options. The third graph illustrates

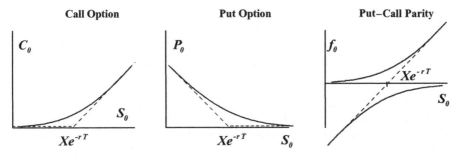

**Figure 2.3**   Option values before maturity

17

the put–call parity relationships with the dotted line representing the value of the forward contract.

One feature should be noted. The dotted lines in the first two graphs look very much like payoff diagrams; but they are not the same. Payoff hockey sticks have a fixed position while these asymptotes drift towards the right over time. They only correspond to the payoff diagrams at maturity.

## 2.3   AMERICAN OPTIONS

In the last section it was seen that the curve of the value of a European option always lies above the asymptotic lines. What of an American option which can be exercised at any time before maturity? Some very general and important conclusions can be reached using simple arbitrage arguments.

(i) First, we establish three almost trivial looking results:

- The prices of otherwise identical European and American options must obey the relationship

$$\text{Price}_{\text{American}} \geq \text{Price}_{\text{European}}$$

  This is because an American option has all the benefits of a European option *plus* the right of early exercise.
- An American option will always be worth at least its payoff value: if it were worth less, we would simply buy the options and exercise them. Conversely, an American option will not be exercised if its value is greater than the payoff, as this constitutes the purposeless destruction of value.
- The price of a stock falls on an ex-dividend date by the amount of the dividend which is paid. The holder of an option does not receive the benefit of a dividend, so the potential payoff of an American call drops by the value of the dividend as the ex-dividend date is crossed. If an American call is exercised, this will therefore always occur shortly *before* an ex-dividend date. By the same reasoning, an American put is always exercised shortly *after* an ex-dividend date.

(ii) *American Calls*: In Section 2.2(ii) we saw that the graph of a call option against price must always lie above the line representing the value of a forward, i.e. $C_{\text{European}} \geq f_{0T} = S_0 - X\,e^{-rT}$. The first point of the last subsection then implies that $C_{\text{American}} \geq f_{0T} = S_0 - Xe^{-rT}$ and if $r$ and $T$ are always positive (i.e. $e^{-rT} \leq 1$) then we must also have

$$C_{\text{American}} \geq S_0 - X$$

If this is true, then by the second point of the last subsection, it can never pay to exercise an American call before maturity; but if an American call is never exercised early, this feature has no value and the price of an American call must be the same as the price of a European call.

(iii) *Dividends*: The last conclusion is summed up by the first of the three graphs in Figure 2.4. However if dividends are introduced, the picture changes. Using the discrete dividend model, the line representing the value of the forward becomes $S_0 - d\,e^{-r\tau} - X\,e^{-rT}$; this line may lie to the right of the payoff line $S_0 - X$, in which case the curve for the American call would cut the payoff line at some point. It would then pay to exercise the American call, i.e. it may pay to exercise if $S_0 - d\,e^{-r\tau} - X\,e^{-rT} < S_0 - X$ or if

$$d\,e^{-r\tau} > X(1 - e^{-rT})$$

This is a condition that the present value of the dividend is greater than the interest earned on the cash that would be used to exercise the option. This clearly makes sense if an extreme example is considered: suppose a company is about to dividend away three quarters of its value; if $S > X$ it makes sense to exercise just before the dividend.

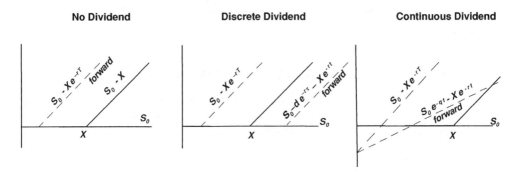

**Figure 2.4**  American calls with dividends

The last of the graphs in Figure 2.4 shows the same issue expressed in terms of the continuous dividend model. The value of the forward is now represented by $S_0\,e^{-qT} - X\,e^{-rT}$. The slope of this line is less than that of the payoff line, so the two lines cross at some point. This happens if $S_0\,e^{-qT} - X\,e^{-rT} < S_0 - X$ or

$$S_0(1 - e^{-qT}) > X(1 - e^{-rT})$$

Once again, the condition is that the dividends earned are greater than the interest on the exercise price. If it might pay to exercise a call before maturity, then clearly the value of the American option must be greater than its European equivalent.

(iv) **American Puts**: The divergence between the values of American and European options is much starker for puts than for calls. By the same reasoning as in Section 2.3(ii), we may conclude that the value of an American put must lie above and to the right of the diagonal line depicting the value of a short position in a forward contract, i.e.

$$P_{\text{American}} \geq -f_{0T} = X\,e^{-rT} - S_0$$

From Figure 2.5 for a non-dividend-paying put, it can be seen that the short-forward diagonal is to the left of the payoff diagonal. The curve for the put option, which is asymptotic to the short forward line, will cut across the payoff line. In the terms of the last couple of subsections, the payoff will be greater than the option price over a substantial region so that the precondition exists for exercise and the American put has a higher price than the European put.

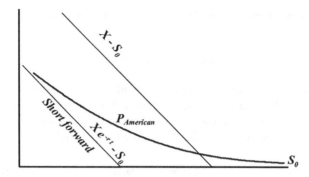

**Figure 2.5**   American put

## 2.4   PUT–CALL PARITY FOR AMERICAN OPTIONS

(i) It will be apparent to the reader that given the more complex behavior of American options, there is no slick formula for put–call parity as there is for European options. However for short-term options, fairly narrow bounds can be established on the difference between American put and call prices.

Consider American options with maturity $T$ which may be exercised at a time $\tau$. The value of the proceeds of each option depends not only on the price $S_T$ at maturity, but also on whether and when it is exercised. If the option is exercised early, the strike price is paid and the time value of this cash has to be taken into account. For example, an American call option might be exercised at any time $\tau$ between now and $T$. After exercise, the stock that we buy under the option will continue to vary stochastically, achieving value $S_T$ at time $T$; but the exercise price would have been paid earlier than final maturity, so that the time $T$ value of the strike price is $X e^{r(T-\tau)}$ where $0 \le \tau \le T$. The generalized payoff value of an American call option assessed at time $T$ may therefore be written as $S_T - X e^{r(T-\tau)}$; the corresponding value for an American put option is $X e^{r(T-\tau)} - S_T$.

Put–call parity relations for American options may be obtained using arbitrage arguments analogous to those for European options. In the analysis that follows, we make the decision ahead of time to hold any American option to maturity. Any short option position may be exercised against us at time $\tau$ $(0 \le \tau \le T)$ and we then maintain the resultant stock position until maturity.

(ii) Let us now compare the following two portfolios:

- A forward contract to sell one share of stock in time $T$ for a price $X$.
- Long one put option and short one call option each on one share of stock, both with strike price $X$ and maturity $T$. Our strategy in running this portfolio is only to exercise the put options on their expiry date. Our counterparty may choose to exercise the call against us before maturity, in which case we invest the cash and hang on to the short stock position until maturity.

Initial and terminal values of these two portfolios are given in Table 2.2. The notation $\{Q, 0\}$ signifies a quantity which could have value $Q$ or $0$, depending on whether our counterparty has exercised the call option or not. A few seconds reflection will convince the reader that the

**Table 2.2** Initial and terminal values of two portfolios

| | Value now | Value at $t = T$ <br> $S_T < X$ | Value at $t = T$ <br> $X < S_T$ |
|---|---|---|---|
| Forward sale <br> of stock at $X$ | $-f_0(X, T) = X\,e^{-rT} - S_0$ | $X - S_T$ | $X - S_T$ |
| Long put; <br> short call | $P_0(X, T) - C_0(X, T)$ | $P_{\text{payoff}} - C_{\text{payoff}}$ <br> $= (X - S_T) - \{S_T - X\,e^{r(T-\tau)}, 0\}$ | $P_{\text{payoff}} - C_{\text{payoff}}$ <br> $= 0 - \{S_T - X\,e^{r(T-\tau)}, 0\}$ |

value of the option portfolio is always equal to or less than the proceeds of the forward share sale, whatever the value of $S_T$. In terms of the present value of the two portfolios, this may be written

$$C_0(X, T) - P_0(X, T) \leq S_0 - X\,e^{-rT}$$

(iii) A very similar argument to that given in the last subsection allows us to establish a different bound. This time we compare the following two portfolios:

- A forward contract to buy one share of stock in time $T$ for a price $X\,e^{rT}$.
- Long one call option and short one put option each on one share of stock, both with strike price $X$ and maturity $T$. Our strategy in running this portfolio is only to exercise the call options on their expiry date. Our counterparty may choose to exercise the put early.

**Table 2.3** Initial and terminal values of two portfolios

| | Value now | Value at $t = T$ <br> $S_T < X$ | Value at $t = T$ <br> $X < S_T$ |
|---|---|---|---|
| Forward <br> purchase of <br> stock at $X\,e^{rT}$ | $f_0(X\,e^{rT}, T) = S_0 - X\,e^{r}$ | $S_T - X\,e^{rT}$ | $S_T - X\,e^{rT}$ |
| Long call; <br> short put | $C_0(X, T) - P_0(X, T)$ | $C_{\text{payoff}} - P_{\text{payoff}}$ <br> $= 0 - \{X\,e^{r(T-\tau)} - S_T, 0\}$ | $C_{\text{payoff}} - P_{\text{payoff}}$ <br> $= (S_T - X) - \{X\,e^{r(T-\tau)} - S_T, 0\}$ |

This time it is obvious that the terminal values of the option portfolio are always greater than or equal to the forward contract proceeds. The inequality may therefore be written

$$C_0(X, T) - P_0(X, T) \geq S_0 - X$$

The results of this section can be summarized to give a put–call parity relationship for American options as follows:

$$S_0 - X \leq C_{\text{American}} - P_{\text{American}} \leq S_0 - X\,e^{-rT} \tag{2.3}$$

This relationship can be generalized to include the effects of dividends by making the normal substitutions $S \to S\,e^{-qt}$ or $S \to S-\text{PV}[D]$.

21

## 2.5   COMBINATIONS OF OPTIONS

This is a book on option theory and many "how to" books are available giving very full descriptions of trading strategies using combinations of options. There is no point repeating all that stuff here. However, even the most theoretical reader needs a knowledge of how the more common combinations work, and why they are used; also, some useful intuitive pointers to the nature of time values are examined, before being more rigorously developed in later chapters. Most of the comments will be confined to combinations of European options.

(i) *Call Spread (bull spread, capped call)*: This is the simplest modification of the call option. The payoff is similar to that of a call option except that it only increases to a certain level and then stops. It is used because option writers are often unwilling to accept the unlimited liability incurred in writing straight calls. The payoff diagram is shown in the first graph of Figure 2.6.

It is important to understand that a European call spread (and indeed any of the combinations described below) can be created by combining simple options. The second graph of Figure 2.6 shows how a call spread is merely a combination of a long call (strike $X_1$) with a short call (strike $X_2$). The third graph is the payoff diagram of a short call spread; it is just the mirror image in the $x$-axis of the long call spread.

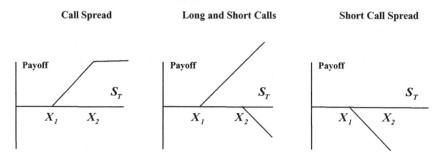

**Figure 2.6**   Call spreads

(ii) *Put Spread (bear spread, capped put)*: This is completely analogous to the call spread just described. The corresponding diagrams are displayed in Figure 2.7.

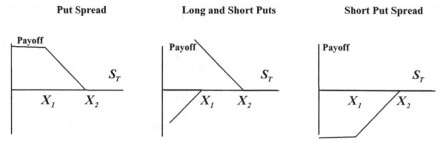

**Figure 2.7**   Put spreads

(iii) In glancing over the last two sets of graphs, the reader will notice that the short call spread and the put spread are very similar in form; so are the call spread and short put spread. How are they related?

All the payoff diagrams used so far have been graphs plotting the value of the option position at maturity against the price of the underlying stock or commodity. But the holder of an option would have had to pay a premium for this position (the price of the option). To get a "total profits" diagram, we need to subtract the future value (at maturity) of the option premium from the payoff value, i.e. the previous payoff diagrams have to be shifted down through the $x$-axis by the future value of the premium. Similarly, short positions would be shifted up through the $x$-axis.

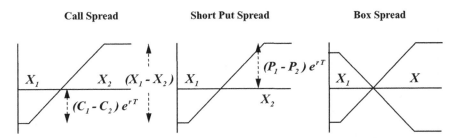

**Figure 2.8**  Equivalent spreads

The effects of including the initial premium on the final profits diagram of a call spread and a short put spread are shown in the first two graphs of Figure 2.8. The notation $C_1, C_2, P_1, P_2$ is used for the prices of call and put options with strikes $X_1, X_2$.

The diagonal put and call payoffs are $45°$ lines, so that the distance from base to cap must be $X_2 - X_1$ as shown. Recall the put–call parity relationship for European options $C + X e^{-rT} = P + S$, from which

$$(C_1 - C_2) e^{rt} + (P_2 - P_1) e^{rt} = X_2 - X_1$$

It follows immediately that these two final profit diagrams are identical. All of these payoffs could be generated using just puts or just calls, and the costs would be the same. This theme is developed further below. Although it is possible to create spreads with American options, remember that the put–call parity *equality* no longer holds; American puts and calls are therefore not interchangeable as are their European counterparts.

(iv) **Box Spread:** The third graph of Figure 2.8 shows an interesting application of the concepts just discussed. By definition, a put spread is perfectly hedged by a *short* put spread; but we have just seen that a European short put spread is identical to a European call spread. Thus a put spread is exactly hedged by a call spread. The combination of the two is called a box spread.

Suppose we buy a call spread for $C_1 - C_2$ and a put spread for $P_1 - P_2$; the put–call parity equality of the last paragraph shows that this will cost $(X_1 - X_2) e^{-rT}$.

Since a box spread is completely hedged, this structure will yield precisely $X_1 - X_2$ at maturity. In other words, a combination of puts and calls with individually stochastic prices yields precisely the interest rate.

There are two purposes for which this structure is used. First, if one (or more) of the four options, bought in the market to make the box spread, is mispriced, the yields on the cash investment may be considerably more than the interest rate. This is quite a neat way of squeezing the value out of mispriced options. Second, gains on options sometimes receive different tax treatment from interest income, so that this technique has been used for converting between capital gains and normal income.

(v) *Straddle*: This is another popular combination of options with the payoff shown in the first graphs of Figure 2.9 . This consists of a put and a call with the same strike price. People invest in this instrument when they think the price of the underlying stock or commodity will move sharply, but they are not sure in which direction. Clearly, this is tantamount to betting on the future volatility of the stock.

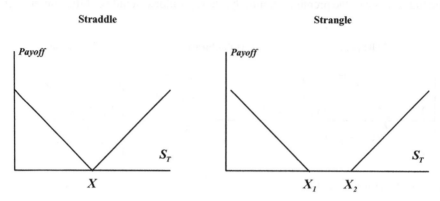

**Figure 2.9**   Straddle and strangle

*Strangle*: A slightly modified version of the straddle is shown in the second graph of Figure 2.9. A straddle is quite an expensive instrument, but by separating the strike prices of the put and the call, the cost can be reduced.

(vi) *Collar*: One of the most important uses of an option is as a hedge against movement in the underlying price. Typically, the owner of a commodity can buy an at-the-money put option; for each $1 drop in the commodity price, there is a $1 gain in the payoff of the put. The put option acts as an insurance policy on the price of the commodity.

   If an insurance premium is too expensive, it can be reduced by introducing an "excess" or "deductible". For example, the owner of the commodity bears the first $5 of loss and the insurance covers any further loss. This would be achieved by buying a put whose strike price is $5 below the current market price.

   Another way in which the insurance cost can be decreased is by means of a collar. In addition to buying a put, the commodity holder sells a call with strike somewhere above the current commodity price. The first graph of Figure 2.10 shows the payoff for a collar. Below $X_1$, the

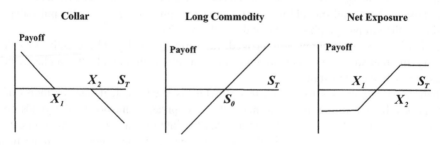

**Figure 2.10**   Collars

24

commodity holder receives $1 from the put for each drop of $1 in the price. Above $X_2$, he pays away $1 under the call option for each $1 rise in the price. If the option positions are combined with his position in the underlying commodity (second graph), the result is his net exposure to the commodity (third graph). Between $X_1$ and $X_2$ he is exposed to movements in the price; outside these limits he is completely hedged. A particularly popular variety is the *zero-cost collar* where the strike prices are arranged so that the receipt from the call exactly equals the cost of the put.

(vii) **Butterfly:** As with simple put and call options, the writer of a straddle accepts unlimited liability. This can be avoided by using a butterfly, which is just a put spread plus a call spread with the upper strike of the first equal to the lower strike of the second. Like the straddle, this instrument is basically a volatility play, but the upside potential for profit has been capped. The payoff diagram is given in the first graph of Figure 2.11.

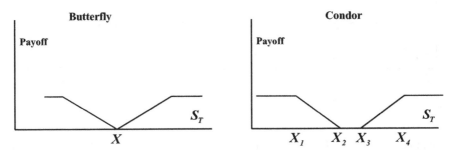

**Figure 2.11**   Butterfly and condor

*Condor*: This instrument is very similar to the butterfly, but has different strike prices for the put spread and call spread.

(viii) In Section 2.5(iii) it was shown how a European spread could be constructed either from puts or from calls; this is equally true of the butterfly and condor. One is occasionally confronted with a very complicated payoff diagram which needs to be resolved into its underlying puts and calls. A condor provides a good example of how to proceed.

- Starting from the left end, move towards the right along the payoff diagram for the condor.
- The first direction change is at $X_1$, where the line bends down 45°. This is achieved with a short call $(-C_1)$.
- Moving on to $X_2$, the line bends up 45°: long call $(-C_2)$.
- At $X_3$, the line bends up 45°: long call $(+C_3)$.
- At $X_4$, the line bends down 45°: short call $(-C_4)$.

The condor could therefore be constructed as $-C_1 + C_2 + C_3 - C_4$.

On the other hand, moving from the right to the left of the diagram, this sort of reasoning would yield a combination $-P_4 + P_3 + P_2 - P_1$. As a further variation, we could conceptually break the condor in two, constructing one half out of puts and the other half out of calls.

These complex payoffs are therefore ambiguous, in that they can be constructed in several different ways. But for European structures, put–call parity always assures that the cost is the same, whatever elements are used to build them.

## 2.6   COMBINATIONS BEFORE MATURITY

(i) The value of a combination of options before maturity is just equal to the sum of the values of the constituent simple options. The evolution of the value of a butterfly at times $T_1$ and $T_2$ before and at maturity is shown in Figure 2.12. Long before maturity, the curve of $f$ is featureless and only loosely acknowledges the direction of the asymptotic lines (see Section 2.3). As time passes, this curve begins to cling more and more tightly to the asymptotes, which are themselves moving towards the right. Finally, at maturity, the curve becomes the payoff diagram.

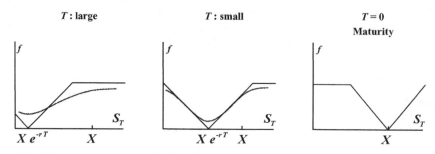

**Figure 2.12**   Derivative value before maturity

(ii) The curvature of $f$ is not uniform. In one region it is concave upwards (in the center); on either side it is convex downwards. Curvature is measured by a quantity called gamma; in the center, gamma is positive; on either side, it is negative.

   The direction of the curvature remains fairly much the same as time elapses. However the sharpness of the curvature changes over time, becoming acute at the corners of the payoff diagram at maturity. Clearly, the size of gamma is related to how sharply the asymptotes change direction. In the center they turn through $90°$ and gamma has the highest (positive) value. On either side, the asymptotes turn through $45°$ and gamma has high (negative) values; at the edges they do not turn and gamma is small.

(iii) The rate at which the value of $f$ changes over time is known as theta. At the center of the butterfly, the curve of $f$ is moving downwards over time so that theta is negative; at the two edges the value is moving up so that theta is positive.

   Some very significant observations can be made purely from the geometry of the graphs.

- At the center: gamma is at its largest and positive. Theta is negative and larger than anywhere else in the diagram. This part of the curve has to go all the way down to reach the bottom of the "V" by maturity.
- At the middle of the sloping sides: gamma is at its smallest since this is where it changes from positive to negative. Theta is small since the curve for $f$ does not have to move far to reach the asymptotes by maturity.
- At the top corners: gamma is negative and fairly large, although not as large as at the center. Theta is positive and fairly large again since the curve has quite a long way to travel to get into the corners by maturity.
- At the extreme edges: gamma is negative but small. Theta is positive and small.

The inevitable conclusion is that gamma and theta are inversely related. If the reader tests this hypothesis with any payoff, he will always come to the same conclusion. The relationship between gamma and theta will be rigorously analyzed later in the course; but it is comforting to know that one of the most important conclusions of option theory can be confirmed by a casual glance at the payoff diagrams.

# 3

# Stock Price Distribution

## 3.1 STOCK PRICE MOVEMENTS

(i) Consider the evolution of a stock price: the prices observed at successive moments in time $\delta t$ apart are: $S_0, S_1, \ldots, S_N$. For simplicity, it is assumed that no dividend is paid in this period. The "price relative" in period $n$ is defined as the ratio $R_n = S_n/S_{n-1}$. This quantity is a random variable and we make the following apparently innocuous but far-reaching assumption: *the price relatives are independently and identically distributed*. If the price relatives are independently distributed, the next move does not depend on what happened at the last move. This is a statement of the so-called weak form market efficiency hypothesis, which maintains that the entire history of a stock is summed up in its present price; future movements depend only on new information and on changes in sentiment or the environment. People who believe in charts or concepts such as momentum for predicting stock prices clearly do not believe in this hypothesis; in consequence, they should not believe in the results of modern option theory.

If price relatives are identically distributed, then their expected means and variances are constant, i.e.

$$E\left[\frac{S_n}{S_{n-1}}\right] = E\left[\frac{S_{n+1}}{S_n}\right]; \qquad \text{var}\left[\frac{S_n}{S_{n-1}}\right] = \text{var}\left[\frac{S_{n+1}}{S_n}\right]$$

The first equation says that the expected growth of the stock remains constant. It will be seen below that the second equation is a statement that the volatility of the stock remains constant.

(ii) Consider the following simple identity:

$$\frac{S_N}{S_0} \equiv \frac{S_1}{S_0}\frac{S_2}{S_1} \cdots \frac{S_N}{S_{N-1}}$$
$$= R_1 R_2 \cdots R_N$$

Taking the logarithm of each side gives

$$x_N = r_1 + r_2 + \cdots + r_N \qquad \text{where} \qquad x_N = \ln\frac{S_N}{S_0}; \qquad r_n = \ln R_n = \ln\frac{S_n}{S_{n-1}} \qquad (3.1)$$

Some very profound conclusions emerge from this trivial-looking equation: if the price relatives $R_n$ are identically distributed and independent, then so are their logarithms, $r_n$. They can be treated as independent random variables, drawn from the same infinite population. It follows that

$$E[x_N] = \sum_{n=1}^{N} E[r_n] = N\,E[r_n] = Nm_{\delta T}$$

$$\text{var}[x_N] = \sum_{n=1}^{N} \text{var}[r_n] = N\,\text{var}[r_n] = N\sigma_{\delta T}^2$$

where $m_{\delta T}$ and $\sigma_{\delta T}^2$ are the mean and variance of the logarithm of the price relatives.

Suppose that two people perform this analysis on the same stock price evolution, but one person considers $N$ successive time increments of length $\delta T$ while the other considers $N/2$ time increments of length $2\delta T$. Slicing up the stock price path is completely arbitrary, but the expectation $E[x_T]$ must be the same in both cases. Explicitly writing out each example:

$$E[x_T] = Nm_{\delta T} \qquad \text{and} \qquad E[x_T] = \frac{N}{2}m_{2\delta T}$$

From which it follows that $m_{2\delta T} = 2m_{\delta T}$, or in other words $m_{\delta T}$ is proportional to the time interval $\delta T$. We may therefore write $m_{\delta T} = m\delta T$; identical reasoning gives $\sigma_{\delta T}^2 = \sigma^2\delta T$. The mean and variance of $x_T$ may now be written

$$
\begin{aligned}
E[x_T] &= mN\delta T = mT \\
\text{var}[x_T] &= \sigma^2 N\delta T = \sigma^2 T
\end{aligned}
\tag{3.2}
$$

Both mean and variance are equal to a constant multiplied by $T$.

(iii) **Central Limit Theorem**: Before going on to derive the key conclusion of this section, we need to make a detour back to the reader's earliest encounters with statistics: suppose we have a random sample $y_1, \ldots, y_N$ taken from an infinite population with mean $m$ and variance $\sigma^2$. The mean of this sample is $\bar{y}_N = (1/N)\sum_{i=1}^{n} y_i$. This sample mean is of course itself a random variable, with expectation $m$ and variance $\sigma^2/N$. Furthermore, the central limit theorem states that whatever the distribution of $y_i$ might be, the distribution of $\bar{y}_N$ tends to a normal distribution as $N \to \infty$.

These results may be summarized as

$$\lim_{N\to\infty} \bar{y}_N \sim N(m, \sigma^2/N) \qquad \text{or} \qquad \lim_{N\to\infty} N\bar{y}_N = \lim_{N\to\infty} (y_1 + \cdots + y_N) \sim N(mN, \sigma^2 N)$$

the sign $\sim$ means "is distributed as" while $N(m, v^2)$ indicates the normal distribution with mean $m$ and variance $v^2$. Applying this last result to equation (3.1) gives the very general result

$$x_T = \lim_{N\to\infty;\, \delta T\to 0} (r_1 + \cdots + r_N) \sim N\left(m_{\delta T}N, \sigma_{\delta T}^2 N\right) = N(m\delta T N, \sigma^2\delta T N) = N(mT, \sigma^2 T)$$

We can reassure ourselves that this result holds simply by notionally slicing the time period into an arbitrarily large number of arbitrarily small segments so that $N \to \infty$ and the central limit theorem holds true.

Finally, an important piece of jargon: if a random variable takes its various values $r_1, r_2, \ldots, r_N$ at successive points in time, it is referred to as a **stochastic variable**.

## 3.2    PROPERTIES OF STOCK PRICE DISTRIBUTION

In the last section we defined $x_T = \ln S_T/S_0$ and showed that $x_T$ is *normally* distributed with mean $mT$ and variance $\sigma^2 T$. $S_T$ is then said to be **lognormally** distributed. Some of the more useful properties of the normal and lognormal distributions are explained in Appendix A.1.

(i) In terms of $x_t$, the stock price is given by $S_t = S_0\, e^{x_t}$ and the explicit probability distribution function for $x_t$ is

$$n(x_t) = \frac{1}{\sigma\sqrt{2\pi t}} \exp\left\{ -\frac{1}{2}\left(\frac{x_t - mt}{\sigma\sqrt{t}}\right)^2 \right\}$$

The various moments for the distribution of $S_t$ may be written

$$E\left[\left(\frac{S_t}{S_0}\right)^\lambda\right] = E[e^{\lambda x_t}] = \int_{-\infty}^{+\infty} e^{\lambda x_t} \, n(x_t) \, dx_t$$

$$= e^{\lambda mt + \frac{1}{2}\lambda^2 \sigma^2 t} \tag{3.3}$$

This result is proved in Appendix A.1(v), item (D).

(ii) **Mean and Variance of $S_T$**: The rate of return $\mu$ of a non-dividend-paying stock over a time interval $T$ is defined by $E\langle S_T \rangle = S_0 \, e^{\mu T}$. Using equation (3.3) with $\lambda = 1$ gives

$$E[S_T] = S_0 \, e^{\mu T} = S_0 \, e^{(m + \frac{1}{2}\sigma^2)T} \tag{3.4}$$

A relationship which simply falls out of the last equation and which is used repeatedly throughout this book is

$$\mu = m + \tfrac{1}{2}\sigma^2 \tag{3.5}$$

Again using equation (3.3), this time with $\lambda = 2$, gives

$$\mathrm{var}\left[\frac{S_T}{S_0}\right] = E\left[\frac{S_T}{S_0}\right]^2 - E^2\left[\frac{S_T}{S_0}\right]$$

$$= e^{2\mu T}\left(e^{\sigma^2 T} - 1\right) \tag{3.6}$$

(iii) **Variance and Volatility**: $x_T$ is a stochastic variable with mean $mT$ and variance $\sigma^2 T$. $T$ is measured in units of a year and $\sigma$ is referred to as the (annual) volatility of the stock. The reader would be quite right to comment that $\sigma$ should be called the volatility of the *logarithm* of the stock price; but the two are closely related and for most practical purposes, the same. To see this, consider a small time interval $\delta T$ (maybe a day or a week) and write $S_{\delta T} - S_0 = \delta S$. Then

$$\mathrm{var}\left[\ln\frac{S_{\delta T}}{S_0}\right] = \mathrm{var}\left[\ln\left(1 + \frac{\delta S}{S_0}\right)\right] \approx \mathrm{var}\left[\frac{\delta S}{S_0}\right] = \mathrm{var}\left[1 + \frac{\delta S}{S_0}\right] = \mathrm{var}\left[\frac{S_{\delta T}}{S_0}\right]$$

where the approximation uses the following standard Taylor expansion for small $a$: $\ln(1 + a) = a - \frac{1}{2}a^2 + \frac{1}{3}a^3 - \cdots$ and we use $\mathrm{var}[\text{constant} + x] = \mathrm{var}\langle x \rangle$. The conclusion is that for small time steps, the variance of $S_T/S_0$ and of $\ln(S_T/S_0)$ are the same.

In practical terms this means that if we estimate volatility from historical stock price data, measuring either daily or weekly price movements, then we get more or less the same result by using either the stock prices themselves or their logarithms. However, these two measures are likely to produce appreciably different results if we use quarterly data.

(iv) In Section 3.1 it was established that $x_t = \ln(S_t/S_0) \sim N(mT, \sigma^2 T)$ where $m = \mu - \frac{1}{2}\sigma^2$. We define a standard normal variate $z_t$ by $z_t = (x_t - mt)/\sigma\sqrt{t}$ so that $z_t$ is distributed as $z_t \sim N(0, 1)$. This can be inverted as $x_t = mt + \sigma\sqrt{t}z_t$, or equivalently

$$S_t = S_0 \, e^{mt + \sigma\sqrt{t}z_t} = S_0 \, e^{mt + \sigma W_t} \tag{3.7}$$

(v) It is worth pondering this last equation for a moment to get an appreciation of what is really meant. The quantity $\sqrt{t}z_t$ is usually written $W_t$ and the study of its mathematical properties has filled many textbooks; but for the moment, it is enough just to understand the big picture. $W_t$ is said to describe a one-dimensional Brownian motion. Brown was the nineteenth century botanist who, studying pollen grains suspended in a liquid, was surprised to observe their erratic movements, caused (as was later discovered) by the buffeting they received from the impact of individual molecules. Most people find it helpful to think of $W_t$ in terms of the physical movement of a particle, rather than the more abstract movement of the logarithm of a stock price. Strictly speaking, we should think of a particle moving backwards and forwards along a one-dimensional line.

Suppose that at time $t = 0$ the particle starts at position $W_0 = 0$. The movement is random so we do not know where the particle will be after time $T$. We merely know the probability distribution of $W_t$. Let us look at a couple of examples.

$z_t$ is a standard normal variate, i.e. with mean 0 and variance 1. From standard tables we know that

$$\Pr[-2 < z_T < +2] \approx 95\%$$

- **Example 1: $T = 2$ years**

$$\Pr\left[-2 < \frac{W_{2\,\text{years}}}{\sqrt{2}} < +2\right] = 95\%$$

$$\Pr[-2.8 < W_{2\,\text{years}} < +2.8] = 95\%$$

- **Example 2: $T = 1$ week**

$$\Pr\left[-2 < \frac{W_{1\,\text{week}}}{\sqrt{1/52}} < +2\right] = 95\%$$

$$\Pr[-0.28 < W_{1\,\text{week}} < +0.28] = 95\%$$

The quantity $W_t$ could take more or less any value. We know that it is proportional to $\sqrt{t}$, but the value could be positive or negative, large or small. Remember that $z_t$ is a standard normal variate: $z_{1000}$ and $z_{0.0001}$ are merely two readings from the same distribution and there is nothing to suggest that one should be larger or smaller than the other.

(vi) **Continuous Dividends**: In Section 1.1 it was seen that a continuous dividend could be accounted for by making the substitution $S_0 \to S_0\,e^{-qt}$ for the stock price. The distribution for $S_t$ at the beginning of this section can therefore be described by

$$\ln \frac{S_t}{S_0} \to \ln \frac{S_t}{S_0\,e^{-qt}} = \ln \frac{S_t}{S_0} + qt \sim N(mt, \sigma^2 t)$$

But if $\ln(S_t/S_0) + qt$ is normally distributed with mean $mt$ and variance $\sigma^2 t$, the term $qt$ merely shifts the mean of the distribution so that

$$\ln(S_t/S_0) \sim N((m - q)t, \sigma^2 t)$$

The effect of a continuous dividend rate $q$ can therefore be taken into account simply by making the substitutions $m \to m - q$ and $\mu \to \mu - q$.

## 3.3   INFINITESIMAL PRICE MOVEMENTS

(i) Let us return to equation (3.7) for the stock price evolution, and consider only small time intervals $\delta t$. We may write that equation as

$$S_t + \delta S_t = S_t \, e^{m\delta t + \sigma \delta W_t} \qquad \text{where} \qquad \delta W_t = \sqrt{\delta t} z_{\delta t}$$

We are dealing with small time periods and small price changes so that we may use the standard expansion $e^a = 1 + a + \frac{1}{2!}a^2 + \cdots$ in the last equation, giving

$$S_t + \delta S_t = S_t \left\{ 1 + (m\delta t + \sigma \delta W_t) + \tfrac{1}{2}(m\delta t + \sigma \delta W_t)^2 + \cdots \right\}$$

Normally, one might expect to drop the squared and higher terms in this equation; but recall the definition $\delta W_t = \sqrt{\delta t} z_{\delta t}$. The term $z_{\delta t}$ is a standard normal variate, taking the values $-1$ to $+1$ for about 67% of the time; values $-2$ to $+2$ for about 95% of the time; values $-3$ to $+3$ for about 99.5% of the time, etc. $\delta W_t$ is therefore not of the same order as $\delta t$ (written O[$\delta t$]); it is O[$\sqrt{\delta t}$]. To be consistent in the last equation then, we need to retain terms up to $\delta t$ together with terms up to $\delta W_t^2$. This gives us

$$\frac{\delta S_t}{S_t} = m\delta t + \sigma \delta W_t + \tfrac{1}{2}\sigma^2 \delta W_t^2$$

(ii) An appreciation of the significance of the last term in this equation is obtained by analyzing the following expectations and variances of powers of $\delta W_t$. First, recall from Appendix A.1(ii) that the moment generating function for a standard normal distribution is $M[\Theta] = e^{\Theta^2/2}$; the various moments are given by $\mu_\lambda = E\langle z^\lambda \rangle = \frac{\partial^\lambda M[\Theta]}{\partial \Theta^\lambda}]_{\Theta=0}$. Using this procedure we get

$$E[\delta W_t] = \sqrt{\delta t} \, E[z_{\delta t}] = 0$$
$$\mathrm{var}[\delta W_t] = E[\delta W_t^2] = \delta t \, E[z_{\delta t}^2] = \delta t$$
$$\mathrm{var}[\delta W_t^2] = E[\delta W_t^4] - E^2[\delta W_t^2] = \delta t^2 \, E[z_{\delta t}^4] - \delta t^2 = 2\delta t^2$$

The quantity $\delta W_t^2$ has expected value $\delta t$ and variance proportional to $\delta t^2$. Thus as $\delta t \to 0$ the variance of $\delta W_t^2$ approaches zero much faster than $\delta t$ itself. But as the variance of $\delta W_t^2$ approaches zero, $\delta W_t^2$ approaches its expected value with greater and greater certainty, i.e. it ceases to behave like a random variable at all. This permits us to make the substitution

$$\lim_{\delta t \to 0} \delta W_t^2 \to E[\delta W_t^2] = \delta t$$

(iii) Using equation (3.5), the process for the evolution of the stock price over a very small time interval can be written

$$\frac{\delta S_t}{S_t} = m\delta t + \sigma \delta W_t + \tfrac{1}{2}\sigma^2 \delta t = \mu \delta t + \sigma \delta W_t \qquad (3.8)$$

With a continuous proportional dividend $q$ this becomes

$$\frac{\delta S_t}{S_t} = (\mu - q)\delta t + \sigma \delta W_t \qquad (3.9)$$

This representation has a great deal of appeal. The model has the stock price growing at a constant rate $\mu$, with random fluctuations superimposed. These fluctuations are proportional to the standard deviation of the stock price and are dependent on a standard normal random variable. This type of process is known as a Wiener process.

For future reference, we quote an often used result obtained by squaring the last result and dropping higher terms in $\delta t$:

$$\left(\frac{\delta S_t}{S_t}\right)^2 = (\mu \delta t + \sigma \delta W_t)^2 \approx \sigma^2 \delta W_t^2 \rightarrow \sigma^2 \delta t \tag{3.10}$$

## 3.4   ITO'S LEMMA

In the last section it was seen that an infinitesimal stock price movement $\delta S_t$ in an infinitesimal time interval $\delta t$ could be described by the Wiener process $\delta S_t = S_t(\mu - q)\delta t + S_t \sigma \delta W_t$. A more generalized Wiener process (also known as an Ito process) can be written

$$\delta S_t = a_{S_t,t} \delta t + b_{S_t,t} \delta W_t$$

where $a_{S_t,t}$ and $b_{S_t,t}$ are now functions of both $S_t$ and $t$. Consider any function $f_{S_t,t}$ of $S_t$ and $t$, which is reasonably well behaved (i.e. adequately differentiable with respect to $S_t$ and $t$). Taylor's theorem states that

$$\delta f_t = \frac{\partial f_t}{\partial S_t} \delta S_t + \frac{\partial f_t}{\partial t} \delta t + \frac{1}{2}\left\{ \frac{\partial^2 f_t}{\partial S_t^2} \delta S_t^2 + \frac{\partial^2 f_t}{\partial S_t \partial t} \delta S_t \delta t + \frac{\partial^2 f_t}{\partial t^2} \delta t^2 \right\} + \cdots$$

where the subscript notation has been lightened a little for the sake of legibility. Substitute for $S_t$ from the generalized Wiener process and retain only terms of order $\delta t$ or lower, remembering that $\delta W_t \sim O[\sqrt{\delta t}]$:

$$\delta f_t = \frac{\partial f_t}{\partial S_t} \delta S_t + \frac{\partial f_t}{\partial t} \delta t + \frac{1}{2}\frac{\partial^2 f_t}{\partial S_t^2} b_t^2 \delta W_t^2$$

Put $\delta W_t^2 \rightarrow \delta t$ as explained in Section 3.3, to give

$$\delta f_t = \left( \frac{\partial f_t}{\partial t} + a_t \frac{\partial f_t}{\partial S_t} + \frac{1}{2}b_t^2 \frac{\partial^2 f_t}{\partial S_t^2} \right) \delta t + b_t \frac{\partial f_t}{\partial S_t} \delta W_t \tag{3.11}$$

This result is known as Ito's lemma and is one of the cornerstones of option theory. It basically says that if $f_t$ is any well-behaved function of an Ito process and of time, then $f_t$ itself follows an Ito process. The function of particular interest in this book is the price of a derivative.

In the case of the simple Wiener process of equation (3.9), Ito's lemma becomes

$$\delta f_t = \left( \frac{\partial f_t}{\partial t} + (\mu - q)S_t \frac{\partial f_t}{\partial S_t} + \frac{1}{2}\sigma^2 S_t^2 \frac{\partial^2 f_t}{\partial S_t^2} \right) \delta t + \sigma S_t \frac{\partial f_t}{\partial S_t} \delta W_t \tag{3.12}$$

# 4

# Principles of Option Pricing

This is the most important chapter in the book and needs to be mastered if the reader is to get a firm grasp of option theory. We start with a simple, stylized example. These examples are often irritating to new students of derivatives who regard them as toy models with little relevance to real-life financial problems. However, the reader is strongly advised not to dismiss them. Firstly, they allow concepts such as risk neutrality or pseudo-probabilities to be introduced in a relatively painless way; introducing such concepts for the first time in a more generalized or continuous context is definitely harder on the reader – trust me. Secondly, as will be demonstrated in a few chapters, simple models which allow only two outcomes can easily be generalized into powerful computational tools which accurately represent real financial markets.

## 4.1 SIMPLE EXAMPLE

(i) Suppose a company is awaiting a crucially important yes/no decision from a government regulator, to be announced in one month. The outcome will radically alter the company's future in a way which is predictable, once we know which way the decision goes. If the decision is "yes", the stock price will rise to $S_{high}$ but for a "no" the price will fall to $S_{low}$. Obviously, $S_{high}$ and $S_{low}$ must be above and below the present stock price $S_0$ (if they were both above, $S_0$ would rise immediately). Let us further assume that everyone knows that given the political climate, the yes probability is 70% and the no probability 30%.

We are equity derivatives investors and are holding an unquoted option on this company's stock which matures immediately after the announcement. The payoff of the option is $f_{1\,month}$, which takes values $f_{high}$ or $f_{low}$ depending on whether the stock price becomes $f_{high}$ or $S_{low}$. How would we go about working out today's value for this option?

(ii) Considering first the stock price itself, the expected value in one month and the expected growth rate over that month $\mu$ are defined by

$$E[S_{1\,month}] = 0.7 S_{high} + 0.3 S_{low} = (1 + \mu) S_0 \tag{4.1}$$

At the risk of emphasizing the obvious, let us be clear on this point: $\mu$ is definitely not the rate by which $S_0$ will grow, since the final stock price will be either $S_{high}$ or $S_{low}$. It is the mathematical expectation of the stock price growth. In this example we can work out $\mu$ from our knowledge of the probabilities of yes and no; alternatively, if we knew $\mu$ at the beginning, we could work out the probabilities.

The expected value for $f_{1\,month}$ is similarly given by

$$E[f_{1\,month}] = 0.7 f_{high} + 0.3 f_{low}$$

which we can evaluate since we know the payoff values. It should not be too hard to calculate the present value, but how? The simplest way might be just to discount back by the interest rate, but remember that this is only valid for finding the present value of some certain future amount; for a risky asset, we must discount back by the rate of return (growth rate) of the particular asset. This is clear from the slightly rewritten equation (4.1):

$$S_0 = \frac{E[S_{1\,month}]}{(1 + \mu)}$$

Maybe the answer is to use $(1 + \mu)$ as the discount factor; but $\mu$ is the growth rate of the underlying equity stock, not the option. There is nothing to suggest that the expected growth rate of the stock $\mu$ should equal the expected growth rate of the option $\lambda$. Nor is there any simple general way of deriving $\lambda$ from $\mu$. This was the point at which option theory remained stuck for many years. At this point, we enter the world of modern option theory.

(iii) Instead of trying to value the option, let us switch our attention to another problem. We could lose a lot of money on the derivative in one month if the stock price moves against us. Is it possible to hedge the option against all risk of loss?

Suppose there were some quantity of stock $\Delta$ that we can short, such that the value of the option plus the short stock position is the same in one month, whether the stock price goes up or down. Today's value of this little portfolio consisting of option plus short stock position is written $f_0 - S_0\Delta$. Note the convention whereby $f_0$ is the price of an option on one share of stock, and $\Delta$ is some negative or positive number which will probably not be an integer. Obviously you cannot buy or short fractions of an equity stock, but the arguments would be exactly the same if we multiplied everything by some number large enough that we only consider integral amounts of stock and derivatives; it is simply easier to accept the convention of fractional $\Delta$.

If this little portfolio is to achieve its stated aim of having the same value in one month whichever outcome occurs, we must have

$$f_{high} - S_{high}\Delta = f_{low} - S_{low}\Delta$$

or rearranging

$$\Delta = \frac{f_{high} - f_{low}}{S_{high} - S_{low}}$$

We have not yet managed to calculate a value for $f_0$, but we *have* devised a method of hedging the position. Note that this makes no reference to $\lambda$ or $\mu$, the growth rates of the derivative and the underlying stock.

(iv) Saying that the derivative is hedged is precisely the same as saying that the value of the portfolio of derivative plus stock is certain and predictable. Its value today is $f_0 - S_0\Delta$ and its value in one month is $f_{1\,month} - S_{1\,month}\Delta$, which is the same whether the stock goes up or down. In Section 1.2 we saw that the return on a perfectly hedged portfolio must be the risk-free rate

$$\frac{f_{1\,month} - S_{1\,month}\Delta}{f_0 - S_0\Delta} = 1 + r$$

or

$$(f_{1\,month} - f_0) + r S_0 \Delta - (S_{1\,month} - S_0)\Delta = r f_0 \qquad (4.2)$$

This is expressed in terms of the general quantities $f_{1\,month}$ and $S_{1\,month}$; more specifically, we can write

$$f_{high} - S_{high}\Delta = f_{low} - S_{low}\Delta = (1 + r)(f_0 - S_0\Delta)$$

A little algebra yields

$$(1 + r)f_0 = p f_{high} + (1 - p) f_{low} \qquad (4.3)$$

where

$$p = \frac{(1 + r)S_0 - S_{low}}{S_{high} - S_{low}}$$

or alternatively

$$(1 + r)S_0 = p S_{high} + (1 - p) S_{low} \qquad (4.4)$$

(v) Let us take a moment to contemplate the last couple of equations. The parameter $p$ is defined by equation (4.4). This is just a number which is made up of a combination of the observable quantities $S_0$, $S_{high}$, $S_{low}$ and $r$. As was pointed out previously, $S_{high}$ and $S_{low}$ lie above and below $S_0$ so that $p$ takes values between 0 and 1. Compare equations (4.1) and (4.4): the first illustrates the connection between the expected return and the probabilities of the stock price moving to $S_{high}$ or $S_{low}$. The second is rather similar in form, but in place of the expected growth rate $\mu$ for the stock, it has the risk-free interest rate $r$; and in place of the probabilities 0.7 and 0.3 it has the numbers $p$ and $(1 - p)$, which have values between 0 and 1. These numbers are called **pseudo-probabilities**, but are not of course the real probabilities of any outcome. Suppose there exists some fantasy world where people are all insensitive to risk. In such a **risk-neutral world**, everybody would be content to receive the risk-free rate $r$ on all their investments. Equations (4.3) and (4.4) would then be equations which connect $r$, the expected return on both the stock and the derivative, to the probabilities of $S_{high}$ or $S_{low}$ being achieved. But remember, this is only a fantasy world and does not describe what is going on in the real world. As the reader becomes more familiar with option theory, he will find that the concept of **risk neutrality** is a very useful tool in working out option prices; but he must remember that this is only an intellectual construction which is a useful way of remembering computational rules. He must not drift into the common trap of forgetting precisely where the real world ends and the fantasy world begins.

(vi) These distinctions are best illustrated with a step-by-step comparison of a derivative pricing in the real world and in a risk-neutral world.

| REAL WORLD | RISK-NEUTRAL WORLD |
|---|---|
| 1. We start with a knowledge of the true probabilities (0.7 and 0.3 in our example). Alternatively, if we only know the expected growth rate we use equation (4.1):<br><br>$$(1 + \mu)S_0 = 0.7 S_{high} + 0.3 S_{low}$$ | Calculate the pseudo-probabilities from equation (4.4) :<br><br>$$(1 + r)S_0 = p S_{high} + (1 - p)S_{low}$$ |
| 2. The probabilities of achieving $S_{high}$ and $S_{low}$ are just the same as achieving $f_{high}$ and $f_{low}$. The true expected value of $f_{1\,month}$ is<br><br>$$E[f_{1\,month}]_{real\,world} = 0.7 f_{high} + 0.3 f_{low}$$ | Pretend that the probabilities of achieving $S_{high}$ and $S_{low}$ (and therefore also $f_{high}$ and $f_{low}$) are the pseudo-probabilities. The pseudo-expectation is then<br><br>$$E[f_{1\,month}]_{pseudo} = p f_{high} + (1 - p) f_{low}$$ |
| 3. The present expected value of the derivative is given by discounting the future expected value by $\lambda$, the expected growth rate of the derivative:<br><br>$$f_0 = \frac{1}{(1 + \lambda)} E[f_{1\,month}]_{real\,world}$$ | Equation (4.3) shows that $f_0$ is just $E[f_{1\,month}]_{pseudo}$ discounted back at the interest rate:<br><br>$$f_0 = \frac{1}{(1 + r)} E[f_{1\,month}]_{pseudo}$$ |
| 4. Unfortunately, neither $\mu$ nor $\lambda$ are known in most circumstances so this method is useless. | This allows us to obtain $f_0$ entirely from observable quantities. |

Astonishingly, we have suddenly found a way of calculating $f_0$ in terms of known or observable quantities, yet only a page or two back, it looked as though the problem was insoluble since we had no way of calculating the returns $\mu$ and $\lambda$. The log-jam was broken by an arbitrage argument which hypothesized that an option could be hedged by a certain quantity of underlying stock. The principle is exactly the same as for a forward contract, explained in Section 1.3. Remember, this approach can only be used if the underlying commodity can be stored, otherwise the hedge cannot be set up: equities, foreign exchange and gold work fine, but tomatoes and electricity need a different approach; this book deals only with the former category.

## 4.2   CONTINUOUS TIME ANALYSIS

(i) The simple "high–low" example of the last section has wider applicability than a reader might expect at this point. However this remains to be developed in Chapter 7, and for the moment we will extend the theory in a way that describes real financial markets in a more credible way. Following the reasoning of the last section, we assume that we can construct a little portfolio in such a way that a derivative and $-\Delta$ units of stock hedge each other in the short term. Only short-term moves are considered since it is reasonable to assume that the $\Delta$ units of short stock position needed to hedge one derivative will vary with the stock price and the time to maturity. Therefore the hedge will only work over small ranges before $\Delta$ needs to be changed in order to maintain the perfect hedge.

The value of the portfolio at time $t$ may be written $f_t - S_t\Delta$. The increase in value of this portfolio over a small time interval $\delta t$, during which $S_t$ changes by $\delta S_t$, may be written

$$\delta f_t - S_t\Delta - S_t q\Delta\delta t$$

The first two terms are obvious while the last term is just the amount of dividend which we must pay to the stock lender from whom we have borrowed stock in the time interval $\delta t$, assuming a continuous dividend proportional to the stock price.

The quantity $\Delta$ is chosen so that the short stock position exactly hedges the derivative over a small time interval $\delta t$; this is the same as saying that the outcome of the portfolio is certain. The arbitrage arguments again lead us to the conclusion that the return of this portfolio must equal the interest rate:

$$\frac{\delta f_t - \delta S_t\Delta - S_t q\Delta\delta t}{f_t - S_t\Delta} = r\delta t$$

or

$$\delta f_t - \delta S_t\Delta + (r - q)S_t\Delta\delta t = rf_t\delta t \tag{4.5}$$

These equations are the exact analogue of equations (4.2) for the simple high–low model of the last section.

(ii) As they stand, equations (4.5) are not particularly useful. However, it is assumed that $S_t$ follows a Wiener process so that small movements are described by the equation

$$\frac{\delta S_t}{S_t} = (\mu - q)\delta t + \sigma\delta W_t$$

We can now invoke Ito's lemma in the form of equation (3.12) and substitute for $\delta f_t$ and $\delta S_t$ into the first of equations (4.5) to give

$$\left(\frac{\partial f_1}{\partial t} + (\mu - q)S_t\frac{\partial f_t}{\partial S_t} + \frac{1}{2}\sigma^2 S_t^2\frac{\partial^2 f_t}{\partial S_t^2}\right)\delta t + \sigma S_t\frac{\partial f_t}{\partial S_t}\delta W_t$$
$$-S_t[(\mu - q)\delta t + \sigma\delta W_t]\Delta - S_t q\Delta\delta t = (f_t - S_t\Delta)r\delta t \tag{4.6}$$

Recall that the left-hand side of this equation is the amount by which the portfolio increases in value in an interval $\delta t$; but by definition, this amount cannot be uncertain in any way because the derivative is hedged by the stock. Therefore it cannot be a function of the stochastic variable $\delta W_t$, which means that the coefficient of this factor must be equal to zero. This gives

$$\frac{\partial f_t}{\partial S_t} = \Delta \tag{4.7}$$

We return to an examination of the exact significance of this in subsection (vi) below.

(iii) **Black Scholes Differential Equation:** Setting the coefficient of $\delta W_t$ to zero in equation (4.6) leaves us with the most important equation of option theory, known as the Black Scholes equation:

$$\frac{\partial f_t}{\partial t} + (r - q)S_t\frac{\partial f_t}{\partial S_t} + \frac{1}{2}\sigma^2 S_t^2\frac{\partial^2 f_t}{\partial S_t^2} = rf_t \tag{4.8}$$

Any derivative for which a neutral hedge can be constructed is governed by this equation; and all formulas for the prices of derivatives are solutions of this equation, with boundary conditions depending on the specific type of derivative being considered. The immediately remarkable feature about this equation is the absence of $\mu$, the expected return on the stock, and indeed the expected return on the derivative itself. This is of course the continuous time equivalent of the risk-neutrality result that was described in Section 4.1(iv).

When the Black Scholes equation is used for calculating option prices, it is normally presented in a more directly usable form. Generally we want to derive a formula for the price of an option at time $t = 0$, where the option matures at time $t = T$. Using the conventions of Section 1.1(v), we write $\partial f_0/\partial t \Rightarrow -\partial f_0/\partial T$ so that the Black Scholes equation becomes

$$\frac{\partial f_t}{\partial T} = (r - q)S_t \frac{\partial f_t}{\partial S_t} + \frac{1}{2}\sigma^2 S_t^2 \frac{\partial^2 f_t}{\partial S_t^2} - rf_t \tag{4.9}$$

(iv) **Differentiability**: For what is a cornerstone of option theory, the Black Scholes differential equation has been derived in a rather minimalist way, so we will go back and examine some issues in greater detail. First, we need to look at some of the mathematical conditions that must be met.

It is clear from any graph of stock price against time that $S_t$ is not a smoothly varying function of time. It is really not the type of function that can be differentiated with respect to time. So just how valid is the analysis leading up to the derivation of the Black Scholes equation? This is really not a simple issue and is given thorough treatment in Part 4 of the book; but for the moment we content ourselves with the following commonsense observations:

- $S_t$ and the derivative price $f_{S_t t}$ are both stochastic variables. In this subsection we explicitly show the dependence of $f_{S_t t}$ on $S_t$ for emphasis.
- Both $S_t$ and $f_{S_t t}$ are much too jagged for $dS_t/dt$ or for $df_{S_t t}/dt$ to have any meaning at all, i.e. in the infinitesimal time interval $dt$, the movements of $\delta S_t$ and $\delta S_{S_t t}$ are quite unpredictable.
- However, partial derivatives are another matter. If you know the time to maturity and the underlying stock price, there is a unique value for a given partial derivative. These values might be determined either by working out a formula or by devising a calculation procedure; but you will be able to plot a unique smooth curve of $f_{S_t t}$ vs. $S_t$ for a given constant $t$, and also a unique curve for $f_{S_t t}$ vs. $t$ for a given constant $S_t$.
- The derivation of the Black Scholes equation ultimately depends on Ito's lemma which in turn depends on a Taylor expansion of $f_{S_t t}$ to first order in $t$ and second order in $S_t$. Underlying this is the assumption that the curves for $f_{S_t t}$ against $t$ and $S_t$ are at least once differentiable with respect to $t$ and twice differentiable with respect to $S_t$.
- A partial derivative is a derivative taken while holding all other variables constant. $df_{S_t t}/dt$ and $\partial f_{S_t t}/\partial t$ mean quite different things. Consider the following standard result of differential calculus:

$$\frac{df_{S_t t}}{dt} \equiv \frac{\partial f_{S_t t}}{\partial t} + \frac{\partial f_{S_t t}}{\partial S_t}\frac{\partial S_t}{\partial t}$$

We have already seen that the first two partial derivatives on the right-hand side of this identity are well defined. However $\partial S_t/\partial t$ is just a measure of the rate at which the stock price changes with time, which is random and undefined; thus $df_{S_t t}/dt$ is also undefined.

- In pragmatic terms, this is summed up as follows: we know that the stock price jumps around in a random way and therefore cannot be differentiated with respect to time; the same is true of the derivative price. However, the derivative price is a well-defined function of the underlying stock price and can therefore be differentiated with respect to price a couple of times. The derivative price is also a well-defined function of the maturity, so that it can be *partially* differentiated with respect to time, while holding the stock price constant.

(v) The concept of arbitrage is the foundation of option theory. It has been assumed that we can construct a little portfolio consisting of a derivative and a short position of $\Delta_{S_t t}$ units of stock, such that the short stock position exactly hedges the derivative for any small stock price movements; this is referred to as an **instantaneous hedge**. The dependence of $\Delta_{S_t t}$ on the stock price is explicitly expressed in the notation. This portfolio has a value which may be written

$$V_{S_t t} = f_{S_t t} - \Delta_{S_t t} S_t \qquad (4.10)$$

The fact that the short stock position hedges the derivative does not mean that the movement in one is equal but opposite to the movement in the other: it merely means that the move in $V_{S_t t}$ is independent of the size of the stock price move $\delta S_t$ over a small time interval $\delta t$. The normal sign conventions are followed when interpreting the last equation, e.g. if $f_{S_t t}$ is negative, a short option position (option sold) is indicated; if $\Delta_{S_t t}$ is negative, so that $-\Delta_{S_t t} S_t$ is positive, a long position is taken in the stock.

At this point it needs to be made clear that there are alternative (but equivalent) conventions used in describing instantaneous hedging. The reader needs to be at home with the different ways of looking at the problem since the approaches in the literature are quite random, with authors sometimes switching around within a single article or chapter.

***Hedging:*** In equation (4.10), $V_{S_t t}$ is the value of the portfolio and is therefore the amount of money paid out or received in setting up the portfolio; but we normally look at the set-up slightly differently. It is easier to keep tabs on values if it is assumed that we start any derivatives exercise with zero cash. If we need to spend cash on a portfolio, we obtain it by borrowing from a so-called cash account; alternatively, if the portfolio generates cash, we deposit this in the same cash account. Equation (4.10) may then be written

$$B_{S_t t} + f_{S_t t} - \Delta_{S_t t} S_t = 0 \qquad (4.11)$$

where $B_{S_t t}$ is the level of the cash account, negative for borrowings and positive for deposits. Except where explicitly stated otherwise, it is assumed that interest rates are constant.

***Replication:*** While option theory can be developed perfectly well with the above conventions, many students find it easier to picture the set-up slightly differently. Rewrite equation (4.10) as follows:

$$f_{S_t t} = \Delta_{S_t t} S_t + B_{S_t t} \qquad (4.12)$$

Instead of thinking in terms of hedging this can be interpreted as representing a replication. We would say that within a very small time interval, a derivative whose price is $f_{S_t t}$ behaves in the same way as a portfolio consisting of $\Delta_{S_t t}$ units of stock and $B_{S_t t}$ units of cash. In this approach it is again assumed that we start with zero wealth so that any cash needed has to be borrowed (indicated by negative $B_{S_t t}$) and any surplus cash is deposited (indicated by positive $B_{S_t t}$). For example, $\Delta_{S_t t} S_t$ is always positive for a call option and always larger than $f_{S_t t}$, so $B_{S_t t}$ is always negative, indicating a cash borrowing. On the other hand, $\Delta_{S_t t}$ is negative for a put option, indicating that the replication strategy requires a short stock position and that $B_{S_t t}$ is positive, i.e. surplus cash is generated by the process.

Replication is perhaps more intuitive as an approach, but people with a trading background tend to be more comfortable with the hedging for obvious reasons. One point which sometimes causes puzzlement should be mentioned: equations (4.11) and (4.12) seem to express the same idea, so where does the sign change in the $B_{S,t}$ term come from? The answer is that the two equations do not represent quite the same thing. In fact hedging an option might be best described as replicating a short option, rather than the option itself. It is completely straightforward to develop option theory using either approach, but the reader is warned that mistakes are likely to occur if it is not absolutely clear which method is being used at a given time.

To illustrate this alternative approach, we now recast the analysis leading up to the Black Scholes equation in terms of replication rather than hedging. The option can be replicated by a portfolio of stock and cash: $f_t = \Delta_t S_t + B_t$, where once again we ease the notation by using the suffix $t$ to indicate dependence on both $t$ and $S_t$. In a small time interval, the change in value is given by

$$\delta f_{S,t} = \Delta_{S,t}\delta S_t + \Delta_{S,t} S_t q \delta t + B_{S,t} r \delta t$$

The middle term on the right-hand side is again the dividend throw-off, while the last term is just the interest earned or incurred on the cash account. Substituting for $B_t$ from equation (4.12) gives

$$\delta f_t = \Delta_t \delta S_t + \Delta_t S_t q \delta t + (f_t - \Delta_t S_t) r \delta t \qquad (4.13)$$

which is just equation (4.5). The rest of the argument is the same as before, leading directly to the Black Scholes differential equation.

(vi) **Graphical Representation of Delta:** In the derivation of the Black Scholes equation (4.7), an important aspect emerged and was quickly passed over. We now return to the equation

$$\frac{\partial f_t}{\partial S_t} = \Delta$$

In the spirit of the last subsection, we assume that we can obtain a formula for $f_t$ as a function of $S_t$; the curve of this function is shown in Figure 4.1. This illustrates the replication approach to studying options which was described in the last section.

$\Delta$ is clearly the slope of the curve of $f_{S,t}$ and the equation of the tangent to the curve is $y = \Delta_{S,t} S_t + B$ where $B$ is some as yet to be defined point on the $y$-axis. Over a very small range $\delta S_t$, the properties of the curve (derivative) can be approximated by those of the tangent (replication portfolio). This is completely in line with the precepts of differential calculus.

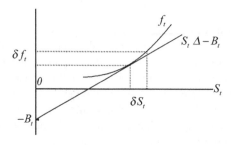

**Figure 4.1**  Delta

(vii) *Risk Neutrality in Continuous Time*: Let the expected return on an equity stock be $\mu$ and the return on a derivative be $\lambda$. The Wiener process governing the stock price movements is

$$\frac{\delta S_t}{S_t} = (\mu - q)\delta t + \sigma dW_t$$

and by definition

$$\frac{E[\delta f_t]}{f_t} = \lambda \delta t$$

Using Ito's lemma [equation (3.12)] for $\delta f_t$ gives

$$E\left[\left\{\frac{\partial f_t}{\partial t} + (\mu - q)S_t\frac{\partial f_t}{\partial S_t} + \frac{1}{2}\sigma^2 S_t^2\frac{\partial^2 f_t}{\partial S_t^2}\right\}\delta t + \sigma S_t\frac{\partial f_t}{\partial S_t}\delta W_t\right] = \lambda f_t\delta t$$

Now use $E[\delta W_t] = 0$ for the only stochastic term in the last equation to give

$$\frac{\partial f_t}{\partial t} + (\mu - q)S_t\frac{\partial f_t}{\partial S_t} + \frac{1}{2}\sigma^2 S_t^2\frac{\partial^2 f_t}{\partial S_t^2} = \lambda f_t$$

This is not of much use in pricing derivatives since we have no way of finding $\mu$ or $\lambda$. However, suppose we now get onto our magic carpet and fly back to the fantasy world described in the last section, where investors are insensitive to risk and therefore accept a risk-free rate of return $r$ on all investments including our derivative and its underlying stock. We would then be able to put $\mu = \lambda = r$ in the last equation to retrieve the Black Scholes equation which can be solved in terms of observable quantities.

This result is just the continuous time equivalent of the result which was obtained for the simple high/low model of Section 4.1. The no-arbitrage condition again leads us to the conclusion that an option price computed in the risk-neutral imaginary world would have the same value as an option price computed in the real world, if we happened to know the values of $\mu$ and $\lambda$. We can formally write this result as

$$f_{S_00} = e^{-\lambda t}\, E[f_{S_t t}]_{\text{real world}}$$
$$f_{S_00} = e^{-rt}\, E[f_{S_t t}]_{\text{risk-neutral world}}$$

(viii) *Approaches to Option Pricing*: The main purpose of the preceding theory is to find a way of pricing options. Two approaches have emerged from this chapter: we derived the Black Scholes equation which applies to any derivative of a stock price. The option price can therefore be obtained by solving this equation subject to the appropriate boundary conditions. The main drawback of this approach is that the equation is very hard to solve analytically in most cases. A later chapter will be dedicated to finding approximate numerical solutions to the equation.

In Section 3.1 the central limit theorem was used to derive a probability distribution function for the stock price in time $S_t$. This was a function of $\mu$, the stock's rate of return. But in the last subsection it was shown that the option may be priced by first making the substitution $\mu \rightarrow r$ and deriving a pseudo-distribution for $S_t$ (i.e. the distribution $S_t$ would have if $\mu$ were equal to $r$). From this pseudo-distribution and a knowledge of the payoff function of the option, a pseudo-expected terminal value can be calculated for the option; if this is discounted back at the risk-free rate $r$, we get the true present fair value of the option.

On the face of it, this seems the simpler approach; it certainly is for simple options, but it will become apparent later in this course that the probability distribution can be very difficult to derive in more complex cases. In fact it is shown in Appendix A.4(i) that deriving a formula for the probability density function is mathematically equivalent to solving the Black Scholes equation.

Other powerful approaches to option pricing are developed later in this book, but for the moment we concentrate on these methods. They are applied to simple European put and call options in the next chapter, but for the moment we continue with the development of the general theory which will be applied throughout the rest of the book.

## 4.3    DYNAMIC HEDGING

In the first section of this chapter we considered a simple one-step model with two possible outcomes. Then in the following section we turned our attention to a more general, continuous model, but we still only considered a single short step $\delta S_t$ over a period $\delta t$. These models not only gave insights into a general approach for solving previously intractable problems (risk neutrality); they also yielded the fundamental differential equation governing all options. We now extend the analysis from one to two steps and in the process we derive the central result which underlies the whole of the modern options industry.

(i) *Beginning of First Step*: We buy an option and hedge it with delta units of the underlying stock. We start with zero wealth so any cash surplus or deficit is borrowed or deposited with a bank. We have already seen from equation (4.11) that our position may be represented by

$$f_{S_t t} - \Delta_{S_t t} S_t + B_{S_t t} = 0 \tag{4.14}$$

Consider two concrete examples

- *A call option valued at 10 when the stock price is 100 which has a delta of 0.5.* The delta of the call is positive so the hedge is to short stock. Putting numbers into the last equation gives

$$10 - 0.5 \times 100 + B_{S_t t} = 0 \qquad \text{or} \qquad B_{S_t t} = +40$$

Shorting the stock means borrowing stock and selling it. This process generates 50 of cash but the option cost us 10; the net of the two is a cash surplus of 40 which we place on deposit.

- *A put option worth 10 when the stock price is 100; delta is −0.5.* The delta of a put is negative, so the hedge is to buy stock. Our equation now becomes

$$10 + 0.5 \times 100 + B_{S_t t} = 0 \qquad \text{or} \qquad B_{S_t t} = -60$$

This time we buy the option for 10 but also need to spend 50 on the stock hedge. Our total outlay is 60 which needs to be borrowed.

(ii) *End of First Step*: Having set up the portfolio described by equation (4.14), we now wait for a period of time $\delta t$ to elapse and then go back to see what happened. The situation is described by a new equation:

$$f_{S_t + \delta S_t\, t + \delta t} - \Delta_{S_t t}(S_t + \delta S_t) - \Delta_{S_t t} S_t q \delta t + B_{S_t t}(1 + r \delta t) = 0 \tag{4.15}$$

- The value of the option changed to $f_{S_t + \delta S_t\, t + \delta t} = f_{S_t t} + \delta f_{S_t t}$ because the stock price and the time to maturity changed.
- $\Delta_{S_t t}$ was the number of shares we held or shorted, and this did not change over the period $\delta t$.

- The stock price changed to $S_{t+\delta t} = S_t + \delta S_t$ over the same period.
- Dividends of $\Delta_{S_t t} S_t q \delta t$ would have been received on a long stock or paid on a short stock position.
- The cash account accrued an amount of interest $B_{S_t t} r \delta t$ in the period.

The portfolio was constructed to be hedged so there could not have been a stochastic jump in wealth. We started at $t$ with nothing, so by the arbitrage principle expressed in the form of proposition 1.2(i), we have nothing at $t + \delta t$; so all the above terms taken together must equal zero.

Subtracting equation (4.14) from equation (4.15) gives

$$\delta f_{S_t t} - \Delta_{S_t t} \delta S_t + (B_{S_t t} r - \Delta_{S_t t} S_t q) \delta t = \delta f_{S_t t} - \Delta_{S_t t} \delta S_t + \Psi \delta t = 0 \qquad (4.16)$$

The term $\Psi_t \delta t$ is usually called the *financing costs*. It is just the cash flows which result from the interest rate and dividend flows, positive if received by us and negative if paid out. This equation may be stated alternatively: over a single hedged time period $\delta t$, the change in the value of the derivative and hedge, net of financing costs, is zero.

(iii) **Beginning of Second Step**: Having moved to time $t + \delta t$ where the stock price is $S_t + \delta S_t$, the stock position no longer hedges the derivative perfectly. The reason is that delta has changed slightly. We wish to remain hedged for a further period $\delta t$ so we change the delta by buying or selling some shares and establish a new, perfectly hedged portfolio corresponding to a stock price $S_t + \delta S_t$ and time $t + \delta t$. The equation corresponding to equation (4.3) is now

$$f_{S_t + \delta S_t \ t + \delta t} - \Delta_{S_t + \delta S_t \ t + \delta t} (S_t + \delta S_t) + B_{S_t + \delta S_t \ t + \delta t} = 0 \qquad (4.17)$$

Again, the left-hand side of this equation is set to zero since arbitrage ensures that our total wealth is always equal to zero. In order to see how the cash account moves when the hedge is rebalanced, subtract equation (4.15) from equation (4.17):

$$-(\Delta_{S_t + \delta S_t \ t + \delta t} - \Delta_{S_t t})(S_t + \delta S_t) + (B_{S_t + \delta S_t \ t + \delta t} - B_{S_t t}) - (B_{S_t t} r - \Delta_{S_t t} S_t q) \delta t = 0$$

Simplifying the notation gives

$$\delta B_t = \Psi_t \delta t + \delta \Delta_t S_{t+\delta t} \qquad (4.18)$$

The relationship expressed by this equation is known as the *self-financing condition*. It is of course totally intuitive (not to say self-evident). In a single period including one rebalancing, the cash flows come from only two sources: the financing costs and the cost of rebalancing the hedge. In other words, our system of derivative, stock and cash account is self-contained: we do not let cash seep in or out.

The above steps may be repeated at successive time intervals $\delta t$, when we repeatedly readjust the hedge by buying or selling shares (changing the delta). The procedure is known as *dynamic hedging*. The values of the deltas which are needed at each step may be obtained from an option model such as the Black Scholes model of the next chapter.

(iv) **Basis of Option Trading**: Returning to our zero-value portfolio of equation (4.14), it is clear that however many times one rebalances the hedge, arbitrage arguments dictate that the value of the portfolio must always remain at zero. At the maturity of the option we must therefore also have

$$f_{S_T T} - \Delta_{S_T T} S_T + B_{S_T T} = 0$$

This looks obvious to the point of being banal, but let us pause for a moment to reflect on what it implies.

Suppose we have somehow been given a call option, but know nothing about option theory; we would have to wait until maturity and see what the payoff is. But suppose instead that we know option theory: specifically, we are able to calculate the value of a call option as a function of stock price and time to maturity; hence we are also able to calculate the delta, its first derivative. The option position is managed as follows.

Set up a portfolio consisting of the following:

- The call option, whose fair value $f_{S_00}$ can be calculated from our knowledge of option theory and the current price of the underlying stock.
- A short position in $\Delta_{S_00}$ units of stock. Again, we know how to calculate $\Delta_{S_00}$, so we borrow this amount of stock in the repo market and sell it to yield $\Delta_{S_00}S_0$ in cash.
- We divide the cash sum into two sums: $f_{S_00}$ is placed in a "value account" and $\Delta_{S_00}S_0 - f_{S_00} = B_{S_00}$ is placed in the "portfolio account"; both accounts bear interest.

The portfolio contains (i) the call option, (ii) the obligations under the stock borrowing and (iii) the "portfolio account". Its value is $f_{S_00} - \Delta_{S_00}S_0 + B_{S_00} = 0$ at the beginning and if we continuously vary $\Delta_{S_t}$ so that the option is perfectly hedged at all times, then its value is also zero at the end. All we are left with then is the "value account" which has accumulated interest to become $f_{S_00}e^{rT}$. By dynamically hedging, we have locked in the value of the option from the beginning, rather than having to rely on an uncertain payoff.

The implications of this for the options industry are enormous. For example, we can sell an option without taking an unknown exposure to stock price movements. If we dynamically hedge this short option position, the hedging process (buying or selling stock and financing costs) will generate a cash sum equal to the fair price of the option sold. Or if we buy an option which is underpriced, we can generate the fair value of the option through a delta hedging procedure and consequently lock in the profit.

The mechanics of what precisely causes this to happen is explained in Section 4.5. However, we first look at a concrete example of delta hedging and its associated cash flows.

## 4.4   EXAMPLES OF DYNAMIC HEDGING

(i) The theory developed in the last section called for rebalancing of the hedge at infinitesimally small time intervals, but this is obviously not possible in practice. The example we consider is a 1-year call option for which we rebalance the hedge once a month; in real life, we would rebalance the hedge more often. The columns of Table 4.1 are as follows.

(A) $S_t$: Assuming the stock price starts at 100, we have generated a scenario of stock prices after 1 month, 2 months, ..., 12 months. These values are calculated from equation (3.7), making the risk-neutral substitution $m = (r - q) - \frac{1}{2}\sigma^2$. In this particular example, we have taken $r = 6\%$, $q = 3\%$, $\sigma = 25\%$ so that

$$S_{\text{month } i+1} = S_{\text{month } i} \exp\left\{3\% \times \frac{1}{12} - \frac{1}{2} \times (25\%)^2 + 25\% \times \sqrt{\frac{1}{12}} z_{i+1}\right\}$$

where $z_{i+1}$ is a random variable drawn from a standard normal population. Such variables are easy to generate in a spreadsheet using formulas discussed in Chapter 10. An infinite number of paths can be generated in this column simply by pressing the button which

**Table 4.1**    Dynamic hedge of a call option (in the money at maturity)

|       | $S_t$  | $\Delta_{S_t t}$ | $f_{S_t t}$ | $\Delta_{S_t t} \times S_t$ | $B_{S_t t}$ |
|-------|--------|-------|-------|----------------------|--------|
| Jan   | 100.00 | 0.58  | 11.01 | 57.91                | 46.90  |
| Feb   | 86.30  | 0.34  |       | 29.52                | 26.53  |
| Mar   | 89.26  | 0.38  |       | 34.13                | 30.19  |
| Apr   | 90.22  | 0.39  |       | 34.94                | 30.70  |
| May   | 92.59  | 0.42  |       | 38.99                | 33.90  |
| Jun   | 87.20  | 0.29  |       | 25.53                | 22.78  |
| Jul   | 87.89  | 0.28  |       | 24.99                | 22.09  |
| Aug   | 91.81  | 0.35  |       | 32.19                | 28.22  |
| Sep   | 106.59 | 0.71  |       | 76.00                | 66.91  |
| Oct   | 111.15 | 0.83  |       | 91.97                | 79.76  |
| Nov   | 103.57 | 0.67  |       | 69.18                | 63.42  |
| Dec   | 106.41 | 0.82  |       | 87.52                | 80.00  |
| Jan   | 118.37 | 1.00  | 18.37 | 118.37               | 101.20 |
|       |        |       | Final Liquidation Value of Portfolio | | 1.20 |

allocates the new set of random numbers for Tables 4.1 and 4.2. We have simply chosen a couple of paths which are good illustrations of the present subject.

(B) $\Delta_{S_t t}$: The deltas shown in the third column are calculated from the Black Scholes model and correspond to the stock prices of column 2 and the time left to maturity.

The last three columns correspond to the portfolio $f_{S_t t} - \Delta_{S_t t} S_t + B_{S_t t} = 0$, which as we have seen should have value zero at every point in time. The first line of this part of the table is constructed as follows.

(C) $f_{S_0 0}$: On day 1, when the stock price is 100.00, we buy an option for its fair value of 11.01. This fair value is obtained from the Black Scholes model.

(D) $\Delta_{S_0 0} \times S_0$: We have already calculated the delta, and this is the number of shares that is shorted to hedge the option. The cash we receive as a result of this short is shown in this column.

(E) $B_{S_0 0}$: The amount of cash available for depositing in the cash account is the difference of the last two items.

The remainder of the last three columns is filled in as follows.

(F) $\Delta_{S_t t} \times S_t$: Each month, observe the new share price and calculate an appropriate delta (columns 2 and 3).

(G) The change in the cash account is the sum of three items:

- Interest on the cash surplus received for the previous month;
- Dividends on the stock borrowed in the previous month;
- Stock bought or sold to readjust the hedge.

Since the portfolio is hedged, the sum of the last three columns should be zero throughout. However there is no need to recalculate the option price at each time step. At maturity, when the stock price is 118.37, we would expect to have 100 in the cash account and a short position of one share; the option value is the payoff of 18.37.

In our example, the numbers are close but not exact. The reason of course is that we did not rebalance at infinitesimal intervals but at 1-month gaps. In fact, the results we have used for illustration have been chosen to be fairly close; with hedging as infrequent as this, the standard deviation of the mismatch between our results and the results obtained from infinitesimal hedging is about 2.25, i.e. one third of the time the error will be greater than 2.25.

(ii) Table 4.2 is a repeat of the previous exercise with a stock price path which finishes out-of-the-money for the option.

**Table 4.2** Dynamic hedge of a call option (out of the money at maturity)

| | $S_t$ | $\Delta_{S_t t}$ | $f_{S_t t}$ | $\Delta_{S_t t} S_t$ | $B_{S_t t}$ |
|---|---|---|---|---|---|
| Jan | 100.00 | 0.58 | 11.01 | 57.91 | 46.90 |
| Feb | 96.31 | 0.52 | | 49.74 | 40.96 |
| Mar | 103.82 | 0.63 | | 65.90 | 53.32 |
| Apr | 106.59 | 0.68 | | 72.31 | 58.07 |
| May | 102.78 | 0.62 | | 63.56 | 52.01 |
| Jun | 97.06 | 0.50 | | 48.87 | 40.96 |
| Jul | 88.59 | 0.30 | | 26.56 | 22.99 |
| Aug | 91.04 | 0.33 | | 30.19 | 25.95 |
| Sep | 86.65 | 0.20 | | 16.92 | 14.18 |
| Oct | 75.39 | 0.02 | | 1.22 | 0.71 |
| Nov | 59.26 | 0.00 | | 0.00 | −0.25 |
| Dec | 61.45 | 0.00 | | 0.00 | −0.25 |
| Jan | 62.93 | 0.00 | 0.00 | 0.00 | −0.25 |
| | | | | Final Liquidation Value of Portfolio | −0.25 |

## 4.5 GREEKS

(i) A deeper understanding of the material of the last couple of chapters is obtained by considering the various partial derivatives of the stock price. Let us return to the Taylor expansion of Section 3.4:

$$\delta f_{S_t t} = \frac{\partial f_{S_t t}}{\partial S_t} \delta S_t + \frac{\partial f_{S_t t}}{\partial t} \delta t + \frac{1}{2} \left\{ \frac{\partial^2 f_{S_t t}}{\partial S_t^2} \delta S_t^2 + \frac{\partial^2 f_{S_t t}}{\partial S_t \partial t} \delta S_t \delta t + \frac{\partial^2 f_{S_t t}}{\partial t^2} \delta t^2 \right\} + \cdots$$

Using the substitution $\delta S_t^2 \to \sigma^2 S_t^2 \delta t$ which is explained in Section 3.3, and retaining only terms of first order in $\delta t$ gives

$$\delta f_{S_t t} = \frac{\partial f_{S_t t}}{\partial S_t} \delta S_t + \left\{ \frac{\partial f_{S_t t}}{\partial t} + \frac{1}{2} \sigma^2 S_t^2 \frac{\partial^2 f_{S_t t}}{\partial S_t^2} \right\} \delta t$$

In Section 4.2(vi) we defined the **delta** of a derivative by $\Delta_{S_t t} = \partial f_{S_t t}/\partial S_t$; two other partial derivatives are now defined as follows.

**Theta:** $\theta_{S_t t} = \frac{\partial f_{S_t t}}{\partial t}$ This is the rate at which the value of an option changes over time.

**Gamma:** $\Gamma_{S,t} = \frac{\partial \Delta_{S,t}}{\partial S_t} = \frac{\partial^2 f_{S,t}}{\partial S_t^2}$ The second derivative is a measure of the rate of change of the slope of the curve of $f_{S,t}$ against $S_t$, i.e. it measures the sharpness of the curvature of the curve.

Lightening up on the notation a little, the Taylor expansion can now be written in Greek letters:

$$\delta f_t = \Delta_t \delta S_t + \left\{ \theta_t + \frac{1}{2}\sigma^2 S_t^2 \Gamma_t \right\} \delta t \tag{4.19}$$

(ii) This last equation is illustrated in Figure 4.2, and may be given the following physical interpretation: in the time period $\delta t$, the stock price moves by $\delta S_t$; over the same interval, the derivative price moves by $\delta f_t = f_{S_t + \delta S_t, t + \delta t} - f_{S,t}$. This is represented by a move from the point A to the point A' in the graph, with the value of $\delta f_t$ represented by the distance A'D. This is made up of three distinct parts, which are easiest to understand if we think in terms of replication of an option rather than hedging.

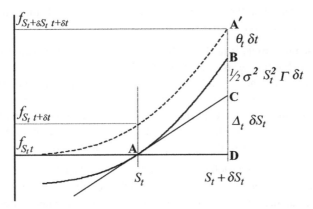

**Figure 4.2** Major Greeks

- A first-order term $\Delta_t \delta S_t$: As a first approximation, the option is replicated by a portfolio consisting of $\Delta_{S,t}$ units of stock plus some borrowing. The movement in value of this portfolio is given by the distance CD in Figure 4.2.
- A second-order term in $\delta S_t$ (equals a first-order term in $\delta t$): The replication is not exact since the graph of $f_t$ is curved. A move up in the stock price causes $f_t$ to move up slightly more than the replicating portfolio. The extra distance moved is given by the distance BC in Figure 4.2. Note that the option value is slightly greater than that of the replicating portfolio, irrespective of whether $\delta S_t$ is up or down.
- A first-order term in $\delta t$: A derivative price is a direct function of time, so that in an interval $\delta t$ the derivative price will change even if $S_t$ remains constant. This change is represented by a shift in the derivative price curve (solid to dotted). In the graph, this is represented by the distance A'B.

(iii) In Section 4.3(iv) it was explained that if we buy an option for fair value and dynamically hedge it until maturity, the process will produce a cash surplus exactly equal to the initial premium of the option (adjusted for the time value of money). This followed from arbitrage arguments, but it was not clear what process or mechanism was causing the positive cash throw-off.

When an option is hedged with underlying stock, there is a slight mismatch between the movements in the value of the option and the value of the hedging portfolio. As just shown, this is due to the curvature of the curve of $f_t$ (the gamma term) and also the fact that the entire curve shifts over time (the theta term). Each of the small gamma gains is positive in our example, and each gain has value $(\theta_t + \frac{1}{2}\sigma^2 S_t^2 \Gamma_t)\delta t$. When added together over the life of the option, these gains accumulate to a sum equal to the future value of the fair value of the option at the beginning of the hedging period.

(iv) **Black Scholes Equation revisited**: If we compare the expansion of equation (4.19) with equation (4.16) we get

$$\left\{\theta_t + \frac{1}{2}\sigma^2 S_t^2 \Gamma_t\right\} = \Psi_t = -(B_t r - \Delta_t S_t q) = -\Delta_t(r-q)S_t + rf_t \qquad (4.20)$$

which is just the Black Scholes equation written in Greek. This is not surprising since the analysis is essentially the same as before: Ito's lemma, which was used when the equation was first derived, is based on the same Taylor expansion and the substitution $\delta S_t^2 \to \sigma^2 S_t^2 \delta t$, which are used in this section

(v) Usually, the financing term $\Psi_t$ is fairly small: $\Delta_t$ can be anything between 0 and 100% so that $\Delta_t S_t$ could be large; but $(r - q)$ is likely to be well below 10% and $rf_t$ will certainly be small. If $\theta_t + \frac{1}{2}\sigma^2 S_t^2 \Gamma_t$ is small, then $\theta_t$ and $\Gamma_t$ will usually have opposite signs. In Figure 4.2, $\Gamma_t$ was positive (curved upwards rather than downwards) and $\theta_t$ was also positive (dotted curve above solid curve). This made the exposition simpler, but in practice if gamma were positive, theta would be negative. This result was deduced in Section 2.6 entirely from the shape of the payoff diagram and the curves of the option prices before maturity.

(vi) **Minor Greeks**: The differentials delta, gamma and theta introduced in this chapter are key concepts for understanding option theory. There are two further differentials which are not central to the theoretical structure, but are nonetheless useful. We list them here for completeness and for future reference.

**Rho**: $\rho_{S,t} = \frac{\partial f_{S,t}}{\partial r}$ This is a measure of the sensitivity of an option value to changes in the interest rate.

**Vega**: $\Lambda_{S,t} = \frac{\partial f_{S,t}}{\partial \sigma}$ This is a spoof Greek letter, although occasionally this differential is referred to as lambda (a real Greek letter). Elementary option theory assumes constant volatility; vega is a measure of the effect of this simplifying assumption breaking down, and is used extensively by practitioners.

# 5

# The Black Scholes Model

## 5.1 INTRODUCTION

In the last chapter, two approaches were suggested for finding the price of an option:

- Use risk neutrality to set growth rates (returns) equal to the interest rate and with these substitutions, work out the expected value of the payoff. The present value of this amount equals the fair value of the option today.
- Solve the Black Scholes equation subject to the appropriate boundary conditions.

Either of these methods can be used to derive the Black Scholes model for the prices of European call and put options, which is the most famous and widely used option model. It consists of a simple formula giving the value of the option as a function of a few parameters; this is called a "closed form solution". Normally, models do not come in such a convenient form, but consist of a set of procedures which are applied in order to get a numerical value for the price of an option; these are the "numerical methods" described in Part 2 of this book.

In the analysis of the previous chapters, a number of restrictive assumptions have been made. They are referred to collectively as the Black Scholes assumptions or a description of the Black Scholes world:

(A) Volatility is constant.
(B) Cash is borrowed or deposited at the same constant rate of interest.
(C) There is no buy/sell spread or sales commission.
(D) It is possible to short stock without charge.
(E) Markets are continuous, so there is always a quote available.
(F) Markets exist for any quantity of stock, including fractions of stock.
(G) Markets are completely liquid, so we get instant execution, in any size, at the quoted price.

## 5.2 DERIVATION OF MODEL FROM EXPECTED VALUES

(i) Risk neutrality tells us that the value at time $t = 0$ of a call option maturing at time $T = 0$ is given by

$$C_0 = e^{-rT} \, E[C_T]_{\text{risk neutral}} = e^{-rT} E[\max[(S_T - X), \, 0]]_{\text{risk neutral}}$$

For notional simplicity, the risk-neutral suffix will be dropped but it must always be remembered that we are dealing with pseudo-probabilities and pseudo-expectations.

The value of the option is zero if it expires out-of-the-money ($S_T < X$), so the expression for the value of the call option at $t = 0$ may be written

$$C_0 = e^{-rT} E[S_T - X : S_T > X]$$

(ii) In order to obtain the expected value we need to multiply the payoff by a probability distribution and integrate over $S_T$. However, it is mathematically much simpler to transform variables: equation (3.7) states that $S_T = S_0 \, e^{mT + \sigma\sqrt{T}z_T}$ where $m = \mu - \frac{1}{2}\sigma^2$ and $z_T$ is a standard normal variate; in a risk-neutral world with dividends, $m = (r - q) - \frac{1}{2}\sigma^2$. The mechanical details of how to evaluate the conditional expectations are given in Appendix A.1(v) The result is

$$C_0 = e^{-rT}\left\{ S_0 \, e^{(r-q)T} \, \mathrm{N}[\sigma\sqrt{T} - Z_X] - X \, \mathrm{N}[-Z_X] \right\}$$

where $Z_X = (\ln(X/S_0) - mT)/\sigma\sqrt{T}$. This result is more usually written as

$$C_0 = e^{-rT}\{ F_{0T} \, \mathrm{N}[d_1] - X \, \mathrm{N}[d_2] \}$$
$$d_2 = d_1 - \sigma\sqrt{T}$$
$$d_1 = \left( \ln(F_{0T}/X) + \tfrac{1}{2}\sigma^2 T \right)/\sigma\sqrt{T} = \left( \ln S_0/X + (r-q)T + \tfrac{1}{2}\sigma^2 T \right)/\sigma\sqrt{T} \quad (5.1)$$

where $F_{0T}$ is the forward price.

(iii) Note that for constant $X$, $\mathrm{E}[X: S_T > X] = \mathrm{E}[X \mid S_T > X]\,\mathrm{E}[S_T > X] = X \, \mathrm{P}[S_T > X]$. It is therefore sometimes stated that the factor $\mathrm{N}[d_2]$ is the probability that $S_T > X$, i.e. that the option will be exercised. But remember that risk neutrality has led to the substitution $\mu \rightarrow r$. Therefore $\mathrm{P}[S_T > X]$ is a pseudo-probability. The true probability that $S_T > X$ is $\mathrm{N}[d_2]$, but with $r$ replaced by $\mu$.

(iv) **General Black Scholes Formula for Put or Call**: Recall the put–call parity relationship of Section 2.2(i):

$$F_{0T} + P_0 \, e^{rT} = X + C_0 \, e^{rT}$$

Substitute from the Black Scholes expression for $C_0$:

$$P_0 \, e^{rT} = X\{ 1 - \mathrm{N}[d_2] \} - F_{0T}\{ 1 - \mathrm{N}[d_1] \}$$

From equation (A1.4), $\mathrm{N}[d] + \mathrm{N}[-d] = 1$, so that

$$P_0 = e^{-rT}\{ X \, \mathrm{N}[-d_2] - F_{0T} \, \mathrm{N}[-d_1] \}$$

The Black Scholes formulas for European put and call options can be combined as

$$f_0 = e^{-rT}\phi\{ F_{0T} \, \mathrm{N}[\phi d_1] - X \, \mathrm{N}[\phi d_2] \} \quad (5.2)$$

where $\phi = +1$ for a call option and $\phi = -1$ for a put.

(v) In manipulating these formulas, we often need an option price at time $t$. Clearly, this is obtained from equation (5.2) merely by making the substitutions $f_0 \rightarrow f_t$; $S_0 \rightarrow S_t$; $F_{0T} \rightarrow F_{tT}$; $T \rightarrow T - t$.

## 5.3    SOLUTIONS OF THE BLACK SCHOLES EQUATION

It has been shown that the same arbitrage reasoning leads both to the risk-neutral stock price distribution (from which we derived the Black Scholes model), and to the Black Scholes equation. The two approaches should therefore lead to the same final conclusions: now comes the acid test.

(i) Stated formally, we seek a solution $C(S_0, T)$ of the equation

$$\frac{\partial C_0}{\partial T} = (r - q)S_0 \frac{\partial C_0}{\partial S_0} + \frac{1}{2}\sigma^2 S_0^2 \frac{\partial^2 C_0}{\partial S_0^2} - rC_0$$

subject to the initial and boundary conditions

- $C(S_0, 0) = \max[0, S_0 - X]$
- $\lim_{S_0 \to 0} C(S_0, T) \to 0$
- $\lim_{S_0 \to \infty} C(S_0, T) \to S_0 e^{-qT} - X e^{-rT}$

(ii) Let us now make the following transformations, suggested by equation (A4.5) in the Appendix:

$$C_0 = e^{-rT'/\frac{1}{2}\sigma^2} e^{-kx-k^2T'} v(x, T'); \qquad x = \ln S_0; \qquad T' = \tfrac{1}{2}\sigma^2 T; \qquad k = \frac{r - q - \frac{1}{2}\sigma^2}{\sigma^2}$$

Substituting in the previous equation and doing the algebra reduces the problem to a solution of the equation

$$\frac{\partial v}{\partial T'} = \frac{\partial^2 v}{\partial x^2}$$

subject to initial and boundary conditions

- $v(x, 0) = \max[0, e^{(k+1)x} - X e^{kx}]$
- $\lim_{x \to -\infty} v(x, T') \to 0$
- $\lim_{x \to \infty} v(x, T') \to e^{(k+1)x+(k+1)^2T'} - X e^{kx+k^2T'}$

(iii) The solution of this problem is demonstrated in the Appendix: using Fourier transforms in equation (A6.5) or using Green's functions in equation (A7.8) we can write

$$v(x, T') = \int_{-\infty}^{+\infty} e^{kx} \max[0, e^x - X] \left[ \frac{1}{2\sqrt{\pi T'}} e^{-\frac{(y-x)^2}{4T'}} \right] dy$$

Without detailing every tedious step, the integral is performed as follows:

- Get rid of the awkward "max" function in the integral, setting the lower limit of integration $y = \ln X$.
- Change the variable of integration $\frac{(y-x)^2}{4T'} \to z$.
- Use the standard integral results of Appendix A.1(v).
- Substitute back for $x$, $T'$ and $k$.

If the reader cares to check all this he will retrieve equation (5.1), the Black Scholes formula.

## 5.4    GREEKS FOR THE BLACK SCHOLES MODEL

(i) *Some Useful Differentials*: The Black Scholes model gives specific analytical formulas for the prices of European put and call options. It is therefore possible to give formulas for the Greeks simply by differentiation. The starting point is the Black Scholes model, but before slogging away at the differentials, we note a couple of general results which much simplify the computations.

(A) From equation (A1.2) we have

$$\frac{\partial N[\phi d]}{\partial \theta} = \frac{\partial N[\phi d]}{\partial (\phi d)} \frac{\partial (\phi d)}{\partial \theta} = \phi n(d) \frac{\partial d}{\partial \theta}$$

where $\phi$ can only take values $\pm 1$ and is independent of $\theta$, and $n(d) = \frac{1}{\sqrt{2\pi}} e^{-\frac{1}{2}d^2}$.

(B) From the definitions of $d_1$ and $d_2$ given in equation (5.1), it follows that

$$d_2 - d_1 = -\sigma\sqrt{T} \quad \text{and} \quad d_2 + d_1 = \frac{2}{\sigma\sqrt{T}} \ln\left(\frac{S_0 e^{-qT}}{X e^{-rT}}\right)$$

so that

$$d_2^2 - d_1^2 = (d_2 - d_1)(d_2 + d_1) = -2 \ln\left(\frac{S_0 e^{-qT}}{X e^{-rT}}\right)$$

Substituting this into the explicit expression for $n(d_2)$ in (A) above gives

$$n(d_2) = \frac{1}{\sqrt{2\pi}} e^{-\frac{1}{2}d_1^2 + \ln\left(\frac{S_0 e^{-qT}}{X e^{-rT}}\right)} \quad \text{or} \quad S_0 e^{-qT} n(d_1) = X e^{-rT} n(d_2)$$

(C) Differentiating the relationship $d_1 - d_2 = \sigma\sqrt{T}$ gives

$$\begin{cases} \dfrac{\partial d_1}{\partial S_0} - \dfrac{\partial d_2}{\partial S_0} = 0 \\[2mm] \dfrac{\partial d_1}{\partial r} - \dfrac{\partial d_2}{\partial r} = 0 \\[2mm] \dfrac{\partial d_1}{\partial T} - \dfrac{\partial d_2}{\partial T} = \dfrac{\sigma}{2\sqrt{T}} \\[2mm] \dfrac{\partial d_1}{\partial \sigma} - \dfrac{\partial d_2}{\partial \sigma} = \sqrt{T} \end{cases}$$

(D) Differentiating the explicit expression for $d_1$ with respect to $S_0$ gives

$$\frac{\partial d_1}{\partial S_0} = \frac{1}{S_0 \sigma\sqrt{T}}$$

The Greeks can now be obtained by differentiating equation (5.2):

$$f_0 = \phi S_0 e^{-qT} N[\phi d_1] - \phi X e^{-rT} N[\phi d_2]$$

$$d_1 = \frac{1}{\sigma\sqrt{T}} \ln\left(\frac{S_0 e^{-qT}}{X e^{-rT}}\right) + \frac{1}{2}\sigma\sqrt{T}; \qquad d_2 = \frac{1}{\sigma\sqrt{T}} \ln\left(\frac{S_0 e^{-qT}}{X e^{-rT}}\right) - \frac{1}{2}\sigma\sqrt{T}$$

(ii) **Delta:**

$$\Delta = \frac{\partial f_0}{\partial S_0} = \phi e^{-qT} N[\phi d_1] + \phi S_0 e^{-qT} n(d_1) \frac{\partial d_1}{\partial S_0} - \phi X e^{-rT} n(d_2) \frac{\partial d_2}{\partial S_0}$$

Using (B) and (C) above gives

$$\Delta = \phi e^{-qT} N[\phi d_1] \tag{5.3}$$

(iii) **Gamma:**

$$\Gamma = \frac{\partial \Delta}{\partial S_0} = \phi^2 e^{-qT} n(d_1) \frac{\partial d_1}{\partial S_0} \quad \text{and} \quad \frac{\partial d_1}{\partial S_0} = \frac{1}{S_0 \sigma\sqrt{T}}$$

so that

$$\Gamma = \frac{n(d_1)}{S\sigma\sqrt{T}}\,e^{-qT}$$

Note that this is independent of $\phi$ so that $\Gamma$ is the same for a put or a call option.

(iv) *Theta*: The differential of the Black Scholes formula with respect to $T$ would measure the rate of increase of the value of an option as its time to maturity increases; but theta is the rate of increase in value as time passes, i.e. as the maturity of the option *decreases*. Recalling the conventions described in Section 1.1(v):

$$\Theta = \frac{\partial f_0}{\partial t} = -\frac{\partial f_0}{\partial T} = \phi q S_0\,e^{-qT}\,N[\phi d_1] - \phi r X\,e^{-rT}\,N[\phi d_2]$$
$$-S_0\,e^{-qT}\,n(d_1)\frac{\partial d_1}{\partial T} + X\,e^{-rT}\,n(d_2)\frac{\partial d_2}{\partial T}$$

Once again using (B) and (C) above gives

$$\Theta = \phi q S_0\,e^{-qT}\,N[\phi d_1] - \phi r X\,e^{-rT}\,N[\phi d_2] - S_0\,e^{-qT}n(d_1)\frac{\sigma}{2\sqrt{T}}$$

(v) *Vega*:

$$\Lambda = \frac{\partial f_0}{\partial \sigma} = S_0\,e^{-qT}\,n(d_1)\frac{\partial d_1}{\partial \sigma} - X\,e^{-rT}n(d_2)\frac{\partial d_2}{\partial \sigma}$$

As before this can be simplified to

$$\Lambda = S_0\,e^{-qT}n(d_1)\sqrt{T} = X\,e^{-rT}n(d_2)\sqrt{T} \tag{5.4}$$

No! The equals sign is not a typo. A direct comparison between this and the expression for gamma gives

$$\Lambda = S^2\Gamma\sigma T$$

(vi) *Rho*:

$$\rho = \frac{\partial f_0}{\partial r} = S_0\,e^{-qT}n(d_1)\frac{\partial d_1}{\partial r} - X\,e^{-rT}\,n(d_2)\frac{\partial d_2}{\partial r} + \phi T X\,e^{-rT}\,N[\phi d_2]$$
$$\rho = \phi T X\,e^{-rT}\,N[\phi d_2]$$

(vii) The specific functional form of the Black Scholes formula leads to a very simple expression for $\Delta$. The value of a call option can be written

$$C_0 = \{e^{-qT}\,N[d_1]\}S_0 - \{X\,e^{-rT}\,N[d_2]\}$$
$$= \Delta S_0 - B_0$$

where the first line is the Black Scholes formula and the second line represents a replicating portfolio. The model can therefore be interpreted as the recipe for replicating a call: buy $e^{-qT}\,N[d_1]$ units of stock and borrow cash of $X\,e^{-rT}\,N[d_2]$.

(viii) *Approximate Option Values*: The relative complexity of the Black Scholes model means that it is quite hard to make a quick intuitive guess at the value of an option. However, practitioners often use the formula $0.4 \times \sigma\sqrt{T}\%$ as the price of an at-the-money-forward option, i.e. one where the strike price equals the forward price.

If $X = F_{0T}$ in equation (5.1), then we have $d_1 = \frac{1}{2}\sigma\sqrt{T}$ and $d_2 = -\frac{1}{2}\sigma\sqrt{T}$. Ignoring the dividends, we have for the price of a call option (or for that matter a put option):

$$C_0 = S_0\{N[+\sigma\sqrt{T}] - N[-\sigma\sqrt{T}]\}$$

The peak of a standard normal distribution is at a height of $1/\sqrt{2\pi} \approx 0.4$ [see equation (A1.2)], so if $\frac{1}{2}\sigma\sqrt{T}$ is small we can write

$$C_0 = S_0 \times 0.4 \times \sigma\sqrt{T}$$

For short-term, low-volatility options this works well, although the robustness of the approximation is surprising, even over a wide range. The exact and approximate call option values for $\sigma = 20\%$, $T = 3$ months are 3.99% and 4.00%; for $\sigma = 40\%$, $T = 4$ years they are 31.08% and 32.00%.

## 5.5 ADAPTATION TO DIFFERENT MARKETS

(i) The objective of this book is to provide the reader with a grounding in option theory, which can be applied to a variety of different markets. Most readers will be interested in one specific market, and it is always easier to read material which is narrowly specific to ones own area of interest, but unfortunately this is not a practicable way to write a book. This section tries to ease the reader's burden of adapting the material to his own specific area of interest.

In much of the forgoing, the market used to develop the theory was the equity market. This was chosen since it is the most straightforward and widely understandable for newcomers to finance theory: everyone understands what the price of one share of stock means and roughly how dividends work; a futures price or convenience yield is more arcane. Where equity failed to provide an adequate example, as in the discussions of arbitrage or futures, we have turned to other markets such as foreign exchange or commodities. At the risk of some repetition, we now summarize how the theory is adapted to other markets.

(ii) *Equities*: This is the easiest, since the theory has been developed largely with reference to this market. It is a very straightforward cash market, i.e. the commodity (stock) is purchased directly with physical delivery as soon as possible after purchase. In most established markets there are traded options on the most important stocks, although forwards and futures on single stocks have not yet become established.

This begs the following question: in the absence of a forward market, can we really price an option using the arbitrage arguments of Section 1.2, which were developed for the foreign exchange market with its large forward market which can be used to execute arbitrage trades? The answer is an emphatic yes; foreign exchange was merely used as a simple illustration of the no-arbitrage principle in its various forms. The notion of a forward can be used in pricing an option, even though no formal forward market exists. The arbitrage that is actually performed if an option is mispriced is not buying spot and selling forward, but extracting the option's fair value through delta hedging.

A formal forward market is not needed to calculate the fair value of an option from the notional forward price; but the delta hedge must exist. In some markets, shorting stock is illegal or restricted to certain categories of market participant, and often stock is just not available for borrowing. This means that positive delta positions (short puts, long calls) cannot be hedged and arbitrage arguments do not apply. The "fair value" is then no more than a hypothetical construction.

The "dividend" $q$ may be different for delta hedging with long or short stock positions. If the stock is held long, $q$ will indeed be the continuous dividend yield; but if the stock is held short, $q$ will be the total cash that needs to be paid out on the short position, i.e. continuous dividend *plus* stock borrowing cost.

(iii) *Prices, Values and Greeks of Forwards and Futures*: Before going on to discuss other markets it is worth briefly recapping on the meanings of the words "price" and "value". In the cash markets (equities, spot FX, spot commodities) the two mean exactly the same: if a stock *price* is $50 its *value* is $50. In the case of options, usage is rather context dependent, but usually price means what someone is prepared to pay, while value is calculated from the price of the underlying commodity using a model.

Confusion arises with forwards and futures contracts, but this is largely a matter of semantics:

- The forward ($F_{tT}$) or futures ($\Phi_{tT}$) *price* is the price at time $t$, at which one agrees to buy a commodity at time $T$ in the future. It was shown in Chapter 1 that if interest rates are constant, then $F_{tT} = \Phi_{tT} = S_t\,e^{(r-q)(T-t)}$.
- If the forward or futures contract is entered into at the prevailing market price (is at-the-money), then its *value* is zero.
- Suppose the contractual purchase price in a forward contract is not equal to the forward price but instead equal to $X$. The value of the contract is then given by equation (1.4):
$$f_{tT} = S_t\,e^{-q(T-t)} - X\,e^{-r(T-t)} = e^{-r(T-t)}(F_{tT} - X).$$
- It follows from the last point that the delta of a forward is $\Delta_{\text{fwd}} = \partial f_{tT}/\partial S_t = e^{-q(T-t)}$.
- A futures contract cannot build up value since it is marked to market daily and $\Phi_{\text{today}} - \Phi_{\text{yetsterday}} = \delta\Phi$ is paid over each day.
- An infinitesimal movement in the underlying price $\delta S_t$ will cause $\delta\Phi_{tT}$ to be paid over at the end of a given day. From the relation $\Phi_{tT} = S_t\,e^{(r-q)(T-t)}$, delta is given by $\Delta_{\text{fut}} = e^{(r-q)(T-t)}$.

Futures and forward contracts both have delta close to 100% but have no gamma. They are often used in place of the underlying stock or commodity to delta hedge options, since they involve no initial cash outlay.

(iv) *Foreign Exchange*: These are the largest and most liquid markets considered in this book. Most of the Black Scholes assumptions of Section 5.1 are fairly realistic, except for constant volatility. In addition to the spot market, foreign exchange is very actively traded between banks using over-the-counter (OTC) forward contracts; also, the important currencies have publicly traded futures markets.

The theory carries over very simply from that developed for equity: the stock simply becomes one unit of the foreign currency. The dividend throw-off is replaced by the foreign currency interest rate. This is a particularly easy substitution to make since interest rates are incurred continuously. In fact the continuous dividend yield Black Scholes model was really first developed for foreign exchange; in that context it is often known as the Garman Kohlhagen model.

Delta hedging of foreign currency options is *not* usually carried out with physical foreign currency. It is much more convenient and less cash consuming to use forward contracts or futures. Note that the forwards or futures do not have to have the same maturity as the option being hedged; the deltas of the option and its hedge just need to match.

(v) **Stock Indices and Commodities**: In theory one can invest in a stock index by buying a prescribed number of shares of each stock in the index. This is obviously too cumbersome to be practical for hedging, but a direct investment in the underlying index is often not possible since no traded instrument exists. In compensation, the futures markets on most major stock indices are very liquid and cheap to deal in, and are the normal source for delta hedges.

Options on commodities may also be analyzed using the Black Scholes methodology developed for equity derivatives. In this case, storage and insurance costs are treated as a *negative dividend* in the Black Scholes formula and in the formula relating the spot price to the futures price. In theory then, we could delta hedge a commodities option by getting the delta from the Black Scholes formula (setting dividends equal to negative storage costs); we would then hedge by buying or selling the right number of futures such that $\Delta_{fut}$ balances the delta of the option. Unfortunately, this does not work well in practice. In the first place, the storage model for commodities futures prices does not describe market prices well; and second, setting futures prices equal to forward prices only really works with constant, or at least uncorrelated, interest rates [see Section 1.4.(iii)].

If we write an option and try to hedge the position in the futures market, we then run the **basis** risk, or risk associated with futures prices deviating from the simple models previously described. However, an alternative approach avoids this problem: instead of writing an option on the spot price of a commodity, write it on the futures price. We turn our attention to these contracts next.

## 5.6   OPTIONS ON FORWARDS AND FUTURES

(i) Following the last section, we now examine what happens if the underlying security is itself a futures contract. For example, it was seen in the last section that a call option on a stock index could be dynamically hedged by buying or selling the appropriate number of stock index futures contracts; now we consider a call option on a stock index *futures price* rather than on the index itself.

The analysis is very similar for forward contracts and futures contracts, so these are treated together, with any divergence in behavior pointed out as we go along. Futures contracts are of course far more important in practice, since these are traded on exchanges, while active forward markets are normally interbank (especially in foreign exchange).

It is critical that the reader has a clear understanding of the concepts and notation of paragraph (iii) of the last section.

(ii) The payoff of an option on a futures or forward contract is more abstract than for a simple stock. Compare the following three European call options maturing in time $\tau$:

| $0$ | $t$ | $\tau$ | $T$ |
|---|---|---|---|
| now | time t | maturity of option | maturity of forward/ futures |

- **Options on the Underlying Stock Price:** the contract is an option to buy one share of stock at a price $X$.

$$\text{Payoff} = \max[(S_\tau - X), 0]$$

- **Options on the Forward Price:** this is an option that at time $\tau$ we can enter a forward contract maturing at time $T$, at a forward price of $X$. The value of this forward contract at time $\tau$ will be $(F_{T\tau} - X) e^{-r(\tau - T)}$.

$$\text{Payoff} = \max\left[(F_{\tau T} - X) e^{-r(T-\tau)}, 0\right]$$

- *Options on the Futures Price:* as in the last case, this is an option to enter a futures contract at time $\tau$ and price $X$; however, futures are marked to market daily so that a profit of $\Phi_{\tau T} - X$ would immediately be realized within one day of time $\tau$.

$$\text{Payoff} = \max[(\Phi_{\tau T} - X), 0]$$

(iii) The forward price is given by $F_{tT} = S_t \, e^{(r-q)(T-t)}$, and if interest rates are constant, we also have $F_{tT} = \Phi_{tT}$. We may therefore write

$$\text{Volatility of } F_{tT} = \text{volatility of } \Phi_{tT} = \sqrt{\text{var} \langle \ln S_t \rangle} = \sigma$$

In general, the volatility of the forward price equals the volatility of the spot price; the volatility of the futures price equals the volatility of the underlying stock if the interest rate is constant.

(iv) **Black Scholes Equation for Forwards/Futures**: We shall now repeat the analysis of Section 4.2(i)–(iii), but with a forward or futures price replacing the stock price of the underlying equity stock. We use the notation $V_{tT}$ to denote the forward/futures *price* and $v_{tT}$ as the *value* of the contract. Using the same construction as before, we suppose that we have a small portfolio containing a forward/futures option plus $\Delta$ units of forward/futures contracts, such that the portfolio is perfectly hedged against market movements. The value of the portfolio is

$$f_t - \Delta_t v_{tT} = f_t$$

The key difference between this and the previous analysis lies in this expression. For a forward contract, $v_{tT}$ is the value at time $t$ of a contract to buy a unit of commodity at time $T$ for a price equal to the time $t$ forward rate; but such a contract has zero value at time $t$. Similarly, a futures contract at time $t$ has zero value.

Now consider an infinitesimal time interval $\delta t$ during which the forward/futures contract changes in value by $\delta v_{tT}$. It follows from Section 5.5(iii) that

$$\delta v_{tT} = \begin{cases} e^{-r(T-t)} \delta F_{tT} & \text{forward} \\ \Phi_{t+\delta t \, T} - \Phi_{tT} = \delta \Phi_{tT} & \text{futures} \end{cases}$$

Either way, we can make the undemanding assumption that $\delta v_{tT} = A(V_{tT}, t)\delta V_{tT}$. The increase in value of the hedged portfolio over time $t$ can now be written

$$\delta f_t - \Delta_t \delta v_{tT} = \delta f_t - \Delta_t A_t \delta V_{tT}$$

The arbitrage condition corresponding to equations (4.5) is

$$\frac{\delta f_t - \Delta_t A_t \delta V_{tT}}{f_t} = r\delta t \tag{5.5}$$

It is assumed that forward and futures prices follow a similar Wiener process to a stock price:

$$\frac{\delta V_{tT}}{V_{tT}} = \mu \delta t + \sigma \delta W_t$$

Substituting this into equation (5.5) and using Ito's lemma for $\delta f_t$ gives

$$\left( \frac{\partial f_t}{\partial t} + \mu V_{tT} \frac{\partial f_t}{\partial V_{tT}} + \frac{1}{2}\sigma^2 V_{tT}^2 \frac{\partial^2 f_t}{\partial V_{tT}^2} \right) \delta t + \sigma V_{tT} \frac{\partial f_t}{\partial V_{tT}} \delta W_t$$

$$- V_{tT} A_t \left( \mu \delta t + \sigma \delta W_t \right) \Delta_t = r f_t \delta t$$

The coefficient of $\delta W_t$ must equal zero, since the portfolio is perfectly hedged, so that

$$A_t \Delta_t = \frac{\partial f_t}{\partial V_{tT}}$$

Substituting this into the remaining terms gives

$$\frac{\partial f_t}{\partial t} + \frac{1}{2}\sigma^2 V_{tT}^2 \frac{\partial^2 f_t}{\partial V_{tT}^2} = r f_t \tag{5.6}$$

(v) **Significance of the Simplified Black Scholes Equation:** The equation which has just been derived holds for forward prices and for futures prices. In the case of futures contracts, it does not depend on the idealized assumptions which were used to equate the forward and futures prices, i.e. constant interest rates.

The equation is simpler than the Black Scholes equation for options on an equity stock. The reason can be traced to equation (5.5): the cost of entering a forward or futures contract is zero, and these instruments have no dividend throw-off. Consequently, the financing costs for the hedge are zero and the financing term reduces merely to the cost of carrying the option itself. This becomes immediately plain by examining the Black Scholes equation written in the form of equation (4.20).

The partial differential equation for forwards/futures has the same form as the general Black Scholes equation for an equity stock, in which one has set $q = r$. This is in line with the properties of forwards and futures with which we are already familiar. Consider first the forward price: from equation (3.4) we have

$$E_t[S_T]_{\text{risk neutral}} = S_t\, e^{(r-q)(T-t)} = F_{tT}$$

where the symbol $E_t[\cdot]_{\text{risk neutral}}$ indicates that the expectation is taken at time $t$ and *risk neutral* means that we have set $\mu \to r$. Then

$$E_t[F_{\tau T}]_{\text{risk neutral}} = E_t\left[ S_\tau\, e^{(r-q)(T-\tau)} \right]_{\text{risk neutral}} = e^{(r-q)(T-\tau)} E_t[S_\tau]_{\text{risk neutral}}$$

$$= e^{(r-q)(T-\tau)} S_t\, e^{(r-q)(\tau-t)} = F_{tT}$$

The risk-neutral expected growth rate of $F_{tT}$ is therefore zero, which is the same as for an equity where $q = r$.

Clearly, this same result would hold for a futures price when $\Phi_{tT} = F_{tT}$, i.e. when interest rates are constant. However the result is more general, and holds for variable interest rates also. The reason is that a futures contract costs nothing to enter so that arbitrage assures that the expected profit from the contract must be zero:

$$E_t[\Phi_{\tau T}]_{\text{risk neutral}} = \Phi_{tT}$$

(vi) **Black '76 Model:** We have established that the Black Scholes equation for an option on a forward/futures price can be obtained from the general equation for an option on the equity price by setting $q \to r$; therefore, the Black Scholes formula for an option on a forward or futures price can be obtained from the general Black Scholes formula by just the same procedure:

$$f_t = e^{-r(\tau - t)} \phi \{ V_{tT} \, N[\phi d_1] - X \, N[\phi d_2] \}$$

$$d_1 = \frac{1}{\sigma \sqrt{\tau - t}} \left\{ \ln \frac{V_{tT}}{X} + \frac{1}{2} \sigma^2 (\tau - t) \right\} ; \qquad d_2 = d_1 - \sigma \sqrt{\tau - t}; \qquad V_{tT} = F_{tT} \quad \text{or} \quad \Phi_{tT}$$

$$(5.7)$$

$$c = e^{-rT} \left[ \ln \frac{F_0}{K} + \frac{\sigma^2}{2} T \right] \cdots \qquad \cdots$$

# 6

## American Options

Apart from a couple of sections in Chapter 2 and a few cursory references elsewhere, this book has so far concentrated on the behavior of European options. These are relatively easy to value and formulas normally exist for calculating prices and hedge parameters; but all of the general option theory that was developed in Chapter 4 applies to *any* derivative which may be perfectly hedged with underlying stock – American as well as European. In view of the widespread use of American options, especially in the exchange traded markets, the pricing of these will now be examined.

It should be stated at the outset that although the material in this chapter throws light on the nature of American options, the most common ways of evaluating these options are dealt with in later chapters. The reader in a hurry may prefer to limit his attention to Section 6.1.

### 6.1 BLACK SCHOLES EQUATION REVISITED

(i) Figure 6.1 shows the curves for the prices of an American and a European put option, each with strike price $X$. The American option has an additional constraint $P_A > X - S_0$ which does not apply to the European put: an in-the-money American put could be exercised at any time, to yield the payoff. In consequence, while the values of the two options might be fairly similar for large values of $S_0$, they might diverge sharply for smaller values of $S_0$, especially below $X$.

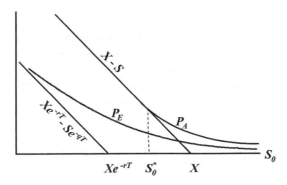

**Figure 6.1**  American vs. European put

(ii) In Section 4.2 the Black Scholes equation was derived from some very general hedging and arbitrage assumptions, and by an application of Ito's lemma. The rather heroic claim was made that the price of any derivative is a solution of this equation, with appropriate boundary conditions. We will test this by substituting the asymptotic values of the options into the Black Scholes equation. But first we re-state equation (4.8) in terms of the time to maturity $T$ by making the substitution $\partial/\partial t \rightarrow -\partial/\partial T$ [see Section 1.1(v)]. Options are valued in terms of today's stock price $S_0$:

$$-\frac{\partial P}{\partial T} + (r - q)S_0\frac{\partial P}{\partial S_0} + \tfrac{1}{2}S_0^2\sigma^2\frac{\partial^2 P}{\partial S_0^2} = rP \tag{6.1}$$

- As $S_0 \to \infty$, $P_E$, $P_A \to 0$; clearly this satisfies the Black Scholes equation for both American and European puts.
- For the European put, as $S_0 \to 0$, $P_E \to X\,e^{-rT} - S_0\,e^{-qT}$. Substituting this asymptotic value of $P_E$ shows that this expression is indeed a solution to the Black Scholes equation.
- For the American put, as $S_0 \to 0$, $P_A \to X - S_0$. Substituting into the equation gives

$$\{r - q\}S = r\{X - S\}$$

This is obviously not true, so that $P_A = X - S_0$ is not a solution of the Black Scholes equation.

(iii) This last conclusion is rather unsettling and needs further investigation. The derivation of the Black Scholes equation depends on two elements: first, Ito's lemma which presupposes that $P(S_0, T)$ is a continuous and well-behaved function of $S_0$ and $T$; second, that a perfect hedge can be constructed over an infinitesimal interval of time.

The second of these assumptions is certainly true; but the first is only half true. Referring to Figure 6.1, the curve of $P_A$ is a function of $T$ and is a solution of the Black Scholes equation for values of $S_0^* < S_0$; but if $S_0 < S_0^*$, then $P_A = X - S_0$ which is neither a function of $T$ nor a solution of this equation.

In summary, the value of an American put may be written

$$P_A = \begin{cases} X - S_0 & S_0 < S_0^* \\ f(S_0, T) & S_0^* < S_0 \end{cases} \tag{6.2}$$

where $f(S_0, T)$ is a solution of the Black Scholes equation and $S_0^*$ is some (as yet unknown) function of $T$. The region $S_0 < S_0^*$ where $P_A = X - S_0$ is the region where the American option should be exercised and $S_0^*$ is known as the **exercise boundary**.

The former conclusion, that the price of an option must satisfy the Black Scholes equation, now needs to be modified slightly: it is indeed true *unless* the option is in a region where it needs to be exercised.

(iv) Figure 6.2 shows how $P_A$ behaves above and below $S_0^*$. Suppose the stock price is exactly $S_0^*$: an American put option (which is in-the-money) is hedged with one share of stock and the value of this portfolio is $P_A + S_0^* = X$. Below the exercise boundary the portfolio has a constant value $X$ so that a fall in the stock price to $S_0^* - \delta S_0$ has no effect on the value of the portfolio. On the other hand, if the stock price rises to $S_0^* + \delta S_0$, the value of the portfolio increases by

$$\left.\frac{\partial f_A}{\partial S_0}\right]_{S_0 = S_0^*} \delta S_0 + \delta S_0$$

This presents a forbidden arbitrage opportunity unless $\partial f_A/\partial S_0 = -1$. The common sense conclusion is that the two parts of $P_A$ join smoothly without a kink or discontinuity. This is known as the "smoothness condition".

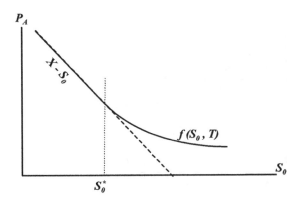

**Figure 6.2**   American put option price

(v) This section might have increased the reader's understanding of the nature of the Black Scholes equation and its application to American options; but unfortunately there is no tidy, analytical solution of the equation available for American options, analogous to the Black Scholes model for European options.

Very general solutions *are* available using numerical techniques (the binomial method) and will be explored in detail in later chapters. These methods are so widely understood and accessible that they have really swept the board as the main tools for evaluating a wide range of American-style options. The one initial drawback was that they took a lot of computing power, but this resource has become cheaper, numerical methods have eclipsed a number of formerly useful and ingenious closed form solutions of the Black Scholes equation which were devised for special cases of American options. However, it is worth briefly looking at a couple of these methods, if only to illustrate the theory developed in the last few pages.

## 6.2   BARONE-ADESI AND WHALEY APPROXIMATION

(i) This method can be applied to continuous dividend puts and calls. We will restrict our analysis to put options where price divergence between European and American options is greater, but the analysis for calls is exactly analogous (Barone-Adesi and Whaley, 1987).

The price of an American put option can be written $P_A = P_E + \varphi$, where $P_E$ is the price of the European option and $\varphi$ is a premium for the possibility of early exercise. This method seeks a way of calculating $\varphi$; the Black Scholes model is used to calculate the values of $P_E$.

$P_A$ is a solution to the Black Scholes equation in the region $S_0^* < S_0$, i.e. above the exercise boundary. Therefore in this region, $\varphi$ is also a solution of the Black Scholes equation. Rearranging from the normal order a little gives

$$\tfrac{1}{2}S_0^2\sigma^2\frac{\partial^2\varphi}{\partial S_0^2} + (r-q)S_0\frac{\partial\varphi}{\partial S_0} - r\varphi - \frac{\partial\varphi}{\partial T} = 0 \qquad (6.3)$$

(ii) Consider the evolution of $\varphi$ over time which is illustrated in Figure 6.3. The key properties of this graph are as follows:

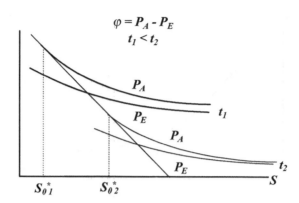

**Figure 6.3**   American put options

(A) The quantity $\varphi$ is defined only in the region $S_0^* < S_0$.
(B) $S_0^*$ is a function of $r$, $q$, $T$ and $\sigma$; it decreases as $T$ increases.
(C) As $S_0 \to \infty$ we expect $\varphi \to 0$ since it is unlikely that the stock price will reach the $S_0^*$ where early exercise occurs.
(D) If $S_0$ is small (but nevertheless above $S_0^*$), $\varphi$ will approach its asymptotic value $(X - S_0) - (X e^{-rT} - S_0 e^{-qT}) \approx X(1 - e^{-rT})$ for small dividend yield $q$.
(E) If $T \to 0$ we must have $\varphi \to 0$ since the early exercise possibility ceases to have any meaning.

(iii) Define a new variable $v = \varphi/(1 - e^{-rT})$; differentiating with respect to $T$ gives

$$-r\varphi - \frac{\partial \varphi}{\partial T} = -\frac{r\varphi}{(1 - e^{-rT})} - (1 - e^{-rT})\frac{\partial v}{\partial T}$$

Substituting this back into equation (6.3) gives

$$\tfrac{1}{2}S_0^2 \sigma^2 \frac{\partial^2 \varphi}{\partial S_0^2} + (r - q)S_0 \frac{\partial \varphi}{\partial S_0} - \frac{r\varphi}{(1 - e^{-rT})} - (1 - e^{-rT})\frac{\partial v}{\partial T} = 0 \qquad (6.4)$$

Consider now the last term in this equation:

• From (C) above, as $S_0 \to \infty$, $\varphi \to 0$ and therefore $v \to 0$; therefore the last term in equation (6.4) goes to zero.
• From (D), when $S_0 \to 0$, $\varphi$, approaches $X(1 - e^{-rT})$; therefore $v$ approaches a constant and the last term in equation (6.4) goes to zero.
• From (E), as $T \to 0$, the expression in brackets in the last term of equation (6.4) goes to zero.

In each of these limits of the variables $S_0$ and $T$, the last term of equation (6.4) may be set to zero. The Barone-Adesi and Whaley (BAW) method assumes that this last term in the equation may *always* be set equal to zero.

(iv) The BAW equation can now be written as

$$S_0^2 \frac{d^2\varphi}{dS_0^2} + bS_0 \frac{d\varphi}{dS_0} + c\varphi = 0 \qquad \text{where} \qquad b = \frac{(r-q)}{\frac{1}{2}\sigma^2}; \qquad c = \frac{-r}{\frac{1}{2}\sigma^2(1 - e^{-rT})}$$

This is a standard differential equation known as the Cauchy linear differential equation. Its general solution is

$$\varphi = AS^{\gamma_1} + BS^{\gamma_2}$$

where $A$ and $B$ depend on the boundary conditions and

$$\gamma_1 = \tfrac{1}{2}\{-(b-1) + \sqrt{(b-1)^2 - 4c}\}; \qquad \gamma_2 = \tfrac{1}{2}\{-(b-1) - \sqrt{(b-1)^2 - 4c}\}$$

(v) $c$ is always negative, so that $\gamma_1$ and $\gamma_2$ must be real; furthermore, $\gamma_1$ must be positive and $\gamma_2$ must be negative. But if $\gamma_1$ is positive, then the boundary condition $\lim_{S_0 \to \infty} P_A \to 0$ means that we must have $A = 0$. We are then left with the following two-part solution:

$$P_A = \begin{cases} X - S_0 & S_0 < S_0^* \\ P_E + \varphi = P_E + BS_0^{\gamma_2} & S_0^* < S_0 \end{cases}$$

These two complementary solutions for $P_A$ must be equal at the point $S_0 = S_0^*$. Furthermore, the smoothness condition of Section 6.1(iv) means that the slopes of the two functions must be the same at this point. This leads to the conditions

$$\left. \begin{array}{l} X - S_0^* = P_E^* + BS_0^{*\gamma_2} \\ \Delta_E^* + B\gamma_2 S_0^{*\gamma_2 - 1} = -1 \end{array} \right\} \qquad \text{or equivalently} \qquad \begin{cases} X - S_0^* = P_E^* + \dfrac{S_0^*}{\gamma_2}\{1 + \Delta_E^*\} \\ B = -\dfrac{1 + \Delta_E^*}{\gamma_2 S_0^{*\gamma_2 - 1}} \end{cases}$$

where $P_E^*$ and $\Delta_E^*$ are Black Scholes values calculated at $S_0 = S_0^*$. The value of $S_0^*$ must be calculated numerically from the implicit equation which is the first on the right-hand side above. The easiest way to do this is to use the Black Scholes formulas for $P_E^*$ and $\Delta_E^*$ and use a "goal seek" function on a spread sheet. Finally, the formula for the price of an American put above the exercise boundary is

$$P_A = P_E - \frac{1 + \Delta_E^*}{\gamma_2} S_0^* \left(\frac{S_0}{S_0^*}\right)^{\gamma_2}$$

(vi) This model is quite ingenious, but the real test is how accurately it prices an option. Table 6.1 gives the prices of put options with $X = 100, r = 10\%, q = 1\%, \sigma = 25\%$ for a range of values of $S_0$ and $T$. BN is the value of an American put calculated with the binomial model using a large number of steps and may be taken as the "right answer". BS is the Black Scholes price of a European put.

The results are fairly good overall, and are in line with the nature of the approximation made: when $T$ is either large or small, subsection (iii) shows that the last term in equation (6.4)

**Table 6.1**   Comparison of models

|  |  | American Put | | European Put |
|---|---|---|---|---|
|  | $S_0$ | BAW | BN | BS |
| $T = 1$ month | 90 | 10.00 | 10.00 | 9.52 |
|  | 95 | 5.58 | 5.61 | 5.42 |
|  | 100 | 2.56 | 2.56 | 2.51 |
|  | 105 | 0.94 | 0.94 | 0.92 |
|  | 110 | 0.27 | 0.27 | 0.26 |
| $S_0^* = 90.31$ | 115 | 0.06 | 0.06 | 0.06 |
| $T = 10$ years | 70 | 30.00 | 30.00 | 5.33 |
|  | 80 | 20.50 | 20.56 | 4.23 |
|  | 90 | 14.34 | 14.35 | 3.40 |
|  | 100 | 10.42 | 10.38 | 2.75 |
|  | 110 | 7.81 | 7.71 | 2.25 |
| $S_0^* = 75.40$ | 120 | 6.00 | 5.87 | 1.86 |
| $T = 3$ years | 70 | 30.00 | 30.00 | 15.49 |
|  | 80 | 20.17 | 20.21 | 11.30 |
|  | 90 | 13.35 | 13.33 | 8.18 |
|  | 100 | 9.08 | 8.96 | 5.88 |
|  | 110 | 6.29 | 6.10 | 4.22 |
|  | 130 | 3.14 | 2.91 | 2.18 |
|  | 150 | 1.63 | 1.45 | 1.13 |
| $S_0^* = 77.40$ | 200 | 0.37 | 0.27 | 0.23 |

may be dropped. For intermediate values of $T$ (we have taken 3 years), this assumption is less justified and the results show that the errors are greater.

## 6.3   PERPETUAL PUTS

(i) The concept of a perpetual option seems bizarre. For European options it is meaningless: a call option may go further and further in-the-money indefinitely, but it cannot be exercised until maturity which is never reached!

For American options, which can be exercised at any time, the concept makes more sense, and we examine the case of a perpetual put. If $r > q$, the expected value of the stock price $S$ (the forward rate) drifts upwards over time so that the option gets indefinitely further out-of-the-money; but in the early stages of this infinitely long process, there is some probability that it will pay to exercise the option. Later, the probability recedes to zero.

(ii) An exact solution to this problem can be obtained using the techniques of Section 6.2. The Black Scholes equation in the region above the exercise boundary can be written

$$\tfrac{1}{2}S^2\sigma^2\frac{\partial^2 P_\infty}{\partial S_0^2} + (r - q)S\frac{\partial P_\infty}{\partial S_0} - rP_\infty - \frac{\partial P_\infty}{\partial T} = 0$$

Since the put is *perpetual*, it cannot be a function of time, so the last term is zero and we are left with Cauchy's equation:

$$S^2\frac{d^2 P_\infty}{dS_0^2} + bS\frac{dP_\infty}{dS_0} + cP_\infty = 0 \qquad \text{where} \qquad b = (r-q)/\tfrac{1}{2}\sigma^2; \qquad c = -r/\tfrac{1}{2}\sigma^2$$

We have already come across the solution to this equation in the last section:

$$P_\infty = AS^{\gamma_1} + BS^{\gamma_2}$$

$$\gamma_1 = \tfrac{1}{2}\{-(b-1) + \sqrt{(b-1)^2 - 4c}\}; \qquad \gamma_2 = \tfrac{1}{2}\{-(b-1) - \sqrt{(b-1)^2 - 4c}\}$$

Again, $\gamma_1$ must be positive and $\gamma_2$ must be negative, so that the boundary condition $\lim_{S_0 \to \infty} P_A \to 0$ gives $A = 0$. We are left with the two-part solution

$$P_\infty = \begin{cases} X - S_0 & S_0 < S_0^* \\ BS_0^{\gamma_2} & S_0^* < S_0 \end{cases}$$

The two solutions and their first differentials must both be equal at $S_0 = S_0^*$ which leads to the conditions

$$\left.\begin{matrix} X - S_0^* = BS_0^{*\gamma_2} \\ -1 = B\gamma_2 S_0^{*\gamma_2 - 1} \end{matrix}\right\} \qquad \text{or equivalently} \qquad \begin{cases} S_0^* = \dfrac{\gamma_2 X}{\gamma_2 - 1} \\ B = -\dfrac{1}{\gamma_2}\left(\dfrac{\gamma_2 - 1}{\gamma_2 X}\right)^{\gamma_2 - 1} \end{cases}$$

The final result may be summarized as

$$P_\infty = \begin{cases} X - S_0 & S_0 < \dfrac{\gamma_2 X}{\gamma_2 - 1} \\ -\dfrac{1}{\gamma_2}\left(\dfrac{\gamma_2 - 1}{\gamma_2 X}\right)^{\gamma_2 - 1} S_0^{\gamma_2} & \dfrac{\gamma_2 X}{\gamma_2 - 1} < S_0 \end{cases}$$

$$\gamma_2 = \tfrac{1}{2}\{-(b-1) - \sqrt{(b-1)^2 - 4c}\} \qquad \text{where} \qquad b = (r-q)/\tfrac{1}{2}\sigma^2; \qquad c = -r/\tfrac{1}{2}\sigma^2$$

(iii) There are no approximations made in this particular model, so accuracy should not be an issue. Taking a put with $S_0 = 100$, $X = 100$, $r = 10\%$, $q = 4\%$, $\sigma = 25\%$, we compare the price of this perpetual put with a binomial put of maturity 200 years with several thousand steps:

$$P_\infty = 13.18$$
$$P_{\text{bin}}(200 \text{ years}) = 13.09$$

## 6.4 AMERICAN OPTIONS ON FUTURES AND FORWARDS

(i) There is a divergence between the behavior of American options on forwards and futures; also between these and American options on the underlying stock.

Recall from the analysis of Section 2.3 that an American call option on a non-dividend-paying stock can be priced as a European option (since it makes no sense to exercise before maturity). The same is *not* true of an American put. This can be summed up as

$$C_A(S_0) = C_E(S_0); \qquad P_A(S_0) > P_E(S_0)$$

If the stock pays a dividend, an American call may of course be more valuable than a European call. Forward and futures contracts do not pay dividends, so can one automatically assume that the behavior follows that of non-dividend-paying stock?

(ii) **Option on Forward Price:** Consider both an American and a European call option with maturity $\tau$ on a forward contract with maturity $T$ ($\tau < T$). We compare the payoff of the American option at time $t$ (if it were exercised at $t$) with the fair value of the European option at the same time. From equation (1.4) the American payoff can be written

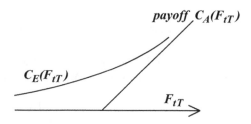

**Figure 6.4**   Option on forward

$$\text{Payoff } C_A = \begin{cases} e^{-r(T-t)}\{F_{tT} - X\} \\ 0 \end{cases}$$

Equation (5.6) (Black '76 model) gives the formula

$$C_E(F_{tT}) = e^{-r(\tau-t)}\{F_{tT}\, N[d_1] - X\, N[d_2]\}$$

As $F_{tT} \to 0$, both these last two expressions tend to zero. As $F_{tT} \to \infty$, $N[d_1]$ and $N[d_2]$ both tend to one; but we always have $\tau < T$ so that the exponential discount factor is smaller for the American payoff than for the value of the European option. It follows that we always have

$$\text{Payoff } C_A(F_{tT}) < C_E(F_{tT})$$

as shown in Figure 6.4.

The arguments of Section 2.3 show that this leads to the conclusion that it would never pay to exercise an American call option on a futures price; but if an American option were never exercised, its value would be the same as that of the corresponding European option. A precisely similar argument can be made to demonstrate that an American put option on a forward price is worth the same as the European option. This is of course in sharp contrast to the result for the options on the underlying stock – where an American put is worth more than a European put. In conclusion

$$C_A(F_{tT}) \le C_E(F_{tT}); \qquad P_A(F_{tT}) = P_E(F_{tT})$$

(iii) **Option on Futures Price:** Let us repeat the analysis of the last section for American and European call options on the futures price rather than the forward price:

$$\text{Payoff } C_A = \begin{cases} \{\Phi_{tT} - X\} \\ 0 \end{cases}$$

$$C_E(\Phi_{tT}) = e^{-r(T-t)}\{\Phi_{tT}\, N[d_1] - X\, N[d_2]\}$$

The difference between this and the previous case is that the futures contract settles daily so that any option payoff is realized immediately; hence the absence of the exponential factor in the American option payoff. This means that as $\Phi_{tT} \to \infty$, the curve for the price of the European option will at some point cut across the payoff line for the American option, as shown in Figure 6.5. The same reasoning also applies to a put option on a futures price. Again using the analysis of Section 2.3, we conclude that

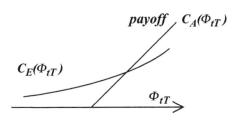

**Figure 6.5**   Option on futures

$$C_A(\Phi_{tT}) > C_E(\Phi_{tT}); \qquad P_A(\Phi_{tT}) > P_E(\Phi_{tT}).$$

# Part 2
## Numerical Methods

# 7

# The Binomial Model

This is one of the most important chapters of this book, so it is worth giving a road map of where we are going.

Section 7.1 introduces the binomial model based on the random walk which is discussed in the Appendix. This converges to the lognormal distribution for stock price movements, when the number of steps is large; the price of an option computed by the binomial model will therefore converge to the analytical formulas based on a lognormal assumption for the stock price movements.

Section 7.2 shows how to go about setting up a binomial tree while Section 7.3 gives several worked examples of the binomial model applied to specific option pricing problems.

The consequences of the binomial model for the derivatives industry have been enormous. It is a powerful and flexible pricing tool for a variety of options which are too complicated for analytical solution. But the impact on the industry goes further than this. Very little technical skill is needed to set up a random walk model; yet these models can be shown to converge reliably to the "right answer" if the number of steps is large enough. This approach has therefore opened up the arcane world of option pricing to thousands of professionals, with an intuitive yet accurate method of pricing options without recourse to advanced mathematics. Without these developments, option pricing would have remained the domain of a few specialists.

## 7.1 RANDOM WALK AND THE BINOMIAL MODEL

(i) The following results are demonstrated in Appendix A.2 for a random walk with forward and backward step lengths $U$ and $D$ and probabilities $p$ and $1 - p$. If $x_n$ is the distance traveled after $n$ steps of the random walk, then

- $E[x_N] = N\{pU - (1 - p)D\}$
- $\text{var}[x_N] = Np(1 - p)(U + D)^2$
- The distribution of $x_N$ is a binomial distribution which approaches the normal distribution as $N \to \infty$.

Consider now the movement of a stock price. It was seen in Section 3.1 that the logarithm of the stock price ($\ln S_t$) follows a normal distribution. If we observe the stock price at discrete intervals of time, we postulate that $x_i = \ln S_i$ follows a random walk. The distribution of $x_i$ then approximates to a normal distribution more and more closely if we make the number of intervals larger and larger. If $x_i$ is the logarithm of the stock price at the beginning of step $i$ then we have $x_{i+1} = x_i + U$ or $x_{i+1} = x_i - D$ (i.e. $S_{i+1} = S_i e^U$ or $S_{i+1} = S_i e^{-D}$) with probabilities $p$ and $1 - p$. In the limit of small time intervals ($N \to \infty$; $U$ and $D \to 0$), $x_N$ is normally distributed and $S_N$ is lognormally distributed.

In the following analysis we switch our attention to the behavior of $S_N$ rather than $x_N$. This actually complicates the algebra a bit, but has the advantage of providing a more intuitive picture; in any case, it conforms with the way most of the literature is written. A condition for

$x_N$ to approach a normal distribution is that $U$ and $D$ are constants; the corresponding condition for $S_N$ to approach the lognormal distribution is that $u = e^U$ and $d = e^{-D}$ should be constant *multiplicative* factors. The progress of $x_N$ is described as an **arithmetic** random walk, while $S_N$ follows a **geometric** random walk.

(ii) **Single Step Binomial Model:** A description of the binomial model starts with the simple one-step example of Section 4.1.

Suppose the stock and derivative start with prices $S_0$ and $f_0$. After a time interval $\delta t$, $S_{\delta t}$ has one of two possible values, $S_u$ or $S_d$, with corresponding derivative prices $f_u$ and $f_d$ (Figure 7.1).

If a perfect hedge can be formed between one unit of derivative and $\Delta$ units of stock, we saw in Section 4.1(iv) that the no-arbitrage condition imposes the following condition:

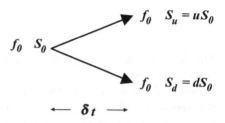

**Figure 7.1** Two possible final states

$$f_u - \Delta S_u = f_d - \Delta S_d = (1 + r\delta t)(f + \Delta S)$$

We find it simpler to manipulate the interest term in continuous form, although many authors develop the theory in the form just given. For small time steps and to first order in $\delta t$, the results are the same. These equations can then be rewritten as

$$S_0 = e^{-r\delta t}(pS_u + (1 - p)S_d); \qquad f_0 = e^{-r\delta t}(pf_u + (1 - p)f_d)$$

$$\Delta = \frac{f_u - f_d}{S_u - S_d}; \qquad\qquad p = \frac{S_0 e^{r\delta T} - S_d}{S_u - S_d} \qquad (7.1)$$

It is critically important to realize that we have *not* started by defining $p$ as the probability of an up-move. We have started from the no-arbitrage equations in which a parameter $p$ appears. It happens to have the general "shape" of a probability and is interpreted as the pseudo-probability (i.e. probability in a risk-neutral world) that $S_0$ moves to $S_u$ in the period $\delta t$.

If continuous dividends were taken into account, we would make the substitution $S_{\delta t} \rightarrow S_{\delta t} e^{-q\delta t}$ in the first equation and $p$ would then be given by

$$p = \frac{F_{0\delta t} - S_d}{S_u - S_d}$$

where $F_{0\delta t} = S_0 e^{(r-q)\delta t}$ is the forward rate.

(iii) **Conditions on Drift and Variance:** Values can be obtained for $u$, $d$ and $p$ from a knowledge of the mean and variance of $S_{\delta t}$. Writing $S_u = uS_0$ and $S_d = dS_0$ and interpreting $p$ as the probability of an up-move in a risk-neutral world, the mean and variance of $S_{\delta t}$ may be written

$$E[S_{\delta t}] = \{pS_u + (1 - p)S_d\} = S_0\{pu + (1 - p)d\}$$

$$\text{var}[S_{\delta t}] = \{pS_u^2 + (1 - p)S_u^2\} - E^2[S_{\delta t}] = S_0^2 p(1 - p)(u - d)^2 \qquad (7.2)$$

Recall the following results derived in Section 3.2(ii) and applied to a risk-neutral world:

$$E[S_{\delta t}] = S_0 e^{(r-q)\delta t} = F_{0\delta t}; \qquad \text{var}[S_{\delta t}] = E^2[S_{\delta t}]\{e^{\sigma^2\delta t} - 1\} \approx F_{0\delta t}^2 \sigma^2 \delta t + O[\delta t^2]$$

Equating these last two sets of equations and dropping terms of higher order in $\delta t$ gives

$$F_{0\delta t} = S_0\{pu + (1-p)\,d\}; \qquad F_{0\delta t}^2\sigma^2\delta t = S_0^2 p(1-p)(u-d)^2 \tag{7.3}$$

These are two equations in three unknowns ($u$, $d$ and $p$), so there is leeway to choose one of the parameters; is there any constraint in this seemingly arbitrary choice?

From the first relationship, it is clear that if $S_u \; (= uS_0)$ and $S_d \; (= dS_0)$ do not straddle $F_{0\delta t}$, then either $p$ or $(1-p)$ must be negative. Since we wish to interpret $p$ as a probability (albeit in a risk-neutral world), we must impose the condition $S_d < F_{0\delta t} < S_u$.

The function $p(1-p)$ has a maximum at $p = \frac{1}{2}$. The second of equations (7.3) above therefore yields the following inequality:

$$\frac{F_{0\delta t}\sigma\sqrt{\delta t}}{S_u - S_d} \leq \frac{1}{2} \tag{7.4}$$

This is really saying that if the spread $S_u - S_d$ is not chosen large enough, the random walk will not be able to approximate a normal distribution with volatility $\sigma$.

(iv) **Relationship with Wiener Process**: Another way of looking at the analysis of the last paragraph is to say that the Wiener process $S_{t+\delta t} - S_t = \delta S_t = S_t(r-q)\delta t + S_t\sigma\sqrt{\delta t}\,z$ can be represented by one step in a binomial process, where $z$ is a standard normal variate so that $E[S_{\delta t}] = S_0(1 + (r-q)\,\delta t)$ and $\text{var}[S_{\delta t}] = S_0^2\sigma^2\delta t$.

We must now choose $u$, $d$ and $p$ to match these, i.e.

$$E[S_{\delta t}] = S_0(1 + (r-q)\delta t) = S_0(pu + (1-p)d)$$

$$\text{var}[S_{\delta t}] = S_0^2\sigma^2\delta t = S_0^2 p\,(1-p)(u-d)^2 \tag{7.5}$$

The reader may very well object at this point since this seems to be the wrong answer; equations (7.3) and (7.5) are not quite the same. But recall that the entire Ito analysis is based on rejection of terms of order higher than $\delta t$:

$$F_{0\delta t} = S_0\,e^{(r-q)\delta t} = S_0\,\{1 + (r-q)\,\delta t\} + O[\delta t^2]; \qquad F_{0\delta t}\,\sigma\sqrt{\delta t} = S_0\,\sigma\sqrt{\delta t} + O[\sqrt{\delta t^3}]$$

To within this order, the results of this and the last subparagraph are therefore equivalent.

## 7.2   THE BINOMIAL NETWORK

(i) The stock price movement over a single step of length $\delta t$ is of little use in itself. We need to construct a network of successive steps covering the entire period from now to the maturity of the option; the beginning of one such network is shown in Figure 7.2.

The procedure for using this model to price an option is as follows:

(A) Select parameters $u$, $d$ and $p$ which conform to equation (7.2). The most popular ways of doing this are described in the following subparagraphs.
(B) Using these values of $u$ and $d$, work out the possible values for the stock price at the final nodes at $t = T$. We could work out the stock value for each node in the tree but if the tree is European, we only need the stock values in the last column of nodes.
(C) Corresponding to each of the final nodes at time $t = T$, there will be a stock price $S_{m,T}$ where $m$ indicates the specific node in the final column of nodes.

(D) Assume the derivative depends only on the final stock price. Corresponding to the stock price at each final node, there will be a derivative payoff $f_{m,T}(S_T)$.

(E) Just as each node is associated with a stock price, each node has a derivative price. The nodal derivative prices are related to each other by the repeated use of equations (7.1). Looking at Figure 7.2 we have

$$f_4 = e^{-r\delta t}\{pf_7 + (1-p)f_8\}$$
$$f_5 = e^{-r\delta t}\{pf_8 + (1-p)f_9\}$$
$$\vdots$$
$$f_2 = e^{-r\delta t}\{pf_4 + (1-p)f_5\}$$
$$\vdots$$

This sequence of calculations allows the present value of the option, $f_0$, to be calculated from the payoff values of the option, $f_{m,T}(S_T)$; this is commonly referred to as "rolling back through the tree".

(ii) **Jarrow and Rudd:** There remains the question of our choice of $u$, $d$ and $p$. The options are examined for a simple arithmetic random walk in Appendix A.2(v); we now develop the corresponding theory for a geometric random walk.

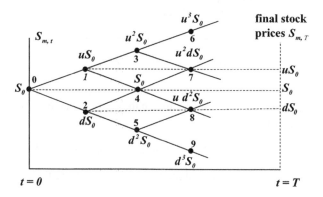

**Figure 7.2** Binomial tree (Jarrow–Rudd)

The most popular choice is to put $u = d^{-1}$, giving the same proportional move up and down. Writing $u = d^{-1} = e^{\Delta}$, substituting in equations (7.5) and rejecting terms higher than $\delta t$ gives $\Delta = \sigma \sqrt{\delta t}$. The pseudo-probability of an up-move is then given by

$$p = \frac{e^{(r-q)\delta t} - e^{-\sigma\sqrt{\delta t}}}{e^{\sigma\sqrt{\delta t}} - e^{-\sigma\sqrt{\delta t}}} \approx \frac{1 + (r-q)\delta t - \left(1 - \sigma\sqrt{\delta t} + \frac{1}{2}\sigma^2\delta t\right)}{\left(1 + \sigma\sqrt{\delta t} + \frac{1}{2}\sigma^2\delta t\right) - \left(1 - \sigma\sqrt{\delta t} + \frac{1}{2}\sigma^2\delta t\right)}$$

$$\approx \frac{1}{2} + \frac{1}{2}\frac{r - q - \frac{1}{2}\sigma^2}{\sigma}\sqrt{\delta t} \tag{7.6}$$

Apart from its simplicity of form, this choice is popular because $u = d^{-1}$. The effect of this is that in Figure 7.2, $S_4 = udS_0 = S_0$. In other words, the center of the network remains at a constant $S_0$. Compare this formula for $p$ with the corresponding result for an arithmetic random

walk given by equation (A2.7). An extra term $\frac{1}{2}\sigma^2$ has appeared in the drift, which typically happens when we move from a normal distribution to a lognormal one.
   Final stock prices merely take the values

$$S_0\,e^{-N\sigma\sqrt{\delta t}},\; S_0\,e^{-(N-1)\sigma\sqrt{\delta t}},\; \ldots,\; 0,\; \ldots,\; S_0\,e^{N\sigma\sqrt{\delta t}}$$

where $N$ is the number of steps in the model.

(iii) **Cox, Ross and Rubinstein**: An alternative, popular arrangement of $S_u$ and $S_d$ is to start the other way round: specify the pseudo-probability as $p = \frac{1}{2}$ and derive a compatible pair $u$ and $d$. Putting $p = \frac{1}{2}$ in equations (7.3) gives

$$S_0\left(\tfrac{1}{2}u + \tfrac{1}{2}d\right) = F_{0\delta t} \qquad \text{or} \qquad S_0(u + d) = 2\,F_{0\delta t}$$

$$\tfrac{1}{2}\left(1 - \tfrac{1}{2}\right)S_0^2(u - d)^2 = F_{0\delta t}^2\,\sigma^2\delta t \qquad \text{or} \qquad S_0(u - d) = 2\,F_{0\delta t}\,\sigma\sqrt{\delta t}$$

The equations on the right immediately yield

$$u = \frac{F_{0\delta t}}{S_0}\,(1 + \sigma\sqrt{\delta t}); \qquad d = \frac{F_{0\delta t}}{S_0}\,(1 - \sigma\sqrt{\delta t}) \qquad (7.7)$$

The binomial network for these values is shown in Figure 7.3. The probability of an up-move or a down-move at each node is now $\frac{1}{2}$. The center line of the network is no longer horizontal, but slopes up. At node 4 in the diagram the stock price is

$$S_{\text{center},2\delta t} = S_4 = ud\,S_0 = S_0\,e^{(r-q)2\delta t}(1 - \sigma\sqrt{\delta t})(1 + \sigma\sqrt{\delta t})$$
$$= S_0\,e^{(r-q)2\delta t}\left(1 - \tfrac{1}{2}\sigma^2 2\delta t\right) = S_0\,e^{(r-q)2\delta t}\left(1 - \tfrac{1}{2}\sigma^2\tfrac{T}{N/2}\right)$$

There are N steps altogether so that $\delta t = T/N$, and the center line $S_{\text{center}}$ has equation

$$S_{\text{center},T} = S_0\,e^{(r-q)T}\left(1 - \tfrac{1}{2}\sigma^2\tfrac{T}{N/2}\right)^{N/2}$$
$$\to \exp\left(r - q - \tfrac{1}{2}\sigma^2\right)T \quad \text{as} \quad N \to \infty$$

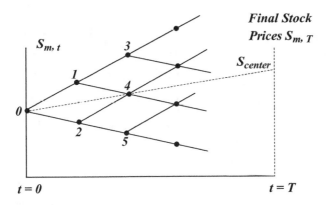

**Figure 7.3**   Binomial tree (Cox–Ross–Rubinstein)

Final stock prices now take values

$$S_0(1 + \sigma\sqrt{\delta t})^N \, e^{(r-q-\frac{1}{2}\sigma^2)T}, \quad S_0(1 + \sigma\sqrt{\delta t})^{N-1}(1 - \sigma\sqrt{\delta t}) \, e^{(r-q-\frac{1}{2}\sigma^2)T}, \ldots,$$

$$S_0(1 - \sigma\sqrt{\delta t})^N \, e^{(r-q-\frac{1}{2}\sigma^2)T}$$

(iv) For completeness, we list a third discretization occasionally used:

$$u = \exp\{(r - q)\delta t + \sigma\sqrt{\delta t}\}; \qquad d = \exp\{(r - q)\delta t - \sigma\sqrt{\delta t}\}$$

Substituting in equation (7.5) and retaining only terms O[$\delta t$] gives $p = \frac{1}{2}(1 - \frac{1}{2}\sigma\sqrt{\delta t})$. The center line of the grid now has the equation $S_{\text{center}} = S_0 \, e^{(r-q)t}$, which is the equation for the forward rate (known as the *forward curve*).

## 7.3   APPLICATIONS

(i) *European Call: Jarrow–Rudd Method* ($u = d^{-1} = e^{\sigma\sqrt{dt}}$)**:** consider the tree shown in Figure 7.4. From the specification of the option and equation (7.6), the following parameters can be calculated:

With three steps $\delta t = 0.5/3$ :     $F_{t\,t+\delta t} = S_t \, e^{(r-q)\delta t} = 1.01005 S_t;$     $e^{-r\,\delta t} = 0.983$

$u = e^{\sigma\sqrt{\delta t}} = 1.0851;$     $d = e^{-\sigma\sqrt{\delta t}} = 0.9216;$     $p = \dfrac{F_{t\,t+\delta t} - S_t \, e^{-\sigma\sqrt{\delta t}}}{S_t \, e^{\sigma\sqrt{\delta T}} - S_t \, e^{-\sigma\sqrt{\delta t}}} = 0.541$

Using these $u$ and $d$ factors, we can start filling in the stock prices on the tree (shown just above each node). The intermediate values of $S_t$ are not really necessary for a European option, since the option payoff only depends on the stock price at maturity; however, they are shown for ease of understanding.

The payoff values of the option are $\max[(S_T - 100), 0]$ and are shown just below the final nodes. The option values at the next column of nodes to the left can be calculated as follows:

$$f(117.74, 4\,\text{months}) = 0.983\{0.541 \times 27.76 + (1 - 0.541) \times 8.51\} = 18.609$$
$$f(100.00, 4\,\text{months}) = 0.983\{0.541 \times 8.51 + (1 - 0.541) \times 0.00\} = 4.43$$
$$f(84.93, 4\,\text{months}) = 0.983\{0.541 \times 0.00 + (1 - 0.541) \times 0.00\} = 0.00$$

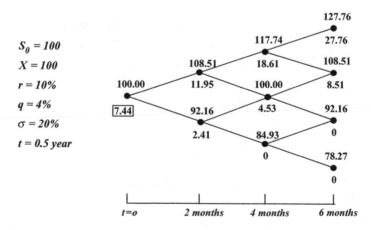

**Figure 7.4**   European call: Jarrow–Rudd discretization

Continuing this process back to the first node ("rolling back through the tree") finally gives a 6-month option value of 7.44. This may be compared to the Black Scholes value (equivalent to an infinite number of steps) of 7.01. This price error is equivalent to using a volatility of 21.6% instead of 20% in the Black Scholes formula.

(ii) **European Call: Cox–Ross–Rubinstein Method** ($p = \frac{1}{2}$): For purposes of comparison, we reprice the same option as in the last section, using a different discretization procedure. Once again we have $\delta t = 0.5/3$ and $e^{-r\delta t} = 0.983$ but now we use $p = \frac{1}{2}$ and equation (7.7), so that

$$u = \frac{F_{t\,t+\delta t}}{S_t}(1 + \sigma\sqrt{\delta t}) = 1.093; \qquad d = \frac{F_{t\,t+\delta t}}{S_t}(1 - \sigma\sqrt{\delta t}) = 0.928$$

The tree is shown in Figure 7.5. This time, only the final stock prices are shown. The procedure for rolling back through the tree is identical to that in the last section, with the simplifying feature that $p = (1 - p) = \frac{1}{2}$. The calculation for the top right-hand step in the diagram becomes

$$0.983 \times \tfrac{1}{2} \times (30.40 + 10.72) = 20.220$$

and so on through the tree. For all intents and purposes, the final answer is identical to that of the last section (more precise numbers are 7.444 previously and 7.438 now).

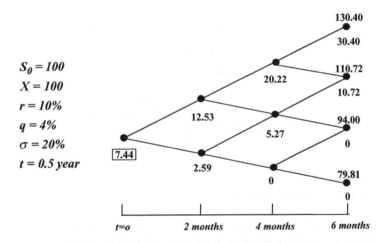

**Figure 7.5**   European call: Cox–Ross–Rubinstein discretization

(iii) **Bushy Trees and Discrete Dividends**: Suppose that instead of continuous dividends, the stock paid one fixed, discrete dividend $Q$. For purposes of illustration, we assume that it is paid the instant before the second nodes. The tree can be adjusted at these nodes by the shift shown in Figure 7.6. $S_t$, whatever its value, simply drops by the amount of the dividend. Unfortunately, this dislocates the entire tree as shown. The tree is said to have become **bushy**.

Let us recall the original random walk on which the binomial model is based. This is described in Appendix A.1, where we see that the tree is recombining by construction since the up-steps $U$ and down-steps $D$ are *additive*. In such a tree, the insertion of a constant $Q$ would not cause a dislocation since everything to the right of this point would move down by the same amount. This would have been the case if we had constructed the tree for $x_i = \ln S_i$. However,

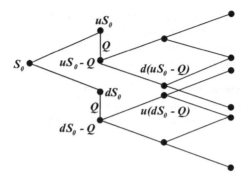

**Figure 7.6** Discrete fixed dividend

we have constructed the tree for $S_i$ directly, so that the sizes of the up- and down-moves are determined by the *multiplicative* factors $u$ and $d$. A discrete dividend must also be multiplicative if the tree is to remain recombining. Instead of a fixed discrete dividend we therefore use a discrete dividend whose size is proportional to the value of $S_t$ at the node in question. This is illustrated in Figure 7.7, where the dividend is $ku S_0$ at the higher node where the stock price is $u S_0$, and $kd S_0$ at the lower node. The effect of this on the following three nodes is immediately apparent: the tree recombines.

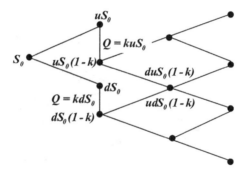

**Figure 7.7** Discrete proportional dividend

This proportional dividend assumption is implicit in the continuous dividend case, where each infinitesimal dividend in a period $\delta t$ is $q S_t \delta t$, i.e. proportional to $S_t$.

We return to the call option and discretization procedure of subsection (ii), except that instead of a continuous $q = 4\%$ (i.e. 2% over the 6-month period), there is a dividend of $2\% \times S_t$ at the second pair of nodes. The parameters are similar to those of subsection (ii) with $q = 0$; $F_{t\,t+\delta t} = 102.020$; $p = 0.582$; $u = 1.0851$; $d = 0.9216$; $e^{r\delta t} = 0.983$.

The terminal values are calculated, taking into account the dividend as shown. Rolling back through the tree shown in Figure 7.8 is exactly the same as before and nothing different needs to be done at the dividend point; this was entirely handled by the adjustment in the stock price. The initial value of the option works out to be 7.297 compared with 7.444 for the continuous dividend case. This difference gradually closes as the number of steps in the model increases. At 25 steps it is only half as big.

The calculation was repeated using a fixed dividend of 2 paid at the same point, so that the tree did not recombine. It is not worth giving the details of the calculations, but the option

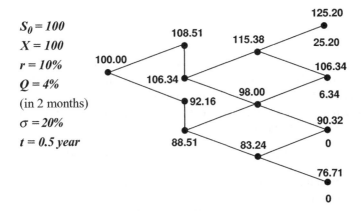

$S_0 = 100$
$X = 100$
$r = 10\%$
$Q = 4\%$
(in 2 months)
$\sigma = 20\%$
$t = 0.5$ year

**Figure 7.8** European call: discrete proportional dividend

value is found to be 7.356. The difference is negligible, justifying the use of the proportional dividend model.

(iv) **American Options:** The European call option could of course have been priced using the Black Scholes model. Binomial trees really come into their own when pricing American options. Consider an American put with $X = 110$ and the remaining parameters the same as for the European call of subsection (i); the same discretization procedure is used as in that section and the results are laid out in Figure 7.9.

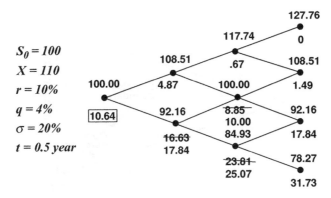

$S_0 = 100$
$X = 110$
$r = 10\%$
$q = 4\%$
$\sigma = 20\%$
$t = 0.5$ year

**Figure 7.9** American put: Jarrow–Rudd discretization

The procedure starts the same as in subsection (i):

(A) Set up the tree and calculate the values of each $S_t$ and the terminal values of the option. This time we need to put in the intermediate stock prices for reasons which become apparent below.
(B) Calculate the terminal payoff values for the put option.
(C) Roll back through the tree calculating the intermediate option values. Starting at the top right-hand corner, we have

$$0.67 = e^{-r\delta t}(p \times 0 + (1 - p) \times 1.49)$$

(D) The next value in this column is

$$8.85 = e^{-r\delta t}(p \times 1.49 + (1 - p) \times 17.84)$$

But an American put option at this point ($S = 100$, $X = 110$) could be exercised to give a payoff of 10.00. The value of 8.85 must therefore be replaced by 10.00. Similarly, at the bottom node in this column, the exercise value must be used.

(E) With these replacement values, the next column to the left is derived. Once again, the bottom node is calculated as

$$16.63 = e^{-r\delta t}(p \times 10.00 + (1 - p) \times 25.07)$$

This is less than the exercise value and must be replaced by 17.84, the exercise value of the American option.

(F) Finally a price of 10.64 is obtained for the option. This compares with a value of 9.29 for a similar European put.

The essence of the matter is summed up in Figure 7.10. In the next chapter we will show that a binomial tree is mathematically equivalent to a numerical solution of the Black Scholes equation. We saw in Section 6.1 that the price of an American option is only a solution of the Black Scholes equation in certain regions. Below the exercise boundary, the value of the American put is simply its intrinsic (exercise) value:

$$\text{American put price} = \begin{cases} f(S_t, t); \text{ solution to BS equation; } S_t \text{ above exercise boundary} \\ X - S_t; \text{ not solution to BS equation; } S_t \text{ below exercise boundary} \end{cases}$$

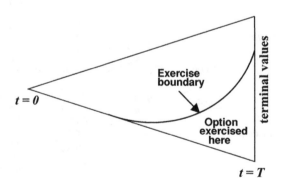

**Figure 7.10**   American puts

(v) While the pricing given in this section is useful for illustration, such a small number of steps would never be used for a real-life pricing. So what *is* the minimum number of steps needed to price an option in the market?

While the answer to this depends on the specific option being priced, solutions are typically distributed as shown in Figure 7.11. The principle features are as follows:

(A) The solid appearance of the left-hand graph comes about because the answers obtained change more sharply in going from an odd number of steps to an even number than they do between successive odd or even numbers of steps. When the option price is plotted against the number of binomial steps, the result therefore zig-zags between the envelopes made up of odd and even numbers of steps.

(B)  The reason for this is intuitively apparent from Figure A2.2 in the Appendix: as $n$ increases from 5 to 6, the way in which the binomial distribution is "fitted" to the normal distribution changes radically. For $n = 5$, the binomial distribution has two equal maximum probability values while for $n = 6$, there is only a single maximum probability; yet when $n$ goes from 6 to 8, the only change is that a couple of extra bars are squeezed in, giving a slightly better approximation to the normal curve. One would therefore expect smooth transitions for the sequences $n = \ldots 5, 7, 9, \ldots$ and $n = \ldots 6, 8, 10, \ldots$ but jumps when going from odd to even to odd.

(C)  In most circumstances, the answer obtained for $n$ steps is improved on by taking the average of the answers of $n$ steps and $(n + 1)$ steps.

(D)  Even when the average of successive steps is taken, the value oscillates, with decreasing amplitude, around the analytical answer. However it is clear that beyond about 50 steps, the answer is close enough for most commercial purposes.

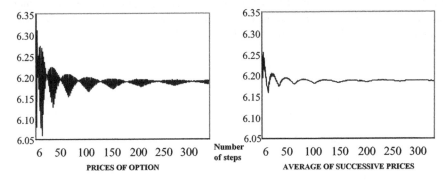

**Figure 7.11**  European call option priced with varying number of binomial steps: $S = 100$; $X = 110$; $r = 10\%$; $q = 4\%$; $\sigma = 20\%$; $t = 1$ year

(vi) **Greeks:** There are two possible approaches to calculating these, depending on the circumstances. Imagine a structured product salesman working on the price of a complex OTC option for a client. He might typically be doing his pricing with a 100-step binomial model programmed into a spreadsheet. After tinkering around for a while he establishes a price, and as a final step he works out the Greek parameters. The easiest way to do this is by numerical differentiation.

His Greeks might then look as follows, putting $\delta S = S/1000$, $\delta t = T/1000$:

$$\Delta = \frac{\partial f(S_0, t)}{\partial S_0} = \frac{f(1.001 \times S_0, T) - f(0.999 \times S_0, T)}{2 S_0} \times 1000$$

$$\Gamma = \frac{\partial^2 f(S_0, t)}{\partial S_0^2} = \frac{f(1.001 \times S_0, T) + f(0.999 \times S_0, T) - 2 f(S_0, T)}{S_0^2} \times 1000^2$$

$$\Theta = \frac{\partial f(S_0, t)}{\partial t} = \frac{f(S_0, 0.999 \times T) - f(S_0, T)}{T} \times 1000$$

This lazy but practical way of finding the Greeks works fine if only one option is being valued. The tree has to be calculated three times, but so what?

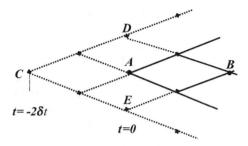

**Figure 7.12** Binomial Greeks

Take instead the case of binomial models which are used to evaluate books containing hundreds of different options. Tripling the number of calculations in order to calculate the Greeks as above may be unacceptably time consuming. An alternative approach is illustrated in Figure 7.12. Suppose the solid part of the tree is the first couple of steps in the calculation of an option price. While leaving the number of steps between now and maturity unchanged, we can add another two steps backward in time; this is the dotted part of the tree. With this small addition, the Greeks can be calculated from a single tree as follows:

$$\Delta_A = \frac{f_D - f_E}{S_D - S_E}$$

$$\Gamma_A = \left\{ \frac{f_D - f_A}{S_D - S_A} - \frac{f_A - f_E}{S_A - S_E} \right\} \Big/ \frac{1}{2}(S_D - S_E)$$

$$\Theta_A = \frac{f_B - f_C}{4\,dt}$$

(vii) Finally, the reader should consider just how powerful a tool the binomial model really is: a few examples should illustrate how we have extended the range of structures that can be priced. These should now be quite within the reader's ability to model:

(A) The strike price could be made a function of time, e.g. an American call with the strike accreting at a constant rate.

(B) The option need not be either European or American but could be Bermudan: e.g. a 5-year option, exercisable only in the first six months of each year.

(C) The payoff may be a non-linear function of the stock price: e.g. an option of the form

$$f = \begin{cases} 0 & \text{if } S_T < X \\ (S - X)^2 & \text{if } S_T > X \end{cases}$$

# 8

# Numerical Solutions of the Black Scholes Equation

## 8.1 FINITE DIFFERENCE APPROXIMATIONS

(i) The object of this chapter is to explain various methods of solving the Black Scholes equation by numerical methods, and to relate these to other approaches to option pricing. We start with the Black Scholes equation in the following form:

$$\frac{\partial f_0}{\partial T} = (r - q)S_0 \frac{\partial f_0}{\partial S_0} + \tfrac{1}{2}S_0^2 \sigma^2 \frac{\partial^2 f_0}{\partial S_0^2} - rf_0 \tag{8.1}$$

where $S_0$ and $f_0$ are the prices of the stock and derivative at a time $T$ before maturity. Using equation (A3.4) of the Appendix, this can be written as a heat equation

$$\frac{\partial u}{\partial t} = \frac{\partial^2 u}{\partial x^2} \tag{8.2}$$

where

$$f_0(S_0, T) = e^{-rT}(e^{-kx-k^2 t}u(x, T)); \qquad x = \ln S_0; \qquad t = \tfrac{1}{2}\sigma^2 T; \qquad k = \frac{r - q - \tfrac{1}{2}\sigma^2}{\sigma^2}$$

We depart from our usual practice of saving the symbol $t$ for time (in the sense of date), although $T$ remains time (to maturity). This saves us having to use obscure or non-standard symbols and should be unambiguous.

(ii) The solution $u(x, t)$ can be envisaged as a three-dimensional surface over the $(x, t)$ plane. The values of $x$ range from $-\infty$ to $+\infty$, and the values of $t$ from 0 to $+\infty$. Imagine that we cover the $x$–$t$ plane with a discrete set of equally spaced grid points, which are $\delta x$ apart in the $x$-direction and $\delta t$ apart in the $t$-direction, as shown in Figure 8.1. At the grid points, we can write $x = m\delta x$ and $t = n\delta t$, where $m$ and $n$ are integers. The coordinates of a grid point can therefore be defined by counting off grid lines from the origin. The notation we adopt for $u(x, t)$ at a grid point is

$$u(x, t) = u(m\delta x, n\delta t) = u_m^n$$

(iii) A first-order approximation of the right-hand side of the heat equation can be written as

$$\frac{\partial^2 u}{\partial x^2} = \frac{\partial}{\partial x}\left\{\frac{\partial u}{\partial x}\right\} \to \frac{1}{\delta x}\left\{\frac{1}{\delta x}\left[(u_{m+1}^n - u_m^n) - (u_m^n - u_{m-1}^n)\right]\right\}$$

$$= \frac{1}{(\delta x)^2}\left\{u_{m+1}^n + u_{m-1}^n - 2u_m^n\right\} \equiv \frac{1}{(\delta x)^2}\hat{\delta}_x^2 u_m^n$$

where the operator $\hat{\delta}_x^2$ is defined by the last identity, and will be used in the interests of brevity. This approximation is symmetric in $u_m^n$ and there is no reason to assume that it is subject to any bias.

The left-hand side of the heat equation, on the other hand, cannot be unambiguously approximated. The following are some of the more common approximations, whose merits are discussed later.

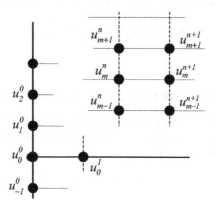

**Figure 8.1** Discretization grid

(iv) *Forward Difference*:

$$\frac{\partial u}{\partial t} = \frac{1}{\delta t}\left(u_m^{n+1} - u_m^n\right)$$

This is the most obvious approximation, but clearly introduces a bias since it is not centered on the time grid points, but half way between $n$ and $n + 1$. Using this approximation, the heat equation gives the following *finite difference equation:*

$$u_m^{n+1} - u_m^n = \alpha\delta_x^2 u_m^n = \alpha\left(u_{m+1}^n + u_{m-1}^n - 2u_m^n\right) \qquad \text{where} \qquad \alpha = \frac{\delta t}{(\delta x)^2}$$

(v) *Backward Difference*:

$$\frac{\partial u}{\partial t} = \frac{1}{\delta t}\left(u_m^n - u_m^{n-1}\right)$$

This looks similar to the forward difference method, except that it is centered half way between time grid points $n - 1$ and $n$, so that the bias is in the opposite direction. The resulting difference equation is

$$u_m^n - u_m^{n-1} = \alpha\delta_x^2 u_m^n = \alpha\left(u_{m+1}^n + u_{m-1}^n - 2u_m^n\right)$$

(vi) *Richardson*: The previous two methods cause forward and backward biases on the time axis, so a simple remedy might be to take the average of the two:

$$\tfrac{1}{2}\left(u_m^{n+1} - u_m^{n-1}\right) = \alpha\delta_x^2 u_m^n = \alpha\left(u_{m+1}^n + u_{m-1}^n - 2u_m^n\right)$$

This seems an appealing solution; but the Richardson method is a standard textbook example of how simple intuitive solutions do not always work. The method has a hidden defect which makes it unusable, as described below.

(vii) *Dufort and Frankel*: This is an attempt to adapt the Richardson method so that it eliminates bias (but also works!). We simply replace the final term $u_m^n$ in the Richardson scheme by the average of $u_m^{n+1}$ and $u_m^{n-1}$, giving

$$\tfrac{1}{2}\left(u_m^{n+1} - u_m^{n-1}\right) = \alpha\left(u_{m+1}^n + u_{m-1}^n - \left(u_m^{n+1} + u_m^{n-1}\right)\right)$$

$$= \alpha\hat{\delta}_x^2 u_m^n - \alpha\left(u_m^{n+1} + u_m^{n-1} - 2u_m^n\right)$$

This method does in fact work, although not especially well, and we will see below that if we are careless in applying the scheme it can lead to quite spurious answers.

(viii) **Crank Nicolson:** This is the most important scheme, and the one that the reader is likely to use if he is going to use the finite difference method seriously. The last two methods tried to overcome the biases which are inherent in the discretization of the time variable. However, there is another approach: when using the approximation for $\partial^2 u/\partial x^2$, use the average of the values at $n$ and $n+1$. The result is simply

$$u_m^{n+1} - u_m^n = \tfrac{1}{2}\alpha\hat{\delta}_x^2\left(u_m^{n+1} + u_m^n\right)$$

This could be regarded simply as the average of the forward difference result, and the backward difference result one time step later.

(ix) **Douglas:**

$$u_m^{n+1} - u_m^n = \tfrac{1}{2}\alpha\hat{\delta}_x^2\left(\left(1 - \frac{1}{6\alpha}\right)u_m^{n+1} + \left(1 + \frac{1}{6\alpha}\right)u_m^n\right)$$

Where on earth did this come from? There is no simple intuitive explanation, but the *really* interested reader will find the derivation in Section A.9 of the Appendix. This scheme takes just about the same effort to implement as Crank Nicholson but can be much more accurate. It can be shown that it is at its most accurate if we put $\alpha = 1/\sqrt{20}$. Note that if we put $\alpha = 1/6$, the difference equation reduces to the forward difference scheme described above.

## 8.2 CONDITIONS FOR SATISFACTORY SOLUTIONS

The six schemes set out in the last section all seem quite reasonable; but are there any tests we can carry out ahead of time, to check that we get sensible answers? It turns out that there are three conditions that must be met which are explained below; but before turning to these, it is worth pointing out to the reader that the numerical solution of partial differential equations is something of an art form, containing many hidden pitfalls. We explain the principles behind the three conditions, but we will not elaborate on the precise techniques used in testing for the conditions. The reader can perfectly well use the discretizations described, taking on trust the comments we make on their applicability. Alternatively, if he wants to be more creative and devise new discretizations, he will have to delve into the subject more deeply than this book allows.

(i) **Consistency:** In simple terms, we must make sure that as the grid becomes finer and finer, the difference equation converges to the partial differential equation we started with (the heat equation), and not some other equation. This may sound rather fanciful, so let us take a closer look at the Dufort and Frankel scheme. On the face of it, we have merely eliminated the biases of the forward and backward methods, without any very fundamental change. But in the limit of an infinitesimally fine grid, we may write

$$\tfrac{1}{2}\left(u_m^{n+1} - u_m^{n-1}\right) \to \delta t\frac{\partial u}{\partial t}; \qquad \alpha\hat{\delta}_x^2 u_m^n \to \alpha(\delta x)^2\frac{\partial^2 u}{\partial x^2}$$

$$\alpha\left(u_m^{n+1} + u_m^{n-1} - 2u_m^n\right) \to \alpha(\delta t)^2\frac{\partial^2 u}{\partial t^2}$$

so that the equation for the Dufort–Frankel scheme in Section 8.1(vii) becomes

$$\frac{\partial u}{\partial t} + \beta^2\frac{\partial^2 u}{\partial t^2} = \frac{\partial^2 u}{\partial x^2}; \qquad \beta = \frac{\delta t}{\delta x}$$

If we decrease the grid size at the same rate in the $x$- and $t$-directions (i.e. keep $\beta$ constant), the Dufort and Frankel scheme converges to a hyperbolic partial differential equation, which is quite different from the heat equation. On the other hand, if we decrease the mesh in such a way that $\alpha = \delta t/(\delta x)^2 = $ constant, $\beta$ would tend to zero and the finite difference equation would be consistent with the heat equation. This constant $\alpha$ convergence is in fact the most common way for progressively making the grid finer.

(ii) **Convergence:** This concept is easy to describe: does the value obtained by solving the difference equation converge to the right number as $\delta x, \delta t \to 0$? Or converge to the wrong number (inconsistent), or oscillate or just wander about indefinitely? Unfortunately, precise tests for convergence are difficult to devise. We therefore move on quickly, and later discover that there is a round-about way of avoiding the whole issue.

(iii) **Stability:** Suppose we have set up some discretization scheme to solve the heat equation; we have calculated all the numbers by hand to four decimal places and are satisfied with the answers. But as a quick last check, we decide to run all the numbers again to one decimal place. To our dismay, we get a substantially different answer. Does this mean that we made an arithmetical slip somewhere? Unfortunately, the answer is "not necessarily". It is in the nature of some discretization schemes that as we move forward in time, a small initial error gets magnified at each step and may eventually swamp the underlying answer. Such a scheme is said to be unstable.

The underlying test we must make of any scheme with $N$ time steps of length $\delta x$ is to let $N \to \infty$ and $\delta t \to 0$ in such a way that $N\delta t = t$ remains finite, and then see if a small error introduced at $t = 0$ could become unbounded by the time it is transmitted to time step $N$. There are two commonly used tests for stability which are quite simple to apply. However, we content ourselves here with merely giving results for the schemes we introduced in the last section.

- The forward difference method is stable only if $\alpha \le \tfrac{1}{2}$.
- The backward difference, Crank Nicholson and Douglas methods are always stable.
- The Richardson method is always unstable.
- Dufort and Frankel is always stable but as we saw above, it may not be consistent with the heat equation.

(iv) **Lax's Equivalence Theorem:** The reader might feel we have tip-toed away from the convergence issue raised in subparagraph (ii) above. However, this theorem states that subject to some technical conditions, stability is both a necessary and sufficient condition to assure convergence, i.e. if we have got the stability conditions right, we can forget about convergence.

Conversely, if a stability condition is even slightly broken, the solutions may fail to converge in quite a dramatic way; an example of this is given later.

## 8.3    EXPLICIT FINITE DIFFERENCE METHOD

(i) The forward difference scheme of Section 8.1(iv) can be written

$$u_m^{n+1} = (1 - 2\alpha)u_m^n + \alpha\left(u_{m+1}^n + u_{m-1}^n\right); \qquad \alpha = \frac{\delta t}{(\delta x)^2} \leq \tfrac{1}{2}$$

This is represented in Figure 8.2, which shows a small part of the total grid. The key point to notice is that each $u_m^{n+1}$ can be calculated from the three values of $u$ to the immediate left, by simple arithmetic combination.

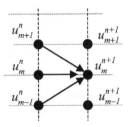

In general, when we use a finite difference method to solve the heat equation, we start off knowing all the values for $t = 0$ along the vertical axis; these are the *initial conditions*. We also know the grid values for certain values of $x$ when $t > 0$; these are the *boundary conditions*. For simple options they consist of known values of $u_m^n$ as $x$ approaches $\pm\infty$.

**Figure 8.2**    Forward difference

If the forward finite difference scheme is used to calculate a particular value for $u(x, t) = u_M^N$, we start with the initial values at $t = 0$ and work across the grid towards the point $(N, M)$. But because of the simple way in which the $u_m^{n+1}$ only depend on the adjacent values to the immediate left, only solutions within the shaded area of Figure 8.3 need to be calculated. This leads to the slightly surprising conclusion that the boundary conditions are redundant.

This method is called the explicit difference method because we start with a knowledge of the $u_m^0$ at the left-hand edge and can explicitly work out any $u_m^n$ from these.

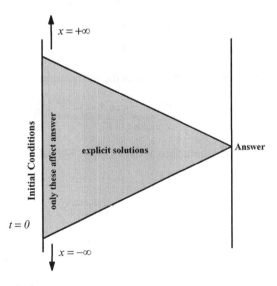

**Figure 8.3**    Explicit method

(ii) We are free to choose whatever value for $\alpha$ we please, subject to the scheme conforming with the stability conditions. If we choose $\alpha = \frac{1}{2}$, the finite difference equation becomes even simpler:

$$u_m^{n+1} = \tfrac{1}{2}\left(u_{m+1}^n + u_{m-1}^n\right) \qquad \text{subject to grid spacing} \qquad \delta x = \sqrt{2\delta t}$$

This scheme looks suspiciously like a binomial model turned back to front. But such a reversal is purely a question of conventions for assigning time. In the conventions of the heat equation, $t = 0$ means "at the beginning" in a calendar sense; this is when the initial conditions (temperature distribution in a long thin conductor) are imposed. In option theory, $T$ means time left to maturity; therefore $T = 0$ means "at maturity". This is why the payoff of an option (value at maturity) is often confusingly referred to as the initial conditions. In Figure 8.3 we can flip the triangular network so that the initial conditions are on the right and the "answer" is at the apex of the triangle on the left. But this now looks just like a binomial tree.

(iii) **Equivalence of Binomial Tree and Explicit Finite Difference Method**: Let us return to equation (8.2) to see how this simple two-pronged discretization scheme looks when expressed in terms of the underlying stock price, rather than its logarithm. The grid spacing relationship becomes

$$\delta x = x_{m+1}^n - x_m^n = \ln\frac{S_{m+1}}{S_m} = \sqrt{2\delta t} = \sigma\sqrt{\delta T}$$

or more simply

$$S_{m+1} = S_m\, e^{\sigma\sqrt{\delta T}}$$

Similarly, we may write

$$u_m^{n+1} = e^{r(T+\delta T)}\, e^{kx + \frac{1}{2}k^2\sigma^2(T+\delta T)}\, f_m^{n+1}$$

$$u_{m+1}^n = e^{rT}\, e^{k(x+\delta x) + \frac{1}{2}k^2\sigma^2 T}\, f_{m+1}^n$$

$$u_{m-1}^n = e^{rT}\, e^{k(x-\delta x) + \frac{1}{2}k^2\sigma^2 T}\, f_{m-1}^n$$

Substituting these into the binomial scheme gives the relationship

$$f_m^{n+1} = e^{-r\delta T}\left\{\tfrac{1}{2}\, e^{\lambda + \frac{1}{2}\lambda^2}\, f_{m+1}^n + \tfrac{1}{2}\, e^{\lambda - \frac{1}{2}\lambda^2}\, f_{m-1}^n\right\}$$

$$\lambda = k\sigma\sqrt{\delta T}$$

Expanding the exponentials and discarding terms of $O[\delta t^{3/2}]$ leads to

$$f_m^{n+1} = e^{-r\delta T}\left\{p f_{m+1}^n + (1-p) f_{m-1}^n\right\}$$

$$p = \frac{1}{2} + \frac{1}{2}\frac{r - q - \frac{1}{2}\sigma^2}{\sigma}\sqrt{\delta T}$$

This is precisely the Jarrow–Rudd version of the binomial model, summed up in equation (7.6). The binomial model and the explicit finite difference solution of the Black Scholes equation are simply different ways of expressing the same mathematical formalism. This conclusion is reinforced by the essential stability condition $\alpha \leq \frac{1}{2}$ mentioned in Section 8.2(iii); again discarding terms of $O[\delta t^{3/2}]$, this may be written in terms of $T$ and $S_T$ as $S_T \sigma \sqrt{\delta T}/2\delta S_T \leq \frac{1}{2}$. To the present order of accuracy in $\delta T$, this is the same condition that was expressed by equation (7.4), and which came from a seemingly unrelated line of reasoning.

This should of course be of no great surprise:

- The binomial model is a graphical way of approximating the probability density function of a stock price (or its logarithm).
- This probability density function is a solution of the Kolmogorov backward equation; therefore the binomial model is a graphical representation of the Kolmogorov equation.
- The explicit difference method was introduced to solve the Black Scholes equation.
- The Kolmogorov and Black Scholes equations are shown in Section A.4(i) of the Appendix to be very closely related.

This duality between the explicit finite difference method and the binomial model is also true of the trinomial model which is examined in a later chapter.

## 8.4   IMPLICIT FINITE DIFFERENCE METHODS

(i) Let us return to the backward difference scheme of Section 8.1(v) which may be written

$$u_m^{n-1} = (1 + 2\alpha)u_m^n - \alpha\left(u_{m+1}^n + u_{m-1}^n\right)$$

and which is represented in Figure 8.4. In this case $u_m^{n-1}$ can be calculated from the adjacent $u$ values immediately to the right. Unfortunately, this is an inconvenient way to proceed. We know the values at the left-hand edge of the grid (initial conditions) and the values at the top and bottom edges (boundary conditions); the solution of the problem is the series of values at the right-hand edge. In order to find these right-hand edge solutions, we need to solve a large array of linear simultaneous equations for all the $u_m^n$; these are not given explicitly in terms of known quantities – hence the name *implicit methods*.

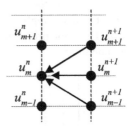

**Figure 8.4**   Backward difference

(ii) As well as producing awkward simultaneous equations to solve, the implicit difference introduces difficult boundary conditions. Compare Figures 8.3 and 8.5, showing boundary conditions for the two methods. The simple nature of the explicit difference method meant that we could ignore all values outside the shaded area, including boundary values. But with the implicit method, boundary values are important.

For a European call option the boundary conditions are

$$\lim_{S_0 \to \infty} f_0(S_0, T) \to S_0 \, e^{-qT} - X \, e^{-rT}$$

$$\lim_{S_0 \to 0} f_0(S_0, T) = 0$$

In terms of $x$, $t$ and $k$ as defined in equation (8.2) this may be written

$$\lim_{x \to \infty} u(x, t) \to e^{rT} e^{kx+k^2t}(e^x - X e^{-rT}); \qquad \lim_{x \to -\infty} u(x, t) \to 0$$

The boundary conditions are set at $x = \pm\infty$, so this would imply that the grid should stretch between these limits. But this would give an infinite number of simultaneous equations to solve!

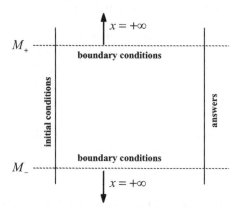

**Figure 8.5**   Boundary conditions

Consider the graph of a European call option shown in Figure 8.6. The upper boundary condition is that $f_0(S_0, T) \to S_0 e^{-qT} - X e^{-rT}$. However this condition does not really need to be applied at $S_0 = \infty$; without appreciable loss of accuracy, it can be applied at $S_0 = U_3$, or $U_2$ or even $U_1$; but if we apply the boundary condition at $S_0 = V$, we start introducing an appreciable error. The same principle applies when we seek a practical implementation of the lower boundary condition.

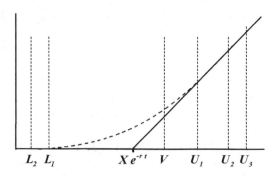

**Figure 8.6**   Effective boundaries for call option

In terms of the boundary conditions in Figure 8.5, we choose a large positive and a large negative $x$ value, $M_{+\infty}$ and $M_{-\infty}$ beyond which we do not extend the grid. The values that we insert at these edges are the effective boundary conditions. Of course, this begs an important question: how do we know that we have chosen $M_{+\infty}$ and $M_{-\infty}$ far enough out that we have not introduced an appreciable error, but not so far that we are doing a lot of redundant computing? The answer is to set up the model on a computer and shift $M_{+\infty}$ and $M_{-\infty}$ about a bit; if the answers do not change much, we are in a safe area.

(iii) At this point, the reader might be wondering why anyone should burden himself with the implicit difference method, when the explicit method is so much easier to solve. The explicit method, cast in the form of the binomial model, is indeed much more popular than implicit methods. After all, for every person who knows how to get finite difference solutions to a partial differential equation, there are 100 guys who can stick numbers into a tree. On the other hand, explicit methods do show an unfortunate tendency to be unstable, while stability is assured over a much wider range by the implicit method.

Recall from Section 8.1 that the forward and backward finite difference schemes are not well centered compared with the Crank Nicolson or Douglas schemes. But these latter two, more stable and accurate schemes are just as easy to implement as the simple implicit method, so they are normally the preferred route if an implicit scheme is used at all. A comparison of the methods is given in Section 8.5.

(iv) The interesting discretization methods laid out in Section 8.1 can be combined into a single formula:

$$u_m^{n+1} - u_m^n = \tfrac{1}{2}\alpha\delta_x^2\big(\theta u_m^{n+1} + (1-\theta)u_m^n\big)$$

Explicit:        $\theta = 0$
Implicit:        $\theta = 1$
Crank Nicolson: $\theta = \tfrac{1}{2}$
Douglas:        $\theta = \tfrac{1}{2}\big(1 - \tfrac{1}{6\alpha}\big)$
Trinomial:      as Douglas with $\alpha = \tfrac{1}{6}$

Written out fully, this formula is

$$(1 + 2\alpha\theta)u_m^{n+1} - \alpha\theta\big(u_{m+1}^{n+1} + u_{m-1}^{n+1}\big) = (1 - 2\alpha(1-\theta))u_m^n + \alpha(1-\theta)\big(u_{m+1}^n + u_{m-1}^n\big)$$

$$(8.3)$$

In the following analysis, we use this in the form

$$-bu_{m+1}^{n+1} + au_m^{n+1} - bu_{m-1}^{n+1} = eu_{m+1}^n + cu_m^n + eu_{m-1}^n$$

This equation is easily expressed in matrix form. A little care is needed with the first and last terms in the sequence (the term $u_{m-1}^n$ is undefined when $m = 1$). Taking these edge effects into account, the above equation may be written as

$$
\begin{pmatrix}
a & -b & 0 & 0 \\
-b & a & -b & 0 \\
0 & -b & a & -b \\
& & & \ddots \\
& & & & a
\end{pmatrix}
\begin{pmatrix}
u_{M-1}^{n+1} \\
u_{M-2}^{n+1} \\
\vdots \\
u_{-M+2}^{n+1} \\
u_{-M+1}^{n+1}
\end{pmatrix}
-
\begin{pmatrix}
bu_M^{n+1} \\
0 \\
\vdots \\
0 \\
bu_{-M}^{n+1}
\end{pmatrix}
=
\begin{pmatrix}
c & e & 0 & 0 \\
e & c & e & 0 \\
0 & e & c & e \\
& & & \ddots \\
& & & & c
\end{pmatrix}
\begin{pmatrix}
u_{M-1}^n \\
u_{M-2}^n \\
\vdots \\
u_{-M+2}^n \\
u_{-M+1}^n
\end{pmatrix}
+
\begin{pmatrix}
eu_M^n \\
0 \\
\vdots \\
0 \\
eu_{-M}^n
\end{pmatrix}
$$

or

$$\mathbf{Ap}^{n+1} = \mathbf{Bp}^n + b\mathbf{q}^{n+1} + e\mathbf{q}^n \qquad (8.4)$$

The square matrices have dimension $(M-2) \times (M-2)$ and the vectors have $M-2$ elements.

(v) We start off knowing the values at the left-hand edge of the grid (initial values $u_m^0$). From the boundary conditions we also know the values at the top and bottom edges of the grid,

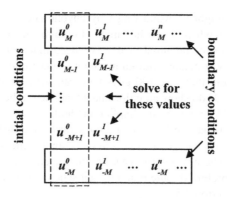

**Figure 8.7**  Solution of implicit method

i.e. we know $u^i_M$ and $u^i_{-M}$. We can therefore calculate the right-hand side of equation (8.4) since we also know the elements of the matrix **B**; this will be designated by the vector $\mathbf{s}^0$. The second column in the grid can therefore be obtained by using the equation $\mathbf{Ap}^1 = \mathbf{s}^0$. And so the process can be repeated across the grid, merely by solving the equations $\mathbf{Ap}^{n+1} = \mathbf{s}^n$. This process is illustrated in Figure 8.7.

The trouble is that inverting a $200 \times 200$ matrix is more than a question of "merely". However, the matrix **A** has a special tridiagonal form which makes the problem fairly easy to solve by using one of several possible tricks; the simplest of these, known as the LU decomposition, is described in Appendix A.10.

Finally, we note that if $\theta = 0$, then the matrix **A** becomes the unit matrix and we have the trivially simple explicit solution explained in Section 8.3.

(vi) **Discretization of the Full Black Scholes Model:** We finish this section with an observation rather than a new method or technique. By a simple change of variables, we can transform the Black Scholes equation into the simple heat equation (8.2); this simplifies the algebra and makes the theory more easily intelligible. However, there is nothing to prevent us from discretizing equation (8.1) directly.

As before we put

$$\frac{\partial f}{\partial S} \rightarrow \frac{1}{2\delta S}\{f^n_{m+1} - f^n_{m-1}\}; \qquad \frac{\partial^2 f}{\partial S^2} \rightarrow \frac{1}{(\delta S)^2}\{f^n_{m+1} + f^n_{m-1} - 2f^n_m\}$$

$$\frac{\partial f}{\partial T} \rightarrow \begin{cases} \dfrac{1}{\delta t}\{f^{n+1}_m - f^n_m\}: & \text{forward difference} \\[2mm] \dfrac{1}{\delta t}\{f^n_m - f^{n-1}_m\}: & \text{backward difference} \end{cases}$$

The Black Scholes equation becomes:

(A) Forward Difference

$$\frac{1}{\delta t}\{f^{n+1}_m - f^n_m\} = \tfrac{1}{2}m(r-q)\{f^n_{m+1} - f^n_{m-1}\} + \tfrac{1}{2}\sigma^2 m^2\{f^n_{m+1} + f^n_{m-1} - 2f^n_m\} - rf^n_m$$

(B) Backward Difference

$$\frac{1}{\delta t}\{f^n_m - f^{n-1}_m\} = \tfrac{1}{2}m(r-q)\{f^n_{m+1} - f^n_{m-1}\} + \tfrac{1}{2}\sigma^2 m^2\{f^n_{m+1} + f^n_{m-1} - 2f^n_m\} - rf^n_m$$

(C) Crank Nicolson. Take the average of (A) and (B) at one time step later

$$a f_{m+1}^{n+1} + b f_m^{n+1} + c f_{m-1}^{n+1} = \alpha f_{m+1}^n + \beta f_m^n + \gamma f_{m-1}^n$$

where

$$a = -\alpha = \tfrac{1}{4} m(r - q)\delta t + \tfrac{1}{4} m^2 \sigma^2 \delta t$$
$$c = -\gamma = -\tfrac{1}{4} m(r - q)\delta t + \tfrac{1}{4} m^2 \sigma^2 \delta t$$
$$(b - 1) = -(\beta - 1) = r\delta t + \tfrac{1}{2} m^2 \sigma^2 \delta t$$

This equation has just the form of equation (8.4), although the coefficients of the $f_m^n$ are not constant. However, this does not prevent us achieving a solution by LU decomposition as described in Appendix A.10(v). It may at first seem slightly puzzling that there is no term in $\delta S$ in the equation, but the price discretization is reflected by the presence of the index number $m$; remember that we are likely to impose an initial condition of the type $f_m^0 = \max[0, (m\delta S - X)]$.

Note that this discretization is not the same as that used in $S_t$ space for binomial trees. In the latter case, the grid spacing is proportional to the stock price while here we have used it equal to $\delta S$.

The reader might be wondering why one would want to go to all the extra bother of discretizing a more complicated equation than necessary. The first reason is simply that it is easier to have an intuitive feel for a calculation if you are dealing with observable quantities rather than with complicated transforms; in any case, once this initial extra algebra is over, this version of the Black Scholes equation is no more difficult to compute than the simple version. Second, we do sometimes run across equations which do not convert easily into a simple heat equation. For example, when we come to look at passport options in Chapter 18, we will see that there is no alternative to discretizing a more complex differential equation.

## 8.5   A WORKED EXAMPLE

(i) In the last chapter we gave an explicit, worked example of how to calculate the price of a European call option using a three-step binomial tree. Both the Jarrow–Rudd and the Cox–Ross–Rubinstein methods were used and it turned out that they gave the same answer. We now look at how to calculate the price of the same option using the Crank Nicolson method. The same example is used as before: a call option, $S_0 = 100$, $X = 100$, $T = 6$ months, $r = 10\%$, $q = 4\%$, $\sigma = 20\%$. The price which was obtained from the three-step binomial model was 7.44 and the Black Scholes price is 7.01.

(ii) The equation that we solve is the heat equation (8.2), so our calculations are performed in terms of $u_m^n$ rather than the option prices directly. The results are illustrated in Table 8.1; before starting the $u$ calculations we set up the exercise with the following steps:

(A) It was decided to choose $N = 3$ time steps, so that $\delta T = 0.5/3 = 0.1667$ years. This is equivalent to $\delta t = \tfrac{1}{2}\sigma^2 \delta T = 0.0033$.

(B) The Crank Nicolson scheme is given by equation (9.3) with $\theta = \tfrac{1}{2}$ We have discretion over the value of $\alpha$ and over the number of grid points in the $x$-direction. In this example we use $\alpha = \tfrac{1}{2}$ and six steps in the $x$-direction; these values are chosen to make the set-up as close as possible to the binomial example of the last chapter.

**Table 8.1**   Crank Nicolson example

| | | | | T = | 0.0000 | 0.1667 | 0.3333 | 0.5000 | |
| | | | | t = | 0.0000 | 0.0033 | 0.0067 | 0.0100 | |
| | | | | | $u_m^n$ | | | | |
| $x = \ln S$ | $S$ | Option Payoff | $m$ | $n =$ 0 initial condition | 1 | 2 | 3 | | $f_0$ |
| 4.85 | 127.76 | 27.76 | 3 | 3545.94 | 3722.36 | 3901.58 | 4083.63 | boundary | 30.10 |
| 4.77 | 117.74 | 17.74 | 2 | 2088.56 | 2242.60 | 2413.97 | 2596.19 | | 20.77 |
| 4.69 | 108.51 | 8.51 | 1 | 923.13 | 1087.05 | 1287.63 | 1476.38 | | 12.81 |
| 4.61 | 100.00 | 0.00 | 0 | 0.00 | 344.88 | 550.20 | 722.67 | | 6.81 |
| 4.52 | 92.16 | 0.00 | -1 | 0.00 | 59.12 | 177.66 | 293.97 | | 3.00 |
| 4.44 | 84.93 | 0.00 | -2 | 0.00 | 9.85 | 42.75 | 92.85 | | 1.30 |
| 4.36 | 78.27 | 0.00 | -3 | 0.00 | 0.00 | 0.00 | 0.00 | boundary | 0.00 |

(C) The grid spacing in the $x$-direction comes from the definition of $\alpha$, i.e. $\delta x = \sqrt{\delta t/\alpha} = \sqrt{0.0033/0.5} = 0.0816$. The first column of the table can now be filled in, starting with $4.61 = \ln 100$ and progressively adding or subtracting 0.0816 to give the remaining values.

The stock price values in the second column are obtained simply by taking exponentials of the first column. Note that the $S$ values in this grid correspond to those of the Jarrow–Rudd scheme of Figure 7.4. If the reader is unsure of the reason for this, he will find the answer in Section 8.3(iii).

(D) The option payoffs are $\max[(S - 100), 0]$ and are listed in the third column.

(iii) The **initial values** $u_m^0$ are simply obtained from the option payoffs of the previous column, using the formula connecting $f(S, T)$ and $u(x, T)$ in equation (8.2). In this case we have $k = 1$ so that as an example, $3545.94 = e^{kx} \times f = e^{4.85} \times 27.76$.

The **boundary conditions** are fixed at the extreme values of $S$ (i.e. at 127.76 and 78.27) in our discretization. As an example, the boundary condition at $S = 127.76$ and $T = 0.1667$ is

$$\lim_{S \to \infty} f \to S\,e^{-qT} - X\,e^{-rT} = 127.76\,e^{-0.04 \times 0.1667} - 100\,e^{-0.1 \times 0.1667} = 28.56$$

$$u = f\,e^{rT}e^{kx+k^2t} = 28.56\,e^{0.1 \times 0.1667}e^{4.85+0.0033} = 3722.36$$

In this particular example we have placed the boundary conditions at the extreme $S$ values. This is because the $\alpha$ value which we selected does not give a very wide spread between maximum and minimum $S$. Normally we construct the grid so that the extreme $S$ values go out at least two or three standard deviations from their starting values. Had we chosen more grid points in the $x$-direction or a smaller $\alpha$ (larger $\delta x$), we might have been in the position of having to make a judgement on where precisely to apply the boundary conditions; but in this case we just do the best we can and acknowledge that the small spread is likely to be a source of error.

The basic Crank Nicolson equation (8.3) is written

$$-\tfrac{1}{4}u_{m+1}^{n+1} + 1\tfrac{1}{2}u_m^{n+1} - \tfrac{1}{4}u_{m-1}^{n+1} = +\tfrac{1}{4}u_{m+1}^n + \tfrac{1}{2}u_m^n + \tfrac{1}{4}u_{m-1}^n$$

In this specific example, equation (8.4) may be written for the elements $u_m^1$ as follows:

$$
\begin{pmatrix}
1\frac{1}{2} & -\frac{1}{4} & 0 & 0 & 0 \\
-\frac{1}{4} & 1\frac{1}{2} & -\frac{1}{4} & 0 & 0 \\
0 & -\frac{1}{4} & 1\frac{1}{2} & -\frac{1}{4} & 0 \\
0 & 0 & -\frac{1}{4} & 1\frac{1}{2} & -\frac{1}{4} \\
0 & 0 & 0 & -\frac{1}{4} & 1\frac{1}{2}
\end{pmatrix}
\begin{pmatrix}
u_2^1 \\ u_1^1 \\ u_0^1 \\ u_{-1}^1 \\ u_{-2}^1
\end{pmatrix}
=
$$

$$
\begin{pmatrix}
\frac{1}{2} & \frac{1}{4} & 0 & 0 & 0 \\
\frac{1}{4} & \frac{1}{2} & \frac{1}{4} & 0 & 0 \\
0 & \frac{1}{4} & \frac{1}{2} & \frac{1}{4} & 0 \\
0 & 0 & \frac{1}{4} & \frac{1}{2} & \frac{1}{4} \\
0 & 0 & 0 & \frac{1}{4} & \frac{1}{2}
\end{pmatrix}
\begin{pmatrix}
2088.56 \\ 923.13 \\ 0 \\ 0 \\ 0
\end{pmatrix}
+ \frac{1}{4}
\begin{pmatrix}
3545.94 \\ 0 \\ 0 \\ 0 \\ 0
\end{pmatrix}
+ \frac{1}{4}
\begin{pmatrix}
3722.36 \\ 0 \\ 0 \\ 0 \\ 0
\end{pmatrix}
=
\begin{pmatrix}
3092.14 \\ 983.71 \\ 230.78 \\ 0 \\ 0
\end{pmatrix}
$$

The details of the solution of this last equation are set out in Appendix A.10. Using the decomposition of Section A.10(i) and the simple iterative formulas of Section A.10(ii) allows us to write

$$
\begin{pmatrix}
1 & 0 & 0 & 0 & 0 \\
-0.167 & 1 & 0 & 0 & 0 \\
0 & -0.171 & 1 & 0 & 0 \\
0 & 0 & -0.172 & 1 & 0 \\
0 & 0 & 0 & -0.172 & 1
\end{pmatrix}
\begin{pmatrix}
1.500 & -0.25 & 0 & 0 & 0 \\
0 & 1.458 & -0.25 & 0 & 0 \\
0 & 0 & 1.457 & -0.25 & 0 \\
0 & 0 & 0 & 1.457 & -0.25 \\
0 & 0 & 0 & 0 & 1.457
\end{pmatrix}
$$

$$
\times
\begin{pmatrix}
u_2^1 \\ u_1^1 \\ u_0^1 \\ u_{-1}^1 \\ u_{-2}^1
\end{pmatrix}
=
\begin{pmatrix}
3092.14 \\ 983.71 \\ 230.78 \\ 0 \\ 0
\end{pmatrix}
$$

or

$$
\mathbf{L} \times \mathbf{Up^1} = \mathbf{s^0}
$$

Writing $\mathbf{Up^1} = \mathbf{t^1}$, we can use the iterations of Section A.10(ii) to give

$$
\begin{pmatrix}
1 & 0 & 0 & 0 & 0 \\
-0.167 & 1 & 0 & 0 & 0 \\
0 & -0.171 & 1 & 0 & 0 \\
0 & 0 & -0.172 & 1 & 0 \\
0 & 0 & 0 & -0.172 & 1
\end{pmatrix}
\begin{pmatrix}
t_2^1 \\ t_1^1 \\ t_0^1 \\ t_{-1}^1 \\ t_{-2}^1
\end{pmatrix}
=
\begin{pmatrix}
3092.14 \\ 983.71 \\ 230.78 \\ 0 \\ 0
\end{pmatrix}
\qquad \text{or}
$$

$$
\begin{pmatrix}
t_2^1 \\ t_1^1 \\ t_0^1 \\ t_{-1}^1 \\ t_{-2}^1
\end{pmatrix}
=
\begin{pmatrix}
3092.14 \\ 1499.06 \\ 487.77 \\ 83.69 \\ 14.36
\end{pmatrix}
$$

99

And finally, using Section A.10(iv) leads to

$$
\begin{pmatrix}
1.500 & -0.25 & 0 & 0 & 0 \\
0 & 1.458 & -0.25 & 0 & 0 \\
0 & 0 & 1.457 & -0.25 & 0 \\
0 & 0 & 0 & 1.457 & -0.25 \\
0 & 0 & 0 & 0 & 1.457
\end{pmatrix}
\begin{pmatrix}
u_2^1 \\ u_1^1 \\ u_0^1 \\ u_{-1}^1 \\ u_{-2}^1
\end{pmatrix}
=
\begin{pmatrix}
3092.14 \\ 1499.06 \\ 487.77 \\ 83.69 \\ 14.36
\end{pmatrix}
\quad \text{or}
$$

$$
\begin{pmatrix}
u_2^1 \\ u_1^1 \\ u_0^1 \\ u_{-1}^1 \\ u_{-2}^1
\end{pmatrix}
=
\begin{pmatrix}
2242.60 \\ 1087.05 \\ 344.88 \\ 59.12 \\ 9.85
\end{pmatrix}
$$

This whole process is now repeated for the next two columns in Table 8.1. The option prices are obtained from the values $u_m^3$ in the final column; for example

$$
f(S_0 = 100, T = 6 \text{ months}) = e^{-rT}(e^{-kx-k^2t}u(x, T))
$$
$$
= e^{-0.1 \times 0.5}(e^{-4.61-0.01} \times 722.67) = 6.81
$$

This is 3% away from the Black Scholes result, which for an absurdly small number of steps is quite surprising. The performance of these finite difference methods as a function of step numbers is examined in the next section.

(iv) **American Options**: The treatment of American options follows the method that was described for the binomial model. We start by recognizing that the value of an American option is only a solution of the Black Scholes equation when the stock price is above the exercise boundary; below this level, the value is simply the exercise value (see Section 6.1). At each grid point, we therefore compare the value $u_m^n$ with a value $v_m^n = e^{rT} e^{kx+k^2t} E$, where $E$ is the exercise value of the option; we adopt the greater of $v_m^n$ and $u_m^n$.

(v) **Discrete Dividends**: Suppose that instead of a continuous dividend, a single dividend is paid between time grid points $n$ and $n + 1$. The standard way of handling this is to make the stock prices $S_m^{n+1}$ drop by an amount $Q$. We assume that the dividend is paid an instant before $t_{n+1}$, so that each of the points $x_m^{n+1}$ drop by an amount $\delta x = \ln S_m^n - \ln(S_m^n - Q) = \ln[S_m^n/(S_m^n - Q)]$. This is a function of $S_m^{n+1}$ so that the grid would no longer maintain uniform spacing in the $x$-direction; practical calculations would become very cumbersome.

The same problem was encountered with the binomial model and was solved by assuming that the dividend is proportional to the stock price, i.e. $Q_m^{n+1} = kS_m^{n+1}$; the grid points then drop by an amount $\delta x = \ln[1/(1 - k)] = \text{constant}$. The whole grid is simply dislocated at the dividend point while retaining the same spacing as before.

## 8.6   COMPARISON OF METHODS

(i) The most straightforward test of the various methods is to see how they compare with an analytical solution. Different methods are therefore applied to a European call option with the following parameters: $S_0 = 100$; $X = 110$; $T = 1$ year; $r = 10\%$; $q = 4\%$; $\sigma = 20\%$.

The graphs that follow show the calculated price of this option plotted against the number of time steps. In each case we have used twice as many grid points in the $x$-direction as in the $t$-direction, and unless otherwise stated, $\alpha = \frac{1}{2}$. In practice, for large values of $N$ this leads to an unnecessarily large spread of $x$ values, which can be truncated without loss of accuracy.

The Black Scholes value of this option is superimposed on the following graphs. The inside (darker) band denotes $\pm 0.1\%$ of the Black Scholes price (6.185), while the outer band is $\pm 0.5\%$. When translated into volatility spreads, these levels of accuracy correspond to volatilities of $20.000 \pm 0.016\%$ and $20.000 \pm 0.081\%$. Any practitioner will realize that even the broader band is well within the tolerances encountered in the options markets.

(ii) **Binomial Model:** This is the simplest model to apply. By definition it has $\alpha = \frac{1}{2}$ (otherwise it becomes a *trinomial model*); but we have seen that an explicit finite difference method is only stable if $\alpha \leq \frac{1}{2}$, i.e. this model hovers uncomfortably at the edge of instability. This is reflected in the zig-zag pattern of Figure 8.8.

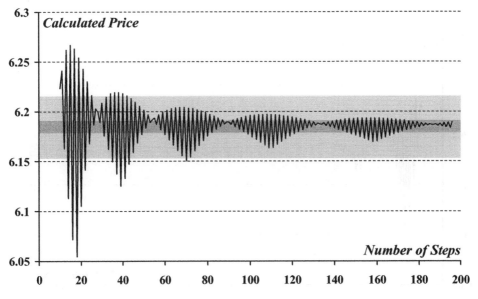

**Figure 8.8**  Binomial method (explicit finite difference method: $\alpha = 0.50$)

(iii) **Instability:** Figures 8.9 and 8.10 illustrate just how sharp the edge between stability and instability really is. Results are shown for $\alpha = 0.51$ and $\alpha = 0.49$ which are immediately adjacent to, but on either side of the stability boundary. Remember that with these values for $\alpha$, the model is no longer binomial. These very slight differences in $\alpha$ make the difference between a wildly unstable model and one which converges fairly quickly.

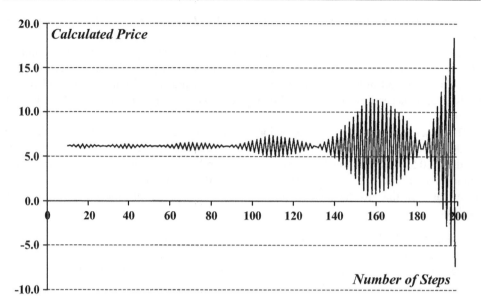

**Figure 8.9**   Explicit finite difference method: $\alpha = 0.51$

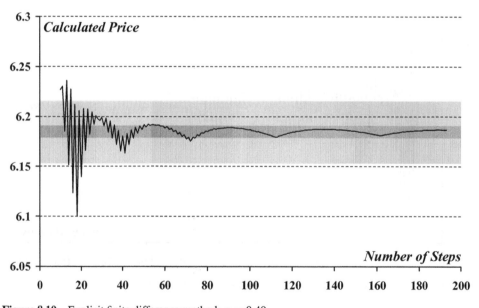

**Figure 8.10**   Explicit finite difference method: $\alpha = 0.49$

(iv) *Trinomial*: The conclusion of the last subsection is that we are more likely to get reliable results by using a trinomial model than with a binomial scheme. In the next subsection it will be seen that there are good reasons for using a trinomial rather than a binomial tree, other than considerations of stability. A popular scheme uses $\alpha = 1/6$ and the results are shown in Figure 8.11.

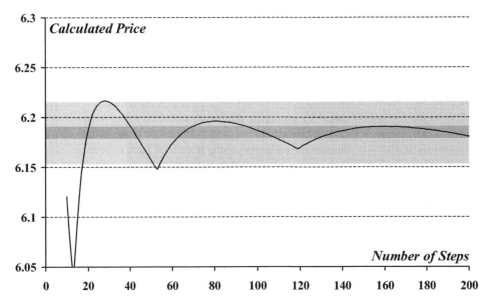

**Figure 8.11**   Trinomial tree

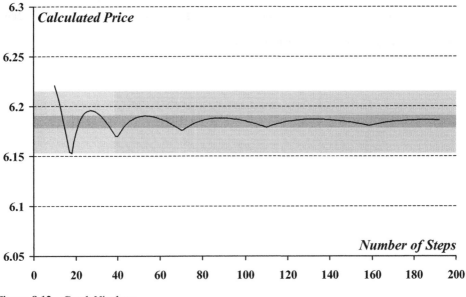

**Figure 8.12**   Crank Nicolson

(v) *Crank Nicolson*: This implicit scheme is illustrated in Figure 8.12. It is clearly the most consistent method illustrated so far. Two other schemes which might be of interest to the reader are not illustrated: the simple implicit method, which in theory should be somewhat less accurate and Douglas, which should be more accurate. But for the option which we have chosen as an example, there is very little difference from the Crank Nicolson result.

(vi) *Average of Successive Binomial*: It was seen in Chapter 7 that we can make a more consistent result from the binomial method by averaging the results obtained using $N$ and $N + 1$ steps. The results are shown in Figure 8.13 and turn out to be surprisingly close in form to the Crank Nicolson results. In a way, this should not be surprising if we look back to Section 8.1(viii) and remember that Crank Nicolson implies an averaging between values at steps $N$ and $N + 1$.

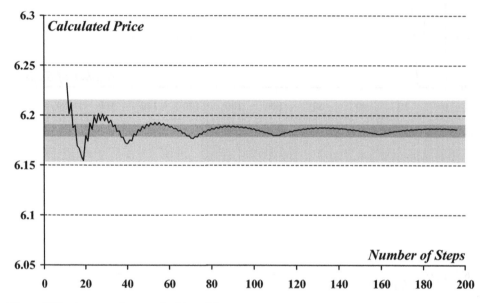

**Figure 8.13**   Average of successive binomial steps

# 9

# Variable Volatility

## 9.1 INTRODUCTION

(i) *Price Volatility*: Apart from a few stray references, option theory has been developed to this point in the book with the assumption that stock price volatility remains constant. But it is very unlikely that a reader would have got this far without having heard that volatility is not constant. Before plunging into the subject we need to spend a couple of pages both defining the jargon and explaining the market observations which cause us to depart from the previous, well-ordered world of constant volatility; also, we define what type of variability we will include in the improved analysis.

Anyone wanting to know the volatility of a stock normally starts with an information service such as Bloomberg, which gives graphs of historical volatility based on data samples of our choice, e.g. measured daily over 3 months or weekly over 1 year. Clearly, the pure sampling process introduces some random fluctuations in the answer we get; but the variability we get in real life far outweighs any sampling error. There is no doubt that the volatility of individual stocks (and indeed the market as a whole) changes over time, often very abruptly: it is not uncommon to see the volatility of a stock suddenly jump from 30% to 40%.

This variability of volatility might arise in a number of ways:

1. There might be an additional random process involving jumps, superimposed on the lognormal distribution of stock price movements. This is clearly sometimes the case: if a stock price suddenly shoots up on the announcement of a merger, there has been a jump. But unfortunately option theory can do little to help us devise a strategy for managing or hedging such events, and the topic will not be pursued further here. Just remember that however much option theory you learn, you still take big risks in the real world.
2. The underlying price process might not be lognormal at all; our attempts to squeeze a nonlognormal process into a lognormal model would make the implied volatility appear to be variable. We will investigate this further below and devise a method of assessing the real underlying distribution, directly from option prices.
3. The volatility itself might follow some unknown stochastic process, completely independent of the stock price process. A mountain of technical literature seeks (with partial success) to describe and explain the underlying mechanisms. We choose not to tackle the subject, which is outside the main objectives of the book.
4. Volatility might be a function of time or of the underlying stock price (or both). We will spend much of the rest of this chapter extending option theory to take account of this dependence.

The reader might be puzzled over our decision to investigate the phenomenon described in point 4 above but not follow the theme of point 3 any further. The reason is that the study of true stochastic volatility, while of great interest in determining future price expectations, does not help us much in working out hedges. On the other hand, we must understand the dependence of volatility on the stock price if we are to price different options on the same underlying stock consistently with each other, i.e. if we are to run books of different options on the same stock. However, we must always remember that the price relationships we derive between different options on the same stock will not be stable through time, as they do not take account of the stochastic movements in volatility which are independent of the price of the underlying asset.

(ii) **Term Volatility**: Consider first a volatility which is dependent only on time. The variance of the logarithm of the stock price after time $T$ can be written $\sigma_T^2 T$. But suppose that over the period $T$, the volatility had been $\sigma_1$ over the first period $\tau$, and $\sigma_2$ over the remaining period $T - \tau$: The volatilities would then have been related as follows:

$$\sigma_T^2 T = \sigma_1^2 \tau + \sigma_2^2 (T - \tau)$$

This is derived from the general property that the variance of the sum of two independently distributed variables is equal to the sum of their variances. The relationship may be generalized to the important result

$$\sigma_{AV}^2(T) = \frac{1}{T} \int_0^T \sigma_t^2 \, dt$$

The jargon for describing these quantities is unfortunately far from standard. For $\sigma_{AV}(T)$ we shall use the expressions *average volatility* or *integrated volatility* or even an expression such as the *2-year volatility*. $\sigma_t$ is called the *instantaneous volatility* or *spot volatility* or *local volatility*.

(iii) **Implied Volatility**: If you ring a broker and ask him the price of an option, he is as likely to give a volatility as he is to give a price in dollars and cents; but securities are bought for money, so what does this quote mean? We have seen that from a knowledge of just a few parameters (including volatility), we can use the Black Scholes equation to calculate the fair value of an option. This process can be inverted so that from a knowledge of the price we can estimate the volatility. A volatility obtained in this way is called an *implied volatility* and this is the volatility quoted by the broker. In the idealized constant volatility world, this volatility would be the observed volatility of the underlying stock.

The reader with any experience of real markets might be very skeptical at this point. Implied volatility is not an objectively measurable quantity; it is a number backed out of a formula. What if the Black Scholes formula is wrong, or even slightly inaccurate? Well, what if it is? As long as everybody agrees on the same formula, we still have a one-to-one correspondence between the option price and the implied volatility. The formula used is always Black Scholes or Black '76 or a tree using Black Scholes assumptions, depending on the type of option and underlying instrument. But what if the interest rates used by two people differ slightly or one uses discrete dividends while the other uses continuous? The answer is of course that before a trade is agreed, both parties must revert to prices in dollars and cents. So why bother to jump through all these hoops rather than just quoting prices directly?

Traded options are quoted with a number of fixed strikes and maturity dates (1 month apart for maturities of less than 3 months and 3 months apart for 3 to 9 months). Clearly it is quite difficult to make immediate, intuitive comparisons between option prices; but comparisons between their implied volatilities will make immediate sense to a professional. There may be individual options that are substantially undervalued compared to others in the same series. This would be immediately apparent by comparing implied volatilities. The process is not dissimilar to comparing different bonds: if we want to compare a 3-year bond with a 12% coupon to a 7-year bond with a 3% coupon, yield comparisons will tell us a lot more than price comparisons.

(iv) In summary, we consider three quantities called volatility and the reader must clearly understand the differences between them:

1. Historic volatility or realized volatility which is the volatility of the underlying stock price observed in the market. The value is obtained by a sampling process, e.g. from day end prices over the previous 1-month period. Although it sounds odd, one occasionally hears expressions like future historic volatility, which means the actual volatility that will be achieved by the stock price in the future.

2. Instantaneous and integrated volatilities, which are idealized mathematical quantities. The first is the factor that appears in the representation of a stochastic process $dx_t = \mu(x_t, t)\, dt + \sigma(x_t, t)dW_t$. We normally write it more simply as $\sigma_t$. The integrated (average) volatility is simply the volatility obtained by averaging the instantaneous volatilities over a period. In any theory of volatility we construct, our average volatility is equated to the historic volatility over a like period.

3. The implied volatility, which is a number backed out of a model (which may or may not be accurate) by plugging in an option price. The previous two types of volatility make no reference to options while this type is obtained from a specific option and a specific model.

(v) **Implied Volatility Skew:** The 1987 stock market crash was of unprecedented abruptness. Its consequences for the real economy were mild when compared with the weaker crash of 1929, but the speed of the fall was much larger. By one well publicized measure at least, this was a 14 standard deviation event. The first reaction to such a figure is to question the probability distribution used for market prices; there is indeed good reason to disbelieve the usual lognormal assumption, and we now examine some of the evidence.

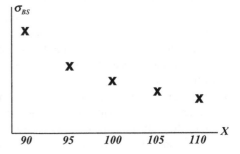

**Figure 9.1**   Volatility skew

The implied volatility depends on the accuracy of the Black Scholes model and hence on the assumptions underlying the model (in particular the lognormal distribution of the stock prices). In Figure 9.1 we plot the implied volatility of a series of traded call options of the same maturity but different strike prices; the stock price was 100. Clearly there is a systematic bias, known as the skew or smile, which indicates that some of the Black Scholes assumptions have broken down. Rather mysteriously, these smiles only started appearing systematically after the 1987 crash.

Given the empirical results shown in Figure 9.1 for European call options, the pattern for European put options must follow from arbitrage arguments. The put–call parity relationship expresses an equivalence between a put and a call with the same strike, given by equation (2.1); it was derived quite independently of any option model or assumption about stock

107

price distributions. Therefore, any mistake or inaccuracy due to model misspecification which appears in the implied volatility of a European call option will also show up in the implied volatility of the corresponding put option. If not, we could arbitrage a put plus underlying stock against the call. In conclusion, when we present implied volatilities plotted against strike prices, it is not necessary to specify whether they are derived from put or call options.

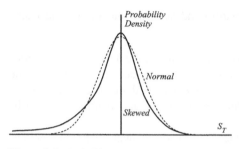

**Figure 9.2**   Volatility skew

If we assume that this skew is due to a departure from lognormality of the underlying stock, what does it imply for the shape of the actual probability function? A normal distribution for the log of the stock price would follow if the curve in Figure 9.1 were flat; but the observed curve shows that put options with a strike of 90 are "overpriced" while call options with a strike of 110 are "underpriced". The implied probability distribution to produce such pricing would have a greater value at lower values of the final stock price. This is illustrated in Figure 9.2.

No convincing single explanation for the skew phenomenon, or why it appeared only after the 1987 crash, has been advanced. However, each of the following is a credible contributory factor:

- Historic volatilities of stocks increase naturally when stock prices fall, because in these circumstances uncertainty and leverage increase for the company. This causes the out-of-the-money puts to be "overpriced" compared to out-of-the-money calls.
- The trading community has permanently learned the lesson that insurance against highly improbable but potentially fatal outcomes makes sense: it is worth buying out-of-the-money puts.
- Empirical observation shows that even if markets follow Brownian motion most of the time, they are nonetheless subject to occasional jumps. If account is taken of this effect, the observed probability distribution appears to become skewed.

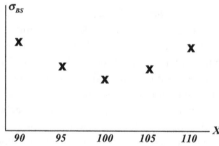

**Figure 9.3**   Volatility smile

(vi) *Smiles:* The skew shown in Figure 9.1 is generally observed for equities and minor currencies. Stock indices also follow the pattern but are distinctly flattened in the region to the right of the at-the-money point. Foreign currency options (on major currencies) have a symmetry imposed by the reciprocal nature of the contracts (a call in one currency is a put in the other). This is reflected in Figure 9.3, which shows the analog of the equity skew, referred to for obvious reasons as the implied volatility smile.

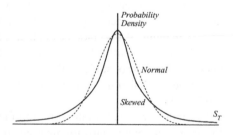

**Figure 9.4**   Volatility smile

The implied probability distribution function takes the form shown in Figure 9.4. Far out-of-the-money puts and calls are now both "overvalued", which implies that the area under the tails of the distribution is higher than it would be for a normal distribution. Such distributions are said to be leptokurtic or fat-tailed.

(vii) *Evolution of Smile/Skew over Time*: Consider the following simple example of two put options with strikes $90 and $87.5 when the underlying stock price is $100. The interest and dividend rates are 6% and 3% and the maturity is 3 months. The market prices and implied volatilities of the options areas follow:

| Strike | Price | $\sigma_{BS}$ |
|--------|-------|-----|
| $87.5 | $1.66 | 33% |
| $90.0 | $1.84 | 30% |

This is consistent with the volatility skew described above. We can go one step further and deduce an important fact about skews and smiles. Suppose the implied volatilities for 1-year options were the same as for 3-month options. The corresponding prices would then be

| Strike | Price | $\sigma_{BS}$ |
|--------|-------|-----|
| $87.5 | $5.84 | 33% |
| $90.0 | $5.77 | 30% |

This gives a higher option price for a put option with a lower strike and the same maturity, which allows a potential arbitrage. The difference between the two implied volatilities for these longer-term options must therefore be less than it was for the short-term options. The general conclusion, which is confirmed by market prices, is that skews and smiles are flattened out as the maturity of an option increases. Most skew/smile studies are confined to options of less than 1 year.

## 9.2   LOCAL VOLATILITY AND THE FOKKER PLANCK EQUATION

In the last section we saw that implied volatilities vary with the strike price and maturity of options. This is tantamount to saying that the Black Scholes model does not quite work. The most straightforward way of getting around this consists of assuming that volatility is a function of both the stock price and of time, which allows us to price options consistently with each other at any given moment in time. This is of course essential if we are ever to use one option to hedge another, or to run them together as a "book" (Skiadopoulos, 1999).

(i) Our starting point is a table of implied volatilities $\sigma_{BS}$ for various values of the strike price and maturity. We can obtain this from the market prices for traded options, which are plugged into the Black Scholes model (or binomial model for American options) to give the implied volatilities. Typically we would have puts and calls for five different maturities (each month for 3 months and then quarterly out to 9 months), and perhaps eight different strike prices. Generally we concentrate on the call options if we can, since traded options are more often American rather than European and we can then use the fact that the American calls can usually be priced using the Black Scholes model; this is not true for put options.

The reader is reminded that the implied volatility is the number squeezed out of a faulty model when we put in observed market data. The implied volatility therefore has no relevance unless it is plugged back into the same faulty model. In this section we seek a continuous function which describes the true volatility for any stock price and maturity. We show below how to obtain this from a knowledge of the market price of an option for any strike price and maturity. But unfortunately, market prices are only quoted for discrete strike prices and maturities, so we will need to interpolate values between real market quotations. Since prices are strongly dependent functions of strike and maturity, it is preferable to interpolate between implied volatilities, which are only weakly dependent on these variables. The continuous function $\sigma_{BS}(X, T)$ is usually referred to as an implied volatility surface. We put to one side the question of what interpolation technique is used to derive this smooth surface and just assume that for any value of $X$ and $T$ we know $\sigma_{BS}(X, T)$. From this smooth implied volatility surface we can immediately derive a smooth "market price" surface simply by using the Black Scholes model.

The question to which we now turn is what information concerning volatility can be obtained from this price surface, that is independent of any specific option model.

(ii) In Appendix A.4 it is shown that the Black Scholes equation can be obtained by multiplying the risk-neutral Kolmogorov *backward* equation by the payoff function of an option, integrating over all terminal stock price values and finally discounting back by the risk-free rate of return. We adopt a similar procedure here, using instead the Kolmogorov *forward* equation (or Fokker Planck equation), which is derived in Appendix A.3 (see for example Jarrow, 1998, p. 429).

The underlying stochastic process is written

$$dS_T = a_{S_T T}\, dT + b_{S_T T}\, dW_T$$

and the associated Fokker Planck equation is

$$\frac{\partial F_{S_T T}}{\partial T} + \frac{\partial (a_{S_T T} F_{S_T T})}{\partial S_T} - \frac{1}{2}\frac{\partial^2 \left(b_{S_T T}^2 F_{S_T T}\right)}{\partial S_T^2} = 0$$

where $F_{S_T T}$ is the transition probability distribution function of a stock price which starts with value $S_0$ at time zero and has value $S_T$ at time $T$. In the rather cumbersome derivations below, this is often written as $F_T$ in the interest of lightening up the notation.

The payoff function is that of a call option, $(S_T - X)^+$. This is of course a non-differentiable function, which we will proceed to differentiate a couple of times. The reader who is troubled by this sloppy approach should consult Appendix A.7(i) and (ii) where a more respectable analysis is given and the following relationships are explained:

$$\frac{\partial (S_T - X)^+}{\partial S_T} = H(S_T - X) = -\frac{\partial (S_T - X)^+}{\partial X}$$

$$\frac{\partial^2 (S_T - X)^+}{\partial S_T^2} = \delta(S_T - X) = \frac{\partial^2 (S_T - X)^+}{\partial X^2}$$

(9.1)

(iii) Let $C(X, T)$ be today's observed market value of a call option with strike $X$ and maturity $T$; again, the arguments of this function are often omitted for sake of simplicity. Equations (9.1) are used to give the following relationships:

- $C(X, T) = e^{-rT} \int_0^\infty F_{S_T T}(S_T - X)^+ \, dS_T$

- $\dfrac{\partial C}{\partial X} = e^{-rT} \int_0^\infty F_{S_T T} \dfrac{\partial (S_T - X)^+}{\partial X} \, dS_T = -e^{-rT} \int_0^\infty F_{S_T T} H(S_T - X) \, dS_T$   (9.2)

- $\dfrac{\partial^2 C}{\partial X^2} = e^{-rT} \int_0^\infty F_{S_T T} \dfrac{\partial^2 (S_T - X)^+}{\partial X^2} \, dS_T = e^{-rT} \int_0^\infty F_{S_T T} \delta(S_T - X) \, dS_T = e^{-rT} F_{XT}$

It is important to appreciate that these relationships do not depend on the Black Scholes model or indeed on any particular assumption for the probability distribution of stock prices. In fact, the last of these relationships gives a method for deriving the probability distribution if we know the option price for all possible strike prices, i.e. if we have an option price surface in $(X, T)$ space.

(iv) While the last subsection applies generally for any distribution $F_{S_T T}$, we now make the standard assumptions

$$a_{S_T T} = (r - q)S_T; \qquad b_{S_T T} = S_T \sigma_{S_T T}$$

where $\sigma_{S_T T}$ is the instantaneous (or spot or local) volatility at $(S_T, T)$.

Multiply the Fokker Planck equation by $e^{-rT}(S_T - X)^+$, substitute these last expressions for $a_{S_T T}$ and $b_{S_T T}$ and integrate from 0 to $\infty$:

$$e^{-rT} \int_0^\infty \left\{ \frac{\partial F_T}{\partial T} + \frac{\partial ((r - q) S_T F_T)}{\partial S_T} - \frac{1}{2} \frac{\partial^2 \left( S_T^2 \sigma_{S_T T}^2 F_T \right)}{\partial S_T^2} \right\} (S_T - X)^+ dS_T = 0$$

Take each term separately and use the relationships in equations (9.1) and (9.2):

- $e^{-rT} \displaystyle\int_0^\infty \frac{\partial F_T}{\partial T} (S_T - X)^+ dS_T$

$\qquad = \dfrac{\partial}{\partial T} \displaystyle\int_0^\infty e^{-rT}(S_T - X)^+ F_T \, dS_T + r\, e^{-rT} \int_0^\infty (S_T - X)^+ F_T \, dS_T$

$\qquad = \dfrac{\partial C}{\partial T} + rC$

- $e^{-rT} \displaystyle\int_0^\infty \frac{\partial ((r - q) S_T F_T)}{\partial S_T}(S_T - X)^+ dS_T$

$\qquad = e^{-rT} \, |(r - q)S_T F_T|_0^\infty - (r - q)e^{-rT} \displaystyle\int_0^\infty S_T H(S_T - X) F_T \, dS_T$

$\qquad = -(r - q)e^{-rT} \displaystyle\int_0^\infty ((S_T - X)^+ + X H(S_T - X)) F_T \, dS_T$

$\qquad = -(r - q)C + (r - q)X \dfrac{\partial C}{\partial X}$

where we have used $S_T H(S_T - X) \equiv (S_T - X)^+ + X H(S_T - X)$.

- $e^{-rT} \displaystyle\int_0^\infty \frac{\partial^2\left(S_T^2 \sigma_{S_T T}^2 F_{S_T T}\right)}{\partial S_T^2}(S_T - X)^+ dS_T$

$$= e^{-rT}\left.\frac{\partial\left(S_T^2 \sigma_{S_T T}^2 F_T\right)}{\partial S_T}(S_T - X)^+\right|_0^\infty - e^{-rT}\int_0^\infty \frac{\partial\left(S_T^2 \sigma_{S_T T}^2 F_T\right)}{\partial S_T} H(S_T - X)dS_T$$

$$= -e^{-rT}\left.\left|S_T^2 \sigma_{S_T T}^2 F_T H(S_T - X)\right|_0^\infty\right. + e^{-rT}\int_0^\infty S_T^2 \sigma_{S_T T}^2 F_T\, \delta(S_T - X)\, dS_T$$

$$= e^{-rT}\sigma_{XT}^2 X^2\, F_{XT} = \sigma_{XT}^2 X^2 \frac{\partial^2 C}{\partial X^2}$$

Substituting these last three results into the previous equation gives

$$\sigma_{XT}^2 = \frac{\dfrac{\partial C}{\partial T} + qC + (r - q)X\dfrac{\partial C}{\partial X}}{\dfrac{1}{2}X^2\dfrac{\partial^2 C}{\partial X^2}} \tag{9.3}$$

Let us be clear about the notation: $C = C(S_t, t; X, T)$ is the price at time $t$ of a call option with strike price $X$, maturing at time $T$. $\sigma_{XT}^2 = E_t[[\sigma_{S_T T}^2]_{S_T=X}]$ is the risk-neutral expectation at time $t$ of the value of $\sigma_{S_T T}^2$ at time $T$ if $S_T = X$. Equation (9.3) is frequently referred to as the Fokker Planck or forward equation, which is really just a piece of shorthand. Furthermore, slightly extravagant claims of its being the dual of the Black Scholes equation should be taken in context: this equation works for a European call or put option; Black Scholes works for any derivative.

(v) Several methods have been used to apply this formula, but we content ourselves with a few general remarks. The first step in the procedure is to obtain a continuous implied volatility surface from a few discrete points. The final answers are very sensitive to the procedures used, which is not very reassuring. The general approaches fall into a few categories:

- Estimation procedures designed to get some statistical best fit for the implied volatility surface as a whole; this has the advantage of eliminating obviously anomalous points which do not reflect a systematic relationship, and it results in regular surfaces. But it does not allow observed market prices to be retrieved and errors may swamp any information content.
- Join the data points up with piecewise polynomials in both the strike and time axes. This is probably the most common method with the cubic spline being the favored approximation, since this can be twice differentiated analytically.
- Observe from equations (9.2) that there is a direct relationship between the probability density function for the stock price and the differentials of the call option price. So equation (9.3) relates the local volatility surface directly to the form of the probability density. Assumptions can be made, for example that the probability density is only a small perturbation from the lognormal form; a series called the Edgworth expansion (analogous to Taylor expansions for analytic functions) can then be used to derive the volatility surface.

- The most direct approach is to recast equation (9.3) in analytical form by performing the differentials on the "Black Scholes" formula for a call option. The inverted commas are used since the formula must use $\sigma_{BS}$ and take into account that this is a function of the strike price. The final formula will then contain first and second differentials of $\sigma_{BS}$ with respect to $X$. These terms may be taken directly from a cubic spline representation of the implied volatility surface.

(vi) Once these local volatilities have been determined, they can be used within a pricing tree and will give results which are consistent with observed short-term option prices in the market. It would be nice if these surfaces were stable over time so that only an occasional check with the market were needed to assure good answers. But unfortunately, this is not the case: the surface is quite unstable and in the real world, daily recalibration is necessary. The reader might wonder if all this effort was really worthwhile, if the only outcome is to obtain a result which will no longer be valid tomorrow. However, it is already a big step to be able to price all short-term options consistently with observed market prices at a given instant in time.

## 9.3   FORWARD INDUCTION

This technique is effort saving and extensively used whenever a tree needs initial calibration prior to calculating prices, e.g. when smiles are being taken into account (Jamshidian, 1991). The underlying principles and the jargon are best explained by starting with the simplest case of a binomial model with constant volatility.

(i) The example we take is that of Section 7.3(i). The exact numbers are written out in that section and the reader is asked to refer back to these. Remember that the essential features of this tree are as follows:

- We chose the Jarrow–Rudd discretization, setting the nodes of the tree at $S_0\, e^{m\sqrt{\delta t}}$ where $m = -3$ to $+3$.
- From a knowledge of the risk-neutral drift $(r - q)$ and variance $\sigma^2$ we calculate the pseudo-probabilities $p$ and $1 - p$ of $S_t$ going up or down.

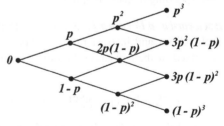

- These pseudo-probabilities describe the time behavior of both the stock and the call option [equation (7.1)].
- The present value of the call option is obtained by rolling the discounted payoffs back through the tree, i.e. making the value of the call op-

**Figure 9.5**   Binomial tree as probability tree

tion at each node equal to the probability weighted sum of the option values at the next nodes, discounted back at the risk-free rate.

(ii) We could of course have performed the calculation in the following mathematically equivalent way. Consider the tree as a probability tree: the probability of reaching each node is shown explicitly in Figure 9.5. The final probabilities $P_i$ are the probabilities of the binomial distribution given in Appendix A.2(i).

The value of an option can now be written as

$$f_0 = f_0^0 = (e^{-r\delta t})^3 \sum P_i f_i^3 = 0.983^3$$

$$\{0.541^3 \times 27.76 + 3 \times 0.541^2 \times 0.459 \times 8.51\} = 7.44$$

Clearly, the answer is the same as we got in Chapter 8, since the mathematical operation is identical, and only the words used in describing the operation are different; but we have now solved the problem by *forward induction*.

This technique could perfectly well be developed for a more complicated case involving variable interest rate and volatility, simply by using the probability tree concept. However, the literature has developed some further jargon and the reader needs to understand this to follow what is going on.

(iii) *Arrow Debreu Securities and State Prices*: An *Arrow Debreu* security is one which pays out $1 if a given node of the tree is reached, and zero otherwise. Take as an example an Arrow Debreu security which pays $1 if the top right-hand node of the tree in Figure 9.5 is reached. In a risk-neutral world, today's value of this security, viewed from the origin of the tree, is just $\lambda_3^3 = (e^{-r\delta t})^3 p^3 \times \$1 = \$0.1504$. This is also known as the *state price* of the particular node (or "state"). Clearly, every single node in the tree has a state price as viewed from the origin. In general, the state price equals the probability of reaching a given node, multiplied by a risk-neutral discount factor. This holds true if the probabilities and interest rates vary throughout the tree, or indeed if the time steps or price spacings of the tree are variable.

(iv) There is yet another, equivalent way of looking at the calculations of subsection (ii). The price of the call option is written $f_0 = \sum \lambda_i^3 f_i^3$, which can be given the following interpretation: if we hold a portfolio of $f_i^3$ units of each of the Arrow Debreu securities corresponding to each of the final nodes (states) of the tree, the payoff of this portfolio is exactly the same as the payoff of a call option. Therefore today's value of the call option must be the same as today's value of the portfolio, i.e. equal to the state prices of the final nodes multiplied by the payoff corresponding to each final node.

(v) *Backward and Forward Trees*: We now turn our attention to a tree with non-constant transition probabilities and interest rates. In Appendix A.3 the Kolmogorov equations are explicitly discussed in their discrete, binomial form. The more common, backward equation can be written

$$P[N, j \mid n, i] = p_i^n P[N, j \mid n+1, i+1] + (1 - p_i^n) P[N, j \mid n+1, i-1]$$

where $P[N, j \mid n, i]$ is the probability that the stock price reaches node level $j$ at time step $N$, assuming it started at level $i$ at step $n$; $p_i^n$ is the probability of an up jump from node $(n, i)$. It is shown in Appendix A.3 that in the limit of infinitesimal step size, this converges to a differential equation; it is further shown in Appendix A.4 that this differential equation is simply the Black Scholes equation, written in a slightly unusual form.

The forward equation (Fokker Planck) is similarly written in binomial form as

$$P[N, j \mid 0, 0] = (1 - p_{j+1}^{N-1})P[N-1, j+1 \mid 0, 0] + p_{j-1}^{N-1}P[N-1, j-1 \mid 0, 0] \qquad (9.4)$$

The state price for node $(N-1, j+1)$ can be written $\lambda_{j+1}^{N-1} = e^{-r(N-1)\delta t} P[N-1, j+1 \mid 0, 0]$ where $e^{-r(N-1)\delta t}$ is the appropriate discount factor back to the origin of the tree, assuming constant interest. Writing the discount factor for a single step as $e^{-r\delta t}$ the forward equation becomes

$$\lambda_j^N = e^{-r\delta t}\left\{\left(1 - p_{j+1}^{N-1}\right)\lambda_{j+1}^{N-1} + p_{j-1}^{N-1}\lambda_{j-1}^{N-1}\right\} \tag{9.5}$$

The interesting point about this is that the state prices for the entire tree can be built up by working across the tree from left to right (assuming we know all the transition probabilities); this explains the expression *forward induction*; the above also explains the assertion that Arrow Debreu prices are discrete solutions of the Kolmogorov forward equation.

The last equation stands in contrast to the equation for *backward induction* which is normally called "rolling backward through the tree". For a dividend-paying stock, this can be expressed as

$$S_i\, e^{(r-q)\delta t} = \left\{p_i^n S_{i+1} + \left(1 - p_i^n\right)S_{i-1}\right\} \tag{9.6}$$

(vi) *Green's Functions and Arrow Debreu Prices*: The reader is reminded that the price of an option is given by

$$f(S_0) = e^{-RT}\int_{\text{all }S_T} f(S_T)\, F[x_T, T \mid x_0, 0]\, dx_T; \qquad x_t = \ln(S_t/S_0)$$

where $f(S_T)$ is the option payoff. Comparing this with a general equation of the form of equation (A7.6), it is clear that $e^{-RT} f[x_T, T \mid x_0, 0]$ is a Green's function. But the probability $P[n, i \mid 0, 0]$ used in the last subsection is just the discrete time analog of the transition density function $F[x_T, T \mid x_0, 0]$. It follows immediately that the Arrow Debreu prices are simply the Green's functions expressed in discrete time.

This section is a little like an elaborate literary reference: it stitches together a number of disparate concepts and allows us to understand what our colleagues are talking about; but it does not really introduce any new concepts – just new words. It has been explicitly pointed out that a tree is a representation of both the forward and backward Kolmogorov equations; that Arrow Debreu prices are solutions of the forward (and backward) equation and can be regarded as a Green's function in discrete time; that by concentrating on the forward equation we can work out state prices from left to right in the tree and use the result to compute an option price. We could of course have just explained forward induction from the fundamental properties of probability trees, but the reader also needs to understand the gratuitous references made in the literature if he is to keep up.

## 9.4 TRINOMIAL TREES

(i) *Binomial Tree with Variable Volatility*: Let us consider a binomial tree of the type studied extensively in Chapter 7. It was assumed that volatility is constant throughout the tree; we now relax this idealized assumption, and consider the case where volatility varies both over time and with stock price. This means that the volatility at each node is different and in consequence, the sizes of steps and the transition probabilities are also variable. In each cell of the tree, there are two relationships corresponding to equations (7.5):

$$1 + (r - q)\delta t = p_i u_i + (1 - p_i)d_i$$
$$\sigma_i^2\, \delta t = p_i(1 - p_i)(u_i - d_i)^2 \tag{9.7}$$

With two equations for three unknowns, we have some discretion. Making the simplifying choice $u_i = d_i^{-1}$ (Jarrow–Rudd) then gives us no further choices; we must have $u_i = e^{\sigma_i \sqrt{\delta t}}$. Unfortunately, if the $\sigma_i$ are different at each node, we would no longer have the nice regular binomial trees of Chapter 7, but something more like the tree of Figure 9.6. Jarrow–Rudd is of course only one of many possible choices. It is possible that some other choice of discretionary variable would give a better looking tree.

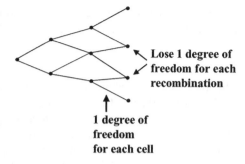

**Figure 9.6**   Binomial tree (variable volatility)

(ii) Let us consider the third column of cells in the diagram. Each of the three cells has a pair of relationships given by equations (9.7), i.e. each cell has one *degree of freedom*, or parameter which we are free to choose. The three cells in the column therefore have a total of three degrees of freedom. We need the tree to recombine if it is to be of any practical use, so there are two constraints that must be imposed: each of the two inside nodes in the final column must be reachable by either an up- or a down-jump. These two constraints eat up a degree of freedom each so that we are left with one degree of freedom for the entire third column of cells. Similar reasoning shows that there is only one degree of freedom for every column in the tree: we have therefore lost nearly all of our flexibility in being able to choose step sizes. The most we can do to improve the appearance of the tree with our one degree of freedom is to line up the central nodes.

One rather desperate solution is to introduce an extra degree of freedom by making the time step length into a variable. We are then able to make the nodes line up horizontally, although at the expense of unequal time step lengths; there is little improvement in terms of ease of computation. Clearly, we need to look for a better type of tree.

(iii) **Trinomial Tree**: We turn our attention to the three-pronged tree which is briefly described in terms of the arithmetic random walk in Appendix A.1(iii). As in the case of the binomial tree, we choose to examine the evolution of the stock price, rather than its logarithm. A single cell in the process is then represented by Figure 9.7. The fundamental equations relating the various parameters to the observed interest rate and volatility [the analogue of equations (9.7)] are simply written:

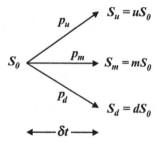

**Figure 9.7**   One cell of trinomial tree

$$1 + (r - q)\delta t = p_u u + p_d d + (1 - p_u - p_d)m$$
$$\sigma^2 \delta t = p_u u^2 + p_d d^2 + (1 - p_u - p_d)m^2 - (1 + (r - q)\delta t)^2 \tag{9.8}$$

The immediate reaction is that we now have an abundance of degrees of freedom: there are five unknowns constrained by two equations. As with the binomial tree, there are an infinite number of ways of choosing our parameters. For computational convenience, it is sensible to make the tree regular by making the following choices:

$$m = 1; \qquad u = d^{-1} = e^{\Delta}$$

With $m = 1$, equations (9.8) become (to $O[\delta t]$)

$$(r - q)\delta t = p_u(u - 1) + p_d(d - 1)$$

$$(\sigma^2 + 2(r - q))\delta t = p_u(u^2 - 1) + p_d(d^2 - 1)$$

(9.9)

Make the substitution $u = d^{-1} = e^\Delta$, expand the exponential and retain only terms of order $O[\delta t]$ and $O[\Delta^2]$. A quick romp through the algebra then yields

$$p_u = \frac{\sigma^2 + \Delta\left(r - q - \frac{1}{2}\sigma^2\right)}{2\Delta^2}\delta t; \qquad p_d = \frac{\sigma^2 - \Delta\left(r - q - \frac{1}{2}\sigma^2\right)}{2\Delta^2}\delta t; \qquad p_m = 1 - \frac{\sigma^2}{\Delta^2}\delta t$$

(9.10)

These are of course the same relationships as we obtained in equation (A2.8) for the three-pronged arithmetic random walk, except with the term $\frac{1}{2}\sigma^2$ which routinely appears when we go from the normal to the lognormal distribution.

It is essential to understand this result compared with its counterpart for the binomial model. In Section 7.2(ii) we put $u = d^{-1}$ to give the Jarrow–Rudd arrangement; this defined the value of $\Delta(= \sigma\sqrt{\delta t})$. However, in the trinomial case we can choose $u = d^{-1}$, and still retain the possibility of choosing $\Delta$ independently. The impact of this extra degree of freedom is immense. When we are confronted with a variable volatility problem, we can fix the numerical value of $\Delta$ to be the same throughout the tree, with the variation in volatility from node to node reflected entirely by variations in the probabilities at different nodes. The geometry of the tree remains fixed and regular.

(iv) *Optimal Spacing (Constant Volatility)*: Before commenting on how to choose $\Delta$ when volatility is variable, consider the choice for a constant volatility tree. We allow ourselves to be prompted by our study of finite difference equations in Section 8.1 and Appendix A.9. It was shown in Section 8.1 that if we solve the Black Scholes equation using a finite difference approach, a particularly efficient solution was obtained using the so-called Douglas discretization. This requires the choice

$$\alpha = \left\{\frac{\frac{1}{2}\sigma^2\delta t}{(\delta x)^2}\right\} = \frac{1}{6}$$

where $x$ is the logarithm of the stock price. With this choice, the finite difference method was shown in Appendix A.9 to be formally equivalent to a trinomial tree. It therefore seems sensible to make the same choice, which in the notation of this section is written as $u = d^{-1} = e^{\sigma\sqrt{3\delta t}}$. Making the substitution $\Delta = \sigma\sqrt{3\delta t}$ in equations (9.10) immediately gives the results

$$p_u = \frac{1}{6} + \left(r - q - \frac{1}{2}\sigma^2\right)\sqrt{\frac{\delta t}{12\sigma^2}}; \qquad p_d = \frac{1}{6} - \left(r - q - \frac{1}{2}\sigma^2\right)\sqrt{\frac{\delta t}{12\sigma^2}}; \qquad p_m = \frac{2}{3}$$

(9.11)

One particular requirement that must be fulfilled if a trinomial tree solution is to be stable is that the probabilities $p_u$, $p_d$ and $p_m$ must not only sum to unity, but must also each be positive. The discretization of equation (9.11) more or less assures that this condition is fulfilled in any real-life case, but it is always worth checking.

117

(v) *Spacing with Variable Volatility*: We cannot of course use equation (9.11) for variable volatility; it would lead to variable $\Delta$ and the whole purpose of this section was to discover a tree with constant step size. Instead, we revert to equation (9.10), and a favorite choice is $\Delta = \sigma_{\text{largest}}\sqrt{3\delta t}$, where $\sigma_{\text{largest}}$ is the largest local volatility encountered in the tree.

## 9.5   DERMAN KANI IMPLIED TREES

There are two common approaches to pricing options in the presence of variable volatilities or interest rates: the first consists of calibrating a trinomial tree using observed market prices of options and then using the same tree to consistently price other, unquoted options (Derman *et al.*, 1996). The second approach uses the Fokker Planck equation (9.3) to extract a continuous expression for the volatility as a function of strike and time to maturity. The results can then be used in a variety of types of computation (trees, Monte Carlo, finite differences). We now examine the first approach.

(i) The procedure is best explained with a concrete example, and we will try to make this as simple as possible. Assume we have a stock with price $S_0 = 100$, interest rate $r = 8\%$ and continuous dividend $q = 3\%$. Prices of call options quoted in the market are as given in Table 9.1.

**Table 9.1**   Quoted European call option prices ($)

| Strike: | 1 month | 4 months | 7 months |
|---|---|---|---|
| 80 | 20.28 | 21.30 | 22.43 |
| 90 | 10.48 | 12.56 | 14.31 |
| 100 | 2.62 | 5.69 | 7.86 |
| 110 | 0.12 | 1.83 | 3.64 |
| 120 | 0 | 0.36 | 1.32 |
| 130 | 0 | 0.04 | 0.37 |

We set ourselves the objective of building a tree to price 6-month options. For the reasons given in the last section, this is best achieved by means of a trinomial tree. We choose a three-step tree, so that the length of each step is 2 months. We further choose the spacing as $e^\Delta$ where $\Delta = 0.25 \times \sqrt{3\delta t} = 0.1786$ or $e^\Delta = 1.1934$. This is in line with the spacings suggested for a tree with variable volatility in the last section. The tree is set out in Figure 9.8; to make the tree fully functional, we need to find out the transition probabilities at all the nodes.

(ii) *State Prices in a Trinomial Tree*: We now apply the analysis of Section 9.3 to a trinomial tree. The state price $\lambda_i^n$ is the value at node zero of an Arrow Debreu security which pays out $1 if (and only if) the node at time $n$ and stock price level $i$ is reached. It was shown that the node zero value of a European option maturing at time step $n$ can be written $f_0 = \sum_i \lambda_i^n f_i^n$, i.e. the payoff multiplied by the state price, summed over all final nodes.

Let us now imagine that we know the market prices of a put or a call option for any strike $X$, maturing in 6 months. We can write the market prices of these options as $C_X^{6m}$ and $P_X^{6m}$; their

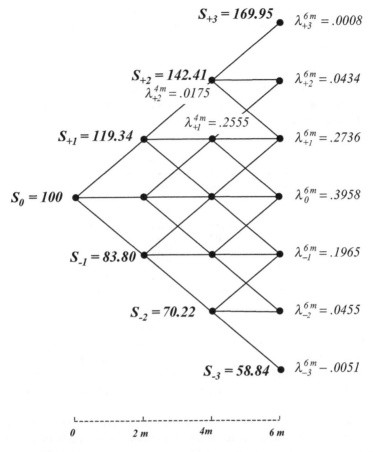

**Figure 9.8**   Trinomial tree

payoffs in 6 months are of course, $\max[S_{6m} - X, 0]$ and $\max[X - S_{6m}, 0]$. Referring back to the trinomial tree of the last subsection, we can write

$$C^{6m}_{142.41} = \sum_i \lambda^{6m}_i \max[S_{6m} - 142.41, 0]$$

The payoffs at all the nodes below the top right-hand one are zero, so this last equation reduces to

$$C^{6m}_{142.41} = \lambda^{6m}_{+3}(169.95 - 142.41)$$

The next state price down in the final column can be obtained from the analogous equation

$$C^{6m}_{119.34} = \lambda^{6m}_{+3}(169.95 - 119.34) + \lambda^{6m}_{+2}(142.41 - 119.34)$$

Since we already know the top state price $\lambda^{6m}_{+3}$ from the previous equation, we can obtain $\lambda^{6m}_{+2}$; and so on down the final column of nodes. We will need one additional relationship to calculate the final node down. This is provided by the normalizing relationship $\Sigma_i \lambda^{6m}_i = e^{-8\% \times 6\,\text{months}}$: remember that the state prices are really probabilities of reaching final nodes multiplied by discount factors, and the probabilities sum to unity.

We have very simply derived the final state prices from observed market prices, and can therefore price any 6-month option whose payoff depends only on the price in 6 months; all this without reference to volatilities or transition probabilities!

(iii) *Interpolations*: The last subsection begs a huge question: where do we get market prices of call options for the precise strikes needed in the trinomial tree? The only practical way of obtaining something useful is by a process of interpolation, starting with the observed market prices quoted in the table.

**Table 9.2**    Implied vols of quoted calls (%)

| Strike: | 1 month | 4 months | 7 months |
|---------|---------|----------|----------|
| 80  | 25.10 | 23.71 | 23.06 |
| 90  | 23.19 | 22.89 | 22.46 |
| 100 | 21.02 | 21.34 | 21.55 |
| 110 | 19.23 | 20.42 | 20.85 |
| 120 | 17.87 | 19.24 | 19.87 |
| 130 | 17.04 | 18.38 | 19.07 |

As was previously explained, interpolation between option prices is best carried out via an interpolation between implied volatilities, since these move slowly with changes in strike price or maturity. The call option prices of Table 9.1 translate into the implied volatilities of Table 9.2 if we apply the Black Scholes formula. In the real world, we would at this point be finessing the data to make sure that there are no obvious anomalies, outliers or mistakes.

Interpolations and extrapolations have to be made in two directions: with respect to time and with respect to stock price. The technique most commonly used in practice is the cubic spline which is described in Appendix A.11, but here we use simple linear interpolation. Our objective is first to obtain implied volatilities and hence option prices, for maturities and stock prices corresponding to the nodes of the trinomial tree. This is done in two steps, first interpolating the rows for maturities 2, 4, and 6 months; then the new columns are interpolated for the specific strikes equal to stock values at the nodes. Finally the interpolated implied volatilities are turned back into "market prices", with the desired strikes and maturities. See Table 9.3.

**Table 9.3**    Interpolations

| Strike: | Interpolated Implied Vols (%) | | | Interpolated "Market Prices" ($) | | |
|---------|----------|----------|----------|----------|----------|----------|
|  | 2 months | 4 months | 6 months | 2 months | 4 months | 6 months |
| 58.84  | —     | —     | 24.72 | —     | —     | 41.98 |
| 70.22  | 26.15 | 24.51 | 23.95 | 30.21 | 30.65 | 31.11 |
| 83.80  | 24.05 | 23.40 | 23.02 | 16.91 | 17.82 | 18.75 |
| 100.00 | 21.13 | 21.34 | 21.48 | 3.84  | 5.69  | 7.19  |
| 119.34 | 18.41 | 19.32 | 19.73 | 0.04  | 0.40  | 1.04  |
| 142.41 | 16.44 | 17.31 | 17.82 | 0     | 0     | 0.02  |
| 169.95 | —     | —     | —     | —     | —     | —     |

(iv) Returning to the theme of subsection (ii) above, we have derived the state prices for each final node of the tree and can therefore price any European option. Obviously, if we were trying to price a European call or put, it would be simpler just to interpolate as we did to find the "market prices". However, there are European options other than puts and calls which may need to be priced. And then there is the matter of American options, which cannot be priced without a knowledge of all the intermediate probabilities in the tree. These are obtained from a knowledge of all the state prices in the tree. The first step therefore is to repeat the calculations of subsection (ii) for each column of nodes in the tree, using the interpolated "market prices" of the call options at each node. The results are given in Table 9.4.

**Table 9.4**   State prices in trinomial tree

| Node Level | $\lambda_0^0$ | $\lambda_i^{2\,months}$ | $\lambda_i^{4\,months}$ | $\lambda_i^{6\,months}$ |
|---|---|---|---|---|
| 58.84 | | | | 0.0008 |
| 70.22 | | | 0.0175 | 0.0434 |
| 83.80 | | 0.1984 | 0.2555 | 0.2736 |
| 100.00 | 1 | 0.6088 | 0.4763 | 0.3958 |
| 119.34 | | 0.1796 | 0.1950 | 0.1965 |
| 142.41 | | | 0.0293 | 0.0455 |
| 169.95 | | | | 0.0051 |

(v) **Transition Probabilities**: Just as we found a simple iterative process for calculating state prices from call option prices, so we can derive the transition probabilities from the state prices. This is illustrated in Figure 9.9, which is a snapshot of the top right-hand corner of the trinomial tree of Figure 9.8. The calculation proceeds in a recursive, two-step process which alternately uses the forward and backward induction described in Section 9.3(v):

(A1) Forward induction connects state prices at successive time steps, and is given explicitly for the binomial tree by equation (9.5). A precisely analogous relationship holds for the trinomial tree: taking the very top branch in the diagram, the formula for $\lambda_3^{6m}$ has the simple form

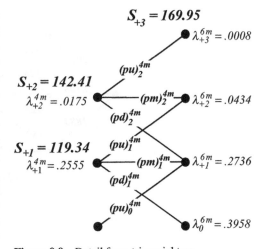

**Figure 9.9**   Detail from trinomial tree

$$\lambda_3^{6m} = e^{-r\delta t}(pu)_2^{4m}\,\lambda_2^{4m}$$

where $(pu)_2^{4m}$, $(pm)_2^{4m}$ and $(pd)_2^{4m}$ are the transition probabilities in 4 months; $e^{-r\delta t} = 0.9868$ is the one-period discount factor. This leads immediately to $(pu)_2^{4m} = 0.0439$ for the top 2-month probability.

(B1) Backward induction (risk neutrality) gives

$$S_2\,e^{(r-q)\delta t} = (pu)_2^{4m}S_3 + (pm)_2^{4m}S_2 + (pd)_2^{4m}S_1$$

$e^{-(r-q)\delta t} = 0.9917$ and probabilities sum to unity: $(pu)_2^{4\,m} + (pm)_2^{4\,m} + (pd)_2^{4\,m} = 1$. Using the result we found for $(pu)_2^{4\,m}$, these last two equations may be solved to give $(pm)_2^{4\,m} = 0.9555$ and $(pd)_2^{4\,m} = 0.0007$.

(A2) Forward induction for the *second* state price down in the last column is

$$\lambda_2^{6\,m} = e^{-r\delta t}\left((pm)_2^{4\,m}\lambda_2^{4\,m} + (pu)_1^{4\,m}\lambda_1^{4\,m}\right)$$

We already know $(pm)_2^{4\,m}$ so we can calculate $(pu)_1^{4\,m} = 0.1066$.

(B2) Backward induction applied to the second cell down gives

$$S_1\,e^{(r-q)\delta t} = (pu)_1^{4\,m}S_2 + (pm)_1^{4\,m}S_1 + (pd)_1^{4\,m}S_0$$

And so on . . . .

The process is continued for the entire column of cells and the same method is used for all columns in the tree, finally yielding the values of all probabilities given in Figure 9.10.

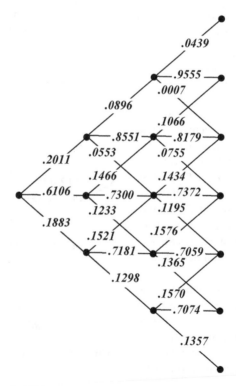

**Figure 9.10**   Transition probabilities

(vi) ***Use of Put Options:*** For most practical purposes, call options are easier to work with than puts. For one thing, American and European calls are usually the same price so that we can use market data on American traded options to build our trees; this is not true of put options. However, from the iterative methods of calculating state prices (and hence probabilities) in subsections (ii) and (v), it is clear that any errors or anomalies in the market price of a call option are transmitted to the calculated probabilities at all the lower nodes. If European put option prices are available it is therefore safer to use these to fill in the lower part of the tree, using precisely the same reasoning as was used for converting call option prices to probabilities.

(vii) **Conclusion:** In this section we have achieved the calibration of a trinomial tree using the observed market prices of options. The tree may then be used to price whatever option we wish. In practical terms, this means that each morning we can feed a set of quoted prices into a machine and use the same machine to price and manage a portfolio of instruments on the same underlying security. Clearly, the machine will need frequent recalibration as the markets move; but this is easily achieved by feeding a new set of market prices into the machine.

## 9.6   VOLATILITY SURFACES

An alternative to the approach of the last section is to use equation (9.3) to obtain the risk-neutral expectation of the local volatility at each point in the $T-X$ plane; this is usually called the volatility surface. The principal difference between this and the Derman Kani approach is that here we are not automatically provided with a procedure for calculating new option prices. We derive the local volatility surface from equation (9.3), i.e. we derive values for the local volatility at a densely packed set of points in the $T-X$ plane. We then use these values in a Monte Carlo program or a tree or a finite difference calculation; the choice is ours. With the Derman Kani method, we are confined to the calibrated tree.

This approach shares a problem with Derman Kani: there are just not enough traded options to give market prices for densely packed points in the $T-X$ plane. We therefore use the same device as before, interpolating implied volatilities and hence using estimated "market prices" for any point we choose. Equation (9.3) calls for first and second derivatives of estimated market prices. The true, observed market prices are likely to be somewhat jerky but our estimating procedures will smooth these sufficiently to obtain sensible results; a concrete example follows.

(i) **Empirical Distribution Functions:** Let us examine the term $\partial^2 C(X, T)/\partial X^2$ which occurs in the denominator of equation (9.3), using precisely the same data that was used in the last section. In addition to being a part of the volatility surface calculation, this term has an interest in its own right: apart from a discount factor, it is the true probability distribution function for the underlying stock price movements.

The starting point for this calculation is the set of interpolated values for the option prices given in Table 9.1, and we will derive values for $\partial^2 C/\partial X^2$ at each of the grid points implied by the table. First, we must make some assumption about the form of the function $C(X, T)$: after all, we have only been given a set of discrete points, not a continuous differentiable function. One of the simplest assumptions to make is the

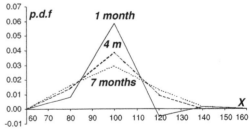

**Figure 9.11**   Empirical stock price pdf

cubic spline assumption, i.e. that $C(X, T)$ is a set of cubic functions between observed data points, arranged so that there are no discontinuities in the first or second differentials at the data points; this is described in detail in Appendix A.11, where it is seen that the first and second differentials of the curve at each point are naturally produced as a by-product of the fitting procedure. The values of $\partial^2 C/\partial X^2$ corresponding to the observed data of Table 9.2 are multiplied by $e^{rT}$ to give the probability distributions and these are plotted in Figure 9.11.

For each maturity we have only taken six points so the curves are fairly grainy; however, the general form is as expected. The slightly negative (and therefore impossible) value arises from the numerical procedures of trying to fit the data points with a piecewise cubic function.

Suppose we now wish to improve on the graph and get a better result for the 4-month maturity. We have no more market prices to use and must therefore rely on the interpolation procedure. It has already been pointed out that option prices vary rapidly with strike price so that it is better to interpolate between implied volatilities. The procedure might therefore be as follows:

- Take the 4-month prices from Table 9.2 and convert these to implied volatilities using the Black Scholes formula.
- Use cubic spline to interpolate between these volatilities.
- Use Black Scholes to convert the interpolated implied volatilities to option prices for $X = 80, 81, \ldots, 130$.
- Use the cubic spline interpolation method of Appendix A.10 to find the value of $\partial^2 C / \partial X^2$ at each point $X = 80, 81, \ldots, 130$.

(ii) *Instantaneous Volatilities*: The steps taken to obtain the values of $\partial^2 C / \partial X^2$ for 4 months to maturity and a relatively dense set of points $X = 80, 81, \ldots, 130$ can be repeated to obtain values of $\partial C / \partial T$ for a densely packed set of points between 1 month and 7 months. Again, interpolation between implied volatilities for market observed prices is recommended as a first step. The result is that we can find the call option prices and their derivatives for a densely packed set of points in the $T$–$X$ plane. This allows us to derive the value for local volatility at any point, using equation (9.3). This local volatility is of course not the same as the volatility for stock price movements between successive points, but the two values converge as the point spacing becomes infinitesimal.

# 10

## Monte Carlo

### 10.1 APPROACHES TO OPTION PRICING

(i) In order to put Monte Carlo techniques into perspective, we recall and classify the techniques that have been used to price options.

1. If we know the form of the payoff and the risk-neutral probability density function of the final stock price $S_T$, then the option price is simply

$$f = e^{-rT} \int_0^\infty P(S_T) \times \phi(S_T)\, dS_T = e^{-rT} \int_0^\infty P(S_T)\, d\Phi_T$$

where $\phi(S_T)$ is the risk-neutral probability density function, $\Phi_T$ is the cumulative probability function and $P(S_T)$ is the payoff; elementary statistical theory allows us to write $\phi(S_T)\, dS_T = d\Phi_T$. In various parts of the book we perform this integral explicitly for European puts and calls, binary options, knock-in options, etc.

2. From a knowledge of the boundary conditions governing the option in question, we may be able to solve the Black Scholes equation. Explicit solutions are given in the book for European puts and calls and for knock-out options.

3. Both of the last two methods yield an analytical answer, i.e. a formula. Although they seem on the surface to be unrelated, they are in fact doing the same thing using different tools. It is shown in Appendix A.4(i) that the Black Scholes equation is just the Kolmogorov backward equation for $\phi(S_T)$, after it has been multiplied by the payoff and then integrated. Unfortunately, these two analytical approaches only succeed in pricing a small fraction of all options.

4. The most common numerical approach to pricing options is to approximate the probability density function by a discrete distribution. The integral of method (1) above then becomes a summation:

$$f = e^{-rT} \sum_i P_i \times \Phi_i$$

In Chapters 7 and 9 we use binomial and trinomial distributions to approximate the normal distribution which we assume to be followed by $\ln S_t$. These methods, known collectively as "trees", vastly expand our ability to price options. Three categories are of particular importance:

- American and Bermudan options are readily soluble.
- Variable volatilities and interest rates can be accommodated.
- A whole range of exotic options can be priced.

5. Numerical methods for solving the Black Scholes equation are an alternative to the tree methods of method (4), and are used to solve broadly the same range of problems. Some of these methods are shown in Chapter 8 to be formally equivalent to trees; others are used because they are computationally more efficient.

6. Another numerical method of calculating $f$ is numerical integration. In its simplest forms ("middle of the range" or trapezium rules), this method amounts to the same thing as method (4) above, i.e. we are adding the areas of a lot of rectangular strips of height $P(S_T)$ and width $\delta\Phi_T$. This last method, numerical integration, has never become particularly popular in option pricing, perhaps because the equivalent tree methods are more intuitive and graphic. Yet all the above numerical methods can be conceptually regarded as methods of numerical integration, by adding the areas of strips under a curve.

(ii) This chapter is about a different approach to numerical integration. Referring to Figure 10.1, there are two methods of finding the area under the curve.

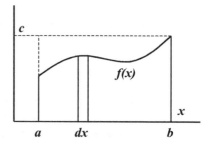

- Divide the $X - Y$ plane into little squares and count how many lie below the curve (perhaps using some correction factor for the squares which overlap the curve).
- Scatter random points across the dotted rectangle and count what fraction lie below the curve. This fraction multiplied by $c \times (b - a)$ is an estimate of the area under the curve.

**Figure 10.1** Numerical integration/ Monte Carlo

The first method is the familiar "adding areas of strips" approach; the second is called Monte Carlo.

When applied to option pricing, the mechanics are simple: calculate an option payoff $P_i$ for a randomly selected path of the stock price between $t = 0$ and $T$. Repeat the operation many thousands of times ($N$), making sure that the random paths are all taken from a distribution which adequately reflects the distribution of $S_t$. The Monte Carlo estimate of the $t = 0$ value of the option is just

$$f = e^{-rT}\frac{1}{N}\sum_i P_i$$

(iii) **The Curse of Dimensionality**: The option pricing approaches (1) to (6) above share a major failing: they cannot handle path-dependent options in a general way. The reader is entitled to be more than a little surprised at this assertion since large chunks of this book are devoted to elegant and efficient methods of pricing knock-outs, look-backs, Asian options, etc. But we are able to price these because we have been able to find a nice regular distribution for variables of interest such as the maximum value or the geometric average of $S_t$ over a given period. This is a long way from solving the general path-dependent problem.

To make this clearer, consider a path-dependent option of maturity $T$ with two monitoring points $t_1$ and $t_2$, e.g. points used for taking an average or testing if a knock-out has occurred. This is represented in Figure 10.2, where the ladders at each point in time are intended to schematically represent the stock prices achievable. The stock prices $S_{t_1}$, $S_{t_2}$ and $S_T$ are three distinct although correlated stochastic variables, so what we have is really a three-asset problem. The correlation coefficients are known exactly, being the square roots of the ratios of the times elapsed [see Appendix A.1(iv)]. The price of any path-dependent option has the general form

$$f = \int \int \int P(S_{t_1}, S_{t_2}, S_T)\,\phi\,(S_{t_1}, S_{t_2}, S_T)\,dS_{t_1}\,dS_{t_2}\,dS_T$$

where $P(S_{t_1}, S_{t_2}, S_T)$ is the payoff and $\phi(S_{t_1}, S_{t_2}, S_T)$ is the joint distribution function. Except for the most trivial examples, a multiple integral of this type would have to be evaluated numerically. The simplest way of doing this is by using a three-dimensional equivalent of the addition of strip-shaped areas: and here we see the beginnings of an intractable problem.

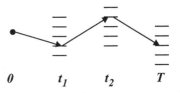

**Figure 10.2**   Path-dependent option as multidimensional option

Suppose we divide the range of integration for each of our stochastic assets into just 10 slices. The number of separate little calculations to perform the integration is $10^3$; no matter, that's what computers are for. But a three-step problem is too simple. A more realistic example might be a 1-year option with weekly monitoring, and we would then be looking at $10^{52}$ separate little calculations. This is what Bellman called the curse of dimensionality.

The position is not improved if we decide to abandon numerical integration and just work with trees. Section 12.6 describes a binomial tree applied to two stochastic assets, and it is immediately apparent from its geometry that the number of calculations increases as $N^2$. Extending to $d$ stochastic assets (dimensions) leads us to exactly the same dead-end that we hit with numerical integration.

The reader should now ask "if it's so difficult, how come we have simple procedures for evaluating knock-out options, either analytically or using a simple (one-dimensional) tree?". The answer is that we have been clever enough to work out distributions for specific quantities such as $S_{max}$ or $S_{max \text{ or } min}$ or $S_{geometric \text{ av}}$; but how would you value a 1-year option with weekly monitoring if the payoff is as follows:

- Knock-out if any sequence of five weekly stock prices has each price greater than the last.
- Otherwise, a call option.

Here we seem to have no choice other than the multiple integral or tree approach; this is where Monte Carlo comes to the rescue.

(iv) **Errors:** Suppose we evaluate the $d$-dimensional integral using a total of $N$ data points, allocating $N^{1/d}$ data points to each of the $d$ variables over which we integrate. Any calculus textbook covering numerical integration will explain how the error arising from the use of either the mid-point rule or the trapezium rule is inversely proportional to the square of the number of data points. The error in our multiple integration is therefore proportional to $N^{-1/d}$.

## 10.2   BASIC MONTE CARLO METHOD

(i) **Stock Price Simulation:** In nearly the whole of this book, it is assumed that the risk-neutral stock price evolution follows equation (3.7):

$$S_t = S_0 \, e^{(r-q-\frac{1}{2}\sigma^2)t + \sigma\sqrt{t}z_i}; \qquad z_i \sim N(0, 1)$$

Obviously, the way in which we use this formula will depend on the specific problem to be solved. In the following subsections we look at three simple examples: a European call, a knock-out call and an Asian option. For the European call, we need only the terminal values, so each simulation will just give us a random terminal value $S_T$.

The other two options are path-dependent so each simulation will need to be an entire random path. This is approximated by a discrete path with successive values given by the same formula in a slightly modified form:

$$S_{t+\delta t} = S_t \, e^{(r-q-\frac{1}{2}\sigma^2)\delta t + \sigma\sqrt{\delta t}z_i}; \qquad z_i \sim N(0, 1)$$

We chose the $\delta t$ to be the time between discrete monitoring or averaging points.

(ii) *Estimates*: The values $z_i$ in the last subsection are standard normal random numbers. Section 10.3 will explain how these are obtained. For each set of random numbers, a stock price path is calculated and the payoff of the option corresponding to this path is calculated; this is a single simulation. The process is repeated a large number of times $N$, and an estimate for the expected value of the payoff is obtained by taking the average of the answers obtained for all the simulations. Finally we must take the present value of this expected payoff to get the option value.

This is in accordance with the following elementary statistical definitions and results:

- If $f_i$ is the option value calculated in a single simulation, then an unbiased estimate of the mean of all possible $f_i$ is equal to the sample average

$$\bar{f} = \frac{1}{N} \sum_i f_i$$

- The unbiased estimate of the variance of all the $f_i$ is

$$\text{var}[f_i] = \text{SD}^2 = \frac{1}{N-1} \sum_i (f_i - \bar{f})^2$$

- The standard error of $\bar{f}$ is

$$\text{SE} = \sqrt{\text{var}\langle\bar{f}\rangle} = \frac{\text{SD}}{\sqrt{N}}$$

- The $\bar{f}$ are normally distributed with mean $f$ (the true option value) and variance $\text{SE}^2$.

(iii) *Errors*: From the last few lines it is obvious that the Monte Carlo method converges to the right answer with an error proportional to $N^{-1/2}$; compare this with the error proportional to $N^{-2/d}$ for numerical integration or trees. The key point is that the Monte Carlo error does not depend on the number of dimensions of the problem. We do not of course know the constants of proportionality for either error, but the variable term for multiple integration shoots up so quickly with $d$ that beyond a very few dimensions, Monte Carlo is more efficient.

It is instructive to look at three simple examples which we use later in this chapter. In each of the three cases (a simple European call, a knock-out call and an Asian call), a 20,000 shot simulation run is already yielding reasonable option prices with errors in the region $\pm 1\%$ of the option prices and running times on a laptop of less than a minute. Now compare the alternative calculation methods for each example:

- The call option is a one-dimensional problem, having no path dependence. The numerical integration alternative would divide the range of integration into 20,000 slices; or we could build a tree with 20,000 steps. Either way, we would have produced an incredibly accurate answer, compared with the $\pm 1\%$ we have produced here. Alternatively, we could have solved the integration analytically: this is called the Black Scholes model.
- The knock-out option has 52 monitoring points. We can derive a continuous distribution for the maximum value of the stock price and hence evaluate a continuously monitored knock-out

option analytically. Alternatively, we can build a simple tree to evaluate the option [not a 52-step tree as this would be too small for accurate answers (see Section 16.5), but some multiple of 52]. We saw in Section 10.1 that this simple knock-out is a "special case".

Suppose instead that we tried to solve this problem by multiple integration or trees, which is what we would have to do if the knock-out feature were more complex. We devote two points to each dimension, i.e. divide the domain of integration into two slices in each dimension or equivalently, construct a multidimensional tree with only two steps for each asset. This would be hopelessly inadequate for an accurate answer, but would still take $2^{52} \approx 5 \times 10^{15}$ calculations. Our Monte Carlo calculations consisted of 20,000 shots where each shot is a path of 52 steps, i.e. about a million calculations.

- The arithmetic average (Asian) option also has 52 monitoring points. Unlike the simple knock-out example, we cannot derive a distribution for a state variable $S_{\text{arithmetic av}}$ and must therefore go straight to the long-winded computation (this is not true for the geometric average option but these are not really traded in the market). Here again the Monte Carlo method takes about $10^6$ calculations to yield an error of around $\pm 1\%$, while numerical integration would take $5 \times 10^{15}$ calculations for an inadequate answer.

So how does Monte Carlo manage to be so much more powerful than numerical integration, which we normally think of as a fairly efficient procedure? The answer is a combination of two parts: first, by its very nature the majority of Monte Carlo paths used in a simulation are the most probable paths. The calculation procedure wastes little time in exploring regions where paths are unlikely to fall. By contrast, tree methods spend equal calculation time on a remote node at the edges as they do on a highly probable node at the center. Similarly, numerical integration spends as much effort on a strip at the edge of a distribution as on one in the center.

The second part of the answer lies in the arithmetic effects of exponentiation. Suppose that in a one-dimensional tree, only 70% of the calculations really contribute appreciably to a pricing. If this is repeated in each of 52 dimensions, then only $0.7^{52} = 0.000001\%$ of the multidimensional tree contributes to the pricing; the rest are wasted calculations.

(iv) **Strengths and Weaknesses of Monte Carlo**: From what has been written in the last couple of pages it is clear that Monte Carlo is the only feasible approach to solving the general multidimensional problem (except for a few special cases). We have described this in terms of general path-dependent options, but there are other multidimensional pricings where Monte Carlo is the method of choice: most particularly spread options involving several assets, for which analytical methods are inadequate.

Quite apart from these theoretical considerations, Monte Carlo has immensely wide appeal. Just about any final payoff can be accommodated and the method can be manipulated by computer programmers with little knowledge of either mathematics or finance. It is the ultimate fall-back method, which works when you cannot think of anything else, or do not have the time or inclination to be analytical. We have all at some time got fed up with working on a problem and instead just switched on the simulator overnight, to find a highly accurate answer on our screens in the morning.

Despite all these advantages, Monte Carlo does have an Achilles heal: American options. Recall the binomial method of calculating an American option price. Starting at the maturity date, we roll back through the tree by discounting the expected option values to previous nodes [see Section 7.3(iv)]. At each node we compare the discounted-back value with the exercise value at that point; if the exercise value is larger, we assume that the American option is terminated at this node, and we substitute the payoff for the option value. The key point is that the method inherently allows us to compare the option value with the payoff value at each point in the tree. With the Monte Carlo method, we can calculate the payoff at each point on our simulated path, but there is no way of comparing this with the option value along the path. Inevitably, methods have been found around this inherent problem and encouraging results have been claimed; but one cannot help feeling that it is better to go with an approach that is intrinsically better suited to American option pricing. Water can be pushed uphill, but why bother if you don't have to?

## 10.3   RANDOM NUMBERS

(i) In the last section we outlined the Monte Carlo method in its simplest form and rather glibly stated that $z_i$ are random numbers taken from a standard normal distribution. What does this mean and where do we get the $z_i$ from? The first question is simple: the $z_i$ are random numbers for which the probability of a number falling in the range

$$z_i \text{ to } z_i + \delta z_i \text{ is } \frac{1}{\sqrt{2\pi}} e^{-\frac{1}{2}z_i^2} \delta z_i.$$

The second question is more difficult and there are several issues which concern Monte Carlo specialists as set out below.

(ii) **Pseudo Random Number Generators:** For most people the starting point is a Rand () function on a PC which purports to produce standard uniform random numbers $x_i$, i.e. evenly distributed from 0 to 1. We show below how to manufacture the standard normal random numbers $z_i$ from these $x_i$. It should be pointed out straight away that a computer cannot produce a set of random numbers. Computers are logical devices and any calculation the machine performs must give the same answer however many times the calculation is carried out. We therefore have to content ourselves with **pseudo-random numbers** which behave as though they are random. In commercial packages these are nearly always produced by the following iterative procedure:

- Generate a set of integers $n_i$ as follows:

$$n_{i+1} = (an_i + b) \bmod N \qquad a, b, N \text{ integers}$$

- The standard uniform random numbers are given by

$$x_i = \frac{n_i}{N}$$

$n \bmod N$ is defined as the integer remainder left over when $n$ is divided by $N$.

A simple example of this procedure for $n_{i+1} = (2n_i + 1) \bmod 5$ is given in Table 10.1. This slightly laborious example is given to illustrate a couple of points:

**Table 10.1**   Random number generator

| | | | | | | |
|---|---|---|---|---|---|---|
| $n_0$ | | $=$ | 1 | $x_0$ | $=$ | 0.2 |
| $n_1$ | $=$ | 3 mod 5 | 3 | $x_1$ | $=$ | 0.6 |
| $n_2$ | $=$ | 7 mod 5 | 2 | $x_2$ | $=$ | 0.4 |
| $n_3$ | $=$ | 5 mod 5 | 0 | $x_3$ | $=$ | 0.0 |
| $n_4$ | $=$ | 1 mod 5 | 1 | $x_4$ | $=$ | 0.2 |
| $n_5$ | $=$ | 3 mod 5 | 3 | $x_5$ | $=$ | 0.6 |

- The sequence of $x_i$ are completely determinate. The same number is always produced given the same starting point $n_0 = 1$. If we started with a different *seed* $n_0 = \frac{1}{2}$ we would get a different set of random numbers. Most computers either start with a seed related to the precise time of day (fraction of day elapsed) or they use the last random number that was generated last time it was used; this way the computer does not keep repeating the same "random numbers". However, there are ways of fixing the seed so that we can repeat the same sequences (see for example the Visual Basic instructions in the Excel help index).
- $n_5$ is the same as $n_1$ and will keep repeating every five iterations – forever. This generator will only produce five different random numbers. We therefore want $N$ to be large.

So how do we find $a$, $b$ and $N$? Unfortunately there is no simple recipe for doing this. We know that we want $a$ to be big and $b$ to be very big. But beyond that it is largely a question of trial and error. Researchers have performed elaborate statistical tests on the random numbers produced by the different combinations of $a$, $b$ and $N$ and have found that there are definitely good combinations and bad combinations. The majority of derivatives professionals just hit the Rand () function and hope for the best. Some fastidious quants go to sources such as Press *et al.* (1992) and copy out well-tested procedures ("RAN2" is recommended). The few who go any further find themselves with a substantial research project on their hands.

(iii) *Normal Random Numbers*: There is a 45% probability that a standard uniform random number will be less than 0.4500. Similarly, there is a 45% probability that a standard normal random number will be less than $-0.1257$: in the notation used elsewhere in this book, $0.4500 = N[-0.1257]$, which could also be written $-0.1257 = N^{-1}[0.4500]$.

We can convert the standard uniform random numbers produced by a random number generator into standard normal random numbers with the transformation

$$\text{RAND}_{\text{normal}} = N^{-1}[\text{RAND}_{\text{uniform}}]$$

There are standard routines to perform this; in Excel it is just the function NORMINV(). The trouble is that this function cannot be expressed analytically and is slow to calculate.

The ultimate objective is usually to *obtain* normal random numbers rather than to make the conversion. There follow two methods for *manufacturing* normal random from uniform random numbers, rather than transforming them one by one.

(iv) *Sum of 12 Method*: The simplest way of producing an *approximately* standard normal random number is as follows:

- Take 12 standard uniform random numbers $x_j$.
- Then $z_i = \left( \sum_{j=1}^{12} x_j \right) - 6$ is a standard normal random number.

The reason for this is straightforward: the central limit theorem tells us that whatever the distribution of $x_j$, the quantity $\sum_{j=1}^{n} x_j$ tends to a normal distribution; furthermore, a simple calculation shows that by choosing $n = 12$, the mean and variance of $z_i$ are exactly 0 and 1. Of course, the central limit theorem also tells us that $\sum_{j=1}^{n} x_j$ only becomes normal as $n \to \infty$, which is quite a lot bigger than 12. Errors are bound to be introduced by this method, but without going into the details, these errors are much smaller than most people suspect from such a small sample.

(v) **Box–Muller Method**: This is the most widespread method for generating standard normal random numbers. If $x_1$ and $x_2$ are two independent standard uniform random numbers, then $z_1$ and $z_2$ are two independent standard normal random numbers, where

$$z_1 = \sqrt{-2 \ln x_1} \, \sin 2\pi x_2; \qquad z_2 = \sqrt{-2 \ln x_1} \, \cos 2\pi x_2$$

At first sight these look a little curious (how do trigonometric functions come into it?), but the connection is easy to demonstrate. We start with the well-known relationship of functional analysis, used for transforming variables: in two dimensions this is written

$$\Phi(z_1, z_2) \, dz_1 \, dz_2 = \Phi(x_1, x_2) \left| \frac{\partial(x_1, x_2)}{\partial(z_1, z_2)} \right| dz_1 \, dz_2$$

Invert the two previous expressions for $z_1$ and $z_2$:

$$x_1 = e^{-\frac{1}{2}(z_1^2 + z_2^2)}; \qquad x_2 = \frac{1}{2\pi} \tan^{-1} \frac{z_2}{z_1}$$

and work out the Jacobian determinant

$$\left| \frac{\partial(x_1, x_2)}{\partial(z_1, z_2)} \right| = \begin{vmatrix} \dfrac{\partial x_1}{\partial z_1} & \dfrac{\partial x_1}{\partial z_2} \\[2mm] \dfrac{\partial x_2}{\partial z_1} & \dfrac{\partial x_2}{\partial z_2} \end{vmatrix} = -\left( \frac{1}{\sqrt{2\pi}} e^{-\frac{1}{2}z_1^2} \right) \left( \frac{1}{\sqrt{2\pi}} e^{-\frac{1}{2}z_2^2} \right)$$

Interpreting $\Phi$ as a probability density function and using

$$\Phi(x_1, x_2) = 1 \quad (0 < x_1 \text{ and } x_2 < 1)$$
$$= 0 \quad \text{(otherwise)}$$

shows that $z_1$ and $z_2$ are independently, normally distributed.

(vi) **Correlated Standard Normal Random Number**: Given that Monte Carlo's really strong suit is multivariate options, it is not surprising that we are frequently called on to construct correlated random numbers, which can be constructed from *uncorrelated* numbers as shown below.

Let $z_1, \ldots, z_n$ be a set of independent standard normal random numbers which can be written in vector form as

$$Z = \begin{pmatrix} z_1 \\ \vdots \\ z_n \end{pmatrix}$$

We can generate correlated standard normal random numbers **y** from these using the transformation $\mathbf{y} = \mathbf{Az}$. Let us take a three-dimensional example for simplicity, and use the general property

$$\mathbf{yy'} = \mathbf{Az(Az)'} = \mathbf{Azz'A'}$$

where a prime signifies transpose. Take the expectation of every element in the last matrix formula:

$$E\langle \mathbf{yy'} \rangle = \Sigma = \begin{pmatrix} 1 & \rho_{12} & \rho_{13} \\ \rho_{12} & 1 & \rho_{23} \\ \rho_{13} & \rho_{23} & 1 \end{pmatrix} = \mathbf{A} \, E\langle \mathbf{zz'} \rangle \, \mathbf{A'} = \mathbf{AA'}$$

$\Sigma$ is known as the variance–covariance matrix of $\mathbf{y}$. The simplest solution for $\mathbf{A}$ is obtained if we write it in lower triangular form. This is called the **Cholesky decomposition**:

$$\mathbf{A} = \begin{pmatrix} a_{11} & 0 & 0 \\ a_{12} & a_{22} & 0 \\ a_{13} & a_{23} & a_{33} \end{pmatrix}$$

It is a question of simple algebra to calculate the $a_{ij}$ in terms of the elements of the variance–covariance matrix: the first few elements are $a_{11} = 1$; $a_{12} = \rho_{12}$; $a_{22} = \sqrt{1 - \rho_{12}^2}$. In the two-dimensional case, we therefore have

$$y_1 = z_1; \qquad y_2 = \rho_{12} z_1 + \sqrt{1 - \rho_{12}^2}\, z_2$$

which is the same result obtained elsewhere by rather different methods [Appendix A.1(vi)]. This decomposition is clearly easy to extend to higher dimensions.

## 10.4   PRACTICAL APPLICATIONS

(i) There is a very large literature on Monte Carlo techniques applied to option pricing, much of it dedicated to techniques for improving on the results obtained by application of the basic method described above. A newcomer to this field is warned to be careful: the field has a large number of Enthusiasts selling their Ideas, and you can waste a lot of time on gushing articles making claims which never seem to produce the same huge benefit when applied to one's own problem; even worse, some touted techniques can either make errors bigger when applied to the "wrong problem" or can introduce biases which are hard to detect.

There are two basic approaches to Monte Carlo: you can use it as a once-off tool rather than for repeat pricing. In this case, you are safer in achieving accuracy by just increasing the number of simulations, rather than trying to stick on some hacker's gimmicks picked up from the trade press. Remember, Moore's law is on your side: your machine is likely to run 20 times faster than the one used by the guy who wrote the article on how to double the speed of your Monte Carlo convergence.

The alternative approach is to use Monte Carlo for multiple pricings in a live commercial situation. In this case, speed of convergence will be critically important. Usually, the best way of achieving this is by means of low discrepancy sequences as described in the next section. If the problem does not allow this approach (usually if the dimensions are greater than 20/30), then there is no alternative to using random number Monte Carlo and finding whatever variance reducing techniques are available; but this will be a serious research project going well beyond the scope of this book.

(ii) *Antithetic Variables (or variates or sampling)*: This is the most popular variance reduction technique, giving improvements in most circumstances. It is also extremely easy to implement and is benign, i.e. even if it does not do much good (see below), it does not introduce hidden biases or other problems. We would be breaking a fundamental rule of the game since $z_1$ and $-z_1$ are not independent of each other. But we *can* do something closely related which *is* allowed: switch our attention from $f(z_i)$ to a new variable $\phi(z_i) = \frac{1}{2}(f(z_i) + f(-z_i))$. The average of these $\phi(z_i)$ for the $N$ different values of $z_i$ is an unbiased estimate of the answer we need; and in most cases we encounter, $\phi(z_i)$ has a much smaller variance than $f(z_i)$. In simple, intuitive terms, if $f(z_i)$ is large, $f(-z_i)$ will be small and vice versa.

In slightly more formal terms, antithetic variables are more efficient than doubling the number of simulations if

$$\text{var}\left[\tfrac{1}{2}(f(z_i) + f(-z_i))\right] < \tfrac{1}{2}\text{var}[f(z_i)]$$

Using the general relationship $\text{var}[a + b] = \text{var}[a] + \text{var}[a] + 2\,\text{cov}[a, b]$, the last condition can be written

$$\text{cov}[f(z_i), f(-z_i)] < 0$$

This is certainly met by a European call, knock-out or Asian option; but it would not be true for a straddle [see Section 2.5(v)], which increases in value as $S_T$ increases *or* decreases. An indication of the effectiveness of this technique is given in Table 10.2 for the following options:

- European Call: $S = 100$; $X = 110$; $r = 10\%$; $q = 4\%$; $T = 1$ year; $\sigma = 20\%$.
- Knock-out Call (weekly sampling): $S = 100$; $X = 110$; $K = 150$; $r = 10\%$; $q = 4\%$; $T = 1$ year; $\sigma = 20\%$.
- Arithmetic Asian Call (weekly sampling): $S = 100$; $X = 100$; $r = 9\%$; $q = 0\%$; $T = 1$ year; $\sigma = 50\%$.

**Table 10.2**    Effect of antithetic variables

|  | 500,000 simulations | 250,000 simulations + antithetic variables |
|---|---|---|
| European Call | $6.179 \pm 0.016$ | $\pm 0.014$ |
| Knock-out Call | $4.035 \pm 0.011$ | $\pm 0.009$ |
| Asian Call | $12.991 \pm 0.030$ | $\pm 0.024$ |

(iii) *Control Variates Applied to Asian Options*: One of the most difficult commonly used options to price is the arithmetic average option. In Chapter 17 it is shown that an arithmetic and a geometric average option have values which are always close in size. Yet a geometric option has an easy analytical pricing akin to the Black Scholes model, while an arithmetic option can only be priced numerically.

This similarity in the two prices can be used to enhance the efficiency of Monte Carlo as follows: rather than focusing on the individual simulation values for the arithmetic average call, let us switch our attention to the variable $\phi(z_i) = f_A(z_i) - f_G(z_i)$; the suffixes A and G indicate the arithmetic and geometric call options. Our best estimate for $\phi$ is the simulation average, i.e. $\hat{\phi} = \bar{\phi}$ or $\hat{f}_A - \hat{f}_G = \bar{f}_A - \bar{f}_G$. Our best estimate of the value of the $f_G$ is just the analytical value, so we may write

$$\hat{f}_A = \bar{f}_A - \bar{f}_G + f_{G\,\text{(analytical)}}$$

The standard error of this estimate can be obtained from

$$\text{var}[\hat{f}_A] = \text{var}[\bar{f}_A - \bar{f}_G] = \text{var}[\bar{f}_A] + \text{var}[\bar{f}_G] - 2\rho\sqrt{\text{var}[\bar{f}_A]\text{var}[\bar{f}_G]}$$

This so-called control variate technique gives an improved result if $\text{var}[\hat{f}_A]$ is less than $\text{var}[\bar{f}_A]$, which we get in a straightforward Monte Carlo run; or equivalently if $\rho > \tfrac{1}{2}\text{SE}_G/\text{SE}_A$. If the standard errors (SE) of the geometric and arithmetic results are approximately the same, the condition for the control variate technique to improve results becomes $\rho > \tfrac{1}{2}$; a correlation with a coefficient of $\frac{1}{2}$ is quite loose and is certainly far exceeded by an arithmetic and a geometric Asian option. If the correlation coefficient approaches unity, we have $SE_{A-G} = SE_A - SE_G$.

Using the same arithmetic Asian call option as in the last subsection, a simple Monte Carlo run with 1 million shots gives a price of $12.994 \pm 0.021$. The analytical value of the corresponding geometric call option is 11.764. Using this as the control variate gives a pricing for the arithmetic call of $13.007 \pm 0.011$ with a mere 25,000 simulation run.

This enormous gain in efficiency is of course due to the very close correlation between arithmetic and geometric prices. Unfortunately, there are no other situations which work remotely as well.

(iv) **Greeks:** So far in this chapter we have referred to pricing options. Equally important for the management of an options book is the calculation of a good estimate for the Greek parameters. The obvious way of doing this is by finite differencing: for example, if $\bar{f}(S_0)$ is the discounted payoff of an option when the stock price is $S_0$, then a single simulation of the delta is written

$$\Delta(S_0) = \frac{f(S_0 + \delta S_0) - f(S_0 - \delta S_0)}{2\delta S_0}$$

An unbiased estimate $\bar{\Delta}(S_0)$ of the delta is then equal to the average of the individual simulation results $\Delta(S_0)$. The critical thing to remember is that the same path (i.e. set of random numbers) *must* be used to generate the $f(S_0 + \delta S_0)$ as are used for the $f(S_0 - \delta S_0)$; otherwise convergence will be too slow to be of any use. Clearly, this method can be used to estimate any of the Greek parameters.

## 10.5   QUASI-RANDOM NUMBERS

(i) Look up on a cloudless night and you see the sky randomly covered with stars: but are they random? Poetic star-gazers over the ages have pointed out the fantastic designs they trace. Less sensitive souls see the patterns less clearly but everyone is agreed that the random stars clump together, leaving some parts of the sky emptier than others (deep comments from astrophysicists or other religious groups are not helpful at this point, thank you).

And so it is with random numbers. If you see pairs of standard uniform random numbers plotted on a plane with the numbers ranging from 0 to 1 on both axes, it is certain that you could "improve" on the random distribution by rearranging some points. So why use random numbers at all? When we did a simulation run with $N$ shots to price a European call, we started with $N$ standard uniform random numbers. Why not start with $N$ numbers equally spaced between 0 and 1. From these we could generate $N$ numbers which lie on the normal curve, bunched together around the peak of the curve. Wouldn't this give a more accurate answer than a random simulation? The answer is of course a resounding "yes: it would be much more efficient".

The reason is that we have effectively gone back to performing a numerical integration of a one-dimensional integral. Furthermore, we have introduced a refinement of the discussion in Section 10.1(iii): having chosen the uniform numbers to be equally spaced, the resultant normal numbers must be in positions such that they describe strips of equal area under the standard normal curve. In other words, the numerical integration procedure which is equivalent to this calculation effectively uses a trapezium rule with strips of equal area. The effect of this is to make the strips thinner (and hence the integration procedure more accurate) in the area of highest probability. This was previously cited as one of the reasons for the high efficiency of the Monte Carlo method.

If we try to extend this to higher dimensions we unfortunately fall under the "curse of dimensionality" once again, e.g. a 10-dimensional grid with only 10 points on each axis gives us 10 billion calculations to do. Furthermore, setting up a grid is not very flexible because of the large jumps in numbers of calculations if we change the numbers of points on each axis: if we are dealing with a 10-dimensional problem, the number of calculation points with two, three or four nodes per axis are $2^{10}$, $3^{10}$ and $4^{10}$, respectively, and i.e. 1000, 60,000 and 1,000,000. What do we do if we want to run a number of simulations lying between these numbers?

We know that we cannot use equally spaced points along each axis for anything but very low numbers of dimensions – maybe four at most. So let us ask a more modest question: can we devise a procedure for packing an $n$-dimensional space with $N$ points more efficiently than with random numbers, so that the simulation results converge more quickly than $N^{-1/2}$ as $N$ increases?

(ii) The answer to the last question is of course "yes"; these are the so-called *low discrepancy sequences* or *quasi-random numbers*. There are several different schemas for manufacturing these sequences known by the names of their inventors: Halton, Fauré, Sobol. The easiest sequence to produce are the simple Halton numbers which we shall use for illustration. Figure 10.3 compares 1000 points plotted in two dimensions for a random distribution and for Halton numbers (bases 2 and 3). There is not much poetry in the Halton diagram but it is obvious that the area is more uniformly covered with dots than the random diagram.

**Random Numbers**                    **Halton Numbers**

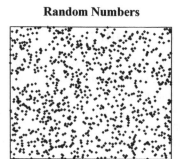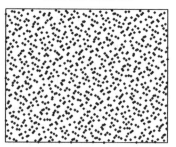

**Figure 10.3**   1000 Pairs of numbers

The speed of convergence of these methods is approximately $\propto c(d)(\ln N)^d / N$, where $d$ is the number of dimensions; $C(d)$ is different for the different methods of producing the low discrepancy sequences.

A lot of jargon and methodology is carried over from true Monte Carlo analysis, but it should be remembered that these are fixed numbers. We have already seen that a computer cannot produce random numbers; but the pseudo-random numbers which we use instead really have the properties of random numbers, e.g. we can start taking our sample from anywhere in a sequence. Quasi-random numbers on the other hand have a definite beginning and order (although no end). By definition they are always the same.

(iii) *Halton Sequence*: Like standard uniform random numbers, these numbers have value 0 to 1. Each one dimensional sequence of Halton numbers is manufactured from an integer base $b$

which can be chosen arbitrarily; normally prime numbers are chosen. The numbers are the following sequence:

$$[0], \frac{1}{b}, \frac{2}{b}, \ldots, \frac{b-1}{b};$$

$$\frac{1}{b^2} + \left(\begin{array}{c}\text{all numbers in} \\ \text{previous row}\end{array}\right), \frac{2}{b^2} + \left(\begin{array}{c}\text{all numbers in} \\ \text{previous row}\end{array}\right), \ldots, \frac{b-1}{b^2} + \left(\begin{array}{c}\text{all numbers in} \\ \text{previous row}\end{array}\right);$$

$$\frac{1}{b^3} + \left(\begin{array}{c}\text{all numbers in} \\ \text{previous row}\end{array}\right), \frac{2}{b^3} + \left(\begin{array}{c}\text{all numbers in} \\ \text{previous row}\end{array}\right), \ldots, \frac{b-1}{b^3} + \left(\begin{array}{c}\text{all numbers in} \\ \text{previous row}\end{array}\right);$$

$$\vdots$$

The first zero, which is inserted in order to express the subsequent numbers simply, is not part of the Halton sequence and is discarded once the sequence has been set up. We take the example of $b = 3$, when the sequence becomes

$$[0], \frac{1}{3}, \frac{2}{3};$$

$$\frac{1}{9} + 0, \frac{1}{9} + \frac{1}{3}, \frac{1}{9} + \frac{2}{3}; \frac{2}{9} + 0, \frac{2}{9} + \frac{1}{3}, \frac{2}{9} + \frac{2}{3};$$

$$\frac{1}{27} + 0, \frac{1}{27} + \frac{1}{3}, \frac{1}{27} + \frac{2}{3}; \frac{1}{27} + \frac{1}{9} + 0, \frac{1}{27} + \frac{1}{9} + \frac{1}{3}, \frac{1}{27} + \frac{1}{9} + \frac{2}{3}; \text{ etc.}$$

Clearly, this is just a way of placing points along a line in an orderly way so that each new point is placed as far away from existing points as possible. On the whole, it is better to use low prime bases rather than high ones.

(iv) *Alternative Representation of Halton Numbers*: The last subsection explained how the interval 0 to 1 is progressively filled with Halton numbers after the base has been chosen. There is an alternative way of describing this, which is less intuitively appealing but easier to code:

- Take the sequence of integers starting with 1 and write these to base b.
- Flip these base $b$ integers over the decimal point as shown in Table 10.3.
- This flipped over fraction, when re-expressed to base 10 is a Halton number.

**Table 10.3**   Manufacture of Halton numbers to base 3

| Integer$_{10}$ | Integer$_3$ | Flipped Integer$_3$ | Flipped Integer$_{10}$ = Halton Number |
|---|---|---|---|
| 1 | $1_3$ | $0.1_3$ | $\frac{2}{3}$ |
| 2 | $2_3$ | $0.2_3$ | $\frac{2}{3}$ |
| 3 | $10_3$ | $0.01_3$ | $\frac{1}{9}$ |
| 4 | $11_3$ | $0.11_3$ | $\frac{1}{9} + \frac{1}{3}$ |
| 5 | $12_3$ | $0.21_3$ | $\frac{1}{9} + \frac{1}{3}$ |
| 6 | $20_3$ | $0.02_3$ | $\frac{2}{9}$ |

(v) *Higher Dimensional Halton Numbers*: Consider a two-dimensional problem needing pairs of "random numbers". If these are true or pseudo-random numbers, we can just pair up random numbers as they come out of the random number generator; but with quasi-random numbers we need to be much more careful. These are deterministic numbers which are built up logically, so undesirable patterns can build up if they are used carelessly: at its most basic, if we take pairs of numbers as they come out of two generators using the same base, all the points will lie along a straight line in the $X - Y$ plane, e.g. $(\frac{1}{3}, \frac{1}{3})$, $(\frac{2}{3}, \frac{2}{3})$, $(\frac{1}{9}, \frac{1}{9})$. The simplest procedure is therefore to use a different prime number for the base of the Halton numbers used for each dimension, e.g. for a three-dimensional sequence, we use the three Halton sequences $H_2$, $H_3$, $H_5$, taking the numbers $H_2(1)$, $H_3(1)$, $H_5(1)$ for the first point, and so on up to $H_2(n)$, $H_3(n)$, $H_5(n)$ for the $n$th point. This simple procedure is adequate for a few dimensions but beyond about six, convergence is not so good.

(vi) **Fauré Sequence:** A slightly more complex method than in the last subparagraph is due to Fauré, and is also made from the Halton numbers; it leads to a sequence which is much more efficient. Halton numbers to a single base are manipulated to obtain the coordinates of multidimensional points, using the following procedure and example:

1. Suppose we wish to obtain a sequence of $d$-dimensional points; our example will take $d = 3$
2. Decide on a base $r$ which is a prime number with $r \geq d$. For our example we choose $r = 3$.
3. We saw above that the Halton numbers are based on ascending integers. Any integer $n$ to base $r$ may be written

$$n = h_m r^m + \cdots + h_2 r^2 + h_1 r^1 + h_0 r^0$$

For example

$$22_{10} = 2 \times 3^2 + 1 \times 3^1 + 1 \times 3^0 = 211_3$$

The Halton number is now written

$$H_r(n) = h_0 r^{-1} + h_1 r^{-2} + h_2 r^{-3} + \cdots$$

In our example

$$H_3(22) = \frac{1}{3} + \frac{1}{9} + \frac{2}{27} = \frac{14}{27}$$

4. The Fauré sequences describe points in $d$ dimensions, i.e. are $d$ parallel streams of numbers. The first stream of numbers is just the simple Halton sequence for $n = 1, 2, 3, \ldots$ The other streams of numbers are obtained by calculating coefficients analogous to the $h_i$ in the last equation. We write the Fauré number from stream $k$ as $\Phi_r^k(n)$, and use the following definitions:

$$\Phi_r^1(n) = H_r(n); \qquad a_i^1 = h_i$$

The $s$ Fauré numbers corresponding to the integer $n$ are then

$$\Phi_r^1(n) = a_0^1 r^{-1} + a_1^1 r^{-2} + a_2^1 r^{-3} + \cdots = H_r(n)$$
$$\Phi_r^2(n) = a_0^2 r^{-1} + a_1^2 r^{-2} + a_2^2 r^{-3} + \cdots$$
$$\vdots$$
$$\Phi_r^d(n) = a_0^d r^{-1} + a_1^d r^{-2} + a_2^d r^{-3} + \cdots$$

In our numerical example

$$\Phi_3^1(22) = 1 \times 3^{-1} + 1 \times 3^{-2} + 2 \times 3^{-3} = \tfrac{14}{17}$$

$$\Phi_3^2(22) = a_0^2 \times 3^{-1} + a_1^2 \times 3^{-2} + a_2^2 \times 3^{-3}$$

$$\Phi_3^3(22) = a_0^3 \times 3^{-1} + a_1^3 \times 3^{-2} + a_2^3 \times 3^{-3}$$

5. The task is now to find the various $a_j^k$. Each row of $a_j^k$ are obtained from the row of $a_j^{k-1}$ preceding it, using the same simple triangular transformation matrix as follows:

$$\begin{pmatrix} a_0^k & a_1^k & a_2^k & \cdots \end{pmatrix} = \begin{pmatrix} a_0^{k-1} & a_1^{k-1} & a_2^{k-1} & \cdots \end{pmatrix} \begin{pmatrix} {}^0C_0 & 0 & 0 & \cdots \\ {}^1C_0 & {}^1C_1 & 0 & \cdots \\ {}^2C_0 & {}^2C_1 & {}^2C_2 & \cdots \\ \vdots & \vdots & \vdots & \ddots \end{pmatrix} \bmod r$$

where ${}^iC_j = i!/j!(i-j)!$ and the modulus $r$ operation is performed on each element after matrix multiplication (mod $r$ is the remainder after dividing by $r$). In our example, we have for $\Phi_3^2(22)$:

$$\begin{pmatrix} a_0^2 & a_1^2 & a_2^2 \end{pmatrix} = \begin{pmatrix} 1 & 1 & 2 \end{pmatrix} \begin{pmatrix} 1 & 0 & 0 \\ 1 & 1 & 0 \\ 1 & 2 & 1 \end{pmatrix} \bmod 3 = \begin{pmatrix} 4 \bmod 3 & 5 \bmod 3 & 2 \bmod 3 \end{pmatrix} = \begin{pmatrix} 1 & 2 & 2 \end{pmatrix}$$

So that

$$\Phi_3^2(22) = 1 \times 3^{-1} + 2 \times 3^{-2} + 2 \times 3^{-3} = \frac{17}{27}$$

(vii) **Normally Distributed Halton Numbers**: Quasi-random numbers are not random; we have seen that they are carefully constructed in groups of $d$, when a point in $d$-dimensional space is specified. Not surprisingly, the "sum of 12" and Box–Muller methods of manufacturing normal random numbers would just scramble their structue and produce meaningless numbers. Each uniform Halton number therefore has to be converted to a standard normal Halton number by using the inverse cumulative normal transformation described in Section 10.2(iii).

(viii) **Correlation**: This is handled using a Cholesky decomposition just as it would be for true random numbers.

## 10.6    EXAMPLES

(i) **Use of Low Discrepancy Sequences**: In the last section we made the distinction between the use of Monte Carlo for an occasional pricing and its routine use for calculating on-line prices or regular revaluation of a book. The same remarks apply to quasi-random numbers. There is no doubt that you need to be a lot more careful when setting up low discrepancy sequences. If you are using simulation for once-off calculations, it might be easier just to let your random number Monte Carlo simulations run for an extra half hour rather than risk the errors that can be made in putting together a quasi-Monte Carlo run. The production of quasi-random numbers and their conversion using an inverse cumulative normal routine takes longer than generating pseudo-random numbers. Furthermore, without wanting to open a large topic, the reader is warned that periodicities in the calculations can emerge in unexpected places and without warning, and yield completely erroneous results.

On the other hand, if you are building a model for repeat use, you should always use quasi-Monte Carlo if possible. Two impressive examples follow in which a 10,000 run with Halton numbers gives results comparable to a 1,000,000 run using random Monte Carlo; on a low-powered laptop, the former takes a fraction of a second while the latter takes half an hour or more. The reason for this speed is not only the smaller number of runs, but the fact that the 20,000 Halton numbers, preconverted to normal form, can be stored in an Excel spread sheet and are instantly available for calculations.

The main drawback of this method is again a matter of dimensionality. There is no universal cut-off and the numbers depend on the specifics of the problem, but the following is an indication:

- The efficiency of quasi-Monte Carlo diminishes with the number of dimensions and it is unsafe to go beyond 20/30 dimensions. The 52-dimension knock-out and Asian calls examined in Section 10.4(ii) are beyond these techniques at present.
- The simple Halton numbers (used in the following examples) should not be used for more than half a dozen dimensions. Any higher, you should use Fauré numbers or preferably Sobol numbers. For an explanation of the latter together with useful code see Press *et al.* (1992) and Jäckel (2002).
- Low discrepancy sequences are prone to suddenly displaying unexpected and spurious results, due to cyclical patterns in the numbers asserting themselves. Single answers should therefore not be relied on, and the convergence towards the answer as the number of data points is increased should be understood. This is not dissimilar to the approach with trees described in Chapter 7. In any case, quasi-Monte Carlo methods do not prescribe an easy method for assessing the error in a calculation, so looking at the convergence is really the only way to have confidence in the result.

Two examples follow for which quasi-Monte Carlo methods are ideally suited. Both models were written in an Excel spread sheet which contained the necessary simple Halton numbers, from 1 to 20,000 in various bases. Once this is set up, the calculations are almost instantaneous. The models were set up to display the pricing using the first $n$ thousand Halton numbers, with $n$ ranging from 1 to 20; that way we can track the convergence of the result to some stable value.

It would have been nice to reanalyze the knock-out and Asian calls which we looked at previously, but 52 dimensions is too high for reliable answers. Better suited alternatives are therefore chosen.

(ii) *European Call on the Spread Between Two Stock Prices*: $S_1(0) = 100$; $S_2(0) = 90$; $X = 10$; $r = 10\%$; $q_1 = 4\%$; $q_2 = 2\%$; $T = 1$ year; $\sigma_1 = 20\%$; $\sigma_1 = 20\%$; correlation $= 0.75\%$:

$$\text{Payoff} = \max[0,\ S_1(1 \text{ year}) - S_2(1 \text{ year}) - X]$$

A simple random Monte Carlo pricing using 1 million simulations gives a price of $6.337 \pm 0.009$ for this option.

The low discrepancy sequence was based on Halton numbers with bases 2 and 3; a graph of the pricing vs. the number of points used is shown in Figure 10.4. Convergence is very rapid, getting to within 0.2% of a 1 million shot Monte Carlo result with just under 10,000 points.

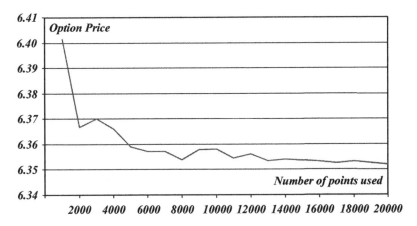

**Figure 10.4**  Pricing spread option with Halton sequence

(iii) *Knock-out Call with Monitoring Every 2 Months*: $S = 100$; $X = 110$; $K = 150$; $r = 10\%$; $q = 4\%$; $T = 1$ year; $\sigma = 20\%$. This is similar to the knock-out option examined previously, but with monitoring every 2 months rather than every week. The Monte Carlo pricing using $\frac{1}{2}$ million simulations with antithetic variates is $4.373 \pm 0.0005$ (Figure 10.5). This is a six-dimensional problem and for each dimension (or equivalently at each node) we use Halton numbers based on the first six prime numbers. Again, satisfactory convergence is achieved in just about 12,000 quasi-simulations.

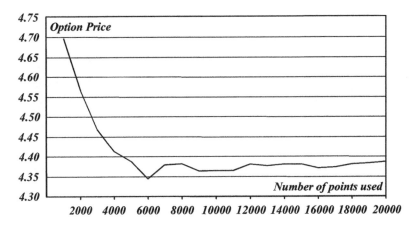

**Figure 10.5**  Pricing knock-out option with Halton sequence

# Part 3
## Applications: Exotic Options

# 11

## Simple Exotics

The purpose of this part of the book is to introduce the reader to the most important types of equity derivatives and to illustrate the pricing techniques which have been introduced in the last two parts. Exotic options can mostly be priced using classical statistical techniques, although we will see in Part 4 of this book that some of the analysis can be simplified (or at least rendered more elegant) using stochastic calculus.

There is no firm definition of an exotic option and we usually take it to mean anything that is not a simple European or American put or call option. We start with a chapter on simple extensions of the Black Scholes methodology, which should really be understood by anyone involved with options, whether or not they have a specific interest in exotics.

## 11.1  FORWARD START OPTIONS

(i) Suppose we buy an option with maturity $T$ which only starts running at time $\tau$. If the strike price is set now, pricing becomes fairly trivial: the price of a European option depends only on the final stock price and the strike price so there is no difference whatsoever between "starting now" and "starting at time $\tau$"; with an American option we must take into account the fact that we cannot exercise the option between now and time $\tau$, but this is easily accommodated within a tree or a finite difference scheme. But the type of options considered here are those that are at-the-money or 20% out-of-the-money at some future starting date.

(ii) *Homogeneous Functions*: This is an important mathematical property of option prices which we use freely in the following chapters. The concept is so intuitive that most people use it instinctively without placing a name to it.

If the reader is already working within a derivatives environment, it is quite likely that his option model has the initial stock price preset to 100; this yields option prices directly as a percentage of the stock price. We know that the initial stock price will not be 100 but we also know that things move proportionately: if an option is priced at 5.5 on our preset model with $S_0 = 100$ and strike price $X = 120$, we know immediately that the price of a similar option with $S_0 = 40$ and $X = 48$ would be 2.2. It is immediately apparent to most people that the strike price has to move in line with the stock price for this reasoning to work, just as it is apparent to most that we *should not* change the time to maturity or the interest rate.

An equally obvious conclusion is reached concerning the number of shares on which an option is written. Suppose we own a call option on one share and the company suddenly declares a 2 for 1 stock split. We know that the share price would fall in half, but we would be kept whole if our call option were replaced by two options of the same maturity, each on one of the new shares, and with the strike price equal to half the original strike price.

Let $f(nS_0, nX)$ be the value of an option on $n$ shares, where $S_0$ is the stock price and $X$ is the strike. The homogeneity condition just described may be written

$$f(nS_0, nX) = S_0 f\left(n, n\frac{X}{S_0}\right) = X f\left(n\frac{S_0}{X}, n\right) = nf(S_0, X) = nS_0 f\left(1, \frac{X}{S_0}\right) \quad (11.1)$$

It should be pointed out that this property holds true for most options we encounter, although sometimes with modification: for example, barrier options are homogeneous in spot price, strike price *and* barrier value. However there are exceptions such as power options which are described later in this chapter.

(iii) **Forward Start with Fixed Number of Shares**: Consider an option starting in some time $\tau$ in the future, maturing in time $T$ and with a strike price equal to a predetermined percentage $\alpha$ of the starting stock price. Using the homogeneity property, the value of this option in time $\tau$ is

$$f(S_\tau, \alpha S_\tau, T - \tau) = S_\tau f(1, \alpha, T - \tau)$$

The term $f(1, \alpha, T - \tau)$ is non-stochastic and may be calculated immediately. If we buy $f(1, \alpha, T - \tau)$ units of stock today at a cost of $S_0 f(1, \alpha, T - \tau)$, the value of this stock in time $\tau$ will be $S_\tau f(1, \alpha, T - \tau)$; but this is the same as the future value of the forward starting option. Today's value of the forward starting option must therefore be

$$S_0 f(1, \alpha, T - \tau) = f(S_0, \alpha S_0, T - \tau)$$

i.e. the value of the forward starting option is the same as if the option started running today, with the time to maturity set equal to the length of time between the start and maturity (Rubinstein, 1991c).

A further refinement is needed if the stock pays a dividend. Remember that if we hold a packet of stock from now to time $\tau$, we will receive a dividend but if we hold an option, we will not. The adjustment to the formula can be made by the usual substitution $S_\tau \to S_\tau e^{-q\tau}$ for continuous dividends to give

$$f_{\text{forward start}} = e^{-q\tau} f(S_0, \alpha S_0, T - \tau)$$

(iv) **Forward Start with Fixed Value of Shares**: The last subparagraph dealt with a forward starting option on a fixed number of shares. But suppose we were asked to price a forward starting option on $1000 of shares. The value of this option in time $\tau$ will be

$$f(n_\tau S_\tau, \alpha n_\tau S_\tau, T - \tau) = n_\tau S_\tau f(1, \alpha, T - \tau)$$

where $n_\tau S_\tau = \$1000$ in our example. Therefore, the value of this option in time $\tau$ is completely determinate (non-stochastic); today's value is simply obtained by present valuing this sum:

$$f_{\text{forward start}} = e^{-r\tau} f(S_0, \alpha S_0, T - \tau)$$

(v) The contrasting results of the last two subsections are well illustrated in the foreign exchange market:

- For an option to buy £1 for dollars, forward start means discounting back by the sterling interest rate.
- For an option to buy sterling for $1, forward start means discounting back by the dollar interest rate.

(vi) *Cliquets (Ratchets)*: As the name implies, this type of option was first used widely in France. It is designed for an investor who likes the basic idea of a call option but is concerned that the stock price might spend most of its time above the strike price, only to plunge just before maturity. In such a case, the cliquet would capture the effect of the early price rise. It is really a series of forward starting options strung together. The option has a final maturity $T$ (typically 1 year) and a number of re-set dates $\tau_1, \tau_2, \cdots$ (typically quarterly). The payoff and re-set sequence is as follows:

- At $\tau_1$, the option pays $\max[0, S_{\tau_1} - S_0]$.
- At $\tau_2$, the option pays $\max[0, S_{\tau_2} - S_{\tau_1}]$, etc.

Clearly, each of these is the payoff of an at-the-money forward starting call option. The fair value is therefore given by

$$f_{\text{cliquet}} = C(S_0, S_0, \tau_1) + e^{-q\tau_1} C(S_0, S_0, \tau_2 - \tau_1) + \cdots + e^{-q\tau_{n-1}} C(S_0, S_0, \tau_n - \tau_{n-1})$$

Common variations on the structure have the effective strikes slightly out-of-the-money, or have the payouts rolled into a single payment at final maturity.

## 11.2 CHOOSERS

(i) The 1990 Kuwait invasion led to a jump in the price of crude oil. Speculators were then faced with a dilemma: if a withdrawal were negotiated, the oil price would fall back; but a declaration of war by the US would lead to a further jump upwards. A ready-made strategy for this situation is the straddle, consisting of both an at-the-money put and an at-the-money call. This has a positive payoff whichever way the oil price moves; but it has the great drawback of being very expensive.

(ii) *The Simple Chooser*: This option has a strike $X$ and a final maturity $T$. The owner of the option has until time $\tau$ to declare whether he wants the option to be either a call option or a put option. The chooser is sold as an option which has the benefits of a straddle, but at a much lower cost. Clearly, at the limit $\tau = T$ the option becomes a straddle while at the limit $\tau = 0$ it becomes a put or call option.

The pricing of this option is surprisingly easy (Rubinstein, 1991b): at time $\tau$, the holder of the option will choose put or call depending on which is more valuable. The payoff at time $\tau$ can therefore be written

$$\text{Payoff}_\tau = \max[P(S_\tau, X, T - \tau), C(S_\tau, X, T - \tau)]$$

Using the put–call parity relationship of Section 2.2(i) gives

$$\text{Payoff}_\tau = \max\left[C(S_\tau, X, T - \tau) + X e^{-r(T-\tau)} - S_\tau e^{-q(T-\tau)}, C(S_\tau, X, T - \tau)\right]$$
$$= C(S_\tau, X, T - \tau) + e^{-q(T-\tau)} \max\left[X e^{-(r-q)(T-\tau)} - S_\tau, 0\right]$$

Taking these two terms separately, the instrument which has a value $C(S_\tau, X, T - \tau)$ in time $\tau$ when the stock price is $S_\tau$ is obviously a call option maturing in time $T$; its value today is $C(S_0, X, T)$.

The form of the second term in the payoff is that of a put option maturing in time $\tau$. Its value today may be written $e^{-q(T-\tau)} P(S_0, X e^{-(r-q)(T-\tau)}, \tau)$. Putting these together gives

$$f_{\text{simple chooser}} = C(S_0, X, T) + e^{-q(T-\tau)} P\left(S_0, X e^{-(r-q)(T-\tau)}, \tau\right)$$

(iii) *Complex Chooser*: The concept of the chooser can be very simply extended so that the put and call options have different strike prices and maturities. Unfortunately, the mathematics of the pricing does not extend so simply and we therefore defer this until Section 14.2.

## 11.3 SHOUT OPTIONS

(i) Like cliquets, these options are for investors who think that the underlying stock price might peak at some time before maturity. The shout option is usually a call option, but with a difference: at any time $\tau$ before maturity, the holder may "shout". The effect of this is that he is guaranteed a minimum payoff of $S_\tau - X$, although he will get the payoff of the call option if this is greater than the minimum.

(ii) *Payoffs*: By definition, the final payoff of the option is $\max[0, S_\tau - X, S_T - X]$. In practice, $S_\tau - X$ is always greater than zero; if not, we would have $S_\tau < X$ which means that the holder of the option had shouted at a time when the effect was to turn the shout option into a simple European call option, for no economic benefit in exchange. The payoff at time $T$ can therefore be written

$$\max[S_\tau - X, S_T - X] = S_\tau - X + \max[0, S_T - S_\tau]$$

At time $\tau$ if a shout is made, the value of this payoff is

$$e^{-r(T-\tau)}(S_\tau - X) + C(S_\tau, S_\tau, T - \tau)$$

(iii) *Shout Pricing*: This option is easily priced using a binomial model as we would for any American option (Thomas, 1993). The final nodes in the tree are $\max[0, S_T - X]$ as they would be for a call option, i.e. if we get as far as the final nodes, it means that no shout took place.

At each node before the final column, the holder has the choice of shouting or not shouting. To decide which, compare the value obtained by discounting back the values of the two subsequent nodes with the time $\tau$ payoff produced by shouting, i.e. $e^{-r(T-\tau)}(S_\tau - X) + C(S_\tau, S_\tau, T - \tau)$; we enter whichever value is greater at that node.

In spirit this is the same as the binomial method for pricing American options which was explained in Chapter 7; in that case we rolled back through the tree and at each node we selected the greater of the payoff value or the calculated discounted average. The present procedure calls for the Black Scholes value of a call option to be calculated at each node. However, with the assumption of constant volatility, the Black Scholes formula only needs to be calculated once for each time step. The homogeneity property described in Section 11.1(ii) says that the price of an at-the-money option is proportional to the stock price, so that for an entire column of nodes we only need to calculate the constant of proportionality $C(1, 1, T - \tau)$ once.

(iv) **Put Shout:** A precisely analogous put option with shout feature can be constructed. A generalized payoff at time $T$ can be written as

$$\max[\phi(S_\tau - X), \phi(S_T - X)] = \phi(S_\tau - X) + \max[0, \phi(S_T - S_\tau)]$$

where

$$\begin{cases} \phi = +1 & \text{for a call} \\ \phi = -1 & \text{for a put} \end{cases}$$

At each node in the tree, a shouted value would be

$$e^{-r(T-\tau)} \phi(S_\tau - X) + \text{Option}(S_\tau, S_\tau, T - \tau)$$

where the option is either a put or a call option.

(v) **Strike Shout:** The shout options described above locked in a minimum payout. Another version of this type of option locks in a new strike price when the shout is made, and is even simpler to price than the previous ones.

The payoff at time $T$ for a calll option with strike shout is

$$\max[0, S_T - X, S_T - S_\tau] = \max[0, S_T - S_\tau]$$

This is the same as in subsection (ii) above, but without the minimum payout. The rest of the analysis is as before.

## 11.4   BINARY (DIGITAL) OPTIONS

(i) Recall the simple derivation of the Black Scholes formula which was given in Section 5.2. In its simplest form, this may be written

$$C(S_0, X, T) = \int_0^\infty F(S_T) \max[0, S_T - X] \, dS_T = \int_X^\infty F(S_T)(S_T - X) \, dS_T$$
$$= S_0 e^{-qT} N[d_1] - X e^{-rT} N[d_2]$$

where $F(S_T)$ is the (lognormal) probability distribution of $S_T$. The two terms in this equation will now be interpreted separately, rather than together as they were before (Reiner and Rubinstein, 1991b).

(ii) **Cash or Nothing Option (Bet):** In the term $\int_X^\infty F(S_T) X \, dS_T$, the factor $X$ appears in two unrelated roles: as a constant multiplicative factor in the integrand and again as the lower limit of integration. The first role is trivial and we will drop $X$ from the integrand. Then $e^{-rT} \int_X^\infty F(S_T) dS_T = e^{-rT} N[d_2]$ is the present value of the risk-neutral probability that $X < S_T$, and can be interpreted as the arbitrage-free value of an option which pays out $1 if $S_T$ is above $X$, and $0 otherwise (Figure 11.1). This option is essentially a bet: "I will give you $1

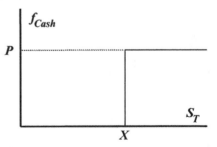

**Figure 11.1**   Cash or nothing option

if the stock price is over $100 in 6 months". Its value is given by the second term in the Black Scholes formula.

(iii) **Asset or Nothing Option**: By the same reasoning as in the last section, the first term in the Black Scholes formula is the price of an option which delivers one unit of stock if the maturity price is above $X$ and nothing otherwise (Figure 11.2).

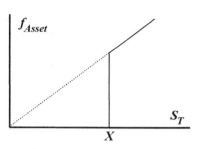

**Figure 11.2**   Asset or nothing option

(iv) **Gap Options**: The last two options can be combined to give the so-called gap options whose price is given by

$$f_{gap} = S_0\,e^{-qT}\,N[d_1] - P\,e^{-rT}\,N[d_2]$$
$$= f_{asset} - f_{cash}$$

There are two special cases of this option which are of interest: first, if $P = X$, we obviously have a European call option; second, if the asset-or-nothing and the cash-or-nothing components have the same value, then the fair value of the gap option is zero, i.e. $f_{gap} = f_{asset} - f_{cash} = 0$. This composite option is known as a **pay-later option** for obvious reasons: the initial premium for the option is zero and any payments either way are made at maturity. The payoff is shown in Figure 11.3.

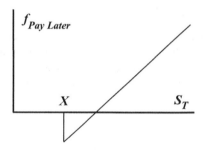

**Figure 11.3**   Pay later option

(v) **Greeks**: The binary option formulas are basically the Black Scholes formula pulled in half; it might therefore seem that there is little new to say about these options. However, in some respects they display pathological behavior which teaches us some important lessons.

Imagine a trader trying to dynamically hedge a short cash-or-nothing option (bet). Shortly before maturity he would be trying to replicate the option shown in Figure 11.4. The trader is sitting with $S_T = X^-$, i.e. just below the strike price. Gamma will be highish positive and delta moderate. $S_T$ starts to rise slightly and gamma shoots up; but more alarmingly, delta goes to astronomical levels. For a simple option, $\Delta$ never rises above 100%; but in this case $\Delta$ can become 1000%. In fact, at the moment of expiry, $\Delta \to \infty$ as $S_T \to X$. It takes quite a brave trader to buy 10 times the underlying stock as a hedge; if the price just zig-zags about $S_T = X$, the trader could lose the entire option premium in transaction costs.

If $S_T$ moves to $S_T = X^+$, things become calmer again. Delta returns to a low level, but the sign of gamma has reversed. At the strike and at the moment of expiry, an infinitesimal move in $S_T$ across $X$ would cause gamma to change from $+\infty$ to $-\infty$; again, not comfortable.

A trader's reaction might be just to sit tight and do nothing as $S_T$ moves from $X^-$ to $X^+$. But then where would he get the payoff from, when the bet is exercised against him? This intense trading activity over a tiny range is what generates the income to make the payoff: hence the occasional need to trade very large quantities of

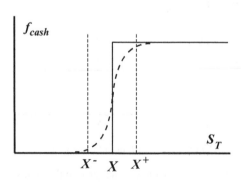

**Figure 11.4**   Hedging a bet

stock in the vicinity of the strike price. In practice, market practitioners tend to avoid bet options in anything but small amounts.

## 11.5  POWER OPTIONS

(i) These may take an infinite variety of forms, but the two most common ones encountered in the marketplace have payoffs given by

$$\{\max[0, S_T - X]\}^2 \quad \text{and} \quad \max\left[0, S_T^2 - X^2\right]$$

In fact, we can write

$$\{\max[0, S_T - X]\}^2 = \begin{cases} 0 & S_T < X \\ (S_T - X)^2 = S_T^2 - X^2 - 2X(S_T - X) & X < S_T \end{cases}$$
$$= \max\left[0, S_T^2 - X^2\right] - 2X\max[0, S_T - X]$$

so the two options are simply connected by a call option.

These options are mostly the domain of leverage junkies and are mathematically rather untidy. Unlike most options we deal with, they are not homogeneous in $S_T$ and $X$. A reflection of this is that the size of the payment depends on the unit of currency used. As an exercise, the reader should try to imagine how the payoff would have been handled in those countries that adopted the Euro during the life of a power option.

(ii) We now look for a formula to price an option whose payoff is $\max[0, S_T^\lambda - X]$. Recall from equation (3.7) that

$$S_T = S_0\, e^{(r-q)T - \frac{1}{2}\sigma^2 T + \sigma W_T}$$

where $W_T$ is a Browian motion. Then

$$S_T^\lambda = S_0^\lambda\, e^{\lambda\{(r-q)T - \frac{1}{2}\sigma^2 T + \sigma W_T\}}$$
$$= S_0^\lambda\, e^{(r-Q)T - \frac{1}{2}v^2 T + v W_T}$$

where

$$Q = \lambda q - (\lambda - 1)\left(r + \tfrac{1}{2}\lambda\sigma^2\right); \qquad v = \lambda\sigma$$

The form of $S_T^\lambda$ is the same as the form of $S_T$ so we can simply use our Black Scholes model, substituting $Q$ for $q$ and $v$ for volatility, while using $S_0^\lambda$ where we would have used $S_0$.

(iii) **Bundles of Call Options**: Suppose we buy a package of call options as shown in Figure 11.5. The package has the following properties:

- Each option on $2 \times h$ shares.
- The strike price of the first option is $X$, and the strike prices of each successive option is $h$ higher than the last.

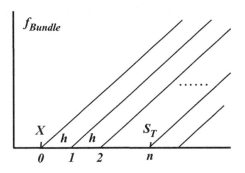

**Figure 11.5**  Equally spaced calls

(The first point implies that $h$ is a pure number while the second implies that it is a dollar amount; this is just another reflection of the dimensional awkwardness of these options.)

Suppose that at the maturity of the bundle, the stock price is $S_T = X + nh$ which is above $X$. If $h$ is small, the payoff of this package is

$$(2h)(h + 2h + 3h + \cdots + nh) = (2h)\frac{n(n + 1)}{2}h$$

$$= (nh)(nh + h) \approx (S_T - X)^2$$

This is the payoff of the first square power option mentioned above. The power option can be simulated by a bundle of options, with the approximation becoming exact as the spacing between the strikes of the options shrinks to zero. Similarly, the second power option is approximated by the same bundle *plus* a single call option with strike $X$, on $2X$ units of stock.

(iv) **Soft Strike Options**: There are high risks associated with hedging an option which is close to maturity, when the stock price is close to the strike price. At this point, gamma blows up. In fact, it is concern over the gamma near maturity that is often the decisive factor when deciding how large an option position can be hedged.

The gamma is the second differential of the derivative price with respect to the stock price; it is therefore constant for a square power option near its maturity.

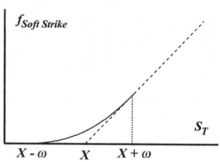

Suppose that a large call option (dotted line in Figure 11.6) is requested by an investor, but the bank is uncomfortable with the potential gamma exposure close to maturity. The bank can instead propose the payoff shown in the graph. For most values of $S_T$ this has the same payoff as a straight-forward call option; but for a distance $\omega$ on either side of the strike price, the call payoff function is replaced by

**Figure 11.6**   Soft strike call

$$f_{\text{soft strike}} = \frac{1}{4\omega}(S_T - X + \omega)^2$$

This option is said to have a *soft strike* over the range $X - \omega$ to $X + \omega$, where it has a constant terminal gamma of $\frac{1}{2}\omega$.

Using the analysis of the last subparagraph, this soft strike option is equivalent to a bundle of call options, with strike prices infinitesimally spaced between $X - \omega$ and $X + \omega$.

# 12

## Two Asset Options

Before plunging into the details of specific options, we need to take a broad overview of the principles underlying this chapter. In Appendix A.1 we set out the most important properties of normally distributed variables. Two general results are of particular importance in this chapter and it is worth repeating them here:

- The sum of two normally distributed variables is itself normally distributed; the mean of the sum of the variables is equal to the sum of the means of the variables.
- The variance of the sum of two normally distributed variables is equal to the sum of the individual variances if the two variances are *independently distributed*. If they are correlated, the variance of the sum is given by

$$\sigma^2 = \sigma_1^2 + \sigma_2^2 + 2\rho\sigma_1\sigma_2$$

where $\rho$ is the correlation coefficient.

Consider two stochastic assets with prices at time $t$ equal to $S_t^{(1)}$ and $S_t^{(2)}$. Since $\ln S_t^{(1)}$ and $\ln S_t^{(2)}$ are normally distributed, $\ln S_t^{(1)} + \ln S_t^{(2)} = \ln S_t^{(1)} S_t^{(2)}$ must also be normally distributed. This means that variables such as $S_t^{(1)} S_t^{(2)}$ and $S_t^{(1)}/S_t^{(2)}$ are lognormally distributed and much of the theory developed for a single stochastic asset can be used in analyzing the composite asset. By contrast, $S_t^{(1)} + S_t^{(2)}$ does not have a simple distribution. This composite asset is therefore extremely difficult to analyze and we have no analytical results, even for apparently simple options such as a call on the sum of two stock prices, with payoff $\max[0, S_T^{(1)} + S_T^{(2)} - X]$.

## 12.1 EXCHANGE OPTIONS (MARGRABE)

(i) Consider an option on two assets whose initial prices are $S_0^{(1)}$ and $S_0^{(2)}$, which has a payoff $\max[0, S_T^{(1)} - S_T^{(2)}]$. This can be interpreted in three ways:

- An option to call a unit of asset 1 in exchange for a unit of asset 2.
- An option to put a unit of asset 2 in exchange for a unit of asset 1.
- A contract to receive a price differential if this is greater than zero.

In general this is referred to as an exchange or a spread or an outperformance option.

A very simple way of pricing this option is as follows (Margrabe, 1978): from the form of the payoff, it is clear that the value of the option $f(S_0^{(1)}, S_0^{(2)})$ is homogeneous in $S_0^{(1)}$ and $S_0^{(2)}$. This condition [see Section 11.1(ii)] can be written

$$f(S_0^{(1)}, S_0^{(2)}) = S_0^{(2)} f(Q_0, 1) \qquad \text{where} \qquad Q_t = \frac{S_t^{(1)}}{S_t^{(2)}}$$

We can interpret $Q_0$ as the price of asset $S^{(1)}$ denominated in units of $S^{(2)}$. $f(Q_0, 1)$ is then just a call option with a strike price of unity. Let us make the arguments more concrete by taking a specific example where $S_0^{(1)}$ is today's \$ price of a barrel of oil and $S_0^{(2)}$ is today's \$ price of an ounce of gold. The quantity $Q_0$ is then today's oil price expressed as ounces of gold per barrel. $f(Q_0, 1)$ is the value (expressed in ounces of gold) of a call option to buy a barrel of oil for 1 ounce of gold (probably not worth a lot at present rates!). In order to price this option we need to first make a short detour and re-examine some fundamental principles.

(ii) Two concepts underlie the notion of risk neutrality: first, which everybody focuses on, is the no-arbitrage principle. The second is so self-evident that it is easy to overlook: if we borrow or deposit cash, then we pay or receive interest. Taking the simplest case of a forward contract, no-arbitrage tells us that if we buy an asset for $S_0$ and sell it forward for a price $F_{0T}$, then the return on the trade must equal the cost of borrowing the cash to buy the asset: $F_{0T}/S_0 = e^{rT}$. Of course, if we were able to borrow money for zero interest rate, then we would simply put $r = 0$ in all our option formulas.

In our current example, prices are denominated in a different form of money: not cash, but ounces of gold. Gold is not like cash: there is no gold-bank where you can deposit 3 ounces of gold and have it grow to 4 ounces a few years later. People hold gold because they expect it to go up in price, not because they can earn interest from it. If you borrow gold, there is no gold-interest charged – merely some handling charge, similar in nature to a stock-borrowing cost. Therefore, if gold is used to denominate the price of a commodity and its derivative, we must set the interest rate equal to zero in our formulas.

Two further points should be made: first, we have not abandoned risk neutrality. We understand that the underlying growth rate in the price of oil (in barrels per gold ounce) is some unknown quantity whose value we do not need to know. We solve our option problem in the usual risk-neutral way, by setting this growth rate equal to the interest rate and present-valuing the option using the interest rate: it just happens that when the money is not cash, the interest rate equals zero.

The second point is that the reader should take care not to confuse the forgoing with the role of dividends. Oil and gold dividends do not make much sense, but these commodities do incur storage charges which as we saw in Section 5.5(v) play a role analogous to dividends. If $S^{(1)}$ and $S^{(2)}$ were company stocks, the usual substitutions $S_0^{(1)} \rightarrow S_0^{(1)} e^{-q_1 T}$ and $S_0^{(2)} \rightarrow S_0^{(2)} e^{-q_2 T}$ can be used to account for continuous dividends.

(iii) **Margrabe's Formula:** An expression for $f(Q_0, 1)$ can immediately be written down using the Black Scholes formula for a call option. In the standard notation of equation (5.1), with $X = 1$ and setting $r \rightarrow 0$:

$$f(Q_0, 1) = \{Q_0 \, N[d_1] - N[d_2]\}$$

One final piece of information is needed: a value for $\sigma_Q$, the volatility of the composite asset $Q_t = S_t^{(1)}/S_t^{(2)} S_t^{(2)}$. An expression for this is derived in Appendix A.1(xi). Generalizing to allow for dividend-paying assets, Margrabe's formula can now be written

$$f_{M \text{ arg rabe}}\left(S_0^{(1)}, S_0^{(2)}\right) = S_0^{(1)} e^{-q_1 T} \, N[d_1] - S_0^{(2)} e^{-q_2 T} \, N[d_2] \tag{12.1}$$

$$d_1 = \frac{\ln Q_0 + \frac{1}{2}\sigma_Q^2 T}{\sigma_Q \sqrt{T}}; \quad d_2 = d_1 - \sigma_Q \sqrt{T}; \quad \sigma_Q^2 = \sigma_1^2 + \sigma_2^2 - 2\rho_{12}\sigma_1\sigma_2$$

(iv) Applying the basic risk-free hedging portfolio arguments of Section 4.2, we would expect to replicate an option on two assets by borrowing cash $B(S_t^{(1)}, S_t^{(2)}, t)$ and investing this in $\Delta_t^{(1)}$

154

and $\Delta_t^{(2)}$ units of each stock, i.e.

$$f\left(S_t^{(1)}, S_t^{(2)}\right) = \Delta_t^{(1)} S_t^{(1)} + \Delta_t^{(2)} S_t^{(2)} - B\left(S_t^{(1)}, S_t^{(2)}, t\right); \qquad \Delta_t^{(i)} = \frac{\partial f_t}{\partial S_t^{(i)}}$$

Euler's theorem [see Appendix A.12(i)] states that if $f(S_t^{(1)}, S_t^{(2)})$ is homogeneous, then we must have

$$f\left(S_t^{(1)}, S_t^{(2)}\right) = S_t^{(1)} \frac{\partial f_t}{\partial S_t^{(1)}} + S_t^{(2)} \frac{\partial f_t}{\partial S_t^{(2)}} = S_t^{(1)} \Delta_t^{(1)} + S_t^{(2)} \Delta_t^{(2)}$$

The last two equations taken together mean that

$$B\left(S_t^{(1)}, S_t^{(2)}, t\right) \equiv 0 \qquad \text{always}$$

We never need to borrow cash, which is of course why $r$ does not appear in Margrabe's formula: we merely borrow the right amount of one stock and exchange it at the current rate for the other stock; we are then automatically hedged for small movements in the price of either stock.

(v) *American Options*: The homogeneity arguments that led to the adoption of a modified Black Scholes model apply as much to an American option as to European options. $f(Q_0, 1)$ can therefore be evaluated using one of the numerical procedures for American options, setting $r \to 0$.

## 12.2   MAXIMUM OF TWO ASSETS

(i) Consider an option whose payoff at time $T$ is $\max[S_T^{(1)}, S_T^{(2)}]$. The value of this option today can be written

$$f_{\max}\left(S_0^{(1)}, S_0^{(2)}\right) = \text{PV}\left[\text{E}\left[S_T^{(1)}: S_T^{(2)} < S_T^{(1)}\right] + \text{E}\left[S_T^{(2)}: S_T^{(1)} < S_T^{(2)}\right]\right]$$

$$= f(1 \max) + f(2 \max) \tag{12.2}$$

From the symmetry of the terms, we only need to find an expression for one of these in order to write down the other (Stulz, 1982). Taking the second term and using the fact that the option price must be homogeneous in $S_0^{(1)}$ and $S_0^{(2)}$:

$$f(2 \max) = S_0^{(2)} \text{PV}[\text{E}[1 \mid Q_T < 1]] = S_0^{(2)} \text{PV}[\text{P}[Q_T < 1]]$$

(ii) $\text{P}[Q_T < 1]$ is the probability that the price of oil is less than 1 ounce of gold per barrel. A quick glance back to Section 5.2 will show that this is the first term (the coefficient of the strike $X$) in the Black Scholes model for a put option. We can therefore lift the formula for this directly from our previous work, remembering that the following points apply in this case:

- The volatility of $Q_t$ is given by $\sigma_Q^2 = \sigma_1^2 + \sigma_2^2 - 2\rho_{12}\sigma_1\sigma_2$, where $\sigma_1$ and $\sigma_2$ are the $ price volatilities of oil and gold; $\rho_{12}$ (or $\rho$) is the correlation between them [see Appendix A.1(xi) and (xii)].
- The interest rate in any formula we use is set equal to zero [see Section 12.1(ii) above].

(iii) The two terms in the expression for $f_{\max}(S_0^{(1)}, S_0^{(2)})$ in equation (12.2) are completely symmetrical and may both be obtained using the first term of the Black Scholes formula for a put option, which is given explicitly in Section 5.2. With a minimal amount of algebra, we get

$$f_{\max}\left(S_0^{(1)}, S_0^{(2)}\right) = S_0^{(1)} \, N[d_{1/2}] + S_0^{(2)} \, N[d_{2/1}]$$

$$d_{i/j} = \frac{-\ln S_0^{(i)}/S_0^{(j)} + \frac{1}{2}\sigma_Q^2 T}{\sigma_Q \sqrt{T}}; \qquad d_{1/2} + d_{2/1} = \sigma_Q \sqrt{T}$$

If the assets pay continuous dividends, we put $S_0^{(i)} \to S_0^{(i)} \, e^{-q_i T}$; $i = 1, 2$.

(iv) **Margrabe Again**: This last formula can be used to re-derive Margrabe's result. Consider the following identity for the payoff:

$$\max\left[0, S_T^{(1)} - S_T^{(2)}\right] = \max\left[S_T^{(1)}, S_T^{(2)}\right] - S_T^{(2)}$$

and find the present value of its expected value:

$$f_{\text{Marg rabe}}\left(S_0^{(1)}, S_0^{(2)}\right) = f_{\max}\left(S_0^{(1)}, S_0^{(2)}\right) - PV[E[S_T^{(2)}]]$$

This formula must be homogeneous in $S_0^{(2)}$ and $S_0^{(1)}$. The first term on the right-hand side was evaluated in the last subsection. The second term is simply the forward rate, but remember that we are working in units which imply a zero interest rate [see Section 12.1(iii)]. The last term can therefore simply be written $S_0^{(2)}$. Using the properties of the cumulative normal distribution given in Appendix A.1 then gives

$$\begin{aligned}
f_{\text{Marg rabe}}\left(S_0^{(1)}, S_0^{(2)}\right) &= S_0^{(1)} \, N[d_{1/2}] + S_0^{(2)} \, N[d_{2/1}] - S_0^{(2)} \\
&= S_0^{(1)} \, N[d_{1/2}] - S_0^{(2)}\{1 - N[d_{2/1}]\} \\
&= S_0^{(1)} \, N[d_{1/2}] - S_0^{(2)} \, N[d_{1/2} - \sigma_Q \sqrt{T}]
\end{aligned}$$

## 12.3    MAXIMUM OF THREE ASSETS

(i) The method of the last section can be extended to three assets. $f_{\max}(S_0^{(1)}, S_0^{(2)}, S_0^{(3)})$ is today's value of an option whose payoff at time $T$ is $\max[S_T^{(1)}, S_T^{(2)}, S_T^{(3)}]$. The value of this option may be written

$$\begin{aligned}
f_{\max}\left(S_0^{(1)}, S_0^{(2)}, S_0^{(3)}\right) &= f(1 \max) + f(2 \max) + f(3 \max) \\
&= PV[E[S_T^{(1)}: S_T^{(2)} < S_T^{(1)}; S_T^{(3)} < S_T^{(1)}] + E[S_T^{(2)}: S_T^{(1)} < S_T^{(2)}; S_T^{(3)} < S_T^{(2)}] \\
&\quad + E[S_T^{(3)}: S_T^{(2)} < S_T^{(3)}; S_T^{(1)} < S_T^{(3)}]]
\end{aligned}$$

This additive pattern reflects a well-known property of probabilities: if three events are mutually exclusive, the probability of all three happening is equal to the sum of the probabilities of any single one happening. As in the two asset case, the option must be homogeneous in $S_0^{(1)}$, $S_0^{(2)}$ and $S_0^{(3)}$, so that the first term can be written

$$f(1 \max) = S_0^{(1)} \, PV[P[Q_T^{2/1} < 1; Q_T^{3/1} < 1]]$$

where $Q_t^{i/j} = S_t^{(i)}/S_t^{(j)}$. As in the last two sections, all quantities on the right-hand side (except $S_0^{(1)}$) are measured in units of commodity $S^{(1)}$. We consequently put $r \to 0$ when we perform our risk-neutral calculations, as explained in Section 12.1(ii). The three terms in the equation for $f_{\max}$ are completely symmetrical so only one of them needs to be evaluated.

(ii) Setting $r \to 0$, the present value discount factor becomes unity, and we see from Appendix A.1 that

$$z_t^{i/j} = \frac{\ln Q_t^{i/j} / Q_0^{i/j} + \frac{1}{2}\sigma_{i/j}^2 t}{\sigma_{i/j}\sqrt{t}}$$

is a standard normal variate. Effecting a change of variables in the manner of equations (A1.7), and using the bivariate normal definitions of equation (A1.12) gives

$$P\big(Q_T^{2/1} < 1; Q_T^{3/1} < 1\big) = \int_0^1 \int_0^1 F_{\text{joint}}\big(Q_T^{2/1}, Q_T^{3/1}\big)\, dQ_T^{2/1}\, dQ_T^{3/1}$$

$$\int_{-\infty}^{d_{2/1}} \int_{-\infty}^{d_{3/1}} n_2\big(z_T^{2/1}, z_T^{3/1}; \rho_{2/1,3/1}\big)\, dz_T^{2/1} dz_T^{3/1} = N_2[d_{2/1}, d_{3/1}; \rho_{2/1,3/1}]$$

$$d_{i/j} = \frac{-\ln Q_0^{i/j} + \frac{1}{2}\sigma_{i/j}^2 T}{\sigma_{i/j}\sqrt{T}} = \frac{-\ln S_0^i / S_0^j + \frac{1}{2}\sigma_{i/j}^2 T}{\sigma_{i/j}\sqrt{T}}; \qquad \sigma_{i/k}^2 = \sigma_i^2 + \sigma_k^2 - \rho_{ik}\sigma_i\sigma_k$$

$$\rho_{i/k,j/k} = \frac{1}{\sigma_{i/k}\sigma_{j/k}}\big\{\sigma_i\sigma_j\rho_{ij} - \sigma_i\sigma_k\rho_{ik} - \sigma_j\sigma_k\rho_{jk} + \sigma_k^2\big\}$$

The last expression is demonstrated in equations (A1.24). Taking all three terms, we have by symmetry

$$\begin{aligned}
f_{\max}\big(S_0^{(1)}, S_0^{(2)}, S_0^{(3)}\big) &= S_0^{(1)} N_2[d_{2/1}, d_{3/1}; \rho_{2/1,3/1}] \\
&+ S_0^{(2)} N_2[d_{1/2}, d_{3/2}; \rho_{1/2,3/2}] + S_0^{(3)} N_2[d_{1/3}, d_{2/3}; \rho_{1/3,2/3}]
\end{aligned} \tag{12.3}$$

As usual, continuous dividends can be accommodated by substituting $S_0^{(i)} \to S_0^{(i)} e^{-q_i T}$ for each asset. An important specific case is an option for the maximum of two stochastic assets or cash. We use equation (12.3) but set

$$S_0^{(3)} e^{-q_3 T} \to X e^{-rT}; \qquad \sigma_X = 0$$

to give

$$\begin{aligned}
f_{\max}\big(S_0^{(1)}, S_0^{(2)}, X\big) &= S_0^{(1)} N_2[d_{2/1}, d_{X/1}; \rho_{2/1,X/1}] \\
&+ S_0^{(2)} N_2[d_{1/2}, d_{X/2}; \rho_{1/2,X/2}] + X e^{-rT} N_2[d_{1/X}, d_{2/X}; \rho_{1/X,2/X}]
\end{aligned} \tag{12.4}$$

where the results of equations (A1.24) give $\sigma_{i/X} = \sigma_{X/i} = \sigma_i$ and

$$\rho_{1/X,2/X} = \rho_{2/X,1/X} = \rho_{12}; \qquad \rho_{X/2,1/2} = \frac{\sigma_2 - \sigma_1\rho_{12}}{\sigma_{1/2}}; \qquad \rho_{X/1,2/1} = \frac{\sigma_1 - \sigma_2\rho_{12}}{\sigma_{2/1}}$$

The adaptations to be made to the $d_{i/j}$ are self-evident.

The techniques of this and the last section can be extended to larger numbers of assets (Johnson, 1987); the formula for $f_{\max}$ will then involve multivariate normal functions of higher order. In practice, correlations between assets tend to be highly unstable – more so than for example volatility. Any derivative which is a function of a correlation therefore needs to be treated with caution. But a derivative whose price is a complicated function of several correlation coefficients probably has little commercial future.

## 12.4   RAINBOW OPTIONS

These are call or put options on the maximum or minimum of two stochastic assets. Their pricing is obtained directly from equation (12.4) (see also Rubinstein, 1991a).

(i) **Call on the Maximum**: This is by far the most commonly encountered rainbow option, and has payoff

$$\max\left[0, \max\left[S_T^{(1)}, S_T^{(2)}\right] - X\right] = \max\left[S_T^{(1)}, S_T^{(2)}, X\right] - X$$

This immediately leads us to the formula

$$C(\max) = f_{\max}\left(S_0^{(1)}, S_0^{(2)}, X\right) - X\,e^{-rT}$$

(ii) **Put on the Maximum**: Regarding $\max[S_T^{(1)}, S_T^{(2)}]$ as an asset in its own right, put call parity gives

$$\text{Put}\left(\max\left[S_T^{(1)}, S_T^{(2)}\right]\right) + \max\left[S_T^{(1)}, S_T^{(2)}\right] = \text{Call}\left(\max\left[S_T^{(1)}, S_T^{(2)}\right]\right) + X\,e^{-rT}$$

which leads directly to the formula

$$P(\max) = f_{\max}\left(S_0^{(1)}, S_0^{(2)}, X\right) - f_{\max}\left(S_0^{(1)}, S_0^{(2)}\right)$$

(iii) **Call and Put on the Minimum**: Suppose you have calls on two different assets, but someone else has a call on you for the larger of the two assets. What are you left with? Simply a call on the smaller of the two assets.

In the notation of this chapter, this is written

$$C(\min) = C\left(S_0^{(1)}\right) + C\left(S_0^{(1)}\right) - C(\max)$$

$$P(\min) = P\left(S_0^{(1)}\right) + P\left(S_0^{(1)}\right) - P(\max)$$

## 12.5   BLACK SCHOLES EQUATION FOR TWO ASSETS

An extension of the Black Scholes differential equation can be derived, which describes an option on two assets. The steps in the derivation follow those of Section 4.2 precisely, and the reader is advised to return to that section in order to follow the amendments below

(i) As in the one asset case, we start with the assumption that a portfolio can be constructed, consisting of the derivative and the underlying stocks, in such quantities that the change in value of the portfolio over a small time interval $\delta t$ is independent of the stock price movements. Otherwise expressed, we can hedge this option with the underlying stocks. The value of the portfolio is written

$$f_t - S_t^{(1)}\Delta_t^{(1)} - S_t^{(2)}\Delta_t^{(2)}$$

where the sign conventions of Chapter 4 are used (negative means a short position). In the small time interval $\delta t$, the value of this portfolio moves by

$$\delta f_t - \delta S_t^{(1)}\Delta_t^{(1)} - \delta S_t^{(2)}\Delta_t^{(2)} - S_t^{(1)}\Delta_t^{(1)}q_1\delta t - S_t^{(2)}\Delta_t^{(2)}q_2\delta t$$

Arbitrage arguments tell us that *if* the portfolio value movement does not depend on the stock price movement, then the rate of return due to this movement (plus any other predictable cash flows) must equal the risk-free return:

$$\frac{\delta f_t - \delta S_t^{(1)} \Delta_t^{(1)} - \delta S_t^{(2)} \Delta_t^{(2)} - S_t^{(1)} \Delta_t^{(1)} q_1 \delta t - S_t^{(2)} \Delta_t^{(2)} q_2 \delta t}{f_t - S_t^{(1)} \Delta_t^{(1)} - S_t^{(2)} \Delta_t^{(2)}} = r\delta t \qquad (12.5)$$

(ii) In order to obtain the generalized Black Scholes equation, we now need to substitute for $\delta S_t^{(1)}$, $\delta S_t^{(2)}$ and $\delta f_t$ in the last equation.

The two stock prices are assumed to follow the following Wiener processes:

$$\delta S_t^{(1)} = S_t^{(1)}(\mu_1 - q_1)\delta t + S_t^{(1)} \sigma_1 \delta W_t^{(1)}$$

$$\delta S_t^{(2)} = S_t^{(2)}(\mu_2 - q_2)\delta t + S_t^{(2)} \sigma_2 \delta W_t^{(2)}$$

which immediately gives us two of the terms to substitute. The third term is obtained from Ito's lemma which needs to be adapted slightly.

(iii) **Ito's Lemma for Two Assets**: As set out in Section 3.4, Ito's lemma is based on two elements:

1. The observation that $(\delta W_t)^2 \to \delta t$ as $\delta t \to 0$. We use this relationship again, but there is an additional relationship, based on precisely the same reasoning, which states that

$$\delta W_t^{(1)} \delta W_t^{(2)} \to \rho_{12} \delta t \quad \text{as} \quad \delta t \to 0$$

where $\rho_{12}$ is the correlation between the two Brownian motions.

2. Taylor's expansion for two assets, making these last substitutions and rejecting all terms of order greater than $O[\delta t]$ becomes

$$\delta f_t = \left\{ \frac{\partial f_t}{\partial t} + (\mu_1 - q_1)S_t^{(1)} \frac{\partial f_t}{\partial S_t^{(1)}} + (\mu_2 - q_2)S_t^{(2)} \frac{\partial f_t}{\partial S_t^{(2)}} \right.$$

$$+ \frac{1}{2}\sigma_1^2 \left(S_t^{(1)}\right)^2 \frac{\partial^2 f_t}{\partial \left(S_t^{(1)}\right)^2} + \rho_{12}\sigma_1\sigma_2 S_t^{(1)} S_t^{(2)} \frac{\partial^2 f_t}{\partial S_t^{(1)} S_t^{(2)}}$$

$$+ \left. \frac{1}{2}\sigma_2^2 \left(S_t^{(2)}\right)^2 \frac{\partial^2 f_t}{\partial \left(S_t^{(2)}\right)^2} \right\}\delta t + S_t^{(1)}\sigma_1 \frac{\partial f_t}{\partial S_t^{(1)}} \delta W_t^{(1)} + S_t^{(2)}\sigma_2 \frac{\partial f_t}{\partial S_t^{(2)}} \delta W_t^{(2)}$$

(iv) Having made the necessary substitutions back into equation (12.5), we set the coefficients of $\delta W_t^{(1)}$ and $\delta W_t^{(2)}$ equal to zero, reflecting the fact that the portfolio is perfectly hedged, to give

$$0 = \frac{\partial f_t}{\partial t} + (r - q_1)S_t^{(1)} \frac{\partial f_t}{\partial S_t^{(1)}} + (r - q_2)S_t^{(2)} \frac{\partial f_t}{\partial S_t^{(2)}} - r f_t$$

$$+ \frac{1}{2} \left\{ \sigma_1^2 \left(S_t^{(1)}\right)^2 \frac{\partial^2 f_t}{\partial \left(S_t^{(1)}\right)^2} + \sigma_2^2 \left(S_t^{(2)}\right)^2 \frac{\partial^2 f_t}{\partial \left(S_t^{(2)}\right)^2} + 2\rho_{12}\sigma_1\sigma_2 S_t^{(1)} S_t^{(2)} \frac{\partial^2 f_t}{\partial S_t^{(1)} S_t^{(2)}} \right\} \quad (12.6)$$

This can be written in more familiar form by making the substitution $\partial/\partial t = -\partial/\partial T$ where $T$ is the time to maturity of an option [see Section 1.1(v)], and setting $t = 0$:

$$\frac{\partial f_0}{\partial T} = (r - q_1)S_0^{(1)} \frac{\partial f_0}{\partial S_0^{(1)}} + (r - q_2)S_0^{(2)} \frac{\partial f_0}{\partial S_0^{(2)}} - r f_0$$

$$+ \frac{1}{2} \left\{ \sigma_1^2 \left(S_0^{(1)}\right)^2 \frac{\partial^2 f_0}{\partial \left(S_0^{(1)}\right)^2} + \sigma_2^2 \left(S_0^{(2)}\right)^2 \frac{\partial^2 f_0}{\partial S_0^{(2)2}} + 2\rho_{12}\sigma_1\sigma_2 S_0^{(1)} S_0^{(2)} \frac{\partial^2 f_0}{\partial S_0^{(1)} S_0^{(2)}} \right\} \quad (12.7)$$

## 12.6    BINOMIAL MODEL FOR TWO ASSET OPTIONS

(i) An extension of the now familiar binomial tree to three dimensions is shown in Figure 12.1. For the sake of simplicity, we use the space variables $x_t = \ln S_t^{(1)}/S_0^{(1)}$ and $y_t = \ln S_t^{(2)}/S_0^{(2)}$, rather than working directly with stock prices. This means that the step sizes (up/down and left/right) are of constant sizes, rather than proportional to the stock values; the first node in the tree has value zero. A tree of this type is described by the basic arithmetic random walk in Appendix A.2. Equation (3.5) shows that if the risk-neutral drift of $S_t^{(1)}$ is $r - q_1$, then the drift of $x_t$ is $r - q_1 - \frac{1}{2}\sigma_1^2 = m_x$, and similarly for $y_t$.

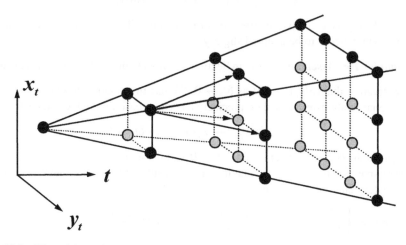

**Figure 12.1**    Binomial tree for two assets

(ii) *Uncorrelated Assets*: Consider the first cell in this tree. Figure 12.2 shows this cell looking at the pyramid from the apex. In the middle of the rectangle we have the starting node with $x_0, y_0 = 0$. From this point we move a time step of length $\delta t$ and $x_0$ and $y_0$ move to one of the four combinations whose values are given at the corners of the rectangle. In this simple case, $x_{\delta t}$ can take two values: $x_u$ and $x_d$; similarly, $y_{\delta t}$ takes values $y_r$ and $y_l$. This means that the movement in asset 2 is the same whether asset 1 moves up or down, i.e. the two asset prices are uncorrelated.

It is shown in Appendix A.2 and in Chapter 7 that with a binomial model for a single underlying asset, we have discretion in choosing nodal values and the probabilities of up- and down-jumps. This is also the case with a three-dimensional tree, and we will choose the transition probability to each corner to be $\frac{1}{4}$ (cf. the Cox–Ross–Rubinstein discretization of the simple binomial tree with $p = \frac{1}{2}$). Our task now is to find each of the nodal values corresponding to these probabilities (Rubinstein, 1994).

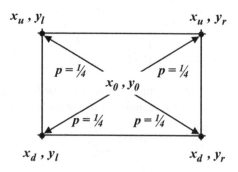

**Figure 12.2**    Single binomial cell: uncorrelated

Using the approach of Section 7.1(iv), the Wiener processes for $x_t$ and $y_t$ are written

$$\delta x_t = m_x \delta t + \sigma_x \sqrt{\delta t} z_1$$
$$\delta y_t = m_y \delta t + \sigma_y \sqrt{\delta t} z_2$$

where $z_1$ and $z_2$ are uncorrelated standard normal variates. Matching local drifts and volatilities to the tree, and using equation (A2.5) of the Appendix means that we can write

$$\mathrm{E}[\delta x_t] = m_x \delta t = \tfrac{1}{2}(x_u + x_d)$$
$$\mathrm{var}[\delta x_t] = \sigma_x^2 \delta t = \tfrac{1}{4}\left(x_u^2 + x_d^2\right) - \mathrm{E}^2[\delta x_t] = \tfrac{1}{4}(x_u - x_d)^2$$

which solves to

$$x_u = m_x \delta t + \sigma_x \sqrt{\delta t}; \qquad x_d = m_x \delta t - \sigma_x \sqrt{\delta t}$$

Similarly

$$y_r = m_y \delta t + \sigma_y \sqrt{\delta t}; \qquad y_l = m_y \delta t - \sigma_y \sqrt{\delta t}$$

(iii) **Correlated Assets:** It is much more difficult to find the nodal values in this case since the value of $y_{\delta t}$ will depend on the value of $x_{\delta t}$. In graphical terms, the grid becomes squashed so that each cell when viewed from the apex turns into the parallelogram of Figure 12.3. As before, we exercise the discretion we are allowed, first by choosing the transition probabilities to each corner to be $\tfrac{1}{4}$, and second by only allowing $x_{\delta t}$ to have two values: $x_u$ and $x_d$. This time, $y_{\delta t}$ takes different values at each corner.

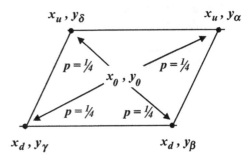

**Figure 12.3**   Single binomial cell: correlated

The Wiener processes can be written

$$\delta x_t = m_x \delta t + \sigma_x \sqrt{\delta t} z_1$$
$$\delta y_t = m_y \delta t + \sigma_y \sqrt{\delta t} z_2 = m_y \delta t + \sigma_y \sqrt{\delta t}\{\rho z_1 + \sqrt{1 - \rho^2} z_3\}$$

where $z_1$ and $z_3$ are independently distributed, standard normal variates [see Appendix A.1(vi)].

A heuristic argument might be made that in the first of these two processes, $x_u$ and $x_d$ are obtained by putting $z_1 \to 1$ and $z_1 \to -1$ respectively. Similarly, putting $z_3$ equal to $\pm 1$ corresponding to each of the values for $z_1$ gives

$$x_u = m_x \delta t + \sigma_x \sqrt{\delta t}; \qquad x_d = m_x \delta t - \sigma_x \sqrt{\delta t}$$

and

$$\delta y_\alpha = m_y \delta t + \sigma_y \sqrt{\delta t}\{\rho + \sqrt{1 - \rho^2}\}$$
$$\delta y_\beta = m_y \delta t - \sigma_y \sqrt{\delta t}\{\rho - \sqrt{1 - \rho^2}\}$$
$$\delta y_\gamma = m_y \delta t - \sigma_y \sqrt{\delta t}\{\rho + \sqrt{1 - \rho^2}\}$$
$$\delta y_\delta = m_y \delta t + \sigma_y \sqrt{\delta t}\{\rho - \sqrt{1 - \rho^2}\}$$

So much for the flaky argument: a proper confirmation that these are indeed the correct expressions is obtained by substituting them in the following defining equations:

$$E\langle\delta y_t\rangle = m_y \delta t \qquad \text{var}\langle\delta y_t\rangle = \sigma_y^2 \delta t \qquad \text{cov}\langle\delta x_t \delta y_t\rangle = \rho\sigma_x\sigma_y \delta t$$

(iv) Payoff values of the option can be calculated for each final node since each of these contains a value for $x_T$ and $y_T$. Discount these back through the tree in the normal way, remembering that the values at four nodes are needed for each step back (rather than two in the single asset tree); probabilities are all set at $p = \frac{1}{4}$. For American options, derivative values at each node are replaced by exercise value if necessary.

(v) **Alternatives to Trees:** It seems that we can extend this tree to higher dimensions to calculate options on three or more assets, but this is not really practical for three reasons:

- Correlations in finance are extremely unstable, except for a very special case discussed in Chapter 14. Calculations involving correlation between the prices of two stocks are useful, but must be treated with extreme caution. Three-way correlation just compounds the instability of results to the point where they have little practical use.
- The mental agility needed to analyze $N$-dimensional trees is discouraging.
- There are deep theoretical reasons why the efficiency of a tree drops off sharply with an increasing number of dimensions: see Section 10.1(iii).

An example is given in Chapter 10 of the pricing of a two asset spread option using quasi-Monte Carlo. This method is very quick and accurate, and can readily be extended to several assets.

# 13

# Currency Translated Options

## 13.1 INTRODUCTION

(i) These options do not require much new theory, yet newcomers tend to find them fairly tricky. It is therefore best to make the analysis as concrete as possible. Consider an international investment bank with offices in New York and Frankfurt. An American customer approaches the bank, looking for a call option on the stock of a German company which is quoted in euros. There are two issues to be decided: first, should the New York or the Frankfurt office handle the business, i.e. is the option better regarded as a euro option or as a dollar option? Second, how is it priced?

We will see that some options can be regarded as either € or $ options, although the analysis is different depending on the approach. But one thing is certain: if there are two approaches, they must give the same answer – apart perhaps from translations at the prevailing spot exchange rate, which have no economic consequence. It therefore makes sense to price the option in whichever framework is simpler (Reiner, 1992).

The following definitions and notation are used:

"Domestic Currency": US$     "Foreign Currency": €

$\phi_t$: Value of €1 in $ (i.e. $ price of the €); $ price $= \phi_t \times $ € price

$\psi_t$: Value of $1 in € (i.e. € price of the $); € price $= \psi_t \times $ $ price

$\psi_t = \phi_t^{-1}$

$S_t$: € price of a German stock;      $B_t^{€}$ : € value of a € zero coupon bond

$P_t = B_t^{€} \phi_t$: $ value of a € zero coupon bond;      $Q_t = S_t \phi_t$: $ value of a € stock

€ $X = $ € strike price;      $ $K = $ $ strike price

$r_{\$}, r_{€}$ and $q =$ interest rates and dividends

(ii) **Foreign Currency Strike; Floating Exchange Rate (Flexo):** The simplest case is when the American customer wants his call option on the € stock to have a € strike price. He pays for the option in $ at the spot rate at the beginning and has the payoff translated into $ at the prevailing rate at maturity. Clearly, this is one for the Frankfurt office, as the option is merely a € option on a German stock, with a € strike price. It is no different from the options routinely sold to the bank's German customers, except there happens to be a spot foreign exchange transaction at the beginning and at the end; it scarcely merits a name of its own.

## 13.2 DOMESTIC CURRENCY STRIKE (COMPO)

Suppose the customer has decided he wants the strike price to be fixed in $. The payoff would have the form max[0, $S_T - $50], where $S_T$ is denominated in €. $ and € denomination is mixed up in a non-trivial way so it is not clear whether we should regard this as a \$ or a € option; nor is it apparent whether the transaction is better handled in Frankfurt or New York. We will examine it from both viewpoints.

(i) *A € View:* The Frankfurt office of our bank sees an option whose payoff is max[0, € $S_T$ − € $K \psi_T$]. This is an option to exchange one € stochastic asset ($K$ times the € price of a dollar) for another (the € stock price); this is just Margrabe's payoff. In Section 12.1 it was seen that the value of this option is

$$€ f_{\text{compo}} = € \{ S_0 \, e^{-q^T} \, N[d_1] - K \psi_0 \, e^{r_\$ T} \, N[d_2] \} \tag{13.1}$$

$$d_1 = \frac{\ln S_0 \, e^{-q^T} / \psi_0 \, e^{-r_\$ T} + \frac{1}{2} \sigma_{S/\psi}^2 T}{\sigma_{S/\psi} \sqrt{T}}$$

$$d_2 = d_1 - \sigma_{S/\psi} \sqrt{T}; \qquad \sigma_{S/\psi}^2 = \sigma_S^2 + \sigma_\psi^2 - 2\rho_{S\psi} \, \sigma_S \sigma_\psi$$

Note that since $\psi_t = \phi_t^{-1}$ we may write $\sigma_\psi^2 = \sigma_\phi^2$; $\rho_{S\psi} = -\rho_{S\phi}$.

From the analysis of Section 12.1(iv), it is apparent that the hedge for this option is to short $e^{-q^T} N[d_1]$ shares of stock; convert enough of the € proceeds of this short position to buy \$$K \, e^{-r_\$ T} N[d_2]$ and deposit these dollars to yield $r_\$$; no € cash is borrowed or deposited.

(ii) *A US\$ View:* While Frankfurt is doing these calculations, the rival team in New York takes a different view: they see a stock price whose terminal value in US\$ is $Q_T = S_T \phi_T$. The payoff of this option is therefore written US\$ max[0, \$$Q_T$ − \$$K$]. In fact, the New York office claims that Frankfurt does not need to get involved at all, since the stock is simultaneously quoted on the Frankfurt *and* New York exchanges. This is no different from any other stock quoted in New York and the fact that the ultimate underlying company is German is irrelevant; the option is therefore no different from any domestic US call option.

The price of this "purely American" call option is given by the Black Scholes formula of equation (5.1):

$$\$ f_{\text{compo}} = \$ \{ Q_0 \, e^{-q^T} \, N[d_1] - K \, e^{-r_\$ T} \, N[d_2] \} \tag{13.2}$$

$$d_1 = \frac{\ln Q_0 \, e^{-qT} / K \, e^{-r_\$ T} + \frac{1}{2} \sigma_Q^2 T}{\sigma_Q \sqrt{T}}; \qquad d_2 = d_1 - \sigma_Q; \qquad Q_0 = S_0 \phi_0 = S_0 / \psi_0$$

In order to price this we use (amongst other parameters) the dividend yield and the volatility:

- Using a proportional dividend yield, the stock is regarded as throwing off a continuous dividend $q \delta t$ in any infinitesimal period $\delta t$. Clearly, if everything is converted from € to US\$ by a variable exchange rate, the *proportional* dividend yield remains unchanged as we move currency.
- The historical volatility of the stock price quoted in New York may be obtained from an information service such as Bloomberg; but if this is not available, a value can be calculated from the volatilities of the stock price quoted in Frankfurt and the exchange rate volatility. The relationship is demonstrated in Appendix A.1(xi):

$$\sigma_Q^2 = \sigma_{S\phi}^2 = \sigma_S^2 + \sigma_\phi^2 + 2\rho_{S\phi} \sigma_S \sigma_\phi$$

Substituting these results in the Black Scholes formula shows that the results obtained using either this US\$ view or the previous € view are identical. In general, the ADR reasoning is more useful as it can be applied more widely than the Margrabe approach, which is limited to European calls and puts.

## 13.3 FOREIGN CURRENCY STRIKE: FIXED EXCHANGE RATE (QUANTO)

(i) **Quantoed Call Option**: Suppose our US customer has changed his mind: he wants a € option on the German stock with a strike price in €; but he is concerned about a possible weakening of € and therefore wants the conversion rate of the € payoff back into \$ to be guaranteed. Note the difference between this and the flexo: the only difference is that the conversion of the € payout was at the prevailing spot rate. If we are to receive a fixed amount of € in the future, we can of course hedge the uncertainty by using the forward foreign exchange rate; but in this case, the size of the € payout is unknown, making the pricing more difficult.

Another way of describing this option is to say that for each € that the stock price has risen in the time $T$, the client receives a fixed number of US\$. This is more akin to the way quantos are often quoted, e.g. a payoff of \$10 for each point that the Japanese Nikkei index exceeds 18,000 at maturity. Alternatively, if the payoff of a euro stock option is €100, the payoff of the corresponding quanto is \$100. This seems an unnatural instrument and is often referred to as an "option in the wrong currency".

Returning to our German stock and American customer, the payoff of the quanto may be written \$max$[0, €S_T - €X] \bar{\phi}$ where $\bar{\phi}$ is the constant exchange rate. This is a curious hybrid quantity, mixing € and \$; but the value of this payoff expressed in € at maturity is a pure € quantity:

$$€\psi_T \max[0, \ S_T - X] \bar{\phi} = \max[0, \ \psi_T S_T - X\psi_T] \bar{\phi} = \max[0, \ U_T - X\psi_T] \bar{\phi}$$

Once again, we have a Margrabe's option: the exchange of stochastic asset $U_T$ for stochastic asset $X\psi_T$. The price of this option is

$$€f_{\text{quanto}} = € \left\{ U_0 e^{-q_U T} N[d_1] - X\psi_0 e^{-r_\$ T} N[d_2] \right\} \bar{\phi}$$

$$d_1 = \frac{\ln U_0 e^{-q_U T} / X\psi_0 e^{-r_\$ T} + \frac{1}{2}\sigma_{U/X\psi}^2 T}{\sigma_{U/X\psi} \sqrt{T}}$$

$$d_2 = d_1 - \sigma_{U/X\psi} \sqrt{T}; \qquad \sigma_{U/X\psi}^2 = \sigma_U^2 + \sigma_{X\psi}^2 + 2\rho_{U/X\psi} \sigma_U \sigma_{X\psi}$$

(ii) What we have described as the unnatural appearance of a quanto becomes apparent at this point. The quantity $U_T = \psi_T S_T$ has no natural physical meaning. $\phi_T S_T$ looks very similar, and is the German stock price translated into dollars; but $\psi_T S_T$ has as much physical significance as the price of oil multiplied by the price of cheese. However, it is a lognormally distributed random variable and we can treat it simply as a mathematical entity. But this begs a critical question: what precisely is the meaning of the "dividend" $q_U$, and can we find a formula for it in terms of observed variables? The answer is given by equation (A1.23) in the Appendix: in terms of the variables of the present section, this can be written

$$q_U = q + r_\$ - r_\epsilon - \rho_{S\psi} \sigma_S \sigma_\psi$$

Substituting this into the last equation and also using the result $\sigma^2_{U/X\psi} = \sigma^2_{S\psi/X\psi} = \sigma^2_S$ from equation (A1.24) allows us to write the final result

$$\text{€} f_{\text{quanto}} = \text{€}\,\psi_0 \left\{ S_0 \, e^{-(q+r_\$-r_\text{€}-\rho_{S\psi}\sigma_S\sigma_\psi)T} \, N[d_1] - X \, e^{-r_\$T} \, N[d_2] \right\} \bar{\phi}$$

(13.3)

$$d_1 = \frac{\ln\left(S_0 \, e^{-(q+r_\$-r_\text{€}-\rho_{S\psi}\sigma_S\sigma_\psi)T}/X \, e^{-r_\$T}\right) + \frac{1}{2}\sigma^2_S T}{\sigma_S\sqrt{T}}; \qquad d_2 = d_1 - \sigma_S\sqrt{T}$$

The US\$ price of this option is obtained simply by dropping the constant $\psi_0$ from the front of the formula. The rule for finding the price of a € call option quantoed into US\$ is therefore simple. Use the formula for a € option (a flexo) but with the following substitutions:

- Replace the euro discount factor by the US discount factor: $e^{-r_\text{€}T} \rightarrow e^{-r_\$T}$.
- Replace the stock dividend $q$ by $q \rightarrow q + r_\$ - r_\text{€} - \rho_{S\psi}\sigma_S\sigma_\psi$.

Finally, if the reader has a feeling of unease with the rather cumbersome arguments for pricing a quanto, he will be relieved to know that this is not the best we can do. The next subsection gives a more elegant and general derivation of the same result and in Chapter 25 we use stochastic calculus to gain further insights.

(iii) **General Quantoed Option**: The material so far in this section has specifically dealt with a European call option. This covers most cases encountered in the market, and a put option could be handled in just the same way; but the results can be generalized to cover any quantoed option, however complicated.

Take a euro option whose value at time $t$ is $\text{€} f_t$ and whose payoff is $\text{€} f_T$. The corresponding quanto (into US\$) can be written $\text{€} f_{\text{quanto}}(t)$ and we previously saw that

$$\text{€} f_{\text{quanto}}(T) = \text{€}\,\psi_T f_T \bar{\phi}$$

Let us define a quantity $F_t$ by

$$\text{€} f_{\text{quanto}}(t) = \text{€}\,\psi_t F_t \,\bar{\phi}$$

Our previous result implies that $F_T = f_T$. This *does not* allow us to write $F_t = f_t$; but if we can set up a Black Scholes type equation for $F_t$, the initial conditions will be the same as they would be for $f_t$. Note that the payoff $F_T(=f_T)$ is completely independent of $\psi_t$ so that $F_T$ is independent of $\psi_T$.

$f_{\text{quanto}}(t)$ is a € asset dependent on two stochastic prices, and so satisfies the Black Scholes equation for two assets in the form given by equation (12.6), with $r \rightarrow r_\text{€}$; $S^{(1)}_t \rightarrow S_t$; $q_1 \rightarrow q$; $S^{(2)}_t \rightarrow \psi_t$; $q_2 \rightarrow r_S$, i.e.

$$0 = \frac{\partial f_{\text{quanto}}(t)}{\partial t} + (r_\text{€} - q)\, S_t \frac{\partial f_{\text{quanto}}(t)}{\partial S_t} + (r_\text{€} - r_\$)\, \psi_t \frac{\partial f_{\text{quanto}}(t)}{\partial \psi_t} - r f_{\text{quanto}}(t)_t$$

$$+ \frac{1}{2}\left\{ \sigma^2_S S^2_t \frac{\partial^2 f_t}{\partial S^2_t} + \sigma^2_\psi \psi^2_t \frac{\partial^2 f_{\text{quanto}}(t)}{\partial \psi^2_t} + 2\rho_{S\psi}\sigma_S\sigma_\psi S_t \psi_t \frac{\partial^2 f_{\text{quanto}}(t)}{\partial S_t \partial \psi_t} \right\}$$

Writing $f_{\text{quanto}}(t) = \psi_t F_t \bar{\phi}$ and remembering that $F_t$ is independent of $\psi_t$, i.e. $\partial F_t/\partial \psi_t =$

$\partial^2 F_t / \partial \psi_t^2 = 0$, allows us to simplify the last equation to

$$0 = \frac{\partial F_t}{\partial t} + (r_{\epsilon} - q + \rho_{S\psi} \sigma_S \sigma_\psi) S_t \frac{\partial F_t}{\partial S_t} + \frac{1}{2} \sigma_S^2 S_t^2 \frac{\partial^2 F_t}{\partial S_t^2} - r_{\$} f_t$$

This is just the single asset Black Scholes equation for the domestic German option, but with the following parameter shifts:

- First put $r_{\epsilon} \to r_{\$}$.
- Followed by $q \to q + r_{\$} - r_{\epsilon} - \rho_{S\psi} \sigma_S \sigma_\psi$.

It was noted above that the initial conditions for $F_t$ are just those for $f_t$, the corresponding domestic (€)option. Thus *any* € option can be quantoed to simply by making the above parameter shifts in the formula for the domestic option. This is the result that was obtained for a call option in the last subparagraph, but this analysis gives the procedures for quantoing any option.

(iv) **Hedging**: The replication equation for a quanto may be written

$$f_{\text{quanto}} = \Delta_S S_0 + \Delta_\psi \psi_0 - B(S_0, \psi_0, T)$$

where $S_0$ and $\psi_0$ are today's stock price (in €) and US\$ price (in €). From equation (13.3), we have for a call option

$$\Delta_\psi = \frac{\partial f_{\text{quanto}}}{\partial \psi_0} = \frac{f_{\text{quanto}}}{\psi_0}$$

which leaves $\Delta_S S_0 = B(S_0, \psi_0, T)$ in the replication equation. The replication strategy for this option may therefore be written:

- Invest a sum of € equal to the value of the quanto, convert this to US\$ and place it on deposit.
- Borrow enough € to buy the equity stock delta of the option.

In practice, this would be executed through the forward foreign exchange market.

## 13.4   SOME PRACTICAL CONSIDERATIONS

(i) If we look at the correlations between currencies and securities, we find that in general they are highly unstable – far more so than volatilities. There are of course exceptions: a German company with a large part of its assets in the US will have a stock price which is strongly correlated with the €/\$ exchange rate. But apart from such obvious cases, the observed correlation coefficient usually flops about, often changing sign as well as magnitude. We have developed nice pricing formulas containing a constant correlation coefficient, while in fact it is a random variable. There are two ways in which this is usually handled:

- Assume the worst case, putting the correlation coefficient equal to $+1$ or $-1$, depending on which leads to the most conservative pricing.
- Ignore the problem: if correlation is generally weak and frequently changing sign, it is often assumed that it will average out at zero over the life of the option. The option seller would then set the correlation equal to zero and pad out the volatility a little to cover any shortfall on the hedging. While this does not have any theoretical foundations, it is often the only way of doing business; pricing by the worst case method is usually uncompetitive.

(ii) **Quanto with $\rho = 0$:** In Section 13.3(iii) it was shown that any option can be quantoed from € to \$ and the effect on the price of the option is accounted for by making adjustments to the € interest rate and stock dividend rate. With $\rho = 0$, the effect of quantoing is to change the present value discount factor from $e^{-r_\epsilon T}$ to $e^{-r_\$ T}$ and the forward rate from $S_0 e^{(-r_\epsilon q)T}$ to $S_0 e^{(r_\$ q)T}$; so the net effect is just to change interest rates.

Most quantos are quantoed into a higher interest rate currency. If an option on a US stock is quantoed into pesos, the Mexican buyer can tell himself that he is not only eliminating FX risk but getting his option cheaper as well!

(iii) **Index Outperformance Options:** These are fairly popular in the investment community and are related to the options analyzed above. Consider an option to take advantage of the outperformance of the US S&P index over the German DAX.

- The payoff might be fixed as

$$€\max[0, \ \phi_T(\text{S\&P})_T - k(\text{DAX})_T] \quad \text{or} \quad \$\max[0, k(\text{S\&P})_T - \psi_T(\text{DAX})_T]$$

Depending on whether the payoff is to be in € or \$; $k$ is just a scaling constant. These are clearly Margrabe options where one of the assets is an ADR type security.
- If the fund manager were neither in Germany nor the US, but in the UK, the payoff might be required in sterling:

$$£\max\left[0, \ (\text{S\&P})_T / \phi_T^{(£/\$)} - (\text{CAC})_T / \phi_T^{£/€}\right]$$

Again, Margrabe is used, but between *two* ADR type securities.
- Alternatively, the payoff may be defined as

$$\max\left[0, k\frac{(\text{S\&P})_T}{(\text{DAX})_T}\phi_T - X\right]$$

Here we use a modification of the Black Scholes equation for the quotient of two \$-securities, $(\text{S\&P})_t$, and $(\text{DAX})_t / \phi_t$. The latter must in turn be decomposed into two lognormal random variables.

Note that each of the above options involves correlations between three or four random variables. Each of these correlations is likely to be unstable over time (although less so for stock indices than for single stocks).

(iv) Each of the above forms expresses the outperformance of the S&P over the DAX. Unfortunately, the most popular type of outperformance investment is a *spread option* whose payoff can be written

$$\$\max[0, [(\text{S\&P})_T - k(\text{DAX})_T / \phi_T]X]$$

While this looks simpler than the above forms, it is actually insoluble analytically. The problem is that the difference of two lognormal random variables is *not* itself lognormal; by contrast, the product *is* lognormal.

The reader is referred to Chapter 10 on Monte Carlo (particularly quasi-Monte Carlo) for quick and efficient numerical methods for pricing these options.

# 14

## Options on One Asset at Two Points
## in Time

In the last two chapters we have looked at various options involving two or more stochastic assets. The resulting pricing formulas involved the correlation between the asset prices and it was observed that in financial markets, correlation is usually highly unstable. We can derive elegant formulas based on the assumption of constant correlation, but in the real world most practitioners handle these products with extreme caution. However, there is one notable exception.

Suppose we have an option whose payoff depends on two prices: but instead of these being the prices of two different assets, they are the prices of the same asset at two different times $\tau$ and $T$ in the future. It is shown in Appendix A.1(vi) that the correlation between $S_\tau$ and $S_T$ (or to be more precise, between the logarithms of the price movements over the periods $\tau$ and $T$) is $\rho = \sqrt{\tau/T}$. This is just about the only case where we can have confidence in the value for $\rho$. The most common options in this category are described in this chapter, although other examples will be encountered in later chapters.

## 14.1 OPTIONS ON OPTIONS (COMPOUND OPTIONS)

(i) **Definitions**: We will consider an option (the **compound** option) on an **underlying** option. Both the compound and the underlying options can be either put or call options, so that we have four options to consider in all. Half the battle in pricing these options is simply getting the notation straight, and this can be summarized as follows:

| 0 | t | $\tau$ | T |
|---|---|---|---|
| now | time t | maturity of compound option | maturity of underlying option |

UNDERLYING STOCK:

$S_t$ and $\sigma$ — Stock price at time $t$ and volatility

UNDERLYING OPTIONS:

$C_u(S_t, X, t); P_u(S_t, X, t)$ — Value at time $t$ of an underlying call/put option. The general case is written $U(S_t, X, t)$

$T; X$ — Maturity date and strike of underlying options

COMPOUND OPTIONS:

$C_C; P_C; C_P; P_P$ — Value at time $t$ of a call on a call, put on a call, etc. The general case is written $\Omega_U(S_t, K, t)$

$\tau; K$ — Maturity date and strike of the compound options

$S_\tau^*$ — Critical stock price at time $\tau$, which determines whether or not the compound option is exercised. It is the value of $S_\tau$ that solves the equation $K = \Omega_u(S_\tau^*, X, \tau)$

(ii) *Payoffs of Compound Options*: Before moving on to pricing formulas, it is worth getting an idea of the likely shape of the curve of the compound price. Let us start with a call on a call. At time $\tau$, the price of the underlying call is given by the curve shown in Figure 14.1. The payoff of the compound call option is defined as

$$C_C(\tau) = \max[C_u(\tau) - K, 0]$$

Define $S_\tau^*$ as the value of $S_\tau$ for which $K = C_U(S_\tau^*, X, \tau)$. Clearly, the payoff diagram is made up of the $x$-axis and that part of the curve $C_U(\tau)$ which lies above $K$. This is shown as the solid line in Figure 14.2, together with the compound option price before maturity (dotted curve).

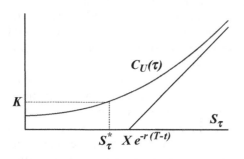

**Figure 14.1**   Underlying option (call)          **Figure 14.2**   Compound option (call on call)

Using the same analysis as for the call on call above, a put option on the underlying stock is represented by the curve shown in Figure 14.3. The payoff of the compound put option, shown in Figure 14.4, is

$$P_P(\tau) = \max[K - P_u(\tau), 0]$$

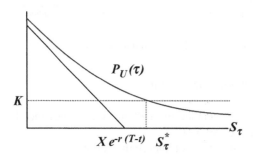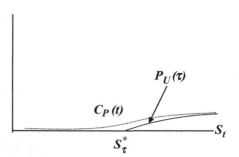

**Figure 14.3**   Underlying option (put)          **Figure 14.4**   Compound option (put on put)

The remaining two compound options have curves shown in Figures 14.5 and 14.6.

(iii) Consider the most common case: a call on a call. In order to calculate the value of this compound option, we use our well-established methodology of finding the expected value of the payoff in a risk-neutral world, and discounting to present value at the risk-free rate; but now, the ultimate payoff is a function of two future stock prices (Geske, 1979):

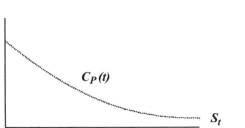

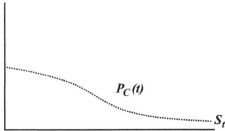

**Figure 14.5**   Compound option (call on put)     **Figure 14.6**   Compound option (put on call)

- $S_\tau$ – *The stock price when the compound option matures.* If this is less than some critical value $S_\tau^*$, it will not be worth exercising the compound option since the underlying option would then be cheaper to buy in the market. This may be written

$$\text{only exercise if } S_\tau^* < S_\tau, \text{ where } S_\tau^* \text{ is the solution to the equation}$$
$$K = S_\tau^* \, e^{-q(T-\tau)} \, N[d_1^*] - X \, e^{-r(T-\tau)} \, N[d_2^*]$$

  $d_1^*$ and $d_2^*$ are the usual Black Scholes parameters with the stock price set equal to $S_\tau^*$.

- $S_T$ – *The stock price when the underlying option matures.* The ultimate payoff at time $T$ is the payoff of the underlying call, if (and only if) the condition $S_\tau^* < S_\tau$ was fulfilled. This ultimate payoff is of course a function of $S_T$.

Since the value of a compound option depends on the expected values of both $S_\tau$ and $S_T$, we must examine their *joint* probability distribution.

(iv) Following the approach of Section 5.2(i) for the Black Scholes formula, the price of this option may be expressed as

$$C_C(0) = PV \left[ E \begin{bmatrix} \text{payoff of underlying option} & \Big| & \text{only if compound} \\ -\text{payment for underlying option} & \Big| & \text{option was exercised} \end{bmatrix}_{\text{risk neutral}} \right]$$

- "Only if compound option exercised" $\equiv S_\tau^* < S_\tau$.
- "Payment for underlying" $= K$ at time $\tau$.
- "Payoff of underlying option" (at time $T$) $= \max[0, S_T - X]$.

Combining this together and simplifying the notation gives

$$\begin{aligned} C_C(0) &= e^{-rT} \, E[\max[S_T - X, 0] : S_\tau^* < S_\tau] - e^{-r\tau} \, E[K : S_\tau^* < S_\tau] \\ &= e^{-rT} \, E[S_T - X : S_\tau^* < S_\tau; X < S_T] - e^{-r\tau} K \, P[S_\tau^* < S_\tau] \end{aligned} \qquad (14.1)$$

These expectations are evaluated explicitly in Appendix A.1(v) and (ix), to give

$$C_C(0) = S_0 \, e^{-qT} \, N_2[d_1, b_1; \rho] - X \, e^{-rT} \, N_2[d_2, b_2; \rho] - K \, e^{-r\tau} \, N[b_2] \qquad (14.2a)$$

where

$$d_1 = \frac{1}{\sigma\sqrt{T}}\left\{\ln\frac{S_0\,e^{-qT}}{X\,e^{-rT}} + \frac{1}{2}\sigma^2 T\right\};\qquad b_1 = \frac{1}{\sigma\sqrt{\tau}}\left\{\ln\frac{S_0\,e^{-q\tau}}{S_\tau^*\,e^{-r\tau}} + \frac{1}{2}\sigma^2\tau\right\}$$

$$d_2 = d_1 - \sigma\sqrt{T};\qquad b_2 = b_1 - \sigma\sqrt{\tau};\qquad \rho = \sqrt{\frac{\tau}{T}}$$

and $S_\tau^*$ is a solution to the equation $K = C_U(S_\tau^*, X, \tau)$. The lower limits of integration in the above-mentioned appendices are the values of $z_\tau$ and $z_T$ corresponding to $S_\tau = S_\tau^*$ and $S_T = X$.

(v) **General Formula**: The put–call parity relationship

$$C_C(0) + K\,e^{-r\tau} = P_C(0) + C_U(0)$$

may be used to calculate the formula for a put on an underlying call. The relationships $N[d] + N[-d] = 1$ and $N_2[d, b; \rho] + N_2[d, -b; -\rho] = N[d]$ [see equation (A1.17)] are used to simplify the algebra, giving

$$P_C(0) = X\,e^{-rT}\,N_2[d_2, -b_2; -\rho] - S_0\,e^{-qT}\,N_2[d_1, -b_1; -\rho] + K\,e^{-r\tau}\,N[-b_2]$$

Similar results are obtained for put and call options on an underlying put option. The four possibilities for compound options can be summarized in the general formula

$$\Omega_U(0) = \phi_U\phi_\Omega\{S_0\,e^{-qT}\,N_2[\phi_U d_1, \phi_U\phi_\Omega b_1; \phi_\Omega\rho] - X\,e^{-rT}\,N_2[\phi_U d_2, \phi_U\phi_\Omega b_2; \phi_\Omega\rho]\}$$
$$- \phi_\Omega K\,e^{-r\tau}\,N[\phi_U\phi_\Omega b_2] \tag{14.2b}$$

where

$$d_1 = \frac{1}{\sigma\sqrt{T}}\left\{\ln\frac{S_0\,e^{-qT}}{X\,e^{-rT}} + \frac{1}{2}\sigma^2 T\right\};\qquad b_1 = \frac{1}{\sigma\sqrt{\tau}}\left\{\ln\frac{S_0\,e^{-q\tau}}{S_\tau^*\,e^{-r\tau}} + \frac{1}{2}\sigma^2\tau\right\}$$

$$d_2 = d_1 - \sigma\sqrt{T};\qquad b_2 = b_1 - \sigma\sqrt{\tau};\qquad \rho = \sqrt{\frac{\tau}{T}};\qquad S_\tau^* \text{ solves } K = \Omega_U(S_\tau^*, X, \tau)$$

$$\phi_U = \begin{cases} +1 & \text{underlying call} \\ -1 & \text{underlying put} \end{cases}\qquad \phi_\Omega = \begin{cases} +1 & \text{compound call} \\ -1 & \text{compound put} \end{cases}$$

(vi) **Installment Options**: When they are first encountered, compound options often look to students like rather contrived exercises in option theory. However they do have very practical applications, as the following product description indicates:

- An investor receives a European call option which expires at time $T$ and has strike $X$.
- Instead of paying the entire premium now, the investor pays a first installment of $C_C$ today.
- At time $\tau$, the investor has the choice of walking away from the deal or paying a second installment $K$ and continuing to hold the option.

This structure clearly has appeal in certain circumstances; it is just the call on a call described in this section, but couched in slightly less dry terms.

## 14.2 COMPLEX CHOOSERS

Recall the simple chooser which was described in Section 11.2: we buy the option with strike $X$ at time $t = 0$ and at $t = \tau$ we decide whether the option which matures at $t = T$ is a put or a call. The complex chooser is similar in principle, but the put and call can have different maturities and strikes (Rubinstein, 1991b). The payoff at time $\tau$ is therefore written

$$\text{Payoff}_\tau = \max[C(S_\tau, X_C, T_C - \tau), P(S_\tau, X_P, T_P - \tau)]$$

For some critical price $S_\tau^*$ at time $\tau$, the value of the put and the call are exactly the same. $S_\tau^*$ is obtained from the equation

$$C(S_\tau^*, X_C, T_C - \tau) = P(S_\tau^*, X_P, T_P - \tau) \tag{14.3}$$

using some numerical procedure or the goal seek function of a spread sheet. For $S_\tau < S_\tau^*$, the payoff is the put option, while for $S_\tau^* < S_\tau$ the call option price is larger. Using the reasoning of Section 14.1(iv) gives

$$f_{\text{complex chooser}} = e^{-rT_C}\, E\langle S_{T_C} - X_C \mid S_\tau^* < S_\tau; X_c < S_{T_C}\rangle$$
$$+ e^{-rT_P}\, E\langle X_P - S_{T_P} \mid S_\tau < S_\tau^*; S_{T_P} < X_P\rangle$$

The first term here is just the first term of equation (14.1) for a call on a call; similarly, the second term is the first term of the formula for a call on a put. Instead of slogging through a bunch of double integrals again, we just steal the answer from equation (14.2b):

$$f_{\text{complex chooser}} = \left\{ S_0\, e^{-qT_C}\, N_2\big[d_1^{(C)}, b_1; \rho^{(C)}\big] - X_C\, e^{-rT_C}\, N_2\big[d_2^{(C)}, b_2; \rho^{(C)}\big] \right\}$$
$$- \left\{ S_0\, e^{-qT_P}\, N_2\big[-d_1^{(P)}, -b_1; \rho^{(P)}\big] - X_P\, e^{-rT_P}\, N_2\big[-d_2^{(P)}, -b_2; \rho^{(P)}\big] \right\} \tag{14.4}$$

$$d_1^{(i)} = \frac{1}{\sigma\sqrt{T_i}}\left\{ \ln\frac{S_0\, e^{-qT_i}}{X_i\, e^{-rT_i}} + \frac{1}{2}\sigma^2 T_i \right\}, \quad i = C \text{ or } P; \qquad b_1 = \frac{1}{\sigma\sqrt{\tau}}\left\{ \ln\frac{S_0\, e^{-q\tau}}{S_\tau^*\, e^{-r\tau}} + \frac{1}{2}\sigma^2\tau \right\}$$

$S_\tau^*$ solves equation (14.3):

$$d_2^{(i)} = d_1^{(i)} - \sigma\sqrt{T_i}; \qquad b_2 = b_1 - \sigma\sqrt{\tau}; \qquad \rho^{(i)} = \sqrt{\frac{\tau}{T_i}}$$

## 14.3 EXTENDIBLE OPTIONS

(i) Consider a European call option with maturity at time $\tau$ and strike price $K$; at maturity, the holder has the choice of exercising or not exercising (Longstaff, 1990). Now suppose that an additional feature is added to this option: the holder is given a third choice at maturity of extending the option to time $T$ at a new strike price $X$, in exchange for a fee of $k$. The payoff of this extendible option at time $\tau$ is

$$\max[0, S_\tau - K, C(S_\tau, X, T - \tau) - k]$$

The issues are best illustrated graphically. Figure 14.7 shows the value of the extended call option $C(S_\tau, X, T - \tau)$ at time $\tau$. This is just a simple graph of a European call option at time

$T - \tau$ before maturity. The points to note on the graph are:

- $X e^{-r(T-\tau)}$ which is the well-known value at which the upper asymptote to the curve for a call option crosses the $x$-axis.
- $S_\tau^*$ is simply defined by $C(S_\tau^*, X, T - \tau) = k$.
- $k + X e^{-r(T-\tau)}$ which is obtained simply by construction as shown.

(ii) Figure 14.8 is a detail of the previous graph (with a shift of the $x$-axis upwards of $k$), together with the dotted line $S_\tau - K$ which is the payoff of the original (unextended) option at time $\tau$. Payoff$_E$ = max$[0, S_\tau - K, C_E - k]$ is represented by the northwest boundary of this composite graph:

- $S_\tau < S_\tau^*$ – The payoff is zero because the other two terms in Payoff$_E$ are less than zero.
- $S_\tau^* < S_\tau < S_\tau^{**}$ – The payoff is $C_E - k$, i.e. the holder would logically choose to extend the option. $S_\tau^{**}$ is defined as the point at which the curve and the diagonal straight line in Figure 14.8 intersect:

$$C(S_\tau^{**}, X, T - \tau) - k = S_\tau^{**} - K$$

- $S_\tau^{**} < S_\tau$ – The payoff is $S_\tau - K$, i.e. a holder would logically take the payoff of the original (unextended) option.

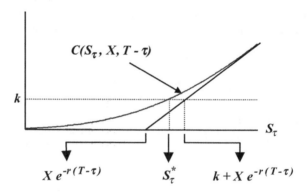

**Figure 14.7**   Call option at $t = \tau$; maturity at $t = T$

(iii) The position of the dotted line in Figure 14.8 depends on the value of the original strike $K$ relative to the extension fee $k$ and the extended strike $X$. In addition to the relative positioning shown in the graph and described in the last subsection, two other configurations are possible. These may be determined at time $t = 0$ when the extendible option is being priced:

- $K < S_\tau^*$ – In this case, an extension would never be economically optimal; therefore, the price of this option is just the same as that of a European call option maturing at time $\tau$.
- $k + X e^{-r(T-\tau)} < K$ – In this case, extending the option would always be preferred to taking the payoff of the original option; therefore, this is just a compound option (call on a call).

Any model we build for an extendible option must therefore test whether $K$ is between $S_\tau^*$ and $S_\tau^{**}$ and if not, just substitute the value of a European call or a compound option. In the remainder of this section we ignore these special cases.

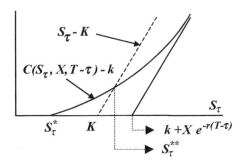

**Figure 14.8**  Detail previous (exercise boundary)

(iv) Using the same approach as for previous options examined in this chapter, today's value of an extendible call is obtained by taking the risk-neutral expectation of the payoff:

$$
\begin{aligned}
f_{\text{ext}}(0) &= \text{PV}[\text{E}[0\colon S_\tau < S_\tau^*] + \text{E}[\text{Payoff } C_E - k\colon S_\tau^* < S_\tau < S_\tau^{**}] + \text{E}[S_\tau - K\colon S_\tau^{**} < S_\tau]] \\
&= e^{-rT}\,\text{E}[S_T - X\colon S_\tau^* < S_\tau < S_\tau^{**}; X < S_T] - e^{-r\tau}\,k\,\text{P}[S_\tau^* < S_\tau < S_\tau^{**}] \\
&\quad + e^{-r\tau}\,\text{E}[S_\tau - K\colon S_\tau^{**} < S_\tau]
\end{aligned}
$$
(14.5)

The terms in this last equation need some dissection; starting with the second and third terms which depend only on $S_\tau$ and using equation (A1.7):

$$
\begin{aligned}
\text{P}[S_\tau^* < S_\tau < S_\tau^{**}] &= \text{P}[S_\tau < S_\tau^{**}] - \text{P}[S_\tau < S_\tau^*] \\
&= \text{N}[-b_2^{**}] - \text{N}[-b_2^*]
\end{aligned}
$$

where

$$
b_2^{**} = \frac{1}{\sigma\sqrt{\tau}}\left\{\ln\frac{S_0\,e^{-q\tau}}{S_\tau^{**}\,e^{-r\tau}} + \frac{1}{2}\sigma^2\tau\right\}
$$

and similarly for $b_2^*$.

$$
\begin{aligned}
\text{E}[S_\tau - K\colon S_\tau^{**} < S_\tau] &\equiv \text{E}[\colon][S_\tau - S_\tau^{**}\colon S_\tau^{**} < S_\tau] + (S_\tau^{**} - K)\text{P}[S_\tau^{**} < S_\tau] \\
&= e^{r\tau}\,C(S_0, S_\tau^{**}, \tau) + (S_\tau^{**} - K)\text{N}[-Z^{**}]
\end{aligned}
$$

where $C(S_0, S_\tau^{**}, \tau)$ is the value of a call option with strike $S_\tau^{**}$ and maturity $\tau$.

The bivariate conditional expectation in equation (14.5), depending on both $S_\tau$ and $S_T$, can be decomposed as follows:

$$
\begin{aligned}
&\text{E}[S_T - X\colon S_\tau^* < S_\tau < S_\tau^{**}; X < S_T] \\
&= \text{E}[S_T - X\colon S_\tau^* < S_\tau; X < S_T] - \text{E}[S_T - X\colon S_\tau^{**} < S_\tau; X < S_T] \\
&= A^* - A^{**}
\end{aligned}
$$

where $A^*$ appears as the first term in equation (14.1) for the value of a call on a call. Just copying the answer from equation (A1.21) of the Appendix gives

$$
A^* = S_0\,e^{(r-q)T}\,\text{N}_2[b_1^*, d_1; \rho] - X\,\text{N}_2[b_2^*, d_2; \rho]
$$

where

$$d_1 = \frac{1}{\sigma\sqrt{T}} \left\{ \ln \frac{S_0 \, e^{-qT}}{X \, e^{-rT}} + \frac{1}{2}\sigma^2 T \right\}; \qquad d_2 = d_1 - \sigma\sqrt{T}$$

and $b_1^*$ and $b_2^*$ are defined as before. There is a similar expression for $A^{**}$.

(v) Equation (14.6) has become a bit of a monster, but each term has now been given explicitly in terms of cumulative distributions. It will be apparent to the reader who has studied Section A.1 of the Appendix that there are different ways of expressing the answers, so a term-by-term comparison with the results quoted in other publications may be difficult: for example, there is a term identical to the value of a call option with strike $S^{**}$ and maturity $T$; some other authors show instead a call option with strike $K$, and with the other terms modified slightly (Longstaff, 1990).

# Barriers: Simple European Options

Barrier options are like simple options but with an extra feature which is triggered by the stock price passing through a barrier. The feature may be that the option ceases to exist (knock-out) or starts to exist (knock-in) or is changed into a different option. These are the archetypal exotics and constitute the majority of exotic options sold in the market (Reiner and Rubinstein, 1991a).

The general topic is a large one and we have chosen to spread it across two chapters (plus a fair chunk of the Appendix), rather than concentrating everything into one indigestible monolith. If the reader is approaching the subject for the first time, he may feel daunted by the sizes of the formulas and by the number of large integrals; but he should make a point of stepping back to understand the underlying principles rather than drowning in the minutiae. There are in fact only a couple of integrals which are just applied over and over again.

This chapter lays out the basic principles and is a direct continuation of the analysis of the Black Scholes model, given in Chapter 5. The following chapter applies these principles to a number of more complex situations; it finishes with an explanation of how to apply trees to pricing barrier options numerically.

## 15.1 SINGLE BARRIER CALLS AND PUTS

(i) The reader should refer to Appendix A.8 which lays out the framework for this chapter. The key result in this context is given by equation (A8.4). Imagine a Brownian particle starting at $x_0 = 0$; the probability distribution function of just those particles that have crossed a barrier at $b$ is

$$F_{crossers}(x_T, T) = \begin{cases} F_{return}(x_T, T) & \text{for } x_T \text{ on the same side of the barrier as } x_0 \\ F_0(x_T, T) & \text{for } x_T \text{ on the other side of the barrier} \end{cases}$$

$F_0(x_T, T)$ is the normal distribution function for a particle starting at $x_0 = 0$ and with unrestrained movement, i.e.

$$F_0(x_T, T)\, dx_T = \frac{1}{\sigma\sqrt{2\pi T}} \exp\left[-\frac{1}{2}\left(\frac{x_T - mT}{\sigma\sqrt{T}}\right)^2\right] dx_T = \frac{1}{\sqrt{2\pi}} e^{-\frac{1}{2}z_T^2}\, dz_T = n(z_T)\, dz_T$$

$F_{return}(x_T, T)$ is the distribution function at time $T$, for those particles starting at $x_0 = 0$, crossing the barrier at $b$ and then returning back across the barrier before time $T$. It is shown in Appendix A.8(iii) that this can be written $F_{return}(x_T, T) = A F_0(x_T - 2b, T)$, where the term $F_0(x_T - 2b, T)$ is the normal distribution for a particle starting at $x_0 = 2b$ and $A = \exp(2mb/\sigma^2)$; $m$ is the drift rate of $x_T$. We can then write

$$F_{return}(x_T, T)\, dx_T = \exp\left(\frac{2mb}{\sigma^2}\right) \frac{1}{\sigma\sqrt{2\pi T}} \exp\left[-\frac{1}{2}\left(\frac{x_T - 2b - mT}{\sigma\sqrt{T}}\right)^2\right] dx_T$$

$$= \exp\left(\frac{2mb}{\sigma^2}\right) \frac{1}{\sqrt{2\pi}} e^{-\frac{1}{2}z_T'^2}\, dz_T' = A n(z_T')\, dz_T'$$

(ii) We will now apply these results to stock price movements. Consider a stock with a starting price $S_T$ in the presence of a barrier $K$. Closely following the Black Scholes analysis of Section 5.2, we write $x_T = \ln(S_T/S_0)$ and note that $x_T$ is normally distributed with mean $mT$ and variance $\sigma^2 T$, where $m = r - q - \frac{1}{2}\sigma^2$. We use the notation $b = \ln(K/S_0)$, so that $A = \exp(2mb/\sigma^2) = (K/S_0)^{2m/\sigma^2}$.

In the remainder of this section, various knock-in options will be evaluated. These will involve a transformation from the variable $S_T$ to either of the variables $z_T$ or $z'_T$, which were defined in the last subsection by

$$S_T = S_0\, e^{mT + \sigma\sqrt{T} z_T} = S_0\, e^{mT + 2b + \sigma\sqrt{T} z'_T}$$

When setting up the integral for evaluating a call option, we integrate with respect to $S_T$ from $X$ to $\infty$. On transforming to the variables $z_T$ or $z'_T$, the integrals will run from $Z_X$ to $\infty$ or from $Z'_X$ to $\infty$, where

$$Z_X = \frac{\ln(X/S_0) - mT}{\sigma\sqrt{T}}; \qquad Z'_X = \frac{\ln(X/S_0) - mT - 2b}{\sigma\sqrt{T}}$$

Analogous limits of integration $z_K$ and $z'_K$ are defined by

$$Z_K = \frac{\ln(K/S_0) - mT}{\sigma\sqrt{T}}; \qquad Z'_K = \frac{\ln(K/S_0) - mT - 2b}{\sigma\sqrt{T}}$$

(iii) **Explicit Calculations:** In this section we calculate two specific examples in order to illustrate how the formulas for prices are obtained. It would be repetitive and boring to do this for every possible knock-in option. However, generalized results for all options are given later in the chapter.

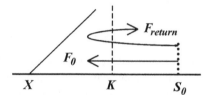

**Figure 15.1**   Down-and-in call; $X < K$

**Example (a): Down-and-in Call; $X < K$.** The option is explained schematically in Figure 15.1. The probability density function $F_{\text{crossers}}$ is different on each side of the barrier as shown.

The price of the option is written

$$C_{d-i}(X < K) = e^{-rT}\int_0^{+\infty} (S_T - X)^+ F_{\text{crossers}}\, dS_T = e^{-rT}\int_X^{+\infty} (S_T - X) F_{\text{crossers}}\, dS_T$$

$$= e^{-rT}\int_X^K (S_T - X) F_0\, dS_T + e^{-rT}\int_K^\infty (S_T - X) F_{\text{return}}\, dS_T$$

The first integral on the right-hand side can be split into two manageable parts as follows:

$$e^{-rT}\int_X^K (S_T - X) F_0\, dS_T = e^{-rT}\int_X^\infty (S_T - X) F_0\, dS_T - e^{-rT}\int_K^\infty (S_T - X) F_0\, dS_T$$

$$= [\text{BS}_C] - [\text{G}_C]$$

The first integral here is just the Black Scholes formula for a call with strike $X$. The second integral is the formula for a gap option which was described in Section 11.4.

To evaluate the second integral in the expression for $C_{d-i}(X < K)$, we make the transformation to the standard normal variate $z'_T$ described in subsection (ii) and use the integral result of equations (A1.7):

$$[J_C] = e^{-rT} \int_K^{\infty} (S_T - X)F_{\text{return}}\, dS_T = e^{-rT} \int_{z'_K}^{\infty} (S_0\, e^{mT+2b+\sigma\sqrt{T}z'_T} - X)An(z'_T)\, dz'_T$$

$$= A\, e^{-rT}\{S_0 e^{2b+(m+\frac{1}{2}\sigma^2)T}\, N[\sigma\sqrt{T} - Z'_K] - X\, N[-Z'_K]\}$$

The value of this option can then be written

$$C_{d-i}(X < K) = [BS_C] - [G_C] + [J_C]$$

***Example (b): Up-and-in Put; $K < X$.*** The reasoning in this example is precisely analogous to that of the last example (see Figure 15.2). The reader is asked to pay particular attention to the signs of the various terms:

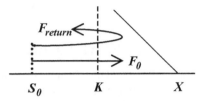

$$P_{u-i}(K < X) = e^{-rT} \int_0^{+\infty} (X - S_T)^+ F_{\text{crossers}}\, dS_T$$

**Figure 15.2**   Up-and-in put; $K < X$

$$= e^{-rT} \int_0^K (X - S_T)F_{\text{return}}\, dS_T$$

$$+ e^{-rT} \int_K^X (X - S_T)F_0\, dS_T$$

The second integral on the right may be written

$$e^{-rT} \int_K^X (X - S_T)F_0\, dS_T = e^{-rT} \int_0^X (X - S_T)F_0\, dS_T - e^{-rT} \int_0^K (X - S_T)F_0\, dS_T$$

$$= [BS_P] - [G_P]$$

As in the previous example, the first term is the Black Scholes formula (for a put option this time) while the second term is again a gap option.

The first integral is solved by making the same transformation as in the last example and using the integral result of equations (A1.7):

$$[J_P] = e^{-rT} \int_0^K (X - S_T)F_{\text{return}}\, dS_T = e^{-rT} \int_{-\infty}^{Z'_K} (X - S_0\, e^{mT+2b+\sigma\sqrt{T}z'_T})An(z'_T)\, dz'_T$$

$$= A\, e^{-rT}\{X\, N[Z'_K] - S_0\, e^{2b+(m+\frac{1}{2}\sigma^2)T}\, N[Z'_K - \sigma\sqrt{T}]\}$$

The value of the option is written

$$P_{u-i}(K < X) = [BS_P] - [G_P] + [J_P]$$

(iv) ***Generalizing the Results:*** If the reader compares the results of the last two examples he will be struck by how similar they are. The essential differences are:

• The first example is for a call while the second is for a put. Each of the terms reflects this difference, which can be accommodated by the use of the parameter $\phi(= +1$ for a call and $-1$ for a put); this was explained in Section 5.2(iv) where we wrote a general Black Scholes formula which could be used for either a put or a call.

- If we make use of the parameter $\phi$, we can almost write a general expression which could be applied to either of the last two examples. There is, however, still a difference in the term [J]: the signs of the arguments of the cumulative normal functions are reversed. This is essentially due to the fact that the limits of integration were $Z'_K$ to $+\infty$ in the first example and $-\infty$ to $Z'_K$ in the second; the difference comes because the stock price had to *fall* to reach the barrier in the first example but *rise* in the second.

Therefore a factor $\psi (= +1$ for rise-to-barrier and $-1$ for fall-to-barrier) multiplying the arguments of the cumulative normal function of [J] would allow us to write a general expression which prices either $C_{d-i}(X < K)$ or $P_{u-i}(K < X)$.

## 15.2   GENERAL EXPRESSIONS FOR SINGLE BARRIER OPTIONS

The reader should now be in a position to derive a formula for any knock-in option. If he really enjoys integration, he can work out the integral results for all the puts and calls with barriers in different positions. Without showing all the detailed workings, we give the results in the next subsection. First, however, we take note of a simple but powerful relationship:

### Knock-in Option + Knock-out Option = European Option

This result is obvious if we consider a portfolio consisting of two options which are the same except that one knocks in and the other knocks out. Whether or not the barrier is crossed, the payoff is that of a European option. This relationship allows us to calculate all the knock-out formulas from the knock-in results.

The following definitions are used:

$$[BS] = e^{-rT} \phi \{ S_0 e^{(m+\frac{1}{2}\sigma^2)T} N[\phi(\sigma\sqrt{T} - Z_X)] - X N[-\phi Z_X] \}$$

$$[G] = e^{-rT} \phi \{ S_0 e^{(m+\frac{1}{2}\sigma^2)T} N[\phi(\sigma\sqrt{T} - Z_K)] - X N[-\phi Z_K] \}$$

$$[H] = A e^{-rT} \phi \{ S_0 e^{2b+(m+\frac{1}{2}\sigma^2)T} N[\psi(Z'_X - \sigma\sqrt{T})] - X N[\psi Z'_X] \}$$

$$[J] = A e^{-rT} \phi \{ S_0 e^{2b+(m+\frac{1}{2}\sigma^2)T} N[\psi(Z'_K - \sigma\sqrt{T})] - X N[\psi Z'_K] \}$$

$$\psi = \begin{cases} +1 & \text{up to barrier} \\ -1 & \text{down to barrier} \end{cases} \qquad \phi = \begin{cases} +1 & \text{call} \\ -1 & \text{put} \end{cases}$$

$$m = r - q - \tfrac{1}{2}\sigma^2; \qquad b = \ln(K/S_0); \qquad A = \exp(2mb/\sigma^2) = (K/S_0)^{2m/\sigma^2}$$

$$Z_X = \frac{\ln(X/S_0) - mT}{\sigma\sqrt{T}}; \qquad Z'_X = \frac{\ln(X/S_0) - mT - 2b}{\sigma\sqrt{T}}$$

$$Z_K = \frac{\ln(K/S_0) - mT}{\sigma\sqrt{T}}; \qquad Z'_K = \frac{\ln(K/S_0) - mT - 2b}{\sigma\sqrt{T}}$$

The formulas for all the single barrier options are given in Tables 15.1 and 15.2.

**Table 15.1**  Single barrier knock-in options

| Calls | Puts | Formula |
|-------|------|---------|
| $C_{d-i}(X < K)$ | $P_{u-i}(K < X)$ | [BS] − [G] + [J] |
| $C_{d-i}(K < X)$ | $P_{u-i}(X < K)$ | [H] |
| $C_{u-i}(X < K)$ | $P_{d-i}(K < X)$ | [G] + [J] − [H] |
| $C_{u-i}(K < X)$ | $P_{d-i}(X < K)$ | [BS] |

**Table 15.2**  Single barrier knock-out options

| Calls | Puts | Formula |
|-------|------|---------|
| $C_{d-o}(X < K)$ | $P_{u-o}(K < X)$ | [G] − [J] |
| $C_{d-o}(K < X)$ | $P_{u-o}(X < K)$ | [BS] − [H] |
| $C_{u-o}(X < K)$ | $P_{d-o}(K < X)$ | [BS] − [G] − [J] + [H] |
| $C_{u-o}(K < X)$ | $P_{d-o}(X < K)$ | 0 |

## 15.3  SOLUTIONS OF THE BLACK SCHOLES EQUATION

(i) The general approach to pricing barrier options has been to use the Fokker Planck equation to derive an analytic expression for the probability distribution function of particles crossing a barrier. This explicit probability density function is then used to calculate an expression for the value of a knock-in option; the knock-out option prices are obtained from the symmetry relationship which states that the sum of the values of a knock-out and a knock-in option equals the value of the corresponding European option.

In Appendix A.4 we discuss the close relationship between the Kolmogorov equations and the Black Scholes equation. A reader might well ask why we bothered to go to the trouble of a two-step solution (first, find the probability distribution function; second, calculate the risk-neutral expected payoff), rather than solving the Black Scholes equation directly. The reason is partly historical: at the time when people first needed to calculate a formula for a barrier option, the expression for the transition probability density function for a Brownian particle in the presence of an absorbing barrier had already been worked out; it was just a question of looking it up in the right book. But there are other good reasons for the approach adopted: it allows a unified approach to all knock-in options with an emphasis on the underlying processes in terms of probabilities. The pure solution of differential equations can be rather sterile, without much reference to underlying processes. Furthermore, in some cases, the boundary conditions for the Black Scholes model are rather hard to apply. We will therefore content ourselves here by sketching out the approach to a relatively easy example: the down-and-out call $(X < K)$ which is the "out" equivalent of the down-and-in call illustrated in Figure 15.1.

The approach is identical to that of Section 5.3 where we solved the Black Scholes equation for a European call option. The fundamental equation is unchanged. We seek a solution in the range $K < S_0 < \infty$ subject to the following initial and boundary conditions:

- $C(S_0, 0) = \max[0, S_0 - X]$;    $X < K$;    $K < S_0 < \infty$
- $\lim_{S_0 \to K} C(S_0, T) \to 0$
- $\lim_{S_0 \to \infty} C(S_0, T) \to S_0 e^{-qT} - X e^{-rt}$

Using the notation and transformations of Section 5.3, the Black Scholes equation becomes $\partial v/\partial T' = \partial^2 v/\partial x^2$ with initial and boundary conditions

- $v(x,0) = \max[0, e^{(k+1)x} - X e^{kx}];$ $\qquad \ln X < b;$ $\qquad b < x_0 < \infty;$ $\qquad b = \ln K$
- $\lim_{x \to b} v(x,T') \to 0$
- $\lim_{x \to \infty} v(x,T) \to e^{(k+1)x+(k+1)^2 T'} - X e^{kx+k^2 T'}$

The solutions of this type of equation are given by equations (A6.8) or (A7.10) in the Appendix:

$$v(x,T') = \int_b^{+\infty} e^{kx} \max[0, e^x - X] \frac{1}{2\sqrt{\pi T'}} \left[ \exp\left[ -\frac{(y-x)^2}{4T'} \right] - \exp\left[ -\frac{(y+x+2b)^2}{4T'} \right] \right] dy$$

We can replace $[0, e^x - X]$ by $e^x - X$ since this is always positive in the range of integration. It then just remains to follow the computational procedures set out in Section 5.3 to work out this integral; unsurprisingly, the answer is the same as that given in Table 15.1.

## 15.4   TRANSITION PROBABILITIES AND REBATES

(i) *First Passage or Absorption Probabilities*: The pseudo-probability of a barrier above being crossed is straightforward to calculate. It is simply the sum of the probabilities of a particle crossing and returning, and a particle crossing and staying across. In terms of equity prices, this is written

$$P_{\text{crossing}} = \int_{-\infty}^{\infty} F_{\text{crossers}} \, dS_T = \int_{-\infty}^{K} F_{\text{return}} \, dS_T + \int_{K}^{\infty} F_0 \, dS_T$$

$$= \int_{-\infty}^{Z'_K} A n(z'_T) \, dz'_T + \int_{Z_K}^{+\infty} n(z_T) \, dz_T = A \, \mathrm{N}[Z'_K] + \mathrm{N}[-Z_K]$$

There is an analogous expression for the pseudo-probability of crossing a barrier below, and the general expression can be written

$$P_{\text{crossing}} = A \, \mathrm{N}[\psi Z'_K] + \mathrm{N}[-\psi Z_K]$$

$$= \exp\left( \frac{2mb}{\sigma^2} \right) \mathrm{N}\left[ -\psi \frac{(b+mT)}{\sigma\sqrt{T}} \right] + \mathrm{N}\left[ -\psi \frac{(b-mT)}{\sigma\sqrt{T}} \right] \qquad (15.1)$$

It should be remembered that this is a pseudo-probability in a risk-neutral world. It is *not* the probability in the real world that an option will be knocked in or out.

(ii) *Knock-in Rebate*: Occasionally, barrier options are structured so that the purchaser receives a lump sum payment if his investment strategy does not work. For example, if he buys a knock-in option and the stock price does not reach the barrier before maturity, he receives a fixed amount $R$ at maturity.

The upfront value of this rebate is simply the present value of $R$ multiplied by the pseudo-probability of the barrier *not* being reached:

$$R_{\text{maturity}} = e^{-rT} R (1 - P_{\text{crossing}})$$

where $P_{\text{crossing}}$ is given in the last subsection.

(iii) *Knock-out Rebate*: More common than for knock-in options, rebates are often given as con-
solation prizes with knock-out options. However, the calculation of this type of rebate is more
complex since the lump sum is paid as soon as the knock-out occurs; we cannot then calculate
the present value just by discounting back over the period $T$.

In Appendix A.8(vii) it is seen that the first passage time $\tau$ (time to first crossing) is a random
variable with a well-defined probability distribution function

$$g_{abs}(\tau) = \frac{\psi b}{\sigma \sqrt{2\pi \tau^3}} \exp\left[-\frac{1}{2\sigma^2 \tau}(b - m\tau)^2\right]$$

By definition, we can write

$$P_{cros\,sin\,g} = \exp\left(\frac{2mb}{\sigma^2}\right) N\left[-\psi \frac{(b + mT)}{\sigma \sqrt{T}}\right] + N\left[-\psi \frac{(b - mT)}{\sigma \sqrt{T}}\right] \tag{15.2}$$

The value of a knock-out rebate of \$1 is given by the following integral:

$$R_{first\,passage} = \int_0^T e^{-r\tau} g_{abs}(\tau)\,d\tau$$

On the face of it, this looks like a very difficult integral to solve: but a little trick helps;
completing the square in the exponential gives

$$e^{-r\tau} g_{abs}(\tau) = \exp\left[-\frac{b(\gamma - m)}{\sigma^2}\right]\left\{\frac{\psi b}{\sigma \sqrt{2\pi \tau^3}} \exp\left[-\frac{1}{2\sigma^2 \tau}(b + \gamma \tau)^2\right]\right\}$$

$$= \exp\left[-\frac{b(\gamma - m)}{\sigma^2}\right] h_{abs}(\tau)$$

where $\gamma = \sqrt{m^2 + 2r\sigma^2}$ and $h_{abs}(\tau)$ is the same as $g_{abs}(\tau)$, but with the replacement $m \to \gamma$.
Using the result of equation (15.2), we can write

$$R_{first\,passage} = \int_0^T e^{-r\tau} g_{abs}(\tau)\,d\tau = \exp\left[-\frac{b(\gamma - m)}{\sigma^2}\right] \int_0^T h_{abs}(\tau)\,d\tau$$

$$= \exp\left[-\frac{b(\gamma - m)}{\sigma^2}\right]\left\{\exp\left[\frac{2\gamma b}{\sigma^2}\right] N\left[-\psi \frac{(b - \gamma T)}{\sigma \sqrt{T}}\right] + N\left[-\psi \frac{(b + \gamma T)}{\sigma \sqrt{T}}\right]\right\} \tag{15.3}$$

## 15.5 BINARY (DIGITAL) OPTIONS WITH BARRIERS

(i) *Recap of Straight Binaries*: Referring back to Section 11.4(iv), a gap option can be written as
(Reiner and Rubinstein, 1991b)

$$f_{gap} = \phi\{S_0[BS]_1 - R[BS]_2\} = f_{asset} - f_{cash}$$

where $[BS]_1$ and $[BS]_2$ are the first and second terms in the Black Scholes formula. $R$ is a cash
sum which may or may not be equal to the strike price $X$; if it *is*, we just have the formula for
a put or a call option. $\phi(= \pm 1)$ differentiates between puts and calls. $f_{asset}$ and $f_{cash}$ are the
prices of asset-or-nothing and cash-or-nothing options with strike $X$.

(ii) Barrier options may be decomposed into digital options in just the same way. This is best illustrated by way of an example. Returning to the example of Section 15.1(iii), the formula for the down-and-in call can be decomposed as described in the last subsection:

$$C_{d-i}(X < K) = \{S_0[BS_C]_1 - X[BS_C]_2\} - \{S_0[G_C]_1 - X[G_C]_2\} + \{S_0[J_C]_1 - X[J_C]_2\}$$

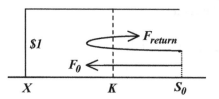

**Figure 15.3** Digital knock in: down-and-in; cash or nothing

Collect together the terms in $-X$; its coefficient $[BS_C]_2 - [G_C]_2 + [J_C]_2$ is the price of an option with the following payoff at time $T$ (Figure 15.3):

- $\$1$, *if* the barrier has been crossed *and* $X < S_T$;
- 0 otherwise.

Similarly, the terms in $S_0$ give the price of an option with the following payoff at time $T$ (Figure 15.4):

- $S_T$, *if* the barrier has been crossed *and* $X < S_T$;
- 0 otherwise.

These last two examples are of course, for specific configurations of $S_0$, $X$ and $K$. Formulas for other configurations can be obtained from Tables 15.1 and 15.2.

(iii) *One Touch Options (Immediate Payment)*: The binary options of the last subsection give a positive payoff if two conditions are met: the barrier is crossed *and* the option expires in-the-money. One touch options are closely related but do not have the second condition. They also pay out as soon as the barrier has been crossed.

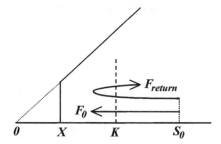

**Figure 15.4** Digital knock in: down-and-in; asset or nothing

The one-touch cash-immediately option with payout $R$ is clearly just the same as the knock-out rebate and is priced by equation (15.3).

The one-touch asset-immediately option is priced in just the same way: at time $\tau$ when the barrier is crossed, $S_\tau$ is equal to $K$; but $S_\tau$ is the payout, so we price this option as a knock-out rebate in which the lump sum payment is equal to $K$.

(iv) *One Touch Options (Payout at Expiry)*: These are simple adaptations of previously obtained formulas:

Cash at expiry: use $e^{-rT} R P_{\text{crossing}}$

Asset at expiry uses the appropriate digital barrier option, putting the strike price equal to zero.

## 15.6 COMMON APPLICATIONS

(i) *American Capped Calls (Exploding Calls)*: These are American call options in which the payout is capped at a certain certain amount $(K - X)$, irrespective of when the option is exercised.

A European capped call is the same as a call spread. If we buy a call with strike $X$ and sell a call with a higher strike $K$, the maximum payoff of the combination at maturity is $(K - X)$.

However, this structure does not carry over to American options because each option holder can choose when to exercise: the person to whom we have sold the call may not wish to exercise when we do.

The American capped call can instead be priced as an up-and-out call, $(X < K)$ with a rebate of $(K - X)$ paid at knock out. A similar approach is used to price an American capped put.

(ii) **Ladders**: When investors buy European call options, it is not uncommon for them to watch the price of the underlying stock soar, and with it the value of the 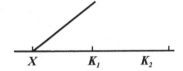 option – only to see both plunge out-of-the-money at maturity. Ladder options have payoffs which capture the effects of such movements.

The simplest form of such a scheme would be a series of one-touch cash-immediately options. The payoffs would be

- $K_1 - S_0$ received as soon as the stock price reaches $K_1$;
- $K_2 - K_1$ received as soon as the stock price reaches $K_2$; etc.

(iii) **Fixed Strike Ladders**: The simple ladder of the last subsection does not really display the features of a call option. There are two commonly used structures which are fundamentally call options but which at the same time capture large up-swings in the stock price (Street, 1992). The fixed strike ladder has the following payoff (we assume for simplicity that the call option is at-the-money, i.e. $S_0 = X$):

- If $S_t$ never reaches $K_1$, we just have a plain call option with strike $X$;
- If $S_t$ gets as far as $K_1$ before maturity, the call payoff has a minimum of $K_1 - X$;
- If $S_t$ gets as far as $K_2$, the minimum payoff is $K_2 - X$; etc.

The combination of options which gives this payoff is summarized below. The analysis is easiest to follow by referring to Figure 15.5.

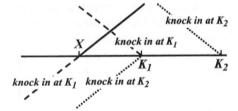

- $C(X)$. Buy a European call option, strike $X$. If $S_t$ never rises above $K_1$, this gives the payoff needed.
- $P_{u-i}(K_1, K_1) - P_{u-i}(X, K_1)$. Buy a knock-in put, strike $K_1$ and sell a knock-in put, strike $X$. If at some point $S_t$ crosses $K_1$ (but not $K_2$), there are two possibilities: if the final stock

**Figure 15.5** Construction of fixed strike ladder

price $S_T$ is between $K_1$ and $K_2$, the two knocked-in puts are out-of-the-money so the payoff comes just from the original call option: $S_T - X$. For $S_T$ anywhere below $K_1$, the payoff is $(K_1 - X)$.

- $P_{u-i}(K_2, K_2) - P_{u-i}(K_1, K_2)$. As in the last step, we have a long put with strike $K_2$ and a short put with strike $K_1$, both of which knock in at $K_2$. We use precisely the same reasoning as for the last step: if at some point $S_t$ crosses $K_2$, there are two possibilities: we have a call option payoff for $K_2 < S_T$ and a payoff $(K_2 - X)$ for all $S_T < K_2$, etc.

(iv) **Floating Strike Ladders:** This structure captures large downward swings in the stock price, by changing the strike price to lower values as barriers are crossed. The payoff is as follows:

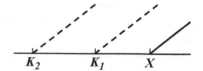

- If $S_t$ never reaches $K_1$, we just have the call option with strike $X$.
- If $S_t$ reaches $K_1$ (but not $K_2$) before maturity, the call option with strike $X$ is replaced by a call with strike $K_1$.
- If $S_t$ reaches $K_2$, the call option with strike $K_1$ is replaced by a call with strike $K_2$, etc.

The structure of the barrier options needed to produce this payoff is simpler to follow than in the last subsection (see Figure 15.6).

- $C(X)$. Buy a European call option with strike $X$. If $S_t$ never falls as far as $K_1$, this gives the payoff we need.
- $C_{d-i}(K_1, K_1) - C_{d-i}(X, K_1)$. Buy a knock-in call option with strike $K_1$ and sell a knock-in call with strike $X$; both knock in at $K_1$. The sold option cancels the original call option of the first step above, and we are left with a new call, strike $K_1$.

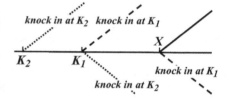

**Figure 15.6**   Construction of floating strike ladder

- $C_{d-i}(K_2, K_2) - C_{d-i}(K_1, K_2)$. Again, the second of these cancels the call option left from the previous step. The net result is that if these two options knock in ($S_t$ crosses the $K_2$ barrier), we are left with a call option, strike $K_2$, etc.

## 15.7   GREEKS

By their nature, barrier options display a sudden increase or decrease in value as the stock price crosses a barrier. We have already seen in the discussion of digital options in Section 11.4(v) that sudden changes in option value for small changes in the price of the underlying stock can cause problems in hedging.

(i) Figure 15.7 shows the value of an up-and-out call option plotted against the stock price. Far from the barrier, the value of the option coincides with that of the corresponding European call option. In this region the probability of a knock-out is remote; but as the barrier is approached, the

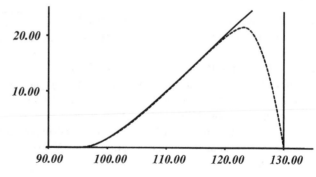

**Figure 15.7**   Up-and-out call option

value of the knock-out option declines sharply. This creates a very pointed peak in the value of the option; put another way, the negative gamma of the option becomes very large. In fact, because of the sharpness of the peak, the negative gamma of this type of option is more pronounced than for any other option commonly encountered in the market. Trading operations would usually avoid dealing in an option of this type except in small size.

All barrier options have some sort of discontinuity: but this does not mean that they are all prone to gamma blow-up. Figure 15.8 shows a down-and-in call where the barrier is out-of-the-money. At high stock prices, the value of the option is small since the probability of knock-in is small. As the price drops, the likelihood of knock-in increases, but at the barrier the underlying call option is out-of-the-money and consequently has small value. This type of option therefore presents less of a problem than the last example; but even in this case, the delta moves from being negative (for

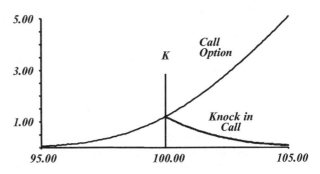

**Figure 15.8**  Down-and-in call option

the down-and-in call) to being positive (European call option) when the barrier is crossed.

## 15.8  STATIC HEDGING

(i) The difficulty of hedging barrier options has led practitioners to try to find alternatives to the standard delta hedging techniques. Dynamic hedging works well for relatively benign options such as standard puts and calls, but can be very risky and expensive for options which have very high gamma over long periods.

Take the example of the down-and-in call option which is illustrated in Figure 15.8. A glance at the graph shows that while the stock price remains above the barrier, the general form of the option price is similar to that of a put option; but as soon as the barrier is touched, the option becomes a standard call option. When these types of option were first introduced in the market, traders soon realized that there is a simple hedging strategy: sell a put option when the option is first taken on; then buy back the put and sell a call if and when the barrier is reached. There are a couple of difficulties with this strategy: first, it assumes that we can exactly exchange the short put for a short call at precisely the point when the stock price hits the barrier; this can be a challenge if the market is lively. Second, what type and amounts of puts and calls do we need? To answer this question we need to make a short diversion.

(ii) **Put-Call Symmetry:** Recall (Carr and Bowie, 1994) from the put–call parity relationship of Section 2.2(i) that if the forward rate equals the strike price ($F_{0T} = X$ or $S_0 e^{-qT} = X e^{-rT}$), then the values of a put and a call option are the same:

$$C_0(S_0, F_{0T}, T) = P_0(S_0, F_{0T}, T)$$

The Black Scholes formula for a call option on one share with strike $X_C$, and a put option on

$n$ shares with strike $X_P$, is taken from equations (5.1) and (5.2):

$$C_0(S_0, X_C, T) = e^{-rT}\{F_{0T}\, N[d_{C1}] - X\, N[d_{C2}]\}$$
$$nP_0(S_0, X_P, T) = n\, e^{-rT}\{X\, N[-d_{P2}] - F_{0T}\, N[-d_{P1}]\}$$

$$d_{i1} = \frac{1}{\sigma\sqrt{T}}\left(\ln\frac{F_{0T}}{X_i} + \frac{1}{2}\sigma^2 T\right); \qquad d_{i2} = d_{i1} - \sigma\sqrt{T}; \qquad i = C\ \text{or}\ P$$

We can easily confirm the put–call parity result previously obtained by using these two pricing formulas and putting $n = 1$, $F_{0T} = X_C = X_P$ (i.e. $\ln F_{0T}/X = 0$) and $N[a] = 1 - N[-a]$.

A further relationship between puts and calls, known as put–call symmetry, may be deduced from the above Black Scholes formulas if we put $n = F_{0T}/X_P = X_C/F_{0T}$. Substituting for $n$ and for $X_P$ from this last relationship into the second Black Scholes formula above gives

$$C_0(S_0, X_C, T) = nP_0\left(S_0, \frac{F_{0T}^2}{X_C}, T\right); \qquad n = \frac{X_C}{F_{0T}}$$

This says that at any time before maturity, a call option with strike $X_C$ is equal in value to $n$ put options with strike $X_P\ (= F_{0T}^2/X_C)$. In the special case where there is no drift (i.e. $r = q$ or $F_{0T} = S_0$), the call option is equal in value to $n = X_C/S_0$ put options with strike $X_P = S_0^2/X_C$.

(iii) **Replication of a Down-and-in Call:** Using the put–call symmetry of the last subsection, we will now devise a strategy to replicate the down-and-in call option illustrated in Figure 15.9.

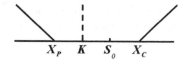

**Figure 15.9** Put–call symmetry; down-and-in call

- If the stock price always remains above $K$, there will be no payoff under the knock-in option.
- Once the stock price has touched the barrier at $K$, the option becomes a call option with strike $X_C$. At the point ($t = \tau$) when the stock price touches $K$ we need to buy a call option with strike $X_C$ and maturity $T$.
- The cost of this call will be $C(K, X_C, T - \tau)$; what instrument can we buy today which will have this value in time $\tau$?
- Let us make the simplifying assumption that the stock price has no drift, i.e. that $F_{\tau T} = S_\tau$. The result given at the end of the last subsection shows that with this assumption, $n = X_C/K$ put options with strike $X_P = K^2/X$ would have precisely the same value as the call option which we need to buy.
- Our strategy is therefore to buy this package of puts for a price $nP(S_0, K^2/X, T)$. If the stock price drops to $K$, these puts would have appreciated to the point where we can afford to buy the call we need.

Note that the above strategy strictly depends on the no-drift assumption; without this condition, the strike price and the number of put options depends on $\tau$. However, for relatively small values of drift the technique remains useful, perhaps augmented by a small amount of delta hedging. Unfortunately, this neat static approach can only be applied to half the barrier options.

# 16

## Barriers: Advanced Options

The last chapter laid out the principles of European barrier option pricing. This chapter continues the same analysis, applied to more complicated problems. The integrals get a bit larger, but the underlying concepts remain the same. Lack of space prevents each solution being given explicitly; but the reader should by now be able to specify the integrals corresponding to each problem, and then solve them using the results of Appendix A.1.

### 16.1 TWO BARRIER OPTIONS

These are options which knock out or in when *either* a barrier above *or* a barrier below the starting stock price is crossed. The analysis is completely parallel to what we have seen for a single barrier option (Ikeda and Kunitomo, 1992).

(i) In the notation of this chapter, $F_0(x_T, T)$ is the normal distribution function for a particle starting at $x_0 = 0$. The function is given explicitly in Section 15.1(i). $F_{\text{non-abs}}$ is the probability distribution function for particles starting at $x_0 = 0$ which have *not* crossed either barrier before time $T$. Two expressions have been derived for this function, which are given by equations (A8.9) and (A8.10) of the Appendix. They are both infinite series although there is no correspondence between individual terms of the two series:

1. $F_{\text{non-abs}}(x_T, T) = \dfrac{1}{\sigma\sqrt{2\pi T}} \sum\limits_{n=-\infty}^{+\infty} \left[ \exp\left( +\dfrac{mu_n}{\sigma^2} \right) \exp\left[ -\dfrac{1}{2\sigma^2 T}(x_T - mT - u_n)^2 \right] \right.$

   $\left. - \exp\left( +\dfrac{mv_n}{\sigma^2} \right) \exp\left[ -\dfrac{1}{2\sigma^2 T}(x_T - mT - v_n)^2 \right] \right]$

2. $F_{\text{non-abs}}(x_T, T) = \exp\left( \dfrac{mx_T}{\sigma^2} \right) \sum\limits_{n=1}^{\infty} \left[ a_n\, e^{-b_n T} \sin\dfrac{n\pi}{L}(x_T + b) \right]$

   $L = a + b; \qquad u_n = 2Ln; \qquad v_n = 2(Ln - b)$

   $a_n = \dfrac{2}{L}\sin\dfrac{n\pi b}{L}; \qquad b_n = \dfrac{1}{2}\left\{ \left(\dfrac{\mu}{\sigma}\right)^2 + \left(\dfrac{n\pi\sigma}{L}\right)^2 \right\}$

(ii) The reasoning of Appendix A.8(iv) and (v) demonstrates that the distribution functions of particles which start at $x_0 = 0$, then cross *either* the barrier at $-b$ or $+a$, and then return to the region $-b$ to $+a$ can be written

$$F_{\text{return}} = F_0 - F_{\text{non-abs}}$$

The total probability distribution function for all those particles that cross one of the barriers can now be written

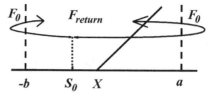

**Figure 16.1**   Double barrier-and-in call

$$F_{\text{crossers}} = \begin{cases} F_0(x_T, T) & x_T < -b \\ F_{\text{return}}(x_T, T) & -b < x_T < a \\ F_0(x_T, T) & a < x_T \end{cases}$$

(iii) As an example, we will look at the knock-in call option shown in Figure 16.1. We do not really need to worry about whether we move up or down to the barrier:

$$C_{ki} = e^{-rT} \int_0^{+\infty} (S_T - X)^+ F_{\text{crossers}}\, dS_T = e^{-rT} \int_X^{+\infty} (S_T - X) F_{\text{crossers}}\, dS_T$$

$$= e^{-rT} \int_X^a (S_T - X) F_{\text{return}}\, dS_T + e^{-rT} \int_a^{\infty} (S_T - X) F_0\, dS_T \tag{16.1}$$

The second integral is completely standard. The first depends on which form of series is used for $F_{\text{non-abs}}$. The sine series is completely straightforward to integrate while the other alternative is handled using the procedures of Section 15.1.

(iv) The question of which of the two series to use and how many terms to retain is best handled pragmatically. Set up both series and see how fast convergence takes place in each case. Both series dampen off regularly, so it is for us to choose how accurate the answer needs to be. We should expect to perform the calculation with one series or the other within four to six terms, and often less.

## 16.2   OUTSIDE BARRIER OPTIONS

The barrier options described so far have been European options which are knocked in or knocked out when the price of the underlying variable crosses a barrier. An extension of this is a European option which knocks in when the price of a commodity other than the underlying stock crosses a barrier. For example, an up-and-in call on a stock which knocks in when a foreign exchange rate crosses a barrier. These options are called outside barrier options, as distinct from inside barrier options, where the barrier commodity and the commodity underlying the European option are the same. The reason for the terminology is anybody's guess (Heynen and Kat, 1994a).

We could repeat most of the material presented so far in this chapter, adapted for outside barriers rather than inside barriers. However, these options are relatively rare so we will simply describe a single-outside-barrier up-and-in call option; the reader should be able to generalize this quite easily to any of the other options in this category.

(i) **Outside Barrier, Up and In**: The general principle remains as before; it is merely the form of some of the distributions that is different. The price of the option is the present value of the risk-neutral expectation of the payoff (Figure 16.2):

$$C_{u-i}^{\text{outside}} = e^{-rT} \int_{S_T=0}^{+\infty} \int_{Q_T=0}^{+\infty} (S_T - X)^+ F_{\text{jo int}}\, dS_T\, dQ_T \tag{16.2}$$

190

where $S_T$ is the maturity value of the stock underlying the call option and $Q_T$ is the maturity value of the barrier commodity. The form of this is the same as for inside barriers; but we need to find an expression for $F_{\text{joint}}$ which is the joint probability distribution for the two price variables. The large topic of derivatives which depend on the prices of *two* underlying assets is attacked in Chapter 12. The material of that chapter and of Appendix A.1 is used to solve equation (16.2).

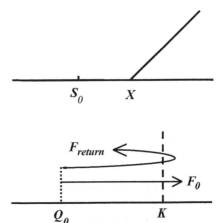

(ii) *Separate Distributions of the Two Variables*: As before, we transform to the logs of prices: $x_T =$

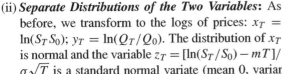

**Figure 16.2**   Outside barrier, up-and-in call

$\ln(S_T S_0)$; $y_T = \ln(Q_T/Q_0)$. The distribution of $x_T$ is normal and the variable $z_T = [\ln(S_T/S_0) - mT]/\sigma\sqrt{T}$ is a standard normal variate (mean 0, variance 1); $\sigma$ is the volatility of the stock and $m - r - q - \frac{1}{2}\sigma^2$.

The variate $y_T$ has a more complex distribution. As explained in Section 13.1(i), $y_T$ is distributed as $F_{\text{crossers}}(y_T, T)$ which has different forms above and below the barrier at $Q_T = K$ or $y_T = \ln(K/Q_0) = b$.

$b < y_T$: $F_{\text{crossers}} = F_0(y_T, T)$ which is the distribution at time $T$ of a particle which started at $y_0 = 0$ and has drift $m_Q = r - q_Q - \frac{1}{2}\sigma_Q^2$ and variance $\sigma_Q^2$. The variable

$$w_T = \frac{\ln(Q_T/Q_0) - m_Q T}{\sigma_Q\sqrt{T}}$$

is a standard normal variate.

$y_T < b$: $F_{\text{crossers}} = F_{\text{return}} = A F_0(y_T - 2b, T)$ where $A = \exp(2m_Q b/\sigma_Q^2) = (K/Q_0)^{2m_Q/\sigma_Q^2}$ and $F_0(y_T - 2b, T)$ is the distribution function for a particle which started at $y_0 = 2b$ and has drift $m_Q$. The variable

$$w'_T = \frac{\ln(Q_T/Q_0) - m_Q T - 2b}{\sigma_Q\sqrt{T}}$$

is therefore a standard normal variate.

(iii) Equation (16.2) may be rewritten

$$C_{u-i}^{\text{outside}} = e^{-rT}\left\{\int_{S_T=X}^{+\infty}\int_{Q_T=0}^{K} A(S_T - X)F_{1\,\text{joint}}\,dQ_T\,dS_T\right.$$
$$\left. + \int_{S_T=X}^{+\infty}\int_{Q_T=K}^{+\infty}(S_T - X)F_{2\,\text{joint}}\,dQ_T\,dS_T\right\}$$

and transforming to the variables $Z_T$, $w_T$ and $w'_T$, this last equation can be written more precisely as

$$
C_{u-i}^{\text{outside}} = e^{-rT} \left\{ A \int_{Z_X}^{+\infty} \int_{-\infty}^{W_K'} (S_0\, e^{mT+\sigma\sqrt{T}z_T} - X) n_2(z_T, w_T'; \rho)\, dz_T\, dw_T' \right.
$$

$$
\left. + \int_{Z_X}^{+\infty} \int_{W_K}^{+\infty} (S_0\, e^{mT+\sigma\sqrt{T}z_T} - X) n_2(z_T, w_T; \rho)\, dz_T\, dw_T \right\}
$$

$$
Z_X = \frac{\ln(X/S_0) - mT}{\sigma\sqrt{T}}; \qquad W_K' = \frac{\ln(K/Q_0) - m_Q T - 2b}{\sigma_Q\sqrt{T}}; \qquad W_K = \frac{\ln(K/Q_0) - m_Q T}{\sigma_Q\sqrt{T}}
$$

$n_2(z_T, w_T'; \rho)$ is the standard bivariate normal distribution describing the joint distribution of the two standard normal variates $z_t$ and $w_t'$, which have correlation $\rho$. $n_2(z_T, w_T; \rho)$ is the standard bivariate normal distribution describing the joint distribution of the two standard normal variates $z_t$ and $w_t$, which have correlation $\rho$.

Note that the correlations between $z_t$ and $w_t'$ are the same as between $z_t$ and $w_t$; $w_T'$ and $w_T$ essentially refer to the same random variable $Q_T$, and differ only in their means, which does not affect the correlations.

Using the results of equations (A1.20) and (A1.21), this last integral is evaluated as follows:

$$
C_{u-i}^{\text{outside}} = A\left\{ S_0\, e^{-qT}\, N[(\sigma\sqrt{T} - Z_X)] - X\, e^{-rT}\, N[-Z_X] \right.
$$

$$
- \left( S_0\, e^{-qT}\, N_2[-(\sigma\sqrt{T} - Z_X), -(\rho\,\sigma\sqrt{T} - W_X'); \rho] - X\, e^{-rT}\, N_2[-Z_X, -W_K'; \rho] \right) \Big\}
$$

$$
+ \left( S_0\, e^{-qT}\, N_2[-(\sigma\sqrt{T} - Z_X), -(\rho\,\sigma\sqrt{T} - W_X'); \rho] - X\, e^{-rT}\, N_2[-Z_X, -W_K; \rho] \right)
$$

$$
\tag{16.3}
$$

## 16.3   PARTIAL BARRIER OPTIONS

In the foregoing it was always assumed that a barrier is permanent. However, the barrier could be switched on and off throughout the life of the option. Such a pricing problem is usually handled numerically, but the simplest case can be solved analytically using the techniques of the last section (Heynen and Kat, 1994b).

This is an option on a single underlying stock at two different times, as described in Chapter 14. The specific case we consider is an up-and-in call of maturity $T$, which knocks in if the barrier is crossed before time $\tau$, i.e. the barrier is switched off at time $\tau$. Its value can be written analytically as

$$
C_{u-i}^{\text{partial}} = e^{-rT} \left\{ \int_{S_T=0}^{+\infty} \int_{S_\tau=0}^{+\infty} (S_T - X)^+ F_{\text{joint}}\, dS_\tau\, dS_T \right.
$$

$F_{\text{joint}}$ is the joint probability distribution of two random variables $S_\tau$ and $S_T$, where $S_\tau$ is subject to an absorbing barrier. This problem is almost precisely the same as the outside barrier option problem solved in the last section. The formula given in equation (16.3) can therefore be applied directly, with the following modifications:

- $Q_0 \to S_0$, $\sigma_Q \to \sigma$ and $m_Q \to m$.
- $T \to \tau$ in the formulas for $w_K'$ and $w_K$.
- The correlation between $S_\tau$ and $S_T$ is shown in Appendix A.1(vi) to be $\rho = \sqrt{\tau/T}$.

## 16.4   LOOKBACK OPTIONS

These are probably the most discussed and least used of the standard exotic options. The problem is that on the one hand they have immense intuitive appeal and pricing presents some interesting intellectual challenges; but on the other hand they are so expensive that no-one wants to buy them. However, this book would not be complete without an explanation of how to price them (Goldman *et al.*, 1979).

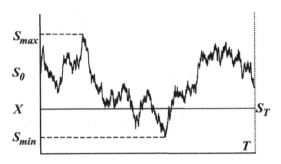

**Figure 16.3**   Notation for lookbacks

(i) *Floating Strike Lookbacks*: Lookback options are quoted in two ways. The most common way is with a floating strike, where the payoffs are defined as follows:

$$\text{Payoff of } C_{\text{fl str}} = (S_T - S_{\min})$$
$$\text{Payoff of } P_{\text{fl str}} = (S_{\max} - S_T)$$

The lookback call gives the holder the right to *buy* stock at maturity at the lowest price achieved by the stock over the life of the option. Similarly, the lookback *put* allows the holder to sell stock at the highest price achieved.

The form of the payoff is unusual in that it does not involve an expression of the form $\max[0, \ldots]$, since $(S_T - S_{\min})$ can never be negative; it has therefore been suggested that this is not really an option at all, although this is largely a matter of semantics. However, it does make the pricing formula straightforward to write out: risk neutrality gives

$$\begin{aligned} C_{\text{fl str}} &= e^{-rT}\{E\langle S_T\rangle - E\langle S_{\min}\rangle\} \\ &= e^{-rT}\{F_{0T} - v_{\min}\} \\ P_{\text{fl str}} &= e^{-rT}\{v_{\max} - F_{0T}\} \end{aligned} \tag{16.4}$$

where $F_{0T}$ is the forward price.

(ii) *Fixed Strike Lookbacks*: As the name implies, these options have a fixed strike $X$. Referring to Figure 16.3, the payoffs of the fixed strike call and put are given by

$$\text{Payoff of } C_{\text{fix str}} = \max[0, S_{\max} - X]$$
$$\text{Payoff of } P_{\text{fix str}} = \max[0, X - S_{\min}]$$

These are sometimes referred to as lookforward options. They give the option holder the right to exercise not at the final stock price, but at the most advantageous price over the life of the option. The payoffs look more like normal option payoffs, containing the familiar "max" function. However, in practice, the payoff can be further simplified, since the options are usually quoted at-the-money, i.e. with $X = S_0$. This implies that $X \leq S_{max}$ or $S_{min} \leq X$, so that

$$
\begin{aligned}
C_{\text{fix str}} &= e^{-rT}\{E\langle S_{max}\rangle - X\} \\
&= e^{-rT}\{v_{max} - X\} \\
P_{\text{fix str}} &= e^{-rT}\{X - v_{min}\}
\end{aligned}
\tag{16.5}
$$

(iii) *Distributions of Maximum and Minimum:* The prices of both floating and fixed strike lookback options depend on the quantities $v_{min}$ and $v_{max}$, which are defined in the last two subsections. It is shown in Appendix A.8(viii) that the distribution functions for $x_{max} = \ln(S_{max}/S_0)$ and $x_{min} = \ln(S_{min}/S_0)$ are

$$
\begin{aligned}
F_{max}(x_{max}, T) = {}& \frac{2}{\sigma\sqrt{2\pi T}} \exp\left[-\frac{1}{2\sigma^2 T}(x_{max} - mT)^2\right] \\
&- \frac{2m}{\sigma^2}\exp\left(+\frac{2mx_{max}}{\sigma^2}\right)N\left[-\frac{1}{\sigma\sqrt{T}}(x_{max} + mT)\right]
\end{aligned}
\tag{16.6}
$$

$$
\begin{aligned}
F_{min}(x_{min}, T) = {}& \frac{2}{\sigma\sqrt{2\pi T}} \exp\left[-\frac{1}{2\sigma^2 T}(x_{min} - mT)^2\right] \\
&+ \frac{2m}{\sigma^2}\exp\left(+\frac{2mx_{max}}{\sigma^2}\right)N\left[+\frac{1}{\sigma\sqrt{T}}(x_{min} + mT)\right]
\end{aligned}
$$

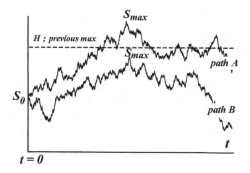

**Figure 16.4**   Previous maximum

(iv) When we derive the formula for the price of an option, we do not usually have to concern ourselves with what happened in the past: if a call option was issued for an original maturity of 3 months, its price after 2 months is exactly the same as the price of a newly issued 1-month option. However, the pricing of a lookback is a little more difficult: after 2 months, the maximum or minimum value of $S_t$ for the whole period may already have been achieved.

Let us assume that a previous maximum $H$ has been established and we wish to find the value of $v_{max}$ at time $t = 0$. Consider the two paths shown in Figure 16.4: path A establishes a new maximum at $S_{max}$ while path B does not make it so that the established maximum remains at $H$. This generalized definition, accommodating a previous maximum, is expressed in the general definition

$$
v_{max} = E\langle\max[H, S_{max}]\rangle = H\,P\langle S_{max} < H\rangle + E\langle S_{max} \mid H < S_{max}\rangle
$$

or

$$v_{max} = H \int_0^H F_{max} \, dS_{max} + \int_H^\infty S_{max} F_{max} \, dS_{max}$$

There is an analogous expression for $v_{min}$ in terms of a previously established minimum $L$.

(v) Expressions for $v_{max}$ and $v_{min}$ can be obtained by using equations (16.6) for $F_{max}$ and $F_{min}$, making the substitution $S_{max} = S_0 \, e^{x_{max}}$. The resulting integrals are performed using the results of Appendix A.1(v), item (E); the algebra is straightforward but very tedious. The expressions can be combined to give the generalized formula

$$v_{max/min} = H \left\{ N[\psi Z_K] - \frac{\sigma^2}{2(r-q)} \exp\left(\frac{2mb}{\sigma^2}\right) N[\psi Z_K'] \right\}$$

$$+ F_{0T} \left\{ 1 + \frac{\sigma^2}{2(r-q)} N[-\psi(Z_K - \sigma\sqrt{T})] \right\} \qquad (16.7)$$

$$b = \ln K/S_0; \qquad Z_K = \frac{(\ln K/S_0 - mT)}{\sigma\sqrt{T}}; \qquad Z_K' = Z_K - 2b$$

for max: $K = H$, $\quad \psi = +1;$ $\qquad$ for min: $K = L$, $\quad \psi = -1$

(vi) **Strike Bonus:** Using equation (16.7) to obtain an expression for $v_{min}$, substituting this into equation (16.4) and rationalizing gives (Garman, 1989)

$$C_{fl\,str} = e^{-rT} \{ F_{0T} N[-(Z_L - \sigma^2 T)] - L N[-Z_L] \}$$

$$+ \frac{\sigma^2 S_0}{2(r-q)} \left\{ e^{-rT} \exp\left[\frac{2(r-q)b}{\sigma^2}\right] N[-Z_L'] + e^{-qT} N[Z_L - \sigma^2 T] \right\} \qquad (16.8)$$

The first term is simply the Black Scholes formula for a call option with strike $X = L$, the previously achieved minimum. At $t = 0$ we consider two possibilities:

- No new minimums are formed below $L$ before the maturity of the option. The payoff of $C_{fl\,str}$ is then equal to the payoff of $C(S_0, L, T)$, i.e. max$[0, S_T - L]$.
- A new minimum is established at $S_{min}$ which is below $L$. The payoff of the option is then max$[0, S_T - S_{min}]$.

Comparing these two possible outcomes, it is clear that the second term in equation (16.8) prices an option to reset the strike price of a call option from $L$ down to the lowest value achieved by $S_t$ before maturity. This option is called the *strike bonus*.

## 16.5    BARRIER OPTIONS AND TREES

(i) **Binomial Model (Jarrow–Rudd):** Binomial and trinomial trees are a standard way of solving barrier option pricing problems which are not soluble analytically, such as American barrier options. However, these methods do display some special features which will be illustrated with the example of a European knock-out call $C_{u-o}(X < K)$. The example uses $S_0 = 100$, $X = 110$, $K = 150$, $r = 10\%$, $q = 4\%$, $\sigma = 20\%$, $T = 1$ year. This is similar to the example examined in some detail in Section 7.3(v) and again in Section 8.6, except for the existence of a knock-out barrier. In the previous investigations we examined the variation of the values obtained from the binomial model, as a function of the number of time steps.

In order to accommodate the knock-out feature in a binomial tree, we simply set the option value equal to zero at each node for which the stock price is outside the barrier. Consider the above knock-out option, priced on a three-step binomial tree. Using the Jarrow–Rudd discretization, there is no node with a stock price higher than 150; therefore there is no node at which we would set the stock price equal to zero. We are therefore unable to price this option – or alternatively put, this model gives the same value for a barrier at $K = 150$ and for $K = \infty$.

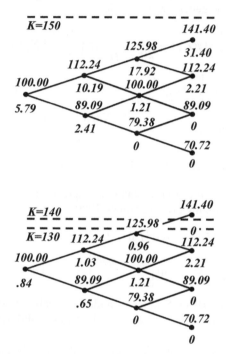

**Figure 16.5**   Knock-out barriers in binomial trees

If we now look at the same model with the barrier at $K = 140$ as in the second diagram of Figure 16.5, we see how the tree is modified, giving a very different value for the option. But the tree would give exactly the same answer for $K = 130$; the barrier would have to be below $K = 125.98$ for the tree to be modified any further. In general, the value of a knock-out option is a step function of the barrier level, with a jump each time the barrier crosses a line of nodes.

(ii) *Price vs. Number of Steps*: Figure 16.6 shows the value of our knock-out call option plotted against the number of steps in the binomial tree; the analytical value of this option is 3.77. It is instructive to compare this graph with Figure 7.11 for a similar option but without a knock-out barrier. The European option shows the characteristic oscillations which are gradually damped away; by the time we reach about 300/400 steps (not shown), the answer obtained is stable enough for commercial purposes. The knock-out option on the other hand shows three different features of interest (Boyle and Lau, 1994):

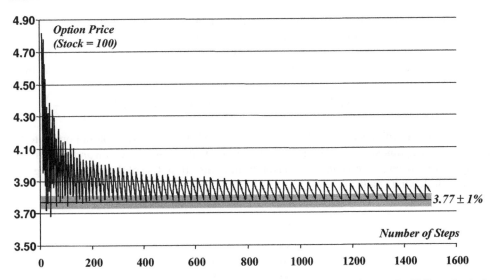

**Figure 16.6**   Up-and-out knock-out call price vs. number of binomial steps (Jarrow–Rudd discretization)

- The graph continues its relentless sawtooth pattern long after the 1500 steps which we have shown. Convergence to the analytical answer is difficult to achieve.
- However, within about 150 steps, we find the bottom of the zig-zags within 1% of the analytical answer; certainly, within 300/400 steps, the envelope of low points gives an almost perfect answer.
- The answers converge to the theoretical answer from above, i.e. apart from a few outliers, the tree always gives answers greater than the analytical value.

We start by turning our attention to the first two features.

In subsection (i) we saw that a knock-out option value calculated with a binomial tree is a step function of the barrier level. This same effect causes oscillations in the calculated value of a knock-out option plotted against the number of steps. If we use the Jarrow–Rudd discretization with $N$ time steps, each proportional up-jump is given by $u = e^{\sigma\sqrt{\delta t}} = e^{\sigma\sqrt{T/N}}$. Therefore as $N$ increases, the spacing between adjacent rows of nodes decreases; the rows of nodes become progressively compressed together and at a certain point an entire row of nodes crosses the barrier. At this point there is a jump in the value of the option calculated by the tree.

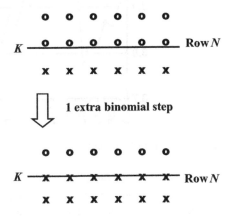

**Figure 16.7**   Effect of increasing number of binomial steps

(iii) As the number of steps $N$ is increased, we would expect the most accurate binomial calculation to occur when a row is just above the knock-out barrier; the option value at these nodes is put at

197

zero. Increasing the number of steps by one would then push the row down through the barrier and change this row of zeros into positive numbers (see Figure 16.7).

Let $N_c$ be a critical number of steps such that row $n$ of nodes in the binomial tree lies just above $K$, i.e. $S_0\, e^{n\sigma\sqrt{T/N_c}}$ is greater than $K$; but $S_0\, e^{n\sigma\sqrt{T/(N_c+1)}}$ is less than $K$. We find $N_c$ from

$$S_0\, e^{n\sigma\sqrt{T/N_c}} < K < S_0\, e^{n\sigma\sqrt{T/(N_c+1)}} \qquad \text{or} \qquad N_c = \text{round down}\left(\frac{n^2\sigma^2 T}{(\ln K/S_0)^2}\right)$$

where "round down" means round down to the nearest integer. Note: It is important to be accurate at this point since $N_c$ will give a *best* answer while $N_c + 1$ gives a *worst* answer.

Figure 16.8 is just a blown up detail taken from Figure 16.6. Use of the formula just given gives the following results:

| $n$ | $N_c$ |
| --- | --- |
| 28 | 190 |
| 29 | 204 |
| 30 | 218 |

which correspond precisely to the jumps in the diagram. The rippling effect of the option values between jumps is the residual effect of the oscillations always observed in binomial calculations.

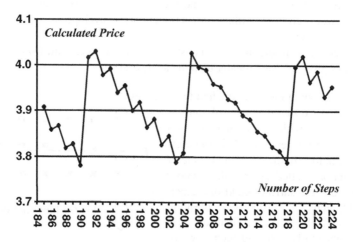

**Figure 16.8**   Knock-out option price vs. steps

(iv) *Alternative Discretizations*: The above sawtooth effect is particularly pronounced when we use the Jarrow–Rudd discretization, since all nodes lie along horizontal levels: entire rows of nodes then cross the barrier at once as the number of time steps is increased. If we use a discretization which does not have horizontal rows of nodes, then only a few grid points cross the barrier each time the number of steps is increased. Figure 16.9 is analogous to Figure 16.6, but using the Cox–Ross–Rubinstein discretization. It continues to display the sawtooth effect, but with much reduced amplitude; the envelope of the low points no longer coincides with the analytical value for the option. The smooth curve which seems to run through the middle of the zig-zags in the diagram is explained later.

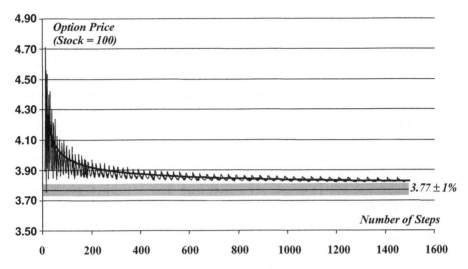

**Figure 16.9**  A: Up-and-out knock-out call price vs. number of binomial steps (Cox–Ross–Rubinstein discretization); B: Discrete barrier correction

(v) The first reaction to the smaller oscillations of Figure 16.9 is to avoid discretizations with horizontal rows of nodes. However, when dealing with variable volatility or interest rates, it is generally necessary to use trinomial trees. There is nothing to say that these must have horizontal nodes, but they are certainly easier to program if they do.

An alternative way of overcoming the zig-zag problem, while still retaining nodes in horizontal rows, is to use interpolation. This method starts with a fixed number of steps and regards the barrier $K$ as a variable. Referring to the diagram of subsection (iii) above, it is clear that the tree calculation will yield the same answer for $K$ anywhere between two neighboring rows of nodes; it is only when $K$ crosses a row that the answer changes. We saw previously that if $K$ is adjacent to (but below) a row of nodes, then we get a "best answer" from a tree. This interpolation method calls for us to calculate two "best answers", for $K$ just below two neighboring rows; a "best solution" for $K$ between these values is an interpolation between the two best answers.

(vi) *Discrete Sampling*: The consideration of binomial price vs. number of steps really involves two quite separate issues. So far in this section, we have focused on issues connected with the stability and geometry of the tree; but there is an even more fundamental issue to consider. Is the option being priced by the binomial tree really the same option that was priced in the last section, using analytical methods? It is now rare to find barrier options which knock in or out if ever the barrier is crossed before maturity: there have been too many disputes about whether the barrier really *was* crossed and whether a bit of market manipulation helped it over. Barrier options contracts now specify a precise time each day (or week) when the market is observed to see if the price is on the other side of the barrier, i.e. the barrier performance is *discretely monitored*. It is of course possible (indeed very probable) that in our example of an up-and-in put, the stock price rises above the barrier only to fall back again before the next discrete monitoring point. A discretely monitored up-and-out call should always be more valuable than one which is continuously monitored. Moreover, the less frequently it is monitored, the more expensive it should be.

The use of a tree to price an option implicitly forces the assumption that the number of monitoring points is equal to the number of time steps in the tree. The trouble is that it is very tricky to separate those effects that are due to discrete monitoring from those which stem from the geometry of the tree. A number of methods have been proposed for estimating the difference between the values of a discretely and a continuously monitored barrier option. The easiest to apply (while at the same time enjoying some theoretical justification) was introduced by Cheuk and Vorst (1996). This shows that a barrier option monitored at equally spaced points has the same value as the corresponding continuously monitored option, but with the barrier shifted from $K$ to a new level $K\,e^{\pm\beta\sigma\sqrt{T/N}}$ where $\beta = 0.5826$ and $T/N$ is the monitoring frequency. The volatility is $\sigma$ and the $\pm$ sign depends on the context: it would be $+$ in our up-and-out call example. This approximation holds fairly well over a wide range and is the heavy curve in Figure 16.9.

Finally, the general form of this correction explains one point which may have puzzled the reader: the binomial results of Figure 16.6 refer to a series of *discretely* monitored barrier options, notwithstanding the zig-zag errors which have already been discussed. How come then, that the lower envelope of the oscillating results corresponds so closely to the theoretical value of a *continuously* monitored barrier option? From the analysis of subsection (iii) it is clear that the difference between a "best answer" and a "worst answer" is the same as the difference caused by moving the barrier a distance equal to the separation of successive horizontal rows of nodes, i.e. moving from $K$ to $K\,e^{\sigma\sqrt{T/N}}$. Moving the barrier half this distance would equate to a move from $K$ to $K\,e^{0.5\,\sigma\sqrt{T/N}}$; but this is remarkably close to a move from $K$ to $K\,e^{0.5826\,\sigma\sqrt{T/N}}$ which is prescribed by Cheuk and Vorst for taking us from a discretely monitored to a continuously monitored barrier option. Therefore, if the center of the sawtoothed pattern in Figure 16.6 is a best estimate of the value of a discretely monitored up-and-out call (Cheuk and Vorst line), then the envelope of the bottom of the sawtooth will approximately give the continuously monitored value.

# 17

## Asian Options

### 17.1 INTRODUCTION

(i) Consider a company which is exporting goods continuously rather than in large chunks. Equal payments are received daily in foreign currency and the exporter decides to hedge these for the next month by buying put options. Compare the following two strategies: (i) the exporter buys a set of put options with strike $X$, maturing on each day of the month; or (ii) he buys a put option on the average exchange rate over the month with payoff $\max[0, X - Av]$.

Clearly, the payoff of package (i) is greater than that of package (ii): simply imagine two successive days on which the exchange rates are $X - 10$ and $X + 10$. The combined payoff for two separate puts would be 10 while the payoff for the put on the average price is zero. An exporter is more likely to be interested in the average exchange rate rather than the rate on individual daily payments. He would therefore execute the cheaper strategy (ii) above.

Options in which the underlying asset is an average price are known as Asian options. They are of most interest in the foreign exchange markets, although they do appear elsewhere, e.g. savings products whose upside return is related to the average of a stock index. In the following, we will continue to use the vernacular of equity derivatives.

(ii) *Average Price and Average Strike*: There are two families of Asian options to consider:

- Average price options with payoffs for call and put of

$$\max[0, Av_T - X] \qquad \text{and} \qquad \max[0, X - Av_T]$$

- Average strike options with payoffs

$$\max[0, S_T - Av_T] \qquad \text{and} \qquad \max[0, Av_T - S_T]$$

Average price options are more intuitively interesting and more common, although the two types are obviously closely related. Both will be examined in this chapter.

(iii) *In-progress and Deferred Averaging*: The underlying "asset" in an Asian option is $Av_T$, the average price up to maturity at time $T$. This is not a tangible asset that can be delivered at the expiry of an option, so these options are cash settled, i.e. an amount of cash equal to the mathematical expression for the payoff is delivered at maturity.

It very often happens that the averaging period does not run from "now" to time $T$. Two cases need to be considered:

- We may be pricing an option that started at some time $\tau$ in the past and the averaging may already have started.
- The option may be only partly Asian, i.e. the averaging does not start until some time $\tau$ in the future.

(iv) *Definition of Averages*: The average of a set of prices is most simply defined as $A_N = (N+1)^{-1} \sum_{n=0}^{N} S_n$. If the averaging does not start until $n = v$ (deferred averaging of the last subsection, then $A_N = (N - v + 1)^{-1} \sum_{n=v}^{N} S_n$. Averaging could be calculated daily, weekly or whatever is agreed. This is the **arithmetic average** and is used for most option contracts. The various $S_n$ are lognormally distributed, but there is no simple way of describing the distribution of $A_N$. Note that by convention, the average includes the price on the first day of averaging, e.g. it would include today's price $S_0$ if averaging started now.

An alternative type of average, defined by $G_N = \{S_0 \times S_1 \times \cdots \times S_N\}^{1/(N+1)}$, is called the **geometric average**. For deferred start averaging, $G_N = \{S_v \times S_{v+1} \times \cdots \times S_N\}^{1/(N-v+1)}$. Taking logarithms of both sides gives

$$g_N = \ln \frac{G_N}{S_0} = \frac{1}{N+1} \sum_{n=0}^{N} \ln S_n = \frac{1}{N+1} \sum_{n=0}^{N} x_n$$

The $x_n$ are normally distributed (see Section 3.1) and we know that the sum of normal random variables is itself normally distributed; the distribution of $g_N$ is therefore normal.

(v) **Geometric vs. Arithmetic Average:** We have the unfortunate situation where options in the market are all written on the arithmetic average while pricing is only easy for the geometric average. Perhaps there is a simple bridge to get from one to the other?

On the right is a set of 20 daily prices of a commodity with a volatility of about 22%. The arithmetic and geometric averages are $A_{20} = 103.95$ and $G_{20} = 103.92$, which are surprisingly close given the very different mathematical forms of the two averages. Given the simplifying assumptions of option theory and the uncertainty surrounding volatility, one is tempted to say that these results are close enough to be taken as being the same.

Could these two averages have come out close by accident? There is a mathematical theorem which states that $G_N \leq A_N$ always; equality occurs if all the $S_n$ are identical. The commodity prices in our list are close in size so the averages are close. Now consider two series in which the numbers being averaged are much more variable, or equivalently stated, prices which are much more volatile:

$$\frac{1}{20}\{1 + 2 + \cdots + 20\} = 10.5; \qquad \{1 \times 2 \times \cdots \times 20\}^{\frac{1}{20}} = 8.3$$

| |
|---|
| 100 |
| 102 |
| 99 |
| 100 |
| 102 |
| 101 |
| 103 |
| 104 |
| 103 |
| 104 |
| 107 |
| 106 |
| 107 |
| 105 |
| 104 |
| 107 |
| 108 |
| 106 |
| 107 |
| 104 |

Even in this case, which is more extreme than price series generally encountered in finance, the difference is only about 25%. It is frustrating to have the arithmetic and geometric results so close, and we describe below how theoreticians have been prompted to devise schemes in which an arithmetic option is regarded as a geometric option plus a correction factor.

(vi) **Put–Call Parity:** Before turning to various explicit models, it is worth pointing out that put–call parity works for European Asian options – strange terminology, but meaning an average option with no payout before final maturity permitted. For either a geometric or an arithmetic average price, we may write

$$C_{av}(T) - P_{av}(T) = Av_N - X$$

Taking risk-neutral expectations and present valuing gives

$$C_{av}(0) - P_{av}(0) = e^{-rT}\{E[Av_N] - X\}$$

which gives the price of an Asian put option in terms of the price of the corresponding call option. Expressions for $E\langle Av_N \rangle$ with different averaging periods can be calculated exactly for both geometric and arithmetic averages. This result means that we can focus on call options, as the put price follows immediately from the above formula.

## 17.2   GEOMETRIC AVERAGE PRICE OPTIONS

(i) **Use of Black Scholes Model for Geometric Average Options**: The notation of Chapter 3 is used and extended for simple or deferred geometric averaging as follows:

$$r_n = \ln \frac{S_n}{S_{n-1}} \qquad E[r_n] = m\delta T \qquad \text{var}[r_n] = \sigma^2\,\delta T$$

| Underlying price: $S_n$ | Geometric average price: $G_n$ |
|---|---|
| $x_n = \ln \dfrac{S_n}{S_0}$ | $g_n = \ln \dfrac{G_n}{G_0}$ |
| $E[x_n] = mT$ | $E[g_n] = m_g T$ |
| $\text{var}[x_n] = \sigma^2 T$ | $\text{var}[g_n] = \sigma_g^2 T$ |
| $E[S_n] = S_0\,e^{(m+\frac{1}{2}\sigma^2)T} = F_{0T}$ | $E[G_n] = G_0\,e^{(m_g+\frac{1}{2}\sigma_g^2)T}$ |

$g_n$ is normally distributed so we can take over the whole barrage of the Black Scholes model to price geometric average price options, using the following substitutions:

- $S_N \rightarrow G_N; \qquad x_N \rightarrow g_N$
- $\sigma^2 \rightarrow \sigma_g^2$ $\hfill$ (17.1)
- $\mu_{\text{risk neutral}} = (r - q) \rightarrow \mu_g = m_g + \frac{1}{2}\sigma_g^2$ $\hfill$ (17.2)

Remember, the term $(r - q)$ only appears in the Black Scholes model as an input into the calculation of the forward rate $F_{0T} \rightarrow S_0\,e^{(r-q)T}$; so equation (17.2) is equivalent to the substitution $F_{0T} \rightarrow S_0\,e^{(m_g+\frac{1}{2}\sigma_g^2)T}$ when using the Black Scholes model. Alternatively, we can describe the substitutions in the Black Scholes model as

- $S_0 \rightarrow S_0; \qquad \sigma^2 \rightarrow \sigma_g^2; \qquad q \rightarrow q_g = r - m_g - \frac{1}{2}\sigma_g^2$ $\hfill$ (17.3)

It just remains to work out expressions for $m_g$ and $\sigma_g^2$. The form of these depends on the precise averaging period being considered and will be given in the next three subsections.

(ii) **Simple Averaging**: We first consider geometric averaging from now until maturity, i.e. neither deferred nor in progress. Using previous definitions in this chapter:

$$\frac{G_N}{S_0} = \frac{1}{S_0}\{S_0 \times S_1 \times \cdots \times S_N\}^{\frac{1}{N+1}} = \left\{ \frac{S_0}{S_0} \times \frac{S_1}{S_0} \times \cdots \times \frac{S_N}{S_0} \right\}^{\frac{1}{N+1}}$$

Take logarithms of both sides:

$$g_N = \frac{1}{N+1}\sum_{n=0}^{N} x_n \qquad (17.4)$$

Using the analysis and notation of Section 3.1(ii) we can further write

$$x_n = \ln \frac{S_n}{S_0} = \ln \frac{S_1}{S_0} \times \frac{S_2}{S_1} \times \cdots \times \frac{S_n}{S_{n-1}} = r_1 + r_2 + \cdots + r_n$$

All the $r_i$ are independently and identically distributed with $E[r_i] = m\delta T$ and $\text{var}[r_i] = \sigma^2 \delta T$. When taking expectations or variances of $x_n$ we can therefore simply write each of the $r_i$ as $r$ and put $x_n \to nr$.

$$E[g_N] = \frac{1}{N+1} \sum_{n=0}^{N} E[x_n] = \frac{1}{N+1} \sum_{n=0}^{N} E[r_1 + r_2 + \cdots + r_n]$$

$$= \frac{1}{N+1} \sum_{n=0}^{N} E[nr] = \frac{m\delta T}{N+1} \sum_{n=0}^{N} n$$

And similarly

$$\text{var}[g_N] = \frac{1}{(N+1)^2} \sum_{n=0}^{N} \text{var}[x_n] = \frac{1}{(N+1)^2} \sum_{n=0}^{N} \text{var}[nr] = \frac{\sigma^2 \delta T}{(N+1)^2} \sum_{n=0}^{N} n^2$$

The following two standard results of elementary algebra

$$\sum_{n=1}^{N} n = \frac{1}{2}N(N+1); \qquad \sum_{n=1}^{N} n^2 = \frac{1}{6}N(N+1)(2N+1)$$

are used to give

$$m_g T = E[g_N] = \tfrac{1}{2} m N \delta T = \tfrac{1}{2} m T$$

$$\sigma_g^2 T = \text{var}[g_N] = \frac{\sigma^2 N \delta T}{3} \frac{(2N+1)}{(2N+2)} = \frac{\sigma^2 T}{3} \frac{(2N+1)}{(2N+2)} \tag{17.5}$$

It is interesting to compare these last two results with the analogous results for the logarithm of the stock price $x_N$ [Section 3.1(ii)]:

- $E[x_N] = mT$ while $E[g_N] = \tfrac{1}{2}mT$. It is no surprise that the expected growth of the average is half the expected growth of the underlying.
- $\lim_{N \to \infty} \text{var}[g_N] = \sigma^2 T / 3$. This is the "square root of three" rule of thumb for roughly estimating the value of an Asian option from the Black Scholes model by dividing the volatility by $\sqrt{3}$, which has long been used by traders.

(iii) **Deferred Start Averaging**: The results of the last subsection need to be adapted if the averaging period is not from "now" to the maturity of the option. We assume that deferred start averaging begins $\nu$ time steps from now. Equation (17.4) becomes

$$g_N = \frac{1}{N - \nu + 1} \sum_{n=\nu}^{N} x_n$$

Using the same analysis as before, we can write (for $n \geq \nu$)

$$x_n = \ln \frac{S_n}{S_0} = \ln \frac{S_\nu}{S_0} \times \frac{S_{\nu+1}}{S_\nu} \times \cdots \times \frac{S_n}{S_{n-1}} = x_\nu + r_{\nu+1} + r_{\nu+2} + \cdots + r_n$$

so that

$$E[g_N] = \frac{1}{N - v + 1} E\left[\sum_{n=v}^{N} \{x_v + r_{v+1} + r_2 + \cdots + r_n\}\right]$$

$$= E[x_v] + \frac{1}{N - v + 1} \sum_{n=v+1}^{N} E[(n - v)r]$$

Use $E[x_v] = E[vr] = vm\delta T$ and $\sum_{n=v+1}^{N}(n - v) = \sum_{n=1}^{N-v} n$ in the last equation to give

$$E[g_N] = vm\delta T + \frac{m\delta T}{N - v + 1}\frac{1}{2}(N - v)(N - v + 1) = \frac{1}{2}m\delta T(N + v) \qquad (17.6)$$

The corresponding expression for variance is given by

$$\text{var}[g_N] = \text{var}[x_v] + \frac{\sigma^2\delta T}{(N - v + 1)^2}\sum_{n=1}^{N-v} n^2 = \sigma^2\delta T\left\{v + \frac{1}{6}\frac{(N - v)(2N - 2v + 1)}{(N - v + 1)}\right\}$$

$$(17.7)$$

In continuous time, with large $N$ and setting $N\,\delta T \to T$ and $v\delta T \to \tau$, the last two equations can be written

$$E[g_N] = \frac{1}{2}m(T + \tau); \qquad \text{var}[g_N] = \frac{\sigma^2}{3}\left\{T + 2\tau - \frac{T - \tau}{2(N - v + 1)}\right\} \qquad (17.8)$$

(iv) **In-progress Averaging:** At some point in its life, every Asian option becomes an in-progress deal. The average then needs to be replaced by the average from now to maturity plus a non-stochastic past-average part. The adaption is straightforward:

$$G_N = \{S_{-v} \times S_{-v+1} \times \cdots \times S_0 \times \cdots \times S_N\}^{\frac{1}{N+v+1}} = \bar{G}^{\frac{v}{N+v+1}}\{S_0 \times S_1 \times \cdots \times S_N\}^{\frac{1}{N+v+1}}$$

where $\bar{G} = \{S_{-v} \times S_{-v+1} \times \cdots \times S_{-1}\}^{1/v}$ is the geometric mean of those past stock prices which have already been achieved. Using the methods of the last two subparagraphs, we have

$$g_N = \frac{v}{N + v + 1}\bar{g} + \frac{1}{N + v + 1}\sum_{n=0}^{N} x_n$$

Using the results of subsection (ii) above immediately gives

$$m_g T = E[g_N] = \frac{v}{N + v + 1}\bar{g} + \frac{N + 1}{N + v + 1}\frac{1}{2}mT \qquad (17.9)$$

$$\sigma_g^2 T = \text{var}[g_N] = \frac{\sigma^2 T}{6}\frac{(N + 1)(2N + 1)}{(N + v + 1)^2} \qquad (17.10)$$

In continuous time these are written

$$m_g T = \frac{\tau\bar{g} + \frac{1}{2}mT}{T + \tau}; \qquad \sigma_g^2 T = \frac{\sigma^2 T}{3}\left\{\frac{T}{T + \tau}\right\}^2 \qquad (17.11)$$

## 17.3 GEOMETRIC AVERAGE STRIKE OPTIONS

The payoff of a call option of this type is $\max[0, S_T - G_T]$; but this is an option to exchange one lognormal asset for another, and can be priced by Margrabe's formula [equations (12.1)] using the substitutions of equation (17.3):

$$C_{\text{GAS}} = S_0\, e^{-qT}\, N[d_1] - S_0\, e^{-q_s T}\, N[d_2] \tag{17.12}$$

$$d_1 = \frac{1}{\Sigma_g \sqrt{T}} \left\{ \ln \frac{e^{-qT}}{e^{-q_s T}} + \frac{1}{2}\Sigma_g^2 T \right\}; \qquad d_2 = d_1 - \Sigma_g \sqrt{T}$$

$$\Sigma_g^2 T = \sigma^2 T + \sigma_g^2 T - 2\,\text{cov}[x_T, g_T]; \qquad q_g = r - m_g - \tfrac{1}{2}\sigma_g^2$$

Expressions for $m_g$ and $\sigma_g^2$ corresponding to different types of averaging were derived in the last section. Now we just need to derive an expression for the covariance term.

**(i) Deferred Start Averaging**: Recall the results from Section 17.2(iii):

$$g_N = \frac{1}{N - \nu + 1} \sum_{n=\nu}^{N} x_n; \qquad x_n = r_1 + r_2 + \cdots + r_\nu + \cdots + r_n$$

and

$$\text{cov}[r_i, r_j] = \begin{cases} \sigma^2 \delta T & i = j \\ 0 & i \neq j \end{cases}$$

to give $\text{cov}[x_N, x_n] = n\sigma^2 \delta T\,(n \leq N)$. Then

$$\text{cov}[x_N, g_N] = \frac{1}{N-\nu+1}\text{cov}\left[x_N, \sum_{n=\nu}^{N} x_n\right] = \frac{\sigma^2 \delta T}{N-\nu+1}\sum_{n=\nu}^{N} n = \sigma^2 \delta T\,\frac{N+\nu}{2}$$

This last may be written $\sigma^2(T + \tau)/2$ in continuous time, and using equation (17.8) for $\sigma_g^2$ gives

$$\Sigma_g^2 = \frac{\sigma^2}{3}\frac{T - \tau}{T}$$

**(ii) In-progress Averaging**: Using the notation of Section 17.2(iv), $\text{cov}\langle \bar{g}, x_N \rangle = 0$ so that

$$\text{cov}[g_N, x_N] = \frac{1}{N+\nu+1}\text{cov}\left[\sum_{n=0}^{N} x_n, x_N\right] = \frac{\sigma^2 \delta T}{N-\nu+1}\sum_{n=0}^{N} n = \sigma^2 \delta T\,\frac{N(N+1)}{2(N+\nu+1)}$$

Once again, the last expression can be written as $\sigma^2 T^2/2(T + \tau)$ which yields the slightly more complicated result

$$\Sigma_g^2 = \sigma^2 \left\{ \frac{T^2}{3(T+\tau)^2} + \frac{\tau}{T+\tau} \right\}$$

## 17.4 ARITHMETIC AVERAGE OPTIONS: LOGNORMAL SOLUTIONS

(i) The analysis of the last two sections on geometric Asian options is satisfyingly elegant; but Asian options encountered in the market are arithmetic, and there are no simple Black Scholes type solutions for these. It was observed in Section 17.1(v) that arithmetic and geometric averages are surprisingly close in value, so that a natural approach is to seek an arithmetic solution expressed as a geometric solution plus a correction term.

The arithmetic average $A_N$ has the following properties:

- $A_N$ is the sum of a set of correlated, lognormally distributed random variables $S_N$, and does not have a simply defined distribution.
- Although the distribution of $A_N$ is ill-defined, exact expressions can be derived for the individual moments, i.e. $E[A_N^\lambda]$ with integer $\lambda$. Expressions for these moments in terms of observed or calculable parameters (volatility of the underlying stock, number of averaging points, risk-free rate, etc.) are given in Section A.13 of the Appendix.
- It has been observed in several fields of technology that the sum of lognormally distributed variables can be approximated by a lognormal distribution, under a fairly wide range of conditions.

These observations lead to various approximation methods. There seems to be a bewildering array of these, but the most important ones are closely related. We have included what we consider the most important approaches and a route map of the subject follows.

1. **Monte Carlo:** The arithmetic average option problem is ideally suited for solution by the Monte Carlo methods using the geometric average price as the control variate [see Section 10.4(iii)]. These can achieve any degree of accuracy we please just by extending calculation times. They are therefore ideal tools for testing or calibrating some faster algorithm to be used for real-life situations.
2. **Exactly Lognormal Models:** All methods explained in the next two sections exploit the fact that the arithmetic average is at least approximately lognormal. If we assume *exact* lognormality with the defining parameters $m_g$ and $\sigma_g^2$ as defined in the last section, we merely reproduce the geometric average results.

   - Vorst's method assumes the distribution of $A_n$ is exactly lognormal, but applies a correction term $E[A_n] - E[G_n]$ to the strike price.
   - The simple modified geometric also assumes that the distribution is exactly lognormal; it assumes that the variance is the same as for the geometric average, but it assumes that the mean $m_a$ equals the exact mean of the arithmetic average.
   - Levy's correction goes one step further than (4) by assuming that both the variance *and* the mean of the lognormal distribution assumed for $A_n$ are equal to the calculated variance and mean of the arithmetic average. Note that the mean and variance are now exactly correct, although the assumption of lognormality may be in error.

3. **Approximately Lognormal Models:** In Section 17.5, we drop the assumption of *exact* lognormality and merely assume the distribution of $A_n$ can be *approximated* by a lognormal distribution. Correction terms to the results of the present section (particularly Levy's method) are obtained in terms of an infinite but diminishing series of observable or calculable terms.
4. **Geometric Conditioning:** In Section 17.6, we examine a very successful method due to Curran, which makes no explicit assumptions about the form of the distribution of $A_N$. It is more awkward to implement than a simple formula, but it is probably the recommended approach at present, giving very accurate answers over a wide range.

(ii) **Vorst's Method:** (Vorst, 1992). Let $C_G$ and $C_A$ be the values of a geometric and an arithmetic average price call option. Given that the payoffs of these options at maturity are $C_A(T, X) = \max[0, A_N - X]$ and $C_G(T, X) = \max[0, G_N - X]$, and also given the general result mentioned in Section 7.1 that $G_N \le A_N$, we have a lower bound for $C_A(0, X)$:

$$C_G(0, X) \le C_A(0, X)$$

This is fairly obvious, but Vorst has also established an upper bound. If $G_N \le A_N$ then we can write

$$\max[0, A_N - X] - \max[0, G_N - X] = \begin{cases} 0: & A_N < X; \;\; G_N < X \\ A_N - X: & A_N > X; \;\; G_N < X \\ A_N - G_N: & A_N > X; \;\; G_N > X \end{cases} \quad (17.13)$$

Note that a fourth possible combination on the right-hand side $(A_N < X; G_N > X)$ is not included because $G_N \le A_N$. Two interesting results are derived from equation (17.13):

1. The equation can be summarized as

   $$\max[0, A_N - X] - \max[0, G_N - X] \le A_N - G_N$$

   Taking present values of risk-neutral expectations gives

   $$C_A(0, X) \le C_G(0, X) + e^{-rT} E\langle A_N - G_N \rangle$$

   This gives an upper bound on the value of $C_A(0, X)$ in terms of calculable quantities: $C_G(0, X)$ is the subject of Section 17.2; the lead-in to equation (17.3) shows that $E[G_N] \to S_0 e^{(m_g + \frac{1}{2}\sigma_g^2)T}$; $E[A_N]$ is derived in Appendix A.13.

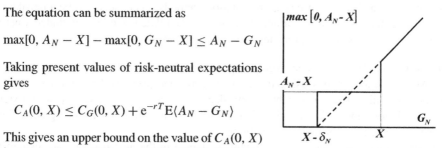

**Figure 17.1**    Vorst approximation

2. Equation (17.13) can be manipulated to a slightly different form:

$$\max[0, A_N - X] = \begin{cases} 0: & A_N < X; \;\; G_N < X \\ A_N - X: & A_N > X; \;\; G_N < X \\ G_N - (X - \delta_N): & A_N > X; \;\; G_N > X \end{cases}$$

where $\delta_N = A_N - G_N$. This payoff is illustrated in Figure 17.1. Recalling that $\delta_N$ is always small, the stepped part of the payoff might be approximated by the diagonal dotted line, prompting the following (Vorst's) approximation for an arithmetic average call option:

$$C_A(0, X) \approx C_G(0, X_\delta); \qquad X_\delta = X - E\langle \delta_N \rangle \quad (17.14)$$

(iii) **Simple Modified Geometric:** Let us assume that $A_N$ is lognormally distributed with the same volatility as $G_N$, i.e. $\sigma_g$. We can write this as $a_N = \ln(A_N/S_0) \sim N(m_a T, \sigma_g^2 T)$, where $a_N = \ln(A_N/S_0)$. It follows that

$$E[A_N] = S_0 e^{(m_a + \frac{1}{2}\sigma_g^2)T} \qquad \text{or} \qquad m_a T = \ln\frac{E[A_N]}{S_0} - \frac{1}{2}\sigma_g^2 \quad (17.15)$$

Expressions for $\sigma_g^2$ under various averaging scenarios were derived in Section 17.2. The corresponding expressions for $E[A_N]$ are derived in Appendix A.13. The net effect of this approach is to use the geometric average model but substitute the known risk-neutral drift of the arithmetic average.

(iv) **Levy Correction**: (Levy, 1992). This is a logical step forward from the last sub section. This time we assume that $a_N \sim N(m_a T, \sigma_a^2 T)$, i.e. the distribution of the arithmetic mean is lognormal; but this time we calculate $\sigma_a^2$ from first principles rather than just approximating it by $\sigma_g^2$.

Equation (A1.8) of the Appendix shows that $E[A_N^\lambda] = S_0^\lambda e^{(\lambda m_a + \frac{1}{2}\lambda^2 \sigma_a^2)T}$ where $\lambda$ is an integer. Therefore we may write

$$\left(m_a + \tfrac{1}{2}\sigma_a^2\right) T = \ln E[A_N] - \ln S_0$$
$$\left(m_a + \sigma_a^2\right) T = \tfrac{1}{2}\left\{\ln E[A_N^2] - \ln S_0^2\right\}$$

These are solved for $m_a$ and $\sigma_a^2$ using the expressions for the moments of $A_N$ given by equations (A13.11)–(A13.13). The value of an arithmetic average price call option can then be written

$$C_A^{\text{Levy}} = e^{-rt}\{E\langle A_N\rangle N[d_1] - X\,N[d_2]\} \tag{17.16}$$

$$d_1 = \frac{1}{\sigma_a\sqrt{T}}\left\{\ln\frac{E\langle A_n\rangle}{X} + \frac{1}{2}\sigma_a^2 T\right\}; \qquad d_2 = d_1 - \sigma_a\sqrt{T}$$

(v) **Arithmetic Average Strike Options**: Using Levy's model, we assume that the arithmetic average is lognormally distributed, so that the analysis is very similar to that given for geometric average strike options in Section 17.3. Again, the price of this option is given by Margrabe's formula:

$$C_{\text{AAS}} = S_0\,e^{-qt}\,N[d_1] - S_0\,e^{-q_a T}\,N[d_2] \tag{17.17}$$

$$d_1 = \frac{1}{\Sigma_a\sqrt{T}}\left\{\ln\frac{e^{-qT}}{e^{-q_a T}} + \frac{1}{2}\Sigma_g^2 T\right\}; \qquad d_2 = d_1 - \Sigma_a\sqrt{T}$$

$$\Sigma_a^2 T = \sigma^2 T + \sigma_a^2 T - 2\,\text{cov}[\ln S_T, \ln A_T]; \qquad q_a = r - m_a - \tfrac{1}{2}\sigma_a^2$$

The term $\text{cov}[\ln S_T, \ln A_N]$ can be calculated from equation (A1.23) which can be written as follows:

$$E[A_N S_T] = E[A_N]E[S_T]e^{\text{cov}[\ln S_T, \ln A_N]T}$$

A formula for each of the expected values is given in Appendix A.13.

## 17.5 ARITHMETIC AVERAGE OPTIONS: EDGEWORTH EXPANSION

(i) It is well known that a function can be expressed by a Maclaurin's (Taylor's) expansion as follows:

$$f(x + \delta x) = f(x) + \sum_{n=1}^{\infty} \frac{1}{n!}\frac{\partial^n f(x)}{\partial x^n}(\delta x)^n$$

It is less well known that if a probability density function $f(A_N)$ is approximated by another distribution $l(A_N)$, then we may write

$$f(A_N) = l(A_N) + \sum_{n=1}^{\infty} \frac{(-1)^n}{n!}\frac{\partial^n l(A_N)}{\partial A_N^n}E_n$$

This is called the Edgeworth expansion and is derived in Appendix A.14.

We assume that the true distribution of $A_N$ has a true density function $f(A_N)$ which is close to but not identical to the lognormal distribution $l(A_N)$; the analytical form of the latter is known so that the derivatives can be evaluated explicitly. The terms $E_n$ are functions only of the differences between the various cumulants under the true distribution of $A_N$, and the corresponding cumulants under the lognormal distribution. Furthermore, the cumulants themselves are functions only of the moments of $A_N$ which may be calculated explicitly for both the true distribution and for the lognormal distribution. All terms on the right-hand side of the Edgeworth expansion are therefore calculable in principle.

(ii) We will restrict ourselves to an investigation of the effects of higher moments up to the fourth term in the Edgeworth expansion:

$$f(A_N) = l(A_N) - \frac{\partial l(A_N)}{\partial A_N} E_1 + \frac{1}{2!} \frac{\partial^2 l(A_N)}{\partial A_N^2} E_2 - \frac{1}{3!} \frac{\partial^3 l(A_N)}{\partial A_N^3} E_3 + \frac{1}{4!} \frac{\partial^4 l(A_N)}{\partial A_N^4} E_4$$

(17.18)

where

$$\delta\kappa_n = \kappa_n^f - \kappa_n^l$$
$$E_1 = \delta\kappa_1; \qquad E_2 = \delta\kappa_2 + (\delta\kappa_1)^2; \qquad E_3 = \delta\kappa_3 + 3\delta\kappa_1\delta\kappa_2 + (\delta\kappa_1)^3$$
$$E_4 = \delta\kappa_4 + 4\delta\kappa_1\delta\kappa_3 + 3(\delta\kappa_2)^2 + 6(\delta\kappa_1)^2\delta\kappa_2 + (\delta\kappa_1)^4$$

The cumulants may be obtained from

$$\kappa_1 = \mathrm{E}[x] = \mu; \qquad \kappa_2 = \mathrm{E}\left[(x - \kappa_1)^2\right] = \sigma^2$$
$$\kappa_3 = \mathrm{E}\left[(x - \kappa_1)^3\right]; \qquad \kappa_4 = \mathrm{E}\left[(x - \kappa_1)^4\right] - 3\kappa_2^2$$

The expectations of the powers of $A_N$ (moments) corresponding to $\kappa_n^f$ are given in Appendix A.13; the moments corresponding to $\kappa_n^l$ (i.e. lognormal) are given by the standard formula $\mathrm{E}[A_N^\lambda] = S_0^\lambda \, \mathrm{e}^{(\lambda m_a + \frac{1}{2}\lambda^2\sigma_a^2)T}$ which was encountered in connection with Levy's method in the last section.

When we say that $l(A_N)$ is a lognormal distribution, this is clearly not enough to define the distribution: we must, for example, specify the mean and variance. Let us select $l(A_N)$ to have mean and variance equal to the true mean and variance of $A_N$, i.e. set these parameters in the same way as for the Levy method. Then by definition, $\kappa_1^f = \kappa_1^l$ and $\kappa_2^f = \kappa_2^l$ so that $E_1 = 0$ and $E_2 = 0$.

This is known as the Turnbull–Wakeham method (Turnbull and Wakeham, 1991). The only remaining inputs which have not been given explicitly are the two partial differentials. But $l(A_N)$ is just the lognormal probability density function

$$l(A_N) = \frac{1}{A_N\sqrt{2\pi\sigma_a^2 T}} \exp\left[-\frac{1}{2}\left(\frac{\ln(A_N/S_0) - m_a T}{\sigma_a\sqrt{T}}\right)^2\right]$$

where $m_a$ and $\sigma_a^2$ are defined in Section 17.4(iv).

(iii) Using this last expansion and equation (A14.8), we can now write for the value of an arithmetic average

$$C_A^{\mathrm{TW}} = C_A^{\mathrm{Levy}} + \mathrm{e}^{-rT}\left\{-\frac{1}{3!}\frac{\partial l(A_N)}{\partial A_N}E_3 + \frac{1}{4!}\frac{\partial^2 l(A_N)}{\partial A_N^2}E_4\right\}_{A_N=X}$$

(17.19)

(iv) In the last subsection, we defined the approximating distribution $l(A_N)$ as having mean and variance equal to the true mean and variance of $A_N$ (always assuming of course that the underlying $S_t$ is lognormal). The effect of this is to make the $E_1$ and $E_2$ terms in equation (17.18) drop out.

We could equally have defined $l(A_N)$ as having skewness and kurtosis equal to the true skewness and kurtosis of $A_N$. Using definitions of the cumulants given in the last subsection, we can then derive the corresponding mean and variance for $l(A_N)$. This approach should give better answers if the true distribution $f(A_N)$ is indeed significantly different from normal due to a high level of skewness and kurtosis. But the computation significantly increases in complexity as none of the terms of equation (17.18) now drop out.

## 17.6 ARITHMETIC AVERAGE OPTIONS: GEOMETRIC CONDITIONING

This is a different approach from that taken in the last two sections, and gives better results over a wider range. In fact, the answers come out so close to the Monte Carlo results that it seems unlikely to be much bettered (Curran, 1994).

(i) **Conditioning**: The underlying technique on which this method is based relies on the following principles: suppose $x$ and $y$ are two random variables which are *not* independent of each other, and let $u(x)$ be some function of $x$. The conditioning principle states that

$$E^x[u(x)] = E^y[E^x[u(x)|y]] \qquad (17.20)$$

We pause to reflect on what this means:

- The left-hand side is easy: we can use the definition $E^x[u(x)] = \int_{-\infty}^{+\infty} u(x)f(x)\,dx$ where $f(x)$ is the probability density function for the variable $x$.
- The term $E^x[u(x)|y]$ is the conditional expectation of $u(x)$, conditional on $y$ achieving a certain value. It may be written $E^x[u(x) \mid y] = \int_{-\infty}^{+\infty} u(x)f(x \mid y)\,dx$ where $f(x \mid y)$ is the conditional probability density function.
- At first glance, the reader is likely to ask how $E^x[u(x)]$ can depend on some arbitrarily introduced variable $y$; but we take the expectation (i.e. integrate) over all $y$ so the $y$-dependence falls away. Alternatively put:

$$E^x[u(x)] = E^y[E^x[u(x) \mid y]] = \int_{-\infty}^{+\infty} E^x[u(x) \mid y]f(y)\,dy$$

$$= \int_{-\infty}^{+\infty} dx \int_{-\infty}^{+\infty} u(x)f(x \mid y)f(y)\,dy \qquad (17.21)$$

- This brings us back to the left-hand side of equation (17.20); in the first bullet point, it was explained that this was an expectation over all $x$, but it could equally have been described as an expectation over all $x$ *and* $y$ (and over all $p$ and $q$ and $r$ as well for that matter!). This is written

$$E^x[u(x)] = \int_{-\infty}^{+\infty} dx \int_{-\infty}^{+\infty} u(x)f(x, y)\,dy \qquad (17.22)$$

Comparing the last two equations gives the general relationship

$$f(x \mid y) = \frac{f(x, y)}{f(y)} \tag{17.23}$$

(ii) Conditioning is now applied with $A_N$ in place of $x$ and $G_N$ in place of $y$:

$$
\begin{aligned}
E^{A_N}[\max[0, A_N - X]] &= E^{G_N}[E^{A_N}[\max[0, A_N - X] \mid G_N]] \\
&= \int_0^{+\infty} E^{A_N}[\max[0, A_N - X] \mid G_N] l(G_N)\, dG_N \\
&= \left\{ \int_0^X + \int_X^{+\infty} \right\} E^{A_N}[\max[0, A_N - X] \mid G_N] l(G_N)\, dG_N = C_1 + C_2
\end{aligned}
$$

where the last equality defines $C_1$ and $C_2$, and $l(G_N)$ is the lognormal distribution function which has previously been shown to apply to $G_N$.

(iii) *Second Integral* ($C_2$): We start with this as it is the easy one. The key observation is that $A_N \geq G_N$ which has already been discussed in this chapter. The integral runs from $G_N = X$ to $G_N = \infty$, so all values of $A_N$ affecting this integral will be greater than $X$. We can therefore dispense with the "max" function in the second integral:

$$
\begin{aligned}
C_2 &= \int_X^{+\infty} E^{A_N}[A_N - X \mid G_N] l(G_N)\, dG_N \\
&= \sum_N \int_X^{+\infty} E^{A_N}[S_n \mid G_N] l(G_N)\, dG_N - X \int_X^{+\infty} l(G_N)\, dG_N \tag{17.24}
\end{aligned}
$$

The exact meaning of the symbol $\sum_N$ in front of the first term depends on the type of arithmetic averaging used. For deferred averaging we would write

$$\sum_N S_n \Rightarrow \frac{1}{N - v + 1} \sum_{n=v}^N S_n$$

On the other hand, for in-progress averaging we would have

$$\sum_N S_n \Rightarrow \frac{v}{N + v + 1} \bar{A} + \frac{1}{N + v + 1} \sum_{n=0}^N S_n$$

It is shown in Appendix A.1(ix), item (D) that if $z_1$ and $z_2$ are two standard normal variables with correlation $\rho$, the conditional distribution $n(z_1 \mid z_2)$ is $N(\rho z_2, (1 - \rho^2))$, i.e. normal with mean $\rho z_2$ and variance $(1 - \rho^2)$. We now make the transformation of variables as previously:

$$x_n = \ln \frac{S_n}{S_0}; \qquad g_n = \ln \frac{G_n}{S_0}; \qquad z_x = \frac{x_n - m t_n}{\sigma \sqrt{t_n}}; \qquad z_g = \frac{g_N - m_g T}{\sigma_g \sqrt{T}}$$

where $t_n$ is the time from now to the point when the stock price is $S_n$. The correlation coefficient between $z_x$ and $z_g$ may now be written

$$\rho_{ng} = \text{cov}[z_x, z_g] = \frac{\text{cov}[x_n, g_N]}{\sigma \sqrt{t_n}\, \sigma_g \sqrt{T}}$$

We will write this correlation as $\rho_n$ for short. The covariance term may be explicitly derived by using the method and notation of Section 17.3(i) as follows:

$$\text{cov}[x_n, g_N] = \frac{1}{N - \nu + 1} \text{cov}\left[x_n, \sum_{i=\nu}^{N} x_i\right]$$

$$= \frac{1}{N - \nu + 1} \sum_{i=\nu}^{N} \text{cov}[(r_1 + r_2 + \cdots + r_n), (r_1 + r_2 + \cdots + r_i)]$$

$$= \frac{1}{N - \nu + 1} \left\{ \nu \sigma^2 \delta T + \sum_{i=\nu}^{N} i \sigma^2 \delta T + (N - n)\sigma^2 \delta T \right\}$$

$$= \frac{\sigma^2 \delta T}{N - \nu + 1} \left\{ \frac{1}{2}(n + \nu)(n - \nu + 1) + N - n \right\}$$

The expectation within the integral $C_2$ may now be written

$$E^{A_N}\langle S_n \mid G_N \rangle = S_0 \int_{-\infty}^{+\infty} e^{z_x \sigma \sqrt{t_n} + m t_n}\, n(z_x \mid z_g)\, dz_x$$

$$= S_0 \int_{-\infty}^{+\infty} e^{z_x \sigma \sqrt{t_n} + m t_n} \frac{1}{2\pi \sqrt{1 - \rho_n^2}} \exp\left[ -\frac{1}{2(1 - \rho_n^2)} \{z_x - \rho_n z_g\}^2 \right] dz_x$$

$$= S_0 \int_{-\infty}^{+\infty} e^{\sigma \sqrt{t_n}(y \sqrt{1 - \rho_n^2} + \rho_n z_g) + m t_n} \frac{1}{\sqrt{2\pi}} e^{-\frac{1}{2} y^2}\, dz_x$$

$$= S_0\, e^{(m + \frac{1}{2}\sigma^2(1 - \rho_n^2))t_n + \rho_n \sigma \sqrt{t_n} z_g} \tag{17.25}$$

where we have changed variable from $z_x$ to $y$ and used the standard results of Appendix A.1. A formula for $C_2$ can now be derived using the further standard results of Appendix A.1(v):

$$C_2 = \sum_N S_0 \int_{Z_g}^{+\infty} e^{(m + \frac{1}{2}\sigma^2(1 - \rho_n^2))t_n + \rho_n \sigma \sqrt{t_n} z_g}\, n(z_g)\, dz_g - X \int_{Z_g}^{+\infty} n(z_g)\, dz_g$$

$$= \sum_N S_0\, e^{(m + \frac{1}{2}\sigma^2)t_n}\, N[\rho_n \sigma \sqrt{t_n} - Z_g] - X\, N[-Z_g] \tag{17.26}$$

where

$$Z_g = \frac{1}{\sigma_g \sqrt{T}} \left\{ \ln \frac{X}{G_0} - m_g T \right\}$$

Note that this derivation has been performed assuming deferred averaging; the modification required for in-process averaging will be left to the reader.

(iv) **First Integral ($C_1$):** We are unable to evaluate this integral exactly and must therefore make a simplifying approximation. The simplest approximation is

$$C_1 = -\int_0^X E^{A_N}[\max[0,\, X - A_N] \mid G_N] l(G_N)\, dG_N$$

$$\approx -\int_0^X \max[0,\, E^{A_N}\langle X - A_N \mid G_N \rangle] l(G_N)\, dG_N \tag{17.27}$$

213

In general, the effect of switching the max[·, ·] and E[·] operators is equivalent to switching between the value of a European put option and its asymptotes, as shown in Figure 17.2. max[0, E[·]] is a lower bound of all possible values of E[max[0, ·]]; one is normally only justified in making the approximation if $\sigma^2 T$ approaches zero. So why do we do it in this case?

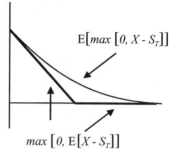

The difference is that in the present case the expectation is conditioned on values of $G_N$ and the final integral over $G_N$ only runs from 0 to $X$. But we have observed several times in this chapter that although in general $A_N \geq G_N$, the difference in size between the

**Figure 17.2**    Effect of switch

two quantities is surprisingly small. So only a very small range of $A_N$ immediately above $G_N = X$ contributes to the calculation.

(v) A solution of this integral now proceeds as follows:

1. From equation (17.25)

$$E^{A_N}[X - A_N \mid G_N] = X - \sum_N S_0\, e^{(m + \frac{1}{2}\sigma^2(1 - \rho^2))T_n + \rho\sigma\sqrt{T_n}z_g}$$

where

$$z_g = \frac{1}{\sigma_g\sqrt{T}}\left\{\ln\frac{G_N}{S_0} - m_g T\right\}$$

2. The form of this function is monotonic decreasing as shown in Figure 17.3. Solve the implicit equation

$$E^{A_N}[X - A_N \mid G_N^*] = 0$$

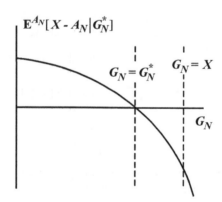

**Figure 17.3**    Geometric conditioning

for $G_N^*$. We can then get rid of the "max" function by changing the upper limit of integration in equation (17.27) to $G_N^*$. This can be quite a substantial numerical task, depending on the number of averaging points, and is performed by some sort of "goal seek" routine.

3. Further use of the standard integrals of Appendix A.1(v) gives

$$
C_1 = - \left\{ X \int_{-\infty}^{Z^*} n(z_g)\,dz_g - \sum_N S_0 \int_{-\infty}^{Z^*} e^{(m+\frac{1}{2}\sigma^2(1-\rho^2))T_n + \rho\sigma\sqrt{T_n}z_g} n(z_g)\,dz_g \right\}
$$

$$
= \sum_N S_0 \, e^{(m+\frac{1}{2}\sigma^2)T_n} \, N[Z^* - \rho\sigma\sqrt{T_n}] - X \, N[X^*] \tag{17.28}
$$

where

$$
Z^* = \frac{1}{\sigma_g \sqrt{T}} \left\{ \ln \frac{G_N^*}{G_0} - m_g T \right\}
$$

## 17.7  COMPARISON OF METHODS

In this chapter, frequent reference has been made to answers being close to each other and distributions approximating each other, but without much quantitative backing. Now the time has come to apply the acid test: how good are the answers obtained from the various methods which have been described?

Table 17.1 gives an abstract from the papers quoted in the footnote. In-progress results are less interesting in the sense that they carry the dead weight of the "average-until-now" and therefore have less optionality than deferred average options; results for in-progress averaging are therefore excluded. Furthermore we only quote results for the rather extreme volatility of 50%. For a volatility of 30%, errors in the answers obtained by the various methods are of the order of one-third of the errors obtained at 50%; at a volatility of 10%, the answers obtained by the different methods are effectively all the same.

Prices are given for two different options in Table 17.1. Both are on a non-dividend-paying stock with a volatility of 50%; the interest rate is 9% and averaging takes place at weekly intervals over 1 year. The "Simple Averaging" option runs for 52 weeks with the averaging starting now; the "Deferred Averaging" option is similar but has the averaging start in 20 weeks and then run for 52 weeks, i.e. it is a 72-week option.

**Table 17.1**  Comparison of models for arithmetic average options

| | Simple Averaging | | | Deferred Averaging | | |
|---|---|---|---|---|---|---|
| Stock Price = 100 | Strike Price | | | Strike Price | | |
| | 90 | 100 | 110 | 90 | 100 | 110 |
| Monte Carlo (±0.03) | 18.14 | 12.98 | 9.10 | 24.17 | 19.38 | 15.44 |
| Geometric | 16.75 | 11.76 | 8.00 | 22.61 | 18.02 | 14.26 |
| Vorst | 18.00 | 12.71 | 8.71 | 23.79 | 19.00 | 15.06 |
| Modified geometric | 18.20 | 12.94 | 8.93 | 24.10 | 19.34 | 15.40 |
| Levy | 18.38 | 13.16 | 9.17 | 24.24 | 19.50 | 15.57 |
| T&W (elementary) | 17.66 | 12.86 | 9.22 | 23.58 | 19.26 | 15.63 |
| T&W (higher moments) | 18.13 | 13.00 | 9.12 | 24.02 | 19.35 | 15.49 |
| Geometric conditioning | 18.14 | 12.98 | 9.07 | 24.10 | 19.37 | 15.47 |

*Note*: Results taken from Levy and Turnbull (1992) and Curran (1992).

A Monte Carlo method has been used to obtain the "right answer" which is quoted with an indication of its accuracy (1 standard deviation). The numbers really speak for themselves but a few comments are worth making:

- Approximating the price of an arithmetic average option by a geometric option price is not nearly close enough for commercial purposes.
- The geometric conditioning method (Curran) wins hands down.
- Modified geometric (adjusted mean only) does quite well, and the more sophisticated Levy correction seems to make things worse rather than better.
- Turnbull and Wakeham in its elementary form (matched mean and variance) is disappointing, given the sophistication of the mathematics and given that it was designed as an improvement on Levy.
- Turnbull and Wakeham is much improved if we match skewness and kurtosis [see Section 17.5(iv)], although it is still inadequate for in-the-money deferred average call options.

# 18

# Passport Options

This part of the book has been devoted to the so-called exotic options, which have varying degrees of importance as commercial instruments in their own right, as well as giving live examples of the application of the theory developed in the first two parts of this book. Broadly, they fall into three categories: correlation options, barrier options and average options. The mathematics used to describe these options has so far been restricted to "classical" methods (statistical distribution theory, differential equations, etc.) In Part 4, we develop the tools for a more "modern" approach using stochastic calculus, and show that the exotic options can be described with greater elegance although at the expense of greater formalism and with few new conclusions.

We leave Part 3 with this short chapter, which is introduced for two reasons: first, the passport option is extremely innovative and interesting. There has been a fairly widely held assumption in the trade since the early 1990s that all the really useful exotics on equities or currencies have already been invented, and future research would merely come up with overcomplicated and impractical ideas. But the passport option is a recent development in a completely new direction, having obvious commercial applicability. Second, the description of these instruments stretches the envelope of the option theory that has been presented in the book so far, and also provides an excellent case study of the complementary nature of classical and modern methods of analyzing options (Andersen *et al.*, 1998).

## 18.1 OPTION ON AN INVESTMENT STRATEGY (TRADING OPTION)

(i) Imagine a trader who specializes in a single asset such as a currency or a stock option; he can only go long or short up to a fixed maximum, and relies entirely on timing to make his profit. The trader's record has been good in the past but his manager is concerned about the general economic outlook for the next 6 months. Therefore, without telling the trader, he buys an option with the following payoff: the cumulative loss made by the trader in the next 6 months, or zero if the trader makes a cumulative profit. This option is called a passport option.

One's first reaction to this option is to question whether it can be sensibly priced at all: after all, the trader could be doing absolutely anything, so how can we ascribe an expected value to his losses. The answer of course is that he cannot do anything; he is constrained in the maximum position he can take and we price the option by assuming that he systematically follows the worst strategy within this constraint. All this presupposes that there exists a worst strategy. One's instinct is that maybe the worst strategy is to maintain a constant short position of 100%, on the grounds that a positive drift $(r - q)$ will ensure that this strategy makes a loss more than 50% of the time; however, this turns out not to be the case.

A "worst" strategy as described above and a "best" strategy are simply the reciprocal of each other, i.e. we just change long positions to shorts and vice versa. The analysis which follows is expressed in terms of "best" or "optimal" strategy.

Our approach will be to derive a differential equation using just the same riskless hedge approach as we used to derive the Black Scholes equation in Section 4.2. The optimum strategy will emerge as a by-product, together with an option replication strategy.

(ii) **The Trading Option**: This is specified as follows. A trader manages a stock position in such a way that he may never be more than one share long or short (fractional shares allowed). He manages according to a strategy $u_t$, where $u_t$ is the amount of shares held at time $t$, and is subject to the constraint $|u_t| < 1$.
Examples of strategies are:

- At the beginning of each day go long or short depending on what would have made money yesterday.
- Go long on odd days and short on even days.
- Take positions that replicate a put option.

An example of a strategy, which we do not consider for obvious reasons, is "go long on days when this produces a profit".

The cumulative profit/loss generated by a strategy between time zero and $t$ is written $w_t$. The trading option is defined as having payoff $\max[0, w_T]$ and the value of this option is given by

$$f = e^{-rT} \, E[\max[0, w_T]]_{\text{risk neutral}}$$

The precise value of $f$ obviously depends on the precise strategy $u_t$ which generates $w_t$, but we keep the argument general for the moment.

(iii) **Partial Differential Equation for Trading Option**: It is assumed that $S_t$ and $w_t$ follow the Wiener processes

$$\delta S_t = (\mu - q)S_t \delta t + \sigma S_t \delta W_t \qquad \text{and} \qquad \delta w_t = u_t \delta S_t$$

Be careful not to confuse $w_t$ and $W_t$: unfortunate, but this is the most common notation.

Assume that we can construct a riskless portfolio consisting of one unit of option and $-\Delta$ units of the underlying stock; its value is $f - \Delta_t S_t$ and its shift in value over a small interval is $\delta f - \Delta_t \delta S_t$. Since it is riskless, its rate of return must equal the risk-free return, so that

$$\delta f - \Delta_t \delta S_t - q S_t \Delta_t \delta t = (f - \Delta_t S_t) r \delta t \tag{18.1}$$

So far, we are headed towards deriving the Black Scholes equation again; but this time, $f$ also depends on $w_t$ so that the Taylor expansion is

$$\delta f = \frac{\partial f}{\partial t} \delta t + \frac{\partial f}{\partial S_t} \delta S_t + \frac{\partial f}{\partial w_t} \delta w_t + \left\{ \frac{\partial^2 f}{\partial S_t^2}(\delta S_t)^2 + 2\frac{\partial^2 f}{\partial S_t \partial w_t}(\delta S_t \partial w_t) + \frac{\partial^2 f}{\partial w_t^2}(\delta w_t)^2 \right\}$$

In addition to the substitution $(\delta S_t)^2 \to S_t^2 \sigma^2 \delta t$ which we previously used for deriving the Black Scholes equation, we now have the following: $(\delta w_t)^2 \to u_t^2 S_t^2 \sigma^2 \delta t$ and $(\delta S_t \delta w_t) \to u_t S_t^2 \sigma^2 \delta t$. Putting these into the Taylor expansion gives Ito's Lemma for this particular problem, analogous to equation (3.12):

$$\delta f = \left\{ \frac{\partial f}{\partial t} + S_t^2 \sigma^2 \left( \frac{\partial^2 f}{\partial S_t^2} + 2u_t \frac{\partial^2 f}{\partial S_t \partial w_t} + u_t^2 \frac{\partial^2 f}{\partial w_t^2} \right) \right\} \delta t + \left\{ \frac{\partial f}{\partial S_t} + u_t \frac{\partial f}{\partial w_t} \right\} \delta S_t$$

Plugging this back into equation (18.1) and setting the coefficient of $\delta W_t$ equal to zero (since the deal is risk-free) gives

$$\frac{\partial f}{\partial t} + S_t^2 \sigma^2 \left\{ \frac{\partial^2 f}{\partial S_t^2} + 2u_t \frac{\partial^2 f}{\partial S_t \partial w_t} + u_t^2 \frac{\partial^2 f}{\partial w_t^2} \right\} + (r-q)S_t \left\{ \frac{\partial f}{\partial S_t} + u_t \frac{\partial f}{\partial w_t} \right\} = rf$$

and

$$\Delta = \frac{\partial f}{\partial S_t} + u_t \frac{\partial f}{\partial w_t} \tag{18.2}$$

This looks like a complex PDE in two "space" variables $S_t$ and $w_t$; but for fixed $u_t$, $S_t$ and $w_t$ have perfect correlation, i.e. they are not really different variables. We now look for a single variable that serves for both.

(iv) **Transformed PDE for a Trading Option**: The homogeneity arguments of Section 11.1(ii) indicate that the trading option price is a homogeneous function of $S_t$ and $w_t$, so that

$$f(t, S_t, w_t) = S_t f(t, w_t/S_t) = S_t v(t, x_t) \qquad \text{where} \qquad x_t = w_t/S_t$$

This change of variable can be applied to equations (18.2) using the following transformations:

$$\frac{\partial f}{\partial S_t} = v - x_t \frac{\partial v}{\partial x_t}; \qquad \frac{\partial^2 f}{\partial S_t^2} = x_t \frac{\partial^2 v}{\partial x_t^2}$$

$$\frac{\partial f}{\partial w_t} = \frac{\partial v}{\partial x_t}; \qquad \frac{\partial^2 f}{\partial w_t^2} = \frac{1}{S_t} \frac{\partial^2 v}{\partial x_t^2}; \qquad \frac{\partial^2 f}{\partial S_t \partial w_t} = -\frac{x_t}{S_t} \frac{\partial^2 v}{\partial x_t^2}$$

so that the equations become

$$\frac{\partial v}{\partial t} + (u_t - x_t)(r-q)\frac{\partial v}{\partial x_t} + \frac{1}{2}\sigma^2 (u_t - x_t)^2 \frac{\partial^2 v}{\partial x_t^2} = qv$$

and

$$\Delta_t = v + (u_t - x_t)\frac{\partial v}{\partial x_t} \tag{18.3}$$

with boundary condition $v(T) = \max[0, x_T]$.

(v) In terms of the parameter $x_t$, the payoff $v(T)$ of the option is given by the usual hockey-stick payoff diagram with $v(t)$ having the general form of the dotted curve in Figure 18.1. The precise form of $v(t)$ will of course depend on the exact form of the strategy $u_t$ employed. However, it is apparent from the general form of the $v(t)$ curve that

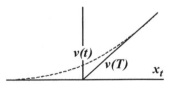

**Figure 18.1** Trading option price

$$0 \le \frac{\partial v(t)}{\partial x_t} \qquad \text{and} \qquad 0 \le \frac{\partial^2 v(t)}{\partial x_t^2} \tag{18.4}$$

## 18.2 OPTION ON AN OPTIMAL INVESTMENT STRATEGY (PASSPORT OPTION)

(i) *The Optimal Strategy*: We now pose the following question: "Is there some optimal strategy which could be followed by our hypothetical portfolio manager, which gives a greater expected return than all others?" If there is, an option on this strategy would be more expensive than options on all other strategies. We therefore turn the question on its head and ask: "what strategy maximizes the value of a trading option?".

Equation (18.3) may be rewritten as

$$v(t) = \frac{1}{q}\{Au_t^2 + Bu_t + C\}$$

where

$$A \equiv \frac{1}{2}\sigma^2\frac{\partial^2 v(t)}{\partial x_t^2}; \qquad B \equiv (r-q)\frac{\partial v(t)}{\partial x_t} - x_t\sigma^2\frac{\partial^2 v(t)}{\partial x_t^2}$$

$$C \equiv \frac{\partial v(t)}{\partial t} - x_t(r-q)\frac{\partial v(t)}{\partial x_t} + \frac{1}{2}x_t^2\sigma^2\frac{\partial^2 v(t)}{\partial x_t^2}$$

Write $U_t$ as the value of $u_t$ for the strategy that maximizes $v(t)$ in the last equation. Some critical points emerge:

- $B$ and $C$ may be positive or negative; but from equation (18.4), we always have $0 \le A$. We assume $0 < q$.
- It follows that $v(t)$ is a maximum if $u_t$ is as large as possible; but remember that $u_t$ is restricted to $-1 < u_t < +1$. The optimal strategy therefore has $U_t^2 = 1$ or $U_t = \pm 1$.
- Switching our attention to the second term in brackets, $v(t)$ is a maximum if $BU_t$ is always positive, i.e.

$$U_t = \text{sign } B = \text{sign}\left\{(r-q)\frac{\partial v(t)}{\partial x_t} - x_t\sigma^2\frac{\partial^2 v(t)}{\partial x_t^2}\right\} \qquad (18.5)$$

where $\text{sign } a = +1(0 \le a), -1(a < 0)$.

This completely defines the optimal strategy. From equation (18.3), the delta of the option is given by

$$\Delta = v(t) + (\text{sign } B - x_t)\frac{\partial v(t)}{\partial x_t}$$

so that the delta jumps each time the sign of $B$ changes.

(ii) *Driftless Solution*: We should now be in a position to solve the partial differential equation, finding an analytical expression for $v(t)$, and hence for the value of a passport option. But disappointingly, equation (18.3) is too hard to solve, except in the driftless case where $r = q$ and $U_t = \text{sign } B = \text{sign } x_t = \text{sign } w_t$ and so

$$\frac{\partial v(t)}{\partial t} + \frac{1}{2}\sigma^2(1 + |x_t|)^2\frac{\partial^2 v(t)}{\partial x_t^2} = qv(t)$$

An analytical solution may be obtained for this using Laplace transforms; however, in view of the restricted applicability, we will not derive an explicit formula here.

(iii) *Intuitive Analysis*: At this point it is worth stepping back to reflect on the optimum solution we have found, and its implications. Confronted with the passport problem for the first time, most people would give the following intuitive analysis:

(A) The Wiener process $\delta S_t = (r - q)S_t \delta t + \sigma S_t \delta W_t$ implies that $E[S_T] = S_0 e^{(r-q)T}$.

(B) The optimum trading strategy should therefore be to stay 100% long if the drift $(r - q)$ is positive, since there is more than a 50–50 chance of an up move. If the drift is negative, stay 100% short.

(C) Price the passport option to correspond to the strategy laid out in the last point, i.e. as a call if the drift is positive and as a put if it is negative.

(D) If there is an accumulated trading profit/loss $w_0$ at $t = 0$, this is merely set aside and accounted for at the end; it will not affect the value of the passport option except in a trivial, additive way.

Point (A) is undisputed. Looking at equation (18.5) shows that point (B) is almost true: the first term in curly brackets is just a restatement of (B) and this term is usually the dominant term; but there is an important second term which the intuitive analysis has missed. It is this term which prevents us from using the recipe in point (C) to price a passport option. The reason why the intuitive analysis does not hold true is that point (D) is false, as is simply demonstrated below.

(iv) Let us examine the driftless case $(r - q = 0)$. The intuitive analysis above would imply that there is no optimal strategy; the expectations of long, short and zero positions are the same. This option could therefore be priced as either a put *or* a call. In the even more restricted circumstance where the accumulated trading profit is exactly zero $(w_0 = 0)$, this is indeed the case. Figure 18.2 shows the well-known symmetry of put and call options with the same strike (at-the-money). But unfortunately, as soon as $w_0 \neq 0$, this symmetry all breaks down.

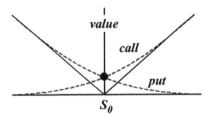

**Figure 18.2** Driftless case with $w_0 = 0$

To see why, consider the following simple, one-period model: instead of a continuous trading strategy, the trader has to decide at $t = 0$ whether to go long or short for the entire period. Depending on whether he goes long or short, the payoff will be

$$\text{Payoff}_{\text{long}} = \begin{cases} \max[0, S_T - (S_0 - w_0)] & w_0 < S_0 \\ w_T & S_0 < w_0 \end{cases}$$

$$\text{Payoff}_{\text{short}} = \max[0, (S_0 + w_0) - S_T]$$

It is already obvious from the asymmetry of the payoffs in this simple model that the option value depends on the initial trading profit $w_0$ in some non-trivial way (i.e. not simply additive). Clearly, in the real world where the trader has the continuous ability to change his position, the value of the passport option will also depend on the cumulative profit. Remember, we are still considering the driftless case, where we had previously advanced the argument that there *is* no optimal strategy.

The underlying reason for the intuitive arguments not working are easy to trace back. In our simple one-period model, the asymmetry was caused by the fact that $S_t$ cannot be less than zero. In fact, the whole issue can be traced back to an alternatively stated description of the same fact, i.e. the skewed nature of the lognormal distribution. If stock prices were normally distributed, the pseudo-intuitive approach would have been correct and it would not have been worth writing this chapter.

## 18.3   PRICING A PASSPORT OPTION

(i) **The PDE:** In the absence of an analytical solution of equation (18.3), we have to use one of the numerical schemes of Chapter 8. The form of the equation makes explicit discretization schemes less stable than for the heat equation, so the Crank Nicolson method is generally used.

We start by putting equation (18.3) into a slightly more familiar format:

$$\frac{\partial v}{\partial T} = (U_0 - x_0)(r - q)\frac{\partial v}{\partial x_0} + \frac{1}{2}\sigma^2(U_0 - x_0)^2\frac{\partial^2 v}{\partial x_0^2} - qv$$

Unlike the Black Scholes equation, this equation cannot be turned into a simple heat equation by a transformation of variables; if it could, we would be able to find an analytical solution. We therefore set up the Crank Nicolson discretization in exactly the manner set out in Section 8.4(vi), item (c) for the untransformed Black Scholes equation. The reader is unlikely to want to share the algebraic slog, but the resultant finite difference equation is

$$af_{m+1}^{n+1} + bf_m^{n+1} + cf_{m-1}^{n+1} = \alpha f_{m+l}^n + \beta f_m^n + \gamma f_{m-1}^n$$

where

$$a = -\alpha = \frac{1}{4}\frac{U_m^n - m\delta x}{\delta x}(r - q)\delta t + \frac{1}{4}\sigma^2\frac{\left(U_m^n - m\delta x\right)^2}{(\delta x)^2}\delta t$$

$$c = -\gamma = -\frac{1}{4}\frac{U_m^n - m\delta x}{\delta x}(r - q)\delta t + \frac{1}{4}\sigma^2\frac{\left(U_m^n - m\delta x\right)^2}{(\delta x)^2}\delta t \qquad (18.6)$$

$$(b - 1) = -(\beta - 1) = +\frac{1}{2}\sigma^2\frac{\left(U_m^n - m\delta x\right)^2}{(\delta x)^2}\delta t + q\delta t$$

The initial and boundary conditions are

$$f(x_0, 0) = \max[0, x_0]; \qquad \lim_{x_t \to -\infty} f(x_t, t) \to 0; \qquad \lim_{x_t \to +\infty} f(x_t, t) \to x_t$$

This equation can be solved using the LU decomposition technique set out in Appendix A.10.

(ii) **Optimal Strategy Values:** A slight problem in solving this finite difference equation is that we must simultaneously ascribe all the correct values of $U_m^n$. The simplest way around this is to use a trial and error approach:

- Make a reasonable (but probably erroneous) guess for all the $U_m^n$. A reasonable start is to use the driftless value $U_m^0 = \text{sign } x_0$. Make a further reasonable guess that $U_m^{n+1} = U_m^n$.
- Use an LU decomposition to calculate all the $f_m^n$.
- Use equation (18.5) in finite difference form to calculate the $U_m^n$, i.e.

$$U_m^n = \text{sign}\left\{\frac{1}{2}(r - q)\left(f_{m+1}^n - f_{m-1}^n\right) - m\sigma^2\left(f_{m+1}^n + f_{m-1}^n - 2f_m^n\right)\right\}$$

Putting in these values for the $U_m^n$, recalculate the $f_m^n$. Keep repeating the last two steps until the $U_m^n$ remain constant. This procedure should only take a few iterations.

(iii) **American Options**: This problem is handled using exactly the same approach as for American call and put options. An American passport option is similar to a European one, except that the option can be exercised at any point to yield $x_t$. The price of this option can therefore be obtained by using the techniques of this section, but replacing each value $f_m^n$ by a value

$$f_m^{n'} = \max\left[f_m^n, \max[0, x_m]\right]$$

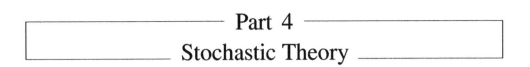

# Part 4
# Stochastic Theory

# 19

## Arbitrage

The concept of arbitrage lies at the heart of option theory. In Parts 1 and 2 of this book, we developed option theory from the concept of arbitrage, mostly using straightforward, classical statistical analysis. The definition of arbitrage was very intuitive and stated in three different ways:

(A) Riskless sequences of transactions cannot yield a profit;
(B) If two riskless portfolios have the same value in the future, they must have the same value now;
(C) The return on a riskless portfolio must be the risk-free rate.

These truths were taken to be self-evident and we used whichever version was the most convenient as we went along. The formulation may have been rather loose, but it enabled us to derive most of the equations, formulas and procedures of modern option theory, at least for equity-type derivatives.

The purpose of this part of the book is to re-state the previous theory in a more precise, elegant and economical way. We start by redefining arbitrage. Some of the concepts may appear unnecessarily precious to the reader, but the results derived in this chapter allow us to apply the whole barrage of stochastic calculus to the study of options.

## 19.1  SIMPLEST MODEL

(i) **States of the World**: We start with the simplest conceivable model: the one-step binomial model. This is the basic element of the binomial tree which was extensively analyzed in Part 2 of this book. The reader may feel that he has seen this stuff a hundred times before and be tempted to jump to the next section; but he is advised against this as the model is used to define and develop some concepts which are the foundations of this part of the book.

When this model is first introduced, it usually refers to a stock price which starts at $S_0$ and at a time $t$ later, either jumps up to a value $S_u$ or drops

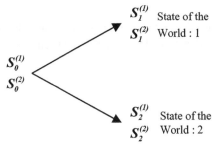

**Figure 19.1**  One-step binomial model

down to a value $S_d$. But for the moment, we will take a slightly more general approach. Suppose there exist two securities $S^{(1)}$ and $S^{(2)}$ whose values at time 0 are $S_0^{(1)}$ and $S_0^{(2)}$. After time $t$, two *states of the world* are possible: state 1 and state 2.

"State of the world" is sometimes referred to as "state of nature" or more usually just as "state"; it is a rather pompous piece of terminology evoking geopolitical tension or global hazard. What it really means is that our model is so restrictive that only two outcomes are permitted after time $t$: either the values of the two securities are $S_1^{(1)}$ and $S_1^{(2)}$ or they are $S_2^{(1)}$ and $S_2^{(2)}$.

So how does this relate to the up–down single step model with which we are already familiar? In that case, we usually consider three securities $S^{(1)}$, $S^{(2)}$ and $S^{(3)}$. The first security is a zero coupon bond which has the same value whether state 1 or state 2 is achieved. $S^{(2)}$ is the underlying stock which may jump up or down. $S^{(3)}$ is a derivative of the stock, whose jump must depend on which way the underlying stock has jumped. We return to this case later in this chapter.

A single step model can obviously be set up using any number of possible states of the world; a single step trinomial model envisages three possible states. The reader should take care not to confuse the number of states with the number of securities.

(ii) **Arrow Debreu Securities**: An Arrow Debreu security is defined as a hypothetical security which has a payoff of $1 when and if a certain state of the world is achieved and zero otherwise. In the binomial model of Figure 19.1, there are two Arrow Debreu securities:

- The value of $\pi_t^{(1)} = \begin{cases} \$1 & \text{if state of the world 1 is achieved at time } t \\ 0 & \text{if state of the world 2 is achieved at time } t \end{cases}$

- The value of $\pi_t^{(2)} = \begin{cases} 0 & \text{if state of the world 1 is achieved at time } t \\ \$1 & \text{if state of the world 2 is achieved at time } t \end{cases}$

These hypothetical securities have calculable values $\pi_0^{(1)}$ and $\pi_0^{(2)}$ at time 0. Although this concept seems a rather artificial construction when first encountered, it will be seen to fall naturally out of arbitrage theory in a couple of pages.

(iii) Consider a portfolio of two stocks in a simple model with two final states. The portfolio contains $x^{(1)}$ and $x^{(2)}$ units of securities $S^{(1)}$ and $S^{(2)}$; in vector notation, the value of the portfolio at time 0 may be written

$$V_0 = \begin{pmatrix} S_0^{(1)} & S_0^{(2)} \end{pmatrix} \begin{pmatrix} x^{(1)} \\ x^{(2)} \end{pmatrix}$$

By time $t$, the world has moved to either state 1 or state 2, so that the value of the portfolio is either $V_1$ or $V_2$. In matrix notation this may be written

$$\begin{pmatrix} V_1 \\ V_2 \end{pmatrix} = \begin{pmatrix} S_1^{(1)} & S_1^{(2)} \\ S_2^{(1)} & S_2^{(2)} \end{pmatrix} \begin{pmatrix} x^{(1)} \\ x^{(2)} \end{pmatrix}$$

or

$$V_t = S_t x$$

At first sight it appears that we could construct a portfolio with any payoff we please (i.e. any values of $V_1$ and $V_2$), just by a suitable choice of $x^{(1)}$ and $x^{(2)}$, the quantities of each security. Once we have decided on the payoff we calculate the quantities from the last equation, rewritten as

$$x = S_t^{-1} V_t$$

However, this is only true if $S_t$ is an invertible (non-singular) matrix. This condition requires the columns (or rows) of $S_t$ to be independent of each other. We could not, for example, have

$S^{(1)}$ and $S^{(2)}$ perfectly correlated with each other since column 1 in the matrix would then be a multiple of column 2. Similarly, the securities could not both be bonds. On the other hand, $S^{(1)}$ as a bond and $S^{(2)}$ an equity stock works just fine. If the condition holds that $\mathbf{S_t}$ is non-singular, we say that the securities $S^{(1)}$ and $S^{(2)}$ form a *complete market*.

If we add further securities to an already complete market, we do not of course destroy the completeness property. In subsection (i) we referred to a market with a bond, a stock and a derivative, so that the above matrix equation would be written

$$\begin{pmatrix} V_1 \\ V_2 \end{pmatrix} = \begin{pmatrix} S_1^{(1)} & S_1^{(2)} & S_1^{(3)} \\ S_2^{(1)} & S_2^{(2)} & S_2^{(3)} \end{pmatrix} \begin{pmatrix} x^{(1)} \\ x^{(2)} \\ x^{(3)} \end{pmatrix}$$

The $3 \times 2$ matrix $\mathbf{S_t}$ is invertible (it has rank 2) and any payoff can be created with a suitable choice of $x^{(1)}$, $x^{(2)}$ and $x^{(3)}$. However the market was already complete before we added the derivative $S^{(3)}$. By the definition of completeness, we can replicate $S^{(3)}$ with a combination of $S^{(1)}$ and $S^{(2)}$:

$$\begin{pmatrix} S_1^{(3)} \\ S_2^{(3)} \end{pmatrix} = \begin{pmatrix} S_1^{(1)} & S_1^{(2)} \\ S_2^{(1)} & S_2^{(2)} \end{pmatrix} \begin{pmatrix} a^{(1)} \\ a^{(2)} \end{pmatrix}$$

In this sense, the derivative $S^{(3)}$ might be called a redundant security in that its payoff can be simulated by a combination of other securities. But of course there is no reason to single out $S^{(3)}$ as the redundant one; any one of $S^{(1)}$, $S^{(2)}$ or $S^{(3)}$ can be manufactured from a combination of the other two.

In this simple model with only two states of the world at time $t$, it is clear that the market is complete if there are at least two independent securities. More generally, the market is complete if the number of independent securities is at least equal to the number of final states of the world; more precisely, $\mathbf{S_t}$ may be inverted if rank $\mathbf{S_t} \geq w$, where $w$ is the number of states of the world.

## 19.2 THE ARBITRAGE THEOREM

(i) The notation introduced in the last section is extended to a model with $n$ securities and $w$ final states. The initial value of a portfolio containing $x^{(1)}, \ldots, x^{(n)}$ units of each security is given by

$$V_0 = \begin{pmatrix} S_0^{(1)} & \cdots & S_0^{(n)} \end{pmatrix} \begin{pmatrix} x^{(1)} \\ \vdots \\ x^{(n)} \end{pmatrix}$$

and its various possible future values, depending on the state of the world which is achieved, can be written as

$$\begin{pmatrix} V_1 \\ \vdots \\ V_w \end{pmatrix} = \begin{pmatrix} S_1^{(1)} & \cdots & S_1^{(n)} \\ \vdots & & \vdots \\ S_w^{(1)} & \cdots & S_w^{(n)} \end{pmatrix} \begin{pmatrix} x^{(1)} \\ \vdots \\ x^{(n)} \end{pmatrix}$$

or

$$V_t = S_t x$$

(ii) **The Arbitrage Hypothesis:** This states that

$$\text{if in } V_t, \text{ all } V_i \geq 0, \text{ then } V_0 > 0$$

This is an extremely economical statement of the principle of arbitrage. It says nothing about interest rates or expected future values. It merely asserts that if you construct a portfolio which gives you a chance of making a positive return in the future but carries no risk of making a loss, then the portfolio must cost something now. This is often known as the "*no free lunch*" principle, and a market which obeys the condition is known as a *viable market.* This statement of the arbitrage hypothesis is so minimalist and obvious that the reader might assume that few interesting consequences could follow from it: wrong!

(iii) **Farka's Lemma:** Before proceeding to the main point of this chapter, we need this standard result which is a piece of pure mathematical formalism and is explained in Appendix A.11. In terms of the matrices used in this chapter, Farka's lemma states that for any non-singular matrix $S_t$ (e.g. representing prices in a complete market), one of the two following mutually exclusive circumstances must hold:

(A)  Either there exists a vector $x$ such that $x'S'_0 < 0$ and all the elements of $x'S'_t \geq 0$.
(B)  Or there exists a vector $\pi$ in the equation $S'_t \pi = S_0$ such that all elements of the vector $\pi$ are positive, i.e. all $\pi_i \geq 0$.

(iii) **The Arbitrage Theorem:** Circumstance (A) can be written in full as

$$x'S_t = x^{(1)}S_0^{(1)} + \cdots + x^{(n)}S_0^{(n)} = V_0 < 0$$

while all the elements of the vector $(V_1 V_2 \cdots V_w)$ are $\geq 0$. But this circumstance is the very thing that is forbidden by the arbitrage hypothesis. Therefore this circumstance cannot hold. The arbitrage theorem is a specific statement of circumstance (B), which must hold instead. This states that if a market is viable and complete, then there exists a vector $\pi$, each of whose elements are positive, such that

$$S'_t \pi = S_0$$

The reader who is fresh to this material is likely to be thinking "is that it then?". But this innocuous-looking little theorem is really the keystone of axiomatic option theory; it is often referred to in the literature as the Fundamental Theorem of Asset Pricing.

## 19.3   ARBITRAGE IN THE SIMPLE MODEL

(i) Returning to a model with three securities and two final states of the world (up and down), the arbitrage theorem can be written as follows:

$$\text{if } \begin{pmatrix} V_u \\ V_d \end{pmatrix} = \begin{pmatrix} S_u^{(1)} & S_u^{(2)} & S_u^{(3)} \\ S_d^{(1)} & S_d^{(2)} & S_d^{(3)} \end{pmatrix} \begin{pmatrix} x^{(1)} \\ x^{(2)} \\ x^{(3)} \end{pmatrix}$$

then the arbitrage theorem says that there exist two positive numbers $\pi_u$ and $\pi_d$ such that

$$
\begin{pmatrix} S_0^{(1)} \\ S_0^{(2)} \\ S_0^{(3)} \end{pmatrix} = \begin{pmatrix} S_u^{(1)} & S_d^{(1)} \\ S_u^{(2)} & S_d^{(2)} \\ S_u^{(3)} & S_d^{(3)} \end{pmatrix} \begin{pmatrix} \pi_u \\ \pi_d \end{pmatrix}
$$

What physical or economic significance might we attach to the numbers $\pi_u$ and $\pi_d$? Suppose that $S^{(1)}$ is an Arrow Debreu security which pays out \$1 if the up-state is achieved and zero for the down-state ($S_u^{(1)} = 1$, $S_d^{(1)} = 0$). Also, let $S^{(2)}$ be the security which does the reverse, i.e. $S_u^{(1)} = 0$, $S_d^{(1)} = 1$. From the last matrix equation we then have

$$
S_0^{(1)} = \pi_u; \qquad S_0^{(2)} = \pi_d
$$

We conclude generally that $\pi_u$ and $\pi_d$ are today's values of the two corresponding Arrow Debreu securities.

(ii) It will cross the mind of the perceptive reader that a state price must reflect two concepts: first, it is today's value of a payoff in the future so that some form of discounting has to take place. Second, a payoff is non-zero only if one specific state of the world occurs, so that the state price must somehow reflect the probability of this one particular state being achieved.

In our simple model we let $S^{(1)}$ be a zero coupon bond. Without loss of generality, it can be assumed that the value of the zero coupon bond is \$1 at time 0 and $B_t$ at time $t$. We can then write $S_0^{(1)} = 1$ and $S_u^{(1)} = S_d^{(1)} = B_t$ since the value of a zero coupon bond will be the same in both states of the world, up and down. By the definition of continuous interest, we could also, write $B_t = e^{rt}$.

The arbitrage theorem in our three-security model then becomes:

$$
\begin{pmatrix} 1 \\ S_0^{(2)} \\ S_0^{(3)} \end{pmatrix} = \begin{pmatrix} B_t & B_t \\ S_u^{(2)} & S_d^{(2)} \\ S_u^{(3)} & S_d^{(3)} \end{pmatrix} \begin{pmatrix} \pi_u \\ \pi_d \end{pmatrix}
$$

The top line of this vector equation is:

$$
1 = B_t \{ \pi_u + \pi_d \}
$$

Define two new variables: $p_u = B_t \pi_u$ and $p_d = B_t \pi_d$; the first two lines of the above vector equation can be combined as

$$
S_0^{(2)} = B_t^{-1} \{ p_u S_u^{(2)} + p_d S_d^{(2)} \}; \qquad p_u + p_d = 1
$$

If the interest rate is constant we have $B_t^{-1} = e^{-rt}$. Introducing the zero coupon bond as the first security suggests that the state prices do indeed contain a discounting and a probability element. Certainly, some sort of discount factor has appeared outside the right-hand side of the last equation and the terms look suspiciously like probabilities. Of course there is nothing to associate the $p_u$ and $p_d$ with actual probabilities of the up- or down-states of the world being achieved: they just look as though they might be candidates.

(iii) We now consider a portfolio consisting of a zero coupon bond, an equity stock and a derivative of that stock. Simplifying the notation to the specific case in hand, the arbitrage theorem states that positive state prices $\pi_u$ and $\pi_d$ must exist such that

$$\begin{pmatrix} 1 \\ S_0 \\ f_0 \end{pmatrix} = \begin{pmatrix} B_t & B_t \\ S_u & S_d \\ f_u & f_d \end{pmatrix} \begin{pmatrix} \pi_u \\ \pi_d \end{pmatrix}$$

Writing $B_t = e^{rt}$ and $p = B_t \pi_u$, this vector equation can be written

$$S_0 = e^{-rt} \{ p S_u + (1-p) S_d \}$$
$$f_0 = e^{-rt} \{ p f_u + (1-p) f_d \}$$

The conclusions to be drawn from these last two equations are as follows:

(A) The present price of the stock $S_0$ can be derived from the two possible future prices $S_u$ and $S_d$ by using a discount-like factor $e^{-rt}$ and two probability-like parameters $p$ and $(1-p)$. We say discount-like and probability-like since the actual returns on the risky assets $S$ and $f$ cannot be the risk-free rate; also, there is nothing to link $p$ with the probability of an up-state occurring. We have of course reinvented risk-neutrality arguments which received extensive discussion in previous parts of this book.
(B) The same discount-like factor and pseudo-probability are used to calculate the present values of both the underlying stock and its derivative.

These conclusions are merely a re-statement of the results of Section 7.1, where a single cell of the binomial model was analyzed. The reader is recommended to flick through those pages briefly to compare the very formalistic derivation here with the rather home-spun arguments used previously. But don't knock them; they yielded precisely the same conclusions and had the advantage of providing an intuitive feel for what is going on. Their disadvantage is that they cannot be readily generalized and extended.

# 20

# Discrete Time Models

In the last chapter an elementary single step model of an option price was built up from a very simple statement of the arbitrage hypothesis. The theoretical concept of state prices was introduced, but otherwise it was purely a matter of mathematics to reach the important conclusions on risk neutrality and pseudo-probabilities.

The logical progression is to string together single steps to form a multistep model, examine the limit as the number of steps becomes very large and finally, extrapolate to the continuous case. The mathematics and jargon are likely to be less familiar to the reader, although we assume that he already has at least an elementary understanding of how the binomial model works. We therefore start by introducing some essential mathematical jargon in the context of a simple, recombining binomial tree.

## 20.1 ESSENTIAL JARGON

Before we start, the reader is introduced to a mantra which starts most technical papers in this field: "The triplet $(\Omega, \mathcal{F}, P)$ is a probability space where $\Omega$ is a sample space, $\mathcal{F}$ is a tribe on $\Omega$ and $P$ is a probability measure." This essentially says "well, here we are: in what follows, we're going to use some of the notation of axiomatic probability theory". Referring to the binomial tree of Figure 20.1, the *sample space* $\Omega$ is the set of all nodal values $S_{ij}$ in the tree together with the set of permitted paths through the tree; we have shown a recombining tree so this latter aspect is self-evident, but in a non-recombining tree we need to define the permitted jumps at each node. The reader will recall that when we build a tree, we have quite a lot of alternatives in the construction: we can decide on the number of steps and we have leeway in deciding the sizes of the up and down steps. They are not completely arbitrary since we must be able to replicate the observed drift and volatility; but subject to this constraint, an infinite number of alternatives are available to us. The most popular are the Jarrow–Rudd and Garman–Kohlhagen schemes described in Section 7.2. The sample space is basically the architecture of the tree, which we chose at our discretion.

The *probability measure* $P$ is the set of probabilities of jumps $(p_{00}, \ldots, p_{22})$ at the various nodes. From his knowledge of trees, or from his reading of Section 19.3, the reader will appreciate that once the sample space has been selected, the probability measure follows from arbitrage considerations. Taken together, $\Omega$ and $P$ define the tree. Looking back at Chapter 7, the reader will recall that in building a binomial tree, one has leeway in choosing the stock prices at the nodes and the probabilities of up or down moves. $\Omega$ and $P$ are the particular choices one makes in constructing such a tree.

In the present context, the *tribe* $\mathcal{F}$ (also known as a *$\sigma$-algebra* or *$\sigma$-field*) can be taken as meaning the information available to us as we move through the tree over time. In Figure 20.1, at time $t_0$ the information we have is designated $\mathcal{F}_0$ and is merely a knowledge of the geometry of the tree; we know this because *we* built the tree (i.e. selected the values at the nodes). $\Omega$ is therefore all that $\mathcal{F}_0$ contains, which is often written $\mathcal{F}_0 = \{\Omega, 0\}$. At time $t_1$

the information available to us is $\mathcal{F}_1$; we know whether the stock price jumped up or down at the first node. $\mathcal{F}_1$ is called a **subtribe** of $\mathcal{F}$. At time $t_3$ in our example, the information is $\mathcal{F}_3$ and we know precisely how the stock price has moved over the entire tree, i.e. we know everything.

It is assumed that information is not "forgotten" so that $\mathcal{F}_2$ includes the information in $\mathcal{F}_1$ and so on. This is written symbolically as $\mathcal{F}_0 \subset \mathcal{F}_1 \subset \mathcal{F}_2 \subset \mathcal{F}_3$. If this condition holds true, the set of **subtribes** $\mathcal{F}_0$, $\mathcal{F}_1$, $\mathcal{F}_2, \ldots$ is called a **filtration**. In our present example, we say that this filtration is **generated** by the specific binomial process shown in Figure 20.1.

A random variable is **$\mathcal{F}$-measurable** if its value at $t_i$ can be determined from $\mathcal{F}_i$. For example, the stock price itself $S_i$ is clearly $\mathcal{F}$-measurable. From his previous knowledge of the binomial model, the reader will realize that the price of a call option is also $\mathcal{F}$-measurable. OK, so what random variable is *not* $\mathcal{F}$-measurable? Well, the average price of the stock between $t_0$ and $t_3$, or the minimum price between $t_0$ and $t_3$.

A **process** is the sequence of values that a random variable can take. It is defined by $\Omega$ above. The process is said to be **adapted** or **consistent** if the random variable is $\mathcal{F}$-measurable.

A variable is **previsible** if its value at time $t_{i+1}$ is known at time $t_i$. An obvious example is a bond, whose payoff at a later date is determined by the interest rate at an earlier date.

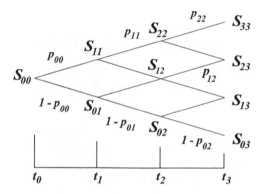

**Figure 20.1**    Binomial tree with variable probabilities

## 20.2  EXPECTATIONS

(i) The concept of conditional expectation has been extensively exploited in previous parts of this book and we merely adapt it here to conform with the new terminology that has been introduced. Continuing with the binomial tree example of the last section, the probability of a random variable achieving value $x_j$ at time $t_j$ given that we know what value it achieved at an earlier time $t_i$ is written as

$$\mathrm{E}^P[x_j \mid \mathcal{F}_i]$$

The notation is similar to what was used previously in the book, but the knowledge of the actual value at $t_i$ is indicated by $\mathcal{F}_i$. Also, a superscript $P$ has been inserted to indicate the set of jump probabilities that are used. Clearly, we draw attention to these probabilities because there are circumstances where we will wish to tinker with them.

(ii) **Conditional Expectations**: These are manipulated extensively in the following pages, so the reader is reminded of some simple rules.

- $E^P[x_j + y_j \mid \mathcal{F}_i] = E^P[x_j \mid \mathcal{F}_i] + E^P[y_j \mid \mathcal{F}_i]$     $t_i < t_j$
- $E^P[x_j y_i \mid \mathcal{F}_i] = y_i\, E^P[x_j \mid \mathcal{F}_i]$     $t_i < t_j$
- $E^P[a_{i+1} x_{i+1} \mid \mathcal{F}_i] = a_{i+1}\, E^P[x_{i+1} \mid \mathcal{F}_i]$     if $a_{i+1}$ is previsible

Note that it is often easier to express a previsible variable $a_{i+1}$ as a straightforward random variable $y_i$, in which case the last two rules reduce to the same thing:

- $E^P[E^P[x_k \mid \mathcal{F}_i] \mid \mathcal{F}_i] \equiv E^P[x_k \mid \mathcal{F}_i]$     $t_i < t_j < t_k$

This last property is the much used **tower property**, and needs a little thought: it says that *today's* expected value of the future value of a random variable cannot depend on knowledge that will be picked up in the future!

(iii) **Martingales**: A random variable $x_i$ is called a **martingale under the measure $P$** (or a **$P$-martingale** for short) if it has the following property:

$$E^P[x_{i+1} \mid \mathcal{F}_i] = x_i \qquad \text{for all possible } i$$

It follows from the tower property that if $x_i$ is a martingale then

$$E^P[x_{i+2} \mid \mathcal{F}_i] = E^P[E^P[x_{i+2} \mid \mathcal{F}_i] \mid \mathcal{F}_i] = E^P[x_{i+1} \mid \mathcal{F}_i] = x_i$$

This may be immediately generalized to give the martingale property:

$$E^P[x_{i+n} \mid \mathcal{F}_i] = x_i$$

A martingale has no tendency to drift, no matter how many steps are considered.

## 20.3  CONDITIONAL EXPECTATIONS APPLIED TO THE ONE-STEP MODEL

The new vocabulary will now be applied to the simple one-step binomial process and some of the results previously derived will be stated formally.

(i) **Martingale Properties**: We should perhaps begin by saying that "the triplet $(\Omega, \mathcal{F}, P)$ is a probability space where $\Omega$ is a sample space, $\mathcal{F}$ is a tribe on $\Omega$ and $P$ is a probability measure". The sample space $\Omega$ is simply an up-move and a down-move, with the size of the move determined by the values of $S_u$ and $S_d$ (Figure 20.2). It was shown in Section 19.3(iii) that if the market is viable, then

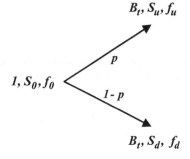

**Figure 20.2**  One-step process

$$S_0 = B_t^{-1}(pS_u + (1-p)S_d)$$
$$f_0 = B_t^{-1}(pf_u + (1-p)f_d) \qquad (20.1)$$

where $p$ and $(1-p)$ are pseudo-probabilities; these are what we call the probability measure. If we vary $\Omega$ by changing the values $S_u$ and $S_d$, we must change the probability measure. In Chapter 7 on the binomial model, various ways were suggested for choosing $S_u$ and $S_d$ on the one hand, and calculating the corresponding values of $p$ on the other; in the present terminology, various sample spaces were selected to correspond to different probability measures.

The variables are indeed $\mathcal{F}$-measurable: at time 0 we know the values of $S_0$ and $f_0$ but do not know whether the jump will be up or down. At time $t$, we know whether the jump was up or down and whether the values become $S_u, f_u$ or $S_d, f_d$. Thus the processes for $S_t$ and $f_t$ are adapted. The random variable $B_t$ is previsible: at time 0 when its value is \$1, we know what the interest rate is and hence that its value at time $t$ will be $e^{rt}$, whether the jump is up or down.

$S_t$ denotes the stock price at time $t$, which in our present model can take values $S_u$ and $S_d$ only; similarly for $f_t$. By the definition of $\mathrm{E}^P$ in terms of pseudo-probabilities $p$:

$$\mathrm{E}^P[S_t \mid \mathcal{F}_0] = pS_u + (1-p)S_d \qquad \text{and} \qquad \mathrm{E}^P[f_t \mid \mathcal{F}_0] = pf_u + (1-p)f_d \qquad (20.2)$$

Substitute equations (20.1) in equations (20.2) and use the previsibility property of $B_t$ and the convention $B_0 = 1$ to give the following key results:

$$\mathrm{E}^P\big[B_t^{-1}S_t \mid \mathcal{F}_0\big] = B_0^{-1}S_0 \qquad \text{and} \qquad \mathrm{E}^P\big[B_t^{-1}f_t \mid \mathcal{F}_0\big] = B_0^{-1}f_0 \qquad (20.3)$$

Remember that the existence of these pseudo-probabilities is a consequence of the arbitrage theorem of the last chapter. We can therefore say that (for the one-step model at least), the arbitrage theorem implies that the discounted price process for the stock is a $P$-martingale; the discounted price process of a derivative of the stock is also a martingale under the same probability measure. These last two points taken together justify the martingale measure being referred to as the *risk-neutral measure*.

(ii) **The Martingale Representation Theorem**: One final result is required before we generalize these results to a multistep binomial model. Suppose $M_t$ is any one-step martingale. The martingale property can be written $\mathrm{E}[M_t \mid \mathcal{F}_0] = M_0$ or alternatively as $\mathrm{E}[M_t - M_0 \mid \mathcal{F}_0] = 0$. If another random variable $H_t$ is defined by

$$H_t - H_0 = a_0(M_t - M_0)$$

where $a_0$ is known at time 0, then $H_t$ is also a martingale. This follows immediately from taking the expected values of both sides of the last equation.

This rather trivial result has a very powerful corollary known as the **Martingale Representation Theorem**. This states that:

If $M_t$ is a $P$-martingale, *any other* $P$-martingale $H_t$ can be expressed as

$$H_t - H_0 = a_0(M_t - M_0)$$

This theorem lies at the heart of the reasoning used in analyzing the multistep binomial model, so it is important to be quite clear about its significance. We will therefore go back to basics and see precisely what underlies the theorem.

(iii) If $M_t$ and $H_t$ are both $P$-martingales, each has sample space ($\Omega$) consisting of an up-move or a down-move; this is illustrated in Figure 20.3. At time 0 we not only know $M_0$ and $H_0$ and also the possible values that could be attained at time $t$, i.e. $M_u, M_d$ and $H_u, H_d$ (in formal jargon, $\Omega$ is contained in the set $\mathcal{F}_0$), we also know that the probabilities $p_u$ and $p_d$ are the same for both processes (both are $P$-martingales). What we do *not* know is whether the actual jump will be up or down.

The critical question posed is the following: is there some unique number $a_0$ which can be calculated ahead of time such that

$$H_t - H_0 = a_0(M_t - M_0) \qquad (20.4)$$

irrespective of whether $M_t$ and $H_t$ turn out to have been up-moves or down-moves? $M_t$ and $H_t$ are both stated to be martingales so that

$$E[M_t \mid \mathcal{F}_0] = p_u M_u + p_d M_d = M_0$$
$$E[H_t \mid \mathcal{F}_0] = p_u H_u + p_d H_d = H_0$$

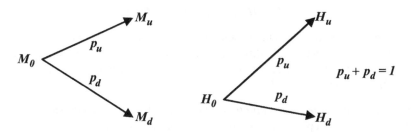

**Figure 20.3**   Two single-step martingales

Substituting these values of $M_0$ and $H_0$ in equation (20.4) and using the identity $p_u + p_d \equiv 1$ gives

$$(p_u + p_d)H_t - (p_u H_u + p_d H_d) = a_0((p_u + p_d)M_t - (p_u M_u + p_d M_d))$$

Simple substitution of either $M_t, H_t = M_u, H_u$ or $M_t, H_t = M_d, H_d$ in this expression yields the same answer:

$$a_0 = \frac{H_u - H_d}{M_u - M_d}$$

Thus a unique number can be calculated for $a_0$ such that equation (20.4) holds true, whichever final state occurs at time $t$. This proves the martingale representation theorem for the one-step case.

## 20.4   MULTISTEP MODEL

(i) Consider a binomial tree, which does not necessarily have to be recombining. The first step in analyzing the tree is to see what general results can be carried over to the multistep case, from the one-step model.

By construction, the multistep model is made up of a sequence of single binomial steps strung together. The arbitrage theorem applies to each of these single steps, so that a probability measure exists for each step. It follows that a probability measure exists for the entire tree. Remember that a probability measure is the set of all branching probabilities, which do not of course need to be uniform throughout the tree.

(ii) Equations (20.3) show that $B_t^{-1} S_t$ and $B_t^{-1} f_t$ are both martingales over a single step. They are martingales over any step (not just the first) so that we may write

$$E[S_i^* \mid \mathcal{F}_{i-1}] = S_{i-1}^* \qquad E[f_i^* \mid \mathcal{F}_{i-1}] = f_{i-1}^*$$

where $S_i^* = B_i^{-1} S_i$ and $f_i^* = B_i^{-1} f_i$. These results will be more useful in the form of martingale differences:

$$E[S_i^* - S_{i-1}^* \mid \mathcal{F}_{i-1}] = 0 \qquad E[f_i^* - f_{i-1}^* \mid \mathcal{F}_{i-1}] = 0 \tag{20.5}$$

It follows immediately from repeated application of these results and from the tower property that

$$E[S_i^* \mid \mathcal{F}_0] = S_0^* = S_0 \qquad E[f_i^* \mid \mathcal{F}_0] = f_0^* = f_0$$

(iii) **Martingale Transformations:** Let $M_i$ be a $P$-martingale. If

$$H_i - H_{i-1} = a_{i-1}(M_i - M_{i-1})$$

then $H_i$ is also a $P$-martingale. This is demonstrated simply by taking expectations of each side. In general, any $P$-martingale difference multiplied by an $\mathcal{F}_{i-1}$ measurable variable is also a $P$-martingale difference. This procedure is called a **martingale transformation** of the martingale $M_i$ to the martingale $H_i$.

(iv) **The Multistep Martingale Representation Theorem:** The above single-step result can be generalized to the multistep model and expressed as follows: if $M_i$ is a $P$-martingale, *any other* $P$-martingale $H_i$ can be expressed as $H_i - H_{i-1} = a_{i-1}(M_i - M_{i-1})$ by a suitable choice of $a_{i-1}$. The latter is a random variable whose value depends on which way previous jumps in the tree have gone; it is $\mathcal{F}_{i-1}$-measurable, i.e. from the geometry of the tree, you can work out its value at node $i-1$ before the next jump occurs.

This theorem is often written as $H_i - H_{i-1} = b_i(M_i - M_{i-1})$ where $b_i$ is a **previsible** random variable, but we feel that our present notation is more explicit and makes the reasoning easier to follow.

## 20.5   PORTFOLIOS

(i) Suppose we are running a portfolio consisting of $\alpha$ units of stock and $\beta$ units of zero coupon bond. We analyze the progress of the portfolio using a binomial tree, so that the values of both the stock and the bond are different at each node. The portfolio is run in accordance with some **trading strategy**, changing the values of $\alpha$ and $\beta$ in response to market movements, according to a set of pre-established rules. The value of the portfolio at node $i$ may be written

$$V_i = \alpha_i S_i + \beta_i B_i$$

where $\alpha_i$ and $\beta_i$ are adapted (or $\mathcal{F}$-measurable) random variables, i.e. the fund manager gets to step $i$, sees what the stock price and zero coupon interest rate are, and rebalances the portfolio following the rules of his strategy by selecting new values for $\alpha_i$ and $\beta_i$.

We now impose two conditions on the portfolio, neither of which is onerous. First, we assume that the market is viable (i.e. that the arbitrage theorem holds). It has already been shown that this implies that $S_i^* = B_i^{-1} S_i$ is a martingale under some probability measure $P$.

(ii) **Discounted Self-financing Portfolios are Martingales:** The second condition imposed on the portfolio is that it should be **self-financing**. By this we mean that no cash is paid into or out of the portfolio; $\alpha$ and $\beta$ are adjusted at each node in such a way that changes in the values of the holdings of the two assets exactly offset each other. The effect of this constraint may be expressed as follows:

$$\alpha_{i-1} S_i + \beta_{i-1} B_i = \alpha_i S_i + \beta_i B_i$$

We arrive at step $i$ having set the holdings of stock and bond at $\alpha_{i-1}$ and $\beta_{i-1}$ one step previously.

In view of the new stock price, we now rebalance the portfolio so that the new holdings of stock and bond are $\alpha_i$ and $\beta_i$. In practice, this is how most real portfolios are run, with some interest-bearing account taking the place of the zero coupon bond. A strategy which is run in accordance with the self-financing condition is called an **admissible** strategy.

The values of the portfolio at times $i$ and $i - 1$ may be alternatively written as follows:

$V_i = \alpha_i S_i + \beta_i B_i = \alpha_{i-1} S_i + \beta_{i-1} B_i$: $\quad\quad$ definition of $V_i$ and self-financing condition

$V_{i-1} = \alpha_{i-1} S_{i-1} + \beta_{i-1} B_{i-1}$: $\quad\quad$ first part of last equation taken one step earlier

Divide the first equation (second part) by $B_i$ and the second equation by $B_{i-1}$ to give

$$V_i B_i^{-1} = \alpha_{i-1} S_i B_i^{-1} + \beta_{i-1}$$
$$V_{i-1} B_{i-1}^{-1} = \alpha_{i-1} S_{i-1} B_{i-1}^{-1} + \beta_{i-1}$$

Use the notation $V_i^* = V_i B_i^{-1}$, $S_i^* = S_i B_i^{-1}$, etc. and subtract the second of these equations from the first to give

$$V_i^* - V_{i-1}^* = \alpha_{i-1}(S_i^* - S_{i-1}^*) \tag{20.6}$$

From equations (20.5), $S_i^*$ is a $P$-martingale and $\alpha_{i-1}$ is $\mathcal{F}_{i-1}$-measurable so that $V_i^*$ must also be a $P$-martingale.

In summary, the value of *any* self-financing portfolio discounted by the value of a zero coupon bond is a martingale under the same probability measure that enforces the arbitrage theorem, i.e. the pseudo-probabilities introduced in the last chapter and discussed in connection with the binomial model.

(iii) **The Fundamental Result of Option Theory**: It was previously shown that $S_i^*$ and $f_i^*$, the discounted prices of the stock and the derivative, are martingales under the same probability measure $P$, which enforces the arbitrage theorem. In the last subsection it was shown that the discounted value of *any* self-financing portfolio $V_i^*$ is also a $P$-martingale. The martingale representation theorem therefore leads us to conclude that there must exist an $\mathcal{F}_{i-1}$-measurable random variable $a_{i-1}$ such that

$$f_i^* - f_{i-1}^* = a_{i-1}(V_i^* - V_{i-1}^*) \tag{20.7}$$

These results form the crux of option theory, so it is worth spelling out the consequences in practical terms. If $f_0$ is today's no-arbitrage price of a derivative which has a payoff at step $N$ of $f_N$, then:

(A) $f_i B_i^{-1}$ is a martingale, which means that $f_0 = E^P[f_N B_N^{-1} \mid \mathcal{F}_0]$. Today's value of the derivative is found by taking the expected value of the discounted payoff, using the probability distribution (probability measure) that applies to the discounted stock price. In the binomial model this means adopting the pseudo-probabilities which fell out of the arbitrage theorem and which are described in Section 19.3.

(B) Equation (20.7) tells us that the derivative price at any point may be replicated by a self-financing portfolio. If the value of this portfolio at the beginning is set equal to $f_0$, a strategy may be followed such that at each node in the tree, the portfolio value is exactly equal to $f_i$. At maturity, the portfolio value will be exactly equal to $f_N$, the payoff of the derivative. This is equivalent to saying that the derivative may be perfectly hedged at all times.

(C)  The replicating portfolio can be written $f_i = a_i S_i + b_i B_i$ and we want to devise a strategy which ensures the replication, i.e. we need to work out $a_i$ and $b_i$. The fact that the portfolio is self-financing allows us to write a martingale difference equation in the same form as equation (20.6). Using the above notation for the replicating portfolio we have

$$f_i^* - f_{i-1}^* = a_{i-1}(S_i^* - S_{i-1}^*)$$

The architecture of the tree (the sample space $\Omega$) is known ahead of time, so an $a_i$ can be calculated for each node of the tree in advance. The analysis of Section 20.3(iii) shows that each $a_i$ is given by an expression of the form

$$a = \frac{f_u - f_d}{S_u - S_d}$$

(D)  The term $b_i$ in the replicating portfolio follows immediately from a knowledge of the $a_i$, using the fact that the portfolio must be self-financing. At each step, we adjust the stockholding to a new value of $a_i$ by buying or selling some stock; the change in $b_i$ is just the amount of cash that has been spent or received on the transaction.

## 20.6   FIRST APPROACH TO CONTINUOUS TIME

The reader with some previous knowledge of options will realize that the central results of discrete time option theory have been developed in the last two chapters in an axiomatic way. Much of the pricing and hedging of options in the commercial world is performed using trees; so this form of analysis should not be regarded as a mere learning tool for grasping the basics before moving on to continuous time models. A binomial tree with enough steps will nearly always yield a sufficiently accurate answer. So why go to the trouble of learning a lot more theory?

The reason is that once these results have been recast in continuous time, there is a whole tool-kit of mathematical techniques available for analyzing the subject: differential, integral and stochastic calculus, to name a few. However, this does not mean that all problems can be solved using these techniques, and we will continue to use trees to solve specific problems. A good example is provided by American options: we would be hard pressed to give a commentary on the relationships between the delta, gamma and theta of such options without using the concepts of differential calculus; yet when it comes to pricing such options, there is rarely an analytical solution available, and it is back to the trees.

As a first step towards option theory in continuous time, we investigate the behavior of the binomial model in the limit of an infinite number of infinitesimally small steps.

(i) It is formally shown in Appendix A.1 that in the limit of an infinite number of steps, the binomial model approaches a continuous time normal distribution. This fact is central to the analysis presented in this part of the book, so that at the risk of a few lines of duplication, we re-state the result using the notation of martingale differences.

Consider a single step in a tree describing a discrete time martingale $H_t$. The martingale starts with value $H_0$, and after one step $H_t$ is equal either to $H_u$ or $H_d$ with probability $p$ or $1 - p$. We will use the following notation:

$$\Delta H_t = H_t - H_0; \qquad \Delta H_u = H_u - H_0; \qquad \Delta H_d = H_d - H_0; \qquad \text{var}[\Delta H_t] = \Delta \sigma^2$$

Remembering that $H_t$ is a martingale allows us to write

$$\mathrm{E}[\Delta H_t] = p\Delta H_u + (1-p)\Delta H_d = 0$$
$$\mathrm{var}[\Delta H_t] = \mathrm{E}\left[\Delta H_t^2\right] = p\Delta H_u^2 + (1-p)\Delta H_d^2 = \Delta\sigma^2 \qquad (20.8)$$

The moment generating function of $\Delta H_t$ is defined as

$$\mathrm{M}(\Theta) = \mathrm{E}[e^{\Theta\Delta H_t}] = p\,e^{\Theta\Delta H_u} + (1-p)e^{\Theta\Delta H_d}$$

In the limit $\Delta H_u$ and $\Delta H_d \to 0$, this can be expanded to second order as

$$\mathrm{M}(\Theta) = p\left\{1 + \Theta\Delta H_u + \tfrac{1}{2}\Theta^2\Delta H_u^2 + \cdots\right\}e^{\Theta\Delta H_u}$$
$$+(1-p)\left\{1 + \Theta\Delta H_d + \tfrac{1}{2}\Theta^2\Delta H_d^2 + \cdots\right\}e^{-\Theta\Delta H_d}$$
$$\approx 1 + \tfrac{1}{2}\Theta^2\Delta\sigma^2: \qquad \text{using equations (20.8)}$$
$$\approx e^{\frac{1}{2}\Theta^2\Delta\sigma^2}: \qquad \text{in the limit } \Delta\sigma^2 \to 0$$

(ii) In a multistep model, the value of a martingale may be written as the sum of martingale differences over $n$ steps, i.e.

$$H_n = \sum_1^n \Delta H_i = \sum_1^n [H_i - H_{i-1}]$$

Quite generally, the moment generating function of a sum of random variables is equal to the product of their individual moment generating functions. Therefore, the moment generating function of $H_n$ is given by

$$\mathrm{M}(\Theta) = \exp\left[\frac{1}{2}\Theta^2 \sum_1^n \sigma_i^2\right]$$
$$= e^{\frac{1}{2}\Theta^2 n\Delta\sigma^2} \qquad \text{for constant variance}$$

But this is the moment generating function for a normally distributed variable with mean zero and variance $n\Delta\sigma^2$. This is the celebrated result that in the limit of a very large number of very small steps, the distribution of a binomial martingale after time $t$ will approach a normal distribution with variance proportional to $t$.

In the following chapters, we will be particularly concerned with the special case where the stochastic variable has expected mean zero and variance equal to $t$. In a tree which simulates this distribution we would therefore write $n\Delta\sigma^2 \to t$. From equations (20.8), the simplest tree is constructed by using the following values:

$$H_0 = 0; \qquad \Delta H_u = H_u = -H_d; \qquad p = \tfrac{1}{2}$$

so that

$$H_u^2 = H_d^2 = \Delta\sigma^2 = \frac{t}{n}$$

If these values are used for $H_u$ and $H_d$, the distribution of our multistep martingale approaches a normal distribution with mean zero and variance $t$ as $n$ approaches $\infty$. The martingale is then said to be a Standard Brownian Motion.

# Brownian Motion

It was shown at the end of the last chapter that in the limit of an infinite number of infinitesimally small steps, the behavior of a discrete time martingale converges to a Brownian motion. This chapter undertakes a review of the properties of Brownian motion. The story of buffeted pollen grains is very familiar by now and the busy reader is probably anxious to move on to the pricing of financial instruments as quickly as possible. However, there are important insights to be gained by considering physical displacements rather than stock price movements. In this chapter we lean rather heavily on such insights, so the description is couched in terms of the movement of a particle in one dimension. We can then exploit physical concepts such as total distance traveled in a certain time, which have no meaning if we consider only stock price movements.

## 21.1 BASIC PROPERTIES

(i) The use of the expressions normally distributed, Gaussian distribution, Wiener process and Brownian motion has been rather casual in previous parts of this book, as indeed in most of the options literature and in practice. The following points should clarify the position:

- Normal distribution refers to the distribution of a single random variable. It is of course possible for two normally distributed variables to be correlated, in which case they enjoy a bivariate normal distribution. A process cannot be said to be normally distributed.
- However, if each of the random variables in a process $H_0, \ldots, H_j$ are normally distributed, the process is called Gaussian.
- A Brownian motion is the continuous Gaussian process which is described in the next paragraph.
- A Wiener process is defined as a continuous adapted martingale whose variance is equal to the time over which the variance is measured. It can be proved that a Wiener process must be a Brownian motion (*Levy's theorem*).

(ii) A continuous random process $W_t$ is a standard Brownian motion if it has the following properties:

(A) It is a martingale starting at $W_0 = 0$.
(B) It is continuous, i.e. no jumps.
(C) It is a *Markov process*: the distribution of $W_t - W_s$ depends only on the value of $W_s$ and not on any previous values.
(D) $W_t - W_s$ is normally distributed with mean 0 and variance $(t - s)$.

Any Brownian motion can of course be constructed from a standard Brownian motion merely by applying a scaling factor for the volatility and resetting the starting point.

(iii) In terms of physical movement, a Brownian particle moves continuously along a line after starting at the point zero. At time $t$ its position is given by $W_t$. Intuition suggests that at time

$t + \delta t$ its position can be expressed as $W_t + \delta W_t$. However, $\delta W_t$ is a random variable with mean zero, which means that at each instant it has an equal chance of being positive or negative and has an unpredictable size. The function $W_t$ is therefore not differentiable at any point. A quick glance at Figure 21.1 confirms this property; it is clear just from the form of the graphs that the first derivative with respect to time is undefined, while the second derivative is infinite, i.e. the function is completely "spiky" at all points.

As an aside, it is interesting to note that although Brownian motion originally referred to a physical phenomenon, the mathematical process defined in this section could never apply to a physical process. The infinite spikiness means that an infinite amount of energy would be needed to get a particle with non-zero mass to follow a Brownian path.

(iv) Figure 21.1 shows a path following a standard Brownian motion. The first graph shows a particular path from time 0 to time 1 year. Suppose we now want to see what is going on in greater detail. We take the part of the year within the dotted box and double it in size, expanding both the $x$- and $y$-axes by a factor of two; this is shown in the second graph. Suppose we again want to examine the path in greater detail. We double half of the second path to give the third graph.

Although the specific paths in the first and third graphs are not identical, they nonetheless have the same general appearance in that they have the same degree of "jaggedness", i.e. they have the same apparent variance. The reason for this is straightforward: the variance of a Brownian motion is proportional to the time elapsed. Thus, expanding both the $x$-axis (which represents time) and the $y$-axis (which illustrates variance) by the same factor will result in paths of similar appearance, despite the fact that the scales of the graph have changed. In a word, Brownian motion is fractal: however many times we select a subsection of a path and magnify it, its variance looks the same. Obviously, the scale of the $x$- and $y$-axes changes as we do this, so that the actual variance of the section of the path chosen is always proportional to the time period over which it is measured. So what, you might say: well, it does have some unexpected consequences.

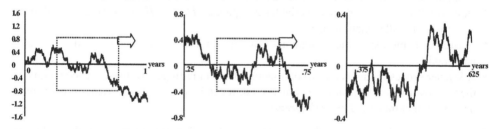

**Figure 21.1**   Fractal nature of Brownian motion

Most people looking at graphs like those in Figure 21.1, would feel intuitively that if the graphs were continued to the right far enough, the Brownian path would cross the zero line quite often. If the $x$-axis were extended to be a billion times longer, the path would cross the zero line very, very often. In fact, it is reasonable to assume that if the length of the time axis increases to $\infty$, then the path will be observed to cross the zero line infinitely often.

Consider a standard Brownian motion at its starting point $W_0 = 0$. We take a snapshot of the beginning of the path and blow it up a billion times. Surprise, surprise: having the fractal property described above, it "looks" just like the original path, although when we look at the scales of the $x$- and $y$-axes, they only cover tiny changes in time and value. But we have already admitted that we believe that if we extended the $x$-axis a billion times, the Brownian path will cross the zero line a very large number of times. We must therefore concede that given the fractal property of the path, it will cross the zero line a very large number of times in the tiny time interval at its beginning. The same must of course hold true any time a Brownian motion crosses the zero line.

Indeed, it can be proved quite rigorously that when a Brownian path touches any given value, it immediately hits the same value infinitely often before drifting away. Eventually, it drifts back and hits the same value infinitely often again – and then it repeats the trick an infinite number of times! These thought games are fun, but might not seem to have much to do with option theory. However, this property of Brownian motion, known as the ***infinite crossing property***, is central to the pricing of options. It will be shown in Chapter 25 that without it, options would be priced at zero volatility.

## 21.2   FIRST AND SECOND VARIATION OF ANALYTICAL FUNCTIONS

The object of the following chapters is to develop some form of calculus or set of computational procedures which can adequately describe functions of a Brownian motion, $W_t$. We really have no right to expect to find such a calculus; after all, classical (Riemann) calculus was evolved with well-behaved, continuous, differentiable functions in mind. $W_t$ on the other hand is a random process; while it is a function of time, it is not differentiable with respect to time at any point. Yet a tenuous thread can be found which links this unruly function to more familiar analytical territory. This thread is first picked up in the following section.

(i) ***First Variation:*** Consider an analytic function $f(t)$ of $t$ which is shown in Figure 21.2. It is most instructive to think of $f(t)$ as the position of a particle on a line, by analogy with the way we consider $W_t$. In this case, however, $f(t)$ is not a random process but some analytical function of $t$. The particle may, for example, be moving like a pendulum or it may have acceleration which is some complicated function of time.

Suppose the $t$-axis is divided into a large number $N$ of equal segments of size $\delta t = T/N$; let $f_i$ be the value of $f(t)$ at $t_i = iT/N$. Define $F_N$ as

$$F_N = \sum_{i=1}^{N} |f_i - f_{i-1}|$$

then the ***first variation*** of $f(t)$ is defined as

$$F \operatorname{var}[f(t)] = \lim_{\delta t \to 0; N \to \infty} F_N = \lim_{\delta t \to 0; N \to \infty} \sum_{i=1}^{N} |f_i - f_{i-1}|$$

(ii) In the case where $f(t)$ is a differentiable function, the mean value theorem of elementary calculus says that

$$f_i - f_{i-1} = f'(t_i^*)\delta t$$

where $t_i^*$ lies between $t_i$ and $t_{i-1}$ and $f'(t)$ is the first differential of $f(t)$ with respect to $t$. Then

$$F \operatorname{var}[f(t)] = \lim_{\delta t \to 0; N \to \infty} \sum_{i=1}^{N} |f'(t_i^*)|\delta t \to \int_0^T |f'(t)| \, dt$$

This last integral can be split into positive and negative segments where $f'(t)$ has positive or negative sign [i.e. portions with +ve and −ve slope of $f(t)$]. In physical terms, the first variation is the total distance covered by the particle in time $T$.

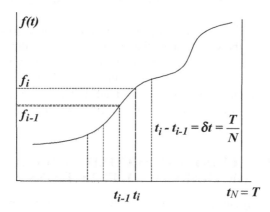

**Figure 21.2**   Variation

(iii) **Quadratic Variation**: Using the same notation as in subsection (i) above, we write $Q_N = \sum_{i=1}^{N} (f_i - f_{i-1})^2$ and then define the **second variation** or **quadratic variation** of $f(t)$ as

$$\text{Qvar}\,[f(t)] = \lim_{\delta t \to 0; N \to \infty} Q_N = \lim_{\delta t \to 0; N \to \infty} \sum_{i=1}^{N} (f_i - f_{i-1})^2$$

Taking again the case of an analytic, differentiable function $f(t)$, and using the same analysis as in the last paragraph, we have

$$\text{Qvar}[f(t)] = \lim_{\delta t \to 0; N \to \infty} \sum_{i=1}^{N} |\, f'(t_i^*)\,|^2 (\delta t)^2 \to \lim_{\delta t \to 0; N \to \infty} \delta t \int_0^T |\, f'(t)\,|^2 \, dt = 0$$

The quadratic variation of any differentiable function must be zero.

## 21.3   FIRST AND SECOND VARIATION OF BROWNIAN MOTION

(i) **Quadratic Variation**: Let us now examine the results of the last section when $f(t)$ is not a differentiable function, but a Brownian motion $W_t$. We first examine the quadratic variation Qvar $[W_t]$. Writing for simplicity $W_{t_i} \equiv W_i$, the variable $\Delta W_i$ defined by $\Delta W_i = W_i - W_{i-1}$ is distributed as N(0, $\delta t$). It follows that

$$\text{E}[\Delta W_i] = 0; \qquad \text{E}\left[\Delta W_i^2\right] = \delta t; \qquad \text{E}\left[\Delta W_i^4\right] = 3(\delta t)^2$$

The first two relationships will be obvious to the reader already, while the third can be obtained simply by slogging through the integral for the expected value using a normal distribution for $W_i$. We define $Q_N$ in the same way as for the analytical function : $Q_N = \sum_{i=1}^{N} (\Delta W_i)^2$, so that the expectations just quoted can be used to give

$$\text{E}[Q_N] = \sum_{i=1}^{N} \text{E}\left[\Delta W_i^2\right] = \sum_{i=1}^{N} \delta t = T$$

$$\text{var}[Q_N] = \sum_{i=1}^{N} \text{var}[\Delta W_i^2] = \sum_{i=1}^{N} E\big[(\Delta W_i^2 - \delta t)^2\big]$$

$$= \sum_{i=1}^{N} E\big[\Delta W_i^4 - 2\Delta W_i^2 \delta t + (\delta t)^2\big] = \sum_{i=1}^{N}\{3(\delta t)^2 - 2(\delta t)^2 + (\delta t)^2\} = 2(\delta t)T$$

In the limit as $\delta t \to 0$ and $N \to \infty$, $Q_N$ becomes the quadratic variation $Q$ of the Brownian path and converges to its expected value $T$. Although $Q$ is a random variable, it has vanishingly small variance. As the time steps $\delta t$ become smaller and smaller, the quadratic variation of any given path approaches $T$ with greater and greater certainty. It is important not to confuse the quadratic variation with the variance of $W_t$. Qvar $[W_t]$ is a random variable and refers to one single Brownian path between times 0 and $T$. On the other hand, var $[W_t] = E[W_t^2]$ is not a random variable; it implies an integration over all possible paths using the normal distribution which governs Brownian motion. The quadratic variation result of this subsection is of course a much more powerful result than the observation that the variance of $W_t$ equals $T$.

This form of convergence, whereby $A_N \to A$ with the variance of $(A_N - A)$ vanishing to zero, is termed ***mean square convergence***. More precisely, a random variable $A_N$ converges to $A$ in mean square if

$$\lim_{N \to \infty} E[(A_N - A)^2] = 0$$

This convergence criterion will be used in developing a stochastic calculus.

(ii) ***First Variation***: Return to the definition $Q_N = \sum_{i=1}^{N} \Delta W_i^2$ where the $\Delta W_i$ are random variables. Suppose $\Delta W_{\max}$ is the largest of all the $\Delta W_i$ in a given Brownian path, then

$$Q_N = \sum_{i=1}^{N} (\Delta W_i)^2 \le |\Delta W_{\max}| \sum_{i=1}^{N} |\Delta W_i| = |\Delta W_{\max}| F_N$$

However, even if it is the largest of all the $\Delta W_i$, we must still have $\lim_{\delta t \to 0} \Delta W_{\max} \to 0$, and $Q_N$ converges to a finite quantity as $N \to \infty$. This implies that

$$\text{Fvar}[W_t] \equiv \lim_{\delta t \to 0; N \to \infty} F_N \ge \frac{T}{\lim_{\delta t \to 0} |\Delta W_{\max}|} \to \infty$$

The first variation of a Brownian motion goes to $\infty$, which is in stark contrast to the result for a differentiable function given in Section 21.2(ii).

(iii) The surprising results for first and second variations of Brownian motion are due to its fractal nature. Imagine a single Brownian path in which we observe the value of $W_t$ only at fixed time points $t_0, \ldots, t_i, \ldots, t_N$. The small jumps $[W_i - W_{i-1}]$ are by definition independent of each other and have expected values of zero. An estimate of the variance of the Brownian motion can be obtained from the sample of observations on this one path:

$$V_N = \text{Est. var}[W_T] = \frac{N}{N-1} \sum_{i=1}^{N} (W_i - W_{i-1})^2 \approx Q_N$$

This estimated variance will be more or less accurate, depending on luck. If we now increase the number of readings 10-fold, we can increase the accuracy of the estimate. But remember that the Brownian path is fractal: we can improve the accuracy of $V_N$ indefinitely by taking more and more readings, until it converges to the variance of the distribution.

The infinite first variation implies that a Brownian motion moves over an infinite distance in any finite time period. It also comes about because of the fractal nature of Brownian motion. We observe the motion of a particle, measuring the distance moved at discrete time intervals. As we zoom in, measuring the distances traveled at smaller and smaller time intervals, the "noisiness" of the motion never decreases. In the limit of infinitesimally close observations, the distance measured becomes infinite. In more graphic terms, the vibration of Brownian motion is so intense that it moves a particle over an infinitely long path in any time period.

# Transition to Continuous Time

## 22.1 TOWARDS A NEW CALCULUS

(i) Our objective is to develop a set of computational rules for Brownian motion, analogous to the differential and integral calculus of analytical functions. The motivation for this search is evident if we pull together some of the results of the last couple of chapters. The martingale representation theorem which was proved in Chapter 20 for a binomial process states that if $x_i$ is a discrete martingale, then any other discrete martingale (under the same measure) $y_i$ can be written as

$$y_i - y_{i-1} = a_{i-1}(x_i - x_{i-1})$$

by a suitable choice of the random variable $a_{i-1}$. By iteration, this last equation may be written

$$y_N - y_0 = \sum_{i=1}^{N} a_{i-1}(x_i - x_{i-1})$$

This relation is quite general for any two martingales under the same measure so we may also write

$$y_N - y_0 = \sum_{i=1}^{N} a_{i-1} \Delta W_i$$

where $W_i$ is a standard Brownian motion $W_t$ at time $t = iT/N, \Delta W_i = W_i - W_{i-1}$ and $a_{i-1}$ is an $\mathcal{F}_{i-1}$-measurable random variable.

So why not simply follow the practice for analytical calculus and write

$$y_N - y_0 = \lim_{N \to \infty} \sum_{i=1}^{N} a_{i-1} \Delta W_i \to \int_0^T a_t \, dW_t \qquad (22.1)$$

Hey presto! We've made calculus for stochastic processes; maybe. If $W_t$ were an analytical function of $t$, the integral in the last equation would be solved by first making the substitution $dW_t \to (dW_t/dt)dt$, so that the variable of integration corresponds to the limits of integration. But what happens when $W_t$ is a Brownian motion?

(ii) Let's take a trip back to pre-college calculus to see what there is in the tool-box that could be of use in dealing with Brownian motion. The study of traditional calculus starts with the following concept:

$$\frac{dy}{dx} = \lim_{\delta x \to 0} \frac{\delta y}{\delta x} \qquad \text{converges smoothly to some value}$$

But as we saw in the last chapter, Brownian motion is random and fractal, so that $dW_t/dt$ is indeterminate. For analytic functions, $dy/dx$ can be considered the slope of the function $y(x)$. This only works if $y(x)$ is smooth and has no "corners". But Brownian motion is a function which is corners everywhere with no smooth bits in between! Alas, traditional differential calculus is not really going to be much use in developing stochastic theory.

(iii) Integral calculus is first introduced to students as the reverse of differentiation. If a Brownian motion cannot be differentiated, it does not seem likely that this approach will help us much in applying integral calculus to stochastic theory.

However, integration may alternatively be approached as a form of summation. In Figure 22.1, $y(x)$ is an analytical function of $x$ and $A(x)$ is the area under the curve of $y(x)$ between 0 and $x$. If $x$ is increased by $\delta x$, $A(x)$ increases by $\delta A$; but from the formula for the area of a trapezium:

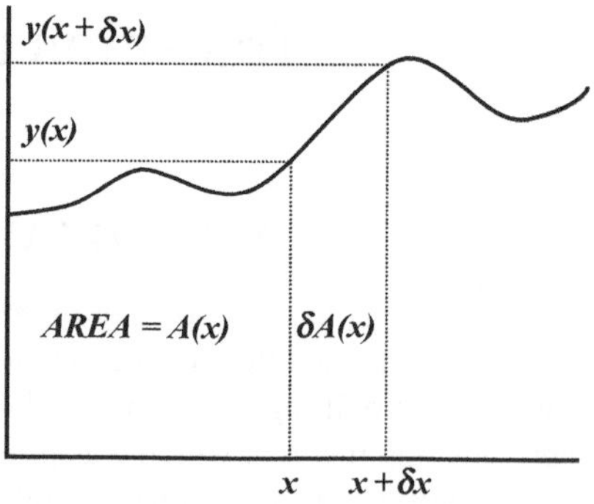

$$\delta A = \tfrac{1}{2}(y(x) + y(x + \delta x))\,\delta x$$

**Figure 22.1**   Analytical calculus

Using $\lim_{\delta x \to 0} y(x + \delta x) \to y(x)$ allows us to write $dA/dx = y(x)$, or reverse differentiating and applying the concept of limits of integration gives

$$A(X) = \int_0^X y(x)\,dx$$

This is basically how we first learned that the area under a curve is obtained by integrating the function of the curve. However, instead of relying on this idea of integration as reverse differentiation, we could approach the problem the other way around. Suppose the area $A(X)$ were sliced up into many trapeziums, each of width $\delta x$. The total area of all these trapeziums could then be written

$$A_N = \sum_{i=1}^{N} \tfrac{1}{2}\,(y(x_i) + y(x_{i-1}))\,(x_i - x_{i-1}) \qquad \text{where} \qquad N = \frac{X}{\delta x}$$

The definite integral could therefore be defined as

$$A(X) = \int_0^X y(x)\,dx = \lim_{N \to \infty; \delta x \to 0} A_N = \lim_{N \to \infty; \delta x \to 0} \sum_{i=1}^{N} \tfrac{1}{2}\,(y(x_i) + y(x_{i-1}))\,(x_i - x_{i-1})$$

For the purposes in hand, this formulation has the great advantage of defining integration without having to use the word "differentiation", which we know is a non-starter for stochastic processes.

(iv) **The Ito Integral:** This last equation is similar to equation (22.1) if we replace the continuous variable $x$ with the Brownian motion $W_t$. The most obvious difference in appearance is that here we have an integrand $\tfrac{1}{2}(y(x_i) + y(x_{i-1}))$ while the corresponding stochastic term is $a_{i-1}$. If the stochastic integral contained a term $\tfrac{1}{2}(a_i + a_{i-1})$, the summation would not be a martingale, and we wish to preserve this useful property. The stochastic integral is therefore defined as follows:

$$I = \int_0^T a_t\,dW_t = \lim_{\delta N \to \infty; \delta t \to 0} I_N$$

where

$$I_N = \sum_{i=1}^{N} a_{i-1} (W_i - W_{i-1}) = \sum_{i=1}^{N} a_{i-1} \Delta W_i \tag{22.2}$$

Such an integral is known as an *Ito integral*. If we had gone with an alternative definition and used the term $\frac{1}{2}(a_i + a_{i-1})$, we would have defined an alternative entity known as a Stratonovich integral, which has uses in some areas of applied stochastic theory but not option theory. It will not be pursued further here.

Figure 22.2 illustrates the term $I_N$ which was defined in the last paragraph as $I_N = \sum_{i=1}^{N} a_{i-1}(W_i - W_{i-1})$. Each slice of area under the graph for $a_i$ is a rectangle whose height is $a_{i-1}$, which is the value at the *beginning* of the time interval. Note the difference between this definition and the areas used either for the Stratonovich integral or the Riemann integral. In the case of the Riemann integral for an analytic function, we actually get the same answer whether we take the height of the rectangle at the beginning, mid-way or ending value of $a_t$ over the interval $(t_i - t_{i-1})$. But in the stochastic case it makes a critical difference: only if we use the beginning value will the martingale property of the integral be preserved.

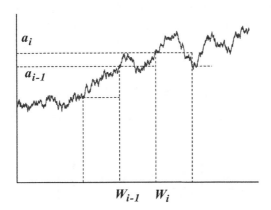

**Figure 22.2** Ito integrals

(v) The fact that we have defined an Ito integral does not in itself move things far forward. It may not converge to anything definite and we have no idea as yet of its properties or rules of manipulation. Certainly, there is no reason to assume that it works the same as Riemann integration; in fact, it does not. The rules of this calculus must be derived by first principles from its definition.

In some ways it is a pity that similar vocabulary is used both for Riemann and stochastic integrals. If the latter were called slargetni, a lot of the confusion that besets a beginner in this field would be avoided. He would always be aware that slargetni are defined as limits of a random process while integrals are the familiar friends of pre-college days. The understandable temptation to think in Riemann terms as soon as an integral sign is spotted would be avoided.

(vi) The first task is to make sure that the expression in equation (22.2) converges to something meaningful. But before we do this, we have to define what we mean by the word "converges". When dealing with analytical functions, the concept of convergence is usually fairly straightforward. But when random variables converge, several different definitions could apply: for example, the random variable $y_{i,N} = [(N-1)/N] x_i$ converges to $x_i$ as $N \to \infty$ in rather the same way that an analytical function converges. Alternatively, $y_{i,N}$ might be said to converge to $x_i$ if $E[y_{i,N}] \to E[x_i]$ as $N \to \infty$. Or again, $y_{i,N}$ might be said to converge to $x_i$ if the limiting probability distribution of $y_{i,N}$ approaches the distribution of $x_i$ as $N \to \infty$.

The particular form of convergence used in defining an Ito integral is the mean square convergence which was encountered in Section 21.3(i) in connection with the quadratic variation of Brownian motion. A more rigorous definition of an Ito integral than was given by equation (22.2) is then as follows:

$$\text{if} \qquad I_N = \sum_{i=1}^{N} a_{i-1} (W_i - W_{i-1}) \qquad \text{and} \qquad \lim_{N \to \infty} E[(I_N - I)^2] \to 0$$

then $I$ is an Ito integral and is conventionally written as

$$I = \int_0^T a_t \, dW_t$$

Why, the reader might ask, use this definition of convergence rather than any of the other possibilities available? The answer, quite simply, is that this rather abstract form of convergence gives some useful results while other, more obvious forms of convergence do not.

## 22.2   ITO INTEGRALS

(i) The simplest Ito integral is the case where the $a_i$ are constant and equal to unity. The Ito integral is then defined by

$$\lim_{N \to \infty} E\left[ \left\{ \sum_{i=1}^{N} (W_i - W_{i-1}) - I \right\}^2 \right] = 0$$

In this trivial case, we can write

$$\lim_{\delta t \to 0; N \to \infty} \sum_{i=1}^{N} (W_i - W_{i-1}) = \lim_{\delta t \to 0} (W_N - W_0) \to W_T - W_0$$

The mean square convergence criterion is clearly satisfied and the stochastic integration rules appear to mirror the Riemann rules, i.e. $\int_0^T dW_t = W_T - W_0$.

(ii) The quadratic variation of a Brownian motion over a single path was shown in Section 21.3(i) to be given by

$$\text{Qvar}[W_t] = \lim_{\delta t \to 0;\, N \to \infty} \sum_{i=1}^{N} (W_i - W_{i-1})^2 = T$$

It was also shown that $\text{var}[\text{Qvar}[W_t]] = E[\{\text{Qvar}[W_t] - T\}^2] \to 0$. Thus in a mean square convergence sense, we can write

$$\int_0^T (dW_t)^2 = T = \int_0^T dt \qquad \text{or maybe} \qquad (dW_t)^2 = dt \qquad (22.3)$$

This relationship looks rather bizarre to students who are unfamiliar with stochastic calculus, but it has been emphasized repeatedly that stochastic calculus is not Riemann calculus with the symbols changed. Remember that it arises because the quadratic variation of Brownian motion is not zero as it would be for an analytic function.

(iii) We now turn our attention to a slightly more complex Ito integral, where the difference between Ito and Riemann rules becomes apparent. Consider the following Ito integral:

$$I = \int_0^T W_t \, dW_t = \lim_{\delta N \to \infty; \delta t \to 0} \sum_{i=1}^N W_{i-1}(W_i - W_{i-1}) \qquad (22.4)$$

A bit of algebra makes this more manageable:

$$\sum_{i=1}^N (W_i - W_{i-1})^2 = \sum_{i=1}^N W_i^2 - 2\sum_{i=1}^N W_i W_{i-1} + \sum_{i=1}^N W_{i-1}^2$$

Using $W_0 = 0$ and $\sum_{i=1}^N W_i^2 = W_N^2 + \sum_{i=1}^N W_{i-1}^2$ on the right-hand side of the last equation gives

$$\sum_{i=1}^N (W_i - W_{i-1})^2 = W_N^2 + 2\sum_{i=1}^N \left(W_{i-1}^2 - W_i W_{i-1}\right)$$

$$= W_N^2 - 2\sum_{i=1}^N W_{i-1}(W_i - W_{i-1})$$

Substituting this result in equation (22.4) simply gives

$$I = \int_0^T W_t \, dW_t = \lim_{\delta t \to 0; N \to \infty} (W_i - W_{i-1})$$

$$= \tfrac{1}{2} W_N^2 - \tfrac{1}{2} \lim_{\delta t \to 0; N \to \infty} \sum_{i=1}^N (W_i - W_{i-1})^2$$

The last term of this equation is just the quadratic variation of a Brownian motion so that we can write

$$\int_0^T W_t \, dW_t = \tfrac{1}{2} W_T^2 - \tfrac{1}{2} T \qquad (22.5)$$

The unexpected term $\tfrac{1}{2} T$ is due to the non-vanishing quadratic variation of the Brownian motion.

(iv) We now consider an Ito integral with a general integrand

$$I = \int_0^T a_t \, dW_t = \lim_{\delta N \to \infty; \delta t \to 0} I_N$$

where

$$I_N = \sum_{i=1}^{N} a_{i-1}(W_i - W_{i-1})$$

The quadratic variation of $I_N$ is the sum of the quadratic variations over each time interval $t_{i-1}$ to $t_i$. But by the construction of an Ito integral, $a_i$ is constant over such an interval so that

$$\text{Qvar}\,[I_i - I_{i-1}] = a_{i-1}^2 \,\text{Qvar}\,[W_i - W_{i-1}] = a_{i-1}^2 \,(t_i - t_{i-1})$$

Summing over all intervals and taking the limit gives

$$\text{Qvar}\,[I] = \text{Qvar}[\lim_{\delta t \to 0; N \to \infty} I_N] = \int_0^T a_t^2 \, dt \tag{22.6}$$

(v) The Ito integral was constructed in such a way that that it is always a martingale. Therefore

$$E[I] = E\left[\int_0^T a_t \, dW_t\right] = 0$$

$$\text{var}[I] = \lim_{\delta t \to 0; N \to \infty} E\left[I_N^2\right] = \lim_{\delta t \to 0; N \to \infty} E\left[\left\{\sum_{i=1}^{N} a_{i-1}(W_i - W_{i-1})\right\}^2\right]$$

$$= \lim_{\delta t \to 0; N \to \infty} E\left[\sum_{i=1}^{N} a_{i-1}^2(W_i - W_{i-1})^2\right]$$

$$+ 2\lim_{\delta t \to 0; N \to \infty} E\left[\sum_{i \neq j}^{N} a_{i-1}a_{j-1}(W_i - W_{i-1})(W_j - W_{j-1})\right]$$

As in the last subsection, the first term in this expression for the variance of $I$ simply gives $\int_0^T a_t^2 \, dt$. The second part, consisting of cross terms, simply drops out because of the tower property and the martingale property of Brownian motion. For example

$$E\,[a_2 a_8\,(W_3 - W_2)\,(W_9 - W_8)|\,\mathcal{F}_0]$$
$$= E\,[a_2 a_8\,(W_3 - W_2)\,E\,[(W_9 - W_8)|\,\mathcal{F}_8]|\,\mathcal{F}_0] = 0$$

We are therefore left with the result

$$E\left[\left\{\int_0^T a_t \, dW_t\right\}^2\right] = E\left[\int_0^T a_t^2 \, dt\right] \tag{22.7}$$

(vi) The construction of the integrals above demands mean square convergence. However, we must guard against one possibility: we could have $\lim_{\delta t \to 0; N \to \infty} E[(I_N - I)^2] \to 0$ while at the same time $E[I_N^2]$ and $E[I^2]$ separately go to infinity in such a way that their divergences cancel out. A supplementary condition is therefore placed on the function $a_t$ if the Ito integral is to be considered sound:

$$E\left[\left\{\int_0^T a_t \, dW_t\right\}^2\right] = E\left[\int_0^T a_t^2 \, dt\right] < \infty \tag{22.8}$$

This is known as the *square integrability condition*. The significance of this condition for option theory is explained in the next section.

## 22.3 DISCRETE MODEL EXTENDED TO CONTINUOUS TIME

The key results of Chapter 20 which were introduced within a discrete time model are now re-stated in the framework of continuous time stochastic calculus.

(i) Recall that the Ito integral was constructed in such a way that it is always a martingale. The martingale difference equations which were written in Chapter 21 in the form

$$f_i - f_{i-1} = a_{i-1}(W_i - W_{i-1})$$

may therefore be extended to continuous time in the form

$$f_T - f_0 = \lim_{\delta N \to \infty; \delta t \to 0} \sum_{i=1}^{n} a(t_{i-1})(W(t_i) - W(t_{i-1})) = \int_0^T a_t \, dW_t$$

In our study of options, we often come across relationships of the following form, known generally as *semi-martingales*:

$$f_T - f_0 = \int_0^T b_t \, dt + \int_0^T a_t \, dW_t$$

Use is frequently made of the fact that in such a relationship, $f_t$ is only a martingale if the integral with respect to $t$ is equal to zero.

(ii) The martingale representation theorem tells us that any martingale $Y_i$ can be written in terms of another martingale $X_i$ as

$$Y_N - Y_0 = \sum_{i=1}^{N} a_{i-1}(X_i - X_{i-1})$$

Of specific interest to us is the fact that any continuous martingale can be written in terms of a Brownian motion. In continuous time this is written

$$Y_T - Y_0 = \int_0^T a_t \, dW_t$$

subject to the square integrability condition.

(iii) In Section 21.4 it was explained how the arbitrage theorem leads to the conclusion that there exists some measure under which both the discounted stock and option prices are martingales. In Section 21.5 it was shown that the discounted value of a self-financing portfolio is a martingale under the same probability measure. The martingale representation theorem of the last subsection allows a discounted option price to be written in any one of the following ways:

$$
f_T^* - f_0^* = \begin{cases} \displaystyle\int_0^T a_t \, dV_t^* \\[2ex] \displaystyle\int_0^T b_t \, dS_t^* \\[2ex] \displaystyle\int_0^T c_t \, dW_t^* \end{cases}
$$

since a discounted portfolio value $V_t^*$, a discounted stock price $S_t^*$ and a Brownian motion $W_t$ are all martingales. Once again, the square integrability condition applies to each of the three integrals.

(iv) *A Fundamental Pricing Formula*: The fact that $f_t^*$ is a martingale leads us to one of the most important results for pricing options. By definition $E^P[f_T \, B_T^{-1}|\mathcal{F}_0] = f_0^*$, or with constant interest rates

$$
f_0 = e^{-rT} E^P [f_T | \mathcal{F}_0]
$$

The superscript $P$ is included to indicate that when moving to the continuous case, we must still make the distinction between pseudo-probabilities and real-world probabilities. This topic merits a chapter of its own later (Chapter 24).

(v) *Free Lunches do Exist*: The square integrability condition should really be stated virtually every time a stochastic integral is mentioned. In practice, most derivatives practitioners simply recite the condition as a mantra whenever seems appropriate. Of course, pure mathematicians find the whole issue rivetingly interesting. So in tangible terms, what sort of thing are we likely to miss if we ignore the condition?

A good illustration is provided by equation (20.6) for the discounted value of a self-financing portfolio in terms of the discounted stock price:

$$
V_t^* - V_{i-1}^* = \alpha_{i-1}(S_i^* - S_{i-1}^*)
$$

The arbitrage theorem tells us that $S_i^*$ is a martingale so that in this discrete case, the expected value of each side of the last equation must be zero. A strategy is a set of rules for changing the $\alpha_i$ at each step depending on the value of $S_i^*$. A *simple strategy* is one where the $\alpha_i$ are changed a finite number of times, i.e. a discrete model. A *non-simple strategy* is one where $\alpha_i$ is changed continuously.

This part of the book has been built on the foundations of the no-arbitrage hypothesis, which says that no simple strategy can produce a free lunch (defined as a situation where $E[V_i^* - V_{i-1}^*] > 0$). But is it possible that in extrapolating to the continuous case, some loophole has been left open which allows us to construct a strategy which *does* produce a free lunch? Surprisingly, the answer is yes.

Consider the following simple betting game: I put up a stake of $1 and flip a coin; if I win I get back $2 and if I lose I forfeit my stake. Play the game repeatedly. My strategy, based on double or quits, is easiest to follow schematically:

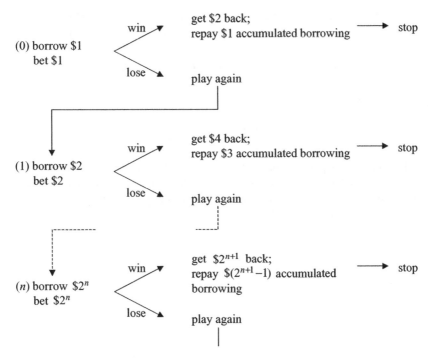

As a matter of linguistic interest, this strategy was popular amongst casino goers in the eighteenth century and was known as The Martingale. Clearly, the potential cumulative profit at each step is only $1 although the cumulative losses grow rapidly. If I can be sure of playing the game forever and I have unlimited borrowing capacity, I can be sure of winning my $1 at some point. The trouble is that my accumulated loss just before my win will be $(2^{n+1} - 1)$. In terms of statistical parameters, we can say that as $n \to \infty$, the expected value of the outcome is a gain of $1, but the variance of the outcome is infinite.

In terms of portfolios and stock prices, we could invent an analogous game. Assuming we start with no funds, the value of a self-financing portfolio in discrete time can be written

$$V_N^* = \sum_{i=1}^{n} \alpha_{i-1}(S_i^* - S_{i-1}^*)$$

Assuming a binomial type of model, one could select $\alpha_i$ at each mode such that in the event of an up-move, all previous debt is repaid and a profit of $1 is left over. In the event of a down-move the procedure is repeated. In the continuous limit and over a time period $T$, this sort of game might be played as follows: structure a leveraged, self-financing, zero-cost portfolio.

- If we are ahead at time $T/2$, stop; otherwise leverage further.
- If we are cumulatively ahead at time $3T/4$, stop; otherwise leverage further.
- If we are cumulatively ahead at time $7T/8$, stop; otherwise leverage further.
- . . .
- If we are cumulatively ahead at time $(2^n - 1) T/2^n$, stop; otherwise leverage further.
- . . .

We would be left with the same result as when we flipped coins, i.e. a free lunch but an infinite variance for $V_T^*$. If we wish to exclude such cases, we impose the condition

$$\text{var}[V_N^*] = \text{E}\left[V_N^{*2}\right] = \text{E}\left[\left\{\int_0^T \alpha_t \, dW_t\right\}^2\right] < \infty$$

or using equation (22.7)

$$\text{E}\left[\int_0^T \alpha_t^2 \, dt\right] < \infty$$

which is the ubiquitous square integrability condition. The reader is left to judge whether any of the derivatives problems he is called on to solve will involve the kind of pathological market strategies just described. Most people in the trade obediently repeat the condition in the right places and give it little further thought.

# 23

## Stochastic Calculus

### 23.1  INTRODUCTION

(i) The last couple of chapters were heavily mathematical with not much reference to option theory. Brownian motion was investigated in some detail and we developed a form of calculus which could be used to analyze this process. We defined the Ito integral $\int_0^T a_t\, dW_t$, which was constructed to be a martingale, and we derived the following three explicit results from first principles:

$$\int_0^T dW_t = W_T; \qquad \int_0^T W_T\, dW_t = \frac{1}{2}W_T^2 - \frac{1}{2}T; \qquad \int_0^T (dW_t)^2 = T \qquad (23.1)$$

The second and third results were rather surprising and reflect the fact that the quadratic variation of Brownian motion is equal to $T$, and not zero as it would be for a differentiable function.

(ii) The reader will be disappointed (or perhaps relieved) to learn that we cannot go very much further in deriving explicit integrals. In classical calculus, virtually any continuous function can be differentiated from first principles, i.e. putting $x \to x + \delta x$ as the argument of a function, expanding and then setting $O[\delta t^2] \to 0$. Not all functions can be integrated analytically; but Riemann integration can be equated to reverse differentiation, so that a large library of standard integrals has been established. Differentiation with respect to time has no meaning in stochastic calculus, so this approach is not available. The reader's first reaction to this news must be to wonder whether it was worth plowing through all the stuff in the last two chapters just to derive a calculus which is so puny that it can only manage three integrals. But thanks to Ito's lemma which is discussed next, some powerful calculation techniques do emerge.

(iii) This brings us to an important definitional point: the whole motivation for these chapters on stochastic theory is that we believe that a stock price movement can be written as $\delta S_t = a(S_t, t)\delta t + b(S_t, t)\delta W_t$. Presumably, in the limit of infinitesimal time intervals, this could be written as the differential equation $dS_t = a(S_t, t)dt + b(S_t, t)dW_t$. The reader might have noticed that books on stochastic theory (including this one) have sections entitled Stochastic Differential Equations, which deal with equations of this type. Yet in the last chapter it was emphasized that differential calculus does not apply to Brownian motion; so what's going on?

Let us ignore the $a_t\delta t$ term for the moment, as this is not where the difficulty arises, and write for $b(S_t, t)$. The position is summarized as follows:

(A) The intuitive relationship $\delta S_t = b_t\, \delta W_t$ is perfectly respectable: a small Brownian motion drives a small movement in $S_t$.
(B) If you want to make $\delta S_t$ and $\delta W_t$ very, very, very small and write this as $dS_t = b_t\, dW_t$, that's OK. You can even write $dS_t/dW_t = b_t$, which is discussed in the next subsection.
(C) You can certainly rewrite this relationship as $S_T - S_0 = \int_0^T dS_t = \int_0^T b_t\, dW_t$. We have, after all, just spent a chapter defining exactly what this integral means.
(D) ***But it is absolutely forbidden*** to put $\int_0^T b_t\, dW_t = \int_0^T b_t \frac{dW_t}{dt}\, dt$.

The punch-line is that when we see the differential equation $dS_t = a_t \, dt + b_t \, dW_t$, what is really meant is

$$S_T - S_0 = \int_0^T a_t \, dt + \int_0^T b_t \, dW_t$$

where the first integral is a Riemann integral and the second integral is the Ito integral which was defined in Chapter 22. The differential form is mere shorthand and should immediately be hidden if a serious mathematician drops by. The justification for this shorthand is that first, it is a simple and intuitive representation of a process and second, everybody else does it. In this spirit of imprecision, we can state that $dS_t = b_t \, dW_t$ is a martingale.

(iv) The next section uses the properties of differentials extensively, so at the risk of belaboring the obvious, it is worth reviewing when differential calculus can be used and when not. A stock price $S_t$ is stochastic, as is the price of the derivative of the stock $f(S_t)$. But despite the fact that they are both stochastic, $f(S_t)$ is a well-behaved, differentiable function of $S_t$. In fact, $\partial f(S_t)/\partial S_t$, is just the delta of the derivative. Similarly, $\partial f(S_t)/\partial t$ is well defined, even though $S_t$ behaves randomly over an infinitesimal time interval $dt$. The reason is that the partial differential is defined as the limit of $\delta f_t$ divided by $\delta t$ while holding $S_t$ constant. Although the partial derivatives of $f(S_t)$ with respect to both $S_t$ and $t$ are meaningful, $dS_t/dt$ does not make the grade. It is impossible to attach a meaning to this when we have no idea whether the next move in $S_t$ will be up or down, or by how much. Similarly, $df(S_t)/dt$ is meaningless; this seems a little surprising since the partial derivative was well behaved, but remember that the total derivative does not hold $S_t$ constant over the infinitesimal time interval. Finally, although $df(S_t, t)/dt$ is not allowed, a close relative defined by

$$\mathcal{A}f(S_t, t) = \lim_{\delta t \to 0} \frac{E[f(S_t + \delta S, t + \delta t) \mid \mathcal{F}_t] - f(S_t, t)}{\delta t}$$

*does* have a respectable place in stochastic calculus. We revisit this in Section 23.8 .

## 23.2   ITO'S TRANSFORMATION FORMULA (ITO'S LEMMA)

(i) In general, a small increment in the price of a derivative may be given by a Taylor expansion as follows:

$$\delta f(S_t, t) = \frac{\partial f_t}{\partial t} \delta t + \frac{\partial f_t}{\partial S_t} \delta S_t + \frac{1}{2} \frac{\partial^2 f_t}{\partial S_t^2} (\delta S_t)^2$$

$$+ \frac{1}{2} \frac{\partial^2 f_t}{\partial t^2} (\delta t)^2 + \frac{1}{2} \frac{\partial^2 f_t}{\partial S \partial t} (\delta S_t)(\delta t) + \cdots$$

In the limit of infinitesimal $\delta t$ we would expect to throw away all terms higher than the first in $\delta t$ or $\delta W_t$. However, if the stock price can be written $dS_t = a(S_t, t) \, dt + b(S_t, t) \, dW_t$, then the third term in the above Taylor expansion will contain a term of the general form $A_t (dW_t)^2$, or in its integral form

$$\int_0^T A_t (dW_t)^2 = \lim_{\delta N \to \infty; \delta t \to 0} \sum_{i=1}^{N} A_i (W_i - W_{i-1})^2$$

This is Brownian quadratic variation, which unlike an analytic quadratic variation, does not vanish to zero in the limit. $(dW_t)^2$ is just not small enough to ignore in the Taylor expansion, and in the limit of mean square convergence, we need to make the replacement $(dW_t)^2 \rightarrow dt$ which was explained in Section 22.2(ii). Our Taylor expansion was of course written in terms of $(\delta S_t)^2$, which leads to additional terms $a^2 (dt)^2$ and $ab \, dS_t \, dt$, but these can be safely dropped as they are $O[(\delta t)^2]$ and $O[(\delta t)^{3/2}]$.

(ii) *Ito's Lemma*: The arguments in the last section have been couched in terms of a derivative which is a function of a stock price. The conclusions apply more generally to any function of a Brownian motion. For future reference, the results can be stated as follows.

If a stochastic variable, driven by a Brownian motion, follows the process

$$dx_t = a(x_t, t)\,dt + b(x_t, t)\,dW_t$$

Then a differentiable function of $x_t$ follows a process which may equivalently be written in either differential or integral form:

$$
df_t = \frac{\partial f_t}{\partial t}dt + \frac{\partial f_t}{\partial x_t}dx_t + \frac{1}{2}\frac{\partial^2 f_t}{\partial x_t^2}(dx_t)^2
$$

$$
= \frac{\partial f_t}{\partial t}dt + \frac{\partial f_t}{\partial x_t}dx_t + \frac{1}{2}b_t^2\frac{\partial^2 f_t}{\partial x_t^2}dt
$$

$$
f_T - f_0 = \int_0^T \left\{ \frac{\partial f_t}{\partial t} + a_t\frac{\partial f_t}{\partial x_t} + \frac{1}{2}b_t^2\frac{\partial^2 f_t}{\partial x_t^2} \right\} dt + \int_0^T b_t\frac{\partial f_t}{\partial x_t}dW_t \qquad (23.2)
$$

Remember that from the definition of an Ito integral, the last term of this second equation is a martingale.

Ito's lemma describes the stochastic process followed by $f_t$, when $f_t$ is a function of a stochastic process $x_t$, which in turn is a function of the Brownian motion $W_t$. A simplified form of the lemma connecting $f_t$ and $W_t$ directly is obtained by putting $a_t = 0$ and $b_t = 1$:

$$
f_T - f_0 = \int_0^T \frac{1}{2}\frac{\partial^2 f_t}{\partial W_t^2}dt + \int_0^T \frac{\partial f_t}{\partial W_t}dW_t \qquad (23.3)
$$

## 23.3   STOCHASTIC INTEGRATION

At the beginning of this chapter it was observed that a stochastic integral cannot be considered the reverse of a stochastic differential with respect to time, simply because the latter does not exist. The result is that stochastic calculus can never build up the battery of standard integrals possessed by analytical calculus. In fact, the store of standard results is so poor that any insights are gratefully received. Ito's lemma confirms in a very simple manner a couple of the results we derived from first principles and gives us a procedure for integrating by parts.

(i) Using equation (23.3), let $f_t = W_t$. Straightforward substitution gives

$$
f_T - f_0 = W_t = \int_0^2 dW_t
$$

which is the simplest integral, derived from first principles in Section 22.2(i).

(ii) A slightly more complex integral, derived in Section 22.2(iii), is obtained by putting $f_t = W_t^2$. Again, substituting this in equation (23.3) gives

$$f_T - f_0 = W_T^2 = \int_0^T dt + \int_0^T 2W_t \, dW_t$$

or

$$\int_0^T W_t \, dW_t = \frac{1}{2}W_T^2 - \frac{1}{2}T$$

(iii) Let $x_t = W_T$ and $f_t = x_t g(t)$ where $g(t)$ is not dependent on $x_t$, i.e. is non-stochastic. Then equation (23.2) becomes

$$f_T - f_0 = W_T g(t) = \int_0^T x_t \frac{\partial g(t)}{\partial t} dt + \int_0^T g(t) \, dW_t$$

which immediately gives a stochastic form of integration by parts

$$\int_0^T g(t) \, dW_t = W_T g(T) - \int_0^T \frac{\partial g(t)}{\partial t} W_t \, dt \tag{23.4}$$

## 23.4    STOCHASTIC DIFFERENTIAL EQUATIONS

(i) The simplest stochastic differential equation (SDE) of interest in option theory has constant coefficients:

$$dx_t = a \, dt + \sigma \, dW_t$$

which may be simply integrated to give

$$x_T - x_0 = aT + \sigma W_T$$

From this very simple expression for $x_T$, it is clear that

$$E[x_T] = x_0 + aT \qquad \text{and} \qquad \text{var}[x_T] = \sigma^2 T$$

(ii) **Stock Price Distribution**: The most frequently used SDE for a stock price movement, which underlies Black Scholes analysis, is the following:

$$dS_t = \mu S_t \, dt + \sigma S_t \, dW_t \qquad \mu, \sigma \text{ constant}$$

Let $f_t = \ln S_t$; then equation (23.2) (Ito's lemma) becomes

$$f_T - f_0 - \ln\frac{S_T}{S_0} = \int_0^T \left(\mu - \frac{1}{2}\sigma^2\right) dt + \int_0^2 \sigma \, dW_t = \left(\mu - \frac{1}{2}\sigma^2\right) T + \sigma W_T$$

or

$$S_T = S_0 \, e^{(\mu - \frac{1}{2}\sigma^2)T + \sigma W_T}$$

which is the well-known result of equation (3.7). The expectation and variance for $S_T$ were found explicitly in Section 3.2 by plugging in the explicit normal distribution and slogging through the integral. We are now able to achieve the same result with a lighter touch by using

Ito's lemma. From the last result

$$E\left[\frac{S_T}{S_0}\right] = e^{(\mu-\frac{1}{2}\sigma^2)T} E[e^{\sigma W_T}] \tag{23.5}$$

Define a new variable $y_t = e^{\sigma W_t}$ and use equation (23.3) to give

$$y_T - y_0 = \int_0^T \frac{1}{2}\sigma^2 y_t \, dt + \int_0^T \sigma y_t \, dW_t$$

Both of the integrals in this equation contain random variables. Take the expectation at time zero of the equation, writing $E[y_t \mid \mathcal{F}_0] = Y_t$, and note that the expected value of the Ito integral is zero (martingale property):

$$Y_T - Y_0 = \int_0^T \frac{1}{2}\sigma^2 Y_t \, dt$$

The random variables have been eliminated from this equation by taking time zero expectations; the solution is $Y_T = e^{\frac{1}{2}\sigma^2 T}$ which can be verified by substituting back in the last equation. Substituting this solution back in equation (23.5) gives

$$E\left[\frac{S_T}{S_0}\right] = e^{\mu T}$$

Precisely the same technique, using an intermediate variable, allows us to write

$$E\left[\frac{S_T}{S_0}\right]^2 = e^{2(\mu-\frac{1}{2}\sigma^2)T} E[e^{2\sigma W_T}] = e^{(2\mu+\sigma)T}$$

giving a variance

$$\text{var}\left[\frac{S_T}{S_0}\right] = E\left[\left(\frac{S_T}{S_0}\right)^2\right] - E^2\left[\frac{S_T}{S_0}\right] = e^{2\mu T}(e^{\sigma^2 T} - 1)$$

From the equation for $\ln S_t/S_0$ at the beginning of this subsection, it is clear that $\text{var}[\ln S_T/S_0] = \sigma^2 T$ precisely. We may, however, make the approximation $\text{var}[S_t/S_0] \approx \sigma^2 \, \delta t$ for small $\delta t$, by expanding the full expression to first order in $\delta t$.

(iii) In the last subsection we looked at the SDE with constant $\mu$ and $\sigma$. Suppose these parameters were functions of $S_t$ and $t$: our results leading to equation (24.3) would simply become

$$S_T = S_0 \exp\left[\int_0^T \left\{\mu(S_t, t) - \frac{1}{2}\sigma^2(S_t, t)\right\} dt + \int_0^T \sigma(S_t, t) \, dW_t\right]$$

(iv) *An Interesting Martingale*: As a further exercise and because we need the result in the next chapter, consider the process

$$dx_t = -\frac{1}{2}\phi_t^2 \, dt - \phi_t \, dW_t$$

Define $\xi_t = e^{x_t}$ and use Ito's lemma to give

$$\xi_T - \xi_0 = -\int_0^T \phi_t \xi_t \, dW_t$$

or in differential shorthand

$$\frac{d\xi_t}{\xi_t} = -\phi_t \, dW_t$$

clearly, $\xi_t$ is a martingale.

(v) **Ornstein–Uhlenbeck Process:** This process, which is of interest in the study of interest rates, has the following SDE:

$$dx_t = -ax_t \, dt + \sigma \, dW_t$$

The stochastic term is the same as before, but the drift term is more interesting: the negative sign and the proportionality to $x_t$ means that the larger this term becomes, the larger the effect of this term in pushing $x_t$ back towards zero.

While it is observed in finance that a stock price is usually well described by Brownian motion, interest rates usually move within a fairly narrow band. We don't often come across interest rates of 50% (at least in markets where we want to do derivatives), but we often see stock prices that start at $10 and after a few years have reached $100. Interest rates are assumed to display **mean reversion**. They do not of course mean revert to zero (as implied by the Ornstein–Uhlenbeck process), but we stick with this most basic process for simplicity of exposition.

Let's try out the function $f_t = x_t \, e^{at}$. Ito's lemma then gives

$$f_T - f_0 = x_T \, e^{aT} - x_0 = \int_0^T \sigma \, e^{at} \, dW_t$$

or

$$x_T = x_0 \, e^{-aT} + e^{-aT} \sigma \int_0^T e^{at} \, dW_t$$

We are not able to solve the integral explicitly, but we can nevertheless obtain some useful results. The integral is a martingale, so taking expectations of the last equation and of its square gives

$$E\left[\frac{x_T}{x_0}\right] = e^{-aT}$$

$$E\left[\frac{x_T}{x_0}\right]^2 = e^{-2aT} + \frac{e^{-2aT} \sigma^2}{x_0^2} E\left[\left\{\int_0^T e^{at} \, dW_t\right\}^2\right]$$

The cross term in this last equation has disappeared on taking expectations. Substituting for the squared integral from equation (22.7) gives

$$E\left[\left(\frac{x_T}{x_0}\right)^2\right] = e^{-2aT}\left\{1 + \frac{\sigma^2}{x_0^2}\int_0^T e^{2at} \, dt\right\}$$

$$\text{var}\left[\frac{x_T}{x_0}\right] = E\left[\left(\frac{x_T}{x_0}\right)^2\right] - E^2\left[\frac{x_T}{x_0}\right] = \frac{\sigma^2}{2ax_0^2}\{1 - e^{-2aT}\}$$

## 23.5 PARTIAL DIFFERENTIAL EQUATIONS

By now, the reader has probably thought to himself that this stochastic calculus is all very well, but there is not much in the way of concrete answers (i.e. numbers) to real problems. One of the main bridges between the rather abstract theory and "answers" is the relationship between stochastic differential equations and certain non-stochastic partial differential equations (PDEs). Partial differential equations may be hard to solve analytically, but they can be forced to yield tangible results using numerical methods.

(i) **Feynman–Kac Theorem:** The basic trick in deriving the PDEs relies very simply on Ito's lemma. Take any well-behaved function $M_t$ of a process $x_t$ whose stochastic differential equation is $dx_t = a(x_t, t)\,dt + b(x_t, t)\,dW_t$. Ito's formula [equation (23.2)] gives the process for $M_t$, and this is a martingale if and only if the drift term (the integral with respect to t) is zero. This implies that

$$\frac{\partial M_t}{\partial t} + a(x_t, t)\frac{\partial M_t}{\partial x_t} + \frac{1}{2}b(x_t, t)\frac{\partial^2 M_t}{\partial x_t^2} = 0 \qquad (23.6)$$

The PDE approach consists of setting up functions which are martingales and then using Ito's lemma to obtain PDEs for these functions.

(ii) The first and most obvious choice for a martingale on which to try out this method is the discounted derivative price $f_t^* = B_t^{-1} f_t$. Substituting $f_t^*$ for $M_t$ in equation (23.6) gives the following PDE for $f_t$:

$$\frac{\partial f_t}{\partial t} + a(x_t, t)\frac{\partial f_t}{\partial x_t} + \frac{1}{2}b(x_t, t)\frac{\partial^2 f_t}{\partial x_t^2} = B_t^{-1}\frac{\partial B_t}{\partial t} f_t$$

Take the Black Scholes case where $x_t = S_t$, $a(x_t,\ t) = r S_t$, $b(x_t,\ t) = \sigma S_t$ and $B_t = e^{rt}$. The last equation then simply becomes the Black Scholes partial differential equation which was first given by equation                                                                                                              $\cdots$

$$\frac{\partial f_t}{\partial t} + r S_t \frac{\partial f_t}{\partial S_t} + \frac{1}{2}\sigma^2 S_t^2 \frac{\partial^2 f_t}{\partial S_t^2} = r f_t$$

Making the drift term $a(x_t, t)$ equal to the interest rate takes a bit of explanation, which is deferred until the next chapter; but all this will be obvious to anyone who is familiar with the risk-neutrality arguments of Chapter 4. This very slick derivation of the Black Scholes equation is shown here in order to demonstrate the power of the PDE approach to martingales.

(iii) **A Martingale Machine:** Having used the most obvious martingale ($f_t^*$) to derive the Black Scholes equation in the last section, where should we go for the next martingale? It turns out that there exists a machine for cranking out martingales on demand.

We are used to making the distinction between a random variable $x_t$ and its expected value $E\langle x_t \rangle$, which is not a random variable. But expectations can be constructed in such a way that they are also random variables: suppose $x_t$ is a stochastic process which we are anticipating at time 0. Then $E[x_t \mid \mathcal{F}_0]$ and $E[x_T \mid \mathcal{F}_0]$ are clearly not random variables; but $E[x_T \mid \mathcal{F}_t]$ definitely is a random variable when viewed from time 0, depending as it does on some future unknown information set $\mathcal{F}_t$.

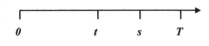

Define the function $f(x_t, t) = E[\phi(x_T) \mid \mathcal{F}_t]$ where $\phi$ is a well-behaved function of $x_T$. From this definition and the tower property we have

$$E[f(x_s, s) \mid \mathcal{F}_t] = E[E[\phi(x_T) \mid \mathcal{F}_s] \mid \mathcal{F}_t] = E[\phi(x_T) \mid \mathcal{F}_t] = f(x_t, t) \qquad (t < s) \qquad (23.7)$$

In other words, your best guess of what your best guess will be in the future has to be the same as your best guess now. Rather obvious perhaps, but it does generate more candidates for the partial differential equation of the last paragraph! An important application of this principle is given next.

(iv) **Kolmogorov Backward Equation:** The general process from which the PDE was constructed was $dx_t = a(x_t, t)\, dt + b(x_t, t)\, dW_t$. In terms of the probability distributions of classical statistics, the conditional expectations of the last subsection may be written

$$f(x_t, t) = E\langle \phi(x_T, T) \mid \mathcal{F}_t \rangle = \int_{\text{all } x_T} \phi(x_T, T) F(x_T, x_t; t)\, dx_T$$

where $F(x_T, x_t; t)$ is the probability density function. Since $F(x_T, x_t; t)$ is the only part of the integral which is a function of $x_t$ or $t$, we can write simply

$$\frac{\partial f(x_t, t)}{\partial x_t} = \int \phi \frac{\partial F}{\partial x_t}\, dx_t; \qquad \frac{\partial^2 f(x_t, t)}{\partial x_t^2} = \int \phi \frac{\partial^2 F}{\partial x_t^2}\, dx_t; \qquad \frac{\partial f(x_t, t)}{\partial t} = \int \phi \frac{\partial F}{\partial \tau}\, dx_t$$

Substituting this back into equation (23.6) immediately gives the backward equation, which was derived using other techniques in Appendix A.3:

$$\frac{\partial F(x_t, t)}{\partial t} + a(x_t, t)\frac{\partial F(x_t, t)}{\partial x_t}\, dx_t + \frac{1}{2}b(x_t, t)^2 \frac{\partial^2 F(x_t, t)}{\partial x_t^2}\, dt = 0 \qquad (23.8)$$

## 23.6   LOCAL TIME

The material in this section is used to analyze the stop-go paradox in Section 25.3 and may be omitted until then.

(i) Let us try to apply Ito's lemma to the function $f_t = \max[0, W_t - X] = (W_t - X)^+$. This is stretching things rather, as one of the preconditions of Ito's lemma is that the function should be "well behaved", i.e. at least twice differentiable with respect to $W_t$. This appears quite at odds with a sharp cornered "hockey-stick" function such as $(W_t - X)^+$. However, the first and second differentials of this function can be defined in terms of Heaviside functions and Dirac delta functions, as shown in equations A.7(ii) and (iii) of the Appendix. The simplified form of Ito's lemma [equation (23.3)] is

$$f_T - f_0 = \int_0^T \frac{\partial f_t}{\partial W_t}\, dW_t + \frac{1}{2}\int_0^T \frac{\partial^2 f_t}{\partial W_t^2}\, dt \qquad (23.9)$$

$$f_T = (W_T - X)^+; \qquad \frac{\partial f_t}{\partial W_t} = 1_{[X < W_t < \infty]}; \qquad \frac{\partial^2 f_t}{\partial W_t^2} = \lim_{\varepsilon \to 0} \frac{1}{2\varepsilon} 1_{[X-\varepsilon < W_t < X+\varepsilon]} = \delta(W_t - X)$$

(ii) The first integral in equation (23.9) appears at first sight to be an adequate representation of the left-hand side of the equation. Does this mean that the second integral, which comes from the quadratic variation term of Ito's lemma, is identically equal to zero? Let us write

$$L_T(X, \varepsilon) = \int_0^T \frac{1}{2\varepsilon} 1_{[X-\varepsilon < W_t < X+\varepsilon]} \, dt \qquad (23.10)$$

and consider $L_T(X, \varepsilon)$ in the context of the Brownian motion shown in Figure 23.1.

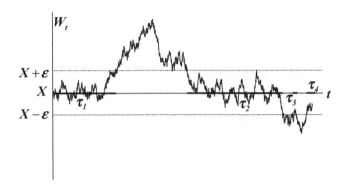

**Figure 23.1**   Total time spent by path in region $X - \varepsilon < W_t < X + \varepsilon$

During those periods when $X - \varepsilon < W_t < X + \varepsilon$, the integrand is just equal to unity; outside this range, it is equal to zero. The effect of the integration is therefore to add up all those time periods $\tau_i$ when the Brownian path is between $X - \varepsilon$ and $X + \varepsilon$.

As $\varepsilon \to 0$ we expect each of the time periods $\tau_i$ to shrink to zero. On the face of it, we might therefore expect $L_T$ to disappear in this limit. But remember the ***infinite crossing property*** of Brownian motion which we described in Section 21.1: as soon as a Brownian path achieves a value $X$, it immediately hits that value again an infinite number of times. Although each $\tau_i$ shrinks to zero, there are an infinite number of them. It may be formally shown that in the limit $\varepsilon \to 0$, $L_T(X, \varepsilon)$ is well defined, unique and non-zero, although the proof goes a bit beyond the scope of this chapter.

(iii) ***Local Time:*** Using the notation $\varepsilon = dX/2$, equation (23.10) may be rewritten as

$$L_T(X)dX = \int_0^T 1_{[X-dX/2 < W_t < X+dX/2]} \, dt$$

where $L_T(X)dX$ is the total time that the Brownian motion spends in the range $X - dX/2$ to $X + dX/2$ in the time interval 0 to $T$. We can generalize the last equation to give the total time spent by a Brownian path between $a$ and $b$ as

$$\int_a^b L_T(X)dX = \int_0^T 1_{[a < W_t < b]} \, dt$$

and we can interpret $L_T(X)$ as a density function describing how long the path spends in the vicinity of $X$. It is called the *local time* of the Brownian motion. It might save the reader some time in the future if he notes that about half the literature uses the notation local time $= L_T(X)$, while the other half uses local time $= 2L_T(X)$.

(iv) Using the Dirac delta function representation above, local time may alternatively be written as

$$L_T(X) = \int_0^T \delta(W_t - X)\, dt$$

If $h(X)$ is any reasonable function of $X$, we can write

$$\int_{-\infty}^{+\infty} h(X) L_T(X)\, dX = \int_{-\infty}^{+\infty} h(X) \int_0^T \delta(W_t - X)\, dt\, dX$$

$$= \int_0^T h(W_t)\, dt \qquad (23.11)$$

where we have made the heroic, but as it happens perfectly valid, assumption that we can switch the order of integration.

(v) *Tanaka's Formula*: In the limit as $\varepsilon \to 0$, the Ito expansion of $f_t$ which was given by equation (23.9) becomes

$$(W_T - X)^+ = (W_0 - X)^+ + \int_0^T 1_{[X < W_t < \infty]}\, dW_t + \frac{1}{2} L_T(X)$$

A precisely analogous investigation of $(W_t - X)^- = \min[0, W_t - X]$ yields the equation

$$(W_T - X)^- = (W_0 - X)^- + \int_0^T 1_{[-\infty < W_t < X]}\, dW_t + \frac{1}{2} L_T(X)$$

Adding the last two equations together gives the result

$$|W_T - X| = |W_0 - X| + \int_0^T \mathrm{sign}(W_T - X)\, dW_t + L_T(X) \qquad (23.12)$$

where

$$\mathrm{sign}(x) \begin{cases} +1 & x > 0 \\ -1 & x \le 0 \end{cases}$$

The literature rather loosely refers to any of the last three equations as Tanaka's formula.

(vi) The local time results derived for simple Brownian motion can be generalized to the semi-martingale process $dx_t = a_t\, dt + b_t\, dW_t$. The reasoning is precisely analogous to the above, and unsurprisingly yields

$$(x_T - X)^+ - (x_0 - X)^+ = \int_0^T 1_{[X < x_t < \infty]}\, dx_t + \lim_{\varepsilon \to 0} \frac{1}{2} \int_0^T b_t^2 \frac{1}{2\varepsilon} 1_{[X-\varepsilon < x_t < X+\varepsilon]}\, dt$$

The last term again results from the quadratic variation term of Ito's lemma and is interpreted as a generalized local time. It is written as $\frac{1}{2} \Lambda_T(X)$ and is subject to the same lack of notational standardization in the literature as simple local time, i.e. some people use $\Lambda_T(X)$ and some $2\Lambda_T(X)$ for the same function.

(vii) Using the Dirac delta function notation

$$\Lambda_T(X) = \int_0^T b_t^2 \delta(x_t - X)\, dt \qquad (23.13)$$

then for any reasonable function $h(x)$ we can write

$$\int_{-\infty}^{+\infty} h(X)\Lambda_T(X)\mathrm{d}X = \int_{-\infty}^{+\infty} h(X) \int_0^T b_t^2\delta(x_t - X)\,\mathrm{d}t\,\mathrm{d}X$$

$$= \int_0^T b_t^2 h(x_t)\,\mathrm{d}t \tag{23.14}$$

(viii) $\Lambda_T(X)$ is by its definition a random variable dependent on $x_t$. The last equation may therefore be used to obtain the expectation of $\Lambda_T(X)$ as follows:

$$\mathrm{E}\langle\Lambda_T(X, x_t)\rangle = \int_{-\infty}^{+\infty} p(x_t, t)\Lambda_T(X, x_t)\,\mathrm{d}x_t$$

$$= \int_{-\infty}^{+\infty} p(x_t, t) \int_0^T b_t^2(x_t)\delta(x_t - X)\,\mathrm{d}t\,\mathrm{d}x_t$$

$$= \int_0^T b_t^2(X)p(X, t)\,\mathrm{d}t \tag{23.15}$$

where $p(x_t, t)$ is the probability density that the Brownian path has value $x_t$ at time $t$.

(ix) Using the same reasoning as in subsection (v), Tanaka's formula for simple Brownian motion becomes the Tanaka–Meyer formula for Brownian motion with drift:

$$|x_T - X| = |x_0 - X| + \int_0^T \mathrm{sign}(x_t - X)\mathrm{d}x_t + \Lambda_T(X) \tag{23.16}$$

## 23.7   RESULTS FOR TWO DIMENSIONS

The results of this section are essential for understanding derivatives of two stochastic assets, but the reader may safely jump ahead until he is ready to tackle this subject.

(i) *Joint Variations for Independent Brownian Motions*: Consider two Brownian motions $W_t^{(1)}$ and $W_t^{(2)}$ which are independent of each other. By analogy with the quadratic variation of the last chapter, the joint variation can be defined as

$$\mathrm{Jvar}\big[W_t^{(1)}, W_t^{(2)}\big] = \lim_{\delta t \to 0;\, N \to \infty} J_N = \lim_{\delta t \to 0;\, N \to \infty} \sum_{i=1}^n \big(W_i^{(1)} - W_{i-1}^{(1)}\big)\big(W_i^{(2)} - W_{i-1}^{(2)}\big)$$

We use the same reasoning as in Section 21.3, writing $W_i^{(1)} - W_{i-1}^{(1)} = \Delta W_t^{(1)}$ and similarly for $\Delta W_i^{(2)}$. Then

$$\mathrm{E}[J_N] = \sum_{i=1}^n \mathrm{E}\big[\Delta W_i^{(1)}\Delta W_i^{(2)}\big] = 0$$

since $W_i^{(1)}$ and $W_i^{(2)}$ are independent with mean zero. And

$$\mathrm{var}[J_N] = \mathrm{E}[J_N^2] = \mathrm{E}\left[\left\{\sum_{i=1}^n \Delta W_i^{(1)}\,\Delta W_i^{(2)}\right\}^2\right] = \sum_{i=1}^n \mathrm{E}\big[\big(\Delta W_i^{(1)}\big)^2\big(\Delta W_i^{(2)}\big)^2\big]$$

where the cross terms of the form $\Delta W_i^{(1)}\Delta W_i^{(2)}\Delta W_j^{(1)}\Delta W_j^{(2)}\,(i \neq j)$ drop out as they are independent with zero means. The $(\Delta W_i^{(1)})^2$ and $(\Delta W_i^{(2)})^2$ terms are independent with expected value $\delta t$ so that

$$\text{var}[J_N] = (\delta t)\, T$$

which vanishes in the limit $\delta t \to 0$. In the sense of mean square convergence, the result corresponding to equation (22.3) is therefore

$$dW_t^{(1)} dW_t^{(2)} = 0 \tag{23.17}$$

(ii) Consider a function $f(x_t^{(1)}, x_t^{(2)}, t)$ which is a function of two independent Brownian motions and may be written as

$$\begin{pmatrix} dx_t^{(1)} \\ dx_t^{(2)} \end{pmatrix} = \begin{pmatrix} a_t^{(1)} \\ a_t^{(2)} \end{pmatrix} dt + \begin{pmatrix} b_t^{(1)} & c_t^{(1)} \\ b_t^{(2)} & c_t^{(2)} \end{pmatrix} \begin{pmatrix} dW_t^{(1)} \\ dW_t^{(2)} \end{pmatrix} \tag{23.18}$$

The Taylor expansion considered is now

$$df\left(x_t^{(1)}, x_t^{(2)}, t\right) = \frac{\partial f_t}{\partial t} dt + \frac{\partial f_t}{\partial x_t^{(1)}} dx_t^{(1)} + \frac{\partial f_t}{\partial x_t^{(2)}} dx_t^{(2)}$$

$$+ \frac{1}{2}\left\{ \frac{\partial^2 f_t}{\partial \left(x_t^{(1)}\right)^2} \left(dx_t^{(1)}\right)^2 + 2\frac{\partial^2 f_t}{\partial x_t^{(1)} \partial x_t^{(2)}} \left(dx_t^{(1)} dx_t^{(2)}\right) + \frac{\partial^2 f_t}{\partial \left(x_t^{(2)}\right)^2} \left(dx_t^{(2)}\right)^2 \right\} + \cdots$$

Substitute for $dx_t^{(1)}$ and $dx_t^{(2)}$ from the first set of equations; to $O[\delta t]$, $(dx_t^{(1)})^2 = (dx_t^{(2)})^2 = dt$ and $dx_t^{(1)} dx_t^{(2)} = 0$, giving a lengthy mess of an equation which is most neatly written in matrix notation:

$$df_t = \frac{\partial f_t}{\partial t} dt + \begin{pmatrix} \dfrac{\partial f_t}{\partial x_t^{(1)}} & \dfrac{\partial f_t}{\partial x_t^{(2)}} \end{pmatrix} \begin{pmatrix} a_t^{(1)} \\ a_t^{(2)} \end{pmatrix} dt$$

$$+ \frac{1}{2} \begin{pmatrix} \dfrac{\partial^2 f_t}{\partial (x_t^{(1)})^2} & \dfrac{\partial^2 f_t}{\partial x_t^{(1)} \partial x_t^{(2)}} & \dfrac{\partial^2 f_t}{\partial (x_t^{(2)})^2} \end{pmatrix} \begin{pmatrix} b_t^{(1)} & c_t^{(1)} & 0 & 0 \\ b_t^{(2)} & c_t^{(2)} & b_t^{(1)} & c_{1t} \\ 0 & 0 & b_t^{(2)} & c_t^{(1)} \end{pmatrix} \begin{pmatrix} b_t^{(1)} \\ c_t^{(1)} \\ b_t^{(2)} \\ c_t^{(2)} \end{pmatrix} dt$$

$$\begin{pmatrix} \dfrac{\partial f_t}{\partial x_t^{(1)}} & \dfrac{\partial f_t}{\partial x_t^{(2)}} \end{pmatrix} \begin{pmatrix} b_t^{(1)} & c_{1t} \\ b_t^{(2)} & c_t^{(1)} \end{pmatrix} \begin{pmatrix} dW_t^{(1)} \\ dW_t^{(2)} \end{pmatrix} \tag{23.19}$$

(iii) The Feynman–Kac analysis of Section 23.5 can be readily extended to two-dimensional Brownian motion. Using precisely the same reasoning as in the one-dimensional case, the right-hand side of equation (23.19) will only be a martingale if the drift term equals zero. Setting the coefficient of $dt$ equal to zero gives the following PDE:

$$0 = \frac{\partial f_t}{\partial t} + \begin{pmatrix} \dfrac{\partial f_t}{\partial x_t^{(1)}} & \dfrac{\partial f_t}{\partial x_t^{(2)}} \end{pmatrix} \begin{pmatrix} a_{1t} \\ a_{2t} \end{pmatrix}$$

$$+ \frac{1}{2} \begin{pmatrix} \dfrac{\partial^2 f_t}{(\partial x_t^{(1)})^2} & \dfrac{\partial^2 f_t}{\partial x_t^{(1)} \partial x_t^{(2)}} & \dfrac{\partial^2 f_t}{\partial (\partial x_t^{(2)})^2} \end{pmatrix} \begin{pmatrix} b_{1t} & c_{1t} & 0 & 0 \\ b_{2t} & c_{2t} & b_{1t} & c_{1t} \\ 0 & 0 & b_{2t} & c_{2t} \end{pmatrix} \begin{pmatrix} b_{1t} \\ c_{1t} \\ b_{2t} \\ c_{2t} \end{pmatrix} \tag{23.20}$$

(iii) *Correlated Brownian Motions*: When applying the above theory to an option dependent on two Brownian motions, the framework is usually set up in a slightly different, but equivalent, way: take two stochastic processes

$$dx_t^{(1)} = a_t^{(1)} dt + b_t^{(1)} dW_t^{(1)}$$
$$dx_t^{(2)} = a_t^{(2)} dt + b_t^{(2)} dW_t^{(2)}$$

where $W_t^{(1)}$ and $W_t^{(2)}$ are not independent but related through a correlation coefficient $\rho$. In Appendix A.1(vi) it is shown that $W_t^{(1)}$ may be written as

$$W_t^{(2)} = \rho W_t^{(1)} + \sqrt{1 - \rho^2} W_t^{(3)}$$

where $W_t^{(1)}$ and $W_t^{(3)}$ are *independent* Brownian motions. With these substitutions, equation (23.17) becomes

$$dW_t^{(1)} dW_t^{(2)} = \rho \, dt \tag{23.21}$$

and Ito's lemma becomes

$$df_t = \left\{ \frac{\partial f_t}{\partial t} + a_t^{(1)} \frac{\partial f_t}{\partial x_t^{(1)}} + a_t^{(2)} \frac{\partial f_t}{\partial x_t^{(2)}} \right\} dt$$

$$+ \frac{1}{2} \left\{ (b_t^{(1)})^2 \frac{\partial^2 f_t}{\partial (x_t^{(1)})^2} + 2\rho b_t^{(1)} b_t^{(2)} \frac{\partial^2 f_t}{\partial x_t^{(1)} \partial x_t^{(2)}} + (b_t^{(2)})^2 \frac{\partial^2 f_t}{\partial (x_t^{(2)})^2} \right\} dt$$

$$+ b_t^{(1)} \frac{\partial f_t}{\partial x_t^{(1)}} dW_t^{(1)} + b_t^{(2)} \frac{\partial f_t}{\partial x_t^{(2)}} dW_t^{(2)} \tag{23.22}$$

The two-dimensional PDE corresponding to equation (23.20) becomes

$$0 = \frac{\partial f_t}{\partial t} + a_t^{(1)} \frac{\partial f_t}{\partial x_t^{(1)}} + a_t^{(2)} \frac{\partial f_t}{\partial x_t^{(2)}}$$

$$+ \frac{1}{2} (b_t^{(1)})^2 \frac{\partial^2 f_t}{\partial (x_t^{(1)})^2} + \rho b_t^{(1)} b_t^{(2)} \frac{\partial^2 f_t}{\partial x_t^{(1)} \partial x_t^{(2)}} + \frac{1}{2} (b_t^{(2)})^2 \frac{\partial^2 f_t}{\partial (x_t^{(2)})^2} \tag{23.23}$$

## 23.8   STOCHASTIC CONTROL

The material in this section is used in the analysis of passport options in Section 26.6. The reader can safely omit the section until he is ready.

(i) *Generator of a Diffusion*: Consider a function $f_t$ of an underlying stochastic process $dx_t = a_t \, dt + b_t \, dW_t$. It was explained in Section 23.1 that no meaning can be attached to the expression

$$\frac{df_t}{dt} = \lim_{\delta t \to 0} \frac{f_{t+\delta t} - f_t}{\delta t}$$

although the expression

$$\frac{\partial f_t}{\partial t} = \lim_{\delta t \to 0} \frac{f_{t+\delta t} - f_t}{\delta t} \bigg]_{x_t \text{ held constant}}$$

is perfectly respectable. We now look at a related expression

$$\mathcal{A}f_t = \lim_{\delta t \to 0} \frac{\mathrm{E}[f_{t+\delta t} \mid \mathcal{F}_t] - f_t}{\delta t}$$

The term $\mathrm{E}[f_{t+\delta t} \mid \mathcal{F}_t]$ is *not* stochastic so there is no reason why this should not follow the behavior of any other analytical function. "$\mathcal{A}$" is known as the ***generator*** of the process $x_t$.

(ii) Ito's lemma can be written

$$\mathrm{d}f_t = \left\{ \frac{\partial f_t}{\partial t} + a_t \frac{\partial f_t}{\partial x_t} + \frac{1}{2}b_t^2 \frac{\partial^2 f_t}{\partial x_t^2} \right\} \mathrm{d}t + b_t \frac{\partial f_t}{\partial x_t} \mathrm{d}W_t$$

Taking expectations at time $t$, the last term is a martingale and drops out, so we have

$$\lim_{\delta t \to 0} \frac{\mathrm{E}[f_{t+\delta t} - f \mid \mathcal{F}_t]}{\delta t} = \mathcal{A}f_t = \frac{\partial f_t}{\partial t} + a_t \frac{\partial f_t}{\partial x_t} + \frac{1}{2}b_t^2 \frac{\partial^2 f_t}{\partial x_t^2} \tag{23.24}$$

From this last result and Ito's lemma in integral form equation (23.2) we have ***Dynkin's formula***:

$$\mathrm{E}[f_t \mid \mathcal{F}_0] = f_0 + \mathrm{E}\left[ \int_0^t \mathcal{A}f_s \, \mathrm{d}s \;\middle|\; \mathcal{F}_0 \right] \tag{23.25}$$

(iii) Suppose a stochastic function is defined by $f_t = \mathrm{E}[\int_t^T g_s \, \mathrm{d}s \mid \mathcal{F}_t]$. Then

$$\mathcal{A}f_t = \lim_{\delta t \to 0} \frac{\mathrm{E}[f_{t+\delta t} \mid \mathcal{F}_t] - f_t}{\delta t}$$

$$= \lim_{\delta t \to 0} \frac{1}{\delta t} \left\{ \mathrm{E}\left[ \mathrm{E}\left[ \int_{t+\delta t}^T g_s \, \mathrm{d}s \;\middle|\; \mathcal{F}_{t+\delta t} \right] \middle| \mathcal{F}_t \right] - \mathrm{E}\left[ \int_t^T g_s \, \mathrm{d}s \;\middle|\; \mathcal{F}_t \right] \right\}$$

$$= \lim_{\delta t \to 0} \frac{1}{\delta t} \mathrm{E}\left[ \int_{t+\delta t}^T g_s \, \mathrm{d}s - \int_t^T g_s \, \mathrm{d}s \;\middle|\; \mathcal{F}_t \right] \qquad \text{(tower property)}$$

$$= -g_t \tag{23.26}$$

Alternatively, if $f_t = \mathrm{E}[h(T, x_T, t, x_t) \mid \mathcal{F}_t]$ we can use the same procedure to write

$$\mathcal{A}f_t = \frac{\partial h(T, x_T, t, x_t)}{\partial t} \tag{23.27}$$

(iv) ***Definition of the Stochastic Control Problem***: Consider a function $G(u_t, x_t, t)$, where $\mathrm{d}x_t = a_t \, \mathrm{d}t + b_t \, \mathrm{d}W_t$. Suppose $G(u_t, x_t, t)$ depends on a parameter $u(x_t)$ which we are free to change in order to change or control the value of $G_t$. We assume that $u_t$ is also a stochastic variable dependent on $x_t$.

The objective of this section is to discover the form of $U_t$, which is the value of $u_t$ which maximizes the value of the expectation $J_0 = \mathrm{E}[g_t(u_t) \mid \mathcal{F}_0]$. We need to be quite clear about the nature of $u_t$: we have discretion to vary this as we wish, although this is likely to be in response to changes in the value of $x_t$; so the expectation $J_0$ depends on whatever we decide the function $u_s$ shall be between times 0 and $t$. On the other hand, $U_t$ depends only on the form of $G_t$ and $x_t$, and can be objectively determined, i.e. we no longer have any discretion to alter parameters. We define the maximum value of $J_0$ as $J_0^{\max}$, i.e. $J_0(U_s) = J_0^{\max}$. $u_t$ is called the ***control variable*** and $U_t$ is the ***optimal control***; $J_0(u_s)$ is the ***cost function*** or ***performance criterion***.

A favorite example makes this more concrete: $x_t$ is a stock price and $G_t$ is the value of a portfolio consisting of just a variable amount of stock and of a bond. $u_t$ is the ratio of the amount of stock and bond in the portfolio. We can change this at will, but our choice is likely to depend on the prevailing stock price. What is the formula for deciding the stock/bond ratio at any given time, which will maximize the expected portfolio value; and what is that maximum expected value?

(v) We assume that $J_t$ has the general form

$$J_t = \mathrm{E}\left[\int_t^T f_s(u_s, x_s, s)\, ds \;\middle|\; \mathcal{F}_t\right] \tag{23.28}$$

The integral term will be affected by the controls (i.e. values of $u_s$) we impose between time $t$ and $T$. Take the time 0 expectation of this last equation and use the tower property to give

$$\mathrm{E}\langle J_t \mid \mathcal{F}_0\rangle = \mathrm{E}\left[\mathrm{E}\left[\int_t^T f_s\, ds \;\middle|\; \mathcal{F}_t\right] \;\middle|\; \mathcal{F}_0\right]$$

$$= \mathrm{E}\left[\int_t^T f_s\, ds \;\middle|\; \mathcal{F}_0\right] = \mathrm{E}\left[\int_0^T f_s\, ds - \int_0^t f_s\, ds \;\middle|\; \mathcal{F}_0\right]$$

$$= J_0 - \mathrm{E}\left[\int_0^t f_s\, ds \;\middle|\; \mathcal{F}_0\right]$$

or

$$J_0 = \mathrm{E}[J_t \mid \mathcal{F}_0] + \mathrm{E}\left[\int_0^t f_s\, ds \;\middle|\; \mathcal{F}_0\right] \tag{23.29}$$

Note the general form of this last equation. Section 23.5(iii) indicates that a term like $J_t$, which is defined as a conditional expectation, should be a martingale. This would indeed be the case if we had $F_s = 0$ in the last equation, i.e. if there were no control variable; but in the situation being considered, we have the ability to intervene by manipulating the control variable, and therefore destroy the natural martingale property of $J_t$.

(vi) $J_t^{\max}$ is the value of $J_t$ if $u_t = U_t$, i.e. if we vary the parameter $u_t$ in such a way that $J_t$ is maximized. If we apply the strategy $U_t$ we are no longer imposing arbitrary values of $u_t$. Equation (23.27) may now be written

$$J_t^{\max} = \mathrm{E}\left[\int_t^T F_s(u_s, x_s, s)\, ds \;\middle|\; \mathcal{F}_t\right] \tag{23.30}$$

The difference between this and equation (23.29) is not trivial as might at first appear. $F_s(u_s, x_s, s)$ is now a well-behaved (albeit stochastic) function, whereas $f_s(u_s, x_s, s)$ was impossible to handle as it could be changed arbitrarily by playing with $u_t$. In other words, all the rules of stochastic calculus can be applied to the functions $J_t^{\max}$ and $F_s(u_s, x_s, s)$ but not to $J_t$ and $f_s(u_s, x_s, s)$; most immediately, we can now use the results of subparagraphs (ii) and (iii) of this section. Equations (23.26) and (23.30) taken together allow us to write

$$F_t(U_t, x_t, t) + \frac{\partial J_t^{\max}}{\partial t} + a_t \frac{\partial J_t^{\max}}{\partial x_t} + \frac{1}{2} b_t^2 \frac{\partial^2 J_t^{\max}}{\partial x_t^2} = 0 \tag{23.31}$$

(vii) The hypothesis that an optimal control exists is equivalent to the condition $J_0^{\max} \geq J_0$. From equation (23.29), this may be written

$$J_0^{\max} \geq \mathrm{E}[J_t \mid \mathcal{F}_0] + \mathrm{E}\left[\int_0^t f_s\, ds \;\middle|\; \mathcal{F}_t\right]$$

By definition, this must always be true, even if we replace $J_t$ with $J_t^{\max}$ on the right-hand side:

$$J_0^{\max} \geq \mathrm{E}\left[J_t^{\max} \mid \mathcal{F}_0\right] + \mathrm{E}\left[\int_0^t f_s \, ds \,\Big|\, \mathcal{F}_0\right]$$

$$\geq J_0^{\max} + \mathrm{E}\left[\int_0^t AJ_s^{\max} \, ds \,\Big|\, \mathcal{F}_0\right] + \mathrm{E}\left[\int_0^t f_s \, ds \,\Big|\, \mathcal{F}_0\right]$$

where Dynkin's formula [equation (23.25)] was used. The last result may be written

$$\mathrm{E}\left[\int_0^t \left(f_s + AJ_s^{\max}\right) ds \,\Big|\, \mathcal{F}_0\right] \leq 0$$

This holds for all values of $t$ from 0 to $t$ so we conclude that $f_s + AJ_s^{\max} \leq 0$.

(viii) **Hamilton–Jacobi–Bellman Equation:** The results of the last two subsections can be summarized as follows. Suppose there exists an optimal control $u_t = U_t$ which maximizes the cost function $J_0 = \mathrm{E}[\int_0^T f_{(u_s,x_s,s)} \, ds \mid \mathcal{F}_0]$; writing $J_0^{\max} = \mathrm{E}[\int_0^T F_{(U_s,x_s,s)} \, ds \mid \mathcal{F}_0]$, the following two conditions then hold:

1. $F_{(U_t,x_t,t)} + AJ_t^{\max} = 0$.
2. The solution given by (1) above corresponds to the *maximum* of the function $f(u_t, x_t, t) + AJ_t^{\max}$.

# 24

# Equivalent Measures

## 24.1 CHANGE OF MEASURE IN DISCRETE TIME

(i) In Section 19.2 the arbitrage theorem was applied to a simple portfolio over a single time step. The analysis led to the concept of pseudo-probabilities, which could be calculated from the starting value of the stock and a knowledge of the two possible values after a single time step. It was emphasized that these pseudo-probabilities are not to be confused with actual probabilities; they are merely computational devices, despite the fact that they display all the mathematical properties of probabilities.

If the concept is extended from a single step model to a tree, there is a pseudo-probability assigned to each branch of the tree. In the simplest trees, there are only two pseudo-probabilities: up and down, which are constant throughout the tree. However, we will keep the analysis more general and consider variable branching probabilities.

Consider a large binomial tree as shown in Figure 24.1. The underlying stochastic variable $x_i$ can take the values at the nodes of the tree which are written $x_m^n$ ($n$: time steps; $m$: space steps from the bottom of the tree). The entire set of values $x_0^0, \ldots, x_N^N$ has previously been referred to as the *sample space* $\Omega$, or the architecture of the tree. The set of probabilities of up or down jumps at each of the nodes is collectively known as the *probability measure P*. From a knowledge of all the branching probabilities (it is *not* assumed that they are constant throughout the tree), we can easily calculate the probabilities of achieving any particular node in the tree; these outcome probabilities can equally be

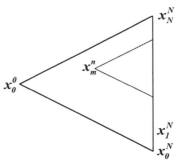

**Figure 24.1** $N$-Step tree (sample space)

referred to as the probability measure, since branching and outcome probabilities are mechanically linked to each other. We use the notation $p_m^n$ to denote the time 0 probability under the probability measure $P$ of $x_i$ achieving the value $x_m^n$ at the $n$th time step. Clearly, we start with $p_0^0 = 1$.

We have already seen that in solving any option theory problem, we have discretion in choosing sample space and probability measure. For example, the Cox–Ross–Rubinstein and the Jarrow–Rudd sample spaces use different probability measures, but yield substantially the same answers when used for computation (see Chapter 7). The purpose of this chapter is to explore the effect of changing from one probability measure to another.

(ii) *The Radon–Nikodym Derivative*: Consider two alternative probability measures $P$ and $Q$, i.e two sets of outcome probabilities $p_0^0, \ldots, p_N^N$ and $q_0^0, \ldots, q_N^N$. Either of these could be applied to the tree (sample space $\Omega$). Let us now define a quantity $\xi_m^n = q_m^n / p_m^n$ for each node of the tree. A new $N$-step tree is shown in Figure 24.2, similar to that for the $x_m^n$ but with nodal values equal to the quantities $\xi_m^n$. This tree ($\Omega$), together with a probability measure, defines a new stochastic process $\xi_i$.

From these simple definitions, we may write

$$E^Q[x_N \mid \mathcal{F}_0] = \sum_{j=0}^{N} x_j^N q_j^N = \sum_{j=0}^{N} x_j^N \xi_j^N p_j^N$$

$$= E^P[x_N \xi_N \mid \mathcal{F}_0] \tag{24.1}$$

And similarly for any function of $x_N$:

$$E^Q[f(x_N) \mid \mathcal{F}_0] = E^P[f(x_N)\xi_N \mid \mathcal{F}_0] \tag{24.2}$$

Simply by putting $f(x_N) = 1$ in this last equation gives

$$E^P[\xi_N \mid \mathcal{F}_0] = 1 \tag{24.3}$$

$\xi_i$ is a process known as the **Radon–Nikodym–derivative** of the measure $Q$ with respect to the measure $P$. The somewhat misleading notation $dQ/dP$ is normally used, but the word derivative (reinforced by the differential notation) must not be taken to denote a derivative as in analytical differential calculus; $\xi_i$ is a stochastic process.

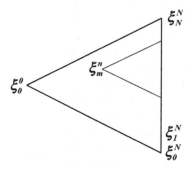

**Figure 24.2**    Sample space or Radon–Nikodym derivative

Care needs to be taken with one point: each of the $\xi_m^n$ is the quotient of two probabilities and if the denominator is zero at any node, then the calculations blow up. We must have either $p_m^n$ and $q_m^n$ both non-zero or both zero for each possible outcome. If the measures fulfill this condition, we say that $P$ and $Q$ are **equivalent probability measures.**

(iii) The Radon–Nikodym process has an additional interesting property which follows from equation (24.3). This equation holds true whatever the value of $N$, and since by definition $\xi_0 = \xi_0^0 = 1$, the process $\xi_i$ must be a martingale.

(iv) It is a trivial generalization to extend equation (24.1) to the following which applies at step $n$:

$$E^Q[x_N \mid \mathcal{F}_0] = E^P[x_N \xi_N \mid \mathcal{F}_0]$$

If we wish to express the expectation of $x_N$ at $\mathcal{F}_0$, subject to the condition that the process $x_i$ has previously hit a node with value $x_m^n$ (or equivalently that $\xi_i$ has previously achieved $\xi_m^n$), then we must introduce the probability of achieving $x_m^n$ on each side of the last equation; but the probabilities must be expressed in the appropriate measure:

$$q_m^n E^Q[x_N; \text{ condition: } x_n = x_m^n \mid \mathcal{F}_0] = p_m^n E^P[x_N \xi_N^N; \text{ condition: } x_n = x_m^n \mid \mathcal{F}_0]$$

$$E^Q[x_N; \text{ condition: } x_n = x_m^n \mid \mathcal{F}_0] = \frac{1}{\xi_m^n} E^P[x_N \xi_N^N; \text{ condition: } x_n = x_m^n \mid \mathcal{F}_0] \tag{24.4}$$

(v) From the foregoing paragraphs, we can distil the following general properties for a Radon–Nikodym derivative:

- $E^Q[f(x_N) \mid \mathcal{F}_0] = E^P[\xi_N f(x_N) \mid \mathcal{F}_0]$
- $E^P[\xi_j \mid \mathcal{F}_i] = \xi_i \qquad i < j \text{ (martingale)}$
- $\xi_0 = 1; \qquad \xi_i > 0$
- $\xi_i E^Q[f(x_N) \mid \mathcal{F}_i] = E^P[\xi_N f(x_N) \mid \mathcal{F}_i]$

## 24.2 CHANGE OF MEASURE IN CONTINUOUS TIME: GIRSANOV'S THEOREM

(i) The probability measure in the tree of the last section was defined as the set of probabilities throughout the tree. In continuous time, the probability measure is the time-dependent frequency distribution for the process. For example, if $W_t$ is a standard Brownian motion, its frequency distribution is a normal distribution with mean 0 and variance $t$. The probability of its value lying in the interval $W_t$ to $W_t + dW_t$ is

$$dP_t = \frac{1}{\sqrt{2\pi t}} \exp\left(-\frac{1}{2t} W_t^2\right) dW_t$$

A change of probability measure which is analogous to changing the set of probabilities in discrete time simply means a change in the frequency distribution in continuous time. A Radon–Nikodym derivative can be defined which achieves this change in probability measure:

$$\xi(x_t) = \frac{dQ_t}{dP_t} = \frac{F^Q(x_t) dx_t^Q}{F^P(x_t) dx_t^P} \tag{24.5}$$

where $F^P(x_t)$ and $F^Q(x_t)$ are the frequency distributions corresponding to the probability measures $P$ and $Q$.

As in the case of discrete distribution, the analysis breaks down if at any point we allow $dQ_t$ to remain finite while $dP_t$ is zero. Therefore only *equivalent probability measures* are considered, which ascribe zero probability to the same range of values of the variable $x_t$. This is illustrated in Figure 24.3.

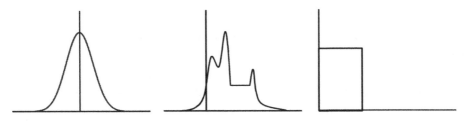

**Figure 24.3** Probability measures

The first frequency distribution is normal. The middle distribution is a little unusual, but is "equivalent" to the normal distribution. The third distribution is a very common one, but is not equivalent to the first, since it ascribes a value 0 outside the square range.

(ii) We now investigate the process $\xi_T$ which is defined by

$$\xi_T = e^{y_T}; \qquad dy_t = -\tfrac{1}{2}\phi_t^2 \, dt - \phi_t \, dW_t$$

It is shown in Section 23.4(iv) that $\xi_T$ is a martingale and that $\xi_0 = 1$ and $\xi_t > 0$. Therefore $\xi_T$ displays the basic properties of a Radon–Nikodym derivative which are set out in Section 25.1(v).

The function $\xi_T$ will be applied as the Radon–Nikodym derivative in transforming a drifted Brownian motion $dx_t^P = \mu_t \, dt + \sigma_t \, dW_t^P$ (defined as having probability measure $P$) to some other stochastic process (defined as having probability measure $Q$). We are interested in discovering what that other stochastic process looks like, for the specific form of $\xi_T$ defined above.

(iii) Before proceeding with the analysis, we recall a result described in Appendix A.2(ii). A normal distribution $N(\mu T, \sigma^2 T)$ has a moment generating function given by

$$M^P(\Theta) = E^P\big[e^{\Theta x_T^P} \,\big|\, \mathcal{F}_0\big] = e^{\mu T \Theta + \frac{1}{2}\sigma^2 T \Theta^2}$$

Furthermore, the moment generating function for the random variable $x_T^P$ is unique, i.e. if $x_T^P$ has the above moment generating function, then $x_T^P$ must have the distribution $N(\mu T, \sigma^2 T)$.

The analogous results for a process $x_t^P$ with variable $\mu_t$ and $\sigma_t$ are obtained from the following modifications:

$$\mu T = E^P[x_T \mid \mathcal{F}_0] = \int_0^T \mu_t \, dt$$

$$\sigma^2 T = \text{var}[x_T] = E^Q\left[\left\{\int_0^T \sigma_t^2 \, dW_t\right\}^2 \,\Big|\, \mathcal{F}_0\right] = \int_0^T \sigma_t^2 \, dt$$

The moment generating function result above can now be written more generally as

$$M^P(\Theta) = E^P\big[e^{\Theta x_T^P} \,\big|\, \mathcal{F}_0\big] = E^P\left[\exp\left[\Theta\left\{x_0 + \int_0^T \mu_t \, dt + \int_0^T \sigma_t \, dW_t\right\}\right]\,\Big|\, \mathcal{F}_0\right]$$

$$= \exp\left[\Theta\left\{x_0 + \int_0^T \mu_t \, dt\right\} + \frac{1}{2}\Theta^2 \int_0^T \sigma_t^2 \, dt\right] \tag{24.6}$$

We will also use the following standard integral result which is a special case of the last equation with $\Theta = 1$:

$$E^P\left[\exp\left[x_0 + \int_0^T \mu_t \, dt + \int_0^T \sigma_t \, dW_t\right]\,\Big|\, \mathcal{F}_0\right] = \exp\left[x_0 + \int_0^T \mu_t \, dt + \frac{1}{2}\int_0^T \sigma_t^2 \, dt\right] \tag{24.7}$$

(iv) The effect of changing to probability measure $Q$ by using $\xi_T$ as the Radon–Nikodym derivative is as follows:

$$M^Q[\Theta] = E^Q\left[e^{\Theta x_T^Q} \mid \mathcal{F}_0\right] = E^P\left[\xi_T\, e^{\Theta x_T^P} \mid \mathcal{F}_0\right]$$

$$= E^P\left[\exp\left[-\frac{1}{2}\int_0^T \phi_t^2\, dt - \int_0^T \phi_t\, dW_t\right]\exp\left[\Theta\left\{x_0 + \int_0^T \mu_t\, dt + \int_0^T \sigma_t\, dW_t\right\}\right]\Big| \mathcal{F}_0\right]$$

$$= E^P\left[\exp\left[\Theta x_0 + \int_0^T \left(\Theta\mu_t - \tfrac{1}{2}\phi_t^2\right) dt + \int_0^T \left(\Theta\sigma_t - \phi_t\right) dW_t\right]\Big| \mathcal{F}_0\right]$$

where we have used $y_0 = 0$ (since $\xi_0 = 1$). Use of equation (24.7) shows that the last equation may be written

$$M^Q(\Theta) = \exp\left[\Theta x_0 + \int_0^T \left(\Theta\mu_t - \tfrac{1}{2}\phi_t^2 + \tfrac{1}{2}\Theta^2\sigma_t^2 - \Theta\sigma_t\phi_t + \tfrac{1}{2}\phi_t^2\right) dt\right]$$

$$= \exp\left[\Theta\left\{x_0 + \int_0^T (\mu_t - \lambda_t)\, dt\right\} + \frac{1}{2}\Theta^2\int_0^T \sigma_t^2\, dt\right] \tag{24.8}$$

where we have arbitrarily defined $\lambda_t = \sigma_t\phi_t$.

Comparing equations (24.6) and (24.8) leads us to the following conclusions which constitute Girsanov's theorem.

The effect on a drifted Brownian motion of changing probability measure by using the Radon–Nikodym derivative $\xi_t$ as defined above is as follows:

- The measure $P$ drifted Brownian motion is transformed into another drifted Brownian motion (with probability measure $Q$).
- The variances of the two Brownian motions are the same.
- The only effect of the change in measure is to change the drift by an instantaneous rate $\lambda_t$ which is defined above.

Formally this may be written

$$W_T^Q = W_T^P - \int_0^T \lambda_t\, dt \qquad \text{or in shorthand} \qquad dW_T^Q = dW_T^P - \lambda_t\, dt$$

The result is subject to the usual type of technical condition (the ***Novikov condition***):

$$E\left[\exp\left(\frac{1}{2}\int_0^T \lambda_t^2\, dt\right)\right] < \infty$$

Girsanov's theorem basically gives a prescription for changing the measure of a Brownian motion in such a way that it remains unchanged except for the addition of a drift. So what, you might ask? You can achieve the same effect by just adding a time-dependent term to the underlying variable $W_t$; what's the big deal? We know already that the value of an option is the expected value of its payoff under some pseudo-probability measure. The value of the theorem is that it provides a recipe for applying this particular measure simply by adding a convenient drift term in the SDE governing the process in question. This procedure is explicitly laid out in the next section.

(v) *Girsanov's Theorem without Stochastic Calculus*: This is a theorem of great power and usefulness in option theory, but it is worth a re-examination from the point of view of someone without a knowledge of stochastic calculus; it leads to an intuitive understanding which does much to demystify the theorem.

Consider a stochastic variable $x_t$ ($x_0 = 0$) distributed as $N(\mu t, \sigma^2 t)$. The probability distribution function of $x_t$ is

$$n(x_t; \mu, \sigma) = \frac{1}{\sqrt{2\pi\sigma^2 t}} \exp\left[-\frac{1}{2}\left(\frac{x_t - \mu t}{\sigma\sqrt{t}}\right)^2\right]$$

and the moment generating function has been shown to be

$$M(\Theta) = \int_{-\infty}^{+\infty} e^{\Theta x_t} n(x_t; \mu, \sigma) \, dx_t = e^{\mu t \Theta + \frac{1}{2}\sigma^2 t \Theta^2}$$

Remember that $M(\Theta)$ uniquely defines a distribution and all its moments can be derived from it. But by pure algebraic manipulation, the last equation could be written

$$M(\Theta) = \int_{-\infty}^{+\infty} e^{\Theta x_t} \, n(x_t; \mu, \sigma) \, dx_t \equiv \int_{-\infty}^{+\infty} e^{\Theta x_t} \left\{\frac{n(x_t; \mu, \sigma)}{n(x_t; \mu', \sigma)}\right\} n(x_t; \mu', \sigma) \, dx_t$$

$$= \int_{-\infty}^{+\infty} e^{\Theta x_t} \left\{\exp \frac{-1}{2\sigma^2 t}((x_t - \mu t)^2 - (x_t - \mu' t)^2)\right\} n(x_t; \mu', \sigma) \, dx_t$$

$$= \int_{-\infty}^{+\infty} e^{\Theta x_t} \exp\left[-\tfrac{1}{2}\phi^2 t - \phi\sqrt{t}\left(\frac{x_t - \mu' t}{\sigma\sqrt{t}}\right)\right] n(x_t; \mu', \sigma) \, dx_t \quad \text{where} \quad \phi = \frac{\mu' - \mu}{\sigma}$$

$$= e^{(\mu' - \phi\sigma)t\Theta + \frac{1}{2}\sigma^2 t\Theta^2}$$

The conclusion to be drawn from this result is that any normal distribution, but always with the same variance $\sigma^2 t$, can be used to take the expectation of a function, but the function must be modified by multiplication by the factor $\exp[-\tfrac{1}{2}\phi^2 t - \phi\sqrt{t}(\frac{x_t - \mu' t}{\sigma\sqrt{t}})]$. Alternatively expressed, an arbitrary choice of normal distribution (but always with the same variance) really only affects the drift term. This may be self-evident, if we remember that a normal distribution is entirely defined by the drift and variance, and it certainly takes some of the mystery out of Girsanov's theorem.

## 24.3 BLACK SCHOLES ANALYSIS

(i) The stochastic differential equation governing a stock price movement is assumed to be

$$dS_t = \mu_t S_t \, dt + \sigma_t S_t \, dW_t^{RW} \tag{24.9}$$

where $\mu_t$ is the drift observed in the real world and the superscript RW indicates that the Brownian motion is observed in the same real world.

Our objective now is to find the measure under which the discounted stock price $S_t^*$ is a martingale; $S_t^* = S_t B_t^{-1}$ where $B_t$ is the zero coupon bond price. The reason we want to find the measure is that the value of an option can be found by taking the expectation of its payoff under this measure.

With variable (but non-stochastic) interest rates, we can define the value of the zero coupon bond in terms of continuous, time-dependent interest rates $r_t$ as $B_t^{-1} = \exp(-\int_0^t r_\tau \, d\tau)$, so that $d(B_t^{-1}) = -B_t^{-1}r_t\,dt$. The process for $S_t^*$ can then be written

$$dS_t^* = d\left(S_t B_t^{-1}\right) = B_t^{-1}\,dS_t + S_t\,d\left(B_t^{-1}\right)$$

$$= S_t B_t^{-1}\left\{(\mu_t - r_t)\,dt + \sigma_t\,dW_t^{RW}\right\}$$

(ii) Girsanov's theorem tells us that we can change the probability measure by changing the drift of the Brownian motion. Writing $dW_t^{RW} = dW_t^{Q} - \lambda_t\,dt$, the last equation becomes

$$dS_t^* = S_t B_t^{-1}\left\{(\mu_t - r_t - \lambda_t\sigma_t)\,dt + \sigma_t\,dW_t^{Q}\right\}$$

where $Q$ is a new measure. This is a $Q$-martingale if the coefficient of $dt$ is zero, i.e. if

$$\lambda_t = \frac{\mu_t - r_t}{\sigma_t} \tag{24.10}$$

The term on the right-hand side of this last equation will be familiar to students of finance theory as the Sharpe ratio. It is normally referred to in option theory as the **market price of risk**.

An important and much used property of $\lambda_t$ is that it is the same for all derivatives of the same underlying stock. Consider a stock whose process is given by $dS_t = \mu_t\,dt + \sigma_t\,dW_t^{RW}$ where $\mu$ and $\sigma$ are functions of $S_t$. Now consider two derivatives; Ito's Lemma means that we can write the processes for these as

$$f_t^{(1)} = \mu_t^{(1)}\,dt + \sigma_t^{(1)}\,dW_t^{RW}; \qquad f_t^{(2)} = \mu_t^{(2)}\,dt + \sigma_t^{(2)}\,dW_t^{RW}$$

Let us construct a portfolio consisting of $f_t^{(2)}\sigma_t^{(2)}$ units of the derivative $f^{(1)}$, and $-f_t^{(1)}\sigma_t^{(1)}$ units of $f^{(2)}$. The portfolio value is

$$\pi_t = f_t^{(1)} f_t^{(2)}\sigma_t^{(2)} - f_t^{(1)} f_t^{(2)}\sigma_t^{(1)} = f_t^{(1)} f_t^{(2)}\left(\sigma_t^{(2)} - \sigma_t^{(1)}\right)$$

A change in the value of this portfolio over an infinitesimal time step $dt$ is

$$d\pi_t = f_t^{(2)}\sigma_t^{(2)}\,df_t^{(1)} - f_t^{(1)}\sigma_t^{(1)}\,df_t^{(2)} = f_t^{(1)} f_t^{(2)}\left(\sigma_t^{(2)}\mu_t^{(1)} - \sigma_t^{(1)}\mu_t^{(2)}\right)\,dt$$

since the $dW_t^{RW}$ terms cancel. But if the return is not stochastic (i.e. is risk-free), then the return must equal the interest rate:

$$\frac{\sigma_t^{(2)}\mu_t^{(1)} - \sigma_t^{(1)}\mu_t^{(2)}}{\sigma_t^{(2)}\sigma_t^{(1)}} = r_t \qquad \text{or} \qquad \frac{\mu_t^{(1)} - r_t}{\sigma_t^{(1)}} = \frac{\mu_t^{(2)} - r_t}{\sigma_t^{(2)}} \qquad (= \lambda_t)$$

(iii) Let us now return to equation (24.9) and rewrite this in terms of the measure $Q$, using the above value for $\lambda_t$. Simple substitution gives us

$$dS_t = r_t S_t\,dt + \sigma_t S_t\,dW_t^{Q} \tag{24.11}$$

In a nutshell, we have changed the real-world SDE by changing to the alternative measure $Q$ which turns the discounted stock price into a martingale; the effect of this switch is merely to replace the real-world stock drift by the risk-free interest rate. The measure is therefore usually referred to as the **risk-neutral measure**. This analysis is simply a sophisticated re-statement of the principle of risk neutrality on which we based the first three parts of this book.

(iv) **Continuous Dividends:** The effect of a continuous dividend rate $q$ is easy to include in the above framework. We use constant rates for simplicity. The effect of a dividend is that the holder of the shares receives a cash throw-off. It was shown in Chapter 1 that this can be incorporated into the calculations by writing the stock price as $S_t \, e^{+qt}$. The discounted share value is therefore

$$S_t^* = S_t \, e^{qt} \, e^{-rt}$$

so that

$$dS_t^* = S_t^* \{ (\mu - (r - q)) \, dt + \sigma \, dW_t^{RW} \}$$

or from the previous analysis

$$dS_t = (r - q) S_t \, dt + \sigma S_t \, dW_t^Q \tag{24.12}$$

(v) *Forward Price*: This can be written $F_t = S_t \, e^{(r-q)(T-t)}$. We saw in the last subsection that $S_t \, e^{-(r-q)t}$ is a $Q$-martingale, i.e. $dS_t^* = S_t^* \sigma \, dW_t^Q$. Multiply both sides by $e^{(r-q)T}$ to give

$$dF_t = \sigma F_t \, dW_t^Q \tag{24.13}$$

Using the results of Section 23.4(iv) gives

$$F_t = e^{-\frac{1}{2}\sigma^2 t + \sigma \, dW_t^Q} \tag{24.14}$$

# 25

## Axiomatic Option Theory

### 25.1 CLASSICAL VS. AXIOMATIC OPTION THEORY

(i) In the first three parts of this book, option theory was developed from a very few key concepts:

(A) *Perfect Hedge:* An option may be perfectly hedged. Previously, it was just assumed that this is possible, and it was shown in Section 4.4 that if such a hedge exists, then it must be a self-financing portfolio. Now, using arbitrage arguments we have shown that a discounted derivatives price is a martingale. It was also shown that the discounted value of a self-financing portfolio consisting of stock plus cash is also a martingale; the martingale representation theorem therefore proves that an option can be perfectly hedged. The reader who has the inclination to play with these two set of arguments as explicitly laid out in Sections 4.3 and 21.5 will quickly realize how closely the two analyses are related. Stochastic theory has just added a lot of fancy words.

(B) *Risk Neutrality:* For discrete models, the derivation of risk neutrality is very closely related in classical and axiomatic option theory. In both cases, we start by examining a single step: in the classical case, we get the result in Section 4.1 by saying that a portfolio consisting of an option plus a hedge must be risk-free and therefore have a return equal to the interest rate; in the axiomatic case, we use the arbitrage theorem to prove the same result.

For continuous models, the arguments appear to diverge rather more. We inferred risk neutrality in the classical case from the fact that the real-world drift does not appear in the Black Scholes equation. In axiomatic theory, risk neutrality falls out of the application of Girsanov's theorem and a consideration of the properties of martingales.

(C) *The Black Scholes Equation:* This was derived in Section 4.2 by constructing a continuous time portfolio of derivative plus hedge and requiring its rate of return to equal the interest rate. In Section 23.5 it appears as a consequence of the fact that the discounted option price is a $P$-martingale, which in turn is a consequence of the arbitrage theorem. Both derivations are critically dependent on Ito's lemma, which was introduced with a lot of hand waving in Section 3.4 and which is of course a central pillar of stochastic calculus. It is not possible to derive an options theory without *some* recourse to stochastic calculus, albeit the very rough and ready description of Ito's lemma given in Chapter 3.

(D) *Risk-neutral Expectations:* Use of these to price options was introduced with a minimum of fuss (or rigor) in Section 4.1. Using the axiomatic approach, it was shown in Section 22.3(iv) to result from the fact that the discounted option price is a $P$-martingale (and hence from the arbitrage theorem).

(ii) At this point the reader faces the awkward question "was it all worth it?" Despite our rather robust approach, stochastic calculus has been seen to be a tool of great subtlety; but we don't seem to have any additional specific results to what we had before.

Without beating about the bush, our view is that if someone is interested in equity-type options (including FX and commodities), he is likely to find most results he needs through the classical statistical approach to option theory. His main problem will be reading the technical literature, which tends to use stochastic calculus whether or not it is needed to explain option theory. But for anyone interested in interest rate options, a knowledge of stochastic calculus is indispensable.

Having said this, the next two sections deal with two topics which demand fairly advanced stochastic techniques. The first is the question of whether an American option is indeed a hedgeable instrument, which is by no means self-evident from the last few chapters. The second is the so-called stop–go paradox, which lies at the very heart of option theory; its resolution is quite subtle and it puzzled theorists for some while. The remainder of the chapter uses stochastic calculus to re-derive a number of previous results more elegantly and sometimes more convincingly.

## 25.2   AMERICAN OPTIONS

The axiomatic option theory developed in this part of the book has so far only examined the case of European options. American options are analytically more difficult to handle; but they are also commercially more common, so we need to be sure that the mathematical rules do not break down when the possibility of early exercise is allowed. For example, if the possibility of early exercise were to destroy the martingale property of the discounted option price, the option might no longer be hedgeable! This subject will need a little bit of a mathematical detour, as we first need to introduce some new concepts.

(i) Consider an American option in a discrete time framework. $f_n$ is the no-arbitrage value of the option at step $n$ and $K_n$ is the exercise value at the same point in time; $f_n^*$ and $K_n^*$ are the discounted values $B_n^{-1} f_n$ and $B_n^{-1} K_n$. Suppose our model has $N$ steps and the option has got as far as step $N - 1$ without being exercised. There are two possibilities at this point:

- It is not worth exercising the option, in which case its value is the same as for the corresponding European option:

$$f_{N-1}^* = E^Q[f_N^* \mid \mathcal{F}_{N-1}]$$

where $Q$ is the risk-neutral probability measure.
- It is better to exercise immediately and receive the payoff $K_{N-1}$.

Taking these two possibilities together gives the price of an American option at $N - 1$ as

$$f_{N-1}^* = \max[K_{N-1}^*, E^Q[f_N^* \mid \mathcal{F}_{N-1}]]$$

Generalizing this to any point in the process gives

$$f_n^* = \max\left[K_n^*, E^Q[f_{n+1}^* \mid \mathcal{F}_n]\right] \tag{25.1}$$

(ii) *Snell's Envelope*: This expression for $f_n^*$ clearly means that the nice martingale property of a discounted option price has been destroyed; this is a little worrying, given the extent to which the martingale property was exploited in the European case.

From its definition in equation (25.1), $f_n^*$ is a *Q-supermartingale*, i.e. $f_n^* \geq E^Q[f_{n+1}^* \mid \mathcal{F}_n]$. Consider this result written in a slightly different format:

$$f_n^* = \begin{cases} E^Q[f_{n+1}^* \mid \mathcal{F}_n] & \text{if } E^Q[f_{n+1}^* \mid \mathcal{F}_n] > K_n^* \\ K_n^* & \text{if } E^Q[f_{n+1}^* \mid \mathcal{F}_n] < K_n^* \end{cases}$$

It is immediately apparent that $f_n^*$ is the smallest conceivable process that is both a super-martingale and also always greater or equal to $K_n^*$. $f_n^*$ is sometimes known as Snell's envelope of the process $K_n^*$.

(iii) **Stopping Times**: We now introduce the important concept of a *stopping time*, also known as a *Markov time*; this is the time at which some event is achieved, e.g. the American option is exercised. The critical property of a random variable called a stopping time $\tau$ is that it is $\mathcal{F}_\tau$-measurable. In non-jargon, this means that $\tau$ can only be a stopping time if you can recognize it as such when a predefined event happens. Take a gambler at a casino: valid stopping times for him might be (a) when his winnings are $1000, (b) when he has lost more than anyone else in the room, (c) at 3.00 a.m.; it cannot be the game before his first loss.

The most elementary stopping time in the study of Brownian motion is the time when the displacement from the origin first achieves a given value. In the context of American options, it is usually the time when it first makes sense to exercise the option. For knock-out options it is usually the time when the option is knocked out.

The most usual notation for a stopping time for a process $y_n$ is $v = \min\{n : y_n = x_n\}$, i.e. $v$ is the earliest time when the stochastic variable $y_n$ achieves a certain predefined value $x_n$.

(iv) The following notation is a little tricky but needs to be absorbed if the rest of the material is to be understood. We are very used to representing a general term in a process by $Y_n$; this obviously means that the variable can take $N$ different time values. Suppose now that there exists a stopping time $v$, which by definition is a random variable. The subscript $n \wedge v$ means that when we consider a variable $Y_{n \wedge v}$, we take 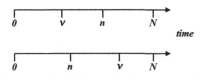 the value $n$ or $v$, whichever is smaller. In other words, $Y_{n \wedge v} \equiv Y_n$ up to the stopping time and $Y_{n \wedge v} \equiv Y_v$ thereafter.

$Y_{n \wedge v}$ can simply be written as the process $Z_n$. It is helpful to compare these processes:

$$
\begin{aligned}
Y_n & \quad : \quad Y_1, Y_2, \cdots, Y_n, \cdots, Y_N \\
Z_n = Y_{n \wedge v} & \quad : \quad Y_1, Y_2, \cdots, Y_v, Y_v, \cdots, Y_v = Y_n 1_{[n<v]} + Y_v 1_{[n \geq v]}
\end{aligned}
$$

It follows from the definitions that $Z_{n+1} - Z_n = (Y_{n+1} - Y_n)1_{[n<v]}$; If $Y_n$ is a martingale, we have

$$
\mathrm{E}^Q [Z_{n+1} - Z_n \mid \mathcal{F}_0] = 1_{[n<v]} \mathrm{E}^Q [Y_{n+1} - Y_n \mid \mathcal{F}_0] = 0
$$

The term $1_{[n<v]}$ is taken out of the expectation operator since by definition a stopping time $v$ is $\mathcal{F}_v$-measurable. This last equation leads to the following important conclusion. If $Y_n$ is a martingale and $v$ is a stopping time, $Y_{n \wedge v}$ is also a martingale; similarly, if $Y_n$ is a super-(or sub-) martingale, $Y_{n \wedge v}$ is also a super-(or sub-) martingale.

(v) **Discounted American Option Price is a Martingale**: Let us now return to our price for an American option which was given by

$$
f_N^* = K_N^*
$$
$$
f_n^* = \max[K_n^*, \mathrm{E}[f_{n+1}^* \mid \mathcal{F}_n]]
$$

and define a new process $Z_n = f_{n \wedge v}^*$ where $v$ is the stopping time at which $f_n^* = k_n^*$ for the first time. $Z_n$ may be written explicitly as follows:

$$Z_n = \begin{cases} E\,[Z_{n+1} \mid \mathcal{F}_n] & n < \nu \\ K_\nu^* = \text{constant} & n \geq \nu \end{cases}$$

By the reasoning of the last subsection, $Z_n$ is seen to be a martingale even though $f_n^*$ has been shown to be a supermartingale. It is a comfort to have found a martingale again, since so much of axiomatic option theory depends on this property.

(vi) **Optimal Stopping**: The question needs to be asked whether an American option should be exercised as soon as the first stopping time is reached, or should we wait for some better stopping time in the future. There

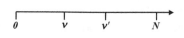

could of course be many occasions when $f_n^* = K_n^*$ and our stopping time $\nu$ is merely the first occasion this happens. Let $\nu'$ be some subsequent stopping time when this condition is fulfilled. Define $Z_n' = f_{n \wedge \nu'}^*$. From $n = 0$ to $n = \nu'$, we have $Z_n' = f_n^*$. But $f_n^*$ is just Snell's envelope of $K_n^*$, i.e. it is a supermartingale. $Z_n'$ is a supermartingale, rather than a martingale which was the case for $Z_n$ where we considered only the *first* stopping time. Thus

$$E\,[Z_n \mid \mathcal{F}_0] = Z_0 = f_0^* \qquad \text{(martingale)}$$
$$E\,[Z_n' \mid \mathcal{F}_0] \leq Z_0 = f_0^* \qquad \text{(supermartingale)}$$

from which $E[Z_n'|\mathcal{F}_0] \leq E[Z_n|\mathcal{F}_0]$.

The first stopping time $\nu$ is called the **optimal stopping time** since the expected value of the underlying process for this stopping time is at least equal to, and sometimes greater than, that for any other stopping time.

(vii) Let us now see what all this means for American options in practical terms.

(A) $f_n^*$ is not a martingale but $f_{n \wedge \nu}^*$ is. By the martingale representation theorem, the latter may be hedged or replicated by a self-financing portfolio containing stock and bond.

(B) The arbitrage theorem implies that there exists a probability measure (set of pseudo-probabilities) which allows us to discount back through the tree using the interest rate. However, the possibility of early exercise means that the value at a node is either the discounted value or the exercise value, whichever is greater. This destroys the martingale property of the discounted option price.

(C) Up to the first stopping time when $f_n^* = K_\nu^*$, we have $f_{n \wedge \nu}^* = f_n^*$. From that point on, $f_n^*$ starts displaying its supermartingale qualities, i.e.

$$E[f_n^* \mid \mathcal{F}_\nu] < f_\nu^*$$

But if the expected future value of $f_n^*$ is less than $f_\nu^*$, any logical person would take $f_\nu^*$ on the day. The economically optimal course of action is for the option to be exercised at the first stopping time.

The conclusions above could of course be recast in the language of continuous time stochastic calculus. However, this does not seem worth doing since it leads to no new insights. It would be great if this analysis led to the holy grail of finding a closed formula for American options, but alas it does not. The essential message to take away from this section is that an American option can indeed be hedged and can be priced using trees, with the proviso that the price at any node is the maximum of the exercise price and the value calculated by rolling back through the tree.

(viii) One topic involving continuous time analysis is of interest and is merely sketched in outline. Recall the reasoning of Section 23.5(ii) where the Black Scholes equation was derived as a direct consequence of the fact that the discounted derivatives price is a martingale. But for American options, the discounted derivatives price is a supermartingale. The Black Scholes equation should therefore be replaced by the inequality

$$rf_t - \frac{\partial f_t}{\partial t} - rS_t\frac{\partial f_t}{\partial S_t} - \frac{1}{2}\sigma^2 S_t^2\frac{\partial^2 f_t}{\partial S_t^2} \geq 0$$

In fact, if we take this last inequality together with

$$f_t \geq Payoff\ value$$

we can say that either the first or the second of these two relationships holds at each point in the price evolution of an American option. If the reader reflects for a moment, he will realize that this is a re-statement of the definition of Snell's envelope. It is also a more formal statement of the intuitive results given in Section 6.1.

## 25.3 THE STOP–GO OPTION PARADOX

(i) Consider the following strategy. Sell a call option for its fair value of $10. As a hedge, use a stop–go strategy of borrowing money and buying 100% of the underlying stock when the stock price $S_t$ reaches the strike price $X$ from below, and selling whenever $S_t$ reaches $X$ from above. In an idealized Black Scholes world of no transaction costs, absolute liquidity and continuous markets, the option is hedged for nothing leading to a $10 profit.

If you ask a crowd of students to explain this paradox, the answers are usually bunched into two groups: there are the banal responses covering liquidity, transaction costs, inability to hit a price exactly, etc., but these have already been covered by the assumption of a Black Scholes world. The second group will more or less precisely point out that the hedge portfolio is not self-financing. This is of course perfectly true but we can (hypothetically) restructure the stop–go strategy using forward contracts. Instead of buying or selling the stock each time its price crosses $X$, we take out or close a forward contract each time the *forward price* crosses $X$. The maturity of each forward contract is the maturity date of the call option being hedged. This time there is no carrying cost for the hedge, but we still appear to have created an arbitrage profit (Kane and Marcus, 1988; Carr and Jarrow, 1990).

(ii) In order to resolve the paradox, we start by defining the strategy precisely. In a Black Scholes world, the stock price is assumed to be described by the following SDE:

$$dS_t = S_t\mu\,dt + S_t\sigma dW_t^{RW}$$

where $\mu$ is the return on the stock and RW indicates a real-world probability measure. A change of measure using Girsanov's theorem allows us to write

$$dS_t^* = S_t^*\sigma\,dW_t^Q; \qquad S_t^* = S_t B_t^{-1} = S_t\,e^{-rt}$$

where $Q$ is the risk-neutral probability measure.

The process for the forward price is given in Section 24.13 as

$$dF_t = F_t\sigma\,dW_t^Q \qquad (25.2)$$

It is immediately apparent that the forward price is a $Q$-martingale.

Suppose we replicate a call option using the following strategy: at each point where the forward price crosses $X$ in the highly stylized Figure 25.1, we buy or sell a forward contract. No cash passes hands when the forward contracts are bought or sold, but the final tally at time $T$ is as follows:

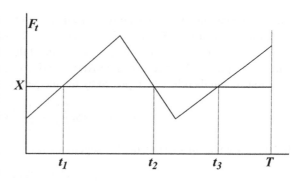

- At $t_1$: enter forward contract to buy stock for $\$X$ at time $T$. No cash exchange.

**Figure 25.1**   Stop–go hedging strategy

- At $t_2$: enter forward contract to sell stock for $\$X$ at time $T$. No cash exchange.
- At $t_3$: enter forward contract to buy stock for $\$X$ at time $T$. No cash exchange.
- At $T$: net, we own one expiring forward contract, valued at $\$(S_T - X)$.

Clearly, if there are a thousand crossings rather than the three shown in the graph, we still come up with the same answer. The strategy does look truly self-financing and always seems to give us a perfect hedge at the end.

(iii) A forward contract has no intrinsic value when it is first entered into at a market rate. However, is does have a value if the market price moves away from the price specified in the contract. Suppose we have a contract to buy one share of stock at price $X$ in time $T - t$ and the present forward price is $F_t$. The value of this forward contract is shown by simple arbitrage arguments in Section 1.3(v) to be given by

$$\text{Value} = (F_t - X)\,e^{-r(T-t)}$$

Our portfolio strategy is to buy or sell forward contracts at the forward price $X$ whenever $F_t$ passes through $X$, i.e. no cash outlay is needed when the forward contracts are bought or sold. The net number of contracts we own at any time is one or zero depending on whether $F_t$ is above or below $X$. We use the notation $1_{[F_t > X]}$ to describe this number. The value of our portfolio at any time $t$ may be written as

$$V_t = 1_{[F_t > X]}(F_t - X)\,e^{-r(T-t)} \tag{25.3}$$

This particular portfolio is self-financing, since no cash is paid or received before maturity. Section 20.5(ii) tells us that the discounted price ($V_t^* = e^{-rt}V_t$) of such a portfolio is a martingale; the martingale representation theorem means that it can be expressed in terms of any other martingale – and specifically in terms of $F_t$:

$$V_T^* = V_0^* + \int_0^T 1_{[F_t > X]}\,dF_t \tag{25.4}$$

Substituting into this last equation from equation (25.3) gives

$$e^{-rT}[F_T - X]^+ = e^{-rT}[F_0 - X]^+ + \int_0^T 1_{[F_t > X]}\,dF_t \tag{25.5}$$

This relationship seems intuitively reasonable *but unfortunately it is the wrong answer!* This becomes immediately apparent if we take the expectation of the last equation to get the value of a call option. Using the fact that the expectation of the integral is zero ($F_t$ is a $Q$-martingale) and $F_T = S_T$ and $F_0 = S_0\,e^{rT}$ gives

$$C_0 = e^{-rT} E_0^Q[[S_T - X]^+] = [S_0 - e^{-rT} X]^+ \tag{25.6}$$

This is indeed the value of a call option, but only if the volatility is zero. So in physical terms, where is the fallacy?

Let's re-examine the strategy, this time being precise to the point of nerdishness. In our description we said that we buy or sell forward contracts each time $F_t$ crosses $X$. Obviously this means that at $F_t > X$, our last move was to buy a contract while at $F_t < X$, our last move was to sell one. Consider what happens when $F_t$ is exactly equal to $X$. Do we both buy *and* sell, or do we do nothing? To a practical, shirt-sleeves, get-the-job-done kinda guy, this question just looks like time wasting. But we'll be more precise and say that as $F_t$ moves upwards across $X$ we buy a forward contract at a price $X + \varepsilon$ and as $F_t$ moves downwards across $X$ we sell a forward contract at price $X$; we then let $\varepsilon$ be infinitesimally small so this really makes no difference to our strategy ... unless ....

In Section 21.1(iv) we examined the infinite crossing property of Brownian motion. As soon as $F_t$ touches $X$, it immediately hits it again an infinite number of times. Each time we buy a forward contract at $X + \varepsilon$ and sell one at $X$ we lose an infinitesimal amount $\varepsilon$, which would not matter if it were not for the fact that we do it an infinite number of times. Contrary to our first intuition, this infinite number of infinitesimal losses leads to a defined, calculable shortfall. This cost must be taken into account in our replication.

(iv) **Black Scholes Model and Local Time:** In Section 23.6(vi), it was seen that the correct form for equation (25.5) should have been

$$e^{-rT}[F_T - X]^+ = e^{-rT}[F_0 - X]^+ + \int_0^T 1_{[F_t > X]}\, dF_t + \tfrac{1}{2} e^{-rT}\, \Lambda_T(X)$$

where the last term is the local time. Having solved the option paradox, it completes the analysis to derive the correct answer from this last, correct equation. Equation (25.6) for the call option price should then be written as

$$C_0 = e^{-rT} E^Q[[S_T - X]^+] = [S_0 - e^{-rT} X]^+ + \tfrac{1}{2} e^{-rT} E^Q[\Lambda_T(X)]$$

The last term in this equation can be evaluated using the result of equation (23.15):

$$E^Q[\Lambda_T(X)] = \int_0^T X^2 \sigma^2 p(X, t)\, dt$$

where $p(F_t, t)$ is the probability density function for the forward rate.

Equation (24.14) gives an explicit formula for the forward rate which implies that $(\ln F_t - \ln F_0 + \tfrac{1}{2}\sigma^2 t) \sim N(0, \sigma^2 t)$. The probability of the forward rate lying within a small interval is therefore

$$dP_t = \frac{1}{\sigma\sqrt{2\pi t}} \exp\left[ -\frac{1}{2} \frac{\left(\ln F_0 - \ln F_t - \tfrac{1}{2}\sigma^2 t\right)^2}{\sigma^2 t} \right] d(\ln F_t)$$

$$= \frac{1}{F_t \sigma\sqrt{2\pi t}} \exp\left[ -\frac{1}{2} \frac{\left(\ln F_0 - \ln F_t - \tfrac{1}{2}\sigma^2 t\right)^2}{\sigma^2 t} \right] dF_t = p(F_t, t)\, dF$$

and the probability density function is

$$p(X, t) = \frac{1}{\sigma X \sqrt{2\pi t}} \exp\left[-\frac{1}{2}\frac{\left(\ln F_0/X - \frac{1}{2}\sigma^2 t\right)^2}{\sigma^2 t}\right]$$

The value of the call option is then

$$C_0 = [S_0 - e^{-rT}X]^+ + \frac{\sigma X e^{-rT}}{2}\int_0^T \frac{1}{\sqrt{2\pi t}}\exp\left[-\frac{1}{2}\frac{\left(\ln F_0/X - \frac{1}{2}\sigma^2 t\right)^2}{\sigma^2 t}\right]dt$$

$$= [S_0 - e^{-rT}X]^+ + \frac{\sigma X e^{-rT}}{2}\int_0^T \frac{1}{\sqrt{t}}n(d_2)\,dt$$

where $n(d_2)$ has the standard definition used for the Black Scholes model in Chapter 5. Although it is not immediately apparent, this result is just the Black Scholes model, written in a rather unusual form. In order to appreciate the connection, the reader is referred back to equation (5.4)

$$\text{vega} = \frac{\partial C_0(\sigma)}{\partial \sigma} = X e^{-rT} n(d_2)\sqrt{T}$$

from which we can write

$$C_0(\sigma) = C_0(0) + X e^{-rT}\int_0^\sigma n(d_2)\sqrt{T}\,ds \qquad \text{where} \qquad d_2 = \frac{\left(\ln F_0/X - \frac{1}{2}s^2 T\right)}{s^2 T}$$

Introducing a new variable $t = s^2 T/\sigma^2$ so that $\sqrt{T}\,ds = (\sigma/2\sqrt{t})\,dt$, the last integral becomes

$$\frac{\sigma X e^{-rT}}{2}\int_0^T \frac{1}{\sqrt{t}}n(d_2)\,dt; \qquad d_2 = \frac{\left(\ln F_0/X - \frac{1}{2}\sigma^2 t\right)}{\sigma^2 t}$$

which is explicitly identical to the equation derived using local time.

## 25.4   BARRIER OPTIONS

In Chapter 15 and Appendix A.8 we obtained pricing and hedging formulas for barrier and lookback options using classical statistical methods: the approach was to solve the Kolmogorov backward equation with appropriate boundary conditions, using the method of images. This gave the appropriate distribution function to work out the risk-neutral expectations of the payoffs. An equivalent but much cooler derivation of the same result is now given using stochastic calculus.

(i) *Reflection Principle for Standard Brownian Motion*: This very slick theorem relies on the symmetry properties of undrifted Brownian motion. In Figure 25.2, a Brownian path starts at $t = 0$ and $W_t = 0$; after crossing a barrier at $b$ for the first time at time $\tau$, the motion continues along *Path A* until a maturity at $t = T$. Consider just that part of the path after $\tau$, i.e. *Path A*. From the symmetry of undrifted Brownian motion, each of the infinity of possible *Paths A* has a possible *Path B* which is the reflection of *Paths A* in the line $W_t = b$. The probability of any *Path A* is equal to the probability of its corresponding *Path B*. Applying this over the totality of all paths, we have the following two intuitive results for the relationships between conditional probabilities:

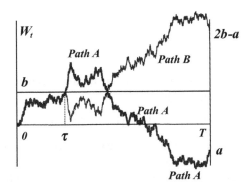

**Figure 25.2**    Reflection principle

- $P[W_T < b \mid \tau < T] = P[W_T > b \mid \tau < T]$
- $P[\tau < T] = P[W_T < b \mid \tau < T] + P[W_T > b \mid \tau < T]$

Substitute the first equation in the second to give $P[\tau < T] = 2P[W_T > b \mid \tau < T]$. In simple layman's terms, if a Brownian particle is at position $W_t = b$, the probability of its being above or below $b$ at some future date is 50/50. The conditional probability term on the right of this last relationship contains a redundancy, since if $W_T > b$ then it must be true that $\tau < T$, i.e. this term can be written as an *unconditional* probability:

$$P[\tau < T] = 2P[W_T > b] \tag{25.7}$$

(ii) *Distribution of First Passage Time for Standard Brownian Motion*: The variable $W_T$ is normally distributed with mean 0 and variance 1, so using the standard integral result given in equation [A1.3] gives

$$P\langle \tau < T \rangle = \frac{2}{\sqrt{2\pi T}} \int_b^\infty \exp\left(-\frac{W_T^2}{2T}\right) dW_T = \frac{2}{\sqrt{2\pi}} \int_{b/\sqrt{T}}^\infty \exp\left(-\frac{x}{2}\right) dx = 2N\left[-\frac{b}{\sqrt{T}}\right] \tag{25.8}$$

We can obtain an expression for the probability distribution function of the first passage time (the stopping time $\tau$) by differentiating this last equation with respect to $T$ and using the relationship

$$g(\tau) = \frac{\partial P\langle \tau < T \rangle}{\partial T}\bigg]_{T=\tau}$$

A little algebra gives

$$g(\tau) = \frac{|b|}{\sqrt{2\pi T^3}} \exp\left(-\frac{b^2}{2T}\right) \tag{25.9}$$

(iii) *Distribution of a Maximum for Standard Brownian Motion*: The condition $\tau < T$ which was used in the probabilities in subsection (i) above could alternatively be expressed as the condition $W_{max} > b$ where $W_{max}$ is the maximum value achieved by $W_t$ between $t = 0$ and $t = T$; viewing the condition in this light leads to some further insights. Referring again to Figure 25.2, the symmetry of *Paths A* and *B* means that if $W_T = a$ for *Path A* then $W_T = 2b - a$ for *Path B*.

Two further reflection relationships can be written as

- $P[W_T < a \mid W_{\max} > b] = P[W_T > 2b - a \mid W_{\max} < b]$     for $a < b$
- $P[W_T < a] = P[W_T < a \mid W_{\max} > b] + P[W_T < a \mid W_{\max} < b]$

where the second of these two relationships is really the same as before. Substituting from the first into the second and rearranging gives

$$P[W_T < a \mid W_{\max} < b] = P[W_T < a] - P[W_T > 2b - a \mid W_{\max} > b] \quad \text{for } a < b$$

The second probability on the right-hand side can be written as the *unconditional* probability $P[W_T > 2b - a]$ since the condition $W_{\max} > b$ is automatically fulfilled if $a < b$ and $W_T > 2b - a$. The left-hand probability is just a *joint* probability and may be written $P[W_T < a; W_{\max} < b]$. The last equation may be written

$$P[W_T < a; W_{\max} < b] = P[W_T < a] - P[W_T > 2b - a]$$
$$= N\left[\frac{a}{\sqrt{T}}\right] - N\left[-\frac{2b - a}{\sqrt{T}}\right] \tag{25.10}$$

where we have used the same method in evaluating the probabilities as was used in deriving equation (25.8).

(iv) Using the methods of Appendix A.1(i), we differentiate equation (25.10) to give the following important results.
**Distribution of $W_T$ below a barrier at $b$:**

$$F[W_T \mid W_{\max} < b] = \frac{\partial P[W_T < a; W_{\max} < b]}{\partial a}\Bigg|_{a \to W_T}$$
$$= \frac{1}{\sqrt{2\pi T}}\left\{\exp\left(-\frac{W_T^2}{2T}\right) - \exp\left[-\frac{(2b - W_t)^2}{2T}\right]\right\} \tag{25.11}$$

**Joint distribution of $W_{\max}$ and $W_T$:**

$$F[W_T; W_{\max}] = \frac{\partial^2 P[W_T < a; W_{\max} < b]}{\partial a \partial b}\Bigg|_{\substack{a \to W_T \\ b \to W_{\max}}}$$
$$= \frac{2(2W_{\max} - W_T)}{\sqrt{2\pi T^3}}\exp\left[-\frac{(2W_{\max} - W_t)^2}{2T}\right] \tag{25.12}$$

(v) **Drifted Brownian Motion:** The results of this section so far might be interesting, but apply only to standard Brownian motion without drift. How can we adapt the results to introduce a drift, which is needed to solve real options problems? This is where Girsanov's theorem comes into its own.

We start by looking at the effect of adding a drift term. From Section 24.2 we know that if we change probability measure from $P$ to $P^\mu$ by using a Radon–Nikodym derivative

$$\xi_T = e^{+\mu W_T - \frac{1}{2}\mu^2 T}$$

then the effect is to give the standard Brownian motion a positive drift $\mu T$. But this is just what we are looking for. Using equation (25.4) we can write

$$F^{P\mu} \, dW_T^\mu = \xi_T F^P \, dW_T$$

or using the probability density function of equation (25.11)

$$P[W_T^\mu < a; W_{max}^\mu < b] = \int_{-\infty}^{a} F^{P\mu}[W_T^\mu \mid W_{max}^\mu < b] dW_T^\mu$$

$$= \int_{-\infty}^{a} \xi_T F^P[W_T \mid W_{max} < b] dW_T$$

(25.13)

$$\int_{-\infty}^{a} e^{+\mu W_T - \frac{1}{2}\mu^2 T} \frac{1}{\sqrt{2\pi T}} \left\{ \exp\left(-\frac{W_T^2}{2T}\right) - \exp\left[-\frac{(2b - W_t)^2}{2T}\right] \right\} dW$$

$$= N\left[\frac{a - \mu T}{\sqrt{T}}\right] - e^{2\mu b} N\left[-\frac{2b - a + \mu T}{\sqrt{T}}\right]$$

The standard results of Appendix A.1(v) have been used to evaluate the integrals.

(vi) The stochastic process underlying the last equation is a shifted Brownian motion which can be written $W_T^\mu = \mu T + W_T$; but we are really interested in a more general process $x_T = \mu T + \sigma W_T$. The transformation from one to the other uses the self-evident fact that

$$P[x_T < a; x_{max} < b] = P\left[\frac{x_T}{\sigma} < \frac{a}{\sigma}; \frac{x_{max}}{\sigma} < \frac{b}{\sigma}\right]$$

Clearly, the general result for the stochastic process of interest is therefore obtained by making the substitutions $a \to a/b$, $b \to b/\sigma$, and $\mu \to \mu/\sigma$ in equation (25.12):

$$P[x_T < a; x_{max} < b] = N\left[\frac{a - \mu T}{\sigma\sqrt{T}}\right] - e^{\frac{2\mu b}{\sigma^2}} N\left[-\frac{2b - a + \mu T}{\sigma\sqrt{T}}\right]$$

(25.14)

This is a slightly more general form of equation (A8.5), and it reduces to the latter equation in the special case where $a = b$. It lies at the center of barrier and lookback option pricing. It is worth noting that the following distributions can be obtained from it:

- Distribution of $x_T$ in the presence of a barrier: differentiate with respect to $a$.
- Distribution of $\tau$, the first crossing time for the barrier: differentiate with respect to $T$.
- Distribution of $x_{max}$, the maximum achieved by $x_T$ before $T$: set $a = b$ and differentiate with respect to $b$.

(vii) The reader may be interested in flicking through Appendix A.7 and comparing that material with what has been presented in this section. Although the branch of mathematics used previously (PDEs solved using Green's functions) seems unrelated to the stochastic calculus of this chapter, the formulas that emerge are very similar; note for example the similarity between the exponential term in front of equation (A8.1) and the Radon–Nikodym derivative used in this section. As we have seen frequently in the book, when there are alternative approaches to a problem, the formulas are the same whichever route we take; just the mathematical dialect is different.

## 25.5 FOREIGN CURRENCIES

In this section we will use stochastic calculus to produce some of the key results of Chapter 13 on currency translated options. In that earlier chapter we used the framework which had been developed for options on two assets, to construct the currency translated pricing models. The reader who has studied that chapter will recall that a fair amount of huffing and puffing was involved in getting the final results. The approach which follows is altogether more graceful.

We use the same notation as previously:

"Domestic currency": US\$;      "Foreign currency": €

$\phi_t$: Value of € 1 in \$ (i.e. \$ price of the €); \$ price $= \phi_t \times$ € price
$\psi_t$: Value of \$1 in € (i.e. € price of the \$); € price $= \psi_t \times$ \$ price
$\psi_t = \phi_t^{-1}$

$S_t$: € price of a German stock; $B_t^{€}$ : € value of a € zero coupon bond

$P_t = B_t^{€} \phi_t$: \$ value of a € zero coupon bond; $Q_t = S_t \phi_t$: \$ value of a € stock
€ $X$: € strike price; \$ $K$: \$ strike price

$r_s, r_{€}$ and $q$: Interest rates and dividends

It is assumed that the currency exchange rates and stock prices follow real-world (i.e. *not* risk-neutral) stochastic processes which can be written

$$d\phi_t = \phi_t \mu_\phi \, dt + \phi_t \sigma_\phi \, dW_t^{\phi;\text{RW}} \tag{25.15}$$

$$d\psi_t = \phi_t \mu_\psi \, dt + \psi_t \sigma_\psi \, dW_t^{\psi;\text{RW}} \tag{25.16}$$

$$dS_t = S_t \mu_S \, dt + S_t \sigma_S \, dW_t^{S;\text{RW}} \tag{25.17}$$

(i) **Domestic Martingale Measure:** The starting point is the Black Scholes analysis of Section 24.3 which uses Girsanov's theorem to find out what drift (or probability measure) will ensure that a discounted stock price is a martingale.

Imagine an American who invests in a euro-denominated zero coupon bond. The euro value of this at time $t$ is $B_t^{€} = e^{r_{€} t}$ and the dollar value is $P_t = B_t^{€} \phi_t$. The quantity $P_t$ is a dollar investment whose price is stochastic; we can therefore apply the analysis of Section 24.3. $P_t^* = P_t / B_t^{\$} = \phi_t e^{(r_{€} - r_{\$})t}$ is a martingale under the risk-neutral measure which precludes arbitrage. And we know that a change of measure can be effected by changing the drift: $dW_t^{\phi;\text{RW}} = dW_t^{\phi;\$} - \lambda_\phi \, dt$.
From equation (25.15):

$$dP_t^* = d\left(e^{(r_{€} - r_{\$})t} \phi_t\right) = P_t^*(r_{€} - r_{\$}) \, dt + e^{(r_{€} - r_{\$})t} \, d\phi_t$$
$$= P_t^*(\mu_\phi + (r_{€} - r_{\$})) \, dt + P_t^* \sigma_\phi \, dW_t^{\phi;\text{RW}}$$

The drift term is zero under the risk-neutral measure, which is achieved if we put $\lambda_\phi = [\mu_\phi + (r_{€} - r_{\$})]/\sigma_\phi$. A short-hand description of this manipulation is to say that we allow the coefficient of $dt$ to $\to 0$ as we make the substitution $dW_t^{\phi;\text{RW}} \to dW_t^{\phi;\$}$ in the last equation. Then

$$dP_t^* = P_t^* \sigma_\phi \, dW_t^{\phi;\$}$$
$$d\phi_t = \phi_t(r_{\$} - r_{€}) \, dt + \phi_t \sigma_\phi \, dW_t^{\phi;\$} \tag{25.18}$$

$W_t^{\phi;S}$ is a Brownian motion under the risk-neutral measure; but an index \$ has been added to indicate that this is only a risk-neutral measure for a person living in a dollar world. It is often referred to as the **domestic risk neutral measure**. The subtlety of this point becomes apparent in the following subsection.

The results have been shown for constant variance, drift and interest rate; but the analysis can be easily generalized to take account of these parameters as functions of asset price and time.

(ii) *Foreign Martingale Measure*: Consider now the "opposite" of the case just described: a European who decides to invest in a dollar zero coupon bond. The value of this investment in euros is $R_t = B_t^\$ \psi_t$ and we look for a risk-neutral measure under which $R_t^* = R_t / B_t^\euro = e^{(r_\$ - r_\euro)t} \psi_t$ is a martingale. As in the last subsection, we have

$$dR_t^* = R_t^*(r_\$ - r_\euro) dt + e^{(r_\$ - r_\euro)t} d\psi t$$

but now we use the relationship $\psi_t = \phi_t^{-1}$, Ito's lemma [equation (24.2)] and equation (25.15) to write

$$d\psi_t = \phi_t^{-1}(-\mu_\phi + \sigma_\phi^2) dt - \phi_t^{-1}\sigma_\phi \, dW_t^{\psi;\$}$$

The symmetry of Brownian motion allows us to write $-W_t^{\phi;RW} \to W_t^{\phi;RW}$, so that

$$dR_T^* = R_t^*(-\mu_\phi + \sigma_\phi^2 + (r_\$ - r_\euro)) dt + R_t^*\sigma_\phi \, dW_t^{\phi;RW}$$

Again, $R_t^*$ is a martingale if the drift term is zero, or if $\mu_\phi \to \sigma_\phi^2 + r_\$ - r_\euro$ as $dW_t^{\phi;RW} \to dW_t^{\phi;\$}$. Then

$$\begin{aligned}
dR_t^* &= R_t^*\sigma_\phi \, dW_t^{\phi;\euro} \\
d\phi_t &= \phi_t(r_\$ - r_\euro + \sigma_\phi^2) dt + \phi_t\sigma_\phi \, dW_t^{\phi;\euro}
\end{aligned} \tag{25.19}$$

Comparing equations (25.18) and (25.19), we seem to have derived two different risk-neutral stochastic processes for the same exchange rate; this is known as *Siegel's paradox* (Dumas, *et al.*, 1995). The reason is that the first martingale measure was defined in terms of domestic currency (dollar), while the second was in foreign currency (euro).

(iii) The price of German stock [whose process is given by equation (25.17)], discounted by the $\euro$ interest rate, is a martingale under the foreign ($\euro$) risk measure. A change in this measure is effected by making $\mu_S \to \mu_\euro$ as $dW_t^{S;RW} \to dW_t^{S;\euro}$. This is just the risk-neutrality principle re-stated yet again. But what would this risk-neutrality relationship look like when viewed by an investor in a \$ framework?

Before answering this question we need to solve an intermediate problem. The value of the foreign stock in dollars is $Q_t = S_t\phi_t$. In Chapter 13 we explain that $Q_t$ could be the price of a traded security such as an ADR (American Depository Receipt). We look for a measure under which $Q_t^* = Q_t/B_t^\$ = e^{-r_\$ t} S_t\phi_t$ is a martingale. $Q_t$ is a function of the two processes given in equations (25.15) and (25.17). We therefore use the two-dimensional Ito's lemma [equation (23.22)] to give

$$dQ_t = Q_t\{(\mu_S + \mu_\phi + \rho\sigma_S\sigma_\phi) dt + \sigma_S \, dW_t^{S;RW} + \sigma_\phi \, dW_t^{\phi;RW}\}$$

We seek the martingale measure for $Q_t^*$, i.e. in $dQ_t^* = -Q_t^*r_\$ dt + e^{r_\$ t} dQ_t$ the drift term should be zero. The change of measure is effected by changing the drifts of the two Brownian motions:

$$dW_t^{\phi;RW} = dW_t^{\phi;\$} - \lambda_\phi dt; \qquad dW_t^{S;RW} = dW_t^{S;\$} - \lambda_S \, dt$$

to give

$$dQ_t^* = Q_t^* \{ (\mu_S + \mu_\phi - r_\$ + \rho_{S\phi}\sigma_S\sigma_\phi - \sigma_\phi\lambda_\phi - \sigma_S\lambda_S)\, dt + \sigma_S\, dW_t^{S;\$} + \sigma_\phi\, dW_t^{\phi;\$} \}$$

For zero drift we have

$$\sigma_\phi\lambda_\phi + \sigma_S\lambda_S = \mu_S + \mu_\phi - r_\$ + \rho_{S\phi}\sigma_S\sigma_\phi \qquad (25.20)$$

Substituting this in the equation for $dQ_t$ gives

$$dQ_t = Q_t r_\$\, dt + Q_t \left( \sigma_S\, dW_t^{S;\$} + \sigma_\phi\, dW_t^{\phi;\$} \right) \qquad (25.21)$$

(iv) We have already seen an expression for $\lambda_\phi$ in the lead up to equation (25.18). This was derived in the context of a zero coupon bond in a foreign currency. But it was shown in Section 24.3(ii) that the market price of risk $\lambda_\phi$ is the same for all derivatives of the exchange rate $\phi_t$. Substituting that previous formula for $\lambda_\phi$ into equation (25.20) gives

$$\lambda_S = \frac{\mu_S - r_\epsilon + \rho_{S\phi}\sigma_S\sigma_\phi}{\sigma_S}$$

Again we use the fact that the market price for risk $\lambda_S$ is the same for all derivatives of $S_t$, as well as for $S_t$ itself. The real-world process described by equation (25.17) can then be expressed in a risk-neutral dollar framework as

$$\begin{aligned} dS_t &= S_t \mu_S\, dt + S_t \sigma_S\, dW_t^{S;RW} \\ &= S_t \mu_S\, dt + S_t \sigma_S\, (dW_t^{S;\$} - \lambda_S\, dt) \qquad (25.22) \\ &= S_t (r_\epsilon - \rho_{S\phi}\sigma_S\sigma_\phi)\, dt + S_t \sigma_S\, dW_t^{S;\$} \end{aligned}$$

(vi) **Compos:** We are now in a position to work out expressions for the various types of currency translated options covered in Chapter 13. The dollar payoff of a compo call option is $\$[S_T\phi_T - K]^+$ where $K$ is the strike price in dollars. More generally, any compo option has the stock price translated at the current exchange rate, but otherwise behaves like a pure domestic option.

The risk-neutral stochastic process for $Q_t = S_t\phi_t$ in a dollar framework is given by equation (25.21). The drift is simply $r_\$$ and the variance is given by

$$\text{var}\left[ \sigma_S\, dW_t^{S;\$} + \sigma_\phi\, dW_t^{\phi;\$} \right] = \left( \sigma_S^2 + \sigma_\phi^2 + 2\rho\sigma_S\sigma_\phi \right) dt = \sigma_{S\phi}^2\, dt$$

Therefore the dollar price of a compo on a European stock is obtained from the formula (or procedure) for pricing a domestic option, with the substitutions

$$r \to r_\$; \qquad S_T \to S_T\phi_T; \qquad \sigma \to \sigma_{S\phi} \qquad (25.23)$$

(vi) **Quantos:** The payoff of a quanto call option is $\$\bar{\phi}(S_T - X)^+$, where $\bar{\phi}$ is a constant. More generally, a quanto is sometimes referred to as a "wrong currency instrument", i.e. it is a purely foreign instrument, except that instead of getting a payoff of a certain number of euros, you get the same number of dollars (this corresponds to $\bar{\phi} = 1$ in the call option above).

The interest rate enters into the calculation of an option price in two ways: first, as a discount factor for present-valuing the expected payout and second, as the drift term in the risk-neutral calculations. Schematically, this is written

$$\text{Value}_0 = e^{-r_{\text{discount}}T} f(F_{0T}(r_{\text{drift}}))$$

where $F_{0T}$ is the stock forward price which depends on $r_{\text{drift}}$; the interest rates used in these two roles are generally the same and we do not give the matter a second thought.

In the case of a quanto, the payoff will be in dollars so that the formula for a quanto must put $r_{\text{discount}} = r_S$. However, the drift for a euro stock in a dollar risk-neutral framework is given by equation (25.22). Therefore, in the formula for a quanto we must have $r_{\text{drift}} = r_\epsilon - \rho_{S\phi}\sigma_S\sigma_\phi$. This corresponds to the procedures given in Chapter 13 for obtaining a quanto price from a pure foreign option formula.

## 25.6 PASSPORT OPTIONS

These options were analyzed in Chapter 18 and there is little to add to the explanation of the computation methods already given. However, the methodology for devising the optimal strategy was perhaps not of the most rigorous, although the formulas produced were correct. These options are usually analyzed using stochastic control theory, and we explain this approach in the following short section. The section should be read in conjunction with Chapter 18, as we have tried to avoid duplication of material (Hyer *et al.*, 1997; Andersen *et al.*, 1998; Henderson and Hobson, 2000).

(i) **The Problem**: The starting point for analyzing these options is the following set of equations:

$$dS_t = S_t(r - q)\,dt + S_t\sigma\,dW_t^Q$$
$$df_t = f_tr\,dt + f_t\varphi_t\,dW_t^Q; \qquad f_t = e^{-r\,(T-t)}\,E[w_t^+ \mid \mathcal{F}_t] \tag{25.24}$$
$$dw_t = u_t\,dS_t = u_tS_t(r - q)\,dt + u_tS_t\sigma\,dW_t^Q$$

The first is just the risk-neutral (measure $Q$) stochastic process for the stock price. The second line expresses the usual relationship for the price of a derivative, given the process for the underlying stock expressed in the previous line. The two parts of this line are alternative statements of the fact that $f_t^* = f_tB_t^{-1}$ is a $Q$-martingale. We do not know the form of $\varphi_t$. The third line is a description of the change in the cumulative portfolio value when $u_t$ is the amount of stock held. We are able to change $u_t$ at will, subject to $-1 < u_t < +1$.

The purpose of this analysis is to find a set of rules for setting $u_t$, which maximizes $f_t$.

(ii **Change of Variables**: $S_t$ and $w_t$ are not independent variables; they are driven by the same Brownian motion $W_t^Q$. The problem is much simplified by the following change of variables:

$$x_t = \frac{w_t}{S_t}; \qquad v_t = \frac{f_t}{S_t}$$

Use of Ito's lemma in two dimensions, in the form of equation (23.22) with $\rho = 1$ and $dW_t^{(1)} = dW_t^{(2)} = dW_t^Q$ gives

$$dx_t = (u_t - x_t)(r - q - \sigma^2)\,dt + (u_t - x_t)\sigma\,dW_t^Q$$
$$dv_t = v_t(q + \sigma^2 - \varphi_t\sigma)\,dt + v_t(\varphi_t - \sigma)\,dW_t^Q \tag{25.25}$$

(iii) **Change of Measure**: The presence of the unknown variable $\varphi_t$ in the drift term is a nuisance. We therefore make a change of measure from the risk-neutral measure $Q$ to an alternative $Q'$, defined by $dW_t^Q = dW_t^{Q'} + \sigma\,dt$. Under this measure, the last two equations become

$$dx_t = (u_t - x_t)(r - q)\,dt + (u_t - x_t)\sigma\,dW_t^{Q'}$$
$$dv_t = v_tq\,dt + v_t(\varphi_t - \sigma)\,dW_t^{Q'} \tag{25.26}$$

Let $v'_t = v_t\, e^{-qt}$. Using Ito's lemma, we can show that $v'_t$ is a martingale; or equivalently expressed:

$$v_t = e^{-q(T-t)} E^{Q'}[v_T \mid \mathcal{F}_t] = e^{-q(T-t)} E^{Q'}[X_T^+ \mid \mathcal{F}_t] \tag{25.27}$$

(iv) The problem can now be presented as a stochastic control problem as follows:

- If $dx_t = (u_t - x_t)(r - q)dt + (u_t - x_t)\sigma\, dW_t^{Q'}$;
- Find the optimal control which maximizes the performance criterion

$$v_t = E^{Q'}\left[e^{-q(T-t)} x_T^+ \mid \mathcal{F}_t\right]$$

We use the Hamilton–Jacobi–Bellman equations of Section 23.8(viii) with slight modification [equation (23.27) used in place of (23.26)] to conclude that:

- The optimal control occurs when the function

$$\frac{\partial v_t}{\partial t} + (u_t - x)(r - q)\frac{\partial v_t}{\partial x_t} + \frac{1}{2}(u_t - x)^2\sigma^2\frac{\partial^2 v_t}{\partial x_t^2} - q v_t$$

  achieves a maximum
- This maximum occurs when

$$\frac{\partial v_t}{\partial t} + (u_t - x)(r - q)\frac{\partial v_t}{\partial x_t} + \frac{1}{2}(u_t - x)^2\sigma^2\frac{\partial^2 v_t}{\partial x_t^2} - q v_t = 0$$

This corresponds to equation (18.3) which was derived using classical statistical methods.

# Mathematical Appendix

There are libraries full of textbooks on applied mathematics and there is no point trying to replicate these here. On the other hand, it can be very frustrating for a reader to spend a lot of time digging out the necessary mathematics when his objective is to understand options as fast as possible. We therefore quickly skim through a few areas which are essential for an understanding of option theory, and present the mathematical tools in a format which is immediately applicable. Many of the mathematical problems of option theory were first solved as physics problems, and the physics vernacular has crept into the options literature. We follow this practice and make no attempt to present the material in a pure or abstract form; in any case, intuitive understanding is often increased by an appreciation of the underlying physical process.

## A.1 DISTRIBUTIONS AND INTEGRALS

(i) *Probability Distribution Functions*: If $F(x)$ is the probability distribution function for a random variable $x$, the probability $P[x < a]$ is given by

$$P\langle x < a \rangle = \int_{-\infty}^{a} F(x)\, dx \qquad \text{or} \qquad F(x) = \left. \frac{\partial P[x < a]}{\partial a} \right]_{a \to x}$$

For two random variables, similar results hold:

$$P\langle x < a; y < b \rangle = \int_{-\infty}^{a} \int_{-\infty}^{b} F(x, y)\, dx\, dy \quad \text{or} \quad F(x, y) = \left. \frac{\partial^2 P[x < a; y < b]}{\partial a\, \partial b} \right]_{a \to x; b \to y}$$

$$(A1.1)$$

(ii) *Normal Distribution*: The expression $x \sim N(\mu, \sigma^2)$ means that $x$ is a random variable (variate), normally distributed with mean $\mu$ and variance $\sigma^2$. A special case of the normal distribution is the *standard normal distribution* which has mean 0 and variance 1. The probability density function for the standard normal variate $z$ is

$$n(z) = \frac{1}{\sqrt{2\pi}}\, e^{-\frac{1}{2}z^2}$$

which is displayed in Figure A1.1.

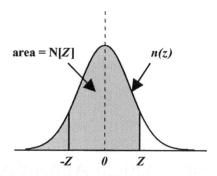

**Figure A1.1**   Normal distribution function

The cumulative distribution function is the shaded area in Figure A1.1:

$$N[Z] = \frac{1}{\sqrt{2\pi}} \int_{-\infty}^{Z} e^{-\frac{1}{2}z^2} \, dz$$

There is no closed form expression for this integral, which must be solved by numerical methods. We will not give an evaluation method for $N[Z]$ here, as it is included as a standard function in spread sheets such as Excel.

The converse formula is also used in this book:

$$\frac{\partial N[z]}{\partial z} = \frac{1}{\sqrt{2\pi}} e^{-\frac{1}{2}z^2} = n(z) \tag{A1.2}$$

(iii) From the symmetry of the normal distribution function about the $y$-axis, we can write

$$N[-Z] = \frac{1}{\sqrt{2\pi}} \int_{-\infty}^{-Z} e^{-\frac{1}{2}z^2} \, dz = \frac{1}{\sqrt{2\pi}} \int_{Z}^{+\infty} e^{-\frac{1}{2}z^2} \, dz \tag{A1.3}$$

Given that the area under the curve must be 1, symmetry also allows us to write

$$N[Z] + N[-Z] = 1 \tag{A1.4}$$

(iv) **Lognormal Distribution:** If $S_t$ is a random variable and $x_t = \ln S_t$ is normally distributed, then $S_t$ is said to be lognormally distributed; this is assumed to be the case for most securities, exchange and commodity prices.

The well-known normal distribution of $x$ is symmetrical about the mean, and $x$ can take either positive or negative values. The position of the normal distribution function is determined by the mean while its shape (tall and thin vs. short and fat) is determined by the variance. However, $\ln S$ is not defined for negative $S$ so that the lognormal distribution is taken as zero for negative values of $S$. This fits rather well with securities which cannot have negative prices. The precise shape of the lognormal distribution function depends on both its mean and variance: a sample of normal distributions with different means (but the same variance) is shown in Figure A1.2, together with their associated lognormal distribution functions.

**Normal Mean : negative**     **Normal Mean : zero**     **Normal Mean : positive**

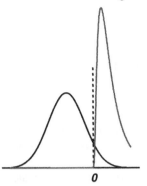

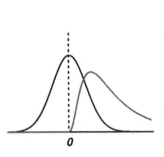

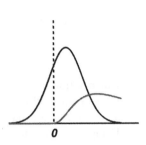

**Figure A1.2**   Normal and lognormal distributions

(v) *Some Useful Integrals*: A number of integrals occur repeatedly in option theory and the most important are given in this Appendix.

(A)

$$I_{-\infty}^{Z}(a) = \int_{-\infty}^{Z} e^{az} n(z)\, dz$$

$$= \frac{1}{\sqrt{2\pi}} \int_{-\infty}^{Z} e^{az - \frac{1}{2}z^2}\, dz$$

$$= e^{\frac{1}{2}a^2} \frac{1}{\sqrt{2\pi}} \int_{-\infty}^{Z} e^{-\frac{1}{2}(z-a)^2}\, dz$$

$$= e^{\frac{1}{2}a^2} \frac{1}{\sqrt{2\pi}} \int_{-\infty}^{Z-a} e^{-\frac{1}{2}y^2}\, dy = e^{\frac{1}{2}a^2} N[Z - a] \qquad (A1.5)$$

(B) The same factorization of terms in the exponential is used in the following:

$$I_{Z}^{+\infty}(a) = \int_{Z}^{+\infty} e^{az} n(z)\, dz$$

$$= e^{\frac{1}{2}a^2} \int_{Z-a}^{+\infty} n(y)\, dy$$

$$= e^{\frac{1}{2}a^2} N[a - Z] \qquad (A1.6)$$

where we have also used equation (A1.1).

(C) Commonly used integrals in option theory are used to evaluate conditional expectations such as $E[S_T - X : X < S_T]$, where $z_T = [\ln(S_T/S_0) - mT]/\sigma\sqrt{T}$ and $m = r - q - \frac{1}{2}\sigma^2$. Four results are given here which come directly from (A) and (B) above

- $E[K : S_T < X] = K\, P[S_T < X] = K\, P[z_T < Z_X]$

$$= K \int_{-\infty}^{Z_X} n(z_T)\, dz_T = K\, N[Z_X]$$

where $Z_X = [\ln(X/S_0) - mT]/\sigma\sqrt{T}$.

- $E[K : X < S_T] = K\, P[X < S_T] = K\, P[Z_X < z_T]$

$$= K \int_{Z_X}^{+\infty} n(z_T)\, dz_T = K\, N[-Z_X]$$

- $\mathrm{E}[S_T : S_T < X] = \mathrm{E}[S_T : x_T < Z_X] = \displaystyle\int_{-\infty}^{Z_X} S_0\, e^{mT + \sigma\sqrt{T}z_T}\, n(z_T)\, dz_T$

$$= S_0\, e^{mT + \frac{1}{2}\sigma^2} N[Z_X - \sigma\sqrt{T}]$$

- $\mathrm{E}[S_T : X < S_T] = \mathrm{E}[S_T : Z_X < x_T] = \displaystyle\int_{Z_X}^{\infty} S_0\, e^{mT + \sigma\sqrt{T}z_T}\, n(z_T)\, dz_T$

$$= S_0\, e^{mT + \frac{1}{2}\sigma^2} N[\sigma\sqrt{T} - Z_X] \tag{A1.7}$$

Our notation uses $Z_X$ which illustrates the origin of the term in square brackets as a limit of integration. A more common notation in the literature uses $d_1$ and $d_2$ where $d_1 = \sigma\sqrt{T} - Z_X$ and $d_2 = d_1 - \sigma\sqrt{T}(= -Z_X)$.

(D) Using the definition $z_T = (\ln S_T/S_0 - mT)/\sigma\sqrt{T}$ (or more precisely its equivalent $S_T = S_0\, e^{mT}\, e^{\sigma\sqrt{T}z_T}$) yields the following frequently used result:

$$\mathrm{E}\{S_T^\lambda\} = S_0^\lambda\, e^{\lambda mT} \int_{-\infty}^{+\infty} e^{\lambda\sigma\sqrt{T}z_T}\, n(z_T)\, dz_T = S_0^\lambda\, e^{\lambda mT} I_{-\infty}^{+\infty}(\lambda\sigma\sqrt{T})$$

$$= S_0^\lambda\, e^{\lambda mT + \frac{1}{2}\lambda^2\sigma^2 T} = F_{0T}^\lambda\, e^{\frac{1}{2}\lambda(\lambda-1)\sigma^2 T} \tag{A1.8}$$

Where $F_{0T}$ is the forward price of the stock.

(E) A related, but slightly more tricky pair of integrals are used in the investigation of lookback options; the first is

$$I_{-\infty}^{Z}(a, b) = \int_{-\infty}^{Z} e^{az}\, N\left[\phi\frac{(z - b)}{\sigma\sqrt{T}}\right] dz$$

$$= \left[\frac{1}{a} e^{az}\, N\left[\phi\frac{(z - b)}{\sigma\sqrt{T}}\right]\right]_{-\infty}^{+Z} - \frac{\phi}{a\sigma\sqrt{2\pi T}} \int_{-\infty}^{Z} e^{az}\exp\left[-\frac{(z - b)^2}{2\sigma^2 T}\right] dz$$

$$= \frac{1}{a} e^{aZ}\, N\left[\phi\frac{(Z - b)}{\sigma\sqrt{T}}\right] - \frac{\phi}{a} e^{ab + \frac{1}{2}a^2\sigma^2 T}\, N\left[\frac{(Z - b - a\sigma^2 T)}{\sigma\sqrt{T}}\right] \tag{A1.9}$$

where we have first integrated by parts and then used equation (A1.5). The same approach gives

$$I_{Z}^{\infty}(a, b) = \int_{-\infty}^{Z} e^{az}\, N\left[\phi\frac{(z - b)}{\sigma\sqrt{T}}\right] dz$$

$$= \left[\frac{1}{a} e^{az}\, N\left[\phi\frac{(z - b)}{\sigma\sqrt{T}}\right]\right]_{Z}^{\infty} - \frac{\phi}{a\sigma\sqrt{2\pi T}} \int_{Z}^{\infty} e^{az}\exp\left[-\frac{(z - b)^2}{2\sigma^2 T}\right] dz$$

$$= -\frac{1}{a} e^{aZ}\, N\left[\phi\frac{(Z - b)}{\sigma\sqrt{T}}\right] - \frac{\phi}{a} e^{ab + \frac{1}{2}a^2\sigma^2 T}\, N\left[-\frac{(Z - b - a\sigma^2 T)}{\sigma\sqrt{T}}\right] \tag{A1.10}$$

(vi) **Bivariate Normal Variables**: Suppose $y$ and $z$ are two **independent, standard, normal variates**. By definition, these have the following properties:

- *Standard*      $\mathrm{E}[y] = \mathrm{E}[z] = 0;$     $\mathrm{var}[y] = \mathrm{var}[z] = 1$
- *Independent*    $\mathrm{cov}[y, z] = \mathrm{E}[yz] = 0$

Let us define another random variable $x$ by the equation $x = \rho y + \sqrt{1 - \rho^2}z$, where $\rho$ is a constant and $x$ has the following properties:

- In general, the sum of two normal variates is itself a normal variate. Thus $x$ is normally distributed.
- $E[x] = 0;$      $\text{var}[x] = \rho^2\text{var}[y] + (1 - \rho^2)\text{var}[z] = 1.$
- Correlation $[x, y] = \dfrac{\text{cov}[x, y]}{\sqrt{\text{var}[x]\text{var}[y]}} = E[xy] = E[\rho y^2 + \sqrt{1 - \rho^2}yz] = \rho.$

Thus $x$ is a standard normal variate which has correlation $\rho$ with $y$. Alternatively expressed, any two correlated standard normal variates $x$ and $y$ can be decomposed into *independent* standard normal variates.

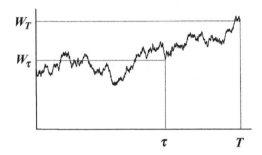

Consider the single Brownian path shown in Figure A1.3. The distance $W_\tau$ moved between time 0 and time $\tau$ is independent of the distance $W_{T-\tau} = W_T - W_\tau$ moved between time $\tau$ and time $T$. On the other hand, $W_T$ and $W_\tau$ are obviously not independent since they overlap. From the definition of a Brownian motion as $W_t = \sqrt{t}z_t$, where $z_t$ is a standard normal variate, we have

**Figure A1.3**   Brownian path

$$W_T = W_\tau + W_{T-\tau}$$
$$\sqrt{T}z_T = \sqrt{\tau}z_\tau + \sqrt{T - \tau}z_{T-\tau}$$
$$z_T = \sqrt{\frac{\tau}{T}}z_\tau + \sqrt{1 - \frac{\tau}{T}}z_{T-\tau}$$

Comparing this with the decomposition we examined immediately before shows that $z_T$ and $z_\tau$ are standard normal variates with correlation $\rho = \sqrt{\tau/T}$.

(vii) *Bivariate Normal Distribution*: Suppose two standard normal variates $z_1$ and $z_2$ have correlation $\rho$. Their joint distribution function is written

$$n_2(z_1, z_2; \rho) = \frac{1}{2\pi\sqrt{1 - \rho^2}}\exp\left[-\frac{1}{2(1 - \rho^2)}\{z_1^2 - 2\rho z_1 z_2 + z_2^2\}\right] \tag{A1.11}$$

In general terms, $n_2(z_1, z_2; \rho)$ can be represented as a bell-shaped hill. The contour lines of this hill are shown in Figure A1.4. If the correlation $\rho$ is zero, this bell is perfectly symmetrical with a circular mouth. If, however, $\rho$ has non-zero value, then the bell is elongated to an ellipse, along an axis at $45°$ to $z_1$ and $z_2$ as shown in the second two graphs. The $45°$ axis used depends on the sign of the correlation: positive slope for positive correlation, and negative slope for negative correlation. The flatness of the ellipse depends on the degree of correlation.

The volume under the bell-shaped hill is unity. The cumulative density function is the volume under the shaded part shown in the first graph of Figure A1.5. It is defined by

$$N_2[a, b; \rho] = \int_{-\infty}^{a} \int_{-\infty}^{b} n_2(z_1, z_2; \rho)\, dz_1\, dz_2 \tag{A1.12}$$

(viii) **Symmetry Properties of $N_2[a, b; \rho]$:** The properties below follow from the symmetry of Figure A1.4.

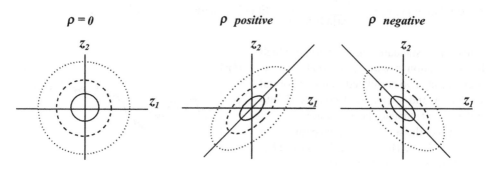

**Figure A1.4** Contours of $n_2(z_1, z_2; \rho)$

(A) Given the symmetry of $z_1$ and $z_2$ in equations (A1.11) and (A1.12), it follows that

$$N_2[a, b; \rho] = N_2[b, a; \rho] \tag{A1.13}$$

(B) Referring to the second graph of Figure A1.5

$$
\begin{aligned}
N_2[\infty, b; \rho] &= \int_{-\infty}^{b} dz_2 \int_{-\infty}^{+\infty} n_2(z_1, z_2; \rho)\, dz_1 \\
&= \frac{1}{2\pi\sqrt{1 - \rho^2}} \int_{-\infty}^{b} \int_{-\infty}^{\infty} \exp\left[-\frac{1}{2(1 - \rho^2)}\{z_1^2 - 2\rho z_1 z_2 + z_2^2\}\right] dz_1\, dz_2 \\
&= \frac{1}{\sqrt{2\pi}} \int_{-\infty}^{b} e^{-\frac{1}{2}z_2^2}\, dz_2 = N[b] \tag{A1.14}
\end{aligned}
$$

where we have made the change of variable $z_1 = \sqrt{1 - \rho^2}\, y + \rho z_2$ and slogged out the integral with respect to $y$, holding $z_2$ constant (i.e. $dz_1 = \sqrt{1 - \rho^2}\, dy$).

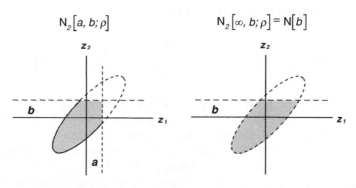

**Figure A1.5** Cumulative bivariate normal function

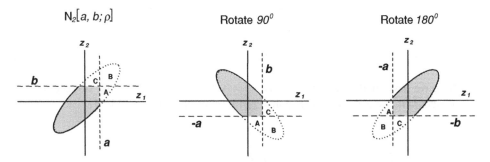

**Figure A1.6**   Cumulative bivariate normal identities

(C) Comparing the first and third graphs of Figure A1.6 shows that

$$\int_{-a}^{\infty} dz_1 \int_{-b}^{\infty} n_2(z_1, z_2; \rho)\, dz_2 = \int_{-\infty}^{a} dz_1 \int_{-\infty}^{b} n_2(z_1, z_2; \rho)\, dz_2 = N_2[a, b; \rho]$$

$$(A1.15)$$

(D) Referring to the first graph and using the fact that the volume of the elliptical bell-shaped "hill" is 1:

$$\text{Shaded volume} = 1 - \text{volume } (A + B) - \text{volume } C$$

$$N_2[a, b; \rho] = 1 - (1 - N[a]) - \text{volume } C$$

$$\text{Volume } C = \int_{-\infty}^{a} \int_{b}^{\infty} n_2(z_1, z_2; \rho)\, dz_1\, dz_2 = N[a] - N_2[a, b; \rho] \quad (A1.16)$$

(E) The second graph is just the first rotated through 90°. Given that the volume of the hill is unity and from property (c) above, we have

$$\text{Shaded volume} = 1 - \text{volume } A - \text{volume } (B + C)$$

$$N_2[a, b; \rho] = 1 - N_2[b, -a; -\rho] - (1 - N[b])$$

$$N_2[a, b; \rho] + N_2[-a, b; -\rho] = N[b] \quad (A1.17)$$

(F) The third graph is the first rotated through 180°. Symmetry and previous results allow us to write

$$\text{Shaded volume} = 1 - \text{volume } (A + B + C)$$

$$= 1 - \{\text{volume } (A + B) + \text{volume } (B + C) - \text{volume } B\}$$

$$= 1 - \{N[-a] + N[-b] - N_2[-a, -b; \rho]\}$$

$$N_2[a, b; \rho] = N[a] + N[b] - 1 + N_2[-a, -b; \rho] \quad (A1.18)$$

(ix) *More Useful Results*:

(A)

$$\int_{Z_2}^{\infty} \int_{Z_1}^{\infty} e^{az_1}\, n_2(z_1, z_2; \rho)\, dz_1\, dz_2$$

$$= \frac{1}{2\pi\sqrt{1 - \rho^2}} \int_{Z_2}^{\infty} \int_{Z_1}^{\infty} \exp\left[az_1 - \frac{1}{2(1 - \rho^2)}\{z_1^2 - 2\rho z_1 z_2 + z_2^2\}\right] dz_1\, dz_2$$

$$= e^{\frac{1}{2}a^2} \frac{1}{2\pi\sqrt{1-\rho^2}} \int_{Z_2-\rho a}^{\infty} \int_{Z_1-a}^{\infty} \exp\left[-\frac{1}{2(1-\rho^2)}\{y_1^2 - 2\rho y_1 y_2 + y_2^2\}\right] dy_1\, dy_2$$

$$= e^{\frac{1}{2}a^2} N_2[a - Z_1, \rho a - Z_2; \rho] \tag{A1.19}$$

where we have made the substitutions $z_1 = y_1 + a$, $z_2 = y_2 + \rho a$ and slogged through the algebra in the exponential. The final result relies on equation (A1.15).

(B)

$$\int_{Z_1}^{+\infty} \int_{-\infty}^{Z_2} e^{az_1} n_2(z_1, z_2; \rho)\, dz_1\, dz_2$$

$$= \int_{Z_1}^{+\infty} e^{az_1}\, dz_1 \left\{ \int_{-\infty}^{+\infty} - \int_{Z_2}^{+\infty} \right\} n_2(z_1, z_2; \rho)\, dz_2$$

$$= \int_{Z_1}^{+\infty} e^{az_1} n(z_1)\, dz_1 - \int_{Z_1}^{+\infty} \int_{Z_2}^{+\infty} e^{az_1} n_2(z_1, z_2; \rho)\, dz_1\, dz_2$$

$$= e^{\frac{1}{2}a^2}\{N[a - Z_1] - N_2[a - Z_1, \rho a - Z_2; \rho]\} \tag{A1.20}$$

where we have used equations (A1.6) and (A1.19) for the last step.

(C) In order to evaluate equation (14.1) for the value of a compound call option (call on a call) or equation (14.5) for an extendible option, we need to evaluate $E[S_T - X : S_\tau^* < S_\tau; X < S_T]$. As in Section A.1(v), item (C) for the univariate case, we write $m = r - q - \frac{1}{2}\sigma^2$ and switch to the more convenient standard normal variates $z_T = [\ln(S_T/S_0) - mT]/\sigma\sqrt{T}$ and $z_\tau = [\ln(S_\tau/S_0) - m\tau]/\sigma\sqrt{\tau}$:

$$E[S_T - X : S_\tau^* < S_\tau; X < S_T] = \int_{Z^*}^{\infty} \int_{Z_X}^{\infty} (S_0 e^{mT + \sigma\sqrt{T}z_T} - X) n_2(z_\tau, z_T; \rho)\, dz_\tau\, dz_T$$

$$= S_0 e^{(r-q)T} N_2[\sigma\sqrt{\tau} - Z^*, \sigma\sqrt{T} - Z_X; \rho] - X N_2[-Z^*, -Z_X; \rho] \tag{A1.21}$$

where we have used the integral results of (A) above with $Z_X = [\ln(X/S_0) - mT]/\sigma\sqrt{T}$, $Z^* = [\ln(S_\tau^*/S_0) - m\tau]/\sigma\sqrt{\tau}$ and $\rho = \sqrt{\tau/T}$. More common notation uses $d_1 = \sigma\sqrt{T} - Z_X$, $d_2 = -Z_X$, $b_1 = \sigma\sqrt{\tau} - Z^*$ and $b_2 = -Z^*$.

(D) A general result for bivariate distributions is $f(z_1, z_2) = f\langle z_1 \mid z_2\rangle f(z_2)$ where the three terms are the **joint**, the **conditional** and the **simple** probability density functions of the random variable $z_1$. From equation (A1.11), we may therefore write for two standard normal variables $z_1$ and $z_2$:

$$n\langle z_1 \mid z_2\rangle = \frac{n_2(z_1, z_2; \rho)}{n(z_2)} = \frac{1}{2\pi\sqrt{1-\rho^2}} \exp\left[-\frac{1}{2(1-\rho^2)}\{z_1 - \rho z_2\}^2\right]$$

$$\sim N(\rho z_2, (1 - \rho^2)) \tag{A1.22}$$

i.e. the **conditional distribution** of $z_1$ is normal with mean $\rho z_2$ and variance $(1 - \rho^2)$.

(x) **Numerical Approximations for the Cumulative Bivariate Normal Function:** Standard spread sheets do not have add-in functions for calculating bivariate cumulative normal functions. A simple algorithm follows (Drezner, 1978).

(A) We start with some definitions: let $a' = a/\sqrt{2(1-\rho^2)}$, $b' = b/\sqrt{2(1-\rho^2)}$ and the function $\Phi(a, b; \rho)$ be defined in the region $a$, $b$ and $\rho$ all $\leq 0$ by

$$\Phi(a, b; \rho) = \frac{\sqrt{1-\rho^2}}{\pi} \sum_{i=1}^{5} A_i \sum_{j=1}^{5} A_j f_{i,j}$$

$$f_{i,j} = \exp\{a'(2x_i - a') + b'(2x_j - b') + 2\rho(x_i - a')b'(x_j - b')\}$$

where the values of $A_i$ and $x_i$ are as follows:

| $i$ | $A_i$ | $x_i$ |
|---|---|---|
| 1 | 0.24840615 | 0.10024215 |
| 2 | 0.39233107 | 0.48281397 |
| 3 | 0.21141819 | 1.0609498 |
| 4 | 0.03324666 | 1.7797294 |
| 5 | 0.00082485334 | 2.6697604 |

(B) In the region $a \leq 0$, $b \leq 0$ and $\rho \leq 0$, $N_2[a, b; \rho]$ is closely approximated by $\Phi(a, b; \rho)$. If these conditions on $a$, $b$ and $\rho$ do not hold, $N_2[a, b; \rho]$ is obtained by manipulation:

• If $0 < a \times b \times \rho$ use the relationship

$$N_2[a, b; \rho] = N_2[a, 0; \rho_{ab}] + N_2[0, b; \rho_{ba}] - \delta_{ab}$$

where

$$\rho_{ab} = \frac{(\rho a - b)\text{sign}[a]}{\sqrt{a^2 - 2\rho ab - b^2}}; \qquad \delta_{ab} = \frac{1 + \text{sign}[a]\text{sign}[b]}{4}$$

$$\text{sign}[a] = 1 \quad (\text{if } 0 \leq x)$$
$$= -1 \quad (\text{if } x < 0)$$

• If $a \times b \times \rho \leq 0$ and

  • $a \leq 0, 0 \leq b, 0 \leq \rho$ use $N_2[a, b; \rho] = N[a] - N_2[a, -b; -\rho]$

  • $a \leq 0, b \leq 0, 0 \leq \rho$ $N_2[a, b; \rho] = N[b] - N_2[-a, b; -\rho]$

  • $0 \leq a, 0 \leq b, \rho \leq 0$ use $N_2[a, b; \rho] = N[a] + N[b] - 1 + N_2[-a, -b; \rho]$

  • $a \leq 0, b \leq 0, \rho \leq 0$ use $N_2[a, b; \rho] = \Phi(a, b; \rho)$

(xi) *Product of Two Securities Prices*: $S_t$ is an asset price (e.g. an equity stock) which we assume to be lognormally distributed, i.e. $x_t = \ln S_t$ is normally distributed. It is shown in Section 3.2 that

$$E[S_T] = S_0\, e^{(\mu-q)T} = S_0\, e^{mT + \frac{1}{2}\sigma^2 T} \qquad (A1.23)$$

where $\mu$ and $q$ are the continuous (exponential) growth rate and dividend yield of the asset; $m = E[x_T]$; $\sigma^2 = \text{var}[x_T]$.

We now examine the behavior of a quantity defined by $Q_t = S_t^{(1)} S_t^{(2)}$, where $S_t^{(1)}$ and $S_t^{(2)}$ are the prices of two lognormally distributed assets. Writing $y_t = \ln Q_t$, the following general results are evoked:

- $\sigma_Q^2 = \text{var}\langle y_t \rangle = \text{var}\left(x_t^{(1)} + x_t^{(2)}\right) = \sigma_1^2 + \sigma_2^2 + 2\rho_{12}\sigma_1\sigma_2$.
- $\text{E}\langle y_t \rangle = \text{E}\left(x_t^{(1)} + x_t^{(2)}\right) = m_1 T + m_2 T = m_Q T$.
- It is a specific property of normal distributions that $y_t$ is also normally distributed.

From the first two of these relationships, an expression for $\text{E}[Q_T]$ corresponding to equation (A1.23) is now written as

$$\text{E}[Q_T] = Q_0\, e^{(\mu_Q - q_Q)T} = Q_0\, e^{m_Q T + \frac{1}{2}\sigma_Q^2 T} = Q_0\, e^{(m_1 + m_2 + \frac{1}{2}\sigma_1^2 + \frac{1}{2}\sigma_2^2 + \rho_{12}\sigma_1\sigma_2)T}$$
$$= Q_0\, e^{(\mu_1 - q_1)T + (\mu_2 - q_2)T + \rho_{12}\sigma_1\sigma_2 T}$$

which is equivalent to

$$\text{E}\left[S_T^{(1)} S_T^{(2)}\right] = \text{E}\left[S_T^{(1)}\right]\text{E}\left[S_T^{(2)}\right] e^{\rho_{12}\sigma_1\sigma_2 T} \tag{A1.24}$$

Alternatively, we could write $\mu_Q - q_Q = (\mu_1 + \mu_2) - (q_1 + q_2) + \rho_{12}\sigma_1\sigma_2$. In the risk-neutral environment in which most of our calculations are performed, each of the "assets" $S_t^{(1)}$, $S_t^{(2)}$ and $Q_t$ enjoys the risk-free return, i.e. $\mu_1 = \mu_2 = \mu_Q = r$; therefore

$$q_Q = q_1 + q_2 - r - \rho_{12}\sigma_1\sigma_2 \tag{A1.25}$$

It follows from the above analysis that any composite price, made up of the product or quotient of lognormally distributed prices, is itself lognormally distributed. The various formulas developed for single prices are therefore easily adapted to describe the behavior of such composite prices; Chapters 12 and 13 are largely based on this technique. By contrast, the sum or difference of two lognormally distributed prices does not have a well-defined distribution and is therefore analytically intractable.

(xii) **Covariances and Correlations of Stock Prices**: It is worth giving some standard definitions and results as referred to in various chapters.

(A) If $x_t^{(1)} = \ln S_t^{(1)}$, we define $\sigma_1$ the volatility of $S_t^{(1)}$ as the square root of the variance of $x_t^{(1)}$:

$$\sigma_1^2 = \text{var}\left[x_t^{(1)}\right] = \text{E}\left[\left(x_t^{(1)} - \bar{x}^{(1)}\right)^2\right] = \text{E}\left[\left(x_t^{(1)}\right)^2\right] - \left(\bar{x}^{(1)}\right)^2; \qquad \bar{x}^{(1)} = \text{E}\left[x_t^{(1)}\right]$$

The covariance of two variables $x_t^{(1)}$ and $x_t^{(2)}$ is defined by

$$\text{cov}\left[x_t^{(1)}, x_t^{(2)}\right] = \text{E}\left[\left(x_t^{(1)} - \bar{x}^{(1)}\right)\left(x_t^{(2)} - \bar{x}^{(2)}\right)\right] = \text{E}\left[x_t^{(1)} x_t^{(2)}\right] - \bar{x}^{(1)}\bar{x}^{(2)}$$

and the correlation between the two stocks is defined by

$$\rho_{12} = \frac{\text{cov}\left[x_t^{(1)}, x_t^{(2)}\right]}{\sigma_1\sigma_2},$$

(B) The volatility of $A S_t^{(1)}$ where $A$ is a constant is given by

$$\sigma_{A1}^2 = \text{var}\left[\ln\left(A S_t^{(1)}\right)\right] = \text{var}\left[\text{const.} + x_t^{(1)}\right] = \text{var}\left[x_t^{(1)}\right] = \sigma_1^2$$

(Note the radical difference from the result $\text{var}[Ax] = A^2\,\text{var}[x]$.)

(C) The volatility of the product of two stochastic prices $S_t^{(1)}$ and $S_t^{(2)}$ is obtained as follows:

$$\sigma_{12}^2 = \text{var}\left[\ln S_t^{(1)} S_t^{(2)}\right] = \text{var}\left[x_t^{(1)} + x_t^{(2)}\right]$$
$$= E\left[\left\{\left(x_t^{(1)} - \bar{x}^{(1)}\right) + \left(x_t^{(2)} - \bar{x}^{(2)}\right)\right\}^2\right] = \sigma_1^2 + \sigma_2^2 + 2\,\text{cov}\left[x_t^{(1)}, x_t^{(2)}\right]$$

or

$$\sigma_{12}^2 = \sigma_1^2 + \sigma_2^2 + 2\rho_{12}\sigma_1\sigma_2$$

Similarly

$$\sigma_{1/2}^2 = \text{var}\left[\ln S_t^{(1)} / S_t^{(2)}\right] = \sigma_1^2 + \sigma_2^2 - 2\rho_{12}\sigma_1\sigma_2$$

or alternatively expressed

$$\sigma_{1/S_t}^2 = \sigma_{S_t}^2; \qquad \rho_{1/2} = -\rho_{1/2}$$

(D) The variances of a number of products and quotients are used in the text and the results are recorded all together here:

- $S_t^{(1)}\left(AS_t^{(2)}\right)$ $\qquad$ $\sigma_{1(A2)}^2 = \text{var}\left[x_t^{(1)} + x_t^{(2)} + A\right] = \sigma_1^2 + \sigma_2^2 + 2\rho_{12}\sigma_1\sigma_2$
- $\left(S_t^{(1)} S_t^{(2)}\right)S_t^{(1)}$ $\qquad$ $\sigma_{(12)1}^2 = \text{var}\left[2x_t^{(1)} + x_t^{(2)}\right] = 4\sigma_1^2 + \sigma_2^2 + 4\rho_{12}\sigma_1\sigma_2$
- $\left(S_t^{(1)} S_t^{(2)}\right)/\left(AS_t^{(1)}\right)$ $\qquad$ $\sigma_{12/A1}^2 = \text{var}\left[x_t^{(2)} - \text{const.}\right] = \sigma_2^2$

## A.2   RANDOM WALK

(i) A drunk leaves a bar one evening and sets out for home. His legs have a will of their own, but follow these rules:

- He takes a step at regular intervals of time $\delta t$.
- Sometimes he steps forward a distance $U$.
- Sometimes he steps back a distance $D$.
- The probability of a $U$-step is $p$ and the probability of a $D$-step is $(1 - p)$.

We are curious to know how far he progresses and what his chances are of reaching home.

The progress of our drunk is a standard example of a *stochastic process* known as a *random walk*. In fact, this is a specific example of a more general class of stochastic processes known as *Markov processes*. In such processes, the next step is completely independent of the distance traveled in the last $n$ steps.

The progress of the drunk can be represented by the grid of Figure A2.1. The distance $x_n$ of the drunk from the bar after $n$ steps is a random variable; but this variable can only assume the discrete values shown, since the forward and backward steps are fixed in length.

The expected position of the drunk after the first step is

$$E[x_1] = pU - (1 - p)D \tag{A2.1}$$

and the variance is

$$\text{var}[x_1] = E\left[x_1^2\right] - E^2[x_1]$$
$$= pU^2 + (1 - p)D^2 - \{pU - (1 - p)D\}^2$$
$$= p(1 - p)(U + D)^2 \tag{A2.2}$$

309

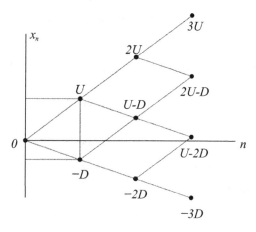

**Figure A2.1**   Random walk grid

Referring to Figure A2.1, consider the probability of reaching the point "$2U - D$" after three steps. This could be achieved with three sequences: $UDD$, $UDU$, or $DUU$. Each path is achieved with equal probability $p^2(1 - p)$ so that the probability of reaching this point is $3p^2(1 - p)$.

Generalizing this approach, the probability of achieving $i$ $U$-steps out of a total of $N$ steps is

$$\frac{N!}{i!(N - i)!} p^i (1 - p)^{N-i}$$

and the distance traveled is $\{iU - (N - i)D\}$. This discrete distribution is known as the **binomial distribution**, and we can directly calculate the expected value and variance for the distance traveled in $N$ steps. However, we can save ourselves a lot of algebra by using the properties of so-called moment generating functions.

(ii) **Moment Generating Functions**: Moment generating functions (MGFs) are much used in theoretical statistics and have the following properties:

1. If $y$ is a random variable, then the MGF $M[\Theta]$ is defined by

$$M(\Theta) = E[e^{\Theta y}]$$

2. The moments of the variable $y$ are given by

$$\mu_\lambda = E[y^\lambda] = \left. \frac{\partial^\lambda M[\Theta]}{\partial \Theta^\lambda} \right|_{\Theta=0}$$

3. If $y_1, y_2, \ldots, y_N$ are *independent* random variables, then the moment generating function of the sum $y_1 + y_2 + \cdots + y_N$ is equal to the product of the individual MGFs.
4. Every distribution has a unique MGF.
5. It may be shown by straightforward integration that the normal distribution $N(\mu t, \sigma^2 t)$ has an MGF given by

$$M(\Theta) = e^{(\mu\Theta + \frac{1}{2}\sigma^2\Theta^2)t}$$

6. An algebraic slog shows that for a standard normal $x$ ($\mu = 0; \sigma^2 = 1$):

$$E[x^{\lambda}] = \begin{cases} 0 & \text{odd } \lambda \\ \dfrac{(\lambda - 1)!}{2^{(\frac{1}{2}\lambda - 1)}(\frac{1}{2}\lambda - 1)!} & \text{even } \lambda \end{cases}$$

(iii) *Moment Generating Function and Random Walk*: The MGFs for a single step is given by

$$M(\Theta) = E[e^{\Theta x}] = \{p\,e^{\Theta U} + (1 - p)\,e^{-\Theta D}\}$$

so that by property 3 of the last subsection, the MGF for the distance traveled in $N$ independent steps is given by

$$M_N(\Theta) = \{p\,e^{\Theta U} + (1 - p)\,e^{-\Theta D}\}^N \qquad (A2.3)$$

Property 2 above yields the following results by simple differentiation:

$$E[x_N] = \frac{\partial M[\Theta]}{\partial \Theta}\bigg]_{\Theta=0} = N\{pU - (1 - p)D\}$$

$$\text{var}[x_N] = \frac{\partial^2 M(\Theta)}{\partial \Theta^2}\bigg]_{\Theta=0} - \left\{\frac{\partial M(\Theta)}{\partial \Theta}\bigg]_{\Theta=0}\right\}^2 = Np(1 - p)(U + D)^2 \qquad (A2.4)$$

Comparing these with equations (A2.1) and (A2.2) leads one to the unsurprising result that the expected value of the distance covered in $N$ steps is $N$ times the expected value of the distance in one step; but it also leads us to the less intuitive result that the variance of $N$ steps is $N$ times the variance of one step.

(iv) *Random Walk and Normal Distribution*: We now examine the case where the number of steps $N$ in a random walk becomes very large, while the time between steps $\delta t$ and the step lengths $U$ and $D$ become very small. $T = N\,\delta t$ is the total time taken by the random walk. Equation (A2.4) may be rewritten in differential format as

$$E[x_N] = N\{pU - (1 - p)D\} \Rightarrow E[x_T] = \frac{T}{\delta t}\{pU - (1 - p)D\} = \mu T$$

$$\text{var}[x_N] = Np(1 - p)(U + D)^2 \Rightarrow \text{var}[x_T] = \frac{T}{\delta t}p(1 - p)(U + D)^2 = \sigma^2 T$$

or

$$\{pU - (1 - p)D\} = \mu\,\delta t; \qquad p(1 - p)(U + D)^2 = \sigma^2\,\delta t \qquad (A2.5)$$

This is of course just another way of writing equations (A2.1) and (A2.2) in terms of instantaneous drift and variance. The reader now needs to watch carefully, while we manipulate the second of these equations into an alternative form which we use later.

It is assumed that $\delta t$ is very small, so that terms $O[(\delta t)^2]$ can be safely ignored. Let us repeat the derivation of equation (A2.2) in the present format:

$$\sigma^2\,\delta t = \text{var}[x] = E[x^2] - E^2[x] = pU^2 + (1 - p)D^2 - \mu^2(\delta t)^2$$

But the last term in this equation is $O[(\delta t)^2]$ and may be dropped, leaving us with the relationships

$$\{pU - (1 - p)D\} = \mu\,\delta t; \qquad \{pU^2 + (1 - p)D^2\} = \sigma^2\,\delta t \tag{A2.6}$$

The second of these equations is clearly not as accurate as the exact forms, and may trouble the reader somewhat; but to $O[\delta t]$ it is perfectly acceptable and we will encounter many other places where terms of $O[(\delta t)^2]$ are ignored.

Return now to equation (A2.3), take the logarithm and substitute $T = N\,\delta t$. Then use the following expansions of $e^a$ and $\ln(1 + a)$ for small $a$: $e^a = 1 + a + \frac{1}{2}a^2 + \cdots$ and $\ln(1 + a) = a - \frac{1}{2}a^2 + \cdots$.

$$\begin{aligned}
\ln M_N[\Theta] &= N \ln\{p\,e^{\Theta U} + (1 - p)\,e^{\Theta D}\} \\
&= \frac{T}{\delta t}\ln\left\{1 + (pU + (1 - p)D)\Theta + \tfrac{1}{2}(pU^2 + (1 - p)D^2)\Theta^2 + \cdots\right\} \\
&= \frac{T}{\delta t}\ln\left\{1 + \left(\mu\Theta + \tfrac{1}{2}\sigma^2\Theta^2\right)\delta t + O[(\delta t)^2] + \cdots\right\} \\
&\approx \left(\mu\Theta + \tfrac{1}{2}\sigma^2\Theta^2\right)T
\end{aligned}$$

or finally

$$M_N[\Theta] = e^{(\mu\Theta + \frac{1}{2}\sigma^2\Theta^2)T}$$

From property 5 of moment generating functions given in Section A.2(ii), the random walk taking a time $T$ converges to the normal distribution $N(\mu T, \sigma^2 T)$. The closer $p$ is to $\frac{1}{2}$ the faster the convergence. Figure A2.2 compares the binomial and normal distributions (using $p = \frac{1}{2}$) for different values of $N$.

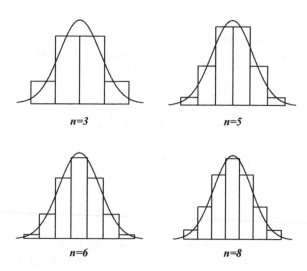

$n=3$ $\qquad$ $n=5$

$n=6$ $\qquad$ $n=8$

**Figure A2.2** Binomial and normal distributions

(v) *Step Lengths and Probabilities*: In the last subsection, the random walk was described in terms of the overall drift $\mu$ and variance $\sigma^2$ rather than step lengths $U$, $D$ and transition probabilities

$p, (1 - p)$. There is *not* a unique correspondence between the choice of the parameters $U, D, p$ and the resultant $\mu$ and $\sigma^2$: for example, a high drift rate $\mu$ could be achieved by having equal probabilities for $U$ and $D$ (i.e. $p = \frac{1}{2}$) together with a large $U$-step compared to the $D$-step; or alternatively by equal $U$ and $D$ but a high probability of up-move $p$. There are in fact an infinite number of choices of $U, D, p$ to produce a given $\mu$ and $\sigma^2$. Two combinations for $U, D$ and $p$ are most commonly used in practice:

- Let $U = D(= \Delta)$: then equations (A2.6) become

$$(2p - 1)\Delta = \mu \, \delta t; \qquad \Delta^2 = \sigma^2 \, \delta t$$

or

$$\Delta = \sigma\sqrt{\delta t}; \qquad p = \frac{1}{2}\left\{1 + \frac{\mu\sqrt{\delta t}}{\sigma}\right\} \qquad (A2.7)$$

- Let $p = \frac{1}{2}$: then equations (A2.5) become

$$U - D = 2\mu \, \delta t; \qquad U + D = 2\sigma\sqrt{\delta t}$$

or

$$U = \mu \, \delta t + \sigma\sqrt{\delta t}; \qquad D = -\mu \, \delta t + \sigma\sqrt{\delta t} \qquad (A2.8)$$

Note that to get these two results, we have used the alternative equations (A2.5) and (A2.6), which are equivalent to $O[\delta t]$.

(vi) If the reader looks around the literature on random walk, he is likely to find alternative treatments of the subject, using a three-pronged process: the drunk takes a step forward, a step back or remains stationary each period. The results obtained using such a process are similar to those using a two-pronged process; this is apparent from Figure A2.3 which shows that a large three-pronged step can be constructed from two two-pronged steps. However a three-pronged tree does give us an extra degree of flexibility which will be very useful when we consider random walks in which the variance $\sigma^2$ and drift $\mu$ are not constant, but depend on the net distance the drunk has traveled and the time he has been going.

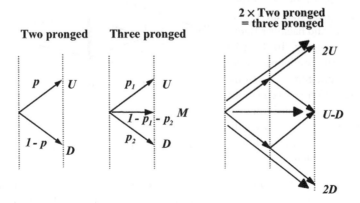

**Figure A2.3**   Binomial vs. trinomial

When we say flexibility we really mean greater ability to choose parameters. Thus in equation (A2.6) we have two equations for three unknowns ($U$, $D$ and $p$); this gives us the flexibility to make the choice between the two alternatives set out in the previous subsection – or indeed, an infinite number of other possible choices. Using the notation of Figure A2.3, the three-pronged analogs of equation (A2.6) are

$$\{p_u U - p_d D + (1 - p_u - p_d)M\} = \mu\,\delta t$$
$$\{p_u U^2 + p_d D^2 + (1 - p_u - p_d)M^2\} = \sigma^2\,\delta t \qquad \text{(A2.9)}$$

This time we have two equations for five unknowns, leaving three degrees of freedom to play with. Most schemas that the reader is likely to encounter impose the conditions $M = 0$ and $U = -D\,(= \Delta)$, so that we may solve for probabilities:

$$p_u = \frac{1}{2}\left\{\frac{\sigma^2}{\Delta^2} + \frac{\mu}{\Delta}\right\}\delta t; \qquad p_d = \frac{1}{2}\left\{\frac{\sigma^2}{\Delta^2} - \frac{\mu}{\Delta}\right\}\delta t \qquad \text{(A2.10)}$$

and we still have a degree of freedom left over!

## A.3 THE KOLMOGOROV EQUATIONS

(i) In the last section we demonstrated that a random walk or binomial process approaches a normal distribution $N(\mu T, \sigma^2 T)$ in the continuous limit, i.e. an infinite number of infinitesimally small steps. This is equivalent to saying that if a particle is at position $x_t$ at time $t$, then the probability that it is between $x_T$ and $x_T + dx_T$ at time $T$ is

$$f\langle x_T, T \mid x_t, t\rangle\,dx_T = \frac{1}{\sigma\sqrt{2\pi(T - t)}}\exp\left[-\frac{1}{2}\left(\frac{x_T - x_t - \mu(T - t)}{\sigma\sqrt{(T - t)}}\right)^2\right]dx_T \quad \text{(A3.1)}$$

This formula for the so-called transition probability density function describes a particle undergoing unrestricted, one-dimensional Brownian motion. But suppose the motion is in some way constrained: suppose in the example of our drunk doing a random walk that there was a deep hole in the road, or that some joker had attached an elastic to his belt; or suppose that the drunk starts sobering up, so that the probabilities of forward and backward steps start gradually changing. To describe these problems (in continuous time) we need the Kolmogorov equations, which are partial differential equations always satisfied by the transition density function; just the boundary conditions change to cater for the constraints of any particular problem.

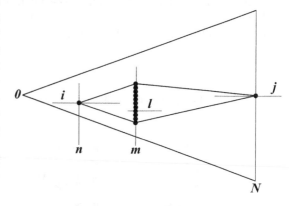

**Figure A3.1** Chapman–Kolmogorov intermediate states

(ii) *Chapman–Kolmogorov Equation*: (The nomenclature for the various equations is not quite standard but we try to use the most common). Imagine a binomial grid of the type shown in Figure A3.1, but with a very large number of steps. Imagine a particle that starts at position

$i$ at time step $n$ and later arrives at position $j$ at time step $N$. The probability of making this particular transition is written $P\langle x_j^N \mid x_i^n \rangle$. Now consider where the particle might have been at time step $m$: it would have been at one of the several positions $l$, which are a subset of all the positions that might be reached by a particle starting at 0. The probability of going from $i$ to $j$ must equal the sum of the probabilities of going via each of the possible $l$ positions, i.e.

$$P\langle x_j^N \mid x_i^n \rangle = \sum_{\text{all possible } l} P\langle x_j^N \mid x_l^m \rangle P\langle x_l^m \mid x_i^n \rangle \tag{A3.2}$$

This is the Chapman–Kolmogorov equation in discrete time.

(iii) Before going on, it is worth repeating a simple point made in several places in this book; if the reader does not get it completely straight here, he will get very mixed up in what follows.

0 is always some fixed "starting point" in time, $T$ is a maturity date (most usually of an option) and $t$ is some variable date. In most options applications, we use $t = 0$ as "now" and $T$ is the time to maturity of the option.

In the following sections, we investigate variations in both $t$ and $T$ and we must be very careful: a small positive change $\delta t$ *shortens* the time to maturity $(T - t)$ while a positive $\delta T$ lengthens it. In virtually everything in the rest of the book, dependence on $t$ and $T$ is deemed to mean dependence on $(T - t)$; we have the following equivalence when differentiating with respect to time:

$$\frac{\partial}{\partial t} \equiv -\frac{\partial}{\partial T}$$

(iv) *Kolmogorov's Equations with Constant $\mu$ and $\sigma^2$*:

(A) Equation (A3.2) (Chapman–Kolmogorov) in the case where $m = n + 1$ is

$$P\langle x_j^N \mid x_i^n \rangle = p\,P\langle x_j^N \mid x_{i+1}^{n+1} \rangle + (1 - p)\,P\langle x_j^N \mid x_{i-1}^{n+1} \rangle$$

This is illustrated in Figure A3.2.

Consider the continuous limit (infinite number of infinitesimal terms) of the last equation and rewrite terms as follows:

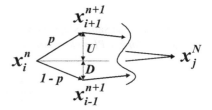

**Figure A3.2**   Kolmogorov backward equation constant $\mu$ and $\sigma^2$

$$
\begin{aligned}
P\langle x_j^N \mid x_i^n \rangle &\rightarrow f\langle x_T, T \mid x_t, t \rangle \, \mathrm{d}x_t \\
P\langle x_j^N \mid x_{i+1}^{n+1} \rangle &\rightarrow f\langle x_T, T \mid x_t + U, t + \delta t \rangle \, \mathrm{d}x_t \\
P\langle x_j^N \mid x_{i-1}^{n+1} \rangle &\rightarrow f\langle x_T, T \mid x_t - D, t + \delta t \rangle \, \mathrm{d}x_t
\end{aligned}
$$

The previous equation can then be written

$$f\langle x_T, T \mid x_t, t \rangle = pf\langle x_T, T \mid x_t + U, t + \delta t \rangle + (1 - p)f\langle x_T, T \mid x_t - D, t + \delta t \rangle$$

We simplify the notation by writing $f\langle x_T, T \mid x_t, t \rangle = f$ and use the following Taylor expansion up to $O[\delta t]$:

$$f\langle x_T, T \mid x_t + \delta x_t, t + \delta t\rangle = f + \frac{\partial f}{\partial t}\delta t + \frac{\partial f}{\partial x_t}\delta x_t + \frac{1}{2}\frac{\partial^2 f}{\partial x_t^2}\delta x_t^2$$

Our equation then becomes

$$0 = \frac{\partial f}{\partial t}\delta t + \{pU - (1-p)D\}\frac{\partial f}{\partial x_t} + \frac{1}{2}\{pU^2 + (1-p)D^2\}\frac{\partial^2 f}{\partial x_t^2}$$

Use the definitions of instantaneous drift and variance given in equations (A2.6) to give

$$\frac{\partial f}{\partial t} + \mu\frac{\partial f}{\partial x_t} + \frac{1}{2}\sigma^2\frac{\partial^2 f}{\partial x_t^2} = 0 \qquad (A3.3)$$

which is known as the **Kolmogorov backward equation**.

(B) Suppose we repeat the calculations of subsection (a) above, but instead start with the intermediate time point as $m = N - 1$. This is illustrated in Figure A3.3. The Chapman–Kolmogorov equation becomes

$$P\langle x_j^N \mid x_i^n\rangle = (1-p)P\langle x_{j+1}^{N-1} \mid x_i^n\rangle + p\,P\langle x_{j-1}^{N-1} \mid x_i^n\rangle$$

and its continuous time equivalent is

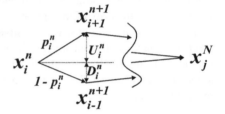

**Figure A3.3** Kolmogorov forward equation constant $\mu$ and $\sigma^2$

$$f\langle x_T, T \mid x_t, t\rangle = (1-p)f\langle x_T + D, T - \delta T \mid x_t, t\rangle + pf\langle x_T - U, T - \delta T \mid x_t, t\rangle$$

Precisely the same steps as before yield the **Kolmogorov forward equation**, also known as the **Fokker Planck equation**:

$$-\frac{\partial f}{\partial T} - \mu\frac{\partial f}{\partial x_T} + \frac{1}{2}\sigma^2\frac{\partial^2 f}{\partial x_T^2} = 0 \qquad (A3.4)$$

Note that the difference between the forward and backward equations is only in the sign of the "convection term", since $\partial f / \partial T = -\partial f / \partial t$.

This derivation was fairly simple, although perhaps not the most rigorous ever seen. A substitution of the probability density function given in Section A.3(i) shows that this function is a solution of both the backward and forward equations. In later sections of this Appendix we will solve the backward equation with other boundary conditions. In Appendix A.4 it is shown that the backward equation is in fact just two steps away from the Black Scholes equation.

(v) **Variable $\mu$ and $\sigma^2$:** In the early part of this book we assume that $\mu$ (with its risk-neutral equivalent $r$) and $\sigma^2$ are constant. Later, we expand the theory to cover a more realistic world. The Kolmogorov equations with variable $\mu$ and $\sigma^2$ can be derived using the same approach as previously, but assuming $U$, $D$ and $p$ to be variable.

Figure A3.4 explicitly shows this variation for the Kolmogorov backward equation. In the derivation of this particular equation in continuous time, there is very little change from what we did in the constant $\mu$ and $\sigma^2$ version. $U$, $D$ and $p$ develop suffixes $n$ and $i$, since their values depend on which node is considered. The instantaneous drift and variance are given by

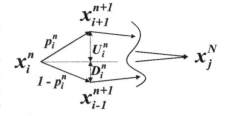

**Figure A3.4**  Kolmogorov backward equation variable $\mu$ and $\sigma^2$

$$\mu_i^n \, \delta t = p_i^n U_i^n - \left(1 - p_i^n\right) D_i^n \quad \text{and} \quad \left(\sigma_i^n\right)^2 \delta t = p_i^n \left(u_i^n\right)^2 + \left(1 - p_i^n\right)\left(d_i^n\right)^2$$

The variable $\mu$ and $\sigma^2$ version of the Kolmogorov backward equation is then given by

$$\frac{\partial f}{\partial t} + \mu(x_t, t)\frac{\partial f}{\partial x_t} + \frac{1}{2}\sigma^2(x_t, t)\frac{\partial^2 f}{\partial x_t^2} = 0 \tag{A3.5}$$

(vi) *Fokker Planck Equation with Variable $\mu$ and $\sigma^2$*: Although the transition from fixed to variable parameters was simple for the Kolmogorov backward equation, it is a lot harder for the forward equation. This is readily understood by examining Figure A3.5. The difficulty is that the two nodes from which a jump is made to the final node have different associated values of $p$, $U$ and $-D$. A little more care is therefore needed in deriving the equation.

Once again, we start with the Chapman–Kolmogorov equation

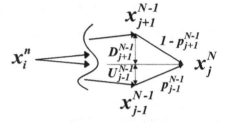

**Figure A3.5**  Kolmogorov forward equation variable $\mu$ and $\sigma^2$

$$P\langle x_j^N \mid x_i^n\rangle = \left(1 - p_{j+1}^{N-1}\right)P\langle x_{j+1}^{N-1} \mid x_i^n\rangle + p_{j-1}^{N-1}\, P\langle x_{j-1}^{N-1} \mid x_i^n\rangle$$

which can be put into continuous time notation using the simplifying notation illustrated in the accompanying diagram:

$$f\langle x_T, T \mid x_t, t\rangle = (1 - p^+)f\langle x_T + D^+, T - \delta T \mid x_t, t\rangle$$
$$+ p^- f\langle x_T - U^-, T - \delta T \mid x_t, t\rangle$$

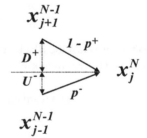

We apply two Taylor expansions on the right-hand side of this equation, one for the function $(1 - p)f$ and the other for the function $pf$, to give

$$f = (1 - p)f - \frac{\partial}{\partial T}\{(1 - p)f\}\delta T$$
$$+ \frac{\partial}{\partial x_t}\{(1 - p)f\}D^+ + \frac{1}{2}\frac{\partial^2}{\partial x_t^2}\{(1 - p)f\}(D^+)^2$$
$$+ pf - \frac{\partial}{\partial T}\{pf\}\delta T - \frac{\partial}{\partial x_t}\{pf\}U^- + \frac{1}{2}\frac{\partial^2}{\partial x_t^2}\{pf\}(U^-)^2$$

or collecting terms

$$-\frac{\partial f}{\partial T} - \frac{\partial}{\partial x_T}\{(pU^- - (1-p)D^+)f\} + \frac{1}{2}\frac{\partial^2}{\partial x_T^2}\{(p(U^-)^2 - (1-p)(D^+)^2)f\} = 0$$

Using equations (A2.6) for the instantaneous drift and variance, with the following approximations:

$$p(x_T, T)U^- - (1 - p(x_T, T))D^+ \approx p(x_T, T)U(x_T, T) - (1 - p(x_T, T))D(x_T, T)$$
$$\rightarrow \mu(x_T, T)\delta T$$
$$p(x_T, T)U^{-2} + (1 - p(x_T, T))D^{+2} \rightarrow \sigma^2(x_T, T)\,\delta T$$

finally gives the Fokker Planck equation as

$$-\frac{\partial f}{\partial T} - \frac{\partial}{\partial x_T}\{\mu(x_T, T)f\} + \frac{1}{2}\frac{\partial^2}{\partial x_T^2}\{\sigma^2(x_T, T)f\} = 0 \qquad \text{(A3.6)}$$

## A.4 PARTIAL DIFFERENTIAL EQUATIONS

(i) **Black Scholes vs. Kolmogorov Backward Equation**: The Black Scholes equation is

$$\frac{\partial u}{\partial T} = (r - q)S_0\frac{\partial u}{\partial S_0} + \frac{1}{2}S_0^2\sigma^2\frac{\partial^2 u}{\partial S_0^2} - ru \qquad \text{(A4.1)}$$

where $u$ is the price of a derivative at time $t = 0$. Let us write $v = u\,e^{rT}$, so that $v$ is the expected future payoff of the derivative in a risk-neutral world. Substituting this in the last equation simply gives

$$\frac{\partial v}{\partial T} = (r - q)S_0\frac{\partial v}{\partial S_0} + \frac{1}{2}S_0^2\sigma^2\frac{\partial^2 v}{\partial S_0^2} \qquad \text{(A4.2)}$$

Let us further make the change of variable $x_0 = \ln S_0$. Substitute this in the last equation and slog through the algebra to give

$$\frac{\partial v}{\partial T} = (r - q - \tfrac{1}{2}\sigma^2)\frac{\partial v}{\partial x_0} + \frac{1}{2}\sigma^2\frac{\partial^2 v}{\partial x_0^2} \qquad \text{(A4.3)}$$

Remember this is just the Black Scholes equation with a change of variable. In the last section we introduced the Kolmogorov equations, which for constant $\mu$ and $\sigma^2$ were written

$$\begin{aligned}
\text{Backward equation:} \quad & \frac{\partial f}{\partial T} = \mu\frac{\partial f}{\partial x_t} + \frac{1}{2}\sigma^2\frac{\partial^2 f}{\partial x_t^2} \\[2mm]
\text{Forward equation:} \quad & \frac{\partial f}{\partial T} = -\mu\frac{\partial f}{\partial x_T} + \frac{1}{2}\sigma^2\frac{\partial^2 f}{\partial x_T^2}
\end{aligned} \qquad \text{(A4.4)}$$

The similarity of the Black Scholes equation written in the form of equation (A4.3) to the Kolmogorov backward equation is striking. This is not really surprising as they are basically the same equation, which can be demonstrated as follows.

- In Section 3.2 it was seen that in a risk-neutral world, $x_t = \ln(S_t/S_0)$ is normally distributed with growth rate $\mu = r - q - \tfrac{1}{2}\sigma^2$ and variance per unit time of $\sigma^2$. The Kolmogorov backward equation can then be written

$$\frac{\partial f\langle x_T, T \mid x_0, 0\rangle}{\partial T} = \left(r - q - \tfrac{1}{2}\sigma^2\right)\frac{\partial f\langle x_T, T \mid x_0, 0\rangle}{\partial x_0} + \frac{1}{2}\sigma^2\frac{\partial^2 f\langle x_T, T \mid x_0, 0\rangle}{\partial x_0^2}$$

- The expected future value of a derivative $v(S_0)$ is defined by

$$v(S_0) = \int_{\text{all possible } S_T} V[S_T]f\langle x_T, T \mid x_0, 0\rangle \, \mathrm{d}x_T$$

where $V[S_T]$ is the payoff of the derivative at time $T$.

- Multiply the risk-neutral Kolmogorov backward equation by $V[S_T]$ and integrate over all $S_T$:

$$\int V[S_T]\left\{-\frac{\partial f}{\partial T} + \left(r - q - \tfrac{1}{2}\sigma^2\right)\frac{\partial f}{\partial x_0} + \frac{1}{2}\sigma^2\frac{\partial^2 f}{\partial x_0^2}\right\} \mathrm{d}x_T = 0$$

$$= \left\{-\frac{\partial}{\partial T} + \left(r - q - \tfrac{1}{2}\sigma^2\right)\frac{\partial}{\partial x_0} + \frac{1}{2}\sigma^2\frac{\partial^2}{\partial x_0^2}\right\}\int V[S_T]f\langle x_T, T \mid x_0, 0\rangle \, \mathrm{d}x_T$$

But the integral is just the future expected payoff so we have

$$-\frac{\partial v(S_0)}{\partial T} + \left(r - q - \tfrac{1}{2}\sigma^2\right)\frac{\partial v(S_0)}{\partial x_0} + \frac{1}{2}\sigma^2\frac{\partial^2 v(S_0)}{\partial x_0^2} = 0$$

which is the Black Scholes equation written in the form of equation (A4.3).

(ii) **The Heat Equation; Simple Form**: The reader might guess that the solution of these PDEs plays an important role in option theory; but he probably does not realize just how important this role really is. Most techniques for calculating option prices, even when they seem on the surface to have little connection with PDEs, can be described as the implied solution of a PDE. This will emerge in the following sections.

The Kolmogorov and Black Scholes equations belong to a class known as *parabolic PDEs*, which were the subject of intense study long before modern option theory was invented. They were of interest to physicists and engineers as they described certain physical phenomena: anyone with any exposure to financial options knows that they were known as the ***heat equations*** or the ***diffusion equations***; on the other hand, surprisingly few people know why in anything but a vague way. We will use a little space to describe the simple underlying physics, as it makes the equations easier to visualize and understand.

Think back to high school physics and the elementary study of "heat" (or "thermal energy" or "internal energy"). Heat flowing into an object makes its temperature go up. The amount by which it goes up depends on how big it is and what material it is made of. The amount of heat needed to make the temperature go up by $1°$ is called the thermal capacity.

Consider a long, thin, straight and well-insulated wire, in which the temperature is not uniform but varies over the length of the wire and over time. Heat will flow from hotter to colder parts of the wire, which is illustrated in Figure A4.1. The notation is as follows:

$\theta(x, T) =$ temperature as a function of position in the wire and time; usually measured in degrees.

$\varphi(x, T) =$ rate of flow of heat along the wire; measured in units such as calories per second.

Fourier's law of heat flow states that the rate of flow of heat is proportional to the temperature gradient in the wire, i.e. $\varphi(x, T) \propto \partial\theta(x, T)/\partial x$. Consider the *increase* over time $\delta T$

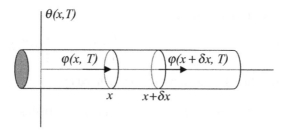

**Figure A4.1**  Heat flow in a wire

of the heat (thermal energy) $\delta E$ within a small element of length $\delta x$. This may be written in two ways:

$$\delta E = [\varphi(x + \delta x, T) - \varphi(x, T)]\, \delta T = \frac{\partial \varphi}{\partial x} \delta x\, \delta T \propto \frac{\partial^2 \theta}{\partial x^2} \delta x\, \delta T$$

where the last step uses Fourier's heat flow law. Alternatively, we may write

$$\delta E = \text{thermal capacity} \times \text{temperature increase}$$

$$\propto (A\, \delta x)\, \delta \theta \propto \frac{\partial \theta}{\partial T} \delta x\, \delta T$$

Equating these two forms gives the heat equation:

$$\frac{\partial \theta}{\partial T} = a \frac{\partial^2 \theta}{\partial x^2}$$

Figure A4.1 can be taken to represent not a heat-conducting wire, but a thin tube of water. A chemical is dissolved in the water but the concentration varies in different parts of the tube. The chemical will diffuse from points of higher to points of lower concentration, at a rate which is proportional to the concentration gradient. Precisely the same reasoning can be applied as before to give a "diffusion equation" which has the same form as the heat equation.

(iii) **The Heat Equation; Alternative Forms:** There are three modifications, each corresponding to a different physical phenomenon, which change the shape of the simple heat equation described in the last subsection.

(A) **Heat Source:** Suppose there is a source producing heat within the thin conducting wire (Figure A4.2). This could for example be produced electrically or chemically. The amount of heat produced in the small segment $\delta x$ in time $\delta T$ is written as $q(x, T)\delta x\, \delta T$, where

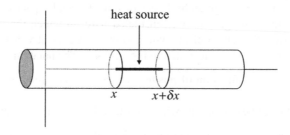

**Figure A4.2**  Heat source

we assume that the heating is proportional to the length of the segment. The heat equation then becomes

$$\frac{\partial \theta}{\partial T} = a\frac{\partial^2 \theta}{\partial x^2} + Q(x, T)$$

(B) **Heat Loss:** In the derivation of the heat equation it was assumed that the thin wire is perfectly insulated so that there is no heat loss from the wire. Now suppose that the insulation is not perfect (Figure A4.3). The effect on the heat flow in the small segment might be the same as the effect of the heat source of the last paragraph, but with the sign reversed. But suppose further that the heat flow across the insulator is proportional to the temperature of the wire; this is Fourier's law of heat flow again. The heat equation would then be written

$$\frac{\partial \theta}{\partial T} = a\frac{\partial^2 \theta}{\partial x^2} + c\theta$$

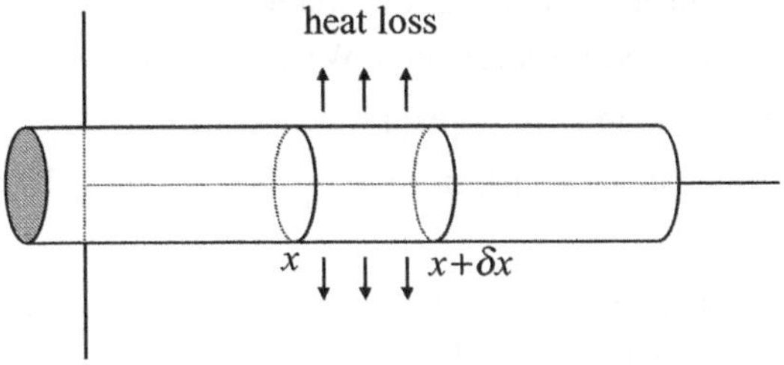

heat loss

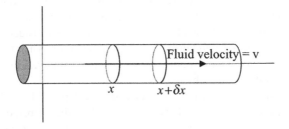

**Figure A4.3**   Heat loss

For heat loss, $c$ would be negative; positive $c$ describes heat gain through the insulator.

(C) **Convection:** Let us turn our attention from the physical properties of heat transfer to diffusion. Suppose that instead of the liquid in the tube being stationary, it is flowing at a speed $v$ (Figure A4.4). An additional term must be added to the diffusion equation, since even if there is no diffusion, the concentration at $x$ would change during the interval $\delta T$ by

$$\delta \theta = \frac{\partial \theta}{\partial x}\delta x = \frac{\partial \theta}{\partial x}\frac{\partial x}{\partial T}\delta T = v\frac{\partial \theta}{\partial x}\delta T.$$

The diffusion equation with convection can therefore be written

$$\frac{\partial \theta}{\partial T} = a\frac{\partial^2 \theta}{\partial x^2} + b\frac{\partial \theta}{\partial x}$$

Fluid velocity = v

**Figure A4.4**   Convection

In summary, a general form of the heat/diffusion equation can be written

$$\frac{\partial \theta}{\partial T} = a \frac{\partial^2 \theta}{\partial x^2} + b \frac{\partial \theta}{\partial x} + c\theta + Q(x, T)$$

where $b$, $c$ and $Q$ can be positive or negative but $a$ must be positive. For reasons which are obvious from the preceding paragraphs, the terms on the right-hand side of this equation are known as the diffusion, convection, heat loss and heat source terms respectively.

(iv) Putting the heat source term to one side for the moment, the heat equation can be written

$$\frac{\partial \theta}{\partial T} = a \frac{\partial^2 \theta}{\partial x^2} + b \frac{\partial \theta}{\partial x} + c\theta$$

This general heat equation can be reduced to the simple form by straightforward transformation of variables.

- The last term can be eliminated by a change of variable $\theta = e^{cT} \psi$, which was used in Section A.4(i) to simplify the Black Scholes equation. We are left with $\frac{\partial \phi}{\partial T} = a \frac{\partial^2 \phi}{\partial x^2} + b \frac{\partial \phi}{\partial x}$.
- Substituting a change of variable $\phi = \psi \exp[-\frac{b}{2a}x - \frac{b^2}{4a}T]$ gives $\frac{\partial \psi}{\partial T} = a \frac{\partial^2 \psi}{\partial x^2}$.
- Finally, the last equation can be transformed to $\frac{\partial \psi}{\partial \tau} = \frac{\partial^2 \psi}{\partial x^2}$ simply by changing the scale of the time variable.

It was assumed that the coefficients $a$, $b$ and $c$ are constant. In a later part of the book we consider cases where these are functions of $x$ and $T$. In that case we cannot achieve the simple transformations, and we really have little hope of solving the heat equation except by numerical methods.

The equation that we are particularly interested in solving is the Black Scholes equation. Using these transformations and the material of subsection (i) we can make the transformation

$$\frac{\partial u}{\partial T} = (r - q)S_0 \frac{\partial u}{\partial S_0} + \frac{1}{2} S_0^2 \sigma^2 \frac{\partial^2 u}{\partial S_0^2} - ru \quad \Rightarrow \quad \frac{\partial \psi}{\partial T'} = \frac{\partial^2 \psi}{\partial x^2}$$

$$u(S_0, T) = e^{-rT} \left\{ e^{-kx - k^2 T} \psi(x, T') \right\}; \qquad x = \ln S_0$$

$$T' = \frac{1}{2}\sigma^2 T; \qquad k = \frac{r - q - \frac{1}{2}\sigma^2}{\sigma^2} = \frac{m}{\sigma^2} \tag{A4.5}$$

## A.5  FOURIER METHODS FOR SOLVING THE HEAT EQUATION

(i) We will focus on the heat equation $\partial \theta / \partial \tau = \partial^2 \theta / \partial x^2$, since it was shown in the last section that more complicated versions of the equation can be reduced to this form by simple transformation. A differential equation can only be solved once we are given the boundary and initial conditions. There are three broad categories of boundary conditions which we consider: first are finite wires of length $L$ where the ends are maintained at fixed temperatures. Then there is a semi-finite wire where one end has a fixed temperature and the other end stretches to infinity; and finally, wires which stretch to infinity in both directions.

When we deal with options we are normally interested in all possible stock price movements between 0 and $\infty$, i.e. values of $x = \ln S$ between $-\infty$ and $\infty$; this corresponds to the boundary conditions for an infinite wire. The semi-infinite solution corresponds to a stock price which is constrained to move only on one side or the other of a fixed level; and the finite wire corresponds to movement constrained between two fixed levels. Some readers might recognize these two latter cases as potentially solving barrier option problems.

The heat equations that interest us particularly are the transformed Black Scholes equation and the corresponding Kolmogorov equation. Referring to equation (A4.5), a couple of observations about the underlying variables $T$ and $x$ are in order. Looking back at the derivation of the heat equation for conduction in a thin wire, it is clear that $T$ is a measure of calendar time: $\theta(x, T)$ is the temperature at position $x$ and time $T$. $\theta(x, 0)$ is the temperature distribution in the wire at the beginning and is used as the initial condition in solving the differential equation. By contrast, $T'$ in equation (A4.5) is a measure of the time to maturity of an option; $T' = 0$ means that the maturity of the option has been reached so that $\psi(x, 0)$ is the (transform of) the final payout of the option. This is the "initial condition" used to solve the equation.

Heat equations with these types of boundary conditions are soluble using two different (but related) techniques: Fourier methods and Green's functions. These are large areas of mathematics in their own right, so we merely give the main signposts showing where the theory comes from and present the major results in a form which is immediately applicable to option theory. Many readers will already be familiar with these techniques, but those who are not will not find themselves at too much of a disadvantage. The fact is that there are only a few European options whose prices can be obtained from an analytical solution of the heat equation: calls, puts and barrier related options. For the most part, numerical approximations must be used to solve the differential equations.

(ii) **Fourier Series**: In general, any periodic function (Figure A5.1) can be represented by an infinite series as follows:

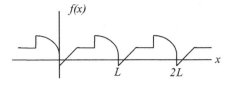

**Figure A5.1**   Periodic function

$$f(x) = \frac{a_0}{2} + \sum_{n=1}^{\infty} \left\{ a_n \cos \frac{n\pi}{L}x + b_n \sin \frac{n\pi}{L}x \right\}$$

$$(A5.1)$$

where the coefficients $a_n$ and $b_n$ are given by Euler's formulas:

$$a_n = \frac{2}{L} \int_0^L f(y) \cos\frac{n\pi}{L}y \, dy; \qquad b_n = \frac{2}{L} \int_0^L f(y) \sin\frac{n\pi}{L}y \, dy \qquad (A5.2)$$

These last two formulas follow immediately if we multiply the Fourier series by $\cos(n\pi/L)y$ or $\sin(n\pi/L)y$ and integrate, using the following elementary results:

$$\frac{1}{\pi} \int_0^{2\pi} \cos n\theta \sin m\theta \, d\theta = \frac{1}{\pi} \int_0^{2\pi} \cos n\theta \cos m\theta \, d\theta = \frac{1}{\pi} \int_0^{2\pi} \sin n\theta \sin m\theta \, d\theta = 1_{[m=n]}$$

where $1_{[m=n]} = 1$ if $m = n$ and 0 otherwise.

(iii) **Fourier Integrals**: The Fourier representation works fine for a function which is periodic. We can also use it to analyze a function defined over a finite range; in this latter case, we use a periodic representation but ignore values outside our range of interest. But the technique cannot be used if our domain of interest is infinite, although the theory can be pushed further to yield the Fourier integral, which is the continuous limit as we allow the periodic distance $L$ to approach $\infty$.

# Mathematical Appendix

The analog of the Fourier series for a non-periodic function is the following Fourier integral:

$$f(x) = \int_0^\infty \{a(\omega)\cos\omega x + b(\omega)\sin\omega x\}\, d\omega$$

where the coefficients $a(\omega)$ and $b(\omega)$ are given by

$$a(\omega) = \frac{1}{\pi}\int_{-\infty}^{+\infty} f(y)\cos\omega y\, dy; \qquad b(\omega) = \frac{1}{\pi}\int_{-\infty}^{+\infty} f(y)\sin\omega y\, dy$$

Substituting these last two expressions into the Fourier integral gives

$$f(x) = \frac{1}{\pi}\int_0^{+\infty} d\omega \int_{-\infty}^{+\infty} f(y)\cos\omega(x-y)\, dy$$

$\cos\omega(x-y)$ is an even function of $\omega$, i.e. function $(\omega) = $ function $(-\omega)$. Therefore, the integral with respect to $y$ is also an even function. But any even function of $\omega$ integrated from 0 to $\infty$ is equal to the same function integrated from $-\infty$ to 0; or equivalently, equal to twice the integral from $-\infty$ to $+\infty$. Thus

$$f(x) = \frac{1}{2\pi}\int_{-\infty}^{+\infty} d\omega \int_{-\infty}^{+\infty} f(y)\cos\omega(x-y)\, dy$$

Odd functions can be written function $(\omega) = -$function $(-\omega)$ which allows us to use the preceding reasoning to write

$$0 = \frac{1}{2\pi}\int_{-\infty}^{+\infty} d\omega \int_{-\infty}^{+\infty} f(y)\sin\omega(x-y)\, dy$$

Using de Moivre's theorem $e^{i\theta} = \cos\theta + i\sin\theta$ gives

$$f(x) = \frac{1}{2\pi}\int_{-\infty}^{+\infty} d\omega \int_{-\infty}^{+\infty} f(y)\{\cos\omega(x-y) + i\sin\omega(x-y)\}\, dy$$

$$= \frac{1}{2\pi}\int_{-\infty}^{+\infty}\int_{-\infty}^{+\infty} f(y)\, e^{i\omega(x-y)}\, d\omega\, dy$$

This is known as the complex Fourier integral.

(iv) **Fourier Transforms**: Rearrange the terms in the complex Fourier integral as follows:

$$f(x) = \frac{1}{\sqrt{2\pi}}\int_{-\infty}^{+\infty} e^{i\omega x}\left[\frac{1}{\sqrt{2\pi}}\int_{-\infty}^{+\infty} f(y)\, e^{-i\omega y}\, dy\right] d\omega$$

We now define the Fourier transform $\Im$ and the inverse Fourier transform $\Im^{-1}$ as

$$\Im[f(x)] = F(\omega) = \frac{1}{\sqrt{2\pi}}\int_{-\infty}^{+\infty} f(x)\, e^{-i\omega x}\, dx \qquad \text{Fourier transform}$$

$$\Im^{-1}[F(\omega)] = f(x) = \frac{1}{\sqrt{2\pi}}\int_{-\infty}^{+\infty} F(\omega)\, e^{i\omega x}\, d\omega \qquad \text{Inverse Fourier transform}$$

These transforms have the following properties which make them useful in solving PDEs:

(A)  For a function $\theta(x, T)$

$$\frac{\partial}{\partial T}\Im[\theta] = \Im\left[\frac{\partial \theta}{\partial T}\right]$$

(B)  If $\lim_{|x|\to\infty}\theta(x, T) \to 0$, integrating by parts gives

$$\Im\left[\frac{\partial \theta}{\partial x}\right] = \frac{1}{\sqrt{2\pi}}\int_{-\infty}^{+\infty}\frac{\partial \theta}{\partial x}e^{-i\omega x}\,dx = i\omega\Im[\theta]$$

$$\Im\left[\frac{\partial^2 \theta}{\partial x^2}\right] = -\omega^2\Im[\theta]$$

(C)  A **convolution** of two functions $f(x)$ and $g(x)$ is designated by the notation $(f \cdot g)(x)$ and is defined by

$$(f \cdot g)(x) = \frac{1}{\sqrt{2\pi}}\int_{-\infty}^{+\infty}f(x - y)g(y)\,dy$$

The Fourier transform of a convolution is

$$\Im[(f \cdot g)(x)] = \frac{1}{\sqrt{2\pi}}\int_{-\infty}^{+\infty}e^{-i\omega x}dx\,\frac{1}{\sqrt{2\pi}}\int_{-\infty}^{+\infty}f(x - y)g(y)\,dy$$

$$= \frac{1}{\sqrt{2\pi}}\int_{-\infty}^{+\infty}dz\,\frac{1}{\sqrt{2\pi}}\int_{-\infty}^{+\infty}e^{-i\omega(z+y)}f(z)g(y)\,dy$$

Let $x - y = z$ so $dx = dz$

$$\Im[(f \cdot g)(x)] = \Im\left[\frac{1}{\sqrt{2\pi}}\int_{-\infty}^{+\infty}f(x - y)g(y)\,dy\right] = \Im[f(x)] \times \Im[g(x)] \qquad \text{(A5.3)}$$

(D)  For a Fourier transform to exist, the function $f(x)$ must approach zero fairly fast as $|x|$ increases. Examples which do not do so are a constant, $\sin x$, or even $e^{-|x|}$; but if the transform does exist, it is unique, i.e. if we know the transform, we can look up the inverse in a set of tables.

## A.6   SPECIFIC SOLUTIONS OF THE HEAT EQUATION (FOURIER METHODS)

In this section we will solve $\partial\theta/\partial T = \partial^2\theta/\partial x^2$ for simple examples of each of the three classes of problem: finite wire, infinite wire and semi-infinite wire.

### (i) *Finite Wire*:

*Boundary Conditions*: Insulated wire of length $L$ has its ends maintained at a temperature $0°$.
*Initial Conditions*: The initial temperature in the wire as a function of position is $\theta(x, 0)$.

Any function defined over a length $L$ can be described as a periodic function for which we ignore values outside the region 0 to $L$. It may therefore be represented by the Fourier series

$$\theta(x, T) = \frac{a_0}{2} + \sum_{n=1}^{\infty}\left\{a_n\cos\frac{n\pi}{L}x + b_n\sin\frac{n\pi}{L}x\right\} \qquad \text{(A6.1)}$$

We assume that the dependence on $T$ is confined to the coefficients $a_n$ and $b_n$. This is broadly equivalent to saying that the temperature profile remains roughly the same as it decays to an eventual zero throughout – rather than having heat pile up unexpectedly in certain areas. See Figure A6.1.

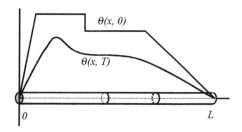

**Figure A6.1** Finite conductor

The first observation is that if $\theta(0, T) = 0$, then $a_n = 0$ for all $n$. Substituting the remainder of the Fourier series into the heat equation then gives

$$\sum_{n=1}^{\infty} \frac{\partial b_n(T)}{\partial T} \sin \frac{n\pi}{L} x = -\sum_{n=1}^{\infty} \left(\frac{n\pi}{L}\right)^2 b_n(T) \sin \frac{n\pi}{L} x$$

Equating individual coefficients of $\sin(n\pi/L)x$ gives

$$\frac{\partial b_n(T)}{\partial T} = -\left(\frac{n\pi}{L}\right)^2 b_n(T) \qquad \text{or} \qquad b_n(T) = b_n(0)\exp\left[-\left(\frac{n\pi}{L}\right)^2 T\right]$$

The initial condition is written $\theta(x, 0) = \sum_{n=1}^{\infty} b_n(0) \sin(n\pi/L)x$ and from equation (A5.2) we have

$$b_n(0) = \frac{2}{L} \int_0^L \theta(y, 0) \sin \frac{n\pi}{L} y \, dy$$

Substituting all this back in equation (A6.1) gives

$$\theta(x, T) = \sum_{n=1}^{\infty} \left[\frac{2}{L} \int_0^L \theta(y, 0) \sin \frac{n\pi}{L} y \, dy\right] \exp\left[-\left(\frac{n\pi}{L}\right)^2 T\right] \sin \frac{n\pi}{L} x$$

$$= \int_0^L \theta(y, 0) \left[\frac{2}{L} \sum_{n=1}^{\infty} \exp\left[-\left(\frac{n\pi}{L}\right)^2 T\right] \sin \frac{n\pi}{L} y \sin \frac{n\pi}{L} x\right] dy \qquad \text{(A6.2)}$$

***More General Result:*** The last result can be generalized to a form which is more useful in option theory. In general, we can change the distance variables $x$ and $y$ by a simple displacement of the distance axis so that

$$\theta(x, T) = \int_M^N \theta(y, 0) \, G(x, y) \, dy = \int_{M-b}^{N-b} \theta(\chi_x + b, 0) \, G(\chi_x + b, \chi_y + b) \, d\chi_y$$

$$= \int_{M-b}^{N-b} \theta'(\chi_x, 0) \, G(\chi_x + b, \chi_y + b) \, d\chi_y = \int_{M-b}^{N-b} \theta'(x, 0) \, G(x + b, y + b) \, dy$$

$$\text{(A6.3)}$$

where the function $\theta'(x, 0)$ reflects the shifted boundary conditions. In the case just considered, the physical problem solved would be to find the temperature distribution in a wire stretching from $-b$ to $L - b$. The boundary conditions are $\theta'(-b, T) = \theta'(L - b, T) = 0$. Making these specific substitutions in equation (A6.2) gives

$$\theta(x, T) = \int_{-b}^{L-b} \theta'(y, 0) \left[\frac{2}{L} \sum_{n=1}^{\infty} \exp\left[-\left(\frac{n\pi}{L}\right)^2 T\right] \sin \frac{n\pi}{L}(y + b) \sin \frac{n\pi}{L}(x + b)\right] dy$$

$$\text{(A6.4)}$$

## (ii) *Infinite Wire*:

*Boundary Conditions*: Insulated wire of infinite length.
*Initial Conditions*: The initial temperature in the wire as a function of position is $\theta(x, 0)$.

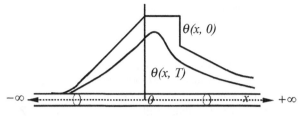

We write the Fourier transform of the solution as $\Im[\theta(x, T)] = \Theta(\omega, T)$. See Figure A6.2. Transform the heat equation and use the properties given in Section A.5(iv), items (A) and (B)

**Figure A6.2**   Infinite conductor

$$\frac{\partial \Theta(\omega, T)}{\partial T} = -\omega^2 \Theta(\omega, T)$$

which solves to

$$\Theta(\omega, T) = \Theta(\omega, 0)\, e^{-\omega^2 T} \tag{A6.5}$$

Our objective is to find $\Im^{-1}[\Theta(\omega, T)]$. But we have the following relations:

By definition   $\Theta(\omega, 0) = \Im[\theta(x, 0)]$

From standard tables, if   $e^{-\omega^2 T} = \Im[f(x)]$   then   $f(x) = \dfrac{1}{\sqrt{2T}} \exp\left(-\dfrac{x^2}{4T}\right)$

so we can write equation (A6.5) in terms of the convolution given in equation (A5.3)

$$\Im[\theta(x, T)] = \Theta(\omega, T) = \Theta(\omega, 0)\, e^{-\omega^2 T} = \Im[\theta(x, 0)] \times \Im[f(x)]$$

$$= \Im\left[\frac{1}{\sqrt{2\pi}} \int_{-\infty}^{+\infty} f(x - y)\theta(y, 0)\, dy\right]$$

Substituting the expression for $f(x)$ gives

$$\theta(x, T) = \int_{-\infty}^{+\infty} \theta(y, 0)\left\{\frac{1}{2\sqrt{\pi T}} \exp\left[-\frac{(x - y)^2}{4T}\right]\right\} dy \tag{A6.6}$$

Note that for $\theta(y, 0)$ of the general form $e^{ay}$, the integral converges; furthermore, $\theta(x, T)$ will have the general form $e^{-bx^2}$ which converges sufficiently fast as $|x| \to \infty$ for the Fourier transform methodology to hold good.

## (iii) *Semi-infinite Wire*:

*Boundary Conditions*: Insulated wire with one end maintained at temperature $0°$ and the other stretching away to infinity.

*Initial Conditions*: The initial temperature in the wire as a function of position is $\theta(x, 0)$, where $0 < x < \infty$.

This standard heat equation problem is usually solved in the textbooks using Fourier sine transforms. These are somewhat simpler than full Fourier transforms and are normally explained first. However we do not go into them here as we are short of space and the result we need can be obtained from the last subsection using a little trick. See Figure A6.3.

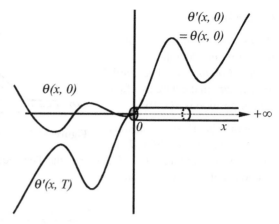

**Figure A6.3** Semi-infinite conductor

The function $\theta(x, 0)$ is only of interest for values $0 < x$; however the function has values for negative $x$ even if these have no physical significance. Let us now define a new odd function as follows:

$$\theta'(x, 0) = \begin{cases} \theta(x, 0) & \text{if} \quad 0 < x < \infty \\ -\theta(-x, 0) & \text{if} \quad -\infty < x < 0 \\ 0 & \text{if} \quad x = 0 \end{cases}$$

Consider the two-way infinite problem of the last subsection if the initial temperature profile had been $\theta'(x, 0)$; from equation (A6.6) we have

$$\theta'(x, T) = \int_{-\infty}^{+\infty} \theta'(y, 0)\left\{\frac{1}{2\sqrt{\pi T}} \exp\left[-\frac{(x-y)^2}{4T}\right]\right\} dy$$

$$= \int_{-\infty}^{0} \theta'(y, 0)\left\{\frac{1}{2\sqrt{\pi T}} \exp\left[-\frac{(x-y)^2}{4T}\right]\right\} dy$$

$$+ \int_{0}^{+\infty} \theta(y, 0)\left\{\frac{1}{2\sqrt{\pi T}} \exp\left[-\frac{(x-y)^2}{4T}\right]\right\} dy$$

Make the variable change $y = -z$ in the first integral, so that it becomes

$$\int_{+\infty}^{0} \theta'(-z, 0)\left\{\frac{1}{2\sqrt{\pi T}} \exp\left[-\frac{(x+z)^2}{4T}\right]\right\} d(-z)$$

$$= -\int_{0}^{+\infty} \theta(z, 0)\left\{\frac{1}{2\sqrt{\pi T}} \exp\left[-\frac{(x+y)^2}{4T}\right]\right\} dz$$

$\theta'(y, 0)$ is only used in the domain 0 to $\infty$ so we may drop the primes on the left-hand side to give

$$\theta(x, T) = \int_{0}^{+\infty} \theta(y, 0)\left\{\frac{1}{2\sqrt{\pi T}}\left(\exp\left[-\frac{(x-y)^2}{4T}\right] - \exp\left[-\frac{(x+y)^2}{4T}\right]\right)\right\} dy \quad \text{(A6.7)}$$

For future reference, identical reasoning shows that for a semi-infinite wire stretching from

$-\infty$ to 0, we have

$$\theta(x, T) = \int_{-\infty}^{0} \theta(y, 0)\left\{\frac{1}{2\sqrt{\pi T}}\left(\exp\left[-\frac{(x-y)^2}{4T}\right] - \exp\left[-\frac{(x+y)^2}{4T}\right]\right)\right\} dy \quad \text{(A6.8)}$$

(iv) *Influence Function*: Each of equations (A6.2), (A6.6) and (A6.7) gives the temperature at a point $x$ on a wire after time $T$. The expression in each case has the general form

$$\theta(x, T) = \int \theta(y, 0)g(x, T; y) \, dy \quad \text{(A6.9)}$$

The term $g(x, T; y)$ is known as the influence function for obvious reasons: it can be interpreted physically as the factor which determines the temperature at position and time $x, T$ resulting from an initial temperature at $y, 0$. This term happens to be the same as the so-called Green's function which emerges from the study of differential equations. We turn our attention to these in the following section.

## A.7   GREEN'S FUNCTIONS

These functions have been popular amongst physicists for a long time. The technique does not normally lead to new solutions (although we will see an exception), but it is elegant and it does provide physical insights; and most important, it has become a standard part of the jargon used in the option theory literature.

(i) *Discontinuous Functions*: Before proceeding to the Green's functions, we need to define a few commonly used functions and their properties:

- The function $1_{[a<x]}$ is defined by

$$1_{[a<x]} = \begin{cases} 1 & \text{if } a < x \\ 0 & \text{if } x \le a \end{cases}$$

  More generally, $1_{[\text{condition}]}$ equals 1 if the condition is fulfilled and 0 otherwise.
- The Heaviside function is defined by

$$H(a-x) = \begin{cases} 1 & \text{if } 0 < a - x \\ 0 & \text{if } a - x \le 0 \end{cases}$$

  Alternatively written, $H(a-x) = 1_{[x<a]}$.
- The payoff of a call option with strike $X$ and underlying price $S_T$ may be equivalently written in any of the following forms:

$$\max[S_T - X, 0] = (S_T - X)^+ = (S_T - X)1_{[X<S_T]}$$
$$= (S_T - X)H(S_T - X)$$

(ii) *Dirac Delta Function*: Consider the discontinuous function shown in Figure A7.1. This consists of a tall thin rectangular strip of width $\varepsilon$ and height $1/\varepsilon$. The function can be written $(1/\varepsilon)1_{[a<x<a+\varepsilon]}$. The area under this "curve" is 1. The limit of this function as $\varepsilon$ becomes infinitesimally small is an infinitely tall spike at $x = a$; The area under the spike remains 1. The

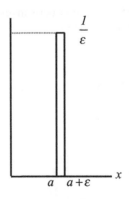

**Figure A7.1**   $\delta(x - a)$

function is denoted by $\delta(x - a)$. It was first used extensively by the theoretical physicist Dirac; 25 years later it was declared respectable by mathematicians.

The key properties of the delta function are summarized as follows:

- $\delta(x - a) = \begin{cases} 0 & x \neq a \\ \infty & x = a \end{cases}$

- $\displaystyle\int_{-\infty}^{+\infty} \delta(x - a)\,dx = \int_{a-\varepsilon}^{a+\varepsilon} \delta(x - a)\,dx = 1$ \hfill (A7.1)

- $\displaystyle\int_{-\infty}^{+\infty} f(x)\delta(x - a)\,dx = \int_{a-\varepsilon}^{a+\varepsilon} f(x)\delta(x - a)\,dx = f(a)$

The delta function was introduced as the limiting case of a rectangle, but it can equally be regarded as the limiting case of certain other functions, most notably the normal distribution function with vanishingly small variance:

$$\delta(x - a) = \lim_{\sigma \to 0} \frac{1}{\sigma\sqrt{2\pi}} \exp\left[-\frac{1}{2}\left(\frac{x - a}{\sigma}\right)^2\right]$$

This is illustrated in Figure A7.2.

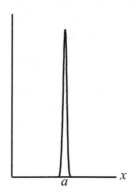

**Figure A7.2** $\delta(x - a)$

(iii) *Some Useful Delta Function Relationships*: Consider the piecewise function $f(x, \varepsilon)$ defined as follows and illustrated in the accompanying graph:

$$f(x, \varepsilon) = \begin{cases} 0 & : \; x < a - \varepsilon \\ \dfrac{1}{4\varepsilon}(x - (a - \varepsilon))^2: & a - \varepsilon < x < a + \varepsilon \\ x - a & : \; a + \varepsilon < x \end{cases}$$

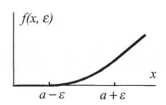

The first and second derivatives of this function may be written as follows:

$$\frac{\partial f(x, \varepsilon)}{\partial x} = \begin{cases} 0 & : \; x < a - \varepsilon \\ \dfrac{1}{2\varepsilon}(x - (a - \varepsilon)): & a - \varepsilon < x < a + \varepsilon \\ 1 & : \; a + \varepsilon < x \end{cases}$$

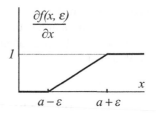

$$\frac{\partial^2 f(x, \varepsilon)}{\partial x^2} = \begin{cases} 0 & : \; x < a - \varepsilon \\ \dfrac{1}{2\varepsilon} & : \; a - \varepsilon < x < a + \varepsilon \\ 0 & : \; a + \varepsilon < x \end{cases}$$

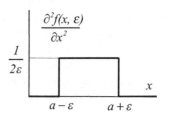

330

It follows from the functional forms that

$$\lim_{\varepsilon \to 0} f(x, \varepsilon) \to (x - a)^+; \lim_{\varepsilon \to 0} \frac{\partial f(x, \varepsilon)}{\partial x} \to H(x - a); \lim_{\varepsilon \to 0} \frac{\partial^2 f(x, \varepsilon)}{\partial x^2} \to \delta(x - a)$$

or in a form which is useful in options analysis

$$\frac{\partial (x - a)^+}{\partial x} = H(x - a); \qquad \frac{\partial^2 (x - a)^+}{\partial x^2} = \delta(x - a) \qquad (A7.2)$$

(iv) **Basic Green's Function Relationship**: The heat or diffusion operator $\hat{L}$ and its conjugate $\hat{L}^*$ are defined by

$$\hat{L}\theta = \frac{\partial \theta}{\partial t} - \frac{\partial^2 \theta}{\partial y^2}; \qquad \hat{L}^*\theta = -\frac{\partial G}{\partial t} - \frac{\partial^2 G}{\partial y^2}$$

A general heat equation with heat source $Q(y, t)$ is therefore written

$$\hat{L}\theta = Q(y, t) \qquad (A7.3)$$

where the boundary conditions depend on the specific problem solved.

Let us now consider the function $\theta \hat{L}^* G - G \hat{L}\theta$ where $\theta$ is a solution of the heat equation and $G$ is not yet defined. Putting in the explicit forms of the operators $\hat{L}$ and $\hat{L}^*$ gives

$$\theta \hat{L}^* G - G \hat{L}\theta = -\left\{ \theta \frac{\partial G}{\partial t} + G \frac{\partial \theta}{\partial t} \right\} - \left\{ \theta \frac{\partial^2 G}{\partial y^2} - G \frac{\partial^2 \theta}{\partial y^2} \right\}$$

$$= -\frac{\partial \{\theta G\}}{\partial t} - \frac{\partial}{\partial y}\left\{ \theta \frac{\partial G}{\partial y} - G \frac{\partial \theta}{\partial y} \right\}$$

or in integral form

$$\int_{t_1}^{t_2} \int_{y_1}^{y_2} \{\theta \hat{L}^* G - G \hat{L}\theta\} \, dt \, dy = -\int_{y_1}^{y_2} [\theta G]_{t_1}^{t_2} \, dy - \int_{t_1}^{t_2} \left[ \theta \frac{\partial G}{\partial y} - G \frac{\partial \theta}{\partial y} \right]_{y_1}^{y_2} dt \qquad (A7.4)$$

where the limits of integration are chosen arbitrarily. Let us now choose $G$ to satisfy the following equation:

$$\hat{L}^* G = \delta(y - x)\delta(t - T) \qquad (A7.5)$$

The boundary conditions have not yet been defined. Clearly, $G$ is a function of two time and position variables and will be written in full as $G\langle x, T \mid y, t\rangle$.

We assume that there is no heat source in the heat equation so that $\hat{L}\theta = 0$. Equation (A7.4) then becomes

$$\theta(x, T) = -\int_{y_1}^{y_2} [\theta(y, t) G\langle x, T \mid y, t\rangle]_{t_1}^{t_2} \, dy - \int_{t_1}^{t_2} \left[ \theta \frac{\partial G}{\partial y} - G \frac{\partial \theta}{\partial y} \right]_{y_1}^{y_2} dt \qquad (A7.6)$$

The left-hand side is essentially the answer we are looking for. The function $G\langle x, T \mid y, t\rangle$ is the so-called Green's function defined by equation (A7.5). Our task now is to define the boundary conditions so that the last equation is reduced to as simple a form as possible. The whole point of the Green's function method is to reduce the original heat equation plus boundary conditions to a conjugate heat equation plus simpler boundary conditions.

(v) Before proceeding to specific solutions for the Green's functions, we need to make a general observation about their structure. Consider the heat equation (A7.3), when the heat source is a delta function:

$$\frac{\partial J}{\partial t} - \frac{\partial^2 J}{\partial y^2} = \delta(y - x)\delta(t - T) \qquad (A7.7)$$

This equation describes a wire in which an infinitely intense but infinitesimally short pulse of heat is introduced at $x, T$. The above equation describes the physics of how the thermal energy spreads in the wire, with $J\langle y, t \mid x, T\rangle$ being the temperature at $y, t$.

There are a variety of different boundary conditions which give different functions for $J\langle y, t \mid x, T\rangle$. One property they all share is that we must have $T < t$, i.e. the equation only describes events after the pulse of energy has arrived. In general we write $J\langle y, t \mid x, T\rangle = 0$ if $t < T$.

Equation (A7.5) for the Green's function looks quite similar to our equation for $J$. The only difference is that the direction of time $t$ is reversed. The equation could therefore be thought of as describing a pulse of energy spreading as time *decreases*. Corresponding to the heat equation condition that $T < t$, we have the property $t < T$ for its conjugate, i.e. envisaging time running backwards from a heat pulse, the Green's function is not defined on the other side of the heat pulse. In general we write $G\langle x, T \mid y, t\rangle = 0$ if $T < t$.

The fact that this visualization is contrary to the laws of physics is not really relevant. The conjugate equation for the Green's function is merely mathematical formalism: it does not pretend to describe any physical process. Our observation is merely a speculation on what sort of process could be described by the conjugate equation.

(vi) **Free Space Green's Function:** The approach we will use is to look for a Green's function which can be written as

$$G = G_0 + G_1$$

where $G_0$ is a general solution of the equation $\hat{L}^* G_0 = \delta(y - x)\delta(t - T)$, but does not necessarily satisfy the boundary conditions we need for equation (A7.6). $G_1$ is a balancing term such that $G$ meets the boundary conditions which will allow this last equation to be solved. It might be a solution to the same equation for $G_0$ or it might solve the equation $\hat{L}^* G_0 = 0$, since the singularity has already been captured once by $G_0$.

$G_0$ is known as a *fundamental* or *principle* solution and is also known as the *free space Green's function*, since it is a solution without tight boundary conditions. It may be derived using Fourier transforms as we did for the heat equation in Section A.6(ii). We write $\overline{G}$ as the Fourier transform of $G$, and using the properties set out in Section A.5(iv). Equation (A7.5) can be transformed to

$$-\frac{\partial \overline{G}_0\langle x, T \mid y, t\rangle}{\partial t} + \omega^2 \overline{G}_0\langle x, T \mid y, t\rangle = \frac{1}{\sqrt{2\pi}}\delta(t - T)\,\mathrm{e}^{-i\omega x}$$

where we have used the standard result that $\mathrm{e}^{-i\omega x}/\sqrt{2\pi}$ is the Fourier transform of $\delta(y - x)$. Now define a new variable $\overline{F} = -\mathrm{e}^{-\omega^2 t}\,\overline{G}_0\langle x, T \mid y, t\rangle$ so that

$$\frac{\partial \overline{F}}{\partial t} = \mathrm{e}^{-\omega^2 t}\left\{-\frac{\partial \overline{G}_0}{\partial t} + \omega^2 \overline{G}_0\right\}$$

Substituting this in the previous equation gives

$$\frac{\partial \overline{F}}{\partial t} = \frac{e^{-\omega^2 t}}{\sqrt{2\pi}} \delta(t - T) e^{-i\omega x} \quad \text{or} \quad \overline{G}_0 = -\frac{1}{\sqrt{2\pi}} e^{-\omega^2(T-t)-i\omega x} + \text{const.}$$

We have already defined $G_0$ (and hence also $\overline{G}_0$) as zero for $T < t$. The last equation can therefore be written

$$\overline{G}_0 = \frac{H(T - t)}{\sqrt{2\pi}} [e^{-\omega^2(T-t)}] \times [e^{-i\omega x}]$$

where $H$ is the Heaviside function. Any table of Fourier transforms shows that

$$e^{-\omega^2(T-t)} = \Im\left[\frac{1}{\sqrt{2\pi}} \exp\left[-\frac{x^2}{4(T-t)}\right]\right]; \quad \frac{1}{\sqrt{2\pi}} e^{-i\omega x} = \Im[\delta(y - x)]$$

So that using the convolution result of equation (A5.3) gives

$$G_0 = \frac{H(T - t)}{2\sqrt{\pi(T-t)}} \int_{-\infty}^{+\infty} \exp\left[-\frac{z^2}{4(T-t)}\right] \times \delta(y - x - z)\,dz$$

$$G_0\langle x, T \mid y, t\rangle = \frac{H(T - t)}{2\sqrt{\pi(T-t)}} \exp\left[-\frac{(y-x)^2}{4(T-t)}\right] \tag{A7.8}$$

(vii) **Infinite Wire:** Let us return to the problem of heat conduction in an infinite wire which was solved in Section A.6(ii). The Green's function approach starts with equation (A7.6):

$$\theta(x, T) = -\int_{y_1}^{y_2} [\theta(y, t) G\langle x, T \mid y, t\rangle]_{t_1}^{t_2}\,dy - \int_{t_1}^{t_2} \left[\theta \frac{\partial G}{\partial y} - G \frac{\partial \theta}{\partial y}\right]_{y_1}^{y_2}\,dt$$

The equation is very general and we can choose the parameters $y_1$, $y_2$, $t_1$, $t_2$ as we wish. We are also at liberty to choose any boundary condition we wish: remember it is we who are defining $G$ (rather than trying to discover it) and we will do so in the most convenient way.

- We will choose $y_1 = -\infty$ and $y_2 = +\infty$ which seem appropriate to the infinite wire problem. At $\pm\infty$ the boundary condition (see Figure A6.2) is $\theta = 0$ and $\partial\theta/\partial y = 0$ so that the second integral in the last equation drops out.
- We choose $t_2$ to be at some arbitrary time greater than $T$, at which point the Green's function equals zero. For notational simplicity we set $t_1 \to t$, in which case the equation becomes

$$\theta(x, T) = \int_{-\infty}^{+\infty} \theta(y, t) G\langle x, T \mid y, t\rangle\,dy$$

- There are no further boundary conditions, so we can take $G = G_0$ the fundamental solution given by equation (A7.8):

$$G_0\langle x, T \mid y, t\rangle = \frac{H(T - t)}{2\sqrt{\pi(T-t)}} \exp\left[-\frac{(y-x)^2}{4(T-t)}\right]$$

This is a slightly more general form of the result we obtained, using Fourier transforms in Section A.6(ii).

333

(viii) **Semi-infinite Wire:** Once again, we solve the problem posed in Section A.6(iii) by imposing appropriate boundary conditions on $G$ in equation (A7.6). The reasoning is parallel to that for the infinite wire.

- This time let $y_1 = 0$ and $y_2 = \infty$; let $t_2$ be some arbitrary time greater than $T$ and set $t_1 \to t$. The first term in equation (A7.6) is therefore similar to the result for the infinite wire.
- The second term is more tricky. The boundary conditions for $\theta$ state that $\theta(0, t) = \theta(\infty, t) = 0$, so that the first term in square brackets drops out. Also $\partial\theta/\partial y]_{y=\infty} = 0$ but there is nothing to suggest that $\partial\theta/\partial y]_{y=0}$ is zero. In order to get the second integral in equation (A7.6) to drop out, we need to impose the condition that $G\langle x, T \mid 0, t\rangle = 0$.

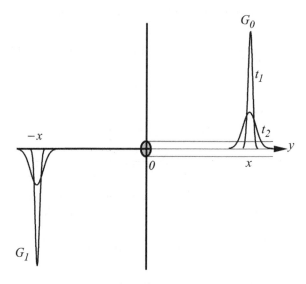

**Figure A7.3**  Green's function with boundary condition $G = 0$ at $x = 0$

Our Green's function will be written $G = G_0 + G_1$ where $G_0$ is the fundamental solution. Let us return to the "Green's function physics" described in Section A.7(ii). The fundamental solution was described as the diffusion of a heat pulse at $t = T$, $y = x$ backwards in time. Clearly, we can make $G$ equal zero at $y = 0$ if $G_1$ were a second (but negative) heat pulse positioned at $y = -x$ and also propagating backwards in time. The positioning of the pulse is shown in Figure A7.3. Using equation (A7.8) for the free space Green's function gives

$$G\langle x, T \mid y, t\rangle = \frac{1}{2\sqrt{\pi(T - t)}}\left(\exp\left[-\frac{(y - x)^2}{4(T - t)}\right] - \exp\left[-\frac{(y + x)^2}{4(T - t)}\right]\right) \quad \text{(A7.9)}$$

and equation (A7.6) becomes

$$\theta(x, T) = \int_0^{+\infty} \theta(y, t)G\langle x, T \mid y, t\rangle\,dy$$

This is the same result as we obtained in Section A.6(iii) using Fourier transforms; it is known as the **method of images**.

***More General Result:*** For future reference, we derive the result for a wire stretching from $-b$ to $+\infty$ by using the transformation of variables used in equation (A6.3)

$$\theta(x, T) = \int_{-b}^{+\infty} \theta(x, t) G\langle x, T \mid y, t\rangle \, dy$$

where

$$G\langle x, T \mid y, t\rangle = \frac{1}{2\sqrt{\pi(T - t)}} \left( \exp\left[ -\frac{(y - x)^2}{4(T - t)} \right] - \exp\left[ -\frac{(y + x + 2b)^2}{4(T - t)} \right] \right)$$

(A7.10)

(ix) ***Finite Wire:*** This case is trickier than the last two, but the approach is very similar to that for the semi-infinite wire. The problem is defined in Section A.6(i) and the starting point is again equation (A7.6).

- Let $y_1 = 0$ and $y_2 = L$; again let $t_2$ be some arbitrary time greater than $T$ and set $t_1 \rightarrow t$. The first term in equation (A7.6) is therefore similar to the result for the infinite wire, apart from the limits of integration with respect to $y$.
- The boundary conditions for $\theta$ are $\theta(0, t) = \theta(L, t) = 0$, so we need to set up the Green's function such that $G\langle x, T \mid 0, t\rangle = G\langle x, T \mid L, t\rangle = 0$.

We achieve the boundary condition for the Green's function using a reflection principle (method of images) similar to that of the last section: we build up the necessary conditions progressively as indicated in Figure A7.4.

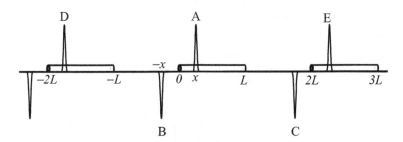

**Figure A7.4**   Green's function boundary condition $G = 0$ at $y = 0$ and $y = L$

- As in the case of a semi-infinite wire, our fundamental solution at A is combined with its reflection at B to give zero at $y = 0$ as in the last section.
- This time, however, we also need the Green's function to be zero at $y = L$, so we add another negative pulse C at $y = 2L - x$. Pulses A and C are equidistant from $y = L$ and being of opposite sign, they cancel to give $G = 0$ at $y = L$.
- But having added pulse C spoils the balance we had achieved at $y = 0$; so we need to add a further pulse D (positive this time) to counteract the effect of pulse C at $y = 0$. Pulses C and D must be equidistant from $y = L$.
- But the addition of pulse D spoils the boundary condition at $y = L$, so we add pulse E.
- And so on.

In terms of an infinite series of fundamental solutions, the Green's function may be written

$$G\langle x, T \mid y, t\rangle = \frac{1}{2\sqrt{\pi(T-t)}} \sum_{n=-\infty}^{n=+\infty} \left( \exp\left[-\frac{(y-x-2Ln)^2}{4(T-t)}\right] \right.$$
$$\left. - \exp\left[-\frac{(y+x-2Ln)^2}{4(T-t)}\right] \right) \qquad (A7.11)$$

where once again

$$\theta(x, T) = \int_0^L \theta(y, t) G\langle x, T \mid y, t\rangle \, dy$$

Unlike the last example, this method does *not* yield the same expression as the Fourier method [equation (A6.2)]. Both methods give the answers as infinite series, but the terms of these series do not have a one-to-one correspondence with each other. In both cases we would seek to truncate the series after a few terms, assuming the remainder to be very small. So which method is best to use?

- Equation (A6.4) shows that the terms in the series damp away very quickly due to the exponential term if $(T-t)/L^2 \gg 1$.
- In Figure A7.4 the free space Green's functions (i.e. the pulses) are singular when $T - t = 0$ and they "spread out" thereafter. Thus the larger $T - t$ becomes, the more terms need to be included in the series in order to satisfy the boundary condition for the Green's function. Therefore it is best to use this series if $(T-t)/L^2 \ll 1$.

***More General Result:*** Just as for the semi-infinite wire in Section A.7(viii), we obtain a general result by a simple change of space variable using equation (A6.3). For a wire stretching from $-b$ to $L - b$, the temperature is given by

$$\theta(x, T) = \int_{-b}^{L-b} \theta(y, t) G\langle x, T \mid y, t\rangle \, dy$$

where

$$G\langle x, T \mid y, t\rangle = \frac{1}{2\sqrt{\pi(T-t)}} \sum_{n=-\infty}^{n=+\infty} \left( \exp\left[-\frac{(y-x-2Ln)^2}{4(T-t)}\right] \right.$$
$$\left. - \exp\left[-\frac{(y+x+2b-2Ln)^2}{4(T-t)}\right] \right) \qquad (A7.12)$$

## A.8 FOKKER PLANCK EQUATIONS WITH ABSORBING BARRIERS

(i) ***General Solution:*** Following the conventions of Appendix A.2, we consider a Brownian particle starting at $x_t$ at time $t$ and later reaching $x_T$ at time $T$. The probability of this happening is written $f\langle x_T, T \mid x_t, t\rangle$ and satisfies both the Kolmogorov equations. The forward equation (Fokker Planck) is

$$\frac{\partial f}{\partial T} = \frac{1}{2}\sigma^2 \frac{\partial^2 f}{\partial x_T^2} - \mu \frac{\partial f}{\partial x_T}$$

Clearly, $f$ and $\theta$ are functions of $x_T$, $T$ and $x_t$, $t$. However, when considering the forward equation, we treat $x_t$, $t$ as constants and consider only $x_T$, $T$ as variables. From the definition of the process, we must have $f\langle y, t \mid x_t, t \rangle = \delta(y - x_t)$.

As a prelude to solving this equation, we simplify the PDE by making the transformation described in Section A.4(iv)

$$f\langle x_T, T \mid x_t, t \rangle = \theta\langle x_T, T \mid x_t, t \rangle \exp\left[\frac{\mu}{\sigma^2}(x_T - x_t) - \frac{\mu^2}{2\sigma^2}(T - t)\right]$$

and rescaling the time variables $t' = \frac{1}{2}\sigma^2 t$ and $T' = \frac{1}{2}\sigma^2 T$ to give

$$\frac{\partial\theta}{\partial T'} = \frac{\partial^2\theta}{\partial x^2}$$

Solutions to this equation have already been found and for the cases considered in this Appendix, take the general form

$$\theta\langle x_T, T' \mid x_t, t' \rangle = \int_{\substack{\text{boundary}\\\text{conditions}}} \theta\langle y, t' \mid x_t, t' \rangle \{ G\langle x_T, T' \mid y, t' \rangle \}\, dy$$

Substituting for $\theta$ in the last equation, using the delta function initial conditions and integrating, gives us the general result

$$f\langle x_T, T \mid x_t, t \rangle = \exp\left[-\frac{1}{2\sigma^2}\{-2\mu(x_T - x_t) + \mu^2(T - t)\}\right] G\langle x_T, T' \mid x_t, t' \rangle$$

Note the primes on the time variable symbols in the Green's function. This merely means that we need to take account of the scaling factor when we use results derived in the last section.

*Fundamental (Free Space) Solutions*: The simplest solution of the Fokker Planck equation is for an unrestricted particle. The Green's function is given by equation (A7.8). Adapting the notation, putting in the time scaling ($t' = \frac{1}{2}\sigma^2 t$) and simplifying the algebra gives

$$f\langle x_T, T \mid x_t, t \rangle = \frac{1}{\sigma\sqrt{2\pi(T - t)}} \exp\left[-\frac{1}{2\sigma^2(T - t)}\{(x_T - x_t) - \mu(T - t)\}^2\right]$$

which is the celebrated formula for a normal distribution. It did not really need the long excursion via Green's function to derive this result; but we now turn our attention to more difficult problems.

*Simplified Notation*: In the remainder of this section we will slightly restrict the generality and simplify the notation of the results, in preparation for their application to option theory. Specifically, we assume that the particle starts at $x_t = 0$, $t = 0$. The notation used is

$$f\langle x_T, T \mid 0, 0 \rangle = F(x_T, T); \qquad G\langle x_T, T \mid 0, 0 \rangle = G(x_T, T)$$

so that the general expression for the probability distribution function in terms of the Green's function becomes

$$F(x_T, T) = \exp\left[-\frac{1}{2\sigma^2}\{-2\mu x_T + \mu^2 T\}\right] G\left(x_T, \tfrac{1}{2}\sigma^2 T\right) \tag{A8.1}$$

(ii) *Absorbing Barriers*: Imagine a particle undergoing a one-dimensional Brownian motion (a diffusion). Instead of the unrestricted motion just considered, there is an absorbing barrier such that if it is touched by the particle, motion ceases. In Appendix A.2 we studied the random walk by looking at the progress of a drunk along a road; the absorbing barrier would correspond to a deep trench dug across the road! The barrier is sometimes referred to as a sticky barrier.

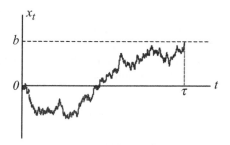

**Figure A8.1**    Absorbing barrier

The progress of the particle is illustrated in Figure A8.1. The Brownian particle, which starts at $x_0 = 0$, $t = 0$, diffuses until time $\tau$ when it first reaches the barrier at $x = b$. The time taken to reach the barrier is known as the first passage time, and is obviously a random variable.

Let $F_{abs}(x_T, T)$ be the probability density function for particles which are absorbed *before* time $T$, i.e. if the particle is very close to the barrier at time $T$, the probability of absorption in the period $\delta T$ thereafter is $F_{abs}(b, T)\delta T$. But the probability of absorption in the period $\delta T$ has to be proportional to the distance moved in $\delta T$; this is proportional to $\sigma \sqrt{\delta T}$ where $\sigma$ is the volatility. This leads us to the unexpected conclusion that $F_{abs}(b, T)\delta T \propto \sigma \sqrt{\delta T}$ or $F_{abs}(b, T) \propto 1/\sqrt{\delta T}$ or $\lim_{\substack{T \to \tau \\ x_T \to b}} F_{abs}\langle b, T \mid b - \delta x_t, T - \delta T \rangle \to \infty$.

In the spirit of the Chapman–Kolmogorov equation (A3.2), we can say that at the outset, the probability of hitting the barrier between times $T - \delta T$ and $T$ is equal to the probability of being adjacent to the barrier at time $T - \delta T$ multiplied by the probability of crossing it in the interval $\delta T$, i.e. the probability of absorption is

$$P_{abs} \propto (F_{non\text{-}abs}\langle b - \delta x_T, \tau - \delta T \mid 0, 0 \rangle \delta x_T) \times (F_{abs}\langle b, \tau \mid b - \delta x_T, \tau - \delta T \rangle \delta T)$$

The left-hand side is finite; we have seen that the second term on the right is singular at $x_T = b$. Therefore we must have $F_{non\text{-}abs}(b, T) = 0$. This is the boundary condition that we need to solve the absorbing barrier problem.

(iii) *Single Barriers*: In the last subsection it was shown that the critical boundary condition for a particle in the presence of an absorbing barrier is that the probability density function for non-absorbed particles is zero at the barrier; but this problem with $F_{non\text{-}abs}(b, T) = F_{non\text{-}abs}\langle b, T \mid 0, 0 \rangle = 0$ has the solution given in equation (A7.10). Using the simplifying initial conditions $x_0 = 0$, $t = 0$ and substituting into equation (A8.1) gives

$$
\begin{aligned}
F_{non\text{-}abs}(x_T, T) &= \frac{1}{\sigma\sqrt{2\pi T}} \exp\left[-\frac{1}{2\sigma^2}\{-2\mu x_T + \mu^2 T\}\right] \\
&\quad \times \left\{ \exp\left(-\frac{x_T^2}{2\sigma^2 T}\right) - \exp\left[-\frac{(x_T + 2b)^2}{2\sigma^2 T}\right]\right\} \\
&= \frac{1}{\sigma\sqrt{2\pi T}}\left\{ \exp\left[-\frac{1}{2\sigma^2 T}(x_T - \mu T)^2\right] \right. \\
&\quad \left. - \exp\left(-\frac{2\mu b}{\sigma^2}\right) \exp\left[-\frac{1}{2\sigma^2 T}(x_T + 2b - \mu T)^2\right]\right\}
\end{aligned}
$$

(A8.2)

We need to take stock for a moment at this point. The Green's function we have just used implicitly assumes values of $x_T$ in the range $-b$ to $+\infty$, i.e. this is the probability density function for a particle starting at $x_0 = 0$ with an absorbing barrier at $-b$. It is more usual (but no more logical) to consider a barrier above the starting point at $+b$, in which case the probability density function is

$$
\begin{aligned}
F_{\text{non-abs}}(x_T, T) &= \frac{1}{\sigma\sqrt{2\pi T}} \exp\left[-\frac{1}{2\sigma^2}\{-2\mu x_T + \mu^2 T\}\right] \\
&\quad \times \left\{\exp\left(-\frac{x_T^2}{2\sigma^2 T}\right) - \exp\left[-\frac{(x_T - 2b)^2}{2\sigma^2 T}\right]\right\} \\
&= \frac{1}{\sigma\sqrt{2\pi T}} \left\{\exp\left[-\frac{1}{2\sigma^2 T}(x_T - \mu T)^2\right] \right. \\
&\quad \left. - \exp\left(+\frac{2\mu b}{\sigma^2}\right) \exp\left[-\frac{1}{2\sigma^2 T}(x_T - 2b - \mu T)^2\right]\right\} \\
&= \{F_0(x_T, T) - F_{\text{ret}}(x_T, T)\}
\end{aligned}
$$

(A8.3)

Notice that $F_{\text{non-abs}}(x_T, T)$ is made up of two parts:

- $F_0(x_T, T)$: a fundamental (free space) distribution for a particle starting at $x_0 = 0, t = 0$.
- $F_{\text{ret}}(x_T, T)$: a fundamental (free space) distribution for a particle starting at $x_0 = 2b$ and $t = 0$, modified by a factor $\exp(2\mu b/\sigma^2)$. It can be written in shorthand as $A F_0(x_T - 2b, T)$.

$F_{\text{non-abs}}(x_T, T)$ is of course not defined on the far side of the barrier.

(iv) **Physical Interpretation**: Let us consider the following experiment: we open a box containing a known number of fruit flies in a room in order to study how they diffuse through a doorway. Two methods are proposed:

(A) Open the door for 10 minutes and then count how many flies are left in the room.
(B) Cover the doorway with a large piece of sticky paper; after 10 minutes, count how many are left in the room.

What is the difference? Simple: (A) gives a bigger fly count in the room since some fly next door and then came back again; in (B) those that hit the doorway do not get the chance to come back. The difference is just the number of flies that go next door and return.

Look at equation (A8.3) again in the context of fruit flies. $F_{\text{non-abs}}(x_T, T)$ corresponds to case (B) above. It is the probability distribution of particles that do not get stuck to the barrier. $F_0(x_T, T)$ is the probability distribution we would have if there were no absorbing barrier. It corresponds to the fruit-fly distribution in (A) above. $F_0(x_T, T) - F_{\text{non-abs}}(x_T, T)$ corresponds to the number that fly out and return again, i.e. $F_{\text{ret}}(x_T, T)$ is the distribution of particles that cross a point and then return to the original side, one or more times.

(v) **Graphical Representation**: The results of the last subsection are illustrated in Figures A8.2 and A8.3. The first shows the free space distribution functions which are combined to make up the distribution function with an absorbing barrier.

$F_0(x_T, T)$ is the distribution of an unrestricted Brownian particle with drift $\mu$ and variance $\sigma^2 T$, starting at $x = 0, t = 0$. $F_0(x_T - 2b, T)$ is the distribution of a similar particle, starting at position $x = 2b, t = 0$. The function $F_{\text{return}}(x_T, T) = A F_0(x_T - 2b, T)$ was shown in the last subsection to have a specific physical interpretation: it is the probability density function of all

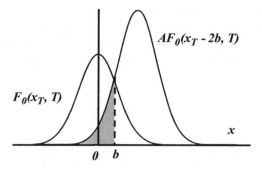

**Figure A8.2** Free space solutions. Shaded area: pdf of particle starting at 0, crossing $b$ and returning before $T$

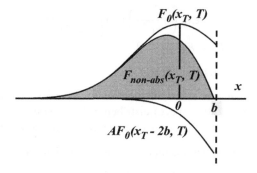

**Figure A8.3** Barrier density. Shaded area: pdf of particle starting at 0, not reaching $b$ before $T$

particles which start at $x = 0$, $t = 0$, cross the point $x = b$, and then return to the original side. The function is only defined on the side of the barrier on which the particle started its progress.

The distribution function for $F_{non-abs}(x_T, T)$ is obtained from equation (A8.3). It is just the difference between the free space distribution centered at zero, and another normal distribution with the same variance but centered at $2b$ and multiplied by the factor $A$, i.e. the difference between the top and bottom curves in Figure A8.3.

Finally, Figure A8.4 shows the overlapping area between the two normal distributions. This is a very specific distribution function: it was seen above that the part of the curve to the

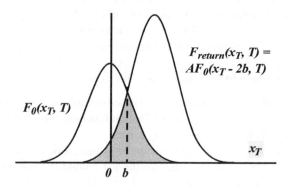

**Figure A8.4** Pdf for particle starting at 0, crossing point $x = b$ before $T$

left of the cusp is the distribution function for particles that cross the barrier but terminate on the original side at time $T$. The shaded part to the right of the cusp is just the distribution function for all those particles that terminate on the right-hand side of the barrier. The two parts taken together are therefore the total distribution function for particles which have crossed the barrier, i.e.

$$F_{\text{crossers}}(x_T, T) = \begin{cases} F_{\text{return}}(x_T, T) & x_T < b \\ F_0(x_T, T) & b < x_T \end{cases} \tag{A8.4}$$

(vi) **Absorption Probabilities:** $F_{\text{non-abs}}(x_T, T)$ is the distribution of particles which have *not* been absorbed by the barrier. The total probability of non-absorption is therefore given by

$$P_{\text{non-abs}} = \int_{-\infty}^{b} F_{\text{non-abs}}(x_T, T)\, dx_T = \int_{-\infty}^{b} \{F_0(x_T, T) - A F_0(x_T - 2b, T)\}\, dx_T$$

$$= N\left[\frac{1}{\sigma\sqrt{T}}(b - \mu T)\right] - \exp\left(+\frac{2\mu b}{\sigma^2}\right) N\left[-\frac{1}{\sigma\sqrt{T}}(b + \mu T)\right]$$

where we have put in the explicit functional form for $F_0$ and used the integral results of Appendix A.1(v).

The functional form of $F_{\text{non-abs}}(x_T, T)$ is the same whether $b$ is above or below zero. If the above calculation is repeated for the case where the particle starts above the barrier, the limits of integration will be changed to $b$ to $+\infty$; the result will be similar but with the signs for the arguments in square brackets reversed. This leads us to the more useful, general result

$$P_{\text{non-abs}} = N\left[\frac{\psi}{\sigma\sqrt{T}}(b - \mu T)\right] - \exp\left(+\frac{2\mu b}{\sigma^2}\right) N\left[-\frac{\psi}{\sigma\sqrt{T}}(b + \mu T)\right] \tag{A8.5}$$

$$\psi = \begin{cases} +1 & 0 < b \quad \text{(barrier approached from below)} \\ -1 & b < 0 \quad \text{(barrier approached from above)} \end{cases}$$

Using the self-evident relationship $P_{\text{abs}} = 1 - P_{\text{non-abs}}$ and the property of cumulative normal distributions $1 - N[a] = N[-a]$, we have

$$P_{\text{abs}} = N\left[-\frac{\psi}{\sigma\sqrt{T}}(b - \mu T)\right] + \exp\left(+\frac{2\mu b}{\sigma^2}\right) N\left[-\frac{\psi}{\sigma\sqrt{T}}(b + \mu T)\right] \tag{A8.6}$$

(vii) **First Passage Time:** Referring back to Figure A8.1, $\tau$ is the time elapsed until the barrier is hit. It is a random variable which may be defined by

$$P[T < \tau] = P[x_T < b] = P_{\text{non-abs}}$$

or

$$P[\tau < T] = P_{\text{abs}}$$

If $g_{\text{abs}}(\tau)$ is the distribution function for the random variable $\tau$, we must have

$$P_{\text{abs}} = P[\tau < T] = \int_0^T g_{\text{abs}}(\tau)\, d\tau \qquad \text{or} \qquad g_{\text{abs}}(\tau) = \frac{\partial P_{\text{abs}}}{\partial T}\bigg|_{T \to \tau}$$

We have given an expression for $P_{\text{abs}}$ in the last subsection, so that with a little algebra and use

341

of equation (A1.2), we get

$$g_{abs}(\tau) = \frac{\psi b}{\sigma\sqrt{2\pi\tau^3}} \exp\left[-\frac{1}{2\sigma^2\tau}(b - \mu\tau)^2\right] \qquad (A8.7)$$

where $\psi$ was defined in the last subsection.

(viii) **Distribution of Maxima and Minima:** The trajectory of a Brownian particle over time $T$ will have a maximum (and a minimum). The value of this maximum $x_{max}$ is a random variable with its own distribution which may be derived from the mathematics of absorbing barriers. Referring to Figure A8.5 we can write

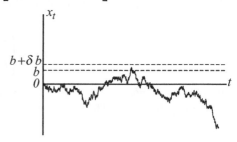

**Figure A8.5** Maximum as a barrier problem

$$P[x_{max} < b + \delta b] = P_{\text{non-abs at } b+\delta b}$$

$$P[x_{max} < b] = P_{\text{non-abs at b}}$$

The probability that $x_{max}$ lies between $b$ and $b + \delta b$ may be written

$$F_{max}(x_{max}, T)\delta b = P_{\text{non-abs at } b+\delta b} - P_{\text{non-abs at b}} \qquad \text{or} \qquad F_{max}(x_{max}, T) = \frac{\partial P_{\text{non-abs}}}{\partial b}\bigg]_{b=x_{max}}$$

Applying this to equation (A8.5) and doing the algebra gives the explicit expression for $F_{max}(x_{max}, T)$. Identical reasoning also gives an expression for the minimum value achieved by the Brownian particle:

$$\begin{aligned}
F_{max}(x_{max}, T) &= \frac{2}{\sigma\sqrt{2\pi T}} \exp\left[-\frac{1}{2\sigma^2 T}(x_{max} - \mu T)^2\right] \\
&\quad - \frac{2\mu}{\sigma^2} \exp\left(+\frac{2\mu x_{max}}{\sigma^2}\right) N\left[-\frac{1}{\sigma\sqrt{T}}(x_{max} + \mu T)\right] \\
F_{min}(x_{min}, T) &= \frac{2}{\sigma\sqrt{2\pi T}} \exp\left[-\frac{1}{2\sigma^2 T}(x_{min} - \mu T)^2\right] \\
&\quad + \frac{2\mu}{\sigma^2} \exp\left(+\frac{2\mu x_{min}}{\sigma^2}\right) N\left[+\frac{1}{\sigma\sqrt{T}}(x_{min} + \mu T)\right]
\end{aligned} \qquad (A8.8)$$

(ix) **Double Barrier:** We now consider an extension of the previous single barrier problem to a situation where we have two absorbing barriers (Figure A8.6), one above and one below the starting point of the particle. As before, the boundary condition used in solving the Fokker Planck equation is that the probability density function is zero at the barriers. The probability density function is given by equation (A8.1) with the appropriate Green's function. In this particular case, the Green's function has been obtained in two different forms: equations (A6.2) and (A7.12).

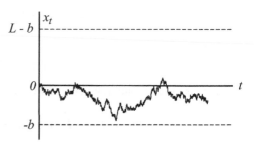

**Figure A8.6** Two absorbing barriers

(A) *Series 1 (Green's Function) Solution*: We start with the second of these which is closely related to the solution for a single barrier:

$$F_{\text{non-abs}}(x_T, T) = \frac{1}{\sigma\sqrt{2\pi T}} \exp\left[-\frac{1}{2\sigma^2}\{-2\mu x_T + \mu^2 T\}\right]$$

$$\times \sum_{n=-\infty}^{+\infty}\left\{\exp\left[-\frac{(x_T + 2Ln)^2}{2\sigma^2 T}\right] - \exp\left[-\frac{(x_T + 2b - 2Ln)^2}{2\sigma^2 T}\right]\right\}$$

This equation is of interest because the terms in the summation go to zero as $n \to \pm\infty$, hopefully leaving just a few contribution terms on either side of $n = 0$. Re-grouping terms and using the symmetry property $\sum_{n=-\infty}^{+\infty} f(n) = \sum_{n=-\infty}^{+\infty} f(-n)$ gives

$$F_{\text{non-abs}}(x_T, T) = \frac{1}{\sigma\sqrt{2\pi T}} \sum_{n=-\infty}^{+\infty}\left\{\exp\left(+\frac{u_n\mu}{\sigma^2}\right)\exp\left[-\frac{1}{2\sigma^2 T}(x_T - \mu T - u_n)^2\right]\right.$$

$$\left. - \exp\left(+\frac{v_n\mu}{\sigma^2}\right)\exp\left[-\frac{1}{2\sigma^2 T}(x_T - \mu T - v_n)^2\right]\right\} \qquad (A8.9)$$

$$u_n = 2Ln; \quad v_n = 2(Ln - b)$$

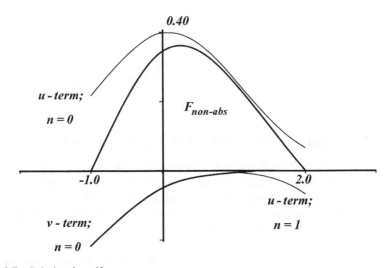

**Figure A8.7** Solution for pdf

The solution is illustrated graphically in Figure A8.7 for $b = 1$, $L = 3$, $v = 1$, $t = 1$, $\mu = 0.1$. Only three terms in the series solution need be retained with the parameters at these levels. Unfortunately, if we feed in parameters typical for barrier options, in the region of six to 10 terms need to be retained to give an accurate solution.

(B) *Series 2 (Fourier) Solution*: Using the solution in the form of equation (A6.2) gives

$$F_{\text{non-abs}}(x_T, T) = \exp\left[-\frac{1}{2\sigma^2}\{-2\mu x_T + \mu^2 T\}\right]$$

$$\times \frac{2}{L}\sum_{n=1}^{\infty}\left\{\exp\left[-\left(\frac{n\pi}{L}\right)^2 T'\right]\sin\frac{n\pi b}{L}\sin\frac{n\pi}{L}(x_T + b)\right\}$$

where $T' = \frac{1}{2}\sigma^2 T$. This may be written more tidily as

$$F_{\text{non-abs}}(x_T, T) = \exp\left(\frac{\mu x_T}{\sigma^2}\right) \sum_{n=1}^{\infty} \left\{ a_n e^{-b_n T} \sin\frac{n\pi}{L}(x_T + b) \right\}$$

$$a_n = \frac{2}{L}\sin\frac{n\pi b}{L}; \quad b_n = \frac{1}{2}\left\{ \left(\frac{\mu}{\sigma}\right)^2 + \left(\frac{n\pi\sigma}{L}\right)^2 \right\}$$

(A8.10)

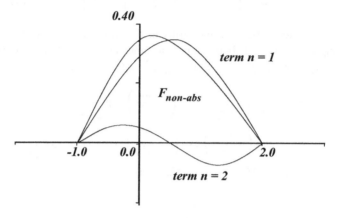

**Figure A8.8** Series 2 solution for pdf

Plotting the first two terms in this series as shown in Figure A8.8 shows that the curve for $F_{\text{non-abs}}(x_T, T)$ can be accurately reproduced for the parameters listed above. If we use parameters typically found in option problems (e.g. $\mu = 0.1$, $\sigma = 0.5$, $L = 0.4$, $b = 0.1$), this series performs far better than the previous one, requiring the retention of only the first couple of terms.

## A.9 NUMERICAL SOLUTIONS OF THE HEAT EQUATION

(i) These Appendices contain 20 or 30 pages describing analytical solutions of the heat equation; but the sad fact is that the vast majority of problems cannot be solved analytically. Chapter 9 describes some of the most popular numerical solutions of the Black Scholes equation in fairly intuitive terms. In this section we set out the various finite difference methods in a more formal way in order to highlight the relationship between them.

The equation to be solved is $\partial u/\partial T = \partial^2 u/\partial x^2$, since more complex parabolic differential equations can be reduced to this form by simple transformation. We shall consider discrete solutions of the equation corresponding to discrete, equally spaced values of $x$ and $t$.

Grid spacings are defined by $x \to m\,\delta x$ and $T \to n\,\delta T$ where $m$ and $n$ are integers; we define the notation $u(x, T) = u(m\,\delta x, n\,\delta T) = u_m^n$.

(ii) **Operators:** We formally define a number of operators and derive some key relationships between them.

(A) In general, the effect of a small change in the value of $T$ is given by the Taylor expansion

$$u(x, T + \delta T) = \left\{ 1 + \delta T\frac{\partial}{\partial T} + \frac{1}{2}(\delta T)^2\frac{\partial^2}{\partial T^2} + \cdots \right\} u(x, T)$$

$$\equiv \exp\left(\delta T\frac{\partial}{\partial T}\right) u(x, T)$$

344

Writing $\hat{L} = \partial/\partial T$, this may be written in terms of discrete grid points as

$$u_m^{n+1} = e^{\delta T \hat{L}} \, u_m^n \tag{A9.1}$$

(B) By just the same reasoning

$$u_{m+1}^n = e^{\delta x \hat{D}} \, u_m^n \tag{A9.2}$$

where $\hat{D} = \partial/\partial x$.

(C) Define the operator $\hat{\delta}_x$ by

$$\hat{\delta}_x u_m^n = u_{m+\frac{1}{2}}^n - u_{m-\frac{1}{2}}^n$$

Applying this operator twice, it follows that

$$\hat{\delta}_x^2 u_m^n = u_{m+1}^n + u_{m-1}^n - 2u_m^n$$

(D) Using equation (A9.2), the last equation may be written

$$\begin{aligned}
\hat{\delta}_x^2 u_m^n &= e^{\delta x \hat{D}} u_m^n + e^{-\delta x \hat{D}} u_m^n - 2u_m^n \\
&= \{e^{\delta x \hat{D}} + e^{-\delta x \hat{D}} - 2\} u_m^n \\
&= \{e^{\frac{1}{2}\delta x \hat{D}} + e^{-\frac{1}{2}\delta x \hat{D}}\}^2 u_m^n \\
&= \{4 \sinh \tfrac{1}{2}\delta x \hat{D}\}^2 u_m^n
\end{aligned}$$

or more usefully

$$\hat{D} = \frac{2}{\delta x} \sinh^{-1} \tfrac{1}{2}\hat{\delta}_x \tag{A9.3}$$

(E) The heat equation in operator notation is $\hat{L}u(x, T) = \hat{D}^2 u(x, T)$, so that we can formally write $\hat{L} = \hat{D}^2$. Using equation (A9.1), we may write

$$u_m^{n+1} = e^{\delta T \hat{L}} \, u_m^n = e^{\delta T \hat{D}^2} u_m^n \tag{A9.4}$$

(F) Let us consider the value $u_\theta$ indicated in the accompanying diagram:

$$u_\theta = u(m \, \delta x, (n + 1 - \theta)\delta T)$$

This can be written in terms of a Taylor expansion, either starting from the value $u_m^{n+1}$ or from the value $u_m^n$, i.e.

$$u_\theta = e^{-\delta T \theta \hat{L}} u_m^{n+1} \qquad \text{or} \qquad u_\theta = e^{\delta T (1-\theta)\hat{L}} u_m^n$$

Using equation (9.4)

$$e^{-\delta T \theta \hat{D}^2} u_m^{n+1} = e^{\delta T (1-\theta)\hat{D}^2} u_m^n$$

or from equation (A9.3)

$$e^{-\alpha\theta (2 \sinh^{-1} \tfrac{1}{2}\hat{\delta}_x)^2} u_m^{n+1} = e^{+\alpha(1-\theta)(2 \sinh^{-1} \tfrac{1}{2}\hat{\delta}_x)^2} u_m^n \tag{A9.5}$$

where $\alpha = \delta T/(\delta x)^2$.

Note that this difference equation is exact. Any approximations are made from this point forward.

(iii) If $u(x, T)$ is a reasonably behaved function, successive terms $\hat{\delta}_x^i u(x, T)$ in an expansion of the last equation diminish in size rapidly. Expanding in powers of $\hat{\delta}_x$ gives

$$\hat{D}^2 = \left(\frac{2}{\delta x}\sinh^{-1}\tfrac{1}{2}\hat{\delta}_x\right)^2 = \frac{1}{(\delta x)^2}\left\{\hat{\delta}_x^2 + \frac{\hat{\delta}_x^4}{12} + \frac{\hat{\delta}_x^6}{90} - \frac{\hat{\delta}_x^8}{560} + \frac{\hat{\delta}_x^{10}}{3150} + \cdots\right\}$$

Substituting this into equation (A9.5), re-expanding the exponentials and retaining terms up to $\hat{\delta}_x^6$ gives

$$\left\{1 - \alpha\theta\hat{\delta}_x^2 + \frac{1}{2}\alpha\theta\left(\alpha\theta + \frac{1}{6}\right)\hat{\delta}_x^4 - \alpha\theta\left(\frac{\alpha^2\theta^2}{6} + \frac{\alpha\theta}{12} + \frac{1}{90}\right)\hat{\delta}_x^6\right\}u_n^{m+1}$$
$$= \left\{1 + \alpha(1-\theta)\hat{\delta}_x^2 + \frac{1}{2}\alpha(1-\theta)\left(\alpha(1-\theta) - \frac{1}{6}\right)\hat{\delta}_x^4\right.$$
$$\left. + \alpha(1-\theta)\left(\frac{\alpha^2(1-\theta)^2}{6} - \frac{\alpha(1-\theta)}{12} + \frac{1}{90}\right)\hat{\delta}_x^6\right\}u_n^m \qquad (A9.6)$$

This is the starting point for deriving the various approximations commonly used.

(iv) **Explicit Methods**: These are obtained by putting $\theta = 0$ in equation (A9.6), so that to sixth order

$$u_m^{n+1} = \left\{1 + \alpha\hat{\delta}_x^2 + \frac{\alpha}{2}\left(\alpha - \frac{1}{6}\right)\hat{\delta}_x^4 + \frac{\alpha}{6}\left(\alpha^2 - \frac{1}{2}\alpha + \frac{1}{15}\right)\hat{\delta}_x^6\right\}u_m^n$$

(A) If we retain only powers up to $O[\hat{\delta}_x^2]$ we have from Section A.9(ii), item (C) above

$$u_m^{n+1} = \left\{1 + \alpha\hat{\delta}_x^2\right\}u_m^n = (1 - 2\alpha)u_m^n + \alpha u_{m-1}^n + \alpha u_{m+1}^n$$

This corresponds to a **trinomial tree** or, if we let $\alpha = \frac{1}{2}$, a **binomial tree**.

(B) If we retain terms to an accuracy $O[\hat{\delta}_x^4]$, we get

$$u_m^{n+1} = \left\{1 + \alpha\hat{\delta}_x^2 + \frac{\alpha}{2}\left(\alpha - \frac{1}{6}\right)\hat{\delta}_x^4\right\}u_m^n$$

which corresponds to a **five-pronged tree**. If we select $\alpha = 1/6$, the last term falls away and we are left with a trinomial tree to compute – but with accuracy to $O[\hat{\delta}_x^4]$.

(v) **Pure Implicit Methods**: These are obtained by putting $\theta = 1$ in equation (A9.6). Up to $O[\hat{\delta}_x^2]$, this gives

$$u_m^n = (1 + 2\alpha)u_m^{n+1} - \alpha\left(u_{m-1}^{n+1} + u_{m+1}^{n+1}\right)$$

(vi) **Intermediate Methods**: The best approaches are hybrid methods which stand somewhere between the purely explicit and purely implicit methods of the last two paragraphs.

(A) **Crank Nicolson Method**: In equation (A9.6), put $\theta = 1/2$ and retain terms up to $O[\hat{\delta}_x^2]$ to give

$$\left(1 - \tfrac{1}{2}\alpha\hat{\delta}_x^2\right)u_m^{n+1} = \left(1 + \tfrac{1}{2}\alpha\hat{\delta}_x^2\right)u_m^n$$

or in terms of grid point values

$$u_m^{n+1} - \tfrac{1}{2}\alpha\left(u_{m-1}^{n+1} + u_{m+1}^{n+1} - 2u_m^{n+1}\right) = u_m^n - \tfrac{1}{2}\alpha\left(u_{m-1}^n + u_{m+1}^n - 2u_m^n\right)$$

(B) **Douglas Method**: Returning to equation (A9.6), we retain terms up to $O[\hat{\delta}_x^4]$ and use the value $\theta = 1/2 - (1/12\alpha)$. Ploughing through the algebra shows that the term containing $\hat{\delta}_x^4$ drops out, leaving

$$\left\{1 - \frac{1}{2}\alpha\left(1 - \frac{1}{6\alpha}\right)\hat{\delta}_x^2\right\}u_m^{n+1} = \left\{1 + \frac{1}{2}\alpha\left(1 + \frac{1}{6\alpha}\right)\hat{\delta}_x^2\right\}u_m^n$$

This scheme is of particular interest because although it involves computations only to $O[\hat{\delta}_x^2]$, it gives results to $O[\hat{\delta}_x^4]$. It may be shown that the value of $\alpha$ which minimizes error is $\alpha = 1/\sqrt{20}$.

A special case arises if we make $\alpha = 1/6$, in which case $\theta = 0$ and this scheme collapses to the trinomial method which we encountered in Section A.9(iv), item (B).

## A.10   SOLUTION OF FINITE DIFFERENCE EQUATIONS BY LU DECOMPOSITION

When we solve the heat equation numerically we first select a discretization scheme and a grid spacing. We then have a series of equations of the form of equation (A9.6) to solve. There are several ways of tackling the problem, falling into two categories: exact methods and iterative methods. The exact methods commonly used are Gaussian elimination and LU decomposition which are mathematically equivalent; the iterative methods include Jacobi, Gauss–Siedel and a variety of further refinements. We shall confine ourselves to LU decomposition, which is probably the easiest to understand and more than adequate for anything the reader is likely to attempt at this stage.

(i) The formal matrix problem posed is to solve for the elements of the column vector $\mathbf{p}$ in the matrix equation $\mathbf{Ap} = \mathbf{s}$, if the elements of $\mathbf{s}$ are known and $\mathbf{A}$ has the tridiagonal form

$$\begin{pmatrix} a & -b & 0 & 0 & 0 \\ -b & a & -b & & \\ 0 & -b & a & & \\ 0 & 0 & -b & & 0 \\ & & & a & -b \\ 0 & & 0 & -b & a \end{pmatrix}$$

The dimensions of the matrix are $n \times n$ and we decompose it into two square matrices $\mathbf{L}$

347

and **U**:

$$\mathbf{A} = \mathbf{L} \times \mathbf{U}$$

$$
\begin{pmatrix}
a & -b & 0 & 0 & 0 \\
-b & a & -b & & \\
0 & -b & a & & \\
0 & 0 & -b & & 0 \\
& & & a & -b \\
0 & & 0 & -b & a
\end{pmatrix}
=
\begin{pmatrix}
1 & 0 & 0 & 0 & 0 \\
l_1 & 1 & 0 & & \\
0 & l_2 & 1 & & \\
0 & 0 & l_3 & & 0 \\
& & & 1 & 0 \\
0 & & & l_{n-1} & 1
\end{pmatrix}
\begin{pmatrix}
h_1 & g_1 & 0 & 0 & 0 \\
0 & h_2 & g_2 & & 0 \\
0 & 0 & h_3 & & \\
0 & 0 & 0 & & 0 \\
& & & h_{n-1} & g_{n-1} \\
0 & & 0 & 0 & h_n
\end{pmatrix}
$$

$$\text{(A10.1)}$$

Our matrix equation can be written

$$\mathbf{Ap} = \mathbf{LUp} = \mathbf{Lt} = \mathbf{s} \tag{A10.2}$$

and is solved for **p** in three steps as follows:

(ii) *Solve for $l_i$, $h_i$ and $g_i$:* From the defining equation (A10.1) we have:

(A) Multiply row $(i-1)$ by col $i$

$$g_i = -b \qquad i = 1, \ldots, n-1$$

(B) Multiply row $i$ by col $(i-1)$

$$h_i l_i = -b \qquad i = 1, \ldots, n-1$$

(C) Multiply row $i$ by col $i$

$$h_1 = a; \qquad g_{i-1} l_{i-1} + h_i = a \qquad i = 2, \ldots, n$$

Substituting from (A) and (B) gives

$$h_1 = a; \qquad h_i = a - \frac{b^2}{h_{i-1}} \qquad i = 2, \ldots, n$$

(iii) *Solve $\mathbf{Lt} = \mathbf{s}$ for $\mathbf{t}$:* This refers to equation (A10.2), when we already know **s**:

$$
\begin{pmatrix}
1 & 0 & 0 & 0 & 0 \\
l_1 & 1 & 0 & & \\
0 & l_2 & 1 & & \\
0 & 0 & l_3 & & 0 \\
& & & 1 & 0 \\
0 & & 0 & l_{n-1} & 1
\end{pmatrix}
\begin{pmatrix}
t_1 \\ t_2 \\ t_3 \\ \vdots \\ \vdots \\ t_n
\end{pmatrix}
=
\begin{pmatrix}
s_1 \\ s_2 \\ s_3 \\ \vdots \\ \vdots \\ s_n
\end{pmatrix}
$$

so that $t_1 = s_1$; $t_i + l_{i-1} t_{i-1} = s_i$; $i = 2, \ldots, n$. Using result (B) in the previous subsection gives

$$t_1 = s_1; \qquad t_i = s_i + \frac{b}{h_{i-1}} t_{i-1} \qquad i = 2, \ldots, n$$

(iv) *Solve* $\mathbf{Up} = \mathbf{t}$ *for* $\mathbf{p}$: Again, writing out the matrix explicitly gives

$$
\begin{pmatrix}
h_1 & -b & 0 & 0 & 0 \\
0 & h_2 & -b & & \\
0 & 0 & h_3 & & \\
0 & 0 & 0 & & 0 \\
& & & h_{n-1} & -b \\
0 & & 0 & 0 & h_n
\end{pmatrix}
\begin{pmatrix}
p_1 \\ p_2 \\ p_3 \\ \vdots \\ \vdots \\ p_n
\end{pmatrix}
=
\begin{pmatrix}
t_1 \\ t_2 \\ t_3 \\ \vdots \\ \vdots \\ t_n
\end{pmatrix}
$$

This time, start at the bottom of $\mathbf{p}$ and work upwards

$$
p_n = \frac{t_n}{h_n}; \qquad h_i p_i - b p_{i+1} = t_i \qquad i = 1, \ldots, n - i
$$

or

$$
p_n = \frac{t_n}{h_n}; \qquad p_i = \frac{1}{h_i}\{t_i + b p_{i+1}\} \qquad i = 1, \ldots, n - 1
$$

This completes the solution of the matrix problem set out in subsection (i).

(v) *General Tridiagonal Matrix*: Consider a more complex matrix in which all elements are different. This has the following form:

$$
\begin{pmatrix}
b_1 & c_1 & 0 & 0 & 0 \\
a_2 & b_2 & c_2 & & \\
0 & a_3 & b_3 & & \\
0 & 0 & a_4 & & 0 \\
& & & b_{n-1} & c_{n-1} \\
0 & & 0 & a_n & b_n
\end{pmatrix}
$$

The LU decomposition still works, but with the $g_i$, $h_i$ and $l_i$ of subsection (ii) now given by

(A) $g_i = c_i$     $i = 1, \ldots, n - 1$
(B) $h_i l_i = a L i + 1$     $i = 1, \ldots, n - 1$
(C) $h_1 = b_1$;     $g_{i-1} l_{i-1} + h_i = b_i$     $i = 2, \ldots, n$

   or

$h_1 = b_1$;     $h_i = b_i - \dfrac{a_i c_i}{h_{i-1}}$     $i = 2, \ldots, n$

## A.11   CUBIC SPLINE

(i) Suppose $y$ is a well-behaved, continuous function of $x$. We are given a series of pairs of data points $(x_i, y_i)$ and wish to create a smooth curve joining these points. The features of the cubic spline method are as follows:

- The total curve is approximated by a series of cubic polynomials in $x$, for each interval $x_i$ to $x_{i+1}$.
- The slopes of successive curves are equal at each $x_i$, i.e. there are no kinks in the total curve.
- The curvatures of successive curves (second derivatives with respect to $x$) are equal at each $x_i$.

349

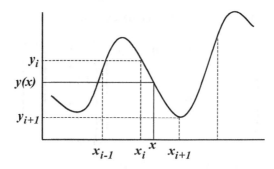

**Figure A11.1**   Cubic spline

The reader should take a look at scatter graphs in an Excel spread sheet. The setting "scatter with data points connected by smoothed lines" is essentially a cubic spline. See Figure A11.1.

(ii) Just suppose for a moment that we were approximating the curve with a series of linear interpolations. In the interval $x_i$ to $x_{i+1}$ we would write

$$y^{\text{linear}}(x) = A(x)y_i + B(x)y_{i+1}$$

where

$$A(x) = \frac{x_{i+1} - x}{h_i}; \qquad B(x) = \frac{x - x_i}{h_i}; \qquad h_i = x_{i+1} - x_i$$

This approximation is not good enough over most of the range $x_i$ to $x_{i+1}$, although it is exact (by definition) at the end points of the range. We now decide to improve the approximation by adding a cubic polynomial $K(x)$ to give

$$y^{\text{cubic spline}}(x) = A(x)y_i + B(x)y_{i+1} + K(x)$$

We drop the "cubic spline" suffix in the following, although it is always implied. The following properties should be noted:

- $\dfrac{\partial^2 y(x)}{\partial x^2} = y''(x) = K''(x)$ because $A(x)$ and $B(x)$ are only linear in $x$.
- $K(x_i) = K(x_{i+1}) = 0$ because $y^{\text{linear}}(x)$ is exact at $x_i$ and $x_{i+1}$.
- $K(x)$ is cubic in $x$ so that $K''(x)$ is linear in $x$ between $x_i$ and $x_{i+1}$. This means that $K''(x)$ can be written

$$K''(x) = A(x)y_i'' + B(x)y_{i+1}''$$

where $y_i'' = y''(x_i)$.

(iii) Taken together, and after some algebraic spadework, these properties lead to the following result:

$$y(x) = A(x)y_i + B(x)y_{i+1} + C(x)y_i'' + D(x)y_{i+1}''$$

$$A(x) = \frac{x_{i+1} - x}{h_i}; \quad B(x) = \frac{x - x_i}{h_i}; \quad C(x) = \frac{h_i^2}{6}(A^3 - A); \quad D(x) = \frac{h_i^2}{6}(B^3 - B)$$

$$\text{(A11.1)}$$

which is confirmed by differentiating and using the results of the previous subsection:

$$\frac{\partial y(x)}{\partial x} = \frac{1}{h_i}(y_{i+1} - y_i) - \frac{h_i}{6}(3A^2 - 1)y_i'' + \frac{h_i}{6}(3B^2 - 1)y_{i+1}'' \tag{A11.2}$$

$$\frac{\partial^2 y(x)}{\partial x^2} = A(x)y_i'' + B(x)y_{i+1}''$$

(iv) Equation (A11.1) would be easy to evaluate if only we were given values for the $y_i''$ and $y_{i+1}''$, as we were for the $y_i$ and $y_{i+1}$. Luckily, we can obtain an expression for these using the condition that the slopes of successive curves must be equal at the points where they join. Equation (A11.2) may be written for the two ranges $x_{i-1}$ to $x_i$ and $x_i$ to $x_{i+1}$, and equated at the point $x_i$ to give

$$h_{i-1}y_{i-1}'' + 2(h_i + h_{i-1})y_i'' + h_i y_{i+1}'' = \frac{6}{h_i}(y_{i+1} - y_i) - \frac{6}{h_{i-1}}(y_i - y_{i-1}) \tag{A11.3}$$

If $i$ runs from 1 to $n$, this is a set of $n - 2$ equations in $n$ unknowns; we need two boundary conditions for these to be soluble. The most common assumption to make, leading to the so-called *natural cubic spline*, is that there is no curvature at the extreme ends of the composite curve, i.e.

$$y_1'' = y_n'' = 0$$

(v) Taking the simplest and most common case of equal $x_i$ spacing $(x_{i+1} - x_i = h)$, equation (A11.3) becomes

$$y_{i-1}'' + 4y_i'' + y_{i+1}'' = \frac{6}{h^2}(y_{i-1} - 2y_i + y_{i+1}) \tag{A11.4}$$

Using the natural cubic spline boundary conditions $y_1'' = y_n'' = 0$, this reduces to the same tridiagonal matrix problem that we encountered in Appendix A.10:

$$\begin{pmatrix} 4 & 1 & 0 & 0 & 0 \\ 1 & 4 & 1 & & \\ 0 & 1 & 4 & & \\ 0 & 0 & 1 & & 0 \\ & & & 4 & 1 \\ 0 & & 0 & 1 & 4 \end{pmatrix} \begin{pmatrix} y_2'' \\ \vdots \\ \vdots \\ \vdots \\ \vdots \\ y_{n-1}'' \end{pmatrix} = \begin{pmatrix} s_2 \\ \vdots \\ \vdots \\ \vdots \\ \vdots \\ s_{n-1} \end{pmatrix}$$

The solution is as before.

## A.12   ALGEBRAIC RESULTS

(i) **Homogeneous Functions:** A function $f(S_1, S_2)$ is defined as homogeneous (and degree one) if $f(\lambda S_1, \lambda S_2) = \lambda f(S_1, S_2)$. Using $\lambda S_1 = v_1$ and $\lambda S_2 = v_2$, it follows immediately that

$$f = \frac{\partial f}{\partial \lambda} = \frac{\partial f}{\partial v_1}\frac{\partial v_1}{\partial \lambda} + \frac{\partial f}{\partial v_2}\frac{\partial v_2}{\partial \lambda} = S_1\frac{\partial f}{\partial v_1} + S_2\frac{\partial f}{\partial v_2}$$

Putting $\lambda = 1$ in this last equation immediately gives **Euler's theorem** for homogeneous functions:

$$f = S_1 \frac{\partial f}{\partial S_1} + S_2 \frac{\partial f}{\partial S_2}$$

(ii) **Farka's Lemma**: A straightforward way of deriving the arbitrage theorem (there are other ways) is to use this standard result of linear algebra, which is demonstrated for the two-dimensional case.

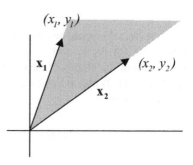

$\mathbf{x_1}$ and $\mathbf{x_2}$ are two fixed vectors which are shown for the two-dimensional case in Figure A12.1. We consider the properties of a position vector $\mathbf{b}$. There are two mutually exclusive possibilities for this vector: either it lies between the vectors $\mathbf{x_1}$ and $\mathbf{x_2}$, somewhere in the shaded area shown in Figure A12.1; or it lies outside this area. We examine the necessary consequences of these two possibilities:

**Figure A12.1**

1. If $\mathbf{b}$ lies between $\mathbf{x_1}$ and $\mathbf{x_2}$, then we must be able to write $\mathbf{b} = a_1 \mathbf{x_1} + a_2 \mathbf{x_2}$ where both $a_1$ and $a_2$ are positive numbers.
2. $\mathbf{b}$ lies outside the shaded area if and only if there exists a vector $\mathbf{c}$ such that

   - $\mathbf{c}$ makes an *acute* angle with $\mathbf{b}$;
   - $\mathbf{c}$ makes an *obtuse* angle with both $\mathbf{x_1}$ and $\mathbf{x_2}$.

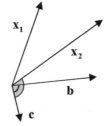

   From the pure geometry, this second condition could not be fulfilled if $\mathbf{b}$ lies between $\mathbf{x_1}$ and $\mathbf{x_2}$. This condition can be expressed in terms of inner products as

   - $\mathbf{c}' \cdot \mathbf{b} < 0$
   - $\mathbf{c}' \cdot \mathbf{x_1} \geq 0$ and $\mathbf{c}' \cdot \mathbf{x_2} \geq 0$

We now use matrix notation to describe these results, with

$$\mathbf{x_1} = \begin{pmatrix} x_1 \\ y_1 \end{pmatrix}; \qquad \mathbf{x_2} = \begin{pmatrix} x_2 \\ y_2 \end{pmatrix}; \qquad \mathbf{A} = \begin{pmatrix} x_1 & x_2 \\ y_1 & y_2 \end{pmatrix}; \qquad \mathbf{a} = \begin{pmatrix} a_1 \\ a_2 \end{pmatrix}; \qquad \mathbf{b} = \begin{pmatrix} b_1 \\ b_2 \end{pmatrix}$$

so that the lemma may be stated more conveniently as follows:

For any matrix $\mathbf{A}$, one of the following two *mutually exclusive* circumstances must hold:

1. Either there exists a vector $\mathbf{a}$ having only positive elements such that

$$\mathbf{Aa} = \mathbf{b}$$

2. Or, there exists a vector $\mathbf{c}$ such that

$$\mathbf{c}' \cdot \mathbf{b} < 0 \text{ and each element of } \mathbf{c}' \cdot \mathbf{A} \geq 0.$$

Farka's lemma is immediately extendible to three dimensions using the same arguments, and does in fact apply to any number of dimensions.

## A.13   MOMENTS OF THE ARITHMETIC MEAN

(i) The arithmetic mean with deferred start averaging is defined in Section 17.1 as

$$A_N = \frac{1}{N - \nu + 1} \sum_{n=\nu}^{N} S_n = \frac{1}{N - \nu + 1} \{S_\nu + S_{\nu+1} + \cdots + S_N\}$$

This may be written in terms of the price relatives $R_n = S_n/S_{n-1}$ as

$$A_N = \frac{S_\nu}{N - \nu + 1} \{1 + R_{\nu+1} + R_{\nu+1} \times R_{\nu+2} + \cdots + R_{\nu+1} \times R_{\nu+2} \times \cdots \times R_N\}$$

$$= \frac{S_\nu L_{\nu+1}}{N - \nu + 1} \tag{A13.1}$$

where $L_{\nu+1}$ is defined by the last equation. The critical point to note here is that using our usual assumption of independently distributed price relatives, $S_\nu$ and $L_{\nu+1}$ are independent of each other, since they are dependent respectively on $R_1, R_2, \ldots, R_\nu$ and $R_{\nu+1}, R_{\nu+2}, \ldots, R_N$. Therefore we may write

$$E[(S_\nu L_{\nu+1})^\lambda] = E[S_\nu^\lambda] E[L_{\nu+1}^\lambda]; \qquad \text{integer } \lambda \tag{A13.2}$$

For the sake of convenience, we will mix discrete and continuous notation, writing $\nu \, \delta T = \tau$ and $N \, \delta T = T$. This reflects common practice, where $S_t$ is assumed to diffuse continuously but averaging is discrete. Equation (A1.8) shows that

$$E[S_\nu^\lambda] \to E[S_\tau^\lambda] = S_0^\lambda \, e^{(\lambda m + \frac{1}{2}\lambda^2\sigma^2)\tau} \tag{A13.3}$$

and with the same reasoning

$$E[R_n^\lambda] = e^{(\lambda m + \frac{1}{2}\lambda^2\sigma^2)\delta T} = a_\lambda \tag{A13.4}$$

where this equation defines $a_\lambda$.

(ii) Consider the term

$$L_{\nu+1} = 1 + R_{\nu+1} + R_{\nu+1} \times R_{\nu+2} + \cdots + R_{\nu+1} \times R_{\nu+2} \times \cdots \times R_N$$

From the form of this expression we can immediately write

$$L_n = 1 + R_n L_{n+1} \qquad \nu + 1 \le n \le N; \qquad L_N = 1 + R_N \tag{A13.5}$$

We simplify the notation by writing $l_n^{(\lambda)} = E[L_n^\lambda]$, where the superscript is written in brackets to distinguish it from a power, i.e. $l_n^{(2)} \ne (l_n)^2$. The following iterative equations follow immediately from the last three equations:

$$l_n = 1 + a_1 l_{n+1}$$
$$l_n^{(2)} = 1 + 2a_1 l_{n+1} + a_2 l_{n+1}^{(2)}$$
$$l_n^{(3)} = 1 + 3a_1 l_{n+1} + 3a_2 l_{n+1}^{(2)} + a_3 l_{n+1}^{(3)}$$
$$l_n^{(4)} = 1 + 4a_1 l_{n+1} + 6a_2 l_{n+1}^{(2)} + 4a_3 l_{n+1}^{(3)} + a_4 l_{n+1}^{(4)} \tag{A13.6}$$

where

$$v + 1 \le n \le N; \qquad l_N^{(\lambda)} = E[(1 + R_N)^\lambda]$$

The various moments (for deferred averaging) are obtained from the expression

$$E[A_N^\lambda] = \frac{E[S_\nu^\lambda]}{(N - \nu + 1)^\lambda} l_{\nu+1}^{(\lambda)}$$

and by a repeated use of the elementary algebraic result

$$1 + x^2 + x^3 + \cdots + x^n = \frac{1 - x^{n+1}}{1 - x} \tag{A13.7}$$

The algebra involved in calculating $l_{\nu+1}^{(\lambda)}$ is simplified appreciably if instead of summing from $\nu + 1$ to $N$ with $l_N^{(\lambda)} = E[(1 + R_N)^\lambda]$, we sum $l_n^{(\lambda)}$ from 0 to $M + 1$, with $l_{M+1}^{(\lambda)} = 1$. At the end of the calculations we retrieve $l_{\nu+1}^{(\lambda)}$ from $l_0^{(\lambda)}$ simply by making the substitution $M \to N - \nu - 1$.

(iii) *Moment 1*:

$$l_n = 1 + a_1 l_{n+1} \qquad 0 \le n \le M + 1; \qquad l_{M+1} = 1$$
$$l_0 = 1 + a_1[1 + a_1(1 + \cdots a_1(1 + a_1 l_{M+1}))]$$
$$= 1 + a_1 + a_1^2 + \cdots a_1^{M+1} = \frac{1 - a_1^{M+2}}{1 - a_1} \tag{A13.8}$$

It is more convenient to rewrite this as

$$l_0 = A_1 + B_1 a_1^{M+1}; \qquad A_1 = \frac{1}{1 - a_1}; \qquad B_1 = -\frac{a_1}{1 - a_1} \tag{A13.9}$$

A more general version of the same equation can be written

$$l_i = A_1 + B_1 a_1^{M-i+1} \tag{A13.10}$$

(iv) *Moment 2*:

$$l_n^{(2)} = 1 + 2a_1 l_{n+1} + a_2 l_{n+1}^{(2)} \qquad 0 \le n \le M + 1; \qquad l_{M+1}^{(2)} = 1$$
$$l_0^{(2)} = 1 + 2a_1 l_1 + a_2[1 + 2a_1 l_2 + a_2(1 + 2a_1 l_3 + \cdots + a_2(1 + 2a_1 l_{M+1} + a_2 l_{M+1}^{(2)}))]$$
$$= 1 + a_2 + a_2^2 + \cdots + a_2^{M+1} + 2a_1 a_2^M + 2a_1\{l_1 + a_2 l_2 + a_2^2 l_3 + a_2^3 l_4 + \cdots + a_2^{M-1} l_M\}$$

Using equation (A13.10) for the $l_i$ gives

$$l_0^{(2)} = 1 + a_2 + a_2^2 + \cdots + a_2^{M+1} + 2a_1 a_2^M$$
$$+ 2a_1\{A_1(1 + a_2 + \cdots + a_2^{M-1}) + a_1^M B_1(1 + (a_2/a_1) + \cdots + (a_2/a_1)^{M-1})\}$$

These series can be summed and simplified to

$$l_0^{(2)} = A_2 + B_2 a_1^{M+1} + C_2 a_2^{M+1}$$

$$A_2 = \frac{(1 + 2a_1 A_1)}{1 - a_2}; \qquad B_2 = \frac{2a_1 B_1}{a_1 - a_2}; \qquad A_2 + B_2 + C_2 = 1 \tag{A13.11}$$

or more generally

$$l_i^{(2)} = A_2 + B_2 a_1^{M-i+1} + C_2 a_2^{M-i+1} \tag{A13.12}$$

Recall that the expression for $l_{\nu+1}^{(2)}$ which is used to calculate $\mathrm{E}[A_N^2]$ is obtained from equation (A13.11) by substituting $M \to N - \nu - 1$.

(v) **Moment 3:**

$$l_n^3 = 1 + 3a_1 l_{n+1} + 3a_2 l_{n+1}^{(2)} + a_3 l_{n+1}^{(3)}; \qquad 0 \le n \le M + 1; \qquad l_{M+1}^{(3)} = 1$$

Slogging out the higher moments is the algebraic equivalent of the salt mines; however, a pattern does emerge after the third or fourth, although happily, we do not use moments higher than these.

$$
\begin{aligned}
l_0^{(3)} &= 1 + 3a_1 l_1 + 3a_2 l_1^{(2)} + a_3 \big[ 1 + 3a_1 l_2 + 3a_2 l_2^{(2)} + \cdots \\
&\quad + a_3 \big( (1 + 3a_1 l_{M+1} + 3a_2 l_{M+1}^{(2)} + 3a_3 l_{M+1}^{(3)}) \big) \big] \\
&= 1 + a_3 + a_3^2 + \cdots + a_3^{M+1} + (3a_1 + 3a_2) a_3^M \\
&\quad + 3a_1 \{ l_1 + a_3 l_2 + a_3^2 l_3 + \cdots + a_3^{M-1} l_M \} \\
&\quad + 3a_2 \{ l_1^{(2)} + a_3 l_2^{(2)} + a_3^2 l_3^{(2)} + \cdots + a_3^{M-1} l_M^{(2)} \}
\end{aligned}
$$

Up to the first series in curly brackets, the calculation is just the same as for the second moment. For the series in the second curly brackets, we now substitute from equation (A13.12). The mechanics are as before, and we can write

$$l_0^{(3)} = A_3 + B_3 a_1^{M+1} + C_3 a_2^{M+1} + D_3 a_3^{M+1} \tag{A13.13}$$

$$A_3 = \frac{(1 + 3a_1 A_1 + 3a_2 A_2)}{1 - a_3}; \qquad B_3 = \frac{(3a_1 B_1 + 3a_2 B_2)}{a_1 - a_3}$$

$$C_3 = \frac{3a_2 C_2}{a_2 - a_3}; \qquad A_3 + B_3 + C_3 + D_3 = 1$$

(vi) **Moment 4:** This is a straightforward extension of the previous three moments, although with the algebra even more long-winded. However the pattern for higher moments now becomes apparent. We merely quote the answer:

$$l_0^{(4)} = A_4 + B_4 a_1^{M+1} + C_4 a_2^{M+1} + D_4 a_3^{M+1} + E_4 a_4^{M+1} \tag{A13.14}$$

$$A_4 = \frac{(1 + 4a_1 A_1 + 6a_2 A_2 + 4a_3 A_3)}{1 - a_4}; \qquad B_4 = \frac{(4a_1 B_1 + 6a_2 B_2 + 4a_3 B_3)}{a_1 - a_4}$$

$$C_4 = \frac{(6a_2 C_2 + 4a_3 C_3)}{a_2 - a_4}; \qquad D_4 = \frac{4a_3 D_3}{a_3 - a_4}; \qquad A_4 + B_4 + C_4 + D_4 + E_4 = 1$$

Again, recall that $l_{\nu+1}^{(4)}$ is obtained by substituting $M \to N - \nu - 1$ in equation (A13.14).

(vii) **In-progress Averaging**: The average is now defined as

$$A_N = \frac{\nu}{N+\nu+1}\overline{A} + \frac{1}{N+\nu+1}\sum_{n=0}^{N} S_n$$

The first term is constant, so the defining equation can be written

$$A_N = K + kA_{\text{simple}}$$

where

$$k = \frac{N+1}{N+\nu+1} \qquad \text{and} \qquad A_{\text{simple}} = \frac{1}{N+1}\sum_{n=0}^{N} S_n$$

$A_{\text{simple}}$ indicates simple averaging from the beginning, i.e. setting $\nu = 0$ in all the previous formulas. Then

$$\mathrm{E}[A_N] = K + k\,\mathrm{E}[A_{\text{simple}}]; \qquad \mathrm{E}\big[A_N^2\big] = K^2 + 2kK\,\mathrm{E}[A_{\text{simple}}] + k^2\,\mathrm{E}\big[A_{\text{simple}}^2\big]$$

$$(A13.15)$$

And so on for higher moments.

(viii) **Cross Moments**: The simplest of these is defined as $\mathrm{E}[A_N\ S_N]$. Using the same notation as before, the deferred averaging case can be written

$$\mathrm{E}[A_N\ S_N] = \frac{\mathrm{E}[(S_\nu L_{\nu+1})(S_\nu \times R_{\nu+1} \times R_{\nu+2} \times \cdots \times R_N)]}{N-\nu+1}$$

$$= \frac{\mathrm{E}[S_\nu^2]}{N-\nu+1}\{1 + R_{\nu+1} + R_{\nu+1} \times R_{\nu+2} + \cdots + R_{\nu+1} \times R_{\nu+2} \times \cdots \times R_N\}$$

$$\times \{R_{\nu+1} \times R_{\nu+2} \times \cdots \times R_N\}$$

$$= \frac{\mathrm{E}[S_\nu^2]}{N-\nu+1}\{a_1^{N-\nu} + a_2 a_1^{N-\nu-1} + \cdots + a_2^{N-\nu}\}$$

$$= \frac{\mathrm{E}[S_\nu^2]a_1^{N-\nu}}{N-\nu+1}\{1 + (a_2/a_1) + (a_2/a_1)^2 + \cdots + (a_2/a_1)^{N-\nu}\}$$

$$= \frac{\mathrm{E}[S_\nu^2]a_1^{N-\nu}}{N-\nu+1}\left\{\frac{1-(a_2/a_1)^{N-\nu+1}}{1-(a_2/a_1)}\right\} \qquad (A13.16)$$

A corresponding equation can be obtained for in-progress averaging using the approach outlined in the last subsection.

## A.14   EDGEWORTH EXPANSIONS

Consider a probability density function $f(x)$ which is close to (but not exactly equal to) a known probability density function $k(x)$. For example, we might be trying to describe a distribution which we know to be close to normal, but which displays slight skewness. Edgeworth expansions express $f(x)$ as an infinite series containing $k(x)$ and its derivatives with respect to $x$; as such it may be thought of as fulfilling a role analogous to a Taylor series.

(i) The reader is reminded of the material on moment generating functions given in Appendix A.2(ii). Two definitions are key:

- The moment generating function is defined by

$$M^f(\Theta) = E^f[e^{\Theta x}] = 1 + \Theta E^f[x] + \frac{\Theta^2}{2!}E^f[x^2] + \cdots$$

$$M^k(\Theta) = E^k[e^{\Theta x}] = 1 + \Theta E^k[x] + \frac{\Theta^2}{2!}E^k[x^2] + \cdots$$

(A14.1)

The term $E[x^n]$ is known as the **nth moment** of the distribution.
- The *cumulants* $\kappa_n$ of a distribution are defined by the following:

$$M^f(\Theta) = \exp\left[\Theta\kappa_1^f + \frac{\Theta^2}{2!}\kappa_2^f + \frac{\Theta^3}{3!}\kappa_3^f + \cdots\right] \quad \text{and}$$

$$M^k(\Theta) = \exp\left[\Theta\kappa_1^k + \frac{\Theta^2}{2!}\kappa_2^k + \frac{\Theta^3}{3!}\kappa_3^k + \cdots\right]$$

(A14.2)

Expand the exponential in the last equation ($e^\alpha = 1 + \alpha + \frac{1}{2!}\alpha^2 + \cdots$) and equate powers of $\Theta$ in this expansion with powers of $\Theta$ in equations (A14.2). Solve the resultant simultaneous equations to give

$$\kappa_1 = E[x] = \mu; \qquad \kappa_2 = E[(x - \kappa_1)^2] = \sigma^2$$

$$\kappa_3 = E[(x - \kappa_1)^3]; \qquad \kappa_4 = E[(x - \kappa_1)^4] - 3\kappa_2^2$$

(A14.3)

The cumulants $\kappa_1, \kappa_2, \kappa_3$ and $\kappa_4$ are called the mean, variance, skewness and kurtosis of a distribution. Higher cumulants will not be considered.

(ii) Dividing $M^f(\Theta)$ by $M^k(\Theta)$ in equation (A14.2) gives

$$M^f(\Theta) = M^k(\Theta)\exp\left[\Theta\delta\kappa_1 + \frac{\Theta^2}{2!}\delta\kappa_2 + \frac{\Theta^3}{3!}\delta\kappa_3 + \cdots\right] \quad \text{where} \quad \delta\kappa_n = \kappa_n^f - \kappa_n^k$$

$$= M^k(\Theta)\left\{1 + \Theta E_1 + \frac{\Theta^2}{2!}E_2 + \frac{\Theta^3}{3!}E_3 + \cdots\right\}$$

(A14.4)

where once again we have expanded the exponential and collected powers of $\Theta$. In terms of $\delta\kappa_n$, the $E_n$ can be written

$$E_1 = \delta\kappa_1; \qquad E_2 = \delta\kappa_2 + (\delta\kappa_1)^2; \qquad E_3 = \delta\kappa_3 + 3\delta\kappa_1\delta\kappa_2 + (\delta\kappa_1)^3$$

$$E_4 = \delta\kappa_4 + 4\delta\kappa_1\delta\kappa_3 + 3(\delta\kappa_2)^2 + 6(\delta\kappa_1)^2\delta\kappa_2 + (\delta\kappa_1)^4$$

(A14.5)

(iii) The objective of this Appendix is to find an approximation to the distribution $f(x)$ which can be written

$$f(x) = k(x) + u_1(x) + u_2(x) + u_3(x) + \cdots$$

where the terms trail off to zero.

From the definition of $M^k(\Theta)$, integrating by parts and assuming that all derivatives of $k(x)$ go to zero as $x \to \pm\infty$, we have

$$M^k(\Theta) = \int_{-\infty}^{+\infty} e^{\Theta x} k(x)\,dx = \frac{1}{-\Theta} \int_{-\infty}^{+\infty} e^{\Theta x} \frac{\partial k(x)}{\partial x}\,dx = \frac{1}{(-\Theta)^2} \int_{-\infty}^{+\infty} e^{\Theta x} \frac{\partial^2 k(x)}{\partial x^2}\,dx = \cdots$$

$$= \frac{1}{(-\Theta)^n} \int_{-\infty}^{+\infty} e^{\Theta x} \frac{\partial^n k(x)}{\partial x^n}\,dx$$

Or more simply

$$\Theta^n M^k(\Theta) = (-1)^n \int_{-\infty}^{+\infty} e^{\Theta x} \frac{\partial^n k(x)}{\partial x^n}\,dx \tag{A14.6}$$

Using this last formula and the definitions of the moment generating functions allows us to write equation (A14.4) as

$$\int_{-\infty}^{+\infty} e^{\Theta x} f(x)\,dx = \int_{-\infty}^{+\infty} e^{\Theta x} \{k(x) + u_1(x) + u_2(x) + u_3(x) + \cdots\}\,dx$$

where

$$u_n(x) = E_n \frac{(-1)^n}{n!} \frac{\partial^n k(x)}{\partial x^n}$$

or equivalently

$$f(x) = k(x) + u_1(x) + u_2(x) + u_3(x) + \cdots \tag{A14.7}$$

(iv) Suppose we wish to find the expectation of the expression $\max[0, S_T - X]$ where $S_T$ has the probability distribution $f(S_T)$ which is close to the lognormal distribution $l(S_T)$. This would arise if we were investigating the value of a call option, knowing that the underlying distribution is slightly skewed and fat-tailed. It also occurs in the investigation of arithmetic average options:

$$E[\max[0, S_T - X]] = \int_X^\infty (S_T - X) f(S_T)\,dS_T$$

$$= \int_X^\infty (S_T - X) l(S_T)\,dS_T + E_n \frac{(-1)^n}{n!} \sum_n \int_X^\infty (S_T - X) \frac{\partial^n l(x)}{\partial x^n}\,dS_T$$

The first term on the right-hand side is just the Black Scholes type expression

$$S_0\, e^{(m+\frac{1}{2}\sigma^2)T}\, N[d_1] - X N[d_2]$$

$$d_1 = \frac{1}{\sigma\sqrt{T}} \left\{ \ln \frac{S_0\, e^{(m+\frac{1}{2}\sigma^2)T}}{X} + \frac{1}{2}\sigma^2 T \right\}; \qquad d_2 = d_1 - \sigma\sqrt{T}$$

In the second term, we use first equations (A1.7) and then the following simplification, obtained by integrating by parts:

$$\int_X^\infty (S_T - X) \frac{\partial^n l(S_T)}{\partial S_T^n}\,dS_T = \left[ (S_T - X) \frac{\partial^{n-1} l(S_T)}{\partial S_T^{n-1}} \right]_{S_T=X}^{S_T=\infty} - \int_X^\infty \frac{\partial^{n-1} l(S_T)}{\partial S_T^{n-1}}\,dS_T$$

$$= \frac{\partial^{n-2} l(S_T)}{\partial S_T^{n-2}} \Bigg]_{S_T=X}$$

Retaining only terms up to $E_4$ we can now write for a call option

$$e^{-rT} E[\max[0, S_T - X]] = e^{-rT} \left\{ S_0 e^{(m+\frac{1}{2}\sigma^2)T} N[d_1] - X N[d_2] \right\}$$

$$+ e^{-rT} \left\{ -E_1 N[d_2] + \frac{1}{2!} E_2 l(X) - \frac{1}{3!} E_3 \frac{\partial l(S_T)}{\partial S_T} \right]_{S_T=X}$$

$$+ \frac{1}{4!} E_4 \frac{\partial^2 l(S_T)}{\partial S_T^2} \right]_{S_T=X} \right\} \tag{A14.8}$$

# Bibliography and References

## COMMENTARY

The purpose of this section is to give the reader a useful guide to further sources, rather than to accredit every wrinkle in the development of the subject. The readers of this book will be much more inclined to look for additional information in other books rather than original papers, as the former are usually far more accessible. There follows a short and very personal commentary on the books available in 2002. This is not comprehensive and certainly does not give proper credit for the historical development of the subject: no "... seminal paper written by Black and Scholes in ... " But it gives the reader a guide of where to look next if he needs more. Part 3 on Exotic Options is perhaps the exception since treatment of the subject in books is thin and the next step is often the original paper.

(i) *General and Introductory Texts*: Hull (2000) has a very special place in any bibliography. It was the first comprehensible *and* comprehensive book on derivative theory and was the introductory text for most people working in the industry today. It remains a model of jargon-free clarity and has been kept reasonably up-to-date in successive editions. However, it is an introductory text and needs to be supplemented for serious quantitative work.

Wilmott (1998) is a romp which some people really enjoy and other less so. It is an introductory text intended for the young-of-heart, and feels more modern than Hull. Wilmott's talent for recycling material means that this book has now metamorphosed to Willmot (2002).

Briys *et al.* (1998) is the most advanced general text and is very useful; but it has many authors and suffers from some consequent weaknesses – unevenness of style and quality, and a tendency to go off at tangents while giving some important topics only cursory treatment. It has a very good bibliography.

The present book is a text on equity-type options, which means that the theory, procedures and formulas can be transferred directly to the analysis of foreign exchange (as well as futures, commodities and stock indices). Anyone who has trouble with this transference is recommended to consult DeRosa (2000).

Finally in this section, we should mention a nice little book called "The Complete Guide to Option Pricing Formulas" (Haug, 1998). Despite the "complete", it does not derive any formulas – just states them. Of course, you can never capture *all* the formulas, but it is a well-edited reference book, and the reader will find it very useful when he writes his own book and needs an aid in hunting for typos in formulas.

(ii) *Numerical Methods*: A number of good, intermediate level texts have appeared in the last four or five years (although there is still room to fill a few neglected areas). The first was Clewlow and Strickland (1998), which covers the material of Part 2 of this book and is used quite widely. It covers both equity-type and interest rate derivatives. The latter part has become dated and unfortunately crowds out the former, which is still valid and could do with expanding.

Recognition that a differential equation can describe any option came early in the development of derivative theory, but as a routine computational approach it was much popularized by Wilmott *et al.* (1993); a more recent version of this book is Wilmott *et al.* (1995). Tavella and Randall (2000) is a good, practical book on numerical solutions of the Black Scholes equation. Shaw (1998) has some very interesting material in the same field, and would have received wider recognition if it had not so closely hitched itself to "Mathematica".

There are three readily available sources for implied trees, volatility surfaces, etc.: Rebonato (1999) which is incisive as one would expect from this author, but can be hard to follow; and two collections of important papers in the field – Broadie and Glasserman (1998) and Jarrow (1988). Jäckel (2002) is the only book dedicated to Monte Carlo for derivatives, but Dupire (1998) is a very useful collection of the most important papers together with some exceptionally good linking commentary.

(iii) *Exotics*: Despite the mountain of papers written on this subject in the 1990s, coverage of the field by dedicated books is surprisingly thin. Zhang (1998) is very detailed and thorough but sticks fairly much to analytical models. Two other books, Nelken (1996) and Clewlow and Strickland (1997), are both collections of essays by different authors and suffer from an absence of unifying methodology. The next stops are chapters in general texts and then back to the original papers.

(iv) *Stochastic Calculus and Derivatives*: This area has progressed from inadequate coverage to supersaturation in five years. The books taken individually are sound and worthy, but taken together there is a lot of repetition and redundancy. A few words might help the reader avoid getting too many duplicates.

1. First come the pure mathematics text books: top of the list is the classic Karatsas and Schreve (1991); its rival, Revuz and Yor (2001) covers more or less the same material and may be slightly more directly applicable to derivatives. The former is an American textbook while the latter is a French textbook written in English, which accounts for differences in style and popularity. Øksendal (1992) again covers mostly the same areas but is a little easier, while still remaining a serious mathematician's book. Anyone without a measure theory background is recommended to look at Ash and Doléans-Dade (2000) before trying these last three books. Alternatively, Cox and Miller (1965) is an old classic which explains stochastic processes in a fairly intuitive way without measure theory – although you will not be able to follow the modern options literature with only this behind you. Local Time is a topic likely to get more attention among option theorists in the future, and is well covered in Chung and Williams (1990).

2. Five years ago, there were just two books dedicated to stochastic theory applied to finance theory: Dothan (1990) and Duffie (1992). The first is a little easier and contains some interesting material, but now looks very dated; the second is still a standard text for specialist graduate students, but Nielsen (1999) and Steele (2001) now compete directly and look a bit more up-to-date.

3. Next come the general derivative textbooks based on stochastic theory, in roughly ascending order of difficulty. Baxter and Rennie (1996) made the first brave attempt to bring stochastic theory and martingales to non-technicians; but while it is very clearly written, it does not give the reader enough to access the serious literature. Neftci (1996) was a little more advanced but suffered from the same drawback; however, the second edition (2000) is much more complete and is recommended. Just a little more advanced is Pliska (1997), which disappoints by what it has left out: it only covers discrete (not continuous) time theory, but does this very well.

   After that, there are many books: Bingham and Kiesel (1998), Musiela and Rutkowski (1998), Elliot and Kopp (1999), Hunt and Kennedy (2000); they all have the same academic approach and vary slightly in level and style.

4. Finally, there are interest rate derivatives books. The first was Rebonato (1998) which remains quite distinctive and the recommended text for practitioners. Others in this category include Martellini and Priaulet (2001) and Brigo and Mercurio (2001), with more to follow soon.

(v) *General Mathematics*: There is a very large number of textbooks to chose from and the following are the author's first choices: for a general mathematics text, Kreyszig (1993) is excellent. There are many introductory mathematical statistics books and we use Freund (1992). Johnson and Wichern (1988) is the standard book on multivariate statistics. Press *et al.* (1992) is indispensable for any quant and is particularly relevant on random numbers, cubic spline and numerical solutions of differential equations.

Partial differential equations are well covered by Kreyszig (1993), Haberman (1987) and Farlow (1993), while the best book on their numerical solution is Ames (1997); Smith (1978) is also good on this latter topic. A highly recommended short monograph on Green's functions (unfortunately temporarily? out of print) is Greenberg.

# BOOKS

Ames W (1977) *Numerical Methods for Partial Differential Equations*, Academic Press.

Ash R and Doléans-Dade C (2000) *Probability and Measure Theory*, Harcourt Academic Press.

Baxter M and Rennie A (1996) *Financial Calculus*, Cambridge University Press.

Bingham N and Kiesel R (1998) *Risk-Neutral Valuation*, Springer.

Brigo D and Mercurio F (2001) *Interest Rate Models*, Springer.

Briys E, Bellalah M, Mai H and de Varenne F (1998) *Options, Futures and Exotic Derivatives*, John Wiley & Sons.

Broadie M and Glasserman P (editors) (1998) *Hedging with Trees*, Risk Books.

Chung J and Williams R (1990) *Introduction to Stochastic Integration*, Birkhäuser.

Clewlow L and Strickland C (1998) *Implementing Derivatives Models*, John Wiley & Sons.

Clewlow L and Strickland C (editors) (1997) *Exotic Options*, John Wiley & Sons.

Cox D and Miller H (1965) *The Theory of Stochastic Processes*, Prentice-Hall.

DeRosa D (2000) *Options on Foreign Exchange*, John Wiley & Sons.

Dothan M (1990) *Prices in Financial Markets*, Oxford.

Duffie D (1992) *Dynamic Asset Pricing Theory*, Princeton.

Dupire B (editor) (1998) *Monte Carlo*, Risk Books.

Elliot R and Kopp P (1999) *Mathematics of Financial Markets*, Springer.

Farlow S (1993) *Partial Differential Equations for Scientists and Engineers*, Dover.

Freund J (1992) *Mathematical Statistics*, Prentice-Hall.

Greenberg MD [ISBN: 0130 38836X] *Application of Green's Functions in Science and Engineering*, Prentice-Hall.

Haberman R (1987) *Elementary Applied Partial Differential Equations*, Prentice-Hall.

Haug E (1998) *The Complete Guide to Option Pricing Formulas*, McGraw-Hill.

Hull J (2000) *Options, Futures and Other Derivatives*, Prentice-Hall.

Hunt P and Kennedy J (2000) *Financial Derivatives in Theory and Practice*, John Wiley & Sons.

Jäckel P (2002) *Monte Carlo Methods in Finance*, John Wiley & Sons.

Jarrow R (editor) (1998) *Volatility*, Risk Books.

Johnson R and Wichern D (1988) *Applied Multivariate Statistical Analysis*, Prentice-Hall.

Karatsas I and Schreve S (1991) *Brownian Motion and Stochastic Calculus*, Springer.

Kreyszig E (1993) *Advanced Engineering Mathematics*, John Wiley & Sons.

Martellini L and Priaulet P (2001) *Fixed-Income Securities*, John Wiley & Sons.

Musiela M and Rutkowski M (1998) *Martingale Methods in Financial Modelling*, Springer.

Neftci S (1996) (2000) *Mathematics of Financial Derivatives*, Academic.

Nelken I (editor) (1996) *The Handbook of Exotic Options*, Irwin.

Nielsen L (1999) *Pricing and Hedging Derivative Securities*, OUP.

Øksendal B (1992) *Stochastic Differential Equations*, Springer.

Pliska S (1997) *Introduction to Mathematical Finance*, Blackwell.

Press WH, Teukolsky SA, Vetterling WT and Flannery BP (1992) *Numerical Recipes in C*, Cambridge University Press.

Rebonato R (1998) *Interest-Rate Option Models*, John Wiley & Sons.

Rebonato R (1999) *Volatility and Correlation*, John Wiley & Sons.

Revuz D and Yor M (2001) *Continuous Martingales and Brownian Motion*, Springer.

Shaw W (1998) *Modelling Financial Derivatives with Mathematica*, Cambridge.

Smith G (1978) *Numerical Solution of Partial Differential Equations: Finite Difference Methods*, Clarendon Press.

Steele J (2001) *Stochastic Calculus and Financial Applications*, Springer.

Tavella D and Randall C (2000) *Pricing Financial Instruments*, John Wiley & Sons.

Wilmott P 2nd version (2002) 2 vol "Paul Wilmott on Quantitative Finance" and 1 vol "Paul Wilmott Introduces Quantitative Finance".

Wilmott P (1998) *Derivatives*, John Wiley & Sons.

Wilmott P, Dewynne J and Howison S (1993) *Option Pricing*, Oxford Financial Press.

Wilmott P, Dewynne J and Howison S (1995) *The Mathematics of Financial Derivatives*, Cambridge.

Zhang (1998) *Exotic Options*, World Scientific.

# PAPERS

Andersen L, Andreasen J and Brotherton-Ratcliffe R (1998) The passport option. *Journal of Computational Finance*, 1(3), 15–36.

Barone-Adesi G and Whaley R (1987) Efficient analytic approximation of American option values. *Journal of Finance*, XLII (2), 301–320.

Boyle PP and Lau SH (1994) Bumping up against the barrier with the binomial method. *Journal of Derivatives*, 1, 6–14.

Carr P and Bowie J (1994) Static simplicity. *Risk Magazine*, 7(8).

Carr P and Jarrow A (1990) The stop-loss start-gain paradox and option valuation: a new decomposition into intrinsic and time value. *The Review of Financial Studies*, 3(3), 469–492.

Cheuk TH and Vorst TC (1996) Complex barrier options. *Journal of Derivatives*, 4, 8–22.

Curran M (1992) Beyond average intelligence. *Risk*, Nov, 60.

Curran M (1994) Valuing Asian and portfolio options by conditioning on the geometric mean price. *Management Science*, 40 (Dec), 1705–1711.

Derman E, Kani I and Chriss N (1996) Implied trinomial trees of the volatility smile. *The Journal of Derivatives*, summer.

Drezner Z (1978) Computation of the bivariate normal integral. *Mathematics of Computation*, 32(14), 277–279.

Dumas B, Jennergren L and Näslund B (1995) Siedel's paradox and the pricing of currency options. *Journal of International Money and Finance*, 14(2), 213–223.

Garman M (1989) Recollection in tranquillity. *Risk Magazine*, 2(3).

Geske R (1979) The valuation of compound options. *Journal of Financial Economics*, 7, 63–81.

Goldman MB, Sosin HB and Gatto MA (1979) Path dependent options: buy at the low, sell at the high. *The Journal of Finance*, XXXIV(5), 1111–1127.

Henderson V and Hobson D (2000) Local time, coupling and the passport option. *Finance and Stochastics*, 4, 69–80.

Heynen R and Kat H (1994a) Crossing barriers. *Risk Magazine*, 7(6).

Heynen R and Kat H (1994b) Partial barrier options. *Journal of Financial Engineering*, 3, 253–274.

Hyer T, Lipton–Lifschitz A and Pugachevsky D (1997) Passport to success. *Risk Magazine*, 10(9).

Ikeda M and Kunitomo N (1992) Pricing options with curved boundaries. *Mathematical Finance*, 2, 275–298.

Jamshidian F (1991) Forward induction and construction of yield curve diffusion models. *Journal of Fixed Income*, 1.

Johnson H (1987) Options on the maximum or the minimum of several assets. *Journal of Financial and Quantitative Analysis*, 10, 161–185.

Kane A and Marcus AJ (1988) The delivery option on forward contracts. *Journal of Financial and Quantitative Analysis*, 23 (Sept).

Levy E (1992) Pricing European average rate currency options. *Journal of International Money and Finance*, 11, 474–491.

Levy E and Turnbull SM (1992) Average intelligence. *Risk*, Feb, 56.

Longstaff FA (1990) Pricing options with extendible maturities: analysis and applications. *The Journal of Finance*, XLV(3), 935–957.

Margrabe W (1978) The value of an option to exchange one asset for another. *Journal of Finance*, XXXIII (1), 177–186.

Reiner E (1992) Quanto mechanics. *Risk Magazine*, 5(3).

Reiner E and Rubinstein M (1991a) Breaking down the barriers. *Risk Magazine*, 4(8).

Reiner E and Rubinstein M (1991b) Unscrambling the binary code. *Risk Magazine*, 4(9).

Rubinstein M (1991a) Somewhere over the rainbow. *Risk Magazine*, 4(10).

Rubinstein M (1991b) Options for the undecided. *Risk Magazine*, 4(4).

Rubinstein M (1991c) Pay now, choose later. *Risk Magazine*, 4(2).

Rubinstein M (1994) Return to Oz. *Risk Magazine*, 7(11).

Skiadopoulos G (1999) Volatility smile consistent models: a survey. *University of Warwick, FORC preprint*.

Street A (1992) Stuck up a ladder. *Risk Magazine*, 5(5).

Stulz R (1982) Options on the minimum or the maximum of two risky assets. *Journal of Financial Economics*, 10, 161–185.

Thomas B (1993) Something to shout about. *Risk Magazine*, 6(5).

Turnbull SM and Wakeham LM (1991) A quick algorithm for pricing European average options. *Journal of Financial and Quantitative Analysis*, 26 (Sept), 377–389.

Vorst T (1992) Prices and hedge ratios of average exchange rate options. *International Review of Financial Analysis*, 1, 179–193.

# Bibliography and References

# Index

Printed and bound by CPI Group (UK) Ltd, Croydon, CR0 4YY

23/04/2025

14660967-0001